Asian Labor in the Wartime Japanese Empire

Asian Labor in the Wartime Japanese Empire
Unknown Histories

Paul H. Kratoska, EDITOR

An East Gate Book

M.E.Sharpe
Armonk, New York
London, England

An East Gate Book

Copyright © 2005 by M.E. Sharpe, Inc.

The EuroSlavic fonts used to create this work are © 1986–2002 Payne Loving Trust.
EuroSlavic is available from Linguist's Software, Inc.,
www.linguistsoftware.com, P.O. Box 580, Edmonds, WA 98020-0580 USA
tel (425) 775-1130.

Library of Congress Cataloging-in-Publication Data

Asian labor in the wartime Japanese empire : unknown histories / edited by Paul H.
Kratoska.
    p. cm.
    "An east gate book."
    Includes bibliographical references and index.
    ISBN 0-7656-1262-3 (hardcover : alk. paper) — ISBN 0-7656-1263-1 (pbk.: alk. paper)
    1. Labor—Japan—Colonies—History—20th century. 2. World War, 1939–1945—
Manpower—Japan—Colonies. 3. Labor policy—Japan—Colonies—History—20th
century. I. Kratoska, Paul H.

HD8726.A825 2005
940.53′1—dc22
                                         2004020822

Printed in the United States of America

The paper used in this publication meets the minimum requirements of
American National Standard for Information Sciences
Permanence of Paper for Printed Library Materials,
ANSI Z 39.48-1984.

∞

BM (c)	10	9	8	7	6	5	4	3	2	1
BM (p)	10	9	8	7	6	5	4	3	2	1

Contents

Part V. Taiwan

Part VI. Indonesia

Part VII. Malaya

Part VIII. Philippines

Part IX. Vietnam

Part X. Memory and Reconciliation

List of Illustrative Materials

Maps

Photographs

Tables

Figures

Acknowledgments

This volume contains articles that deal with labor in the territories occupied by Japan during the Pacific War of 1941–45. Most were originally prepared for this collection, but four are English translations of articles first published in other languages. The piece by Ju Zhifen was written in Chinese and translated by Chang Yueh Siang, a postgraduate student in history at the National University of Singapore. The chapters by Harry Poeze, Henk Hovinga, and Remco Raben were first published in Dutch. Those by Harry Poeze and Henk Hovinga were translated by Frank Dhont, a Belgian who was at the time a postgraduate student at Gadjah Mada University. Remco Raben prepared the English version of his own article. The chapter by Chin Sung Chung is an edited version of her article published in the journal *Positions* in 1997.

I am very grateful to the many people who have contributed to the preparation of this book. Apart from the authors themselves, and the translators mentioned above, I would particularly like to mention Greg Clancey, Goto Ken'ichi, Hara Fujio, Yasuko Kobayashi, Elly Touwen-Bousma, Mika Toyota, and Geoff Wade. Michiko Nakahara called my attention to the photographs by Rumiko Nishino that are included with chapter 10, and I am very grateful to Ms. Nishino for agreeing to let me use them, and for providing copies of the pictures. The maps were prepared by Lee Li Kheng, a cartographer with the Department of Geography at the National University of Singapore. Excerpts from Tan Malaka's *From Jail to Jail* in chapter 8 are taken from the translation by Helen Jarvis and are used with permission from Ohio University Press.

Introduction

Paul H. Kratoska

The mobilization of labor was a major feature of the Japanese empire in the 1930s and 1940s, and the number of people forced to work for the Japanese across Asia ran well into the millions. Japan needed soldiers, and it needed workers to produce military equipment and construct airfields and other military facilities, and to grow food for the armed forces and the civilian population. As Japan expanded into China and then into Southeast Asia, the demand for labor increased and people from these regions began to be pressed into service, some on a short-term basis but others for periods lasting months or even years. The prewar economy had collapsed, causing widespread unemployment, and workers initially responded positively to promises of generous wages and benefits. By 1944 labor reserves had been used up, and the Japanese turned to forced recruitment. Many workers were sent to distant locations, and a considerable number of them did not return. Theirs is a story of death and dislocation of holocaust proportions, and remarkably it is a story that has received little attention from historians.

Conditions at the Japanese work sites were often extremely bad, with rudimentary housing, inadequate diets, little or no medical care, and strict labor regimens that showed scant concern for the loss of human life. Malaria and dengue fever were endemic at many project sites, and laborers brought in from other places often had little resistance to these diseases. Moreover, workers suffered from malnutrition, which left them weakened and lacking physical stamina. Bringing large numbers of unskilled workers to work sites with inadequate prior planning for sanitation resulted in outbreaks of dysentery, cholera, and other diseases. Laborers also developed debilitating tropical ulcers, leading in some cases to amputation of limbs or death. Finally, infractions of the rules or failure to work hard brought harsh corporal punishment, worsening the physical deterioration of the workers. Mortality rates of 30 to 40 percent appear to have been common, but there are few statistics, or even remotely reliable estimates, to indicate how many people died. It is certain from firsthand observations and anecdotal evidence that the numbers were very large.

Grief and despair find little place in most historical accounts and are absent from most of the source materials historians use, but the hundreds of thousands who died were sons, husbands, and fathers, or sometimes daughters, wives, and mothers, and had families awaiting their return. In some cases their departures were recorded ceremoniously, with laborers affixing signatures or thumbprints to documents showing their home addresses and the names of their next of kin, and acknowledging advances of cash against future wages. Deaths often went unrecorded. Coolies too sick to work were placed in death houses where they spent their final hours in accumulated filth—mud and the vomit and excrement produced by those who had died before them—without food or medicine, and certainly without hope. Their corpses were thrown into unmarked graves, or burned, or abandoned in the forest, or tossed into rivers. Their families received no information and eventually had no choice but to presume the worst.

The sufferings of European prisoners of war forced to work for the Japanese, most famously on the Thailand–Burma railway, have been well chronicled, but the experiences of Asian laborers remain unstudied. There are many reasons for this omission. Most of the workers were illiterate, and those who had some education lacked the traditions of writing and publication that produced vivid accounts of European POW labor and of the Holocaust in Europe. Moreover, historians have little material with which to work because the Japanese destroyed the records of their wartime administration immediately after the conflict ended in August 1945. The materials that do exist are in several languages—authors in the present collection have drawn on documents in Japanese, Chinese, Malay, Indonesian, Filipino, Thai, Vietnamese, Burmese, Dutch, and English—and are kept in a very wide range of locations.

To some degree oral sources can make up for the absence of written records. The initial effort to assemble first-hand information about the occupation took place immediately after the war in connection with war crimes trials. This material is found in various archives and in transcripts of the trials. There have been later efforts to develop a record of the war by interviewing people about their experiences, notably in Singapore where a large collection of tapes and transcripts is available to the public.[1] In Taiwan, Hui-yu Caroline Ts'ai has interviewed several hundred people about their wartime experiences. Indonesian researchers in Central Java have interviewed former laborers, or *rōmusha*, and in 1999 P. J. Suwarno published some of the results in an Indonesian-language book entitled *Romusa*.[2] A Burmese-language book published in 1968 by Lin Yone Thit Lwin describes the experiences of workers recruited in Burma.[3] In Japan the Toyota Foundation has funded projects to assemble and preserve materials relating to the war and occupation in Burma, Indonesia, Malaya, and the Philippines.[4] However, many of these efforts were carried out long after the war ended, when memories had faded and key participants had already died. Much of what happened will never be known.

The contributors to this volume examine labor in different parts of Japan's wartime empire. The coverage is not comprehensive, but the collection provides a representative sampling of Japan's labor policies, and it shows the importance the Japanese attached to labor in their war effort. It also offers a harrowing look at the experiences of those recruited to work on Japanese projects. More remains to be done, and it is to be hoped that this volume will prompt further study of the issues it raises. That, however, is not its purpose. The articles assembled here are not anodyne accounts written to fill gaps in the historical record, but compelling stories of a great human tragedy that force readers to consider the war and occupation in a new light.

Some of the events the authors describe grew out of the culture and social expectations of the Japanese and the people they ruled during the war. Others, however, arise from the insidious demands of war and occupation, a complex of events that, once set in motion, can as easily destroy its creators as those against whom they fight. Japan's war effort began as a struggle for dominance, but for all those drawn into the conflict it became a struggle for survival.

An Allied Labor Force: The Indian Pioneer Corps

This book concerns the use of Asian labor by Japan as part of its war effort in East and Southeast Asia, but labor is essential to any military effort, and the Allies also recruited Asian workers to support the military effort.[5] To meet its manpower requirements Admiral Mountbatten's South East Asia Command made use of workers provided by the Indian Auxiliary Pioneer Corps (later called the Indian Pioneer Corps). Created early in the war, the Corps was organized in companies, paralleling the military services. Companies belonging to the Corps initially worked in the Middle East and in India, where each battalion was assigned four labor companies consisting of 417 men each. In 1943 the Corps was restructured under a group headquarters, which began assigning companies individually according to need. The Japanese thrust into Southeast Asia brought the creation of additional civil labor units in the form of state and provincial labor units, a Porter Corps, and Indian Tea Association labor forces. Prior to January 1945, when ALFSEA (Allied Land Forces, South East Asia) Headquarters consolidated these workforces, there was considerable overlap among these bodies. After the reorganization, Pioneer group commanders became responsible for all labor employed within specified territorial zones. When Allied forces returned to Southeast Asia, labor companies were sent to Singapore and Malaya, Java, Siam, French Indochina, Hong Kong, and Borneo.

The workforce reached a very substantial size. In April 1945 ALFSEA operations included thirty-four Pioneer Group Headquarters and 266 companies, and the Pioneer and Labor (P and L) Directorate controlled 523,304 men. Following the Japanese surrender, local civilian labor replaced Pioneer Corps workers. By February 1946 the number of companies operating in Southeast Asia had been reduced by 50 percent, replaced by some 305,190 locally recruited civilians.

Pioneer labor companies carried out a wide range of activities, building roads, bridges, railways, and airfields, laying pipelines and signal wire, unloading ships, and manning storage depots. For example, nearly fifty-four thousand workers took part in constructing airfields in Assam for supply missions to China, building the Ledo road, and laying pipelines in northern Burma.

Many of the laborers were Nepalese, and they performed impressive feats of endurance, marching as much as thirty miles a day to carry stores to the front lines, and carrying back wounded soldiers. Pioneers often worked under fire, but they were neither armed nor expected to fight. Late in the war, in June 1945, the teams were "combatized," receiving rifles and training and a corresponding adjustment in pay. Following the Japanese surrender, Pioneers served as guards for working parties made up of Japanese "surrendered personnel," rode goods trains to protect shipments of supplies in Malaya, and guarded storage depots in Burma.

List of Abbreviations

ALFSEA	Allied Land Forces South East Asia
BMA	British Military Administration
BP3	*Badan Pembantu Prajurit Pekerja* (relief organization for "work soldiers")
CEA	Civilian Emergency Administration (Philippines)
CEBREJA	Central Bureau for Repatriation of Javanese and Other Indonesians
CER	Chinese Eastern Railway
DPWC	Department of Public Works and Communications (Philippines)
EC	Philippine Executive Commission
EC *OG*	Executive Commission *Official Gazette* (Philippines)
FBIS	Foreign Broadcast Intelligence Service
IC	Indische Collectie (Netherlands Institute for War Documentation, Amsterdam)
ISPS	Association of Imperial Subjects for Patriotic Service (Taiwan)
JFMA	Japan Foreign Ministry Archives
JMA	Japanese Military Administration
Kalibapi	*Kapisanan sa Paglilingkod sa Bagong Pilipinas* (Association for Service for the New Philippines)
KNIL	Kononklijk Nederlandsch-Indisch Leger (Royal Dutch East Indian Army)
LRA	Labor Recruitment Agency (Philippines)
MCA	Manchuria Construction Association
MCS	Malayan Civil Service
MJCA	Manpower in Japan and Occupied Areas
MKG	*Manshū kenchiku gaisetsu* (Survey of Manchurian Architecture)
MLA	Manchuria Labor Association (*Manshū rōko kyōkai*)
MMMJ	Manpower Mobilization Measures in Japan
MPSI	Movement for Patriotic Services in Industry (Taiwan)
MSK	*Manshū seifu kōhō* (Manshū-koku Empire, Official Gazette)
NCCD	North China Coordinations Department

NCLA	North China Laborers Association
NEBUDORI	Netherlands Bureau for Documentation and Repatriation of Indonesians
NEFIS	Netherlands Forces Intelligence Service
NEI	Netherlands East Indies
NICA	Netherlands Indies Civil Administration
NIDS	National Institute for Defense Studies
OJJMA	Official Journal of the Japanese Military Administration (Philippines)
OSS	Office of Strategic Services
PAC	Prosper Asia Court
PETA	Pembela Tanah Air (Indonesia; a Japanese-sponsored local military force)
PKI	Indonesian Communist Party
PMI	Indonesian Red Cross
PRO	Public Record Office
PSYC	Patriotic Service Youth Corps (Taiwan)
RAPWI	Organization for the Recovery of Allied Prisoners of War and Internees
R&A	Research and Analysis
RG	Record Group (in the U.S. National Archives, College Park, Maryland)
RP *OG*	Republic of the Philippines *Official Gazette*
SMR	South Manchuria Railway
UNCHR	United Nations Commission on Human Rights
USNA	U.S. National Archives, College Park, Maryland

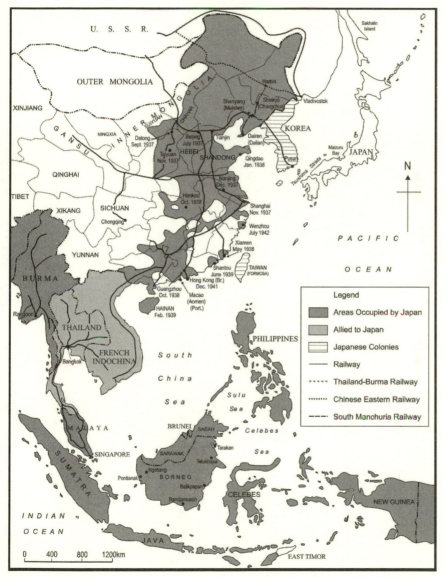

Eastern Asia

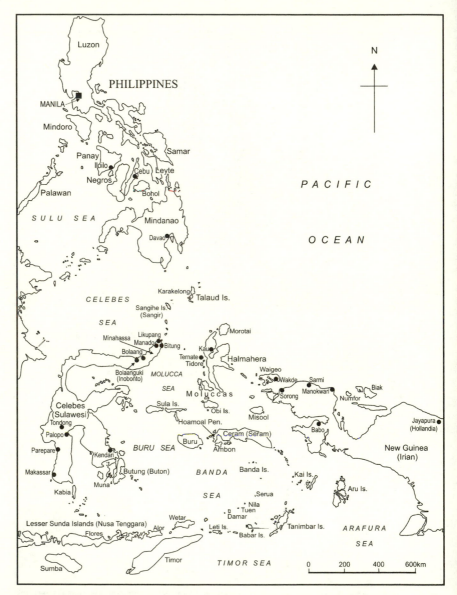

Eastern Indonesian Archipelago

Part I

Japan

1

Labor Mobilization in Japan and the Japanese Empire

Paul H. Kratoska

Between 1937 and 1945 imperial Japan utilized the skills, energy, and physical strength of millions of human beings to prosecute a war of conquest across East and Southeast Asia. Japan needed manpower to staff the military services, manufacture war matériel and consumer goods, construct military facilities, roads, and railways, and produce minerals and agricultural products. The population of Japan proper, around 100 million people, was systematically mobilized. Korea supplied soldiers, civilian workers for the military, and "comfort women" for brothels used by the troops. Millions of people in northern China worked for the Japanese in agriculture and construction, with some being sent to Manchukuo, Mongolia, and Tibet. There was also widespread recruitment of civilian labor in Taiwan and the occupied territories of Southeast Asia. Although most workers were nominally hired as paid contract laborers, many were recruited under duress, and there was some use of forced labor. The process caused a massive dislocation of people and resulted in a huge death toll.

For Japanese men, military recruitment took precedence over all other activities, and civilian employers—including war industries—lost experienced workers to the military. Employers replaced these workers with people who had fewer skills and less physical strength—former shop assistants, women, students, Koreans, farm laborers, and others who did not meet the military's physical requirements.[1]

In Japan and throughout the Japanese empire, economic disruption caused by the war threw substantial numbers of people out of work, creating a pool of labor that Japan was able to tap. Once surplus labor had been absorbed, the Japanese recruited workers through newly created patriotic associations, community organizations, religious sects, schools, and local government. When these sources were exhausted, the authorities diverted labor from jobs deemed nonessential to war-related activities, and shifted workers from populous and labor-rich areas such as North China and Java to places where the existing labor force was insufficient to carry out military projects. There were also efforts to draw women and students into the workforce, and to obtain labor from marginal sources, such as people who already held jobs but could do additional work in their spare time. Increasingly, an element of coercion crept into the recruitment process, and eventually the Japanese turned openly to the use of forced labor.

Transporting, housing, and feeding workers who were moved to strategically important locations greatly overtaxed Japan's resources. Accommodations were rudimentary, diets inadequate to maintain good health, sanitary facilities lacking, and medical care poor or nonexistent. The last point is particularly significant because workers were exposed to endemic diseases for which they had no immunity, and the presence of large numbers of people with limited resources and little knowledge of sanitary facilities was an additional source of illness.

These circumstances are explicable, if not excusable. It is more difficult to understand the harshness of the work regime, which contributed to the physical deterioration of the workforce and was counterproductive given the need to complete projects as quickly and efficiently as possible. Laborers were subjected to brutal corporal punishment for minor infractions, and in some cases to vicious and gratuitous acts of cruelty. A number of explanations can be suggested for this behavior. First, corporal punishment was common within the Japanese military, where low-ranking soldiers were often struck for real offenses or simply to instill discipline, and this treatment was extended to civilian workers. Second, many of the people employed as guards or supervisors were poorly educated and of working-class origins. Their own life experiences were often brutal, and this, combined in some cases with feelings of racial superiority, led to harsh treatment. To this must be added differences of language and culture, and misunderstandings arising from communication problems. Third, the tasks being done were ordered in the name of the emperor and treated as vital to the war effort, which overrode all other considerations. In the circumstances, laborers were expendable and could be replaced. Finally, there can be little doubt that many people did not work particularly hard. Recruited under duress and sent to places they did not want to be, laborers lived and worked in abysmal conditions for wages that were often not paid on time or in full. They did not share the feelings of loyalty or patriotism that might have inspired Japanese workers, and while the Japanese made efforts to instill Japanese spirit (*seishin*) in their employees, there could be no realistic expectation that non-Japanese would be willing to sacrifice themselves for the emperor. The impetus for work had to lie elsewhere, in fear and in a desperate effort to survive.

In the final year of the conflict, Japan's labor system broke down. Record keeping deteriorated, and the system of registration and control collapsed as the government evacuated cities and dispersed industries into the country-side. Air raids caused widespread destruction of factories, and there was a shift in emphasis from manufacturing to agriculture and repair of existing equipment.[2] When the war ended, many hundreds of thousands of Japanese and Allied soldiers awaited repatriation, and resources for welfare activities were limited. Workers who had been relocated from their homes received some assistance, but a great many were left to their own devices, with little money and now with no jobs.

This chapter offers an overview of Japan's system of wartime mobilization of labor based on wartime intelligence materials[3] together with a discussion by Jerome B. Cohen in his 1949 book *Japan's Economy in War and Reconstruction*.[4] The intelligence services gathered information by monitoring radio broadcasts, interviewing people from occupied territories who happened to fall into their hands, and collecting scraps of information from documents found on enemy soldiers who were killed or captured. By piecing together such materials they created a picture of conditions in Japan and throughout the Japanese empire. Cohen's work uses these and other documentary sources along with postwar interviews with Japanese involved with labor matters.

Unemployment and Labor Surpluses

Japan's economic development was built on abundant cheap labor, and the country had enough workers to meet its needs throughout the war years. The economy was weighted toward handicrafts and agriculture, with large numbers of workers gaining a livelihood from very small companies or from small farms. According to a wartime calculation, Japan's small-scale irrigated farms required twelve times as many workers as the farms in Great Britain,[5] and eventually enough labor was drawn from rural areas to cause a decline in agricultural production.

Historically, Southeast Asia was a labor-deficit region, and the region's export economy depended on workers from China and India. The Japanese invasion caused widespread unemployment. Large numbers of people depended for their livelihoods on the export of primary products such as rice, rubber, tobacco, palm oil, tin, abaca, coconuts, sugar, and coffee, and the invasion abruptly severed connections with principal markets in Europe and the United States. Movement of these products within the Japanese empire was limited by a severe shortage of transport, and in any case regional demand did not keep up with prewar levels of production. Both laborers and white-collar workers—clerks, teachers, and civil servants—found themselves out of work. In Manila, for example, the Commissioner of the Interior (Jose P. Laurel) estimated in February 1943 that one-fourth of the city's population was unemployed.[6]

These difficulties seemed likely to cause unrest, and since the Japanese authorities could do little to alleviate the situation, they relied on terror and draconian punishments to maintain order. As shortages worsened, some of those without work began to grow food for their own consumption, a development the Japanese strongly encouraged. However, the military was beginning to undertake construction projects that required significant inputs of labor, and unemployed workers were a major source of additional labor. Because these projects offered fixed-term contracts and generous wages and benefits, many people were happy to accept offers of jobs. However, few laborers returned after the contractual period was up, and those who did manage to get back brought tales of terrible working conditions, callous brutality from supervisors, malnutrition, malaria, and tropical ulcers. Moreover, the promised wages and allowances were paid irregularly, or not at all, and inflation caused by excessive printing of currency greatly reduced the value of the money workers did receive. As these stories spread, recruitment became progressively more difficult.

Military Recruitment

Japan passed a military conscription law in 1872, shortly after the Meiji Restoration, and it remained in force at the time of the Pacific War. During the 1930s all males between the ages of seventeen and forty were subject to conscription for military service. Boys underwent a physical examination at the age of nineteen and began military training after turning twenty. Toward the end of 1943, the age for active military service was lowered to nineteen, and in October 1944 boys between seventeen and nineteen began to receive preconscription training. The minimum requirement for military service was a height of five feet and good physical condition. Boys who did not meet this standard went into a conscript reserve or else were declared unfit for service. Japanese living outside of Japan, apart from those in Manchukuo or China, were not liable for military service before the war, but this exemption ended in 1943, and in May 1944 Japanese civilians in the southern regions began undergoing physical examinations prior to conscription.[7] Japan was extremely cautious about giving military training to Koreans and Taiwanese, fearing that this might facilitate anti-Japanese nationalist activity in the two territories, but Koreans became subject to military service in 1944 and

Taiwanese in 1945. Recruits were grouped according to their age and military experience. The First National Army consisted of men from the First Reserve or the conscript reserves who were at least partially trained. The Second National Army consisted of men fit for limited service, and boys between seventeen and nineteen. In peacetime the navy had relied almost entirely on volunteers, enlisting young men who wished to avoid being drafted into the army, but during the war the navy, like the army, used conscripts to fill its ranks.[8]

The armed forces absorbed a large number of young men from Japan proper. The number of men in the military services increased from 243,000 in 1930 to 1,694,000 in 1940 (4 percent of the male population), and to 3,980,000 in February 1944 (10 percent of the male population). Between February 1944 and August 1945 large numbers of new recruits were inducted into military service, and the strength of the army and navy at the time of Japan's surrender was 7,193,000.[9]

The Japanese created military forces in China and throughout Southeast Asia. These bodies served a number of functions—helping maintain order, assisting regular Japanese forces by carrying out air-raid and coastal surveillance duties, and preparing to resist a possible Allied invasion. These forces also provided a living for unemployed young men who might otherwise become security threats. There were three basic types of military organization, with local variations. The first was a volunteer army, a regular military force trained by the Japanese army and provided with arms and uniforms.[10] The second was a volunteer corps, described (in Malaya) as "an army (troops) of semi-soldiers and semi-farmers" formed into "small units . . . for the maintenance of peace and order and the performance of defence measures."[11] The third was the *heiho*, auxiliary soldiers who were inducted into the Japanese army or navy as noncombatants and provided labor for the military.[12] The Japanese also used local people to staff auxiliary police forces and quasi-military organizations that carried out duties connected with air-raid protection and prevention of sabotage. Table 1.1 shows some of the military forces created or supported by the Japanese.

In developing these military organizations the Japanese invoked local nationalisms rather than the defense of Greater East Asia. The purpose of the Burma Defense Army was "to establish a home front for defense of the national domain with its own nation as the actual battlefield."[13] The Malayan Volunteer Army responded to "the desires of the Malaian [sic] local inhabitants for the defense of their native land,"[14] the Bali Volunteer Defense Army consisted of those "who have applied for voluntary service in the defense of their homeland," and the Nias Volunteer Home Defense Force was made up of people "determined to defend their country, bound with Japan."[15]

Table 1.1

Japanese-Sponsored Military Forces

Location	Name of armed body
Burma	Burma Independence Army Burma National Army (later Burma Defense Army)
Malaya	Volunteer Army Volunteer Corps
Sumatra	Chinese Passive Defense Corps Police Corps Volunteer Corps
Java	Java Volunteer Defense Corps (Sukarela Pembela Tanah Air, or PETA) Special Home Defense Corps Women's Defense Corps
Bali	Bali Volunteer Defense Army (PETA)
Nias	Volunteer Home Defense Force
Borneo (Bandjarmasin)	Special Defense Service
Philippines	Makapili (Kelipunang Makabayan ng mga Pilipinas, the Patriotic League of Filipinos) Philippine Constabulary
Malaya, Thailand, Burma	Indian National Army

Sources: Office of Strategic Services Research and Analysis Branch Assemblage 45, "Manpower in Japan and Occupied Areas," extracts from short wave Radio Tokyo and affiliated stations from December 1941 to July 15, 1944, vol. 2; Joyce Lebra, *Japanese-Trained Armies in Southeast Asia* (New York: Columbia University Press, 1977).

Civilian Labor

Mobilization Procedures

In 1938 a National General Mobilization Act gave the Japanese government broad powers relating to the conscription and control of civilian labor both in Japan proper and throughout the Japanese empire.[16] The term "conscription" is widely used in connection with wartime labor and military service, but in the Japanese context it referred not only to drafting people into the military or the workforce, but also to freezing people in their existing jobs. Large numbers of workers were locked into their current positions, but conscription in the sense of compulsory government requisitioning of manpower accounted for only a small proportion of the wartime labor force. In 1944 just 8 percent of the civilian male workforce had been recruited through conscription.[17] However, pressures arising from these and other wartime measures (such as restricting opportunities for education) forced many people to enter the workforce "voluntarily."

Responsibility for the process of national mobilization rested with a National General Mobilization Council, established in May 1938. The mobilization law allowed the government to

> require Japanese subjects to engage in war work; regulate the employment and dismissal of workers, wages and hours, and other conditions of work; prohibit labor disputes, and certain methods of labor controversies; require Japanese workers or their employers to give particulars of workers' vocations qualifications; require schools, factories, and other institutions to provide technical and vocational training in order to insure the necessary supply of skilled labor; and compel employers to use labor more efficiently. In the 6 years which have elapsed since the passage of the Act, the Government has issued ordinances pertaining to almost every one of the above subjects.[18]

Cohen described this enactment as the "basic enabling act for labor control" and the basis for the mobilization of labor. Subsequent ordinances issued under the enactment allowed the government to fix wages, deal with turnover and hoarding of labor, control the use of labor and direct workers toward essential industries, and carry out a process of national registration and comprehensive national mobilization.[19]

Japan launched a National Register of Vocational Abilities in January 1939, based on an examination that used both practical tasks and written questions to establish the skill level of individual workers. Similar registers listed doctors, dentists, pharmacists, hospital attendants, scientists, and technicians. A law passed in July 1939 authorized conscription of registered workers, but it was not enforced until 1942, when the government approved mobilization of young men between the ages of seventeen and twenty to provide labor service. Toward the end of 1943 a general registration of the population took place as a prelude to mobilizing unskilled labor, a process that began in 1944. Men between sixteen and forty years of age (later raised to forty-five), and unmarried women between sixteen and twenty-five years of age, had to register and list their occupational skills. In February 1944 the government broadened the age ranges still further, to between twelve and sixty for men, and between twelve and forty for unmarried women and widows.

Photograph 1.1. A wartime Japanese woman in an aircraft factory. (Photograph courtesy of the *Mainichi Shimbun*.)

Students, previously exempt from registration, were also included in this exercise. The registers were used sparingly, but critical industries needed additional labor urgently, and by the end of 1944 the coal mining, aircraft construction, and shipbuilding industries were relying heavily on this system to secure workers.[20] Local officials operating out of labor mobilization offices situated within the police bureaus did the actual work of recruitment by selecting names from the registers, starting with those who were unemployed or working in nonessential industries, and taking into consideration special skills and family obligations.

During the war years the Japanese government prepared an annual Labor Mobilization Plan (later known as the National Mobilization Plan) that outlined labor requirements and analyzed the available supply of labor. Individual firms submitted estimates of their needs, and the respective ministries compiled this information for the planning board, although requests for workers always exceeded the supply and were adjusted downward before reaching the board. In principle, responsibility for recruitment and allocation of labor lay with the Welfare Ministry (Koseisho). In practice, it proved difficult to achieve centralized control over labor matters. Cohen wrote that

> labor control was spread over all the Ministries—agricultural and forestry labor in the Ministry of Agriculture and Forestry, merchant marine, communications and railroad labor in the Transportation ministry, munitions company labor in the munitions Ministry, ordnance and arsenal, air depot

Table 1.2

Labor in Japan: Supply and Demand (thousands of people)

Year	Demand	Supply
1939	1,095	1,139
1940	1,470	1,540
1941	2,212	2,213
1942	1,967	1,967
1943	2,396	2,396
1944	4,542	4,542

Source: *Nippon Times,* September 8, 1945, as cited in Jerome B. Cohen, *Japan's Economy in War and Reconstruction* (Minneapolis: University of Minnesota Press, 1949), p. 306.

and defense construction project labor in the Army and Navy, labor for industries run by the Monopoly Bureau in the Finance Ministry, labor for colonization purposes in Manchuria and China in the greater East Asia Ministry—coordinated only by a loose Ministerial conference system at the national government level. Army and Navy labor demands could not be questioned. Neither they nor the Munitions Ministry would supply the Welfare Ministry with production figures so that labor requirements might be judged more exactly.[21]

In 1943 the Munitions Ministry and the Industrial Control Associations responsible for key industries (iron and steel, coal, shipbuilding, light metals, aircraft) received authorization to conscript workers without going through the Welfare Ministry, and factories involved in war production could requisition labor from plants engaged in nonessential work. War industries appear to have absorbed far more workers than they required, to the detriment of civilian production, but other agencies were not allowed to investigate staffing levels or reassign these workers.[22]

A report prepared by the Welfare Ministry showed data for the supply and demand of labor during the war, based on figures drawn from the labor mobilization plans (see Table 1.2).

The Japanese administration carried out registration exercises in some of the occupied territories as well. The Syonan (Singapore) Labor Office set up a register of unemployed workers in April 1943, and on January 1, 1944, began to register all workers on the island.[23] Registration also took place in Malaya, while in the Philippines an executive order issued in May 1943 stipulated that "no worker or peasant who is not registered in the census of unemployed [made] by the provincial governor or city mayor can be employed by any person, firm or corporation . . . or in any public construction work carried out by the government."[24] However, recruitment and allocation of labor in these and other occupied territories were much less systematic than in Japan.

Patriotic Associations and Labor Mobilization

A wide range of patriotic associations assisted with the mobilization and control of labor in Japan. The Great Japan Patriotic Industrial Association (Dai Nippon Sangyo Hōkoku Kai), created at the end of the 1930s, placed factory workers in a militaristic body intended to eliminate tensions between capital and labor. The association, which received a substantial government subsidy, set up branches in major industrial facilities, and regional organizations in every prefecture and in large urban areas. Similar bodies organized workers in agriculture (Nogyo [Farm] Hōkoku Kai), railways, communications (Sangyo Kokoku Kai), and commerce (Shogyo [Commerce] Hōkoku Kai). In 1942 all these associations became affiliates of the Imperial Rule Assistance Association. Day laborers could join the Dai Nippon Romu Hōkoku Kai, which had an estimated 2 million members. The government mobilized workers for part-time or short-term work through a Patriotic Labor Service Corps (the Kokumin Kinro Hōkoku Tai), created in November 1941.[25]

In Southeast Asia there was some trade union activity before the war, particularly in the Philippines and Java, while secret societies and clan or dialect associations gave assistance to Chinese workers. Japanese military administrations dissolved these organizations, replacing them with centralized patriotic and communal associations under Japanese control, which were used to maintain order and to mobilize labor. Table 1.3 lists some of the organizations set up in occupied territories across Asia.[26]

Training Programs

Japan's workforce included only a small number of experienced engineers and technicians, and there was a shortage of technically competent supervisors and workmen throughout the empire. To overcome this deficiency, the Japanese operated training programs to teach technical skills, both on the job and in specially created institutes. The government also required schools and universities to change their programs of instruction to give increased emphasis to engineering and technical subjects.[27] Japanese administrations throughout the occupied territories likewise operated programs to teach skills needed to meet wartime needs. Table 1.4 lists some of the Japanese-sponsored wartime training schemes.

Table 1.3

Patriotic Associations

Location	Associations
China	North China Labor Association Imperial Rule Assistance Association Hsin Min Youth Corps Industrial Construction Corps North China Labor and Industry Association Compulsory National Labor Battalion North China Patriotic Labor Service National Development Corps
Manchuria	Concordia Society People's Patriotic Labor Service Association Skilled Workers' Mobilization Council
Burma	National Labor Service Corps Young Men's League of East Asia
Malaya	Labor Service Corps (Seicho) Free Labor Corps Chinese Labor Service Corps Indian Independence League Malay Welfare Association (Free Labor Service Corps)
Sumatra	Native Service Corps Native Maritime Service Association East Indies Central Federation
Java	Patriotic Service Association People's Sacrificial Service Association People's Strength Concentration (Pusat Tenaga Rakyat) Civilian Labor Organization Surabaya Labor Association New Djawa Service Organization Indonesian Economic Progress Association Young Men's Association Village and neighborhood associations
Borneo	Labor Service Organization Youth Corps
The Celebes	Labor Service Corps Patriotic Service Corps Naval Central Labor Association Students Providing Volunteer Labor Service
Philippines	Patriotic Labor Service Association Volunteer Labor Corps Committee to Help Win the War Tanauan Youth Movement Student Volunteer Corps Sunday Service Volunteer Corps

Source: Office of Strategic Services Research and Analysis Branch Assemblage 45, "Manpower in Japan and Occupied Areas," extracts from shortwave Radio Tokyo and affiliated stations from December 1941 to July 15, 1944, vol. 2.

Table 1.4

A Partial List of Japanese-Sponsored Training Programs

Location	Training program
Burma	Greater East Asia Training Institute Agricultural University Training in cotton spinning and weaving
Malaya and Singapore	Shonan Industrial School Malai Fisheries Training Institute Seamen's Training Institute Perak Seamen's Institute Naval aircraft schools
Sumatra	Nautical Training School (Padang)
Java	Vocational schools School for aquatic experts at the Aquatic Industrial Research Institute (Bogor) Native Seamen Training School (Surabaya) Land transportation training station
Madura	Seaman's School
Borneo	Agricultural training Training of seamen
The Celebes	Agricultural school Industrial technical schools Naval and Seamen's Training Institute
Philippines	Land Transportation Management Bureau training for railway labor Seamen's Training Institute Provincial agricultural schools

Source: Office of Strategic Services Research and Analysis Branch Assemblage 45, "Manpower in Japan and Occupied Areas," extracts from shortwave Radio Tokyo and affiliated stations from December 1941 to July 15, 1944, vol. 2.

The Agricultural Workforce and Food Production

The agricultural sector in Japan accounted for 47 percent of the country's total workforce in 1930 (14,130,000 of 29,620,000 workers, including 6,400,000 women). A further 5,810,000 people worked in agriculture on a part-time basis. During the 1930s there was considerable surplus labor capacity in agriculture, which caused a good deal of poverty in rural areas. The mobilization that took place in 1937 in connection with the Sino–Japanese War drew large numbers of men into the military for service in

China, with 70–80 percent of them coming from farming villages. In addition, Japan drew substantial numbers of men from the industrial sector to work in munitions factories or to go to China as civilian laborers to assist in "reconstruction." Factories hired replacements from agricultural areas, and in 1940 the Ministry of Agriculture estimated that the number of individuals engaged in farm labor had declined by 16 to 20 percent. In the northeastern part of the country some villages were depopulated to such a degree that not enough people remained to plant and harvest the crops. Similarly, migratory labor gangs that normally moved in time with the harvest from the south to the north of Japan largely disappeared, as the workers found jobs in factories. In an effort to maintain agricultural production, the Ministry of Agriculture and Forestry proposed a number of reforms: using students and schoolchildren to provide seasonal labor, employing migratory gangs of laborers, setting up village day-care centers to care for children so that women could provide additional labor, and doing tasks on a communal basis. There was some attempt to overcome labor shortages through mechanization, but restrictions on fuel limited this option, and in any case the topography and cultivation patterns of the countryside were poorly suited for existing machinery.[28]

Japanese military administrations in Southeast Asia placed a strong emphasis on food production. Although Southeast Asia was the major rice-exporting region in the world before the war, production was unevenly distributed, and substantial numbers of people lived in food-deficit areas. Lower Burma, the central plains of Thailand, and Cochin China produced rice on a large scale for export, and other places (such as the Malay state of Kedah, Nueva Ecija and Tarlac on Luzon, Bali, and Lombok) supplied rice to nearby deficit areas. Indian and Javanese workers in the plantation zones along the west cost of Malaya and in Sumatra's East Coast Residency consumed rice imported from Burma almost exclusively; and during the 1930s well over half the rice consumed in both territories was imported. Japan did not have the capacity to transport large quantities of rice, and strongly encouraged local production of food to meet local food needs and to supply Japanese garrison forces, pressing farmers to increase their output and urging people who had lost their jobs to begin planting vegetables. The Japanese also needed large quantities of certain nonfood crops that had industrial uses, and in some places forced farmers to plant oil- or fiber-producing plants on land normally used for food.[29]

In the latter stages of the war, many urban residents were encouraged to move to the country where they could contribute to food production. In Malaya the administration created more than thirty agricultural settlements for residents of Singapore and other cities in the peninsula, while authorities in Java made tentative efforts to relocate people from central Java to the

Photograph 1.2. Women assisting men working on a coal face in a mine in Japan. (Photograph courtesy of the *Mainichi Shimbun.*)

Lampongs in southern Sumatra, to develop agricultural settlements and grow food for Java.[30] At the same time, however, there were countervailing pressures to draw labor out of agriculture and into war production. For example, an English-language radio broadcast from Tokyo indicated that in Indonesia "most of the native islands were engaged in farming" before the war and the residents "were content with a low level of living," but the "Sunda natives" had shown a desire to improve their standard of living and were working in "vital war industries."[31]

Women in the Labor Force

In 1930 women constituted 36 percent of Japan's workforce, a figure that increased to 42 percent by 1944.[32] The 1930 figures show that women made up 46 percent of the agricultural workforce but just 28 percent of the labor force in the nonagricultural sector.[33] Factory girls (*joko*) had a poor reputation, and many women were reluctant to work in factories, but the situation would change during the war because soldiers on active duty received low wages, and their wives needed paid employment to support themselves and their children. Accordingly, women entered the industrial workforce in growing numbers.

In 1942 the Japanese government repealed laws that had prevented employment of women in mines, although the new regulations allowed them to work only on levels near the surface and only on tasks that did not involve excessively hard labor. In 1943 women became liable to labor conscription,

Photograph 1.3. Women doing track repair work in wartime Japan. (Photograph courtesy of the *Mainichi Shimbun*.)

but the government moved circumspectly on this highly sensitive issue. Prime Minister Tojo stated in February 1943 that there would be "positively no conscription of women for industrial work at the present time," and he reiterated the point a year later, in February 1944, when he said that women were so important to the nation that he would not allow them to be subjected to a program of labor service.[34] The government relied on persuasion and assistance to draw women into the workforce, although an intelligence analyst wrote that Japan's "voluntary inducement . . . would be called compulsory labor in another country." Mobilization took place through a Women's Labor

Service Corps that arranged for women to work in factories or in agriculture for short periods of time, normally at locations near their homes.[35]

In September 1943 the Japanese cabinet decided to control or ban the hiring of men between the ages of fourteen and forty to fill certain jobs that could be handled by women. The jobs concerned included the following:

> all office help, cashiers, messengers, office boys, receptionists, store salesmen, peddlers, traveling salesmen and canvassers, bill collectors, telephone operators, ticket collectors, certain classes of conductors, certain crossing guards, elevator operators, clerks and barkers, waiters, cooks, barbers, hairdressers and beauty operators, baggage clerks, ushers and shoe and clog checkers.[36]

Implementation of this ruling took place early in 1944. The women expected to take over these jobs were recent school graduates, unmarried girls over age fourteen, students, and women wanting to change jobs "in conformity with the industrial adjustment."[37] Also in September 1943, the government lifted restrictions that had prevented women from performing light tasks in munitions factories and announced that recent female high school graduates would be hired in solid groups to fill jobs vacated by men for periods of one or two years.[38]

The Women's Labor Service Corps failed to meet the needs of the military production program, and the labor mobilization plan for 1944 emphasized the need to increase the number of female workers.[39] In March a new Women's Volunteer Labor Corps, operating with police support, began recruiting unmarried women to work in industrial facilities, especially aircraft manufacturing plants. The corps operated through local officials, schools, and various women's organizations. Women were organized into groups of between twenty and fifty individuals for assignment to factories where they were to remain for one year. In August 1944 a Women's Labor Ordinance allowed the government to issue conscription orders to women listed on various registers, although this law appears to have done no more than codify existing arrangements. The law provided for prison terms or fines for women who failed to respond when ordered to work, but the government in the end did not carry out compulsory drafts of female workers. However, in October 1944 working women were frozen in the jobs that they currently held.[40]

In Southeast Asia the Japanese military administrations disregarded women in the early stages of the occupation but later paid more attention to female labor. In 1944 Malayan newspapers highlighted the contributions of women to the workforce, and at the end of the year the Malayan administration began enforcing a previously introduced Change of Trade ordinance similar to the one used in Japan. As in Japan, the government emphasized that women were being encouraged but not compelled to work.[41] Similarly the Women's Association in Makassar, in the Celebes, encouraged labor service among women, while in the Philippines the Women's Bureau of the Kalibapi (*Kapisanan sa Paglilingkod sa Bagong Pilipinas,* the Association for Service for the New Philippines) promoted "the orientation of Filipino women so that they may play a more important role in the establishment of the new order."[42]

Mobilization of Students and Young People

In 1938 Japanese students performed compulsory labor service for five days during the summer vacation. By 1941 the requirement had been increased to thirty school days in addition to all holidays and after-school periods, and by 1944 the requirement had grown to four months a year. Young people not mobilized through educational institutions were brought into the workforce through a Japanese Youth Corps, established in 1941 and placed under the Imperial Rule Assistance Association in 1943.

In March 1944 the cabinet approved a requirement that all students provide labor service for an entire year, working in factories and receiving a limited amount of instruction in academic subjects on the factory premises. In the same year the Ministry of Education shut down courses of study deemed nonessential and told schools to limit their enrollments to one-third of the number of students registered in 1943. The duration of courses of study for girls was reduced and summer and winter vacations suspended. During 1944 some 2 million students were mobilized, and by February 1945 the figure had reached 3 million.[43] Students from industrial schools worked in factories, and those studying other subjects assisted with tasks such as land reclamation and farming.

In Java the recruitment of student labor began in earnest in 1944. Student mobilization plans produced by the Education Division of the Japanese military administration in Java took effect on June 1, and by the end of the year the Japanese were reporting that around 1 million students from Jakarta were digging bomb shelters and doing other tasks. Plans called for the mobilization of "several million students" across Java to work on "grass cutting, cultivation, land improvement, increased food production, machinery cleaning, blacksmithing, making of wooden boxes, care of military clothing, drafting, construction of defense installations, shipbuilding, etc."[44] Similar programs operated in Bali, Borneo, the Celebes, and the Philippines, in most cases starting around the same time.[45]

Relocation of Workers

During the war, Japan shifted substantial numbers of workers from labor-surplus areas to places where labor was in short supply. The principal sources of labor included Korea, North China, and Java, but there was also significant movement of workers out of Taiwan, Malaya, and islands in the eastern part of the Indonesian archipelago.

At the start of the war about 1.4 million Koreans lived in Japan, slightly more than half of them working in the construction industry, in mining or manufacturing, or as unskilled laborers. During the war years, some 660,000 more Koreans came to Japan on labor contracts, many to work as coal miners. In December 1941 there were 41,566 Koreans working as coal miners in Japan (12 percent of the mining workforce), and 133,751 in March 1945 (33 percent). The Japanese wanted to bring more Korean workers to Japan, but the colonial governor-general of Korea objected that the movement of workers to Japan was interfering with war production in Korea.[46]

North China and Java were particularly rich sources of cheap labor. Workers from North China were sent both to Japan and in large numbers to Manchukuo, Mongolia, and Tibet, to carry out construction projects or to work in agriculture. Some of the workers recruited in Java, known as *rōmusha*, were sent to Malaya, Cambodia, Vietnam, northern Borneo, and the Andaman Islands, but still more were deployed at work sites within the archipelago. In 1951 the Indonesian government estimated that 4.1 million Indonesians had been forced to work for the Japanese,[47] but the numbers involved are a matter of conjecture. Although the Japanese registered workers at their point of departure, work-site records for Asian labor were poor, and in any case the Japanese destroyed these materials at the end of the war. One of the largest projects in Southeast Asia was construction of a railway line between Thailand and Burma, and estimates of the number of Asian laborers involved range from 180,000 to 270,000. There were, however, many other projects that employed Asian labor—railways built in southern Thailand, in southwestern Sulawesi, across Sumatra, and in South Banten,[48] along with airfields and defensive works, shipyards, agricultural colonies, and ports. In August 1943 representatives from the Japanese military services and the labor department met in Singapore to discuss issues relating to labor recruitment and decided to increase the export of Javanese workers to Malaya, Borneo, and Sumatra.[49]

Conclusion

Shortages of labor plagued Japan throughout the war, and toward the end of the conflict the labor situation became very serious. On balance the Japanese handled the situation very inefficiently. In Japan proper the machinery for labor mobilization was comprehensive and effective, but induction of skilled workers into the military seriously disrupted production of military and consumer goods. In occupied territories, the mechanisms for labor recruitment were much less effective. While the Japanese population displayed a loyalty to the emperor and responded to appeals to patriotism, people in the occupied territories could not be expected to make extraordinary sacrifices for Japan. The Japanese promoted the idea of a Greater East Asia built on a shared Asian identity and called for short-term sacrifices in return for long-term mutual benefits, or "coprosperity." However, Japanese military administrations seem to have had little confidence in the efficacy of such appeals and used a combination of generous wages and benefits and draconian recruitment measures to secure the labor that was needed. The process caused severe disruption and cost many hundreds of thousands of lives.

Part II

Manchuria

2

Labor Policy and the Construction Industry in Manchukuo

Systems of Recruitment, Management, and Control

David Tucker

As the Japanese empire attacked a succession of foes in the 1930s and 1940s, it confronted the disparity between its own limited resources and the resources of its enemies. Strengthening the empire by securing areas of strategic resources was a major motivation for war, and one of the most important locations for Japanese planners was Manchuria, with its soybeans, coal, and iron ore. In 1931, the Guandong Army, which had the mission of defending Japan's colonial South Manchuria Railway (SMR) and Guandong Leasehold, moved to seize the rest of Manchuria. It then set up the puppet state of Manchukuo to control Manchuria and develop it as a base of strategic production. Labor resources were essential to these plans.

To develop Manchukuo, Japanese military and civil managers undertook a vast program to build factories and mines, roads, railways and harbors, communications infrastructure, towns, housing, and fortifications, all requiring enormous numbers of skilled and unskilled labor.

Unlike the areas Japan seized after 1937, Manchukuo was under Japanese rule for several years before the wider war began, and Japan could draw on well-established systems of colonial labor procurement and management. Yet the Japanese rulers of Manchuria were unable to manage these huge labor resources to bring their strategic project to fruition. Why did they fail in a place they thought vital, where they had control, time, resources, and organization?

Their first advantage was a large Chinese population, both in Manchuria and in nearby North China. Second was a long-established pattern of seasonal and long-term labor migration to Manchuria from Hebei and Shandong in North China. At the start of the twentieth century in Manchuria, Russian construction of the Chinese Eastern Railway (CER), Harbin, Dalny, and Port

Arthur both attracted North Chinese labor and created the transportation system that made increased migration possible. Japan took the railway between Port Arthur and Changchun as a prize of the Russo-Japanese War in 1905 and set up the SMR as a colonial corporation to develop the region. The third Japanese advantage was control and extension of this port and railway network, which made it possible for millions of North Chinese to go to Manchuria and provide the labor for Japanese regional development.

Fourth, along with transport facilities, organizational structures were in place to recruit, relocate, and manage large numbers of workers. Fifth, this was cheap labor, tolerant of low living standards. Because many workers were outsourced, labor costs could be kept low. There often was need to support only single male workers. Housing costs for construction workers were particularly low, as many of them lived in temporary shelters at construction sites and returned to North China in the winter. Sixth, the Japanese army had means to gather and transport forced labor made up of captured troops and conscripted farmers and urban dwellers.

In short, the Japanese military and Manchukuo regime had access to abundant and cheap supplies of labor and had robust mechanisms for labor recruitment and management, but they were unable to overcome problems of wartime labor supply, control, and management. Nevertheless, even as the military prepared to attack the United States and Britain in 1941, Japan's projects in Manchukuo suffered labor shortages. Labor, like material shortages and production difficulties, became one more unsolved problem that contributed to the defeat of 1945.

The labor problem actually was a collection of problems—recruitment, transport, management, skills, high turnover, competition from other firms and administrative organizations, rising costs, increasing labor demand, and worker resistance and flight. As difficulties mounted, the Japanese army and Manchukuo regime turned increasingly to a variety of coercive recruiting and management methods and to compulsory labor.[1] Coercion and compulsory labor did not completely supplant the older colonial labor methodology, nor did they produce a new, coherent, and functional system. Instead, these practices pulled increasingly marginal labor sources and harsh management regimes into a poorly integrated mix. Forced labor had to be assembled, transported, fed, housed, and clothed, and using forced labor did not eliminate the high expenses of recruitment, transport, and pay. The older colonial labor system had already pushed its recruiting and management costs down to what must have been minimal levels. High labor costs reflected not high wages but the increased expenses associated with finding and transporting workers and keeping them alive under wartime pressures, costs shared by forced labor regimes.

Manchurian Construction

This chapter examines the Manchukuo labor system and ongoing attempts to maintain access to adequate labor supplies and to develop a coherent labor policy in response to economic and ideological demands. I concentrate on construction labor because it was a major and representative part of the Manchurian economy and absorbed a large part of the domestic (Manchurian) and immigrant labor force. Ideologically and materially, construction was a vital part of the Manchukuo project, and it was not accidental that construction served as a central metaphor for Manchukuo's colonial rulers. The SMR, involved in almost every type of construction in Manchukuo, boasted in 1936: "Construction is the synonym of Manchuria today," and the regime took an active role in construction labor affairs. The construction industry was part of the development of Manchuria's labor procurement and management system from its inception during the Russian colonial occupation to the collapse of Manchukuo almost half a century later. Construction relied on, and helped to form, the typical Chinese worker in Manchuria, and it illustrates the problems Japanese managers and labor researchers had in conceptualizing and managing Chinese labor—which they referred to as "coolie" labor. "The coolie migrating from Shandong Province is the most welcome person for the construction community," noted a Japanese firm's 1936 yearbook. "To understand the coolie's essence and how to use him is the chief cause of a successful project."[2] Finally, the failure of the Japanese army, the Manchukuo regime, and the construction industry to solve labor problems shows their inability to create a Japanese Manchuria, separate from China.

The construction industry reflected the development of both the Manchurian economy and its Japanese colonial management. In the 1920s, agriculture accounted for about half, and the secondary sector well under a fifth, of GDP. In 1932, the new Manchukuo regime began a program of industrialization, and a building boom followed. The value of construction more than doubled from 1929 to 1941, and its share of GDP increased to 5.4 percent—more than a quarter of the secondary sector.[3] Construction employment grew accordingly, quadrupling from 34,430 in 1931 to 143,706 in 1932, then more than doubling again to 292,937 between 1932 and 1934. Restrictions on migration and economic disorder reduced this figure to 232,485 by 1937, but the expanded military and industrial projects covered by Manchukuo's First Five-Year Plan pushed construction employment to 487,000 in 1939. Of the 5.5 million nonagricultural workers in Manchukuo in 1940, about 500,000 were in construction.[4]

Like mining and transport, Manchukuo's construction industry demanded large numbers of cheap workers but faced a structural labor shortage. After decades of one of modern history's largest in-migrations, Manchuria remained much less populous than China proper, with more than twice as much cultivated land per capita. This available land attracted almost half a million people a year between 1891 and 1942, with a net gain of more than 8 million. Between 1890 and 1930 these immigrants opened to cultivation more than 5 million hectares of new land and fueled rapid development.

Manchuria's 1910 urban population of about 1.4 million was less than 10 percent of its total population. By 1940 the total population had almost tripled to about 45 million, and was 20 percent urban. Even with rapid population increase, labor within Manchuria was largely absorbed by agriculture, and growth in construction and industry required immigrant labor. The expanding network of railways and steamships allowed people to move quickly from North China to even remote areas of Manchuria, increasing potential working days and reducing nonremunerative and expensive travel time. Since many workers returned to North China, improved transport was essential to sustaining labor traffic.[5]

To construct the CER and the port of Dalny (renamed Dairen after Japanese occupation) at the beginning of the twentieth century, the Russians relied on cheap Chinese labor. This pattern continued after Japan acquired the Guandong Leasehold and the SMR in the Russo–Japanese War. The SMR sought to consolidate Japan's hold on Manchuria through rapid development of mines, factories, and towns. This process, which continued almost until the collapse of Japanese rule in 1945, combined capital-intensive investment and advanced technology with cheap Chinese labor and almost feudal labor management. Manchurian development was both extravagant and parsimonious. The SMR threw money into the dream of Manchurian development and justified Manchuria's seizure by the "blood and treasure" spent there, but the hands that threw so many yen and lives after this dream were close-fisted when paying the Chinese workers who built it.

The Coolie and the *Batou* System

The construction industry was one of the largest employers of this cheap labor, relying on methods to procure and use it that had matured long before Manchukuo's 1932 establishment. The importance of low-wage Chinese workers is reflected in such publications as the Manchurian Architectural Association's (*Manshū kenchiku gakkai*) 1940 builder's handbook *Manshū kenchiku gaisetsu* or *Manchurian Construction Survey (MKG)*, which had extensive explanations of Manchurian labor conditions and labor management. In the early years after the Russo-Japanese War, Japanese made up a substantial part of the construction workforce, although they earned double or more the wages of Chinese workers. Therefore employers replaced them once enough Chinese workers who met specialized skill requirements were available. The *Manchurian Construction Survey* saw the process of skill re-orientation and specialization, as a kind of technology transfer, in which, like the Japanese introduction of new materials like cement, steel and paint, Chinese work skills increased under Japanese "guidance." It said, for instance, that the profession of plasterer, or *ni jiang*, had not existed in China. Instead, plastering, along with bricklaying and roof-tiling had been part of the work of *wa jiang*. Therefore that Manchurian workers were *ni jiang* was "something learned from Japanese."[6]

The *Manchurian Construction Survey* saw the construction of barracks at the Anshan ironworks in 1919 as a significant marker in the development of construction labor because thousands of skilled Chinese workers were available in the SMR zone for the project. In 1908 there had been "absolutely no skilled workers available" at the SMR coal mines in nearby Fushun, one of the first major Japanese construction projects in Manchuria. It had been necessary to bring workers from Tianjin in North China, including one hundred carpenters, even though they were not considered adequately skilled. Many of them stayed on, adjusted to Japanese builders' requirements, and provided a core of skilled workers for the Anshan project.[7]

By the time of the Anshan construction, Japanese enterprises had become heavily dependent on Chinese labor and the *batou* system, an arrangement that integrated labor procurement, management, and care.[8] In the *batou* system, a Chinese intermediary—the *batou,* or coolie boss—recruited and delivered workers to employers. The *batou* generally received workers' wages from the employer, deducted a percentage, and then distributed them. Japanese firms at the Anshan project depended on a small number of *batou* who supplied and managed several thousand workers. In June 1918, the firms were unable to meet pay schedules, and in the dispute that followed, about three thousand coolies attacked the house of the largest *batou,* Cui Qinglin, who had supplied more than five thousand workers to the major regional construction firm Sakakiya gumi. Cui's guards killed eight workers and wounded seven others, and the Sakakiya gumi took Cui into the SMR zone for Japanese police protection. To settle the dispute in a way that protected Cui required days of negotiation by junior *batou* to persuade workers to return to work, along with the involvement of the Japanese Consul in Liaoyang and Consul-General in Shenyang, and the threat to use Japanese troops against the Chinese police who had surrounded the local Japanese police. Sakakiya gumi's head, Sakakiya Senjirō, said that Cui "absolutely could not be turned over" because a *batou* who could manage "over 5,000 men" was irreplaceable. The project could not be completed without him. Japanese construction had become dependent on Chinese labor and, with it, the *batou*.[9]

Because the Japanese colonial regime lacked political and legal authority outside the SMR zone and Guandong Leasehold, it depended on the cooperation of Chinese authorities, who were not always pliable, as Cui's case demonstrates. The Guandong Army's seizure of all of Manchuria and the establishment of Manchukuo launched a Chinese puppet regime (with Japanese officials in key administrative positions) firmly under Japanese control. But political control of Manchuria did not bring direct control of workers. Japanese enterprises continued to depend on indirect labor management through the *batou* system.

The basic unit of the *batou* system was a squad of about fifteen workers, even in the largest *batou* organizations that managed thousands of workers through hierarchies of sub-*batou*. Each squad was in the charge of a Number 2 *batou,* or master (*kogashira* in Japanese), and two or more squads formed a larger unit managed by a chief *batou* (also called a master). Once a *batou* organization had about two hundred workers, the fully articulated management hierarchy appeared. Squad bosses were now called Number 3 *batou,* or third masters. Between them and the chief *batou* was a layer of what were now called Number 2 *batou,* or second masters, each directing several Number 3 *batou* and their squads. A large organization had other functionaries as well, such as a *xiansheng* or *sensei* (who was clerk, accountant, and paymaster), cooks, and runners.

The system offered advantages to enterprises that employed workers and to the workers themselves, and both sides were willing to grant considerable authority and latitude to *batou*. *Batou* delivered workers as a group to enterprises for limited periods, offering the advantages of a temporary employment agency to an industry that undertook many seasonal and temporary projects. They also managed worker direction, care, communication, discipline, and firing, and were especially useful to those Japanese managers who spoke little Chinese.

The system offered security to the workers. As the *Manchurian Construction Survey* noted, workers without a *batou* might be forced into the casual labor market and become "lumpen." *Batou* often had strong recruiting relations, even family connections, with certain villages or districts in North China. To a North Chinese about to travel hundreds of miles with few possessions to an uncertain future in Manchuria, the *batou* could offer advance pay and a job, transport, the companionship of travel and work with acquaintances, medical care, and some protection against the arbitrary authority of foreign enterprises. Some also remitted money to workers' families in North China, settled debts, or provided cooked food (deducting costs from wages) and health care for workers who fell ill or were laid off. Japanese researchers saw this deep reach into workers' lives as the basis of the *batou*'s almost absolute power over them. *Batou* had many advantages over Japanese managers, who pointed to the *batou*'s understanding of psychology and Chinese custom to explain its importance. "A good *batou* is like money in the bank," concluded the *MKG*.[10]

Enterprises had other means of labor recruitment, including sending agents to recruiting areas, or turning to labor contractors, worker self-recruitment, and the casual labor market. But they saw advantages in letting "Chinese hire Chinese" and in having *batou* "take all responsibility." Similarly, the *batou*'s provision of food, temporary housing, and even recreation to workers relieved enterprises of those matters. Even pay schedules led managers to favor using *batou*. Wages were low enough that workers expected to be paid daily, a time-consuming task performed by the *batou*'s staff. Late pay was "absolutely something to avoid" (as the Anshan project demonstrated), even if a high-interest loan was required to meet a payday. *Batou* were cushions between enterprise and worker, saving firms time and expense.[11]

Japanese in the construction industry and SMR researchers found the *batou* system familiar—very like the *oyabun-kobun* or *oyakata* patronage system in Japanese industries such as construction and forestry. The *MKG* referred to *batou* as *oyakata,* emphasizing the *batou*'s parentlike role and the function of reciprocal obligation in the *batou* system. It explained that the Chinese family system was part of Chinese society's "fundamental structure" and therefore had to be understood. The *batou* system was a similarly "medieval, feudal phenomenon." Pragmatic contractors thought the institution realistic and necessary for management of Chinese labor, and defended it.[12]

In some SMR construction projects, firms organized and paid workers directly but still relied on *batou* to manage workers. In some circumstances the SMR also attempted to replace the *batou* system with direct hiring and pay, and to develop worker loyalty to the firm rather than the *batou*. Two examples were its subsidiaries, the Fushun coal mines and Dairen's Hekizanzo labor compound, which housed between eight and ten thousand cargo handlers, but neither Fushun nor Hekizanzo eliminated *batou* entirely. Workers were hired directly, but *batou* supervised them. Furthermore, Fushun had notoriously low worker loyalty, and the turnover rate exceeded 100 percent in some years. High turnover plagued enterprises throughout the Manchukuo period and grew more severe in the late 1930s. *Batou*-supplied workers gave enterprises more labor security than did directly hired workers. As Eda Kenji points out, direct management of labor was premised on labor abundance, and Manchuria's labor shortages intensified with the expansion of war in China in the late 1930s. *Batou* labor management consequently revived within SMR enterprises that had attempted direct management, although with modifications, while in the construction industry direct management had little impact.[13]

Understanding the Coolie

The *batou* system, as well as direct hiring and management, presented problems of understanding and evaluation for both labor and management. The SMR and builders carried out extensive research to try to understand Chinese workers, but while they often characterized Chinese as individualistic (at the same time they saw them as enmeshed in a feudal family system), Manchukuo's labor studies rarely presented Chinese workers as individuals. The typical worker was simply a coolie—part of a mass. SMR experts thought modern management required greater knowledge of workers. In an attempt to rationalize labor recruitment and management, the SMR commissioned Wada Toshio, director of the Daitō Psychology Institute of Hiroshima and Dairen, to produce standardized "simple aptitude tests for general Chinese employees," whom SMR managers considered likely to be "ignorant and dishonest." Wada's "scientific tests" drew from a variety of sources— experimental psychology, character analysis, anthropology, physiology, and phrenology—and relied heavily on physiognomy, or *kansō gaku*. Observers evaluated such features as the shape of the jaw or the distance from the eye to the ear to determine character and ability. Wada devised cards with characteristics to be checked off in order to improve and standardize evaluation efficiency, based on more than twenty such observations per individual.[14]

Wada's method was to note individual differences carefully but to link them explicitly with racial characteristics: "If we look at Chinese one by one, there are thousands of differences in the face and appearance," he wrote, "but, when we look at a group as a group, then we recognize the special characteristics of each group." Of the various Chinese populations, three were relevant to Wada: those from Shandong, those from Hebei, and those born in Manchuria. Each had distinct characteristics—although as "Manchurians" were descended from a "mixture of immigrant groups," Wada thought them harder to define. Shandong people generally were a "thick-skulled people of low culture and ability" with strong backs and powerful grips. He thought these and other characteristics—a large jaw, a cranial circumference of 55 centimeters, a facial length from 1.35 to 1.4 times the line of the lower jaw, prominent cheekbones, stupidity, big teeth, a bridge of the nose that indicated docility and submissiveness, barbarity—made them the "most suitable people for physical labor."[15]

People from Hebei were also "first-class physical workers" and could be even better than Shandong laborers. Of 155 Shandong and 70 Hebei coolies in one Wada survey, 68 percent of Shandong coolies and 76 percent of those from Hebei had noses that indicated good performance ability. Hebei people, Wada said, made good skilled workers because they were more advanced intellectually, with an "anthropologically superior" head shape and average cranial circumference up to 6 millimeters greater than Shandong people. However, Wada concluded that Shandong workers were easier to use. "Manchurians" were also suited for skilled labor, as they were quicker than Shandong people, and although not as quick as those from Hebei, they had a greater learning capacity.

Attitudes similar to these expressed by Wada and the SMR were not unusual in the construction community. The *MKG* characterized Shandong workers as good only for physical labor, but the "best in the world at this work." Hebei, at a higher cultural level, produced more carpenters and plasterers. Despite these attitudes, Shandong residents, who typically made up more than half of Chinese migrants to Manchukuo, were vital to construction (as the yearbook of the construction company *Manshū Shimizu gumi* noted) and to Japanese enterprise generally in Manchuria.[16]

To many Japanese concerned with Manchurian labor management, the coolie was the representative Chinese worker. They often used *kūrī* (coolie) interchangeably with *rōdōsha* (worker or laborer), even though they held *kūrī* to have a more specific meaning.[17] The 1934 SMR study *Manshū no kūrī* took pains to define coolies as a limited group—not all of the many "shabbily dressed" Manchurians were coolies. Rather, coolies were a social grouping of Chinese or Manchurian wage laborers who did outdoor physical jobs and had very difficult lives. (A self-employed rickshaw puller was not a coolie even though working outside.) Ethnicity was a central attribute. Japanese writers employed approximate Japanese synonyms for coolie (for example, *nimpu* or *dokō*) but reserved "coolie" for Chinese (including Manchus) and did not use the word for Japanese or Koreans in Manchuria (Korean laborers were "absolutely not" coolies.) They recognized that *kūrī* had negative connotations for Chinese workers. As *Manshū no kūrī* noted without apparent irony: "It is not appropriate to use this word to refer to the coolies settling in today's Manchuria where we are building up Manchukuo." Still, the word was in common use. *Manshū no kūrī* itself did not observe the distinction it made between coolies and other workers but listed more than fifteen kinds of coolies, including ironworkers, miners, and workers in the chemical and machine tool industries.[18]

The distinction between skilled and coolie labor was also blurred on the construction site. Construction relied heavily on animal and human power, often massed human labor, and older technology was much in evidence. Sawyers produced lumber on site, some workers nailed with hatchet heads, axes were still in use, and planes had not completely displaced broadaxes. Skilled construction workers might earn 75–100 percent more than laborers, have better clothing (even Western clothing for days off), possess greater self-confidence, and own their own tools. But the distinction was relative: a "15–20 yen set of carpenters' tools might seem great wealth compared to a coolie's life," but for craft workers, a set of tools was the "only considerable property" they owned, and it was not so considerable. A 1939 set of tools cost a carpenter about ten days' wages. The distinction between skilled worker and laborer often was not great.[19]

Both skilled workers and laborers were part of a large cheap labor pool and were often members of *batou* groups, far from their families. They generally lived in temporary huts on-site and sometimes had only one set of clothes. For Japanese builders, coolies and skilled workers shared qualities and attitudes, notably fatalistic indifference. For managers, coolies were strong and diligent, followed orders, accepted low pay, did not drink to excess, and, when supervised, worked from dawn to dusk. In high summer this was from about 4:00 AM to 9:30 PM—with breaks, thirteen to fourteen hours of physical labor. On the other hand, some writers saw coolies as thieves and gamblers, migratory and irresponsible, lacking in initiative or interest in improving skills, and at a low cultural level. Even their endurance (or lack of alternatives to endurance) troubled one Japanese manager, giving him a "mysterious feeling" that coolies were "not human."[20]

The coolie's life was not easy for some to contemplate, but Japanese builders felt they must grasp it to manage Chinese workers successfully. They saw workers who lived in shacks, were uninterested in bathing, were indifferent to basic sanitary precautions, and calmly brushed away the flies that blackened their food. They saw workers who labored tirelessly but took unpredictable holidays and refused to work in rain no matter how threatened. One response was to say it was necessary to understand their poverty to manage coolies. Another was disdain: "Ha ha; the coolies are eating dandelions." Some were discomfited at the contempt of other Japanese for Chinese poverty and the benefits it produced: "Many of them are shipped in SMR freight cars used for horses and cattle . . . is this a comprehensible life? When we hear that shipping coolies in cattle cars has a big effect on SMR profits, can't we imagine how many there are?" Some attributed workers' conditions and behavior to ethnic custom, necessitating understanding their racial nature: "If you want to employ Manchurians, until you really understand their racial characteristics, you must respect their customs and be careful to properly guide their racial feelings."[21]

These expressions of the desirability of sympathy and understanding are the more attractive aspects of what might be called "management by ethnicity" in the construction industry, and resemble the Manchukuo regime's own emphasis on *minzoku kyōwa*, or "racial harmony," and cooperation as a principle of the state. As the regime stated, it intended racial harmony as a countermeasure to the "overbearing attitude" of the Han Chinese that had been "one of the chief causes of the social unrest and disorder in Manchuria in the past." It argued that Chinese were not native to the region, but had "deemed themselves the absolute masters of Manchuria, and conducted themselves accordingly." It tried to dilute the prominence of the Han Chinese, who made up over 90 percent of the population in an interesting double move. On the one hand, it advanced the idea that the Han were just one of Manchukuo's five races (Manchu, Mongol, Japanese, Korean and Han), even though the populations of the other ethnic groups were very small in comparison to the Han, and it gave prominence to the other groups, especially the Manchus (in Manchukuo's name, for instance.) On the other hand, for statistical and other purposes, it often categorized the Manchus, Mongols, and Han as members of a single group, which it named Manchu or Manchurian. The *Manchurian Construction Survey* provides a good example of this circular logic. In the beginning of its section on labor, for instance, the *Manchurian Construction Survey* reported that Manchukuo's population was 1.9 percent Japanese, and 98 percent *Manshūjin* (this may be understood as either Manchurian or Manchu). It then noted that the great majority of *Manjin* (also Manchu or Manchurian) were Han Chinese, and there were "decidedly few Mongols or *Manshūjin* (aborigines)." There were real consequences to this division. As the *Survey* immediately noted, the Japanese had a "leading place" in Manchukuo's structure, and in the same way they held a "leading place in construction labor." Japanese continued to earn wages about twice those of Chinese, while the wages of Koreans in Manchuria, who were Japanese subjects, fell in between.[22]

Labor Control

Japanese firms dominated construction in Manchukuo. The major industry association was the Manchuria Construction Association (MCA), which was active in labor recruitment and negotiated industry interests with the SMR, army, and Manchukuo regime. By 1932, the MCA already had a key recruiting role and long-established links to North China. As the new regime began to develop labor policy, the MCA worked to maintain access to North Chinese labor and control recruitment costs. During the 1930s, it became integrated into the Manchukuo regime's labor control systems, where its ability to advance the interests of the industry was enhanced by its very active chief, Sakakiya Senjirō, head of the Sakakiya gumi construction company.[23]

The disorder that accompanied the establishment of Manchukuo discouraged migration of North Chinese workers, and North Chinese authorities who opposed the Japanese occupation of Manchuria also obstructed access to recruiting areas. The result was a sharp drop in immigration from North China, from over a million in 1929 to about 400,000 in 1932.[24] At the same time, the Guandong Army and Manchukuo regime sought to limit immigration from North China and increase labor immigration from Japan, considering many Chinese immigrants potentially hostile to the new regime, or subversives in disguise. They also believed that reliance on North Chinese labor would create vulnerability in an emergency and so planned to protect and develop domestic labor, even though it was less efficient than North Chinese, by limiting Chinese immigration. The domestic labor supply seemed adequate because a Manchurian agricultural depression had increased unemployment. Authorities also worried about the outflow of money that migrants carried back to North China and wanted to prevent the increased sinicization of Manchuria that Chinese immigration brought. "Aiming at the strengthening of the racial ties between Japan and Manchukuo," they encouraged Japanese and Korean migration and began to organize a Labor Control Committee (*Rōdō tōsei iinkai*).[25]

The MCA, however, wanted more, not fewer North Chinese workers, and control over wages and recruiting costs. In November 1932 Sakakiya met with Guandong Army Chief of Staff Koiso Kuniaki to discuss rapidly rising wages and an increasingly difficult labor situation. Koiso, who served as chair of the new Labor Control Committee, established in December, was receptive, and the makeup of the committee shows the importance of labor policy and its security implications for Japanese authorities. There were ten members, four from the Manchukuo government and the remainder from the Guandong Army staff, the Japanese embassy, the Korean and Guandong governments, and the SMR's research and planning bureau, the Economic Research Association, or *keizai chōsakai*.[26]

During 1933, the MCA opposed immigration limits, arguing that domestic supplies of skilled carpenters and plasterers were inadequate. At the first formal meeting on January 9, 1934, Sakakiya, the head of the MCA, criticized immigration limits for an hour, arguing that there were clearly not enough coolies in Manchukuo and that Shandong coolies received two-thirds the wages of indigenous (*dōchaku*) workers but were three times as efficient. At the second meeting, on March 12, firms continued to oppose immigration restrictions because of North Chinese labor's efficiency and wage advantage.[27]

The army, concerned about subversive immigrants, was unconvinced. As disorder eased and economic and construction activity increased, North Chinese immigration rose sharply, to 630,000 in 1933 and 695,000 in 1934. In 1934, the Manchukuo regime gradually strengthened immigration restrictions in cooperation with the Guandong Territory, which included Dairen, the major port of entry for North Chinese workers. In addition, it set up the

Photograph 2.1. Migrants waiting after landing at Dairen. (From *Manshū no Kūrī*, see note 8 for more information.)

Dadong Company in Tianjin to interview immigrants and to issue identity papers necessary for those approved to enter Manchukuo.[28]

In 1935, the Labor Control Committee decided that Manchukuo and the Guandong Territory (both represented on the committee) should coordinate legislation to strengthen controls. The Guandong Territory Foreign Worker Control Law of March 9, 1935, and the Manchukuo Foreign Worker Control Law of March 21 followed. The Dadong Company was reorganized in February 1935 as a limited-stock corporation with headquarters in Manchukuo's capital, Shinkyō, and branches in Dairen (Guandong Territory) and Tianjin (North China), so it now operated in all three relevant jurisdictions. Its function was to recruit Chinese workers to Manchukuo, provide them identity papers, and arrange transport.[29]

Several features of Manchukuo's labor problem took root in its early years. Authorities from competing and overlapping governmental and extragovernmental agencies within and outside Manchukuo (including the army, SMR, Guandong territorial government, Korean government-general, Japanese foreign ministry, and Manchukuo government) attempted to control migration, but with limited effect. Although labor control was centralized, it was incompletely consolidated, with actively competing bureaucracies. Labor policy was exhortative, arbitrary, legalistic, and highly bureaucratized. Pragmatic firms accepted labor control mechanisms but insisted on access to

North Chinese workers because domestic labor was insufficient and inefficient and attempts to recruit Korean labor were unsatisfactory. Although migration decreased due to disorder and limitations by both Manchukuo and its
Republic of China opponents, hundreds of thousands of Chinese still migrated to Manchuria each year.

Manchukuo's attempts to restrict Chinese immigration also served to increase opportunities for Japanese workers. Manchukuo was the focus of various immigration schemes designed to relieve Japanese social problems,
including plans for poor Japanese farmers to emigrate under a Millions for
Manchuria program.[30] In the mid-1930s the Japanese Home Ministry's Social Bureau coordinated efforts with the War, Navy and Colonization ministries, the Central Employment Bureau, the municipal and prefectural offices
of Tokyo, Osaka, and Fukuoka, and agencies in Manchukuo to promote migration of Japanese urban workers to Manchukuo. The Social Bureau argued
that Manchukuo's construction program required a large labor supply and
insisted that Japan and Manchukuo's existence and prosperity depended on
their unification and on controls over the economy and particularly the allocation of labor. Accordingly, Japanese employment in Manchukuo needed to
increase, although the Social Bureau anticipated that migrants would require
subsidization and bureaucratic negotiation to deal with climate, custom, language, and work conditions, as well as transport difficulties, training, pay,
and work relations.[31]

The Social Bureau overlooked a more basic difficulty—Japanese labor's
complete inability to compete with Chinese workers receiving low wages.
Their eagerness to integrate Japan and Manchuria blinded bureaucrats to the
reality that the region was already demographically Chinese. The true Millions for Manchuria phenomenon was North Chinese migration rather than
the comparative trickle of people from Japan, and Manchukuo's accelerated
development program would attract Chinese migrants and increasingly
sinicize rather than Japanize Manchuria. Unable to comprehend the scale of
Manchuria's dependence on Chinese labor, the Social Bureau pursued a fan-
tasy of the region as an empty space awaiting Japanese settlement.

To promote and coordinate Japanese employment in Manchukuo, the Social Bureau planned to develop organizations based on and bearing the name
of the original Japanese–Manchuria Labor Association, *Nichi-Man rōmu
kyōkai*. This organization, founded in Osaka in 1934, reached an agreement
with the MCA in June of that year to send Osaka construction workers to
Manchuria, including more than 150 carpenters, plasterers, and other craft
workers, and, improbably, more than 100 laborers, all meeting specified standards of age and skill. The *rōmu kyōkai* agreed to recruit workers, make
travel arrangements, and advance travel funds, and it negotiated relatively

favorable wages and work conditions. The process was expensive, and the results modest. By summer of 1935, only 130 Osaka carpenters had been placed in Manchuria.[32]

Nevertheless, the Social Bureau wanted to continue subsidized worker migration to Manchuria to help ease unemployment in Japan. Local *rōmu kyōkai* were to select and train workers, advance travel funds, provide medical care and entertainment en route, find employment, and conduct research on work conditions and efficiency. In the summer of 1935, the Tokyo government sent representatives to Manchukuo for discussions with the MCA and with major builders, intending to place some of the large surplus of Tokyo-area carpenters and plasterers remaining after the collapse of the reconstruction boom that had followed the 1923 earthquake, but they found Manchurian construction firms unwilling to participate further in the scheme. While generous Manchukuo government contracts had allowed them to absorb a few high-cost Japanese workers in the past, there were now fewer contracts, and competitive sealed bidding had replaced a contract allocation system, leaving little surplus to maintain Japanese workers on a year-round payroll. Chinese workers could be hired seasonally and easily dismissed. Moreover, the pay discrepancy between Japanese and Chinese was so large that one builder claimed Japanese workers hired Chinese substitutes and pocketed the difference. The builders were blunt in saying that any Japanese advantage in skill or efficiency could not overcome this wage disparity.[33] This expensive program was not capable of supplying enough workers to builders, nor could it reduce Chinese immigration. In 1934, as the Japanese government struggled to send 130 subsidized carpenters to Manchukuo, almost 700,000 North Chinese migrated there.

In the mid-1930s immigration controls and the Nationalist Chinese government's policies discouraging emigration to Manchukuo did impede Chinese immigration, which dropped from 695,000 in 1934 to 491,000 in 1935; 399,000 in 1936; and 362,000 in 1937. The Dadong Company claimed to have screened and issued identity papers for almost all immigrants, and the Guandong Army seems to have been able to override any opposition to its labor immigration policy. However, the policy had to be followed not only by government but also by recruiters and firms. The construction industry occupied a critical place in Manchukuo's labor structure and actively pursued continuing access to sufficient Chinese workers and the lowest possible wages. Because of its size and organization, and the assertive behavior of its president, Sakakiya, the MCA remained involved in discussions of labor policy. At the January 13, 1936, meeting of the Labor Control Committee at Guandong Army Headquarters, committee chair and army Chief of Staff Nishio Toshizō reviewed the 1935 immigration quota of 450,000 workers (including 120,000 for construction) and announced a 1936 plan of 500,000. Rather than directly challenge this, Sakakiya emphasized that the construction industry had promoted labor stability with wage unification while other industries had attempted to lure workers from difficult work conditions, such as construction, by offering higher wages.[34]

In 1936 contradictions in the policy of restricted immigration emerged more sharply. The immigration figure for the year (399,000) fell short of the quota by more than 100,000. The 1937 figure of 362,000 can be attributed to the outbreak of war in North China, with most of the decline involving reduced migration from northern Shandong. Even as the supply fell, the demand for labor grew. In June 1936, the Japanese army general staff began to plan for rapid expansion of Manchukuo's economy to help achieve Japanese military self-sufficiency. By October, the Guandong Army, Manchukuo government, and SMR were preparing a five-year plan for industrial development. Published in June 1937, the plan projected large Manchukuo production increases supported by a large expansion of infrastructure, something that would require additional labor. One estimate suggested that the supply of labor needed for 1938 was double the level for 1937, which would involve an increase in North Chinese labor migration. However, this requirement was contrary to an associated plan that called for the Japanese share of Manchukuo's population to increase from less than 2 percent to 10 percent by 1956.[35]

Greatly increased labor demands led Manchukuo authorities to abandon limits on immigration while continuing labor controls, and to increase domestic and North Chinese labor supplies. There had already been attempts to introduce coercive recruitment methods, and the Guandong Army now took steps to formalize requisition of domestic labor and to establish general labor service. The May 13, 1937, Military Supplies Requisition Law established legal military authority for both the Japanese and Manchukuo armies to expropriate and use materials, land, and facilities, and to conscript labor. This broad authority was not limited to warfare, but also covered "bandit suppression," guarding, and "other defensive measures."[36]

The National Mobilization Law of February 26, 1938, allowed the Manchukuo government to conscript its subjects for labor, to extend its authority over labor supply enterprises, and to register technical experts and laborers.[37] The Defense Law of March 10, 1938, and two April 20, 1939, imperial ordinances issued gave military courts great authority over civil offenses and established military supervisory authority over factories supplying military goods. They also set up defense commissions with extensive powers over Manchukuo subjects, to be exercised by the Japanese army. On the same date, the committee studying universal national service issued a report advocating compulsory military service, and for males not serving in the army, one month's public service annually for three years, followed by entry into a voluntary service corps.[38]

The regime also began to reorganize the administration of labor recruitment. On August 23, 1937, representatives of the army, Manchukuo, SMR, MCA, and special companies met to plan the establishment of the Manshū rōkō kyōkai, or Manchuria Labor Association (MLA). The organization was to coordinate labor recruitment and administration, have authority over labor recruitment and transport, regulate labor supply and demand, and unify wages. Sakakiya strongly supported its establishment, pointing to annual 20–30 percent wage increases that had raised wages to twice the pre-Manchukuo level. The regime formally established the MLA on January 8, 1938, placing it under the Department of People's Welfare. The Manchukuo government, and companies and associations that used or supplied labor, provided financing. The MCA was the fourth largest supplier of capital, and Sakakiya became an MLA director.[39]

At first, the MLA focused on domestic labor, and the Dadong Company continued to supervise North Chinese labor migration. However, the MLA took part in efforts to increase labor supply by increasing immigration, moving Manchurian farm labor into mines and industry, and replacing lost male farm labor with female labor. It also tried to make recruiters and employers adhere to labor control agreements, gradually took control of recruiting, and administered regulations enacted on January 30, 1938, for fingerprinting workers. After June 1938, the MLA issued labor cards as part of the labor registration process, registering 570,000 workers in 1938 and about 700,000 in 1939.[40]

As the MLA was beginning operations in early 1938, Manchukuo authorities strengthened labor controls in coordination with the revision of the Five Year Plan. On February 8, the general staff of the Guandong Army asked for increased labor training and more specific planning of labor distribution. On May 7, the old Labor Control Committee was dissolved and a new labor committee, called *rōmu i-inkai,* was established as a subcommittee of the Manchukuo State Council Planning Committee, *Kokumu-in kikaku i-inkai.* The new labor committee produced an outline of labor control that provided the basis of the December 1, 1938, Labor Control Law, which together with the February 1938 General Mobilization Law, established the regime's principles of labor control. Problems of labor shortages, which were aggravated by dangerous wartime conditions in recruiting areas, and of wage inflation were to be addressed through control agreements and by expansion of the Manchuria Labor Association. The latter body would absorb the Dadong Company and open more than 150 branches and offices in Manchuria and

North China. Finally admitting that North Chinese labor was essential to Manchukuo's economy, the regime and army were now attempting to extend Manchukuo labor administration beyond its borders into North China.[41]

Despite Japanese army control over much of North China, labor administration remained poorly coordinated. On the one hand, the regime increased its role in labor recruitment. The clauses of the Labor Control Law governing recruitment were very similar to the Mobilization Law and blurred the distinction between voluntary recruitment and forced mobilization. On the other hand, the Labor Control Law left significant control over employment arrangements and working conditions in the hands of private companies. The primary instruments used to regulate wages were control agreements and agreements against labor competition.[42]

These changes—the reorganization of labor administration, extension of labor controls, and provision for forced recruitment—were responses to the deteriorating labor situation. Labor shortages were severely aggravated by the five-year plan, which required many more skilled workers than existed. Despite the plan's emphasis on capital plant and skilled manufacturing labor, much of the attempt to increase production depended on cheap unskilled labor, further increasing demand for immigrant workers. The problems faced by firms did not end with recruitment. Competition among employers for workers increased, and turnover rates became very high. Severe price and wage inflation accompanied the plan's large spending increases.[43]

Immigration from North China increased dramatically at the end of the 1930s but did not meet labor demand. From 573,000 in 1938, it almost doubled to 1,123,663 in 1939, and rose to 1,475,158 in 1940, before falling to 1,066,284 in 1941. Relatively higher incomes in Manchuria during the early twentieth century had attracted North Chinese workers.[44] Higher Manchurian wages in the late 1930s, however, did not attract as many workers as the regime required. Even as immigration nearly doubled in 1939, recruiters faced increasing difficulties in North China, illustrated by the responses of the MCA in late 1938 and 1939 to changes in labor supply, demand, and administration. By 1938, Sakakiya's complaints about increased recruiting costs and declining worker quality had become routine. He accepted the need for expanding labor recruitment within Manchukuo, even though construction *batou* and recruiters had weaker networks there, but the MCA was skeptical of plans to increase direct Dadong Company and MLA involvement in recruiting, something Sakakiya criticized as "academic" and "dangerous" in a November 1938 meeting with army, government, and Dadong Company officials. The MCA proposed a compromise to keep the Dadong Company out of direct recruiting: it would supervise the process, and the MCA would be more active in controlling recruitment. The government agreed in December 1938,

Photograph 2.2. Migrants entering Manchukuo at Shanhaikwan, where the Great Wall meets the sea. (From *Manshū no Kūrī*, see note 8 for more information.)

and the MCA began to prepare a recruitment schedule and plan for spring inspection of the recruiting grounds.[45]

At the end of 1938 a meeting of the Manchukuo government, Guandong Army, MCA, and SMR concluded that it was necessary to increase labor supply by more than 30 percent. In January 1939 the MCA negotiated "coolie" control, wage levels, and rail car allotments with the army, government, Dadong Company, and SMR, and fixed the recruiting schedule. The construction industry would recruit 25,000–30,000 in February, 80,000 in March, 70,000 in April, and 70,000 in May—to be divided among 140 firms. Since Manchukuo's recruitment goal for 1939 was 600,000 (as many as 300,000 unrecruited North Chinese were expected to account for the 900,000 needed) the construction industry would receive almost half of the recruited workers. Daily wages of 1.58 yen for Chinese workers and from 5.5 to 6 yen for Japanese were proposed. By January 14, 1939, builders were already negotiating recruitment allotments by submitting inflated requests that Sakakiya objected to as twice their actual needs. Finding construction workers had become difficult and complicated.[46]

North China Army staff told Sakakiya that they planned "subjugation" operations in Shandong in the last ten days of March, after which recruiting should be safe, but refused his request to begin recruiting operations in the middle of the month. On January 31, Sakakiya carried out an assessment of North China construction projects with the army, arranged SMR freight car allocation for worker transport, and consulted with military police and the North China Construction Association about projects and recruitment. After several days of consultations he concluded that dangers in recruiting areas made North China Army cooperation essential and asked General Doihara Kenji for recruiting aid.[47] Furthermore, Manchurian and North Chinese construction costs and wages were about equal. Although recruiters paid advances and expenses and transported workers to Manchuria, unless North Chinese wages were lowered, workers would return, as it was pointless to stay in Manchukuo if they could earn as much nearer home.[48]

By February 1939, early Tianjin recruiting reports indicated that the first controlled recruitment of North Chinese construction workers was going badly. Army cooperation was suspect. Flood repair work in North China provided good wages and absorbed many workers. Nationalists threatened workers who migrated to Manchuria, recruiting-area security was poor, and there was a shortage of boats and trains for transport. Construction recruiting was particularly vulnerable to this situation. Like miners, construction workers typically were recruited in groups that recruiters had to lead out of recruiting areas, and such parties were vulnerable to attack.[49]

At an eight-hour Shinkyō meeting on February 13, more than four hundred builders, *batou,* and recruiters, along with army, military police, and government authorities, discussed the MCA's controlled recruitment methods. For ninety minutes Sakakiya explained the regulations, violations of which could cause builders to be banned from recruiting. Each firm had a fixed total of new and unfinished contracts, and would be allowed to recruit workers at a ratio of five hundred workers per million yen in building contracts, and one thousand per million yen in labor-intensive civil engineering contracts. The following day a group of about 150 builders and recruiting contractors' representatives received more detailed instruction. Recruiters were to seek workers for their own companies but would be paid by the MCA from assessments it made on each firm based on an average recruiting fee and the firm's recruiting allotment. Firms that exceeded their allotment were to share workers with those recruiting in difficult areas. This highly bureaucratized system was intended to reduce competition and direct the limited labor supply to firms and projects given priority by the authorities.[50]

A conference of 324 builders and officials held on March 3 reviewed the recruiting situation and coolie problem, and other meetings followed. By April, well into the recruiting season, controlled recruitment's poor results were becoming evident. Many companies had obtained less than half their allotment of workers, and some less than a quarter. Transport delays stranded recruits in North Chinese staging areas where firms fed them at an expensive 0.35 yen per day. The North China Army was uncooperative, recruiting security was poor, and the demand for labor in North China remained high. By the end of April, recruiting-area reports indicated that goals for 1939 would not be met. The April 28 labor committee meeting found that less than half the planned number had been recruited, and construction projects were falling behind schedule. Sakakiya estimated North China recruiting costs at 40 to 55 yen per capita, up from about 15 yen in 1927 and 20 yen in 1934. In 1938 floods and fighting disrupted the recruiting areas around Yanshan and Changzhou in southeast Hebei, forcing recruiters into more distant Jining in southwest Shandong, where poor transport and greater distance increased recruiting costs. As for making up the shortfall with domestic labor, Sakakiya argued that Manchurians resisted poor living conditions tolerated by North Chinese recruits.[51]

As recruitment suffered, Manchukuo authorities continued attempts to unify labor immigration controls. At the end of June 1939, the Manchuria Labor Association absorbed the Dadong Company, expanded domestic operations, and opened a main North China office in Tianjin. This branch, the North China Labor Association, Hokushi rōkō kyōkai, was to receive a third of the Manchuria Labor Association's budget of 600,000 yen to recruit and supply labor. The scheme failed to inspire confidence among builders. In November in Beijing, Sakakiya met with representatives of two of the largest Manchurian builders, Shimizu and Ōmori, and they agreed that 1939 had been construction's worst year since the establishment of Manchukuo, despite an increase in projects under the Five Year Plan. Sakakiya saw no solution to the labor shortage but to force down North Chinese living costs to reduce North China wages, a task beyond the industry's power that would require the efforts of the Japanese army and authorities in North China.[52]

Manchukuo's construction industry faced a dilemma. Contractors wanted low labor costs, and authorities pressed them to contain wages and avoid wage competition. In late 1939, some Guandong Army officers even hoped to force down Manchurian project costs and wages, which Sakakiya pointed out would threaten the workers' very survival unless rising living costs were stabilized. Moreover, containing Manchurian wage increases decreased competitiveness with wages in North China, aggravating Manchukuo's labor shortage and increasing upward pressure on wage rates. Meanwhile, inflation grew worse in Manchukuo and North China. A wholesale price index for Shinkyō based on 100 in 1933 was 149.8 in 1938, and 249.7 in September 1941. Shinkyō's general cost-of-living index had increased even more rapidly—at 100 in 1936, it reached 261.77 by October 1941. The wholesale price of a pound of flour was 3.3 yen in 1934, more than twice a Shinkyō carpenter's daily wage of 1.38 yen and 4.7 times a Shinkyō laborer's 1935 average wage of 0.7 yen, and cost 9.38 yen in September 1941—more than seven times the 1941 laborer's wages as reported by Sakakiya. This situation, combined with high turnover and competition from other enterprises that lured away workers, made it difficult to hold down wages.[53]

Inflation in North China was even greater. The Manchukuo government reported that the Tianjin index, at 91.3 in 1934, reached 506.5 in September 1941. Despite North China's inflation, there were also disincentives for workers to go to Manchuria. In February 1941, Sakakiya reported that wages in Manchukuo were lower than in North China, while living expenses were more than twice as high. The shorter work year in, and travel time to, Manchukuo further reduced income. By November 1941, Manchukuo and North China wages had both increased and there was little difference between them. Even in the construction-recruiting area of Jinan in Shandong, with high wages because of high food costs, there was little difference in a year's earnings if a worker went to Manchukuo. Once lost time and other expenses were calculated, going to Manchukuo was less attractive. Recruiting thus grew more difficult and expensive and became a significant factor in labor unit costs. Sakakiya calculated that recruiting represented as much as a quarter of 1941 construction labor costs.[54]

Other observers cited additional obstacles to migration. Anti-Japanese resistance continued to threaten recruits. A shortage of boats and trains forced delays in Tianjin that averaged a week, a significant expense for recruiters and those workers who financed their own travel. Japanese authorities required additional payments from some migrants, including labor permit fees. Workers paid in Japanese-controlled currencies might lose money in exchanges. On June 24, 1940, Manchukuo strengthened currency controls and reduced to 50 yen the amount of money returnees to North China could carry, in addition to 50 yen they were allowed to send. Currency controls may have encouraged out-migration from Manchukuo, which more than doubled in 1940 to 965,102. In an SMR survey of 800 workers leaving Manchukuo from June 13–23, 1940, none mentioned currency limitations as a reason for leaving, but in an August 7–16 survey of 1,000 workers, currency controls were cited by 43.5 percent as the reason they left Manchukuo during the work season, presumably because they had already saved as much as they were allowed to carry back to China. Workers devised other ways of returning their earnings to China. Some bought goods to carry back. Some purchased certificates at stores in Manchukuo that could be converted in their North Chinese branches. In November Manchukuo raised the limits to 60 yen for unskilled workers and to 120 yen for skilled workers, and in May 1941 eliminated limits on money remitted to China.[55]

The North Chinese labor shortage and the unfavorable exchange situation with North China led Manchukuo authorities again to try to reduce their dependency on North Chinese labor. They tried to increase the supply of labor from other sources and to control labor demand through increased efficiency or by moving workers away from less vital activities, particularly construction, into priority production. Limitations on construction and rationing of construction materials, already in effect in Japan, were applied to Manchukuo under a May 22, 1940, Construction Control Law, *Doboku kenchiku tōsei hō*, and the Manchuria Construction Association Law, *Manshū doboku kenchiku gyōkai rei*. On May 23, the MCA was re-formed and moved to Shinkyō, marked by a ceremony attended by the Manchukuo premier and addressed by a representative of the Guandong Army commander on "the true significance of continental construction." The general purpose of the reorganization, according to both Sakakiya and the articles of incorporation, was to control construction companies.[56]

The reformed MCA was to act as intermediary in obtaining or distributing financing, contracts, materials and equipment, and food for workers, and would also control worker recruiting and transport, balance labor supply and demand, provide training, and unify construction expenses, material costs, wages, and the price of foodstuffs. It was to encourage migrant workers to settle in Manchukuo (reducing currency outflows), to promote better working conditions, and to direct surplus and winter-idled construction labor to coal mining firms.[57]

Manchukuo's labor situation grew worse as competition for workers in North China continued and competition for workers increased among firms. Five Year Plan production goals required more labor and higher productivity, but productivity actually decreased, in part because of bad, even draconian, working conditions, especially on military construction sites in the northern frontier areas. Labor policy, which aimed to "achieve perfect labor control," moved in different directions to eliminate "the rampancy of undesirable workers," even as expanded (and more costly) recruitment was netting growing numbers of less desirable workers. The Manchuria Labor Association attempted to secure an "unprecedented supply of workers" with an announcement that it wanted to "rectify the conception of coolies," improve their treatment, and prevent labor mobility with protective regulations that would urge employers "to treat their employees better." At the same time, however, the regime was increasing the use of coerced labor.[58]

In November 1940, the Manchukuo government announced *Doboku kenchiku rōdōsha hogo kisoku*, or Regulations for the Protection of Construction Workers, along with regulations to "extend paternal care" to workers, which were to apply to construction, mining, and other industries. The

Photograph 2.3. Construction-worker housing in Jehol Province in southwestern Manchukuo. One type, probably illustrated by the structure in the foreground, was an A-frame built of unsawn timber or branches and covered with rush matting, with drainage trenches at the bottom edges. Inside, an earth-floored walkway ran down the middle, separating low platforms for resting. These could be as simple as mat-covered branches stuck into the wall, and supported by stakes. (See Matsu'ura, p. 1210.) (From *Manshū no Kūrī*, see note 8 for more information.)

Manchukuo government and MCA discussed various draft regulations intended to borrow the best features of German and Japanese labor law. Sakakiya, wanting more practical laws, strongly objected to these efforts as "academic." His objections indicate the gap between the aims of regulations and actual conditions, as shown by the regulations themselves, which state that there should be an "assured supply of daily necessaries such as food," and "lodgings are to be designed so as to be adapted to the climate." The generous space, lighting, ventilation, and sanitary standards prescribed for worker housing bore little resemblance to the huts described by Matsu'ura and others. Furthermore, temporary construction projects between April 1 and September 30—the main construction season—were exempted. Japanese officials in "direct contact" with workers were to receive instruction in the Chinese language, while workers would learn Japanese "for perfect understanding between them." How those who worked from dawn to dusk would find time for language study was left unexplained.[59]

Workers who deserted or registered improperly were to be punished, and wage standards were imposed to prevent "abnormally high wages" which were "harmful to workers themselves." New regulations introduced on July 1, 1940, fixed standard wages for a twelve-hour workday at Shinkyō at 1.0 yen, supposedly four to six times minimal food costs. The standard varied from 0.75 yen in Rehe to a high of 1.30 yen and was adjusted upward for certain categories of workers. Excavation workers were allowed 120 percent, carpenters and bricklayers 185 percent, and sawyers and roofers 195 percent of the standard. These variations were intended to compensate for local living cost differences, but according to the MCA, which asked for revisions to the scheme, they simply caused workers to "move on to the higher paid places."[60]

Labor Mobilization

As well as trying to move labor to essential projects and decrease worker turnover, authorities looked for alternative supplies as they confronted the reality that voluntary recruitment increasingly failed to provide enough workers. Recruiting remained poor in North China. In February 1940 the MCA, hoping to recruit 300,000 domestic and 300,000 North Chinese workers, met with the MLA seeking to obtain a small part of these—10,000—from the Guandong Territory. The Guandong Labor Recruiting Committee, *Kantōshū rōryoku boshū i-inkai*, answered that it could not help, as the labor supplies for the Guandong Territory itself were not adequate. Authorities also hoped to increase Korean immigration, despite labor shortages there.[61]

The regime then turned to coercive and controlled recruitment to increase domestic labor supplies, and to a variety of forms of mobilized and coerced labor. These included the labor service corps described below, students from elementary school through university, forced labor from within Manchukuo (prisoners, prisoners of war, vagrants, and the floating urban population), and forced labor imported from North China. The regime intended labor mobilization to pull all available young males into the workforce and to mobilize other groups directly and indirectly. Capturing "surplus agricultural labor" was a major goal, in the hope that women would replace mobilized male farm workers.[62]

Manchukuo's compulsory labor service was a product of the April 1940 National Army Law, *Kokuhei hō*, and related laws that provided for a national registration system, physical examinations to establish fitness, and conscription as part of universal service. The initial plan was for conscription of 10 percent of the fit. The Guandong Army's 1941 expansion of the northern frontier area fortifications required an increased labor supply, and

Photograph 2.4. A migrant worker accompanied by family. (From *Manshū no Kūrī,* see note 8 for more information.)

the government broadened mobilization by organizing a national labor service system in which "all subjects were workers." The new labor system, decided upon in autumn 1941, required all male subjects to undergo the army physical examination at age nineteen. Those recorded as fit who did not serve in the army were to volunteer for twelve months in the national labor corps, *rōdō hōshitai,* between the ages of twenty and twenty-three and work in military construction, essential industries, or local production. There were also proposals for technical and spiritual training and proposals to increase production through the "spirit of racial harmony" or the spirit of the "enterprise as a family."[63]

The same fall, the regime increased its participation in labor mobilization by introducing "controlled recruitment" (*kokumin kairō*). The Manchukuo cabinet adopted an Outline of the Establishment of the New Labor System (*Rōmu shintaisei kakuritsu yōkō*) in September. On October 2, a Manchukuo imperial edict dissolved the MLA and established the *rōmu kōkokukai,* intended to serve as an employment agency as well as be a movement to instill consciousness of national service. In February 1942, the Manchukuo Welfare Department promulgated emergency regulations that gave it legal authority to draft subjects into labor service. On April 1, 1942, the Manchukuo government issued a directive requesting a doubling of labor power, increased productivity, scientific wage control, and abolition of wage competition, with the minimum cost of living taken as the basis for wage levels. All these were long-standing policies. The problems they addressed—shortages of both general and skilled labor, inefficiency and low productivity, labor and project cost inflation, and keeping wages as close as possible to survival level—had been central concerns during most of the existence of Manchukuo. It was not clear how mass mobilization would solve them.[64]

Mass labor mobilization was implemented inefficiently and slowly as local officials assessed labor supplies and needs then matched them to central government directives, but by 1944 the government claimed to have mobilized 2.56 million out of a planned 3 million workers. To accomplish this, officials turned to marginal labor sources, assigning older people as well as children to construction projects. Mass labor mobilization could generate numbers, but did not produce a skilled, motivated workforce. Complaints of low productivity continued, and in 1944 the problem of high labor turnover remained unresolved. Mobilization threw many workers into difficult conditions, such as those associated with military projects in the very cold northern regions. High rates of accidents, desertion, sickness, and death indicate that mobilized labor experienced even worse conditions than recruited construction workers.[65]

Mass labor mobilization within Manchukuo was not sufficient to supply the needs of construction companies, who continued to rely on high-quality North Chinese labor. Even as Manchukuo elaborated its system of national mobilization, Sakakiya noted on March 3, 1941, that the labor problem remained "the focal point for the construction world." A construction recruiters' conference in Tianjin at the end of February concluded that they would recruit only half of the 270,000 desired by the Japanese. By early April 1941 Sakakiya further reduced that figure to 90,000. He met an army vice chief of staff and other officers in Beijing on April 4 and 5, and requested their help in recruiting 150,000 more workers. Sakakiya proposed army operations to "subjugate" recruiting areas in Changzhou, Yanshan, Jinan, and Qingdao, and the officers agreed to begin operations in about ten days.[66]

North Chinese recruiting in 1941 was not good. Sakakiya concluded that solving labor problems required control of construction firms. Recruiting expenses continued to rise. The 16 million yen spent recruiting 103,000 construction workers in North China meant an average cost of 155 yen, although there were considerable variations. Some companies spent more than 200 yen per worker recruited, while Sakakiya's company reported about 50 yen each. These figures were well above those of the past and amounted to months of actual wages. The combination of insufficient transport and inflation made recruiting more time-consuming and more expensive. Food cost more, and

Photograph 2.5. Fourth class passengers entering Dairen harbor. (From *Manshū no Kūrī*, see note 8 for more information.)

more food was needed to sustain recruits waiting longer periods for trains and boats. Increased competition for recruits also meant larger advances. The MCA requested the Guandong Army and SMR to absorb half the cost increase, with the remainder divided among construction firms. After months of negotiation, the army and SMR agreed to contribute over a third, a total of 6 million yen.[67]

These trends continued. As recruiters widened their searches, recruit quality declined and productivity worsened, further increasing the pressure to find labor—reflected in early 1942 projections that construction activity would remain about the same while labor needs would increase—but North Chinese recruitment proved disappointing. In December 1943, Sakakiya asked officials to obtain 2,000 North Chinese coolies for a hydroelectric project, arguing that he had used Shandong and Yanshan workers for thirty-five years because their experience made them productive and they were able to educate and increase productivity of domestic workers. The following May, he was still complaining of the "complete failure" of North China recruiting.[68]

From the end of 1941, Manchukuo construction relied on three problematic major labor sources. The quality of North China labor, which had been the basis of the industry, declined as recruiters scoured the region for additional workers. The next choice, voluntarily recruited Manchukuo labor, was also inadequate, and as demand increased, the physical condition of recruits worsened. The least satisfactory source was state-delivered mobilized labor. Indeed, a December 1942 article by Yukawa Hiroshi on Manchukuo construction labor management advised that the image of the coolie as the perfect worker who existed on the coarsest food but was as strong as a horse was no longer applicable. More than half of the workforce, he claimed, was made up of children and elderly people incapable of hard work, although fortunately the number of opium addicts was limited. Most of the people delivered had been farmers, who were slow and lacked skills. Their performance was inefficient but significant in the aggregate, and so required careful management.[69]

"They must never be treated like animals" might seem obvious advice, but Yukawa found it useful to make the point, even as he indicated more subtle problems some managers overlooked. Farmers delivered by the state might get the same cheap food, clothing, and shelter as coolies, and lack their skills and efficiency, but they regarded coolie status as below a beggar's and did not want it, a concern that managers needed to treat carefully. He felt that public welfare institutions were desirable but impossible to introduce because Chinese custom and the Manchurian situation would not allow them. Temporary construction sites did not allow permanent facilities, and workers preferred huts and chose old Chinese rather than modern medical treatment.[70] Yukawa noted that the *batou* system persisted and should not be bypassed, that managers should avoid direct punishment, allow communication through *batou,* and maintain *batou* prestige to ensure harmony. Even within the system of mobilized labor, a *batou*-like system emerged as local leaders and their subordinates adopted *batou* roles.[71]

Labor mobilization could deliver supplies of forced labor for Manchukuo's large construction projects, such as the fortification of the northern frontier. One hydroelectric project, for instance, used about 15,000 workers a day. But forced labor did eliminate basic expenses and problems of labor management. Prison labor could be cheaper than recruited workers. The *MKG* had shown this in a comparison of labor costs of prisoners and ordinary construction workers based on research between 1931 and 1938, and found prison labor cheaper. But mobilized workers were not without costs. Workers had to be fed, housed, clothed, transported, and guarded, and there were administrative burdens and inefficiencies. Managers had to motivate mobilized workers and sometimes work to maintain their dignity, and the *batou* system persisted.[72]

Transport, food, and shelter added to the cost of paid labor as well. The colonial system of Chinese migrant labor that had long sustained the Japanese "construction" of Manchuria successfully transferred some costs of worker livelihood back to the North Chinese homes where many workers spent their winters. Individual workers living in temporary shelters were less expensive to maintain than those who had brought families with them. On the other hand, pay had to be high enough for workers to save something to take or send back to North China, or they would have no motivation to go to Manchuria. For many decades, builders had paid low wages to a skilled migrant workforce, and they attempted to maintain this arrangement even as the system of migrant labor disintegrated. As Sakakiya noted, he had long relied on the skills of workers from Shandong, who were as essential to his company in 1943 as they had been in 1918.[73]

By 1943, Japanese management of Manchuria was increasingly unable to sustain itself. Manchukuo was a conflicted program that aimed first at severing links between North China and Manchuria in order to bind Manchuria to Japan, and then at expanding Japanese rule into North China. Neither goal was feasible. Labor policy was shaped by the desire to shift Manchuria away from China, but the demographic reality was that Japanese development activity increased the sinicization of Manchuria. From the time of Manchukuo's founding until its collapse, its managers struggled with problems of labor supply, quality, and cost. Their solution was to create organizations to coordinate recruitment of labor and to balance competing interests and aspirations. While enterprises and industries competed for workers, bureaucratic controls denied builders unrestricted access to North Chinese labor. Businesses wanted to reduce wages but had to pay enough to enable migrant workers to remit money to North China. Manchukuo competed for labor with North China, the Guandong Territory, and Korea. In particular, attempts to use North China as a source of labor for Manchukuo conflicted with the goal of developing North China. The Japanese failed to resolve these contradictions, and in Manchukuo they operated a labor procurement system unable to support development activities, or even to sustain itself.

Conclusion: Manchukuo's Labor Regime and Its Contradictions

Japanese authorities and enterprises in Manchukuo faced intractable problems in their efforts to build a strategic power base for Japanese security and to establish a profitable, ongoing construction program. Manchuria and North China had enormous labor resources, but the workforce had to be developed and integrated into the Manchurian economy and fit into the programs of Japanese authorities. Wartime labor demands overwhelmed existing recruiting and management capabilities, and the use of forced labor did not provide a solution. This was especially evident in the construction industry, even though construction projects seemingly were among the most amenable to forced, massed labor.

A fundamental feature of the colonial labor regime, which had flexibly supported Japanese development and management of Manchuria, was the *batou* system, which transferred much of labor recruitment, development, and management to Chinese intermediaries. The "feudal" *batou* system conflicted with SMR and regime efforts to "rationalize" labor arrangements by establishing direct labor management and control, but even within SMR enterprises and in conditions of forced labor the use of *batou* persisted. The construction industry, which tended to rely on *batou* recruitment and management, also wanted tighter labor controls to improve recruitment, stabilize wages, and reduce labor turnover, but its primary goals were low-cost and easy recruitment of a skilled labor force that did not have to be retained at the end of the construction season. Moves to achieve stability could not prevent competition for labor among firms and between the construction industry and other industries. Fundamentally, the construction industry depended on the skilled and flexible migrant labor force that the *batou* system of recruitment and management provided. Wartime conditions and greatly increased labor demands enormously strained the recruiting grounds and the whole *batou* system for the construction industry.

In Manchukuo's early years, Japanese military and civilian authorities aimed to make Manchuria more Japanese by increasing its separation from China, promoting Japanese immigration, and restricting immigration from North China. But the construction industry depended on cheap, skilled, and compliant North Chinese labor, and attempts to control the construction industry and the labor force conflicted with the industry's desire for cheap labor and higher profits. When the Japanese army decided to press for a substantial increase in production under Manchukuo's 1937 Five-Year Plan, it abandoned efforts to restrict Chinese immigration and attempted to increase the flow of workers from North China, while tightening controls over migrant and domestic labor. This brought existing and new contradictions to the fore.

One strength of the colonial labor migration regime was that it met the needs of contractors for cheap, reliable labor while increasing North Chinese income. The *batou* system delivered large numbers of skilled, well-managed workers to builders for limited and flexible periods of time. Firms generally did not need to provide housing and other social facilities for workers' families, who remained in North China, but they did have to pay enough to make it worthwhile for workers to travel to Manchuria. The balance between cheap wages and the efforts of Chinese workers to transfer money to North China came under strain as war widened and as the regime attempted to limit worker remittances.

Photograph 2.6. Migrants heading north on foot. (From *Manshū no Kūrī*, see note 8 for more information.)

The Japanese occupation of Manchuria and creation of Manchukuo had already damaged labor migration by increasing nationalist and anti-Japanese feeling in North China. Japan's invasion of North China in 1937 increased anti-Japanese resistance and interference with labor recruitment. The harsh suppression of North China by the Japanese army hardened this resistance and impeded voluntary migration to Manchukuo. At the same time, the Japanese occupation of North China created its own labor needs that conflicted with those of Manchukuo and reduced cooperation between the Japanese army in North China and that in Manchukuo. North Chinese flood repair and military construction, as well as mining and civilian construction projects, absorbed labor and raised wages. Inflation accompanied the chaos of war in North China and increased uncertainty about the profitability of migration. Was it worth the dangers and difficulties of migration if a worker could earn comparable amounts nearer home?

Manchukuo's labor policies depended on a balance between nurturing Chinese labor migration and controlling and restricting it while reducing wages and remittances to minimal levels. The intensification of war and increasing economic difficulties after 1937 sharpened these contradictions. Brief attempts to restrict remittances were abandoned when migration fell. Labor turnover, raiding, and competition increased along with inflationary pressures on firms. The colonial labor migration system, which remained the basis of construction labor in Manchukuo, was incapable of meeting the large labor demands made by the Manchukuo and Japanese regimes in North China after 1937.

Japanese authorities resorted to various forms of forced labor, not because they had exhausted the bounty of labor that could easily be plucked in North China, but because of the limitations of the colonial labor system. North China was a vast reservoir of labor, but it proved excruciatingly difficult for Manchukuo to tap more than a small portion of it. Forced labor was not free, but expensive. Recruitment costs, expenses for transport and food, labor management, turnover, labor flight, resistance, and sabotage were new versions of costs incurred under the older system, but forced labor brought added problems of poor skills, low productivity, and inefficiencies.

Expanded warfare disrupted the stable colonial system of labor recruitment. This stability was, of course, predicated on the continued Japanese colonial development of Manchuria, and the inability of Japanese colonialism—which involved only limited Japanese direct colonial control of a small part of Manchuria—to accommodate itself to Chinese expansion, and resistance in Manchuria led the Guandong Army to seize all of Manchuria and attempt to control it through the Manchukuo regime. The colonial labor system was an important prop for that regime, but the Guandong Army and Manchukuo regime could not tolerate that system as it was and were unable to create out of it a system for delivery and management of labor equal to their ambitions.

Part III

North China

3

Northern Chinese Laborers and Manchukuo

Ju Zhifen

The Japanese System of Expropriating Labor in North China

The Japanese system of expropriating labor in North China went through two phases after the Marco Polo Bridge Incident (or China Incident) on July 7, 1937. The first was a period of recruitment of labor through deceit prior to the establishment of the North China Labor Association in July 1941. The second was a period of total domination and forced conscription, with the association acting as an administrative and executive organ of the Japanese.

In the November 1942 issue of *North China Labor Times,* Kawai Masahisa wrote: "The Japanese system of organizing labor in North China depends on the Military based in North China in association with the Asian Development Board at the center, and with various levels of Special Operations and their subsidiary 'Committees for the Administration of Labor Matters' at the regional level."[1] There are two major sources of information on the labor situation during this period, and both corroborate his statement. The first is a comprehensive study, intended for use by policy makers, of labor-related organizations in North China from the start of Japanese rule that was carried out by the Division of Labor Affairs of the North China Coordination Department (NCCD) of the Asian Developmeant Board. Established in September 1940, the NCCD was one of the policy-making organs involved in the Japanese system of expropriation,[2] and the report, entitled "A Summary of Questions Regarding North China Labor," contains data pertaining to Japanese activity prior to 1940 that is complete and generally accurate. The second source, which is reliable and comprehensive, is a 1943 report entitled "A Summary of the Post-Confrontation North China Economy and Matters Pertaining to the Mining Industry and Labor." This top secret report was prepared by the North China Institute of Research, a joint undertaking of the Office of Research within Japan's North China Development

Company and the Manchurian Railway's Institute of North China Economic Research, which provided political, economic, and cultural information and intelligence to the Japanese military based in North China.[3]

During the period July 7, 1937, to July 8, 1941, local demand for labor was not great in North China because Japanese rule over territories it had occupied was not yet well organized and the economy was recovering from the effects of the Sino–Japanese War. The war and large-scale flooding had caused large numbers of North China refugees and unemployed workers to flee to Manchuria and Meng Jiang.[4] The recruitment of additional laborers for Manchuria was handled mainly by the Great Eastern Company (Dadong Gongsi) under a commission issued by the Manchuria Labor Organization Committee, with the assistance of local recruitment offices set up by the Manchuria Labor Association that distributed identity passes and work permits and arranged transport. Initially, owing to the large numbers of workers being recruited, the Japanese commissioned private recruitment offices in North China to assist in the process, but the appearance of growing numbers of fraudulent private recruitment companies claiming to hold such commissions prompted the Japanese to take over recruitment activities beginning in June 1938 and establish their own recruitment associations in Beijing, Tianjin, Baoding (Hebei), and Kaifeng (Henan). Operating through the New People's Associations (Xinminhui) in these provinces and cities, the Great Eastern Company induced large numbers of workers to go to Manchuria.[5]

In July 1939 the Japanese established a Directing Committee for Labor at the Mongolian border that moved laborers from North China into Mongolia. Because North China was under military administration, the headquarters of the New People's Associations and the Mongolian Border Joint Committee signed an "Agreement regarding the assignment of North China Laborers at the Mongolian Border" stipulating that all such workers came under the administration of the New People's Association, which carried out personnel checks and issued work permits.[6] In Shandong, in October 1938, the North China military administration ordered the Jinan Land Forces' Special Operations Unit to establish the Shandong Company for Labor Matters, which became responsible for recruitment throughout the province and for the dispatch and transport of those recruited to Manchuria. Qingdao, administered jointly by the Japanese army and navy, had a substantial population of Japanese residents and a concentration of Japanese capital and enterprises that required a large supply of labor. It was also the main port for the transport of laborers from Shandong to Manchuria. To balance Qingdao's local labor requirements with the distribution of manpower to other locations, the army's Special Ground Troops and the navy's Special Operations Unit collaborated with various Japanese-operated secret societies in Qingdao and organized the Shandong Laborers' Welfare Office, which supplied labor to Qingdao and assisted in the recruitment and dispatch of workers to other places.[7]

In March 1939 the Japanese established the North China Communications Department in Beijing, a move that reflected the Japanese government's imperialist domination of the politics, economy, and culture of the occupied territories. However, the administration of the region was shared between the Japanese government's Asian Development Board and its North China military administration.[8]

The military headquarters in North China set up a fourth section in the planning division to oversee political and economic developments, including labor matters. Locally, the Special Operations section of the army in various parts of North China took charge of the approval of recruitment and dispatch of laborers. At this point, the Japanese Military Administration clearly dominated the recruitment of labor in North China, but there was a lack of coordination among Japanese agencies.[9]

In the second half of 1939, large numbers of workers were required simultaneously in Manchuria and at the Mongolian border, creating a clash of interest between the labor requirements of local enterprises and the military in North China. Various Japanese authorities demanded a unified system of allocation of labor, and to this end a North China Labor Association (NCLA) was created in September. Owing to the intervention of the Fourth Section of the North China Military and the NCCD, urgent negotiations took place for about half a year among the various coordinating units for the conscription of labor in Manchuria, Meng Jiang, and North China, which resulted in a unified system of conscription through the NCLA. The association insisted on having "Subsidiary of North China Temporary Government" and "Chinese Financial and Legal Corporation" as part of its nomenclature, but in fact was jointly administered by the Japanese military in North China and the NCCD. The main beneficiaries were the Japanese. The temporary government had to finance this body, but its committee leader, Wang Kemin, objected to this arrangement, halting Japanese plans to launch the NCLA in 1940.

In September 1940 the NCCD set up an Administrative Office for Labor Affairs and an internal Central Governing Committee for Labor Affairs to handle the daily business of recruitment. With the establishment of the Wang Jingwei puppet government in March 1940 and the consequent abolition of the North China temporary government and establishment of the North China Administrative Committee, Wang Kemin resigned and the traitor Wan Yitang became committee chairperson. At this point the Japanese master plan was adopted in its entirety, and the NCLA was finally established on July 8, 1941.[10]

Hitherto, the Japanese system of expropriating labor had been neither methodical nor thorough. After the establishment of the NCLA, the system

64   CHAPTER 3

Figure 3.1 **Japanese System of Enforced Conscription in North China before July 1941**

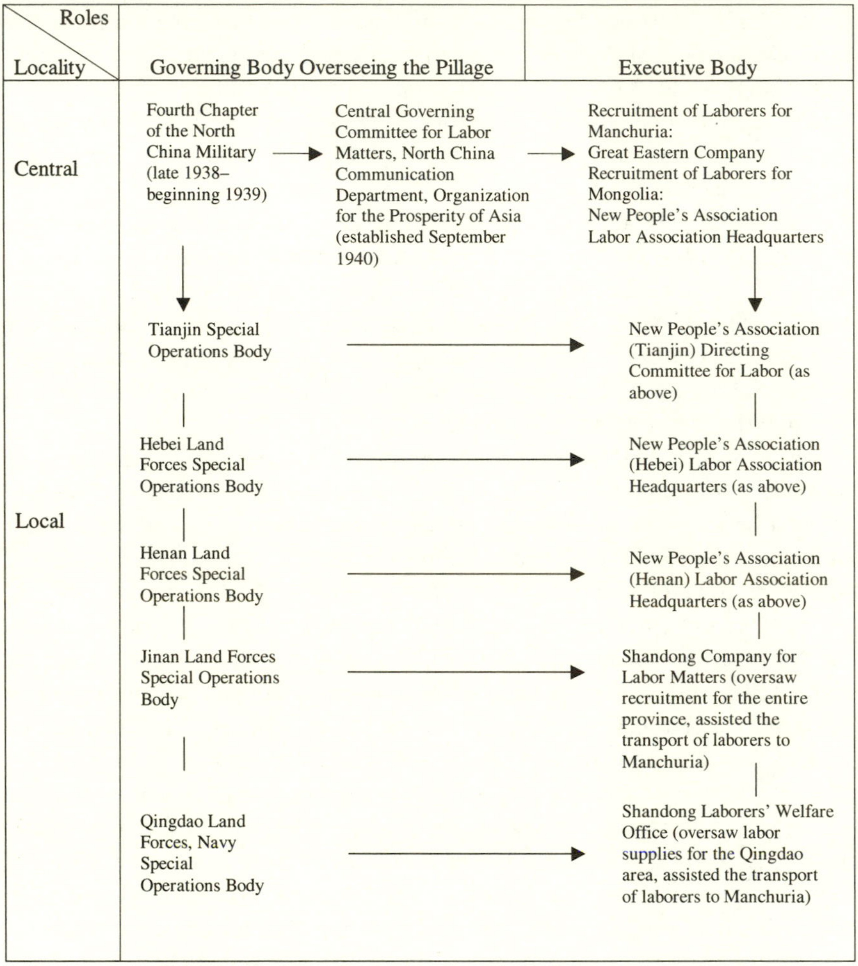

Roles / Locality	Governing Body Overseeing the Pillage	Executive Body
Central	Fourth Chapter of the North China Military (late 1938–beginning 1939) → Central Governing Committee for Labor Matters, North China Communication Department, Organization for the Prosperity of Asia (established September 1940) →	Recruitment of Laborers for Manchuria: Great Eastern Company Recruitment of Laborers for Mongolia: New People's Association Labor Association Headquarters
Local	Tianjin Special Operations Body ———————————→	New People's Association (Tianjin) Directing Committee for Labor (as above)
	Hebei Land Forces Special Operations Body ———————————→	New People's Association (Hebei) Labor Association Headquarters (as above)
	Henan Land Forces Special Operations Body ———————————→	New People's Association (Henan) Labor Association Headquarters (as above)
	Jinan Land Forces Special Operations Body ———————————→	Shandong Company for Labor Matters (oversaw recruitment for the entire province, assisted the transport of laborers to Manchuria)
	Qingdao Land Forces, Navy Special Operations Body ———————————→	Shandong Laborers' Welfare Office (oversaw labor supplies for the Qingdao area, assisted the transport of laborers to Manchuria)

Note: ——▶ indicates supervisory relationship; ——— indicates equal relationship.

became more comprehensive, and coordination improved. In December 1943, when the Third Convention of North China, Manchurian, Mongolian, and Central China Labor passed and implemented a program to identify sources of labor supply, the Japanese system of expropriating labor became complete and entrenched. Figure 3.1 summarizes its structure.

At the heart of the Japanese system was the Fourth Section of the North China military and the NCCD's Office for Labor Affairs (under the joint direction of the political and economic units). These were the policy- and decision-making bodies in North China labor affairs. The latter was responsible for the daily business of labor matters—determining labor requirements, assigning workers, dealing with laborers' salaries, raising funds, and so on. In November 1942 the NCCD was eliminated, and the Great Eastern Company's office at the Beijing embassy assumed its duties.[11]

The headquarters of the NCLA was responsible for executing labor policies. Its public identity was the China Financial Group's legal section, which fell under the Department of Labor within the North China Administration Committee. Its organization, personnel, and business were, according to the North China Institute of Research, "all the while supervised and administered by the North China Military and North China Communication Department, and very reasonably so." Two of the four councilors were Japanese and the other two Chinese. The first president (Yin Tong) was assistant chairman of the New People's Association, but he seldom attended meetings and died of illness early in 1943. Effectively the Japanese councilor charged with its overall supervision ran the operation.[12]

Regional labor affairs in North China were overseen by various units of the North China Military along with Special Operations Units of the army and its subsidiary Committees for Labor Affairs. The NCCD was in charge of political and economic affairs, but other than a special office at Tsingdao that coordinated the activities of the Japanese army and navy, it had no subordinate offices. Thus one may conclude that the organization behind the systematic expropriation of North China labor was entirely controlled and directed by the Japanese. According to the findings of the North China Institute of Research, before October 1943 the Special Operations Units of the army in special cities with important properties and areas of labor concentration set up Committees or Branch Committees for the Regulation of Labor Matters.[13] These committees were responsible for the guidance and supervision of the different kinds of policy and planning carried out by the labor associations and their offices in various localities. They also handled the allocation of human and other necessary resources in these areas and took disciplinary action against laborers who violated regulations. Their activities reflect the total control of the Japanese military in North China over local labor conscription.

In conjunction with this arrangement, the NCLA established offices in eight major cities (Beijing, Tianjin, Qingdao, Jinan, Baoding, Taiyuan, Kaifeng, and Xuzhou) and branch offices in fourteen small and medium-size cities with important properties and concentrations of manpower, and in ports such as Shimen, Zhangdian, Weixian, Tangshan, Tanggu, Xinxiang, Guide, Haizhou, Gubeikou, Weihaiwei, and Longkou. Starting in January 1944, a series of sixteen provincial offices were established on a trial basis to carry out systematic recruitment in Hebei and Shandong provinces, and the number was increased to forty (in Hebei, Shandong, Henan, and Jiangsu provinces). The report of the North China Institute of Research admits that while the leaders and various officeholders of these bodies were local men, they occupied dummy positions: "The real Executive positions were filled entirely by the Japanese." The report states: "Because North China was at present a battlefield," it was "inevitable and necessary to tap the knowledge and experience of the Japanese for the task of reinforcement."[14]

Based on the above account, it is possible to develop a chart indicating the organization of Japanese labor recruitment in North China. Figure 3.2 shows that until the end of 1943, Japanese forced conscription in North China became increasingly systematic and complete, as well as uniform and secretive.

The Japanese Invasion and the Movement of North China Labor after 1942

With the outbreak of the Pacific War at the end of 1941 and the expansion of Japan's military presence, the demand for labor in occupied territories throughout East and Southeast Asia greatly increased. North China laborers were needed not only for local enterprises and the mining industry, but also to work in Manchuria, the Mongolia–Xinjiang territories, Central China, the northern Korean peninsula, and Japan. North China became the "Wellspring of Labor in East Asia."[15] Between January 1942 and August 1945 Japan relocated a total of 2.625 million people throughout East Asia, a figure that can be substantiated in detail from Japanese archival materials.[16] This chapter will discuss the coercive policies and methods adopted by the Japanese in mobilizing this workforce.

After 1942, the Japanese divided responsibility for labor in the conquered territories. The NCLA, for example, implemented a Division of Territory and Duties expansionist scheme from January 1942 to August 1944 and a system of Coercive Administration and Supply between September 1944 and August 1945 under the North China Administrative Committee. I will explain the main policy first.

The decision to export laborers beyond the borders of North China under the Division of Territory and Duties scheme was made at the end of 1941, during the First Convention of North China, Manchurian, and Mongolian Labor Affairs. Two documents summarized the main elements of this decision: "Key Points Regarding the Temporary Measures Taken in Recruitment and Management of North China Labor" and "Key Points Regarding Allocation by Territory in the Recruitment of North China Labor."

Figure 3.2 **Japanese System of Enforced Conscription in North China after July 1941**

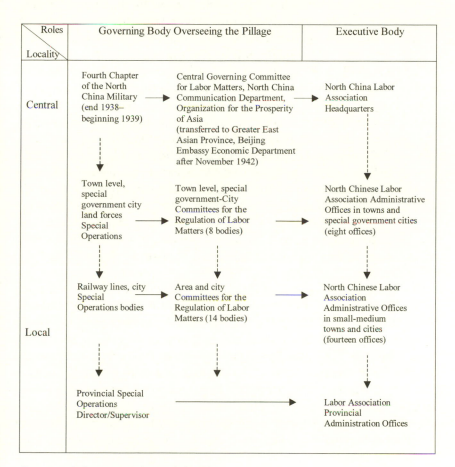

Note:——▶ indicates supervisory relationship.

The former stipulated that all workers sent for employment beyond the borders of North China, no matter how large their numbers, had to have proof of recruitment through the conscription machinery of the various border and Japanese authorities. These arrangements were handled directly by the headquarters of the NCLA, and their implementation required approval from the North China military command.[17] In short, workers exported from China after 1942 were under the direct charge of the North China military administration. The second document detailed procedures under the Division of Territory and Duties scheme:

1. By December 20 of each year, units or headquarters beyond the borders of North China had to submit plans for the coming year that included the targeted region for labor recruitment and a projection of the numbers expected from each area, along with the actual numbers and details of labor recruited in the current year.

2. The NCLA headquarters used these reports to mark out the areas where conscription would take place and to specify the numbers required and the time needed for the process. This calculation took into account local labor requirements, the law-and-order situation, the level of desolation and destruction experienced, and the success of the harvest. An application was then submitted to the North China military for final approval, and once approval was obtained, the local recruitment stations concerned had to be notified before January 10.

3. The NCLA granted permits to extraterritorial recruiting offices to operate in their areas of jurisdiction, and liaised with the military and police on their behalf. Changes in the area of recruitment or extensions of time required approval from the North China military.[18]

The North China Institute of Research reported in October 1943 that the NCLA had issued a set of directives regarding the allocation of labor resources to Manchuria, Mongolia, and central China in 1942 and 1943. Workers recruited from Manchuria were assigned to nearby locations, such as the Jinpu Transport Lines, the Shandong Provincial Transport Lines, and the Longhai Road Transport Lines.[19] Those recruited from the Mongolian region were allocated to the nearby Yanjing Railway Line, the Jinghan Road Transport Line, and the North Henan Railway (except for areas where the coal mines were concentrated), while those recruited from central China went to the Subei Railway Line, Yudong Railway in Xuzhou, and Caozhou Railway in Shandong.[20]

Toward the end of 1943 and in 1944, following the formation of provincial offices and village chapters as foundation units of the NCLA, the Japanese sought to exploit networks formed at the village level. They set up permanent (or at least long-term) bases for the forced mobilization, organization, training, and transport of labor.[21] However, from the second half of 1944, the Allies' eventual triumph in the Pacific could be foreseen, and the Japanese began a large-scale withdrawal from northern China. In the absence of support from the North China military, the labor scheme was aborted and replaced by a system of coercive administration and supply operated by the North China Administrative Committee. The committee allocated labor resources to various provinces, special municipalities, counties, and villages with support from the Japanese military, government administration, police, vanguard, special operations unit, labor association, and New People's Association.[22]

To carry out their expansionist policies after establishing their system of coercive recruitment of North China labor, the Japanese made use of a number of ruses and devices. On April 5, 1941, the Japanese Army in Guandong and the North China Military ratified a treaty regarding laborers sent to Manchuria that included emergency measures to conscript laborers from North China. It linked conscription with maintaining law and order in the region. The North China Military used force to capture laborers and send them to Manchuria. North China residents forced to move to Manchuria for reasons of security or law and order had priority in arranging passage into Manchuria.[23] The Military History Department of the China Institute of Military Science records in works such as "The Military History of China's War of Resistance" that about 80,000 local civilians were seized and transported to the Northeast as laborers in the course of raids conducted by Japanese forces against Kuomintang and 8th Route Army bases of anti-Japanese resistance between the spring of 1941 and the summer of 1942. This was in addition to the estimated 80,000 prisoners of war (POWs) captured in combat with the Kuomintang and the 8th Route Army. The breakdown is as follows: 20,000 local civilians were taken in the northern Yue area from the anti-Japanese resistance bases of Shanxi, Chahar, and Hebei in autumn 1941; 10,000 local civilians were taken during the winter of 1941 from the Shandong-based resistance; and about 50,000 civilians were taken as laborers during the May First Raid in 1942 against the central Hebei resistance.

To "contain" and "suppress" the 8th Route Army's base area, the Japanese enforced a "concentration of families and villages" at the border between the plains and mountains of Hebei and Shanxi between the autumn of 1941 and the autumn of 1942. This created a no-man's-land and in effect amounted to a policy of isolation. In the process of burning tens of thousands of villages and moving the people into "human circles" that resembled concentration camps, the Japanese forced about 100,000 able-bodied young men and their families to go to Manchuria to be laborers. According to a report published in April 1943 by the NCLA's Planning Division, in ten districts in Luan County alone, several hundred villages were destroyed in the creation of the no-man's-land after November 1942, and about two to three hundred families (more than a thousand people) were taken to Manchuria as "Special Labor."[24]

The Japanese also utilized the North China Transport Office's Police Department (the Railway Police Department), one-third of which consisted of Japanese soldiers,[25] to conscript laborers by force from so-called "Villages of Care" along the North China Railroad. According to the Fushun coal mine archives, the Manchurian Railway, the Manchurian Heavy Industries Company, and the North China Transport Company determined the main policies and procedures for conscription from these villages as early as April 1941. The villages had about 30 million residents, all living within ten miles of the railroad, and the Japanese planned to draw 180,000 men from the 10 million who were the most stable, that is, those living within three miles of the line. These workers were to be supplied to the Manchurian Railway Company and the Manchurian Heavy Industries Company for key enterprises and the mines. However, because the North China Army had just begun a large-scale war of pacification, the implementation of this coercive scheme did not go smoothly, and in the end the North China Transport Company managed to provide only about 3,500 men for all the coal mines in Manchuria, including the Fushun Coal Mine. In 1942, the Japanese attempted to cull 300,000 men from the Villages of Care, this time with better results. During the year the North China Army had carried out several large and cruel attacks to subjugate the 8th Route Army's base and had implemented its barbaric "burn all, kill all, plunder all" policy. Moreover, the people had to contend with a drought, and these conditions gave the Japanese forces greater success in conscripting laborers.[26] In 1943 the Manchurian Railway Company forcefully conscripted 6,000 men, and in 1944 another 2,000 through the North China Transport Police Department.[27]

After determining the location of the recruitment centers and the numbers to be sent abroad, the military, the civilian police, and the military police (the Kempeitai) enforced the distribution of these men to various counties, localities, and villages, with the backing of the Japanese Special Operations Unit. According to the *Jin Cha Ji Ribao* (the Shanxi-Hebei Daily), the Japanese seized 5,000 men during a raid in Handan County (an average of three men per village) and 6,000 in Bo Ai County, while in Quyang County every village had 5–6 men taken, a total of several thousand workers. The Japanese also used institutions such as the Long Hua Refugee Shelter as a cover for forced conscription, which was carried out under the guise of "relief work."[28]

The above describes the deceptive methods adopted by the Japanese to supply large numbers of workers to Manchuria, Mongolia–Tibet, and Central China after 1942. However, the measures used to export labor to Korea were different.

According to a report prepared by the North China Institute of Research, the labor supplied to the Korean peninsula was exclusively used for military engineering repair work in the North. Around 1,500 men were exported in 1941, and another 1,177 in 1942.[29] According to a report in the *North China Labor Times,* through the first half of 1943 the laborers sent to northern Korea were divided into two batches (1,187 men in the first half of 1942 and 628 in the first half of 1943) totaling 1,815 men; all were civilians seized by the Japanese, forcibly assembled, and transported to Korea.[30]

As for laborers to be used in Japan itself, the "Document for Transfer of Chinese Labor into the Interior" issued by the Japanese Ministry of Internal Affairs stipulated: "As far as possible, make use of laborers that already have the required skills and training, as well as POWs who have undergone training." About half of those sent to Japan were KMT and 8th Route Army POWs collected from concentration camps and put through exhaustive training. According to the inaugural speech given in December 1943 by its secretary, Okamura Neiji, the NCLA could train a thousand men a month to be sent to Japan, drawing on the POW concentration camps of Shimen and Jinan.[31] Other than POW labor, the Japanese government also requested experienced and technically trained North China laborers. However, after 1944 there was a shortage of skilled labor, and those available were not willing to go to Japan, so the Japanese recruiters and the NCLA used deception to seize workers.

For example, between July and August of 1943, with the approval of the Japanese Embassy in Nanjing, the East Japan Shipbuilding Company, the Japanese Trade and Labor Congress, and other units took out a joint advertisement at Lushui to recruit two batches of 432 carpenters and shipbuilders under the pretext of making ships in Japan under a one-year contract, with a promised remuneration of savings vouchers worth 1,200 to 1,600 yuan. Upon reaching Japan, these laborers were transferred to Hokkaido to work as miners in the worst possible conditions. In January 1945 the representatives of the Shanghai Steamship Carpenters' Union approached Wang Jingwei's foreign ministry to ask the Japanese to repatriate these workers, but the Japanese ambassador rejected the request on grounds that all the workers were willing to renew their contracts.[32]

In June 1944, the NCLA office in Tianjin tried to recruit 1,500 men for projects in Nagasaki and Qingdao, and when there were no takers they asked the Tianjin municipality for permission to seize odd-job laborers for the purpose. At the start of 1945 the Qingdao municipality, following instructions from the Japanese commission at Qingdao, began giving training to beggars, vagrants, petty criminals, and "elements who disturbed the peace" arrested by the Japanese police and the Kempeitai, preparatory to sending them to Japan as laborers.

Between July and September 1944, the Japanese government, acting under the Sino–Japanese Labor Association and working through the Japanese Embassy in Shanghai, conscripted 1,500 Chinese laborers in Nanjing, Shanghai, Hangzhou, Bengbu, and other places to work in the mines and at the docks in Hokkaido and Fukuoka. The men were promised savings vouchers worth 3,000 yuan as remuneration. Shortly after their arrival, seven of these men, led by Lin Shaomei and Bao Chenglong, escaped due to "harsh working conditions, insufficient food supplies, and mistreatment" and approached Wang Jingwei's embassy at Kawasaki to ask for the mediation of Wang's government in exposing "the cruelty of the Japanese."[33]

Table 3.1

Distribution of Labor in North China, 1941 (in thousands)

Labor supplied from North China	665
Labor supplied from Manchuria	1,200
Labor supplied from Mongolia–Tibet	100
Total	1,965

From 1941 to August 1945, the number of forced laborers employed in the Japanese war economy in North China numbered 3 million. This figure has been assembled from information found in several sources. First, in June 1940 the NCCD published "Table of the Number of Laborers in the Major North China Industries" that showed 550,000 workers employed in ten major industries.[34] However, in 1940, the Japanese had not taken control of the industries and mining resources of North China, so the workers listed on this table cannot be considered forced labor. It is possible to talk about forced labor only in connection with workers conscripted from 1941 onward.

A second source of information concerning the number of workers is the Asian Development Board's table "Distribution of Labor in North China, 1941." Table 3.1 summarizes information from this source.[35]

The plan, which was formulated at the end of 1940, included an estimate of the security and labor needs for 1941 that was inaccurate and overly optimistic in estimating the total number of laborers that could be secured from North China. For instance, the figure for Manchuria was originally 1.2 million men, later reduced to 1.1 million, but at the end of the year the number working in Manchuria was 949,000, just 86 percent of the revised projection. The number sent to Mongolia–Tibet was 35,000—35 percent of the original projection.[36] The figure of 665,000 allocated in this table to North China industries in 1941 is probably inflated as well.

The Asian Development Board created a third document, "Table of Projection of Numbers of North China Laborers," prior to the outbreak of the Pacific War when it was planning the mobilization of resources for 1942–46.[37] This calculation was based on the twelve main industries in the war economy in North China in 1941, which accounted for all the conscripted workers. In 1941 these twelve industries employed 400,000 conscript laborers. Each industry's labor force grew at different rates in 1942, but the average growth was 8.8 percent, and at the end of that year these twelve industries collectively employed 435,000 men. Subsequently the average growth of the labor force was about 10.4 percent, and planning documents called for 480,000 workers in 1943; 530,000 in 1944; and 580,000 in 1945. Because the plan was drafted after 1941, the figures are more accurate than those in the documents described previously. With regard to the new labor demands on local industries in North China in 1942, Kawai Masahisa, the Japanese representative of the North China Labor Association, pointed out in the November issue of the *North China Labor Times* that the numbers supplied to local industries in North China, Mongolia–Tibet, and central China did not exceed 550,000. When the 100,000 originally intended for Mongolia–Tibet and Central China are subtracted, the numbers recruited for local North China industries would not have exceeded 450,000 men. This assessment is consistent with a figure of 435,000 projected for 1942 that appeared in the table. At the beginning of 1943, the North China Development Company and the fictitious North China Development Authority and other units created a document entitled "Estimate of the Number of Men Required for North China Industries for 1943." In it they announced a requirement for 460,000 men, close to the figure of 480,000 in the plan for 1943. Thus, this third document shows clear evidence of the extent of Japanese exploitation of labor in North China industries between 1941 and 1943. It appears that Japanese manpower demands in North China between 1941 and 1943 did not exceed 500,000 workers annually and that the total number used during these three years was around 1.5 million men.

However, in 1944, owing to gross expansion of Japanese "defense properties" in North China, the demand for labor in local industries increased phenomenally. The Third Convention of North China, Manchurian, Mongolian, and Central China Labor held at the end of 1943 approved a projected requirement of 900,000 men to meet the needs of local industries in North China. Accordingly, with the approval of the Japanese Embassy in Beijing, the NCLA reassigned 400,000 men originally bound for nonessential work in Manchuria to local industries. The recruitment plans for North China adopted by the First East Asia Convention for Labor Matters in 1945 still called for 900,000 men,[38] but the Japanese subsequently scaled back their requirements for local labor to about 500,000 men.

In conclusion, during the four years and eight months from 1941 to August 1945, the total number of men that the Japanese conscripted by force stood at around 3 million.

Forced Labor in Japanese Military Engineering Works in North China

The Japanese carried out large-scale construction and engineering works from 1940, building roads, railways, military bases, and fortifications.[39] They planned to use roads and railways as "chains" and military facilities as "locks" to divide, surround, and destroy the various bases of the 8th Route Army.

According to a survey carried out in June 1940 by the Sixth Division (Labor) of the Asian Development Board's Designated Committee of the North China Development Plan, the number of laborers employed on military engineering works (that is, Special Labor Forces) was about 200,000 men.[40]

Early in 1941, after the Battle of the Hundred Regiments, the Japanese army began to implement a bloody policy of "burn all, kill all, and plunder all" across North China. In connection with the "cleanup" and "containment" taking place, the pace of military building projects increased greatly. According to Manchurian Railway authorities, in November 1941 around 200,000 men were being used to build roads, camouflage trenches, and perform other tasks.[41] After the Japanese had completed their "sweep" of anti-Japanese bases in central and east Hebei, the number of laborers employed grew sharply.

Battle to Pacify North China, a volume edited by the Office of War History of the Japanese Ministry of Defense, quotes one of the leaders of the North China campaign as saying, "the total length of trenches dug in both the pacified and nonpacified areas [this year] was 11,860 kilometers, and fortifications built to contain the mischief of enemy forces exceeded 7,700." How many laborers were forced into this massive scheme, nicknamed "the other Great Wall of China"? The Japanese Ministry of Defense provides only partial information in *Battle to Pacify North China*. For instance, the troop records of the Japanese forces stationed in East Hebei reveal the following:

> Completed the planned work of this unit and other units before the stipulated deadline of 6 November (1942). Built 245 kilometers of trenches, linked with other lines of 74 kilometers, total length 319 kilometers. Built 132 bunkers, 3 fortifications, 18 walls, 2 checkpoints, total number: 155. This project took 52 days to complete, and used as many as 1,957,000 man-days.[42]

The conclusion of a report by a unit stationed in Central Hebei concerning the preparatory work undertaken for the "cleanup" of May 1 states,

> a blockade line of several kilometers was built at the foot of the Xishan Yue area, along the Jinghan Railway (the line consisted of stone walls and fortifications; the stone wall was 2 meters tall, and about 1 meter thick at the base, and was used to cut supply lines from West Hebei to Central Hebei). This project, combined with the construction of another more direct line of blockade measuring 90 kilometers, took 70 days to complete, and required 100,000 men.[43]

Projects undertaken by the Japanese normally required 1–3 months to complete, and Commander Nie Rongzhen (in charge of Shanxi, Chahar, and

Hebei provinces), estimated in December 1942 that the Japanese had used at least 45 million man-days to carry out military engineering works that included trench digging, road building, and the preparation of fortifications in North China.[44] This translates to 7–800,000 men working for periods of two months each. Taking into consideration laborers employed in 1940–41, the indications are that between 1940 and 1942 more than a million North China laborers were employed on large-scale military construction projects. These men were unpaid "voluntary" workers, in other words, forced labor. According to the report by the Manchurian Railway authorities, this type of labor "mainly depended upon the supply of manpower provided by the Villages of Care (on both sides of the Railway) . . . even during periods and seasons when farmhands were much needed for farm work, they had to continue to meet the demand for laborers." The Chief Secretary of Japan's North China Army acknowledged this when he said on September 30, 1942, "in the pacified areas and the non-pacified areas, the digging of trenches" depended entirely "on the sacrifices made by the farmers, when they provide voluntary service."

Correspondence between the clerk of Changping County, Ji Zhaobin, Li Shaowei of the Yanjing Railway and the North China committee concerning Japanese forced conscription to build the Trench for the People's Benefit shows the miserable working conditions the men employed by the Japanese for military construction had to endure. In a message dated June 5, 1942, Ji wrote:

> Spring was dry this year . . . since the seedlings have dried in the fields, there is no hope for harvest in autumn, given these circumstances . . . from May 27th we have to commence with the digging of the Trench for the People's Benefit, and try to finish it by the end of June. This means work lasting 35 days, so we need about 15,000 men daily. . . . But the food that some of these men bring for meals is so poor that among the worst of them, their meals consist of a porridge mixed with leaves and bark. And then the men try to labor under the harsh sun in these plains . . . it is truly a sad sight to behold.[45]

After 1943, the Japanese no longer organized projects on such a massive scale. The work now involved maintenance and repair of completed works, and the numbers recruited were smaller. Toward the end of 1944 the Japanese began a massive retreat from North China, concentrating along the railways, commercial centers, and larger cities. During this period, most military construction and engineering work took place within military air bases or bases used for secret operations, although there were also some ad hoc projects. Generally, large cities such as Beijing, Tianjin, Qingdao, and Jinan each required a labor force of around 20,000 men for these purposes.

Forced Labor on Japanese Military Engineering Projects in Mongolia–Tibet

Japan's control of labor affairs in the Mongolia–Tibet region began in 1939, when the Japanese implemented the Properties and Development Three-Year Plan (1939–41) and began to increase their exploitation of the Dadong coal mines, Xuan Hua Long Yan iron mines, and other mineral production.[46] At the same time, military construction began along the borders of Mongolia and Tibet, causing a great surge in the number of laborers needed. The Mongolia–Tibet area was sparsely populated, and only a small number of workers could be recruited locally. Moreover, many of the local inhabitants were opium addicts and lacked the physical capacity to undertake physically demanding work for a prolonged period of time. For this reason the required labor force was recruited through deceit from nearby territories in North China. On May 29, 1939, under the direction of the North China Army,[47] the Mongolia–Tibet Joint Committee signed an "Agreement Regarding the Distribution of North China Laborers" that made the New People's Associations responsible for acquiring workers. On July 10 of the same year, the Mongolia–Tibet Joint Committee's Department of the People's Affairs established the central Committee for Mongolian–Tibet Labor Matters, and distributed a "Guide to Administration of Labor" for Mongolia–Tibet, while the autonomous government of North Shanxi set up the North Shanxi Labor Association. The rules called for tighter control over North China laborers in matters relating to recruitment, employment, and distribution of workers, and the terms and conditions of work. The rules also prevented laborers from escaping, hiding, or moving freely. Laborers from North China could not cross the border without a permit issued by the New People's Association's Labor Association.[48] Those who went to Mongolia–Tibet thus immediately lost their freedom and mobility and became forced laborers.

On September 1, 1939, an autonomous Mongolian government replaced the Mongolia–Tibet Joint Committee and the North Shanxi Autonomous Government. This change brought suggestions for a corresponding centralization of labor affairs. Moreover, as Japanese industries in Mongolia–Tibet expanded, they sought assistance from the various authorities responsible for labor matters to increase the supply of workers and improve the infrastructure for training them. In response to these requests, the Mongolia–Tibet Labor Association was created on May 10, 1940, under the direction of the Autonomous Mongolian Government to oversee the finance, organization and laws relating to manpower. In August the "Guide to Administration of Labor" transferred the duties of the former Committee for Mongolia–Tibet Labor Matters to the Department of People's Affairs and dissolved both the Committee for Labor Matters and the North Shanxi Labor Association. The Mongolia–Tibet Labor Association now handled recruitment, administration, management, and training, although "under extreme necessity (in the area of public works)" it could seek laborers through the local government office in charge of a project. It was then up to senior local officials to allocate the workforce recruited in the areas under their jurisdiction. The law stated that these laborers should be cared for with great consideration,[49] but the Japanese were already using force to obtain local laborers and workers from North China.

By the end of 1941, an acute shortage of labor in North China made it necessary for Mongolia–Tibet and Manchuria to carry out campaigns of forced conscription within their own territories. Local workers were required to participate in projects on a rotating basis, with groups of 1,000 men working in shifts of three months in the coal mines and other important industries in North Shanxi and Ba Meng as part of so-called Diligent Nationalist Teams. In 1943, groups of 3,000 men served for periods of six months in the mines of ten counties in the Dadong coal mine area under the rubric Diligent Youth Teams.[50] Overall, North China laborers made up 60 percent, and local laborers 40 percent, of the workforce in the mines, industries, and military construction projects in Mongolia–Tibet.[51]

This information makes it possible to develop a more accurate estimate of the numbers of Chinese forced laborers exploited by the Japanese in the Mongolia–Tibet region between 1939 and 1944. The projected number of North China laborers required in 1939 was 61,000, including 50,000 for military works, 8,000 for the Dadong coal mines, 2,000 for the Longyan iron mines, and 1,000 for other mines.[52] However, the great flood in North China that year threw these plans into disarray, and actual figures are unavailable. According to the government, 45,000 laborers arrived from North China, but records of the New People's Association show that it issued just 4,000 employment passes, and this is the only figure that can be verified. Other figures from the Mongolia–Tibet Department for the People's Affairs suggest that the number of laborers working in the mines and industries of Mongolia–Tibet could not have exceeded 11,700.[53]

The plan for 1940 called for the export of 120,000 workers from North China to Mongolia–Tibet, but the number sent was just 50,845.[54] For 1941 and 1942 the plan called for sending 100,000 and 30,000 men, respectively, but the actual numbers were 32,000 and 40,796. For 1943 the figure sent rose to 83,093.[55] In 1944, the planned figure for Mongolia–Tibet was 100,000 men,[56] but according to the NCLA the actual number was 47,275. In 1945, plans called for transporting 70,000 laborers from North China to Mongolia–Tibet,[57] but the actual figure cannot be determined because the NCLA abruptly halted operations in July 1945.

These sources provide evidence that the Japanese used about 254,000 forced laborers from North China in Mongolia–Tibet. Information from sources cited previously shows an additional 169,000 workers from North China (based on the assumption that 60 percent of the labor force came from North China and 40 percent consisted of local labor). Combining these figures suggests that the total number of laborers employed by the Japanese in the Mongolia–Tibet region during the war was around 400,000.[58]

Part IV

Korea

4

Japan's Korean Soldiers in the Pacific War

Utsumi Aiko

The Invisible Korean Soldier

The armed forces of the Japanese empire during the Pacific War included soldiers from Japan's colonial territories in the same way that the U.S. armed forces included Filipino troops and the British Empire and Commonwealth forces included Indian soldiers. However, the Japanese military did not create units made up exclusively of Koreans or of Taiwanese, but placed them in Japanese units so that their presence would not stand out. In deciding where to assign Korean soldiers, and in what numbers, the Japanese military applied the following criteria and quotas: frontline combat forces, up to 20 percent; rear echelon troops responsible for logistical support (securing transport and supplying matériel) and other duties, up to 40 percent; and rear units responsible for field hospitals, the internment of prisoners, and so on, up to 80 percent. Thus, more Korean soldiers were assigned to support activities at the rear than to combat duties at the front.[1] This chapter examines the mobilization of Koreans to serve as soldiers.

Although the Japanese army combined different ethnic and national elements, there was no special nomenclature, such as "Japan–Korea Army," to designate this force. Japan's colonial policy aimed at the assimilation of Koreans, and until the end of the war it was official policy to regard Korean soldiers as Japanese. After Korea became independent, many Koreans who had served in the Japanese army concealed the fact because they faced possible censure and even social ostracism. The historical reality of Korean soldiers in the Japanese army was ignored or denied by both the Japanese and Korean sides, and Korean soldiers became invisible to history. In Indonesia, Japanese-trained Indonesian troops cut a bright swathe in that country's war of independence. The position of Koreans who had served in the Japanese army was very different.

Fifty years after the war ended, former Korean soldiers started to speak out.

In Japan, too, researchers studying the period of the Pacific War were taking an interest in the presence of Korean and Taiwanese officers and men in the Japanese military. The figure of the Korean soldier in the Japanese army has, little by little, begun to emerge, and it is now clear that the attack corps of the Japanese military included Korean officers. Moreover, some of the Japanese judged to have committed war crimes were actually Korean or Taiwanese.

Although the presence of Korean soldiers in the Japanese army was until recently not widely known in either Japan or Korea, it has been a topic of discussion since the end of the war in the Philippines, where some people seem to have thought the Korean soldiers were part of a separate Korean army. People who experienced the war sometimes remark, "The ones who were cruel during the Occupation were not the Japanese but the Koreans," a comment I have heard personally from Filipinos many times. The collective memory of the people of the Philippines includes a figure of the "cruel Korean," reinforced by stories that continue to be handed down even today. Moreover, Allied records contain many accounts testifying to the brutality of individual Korean guards and supervisors.

The Road to Conscription

Because the Japanese army was an element of the Japanese empire and responsible to the emperor, it was called an "imperial army." The army's internal regulations, contained in the *Guntai Techō* (Military Handbook), carried by every serving officer and soldier at all times, included the following passage: "The essential mission of the Army, under the direct leadership of the Emperor, is to expand the basis on which the Emperor rules the nation and to demonstrate clearly the nation's strength . . . the true aim of leadership of the Army is to unite the hearts and minds of officers and men through loyalty to the Emperor so that officers and men may be aroused to serve the true purpose of the Army."

Under the Meiji Constitution the word *naichi* referred to Japan's home territory, and the Japanese who lived there had their status recorded in the *Naichi-kōseki,* the Domestic Family Register. Korea and Taiwan, on the other hand, as territories recently acquired by Japan, had the status of colonies and were known as *gaichi,* "external territories." Details of the populations in those territories were recorded in the *Chōsen-koseki,* Korean Family Register, or the *Taiwan-kōseki,* Taiwanese Family Register, collectively known as the *Gaichi-kōseki,* the External Family Register. Thus there were two categories of Japanese national: those listed in the Domestic Family Register and those listed in the External Family Register, although they were both called Japanese. People had no choice about which register contained their names.

For many years the right to enlist as a soldier in the army of the emperor of Japan was restricted to Japanese from the *naichi,* the "internal lands" or "home territory" of Japan, that is, to those Japanese recorded in the Domestic Family Register. With the invasion of China in 1937, it became obvious that there would be a future shortage of combat troops if only *naichi* Japanese were eligible to serve, and the War Ministry turned to *gaichi* Japanese, the Koreans and Taiwanese recorded in the External Family Register, to make up the numbers. However, recruiting and training soldiers from Korea, where there was a strong national independence movement, involved considerable risks, and the Japanese government implemented a rigorous policy calculated to make Koreans into Japanese "retainers" serving the emperor. One manifestation of this scheme was an amendment to the Education in Korea Law that banned the use of the Korean language in Korean schools, forced Koreans to adopt Japanese-style names (*sōshikaimei*), and required students and adults to sing in unison an oath of allegiance as *Kōkoku-Shinmin* (a retainer people of the imperial nation)—in contrast to "a people who follow the emperor" (*naichi* in Japanese). This policy was known as *Naisen-ittaika,* the incorporation of Korea as an "imperial nation," and its purpose was to turn Koreans physically and mentally into a people serving the emperor. Koreans "converted to an imperial people" joined the army as volunteers and later as conscripts following the introduction of national conscription in Korea.

Voluntary Enlistment by Koreans

On April 3, 1938, an "army special volunteer system" allowed Koreans to enlist in the Japanese armed forces for the first time. An illustrated magazine edited by the Cabinet Information Office claimed to express Korean feelings: "As our bodies surged with deep emotion, we sealed with our thumbs the mark on the oath [of military service], and from that very instant there arose in our bodies, now dedicated to the land of the Emperor, that great Japanese Spirit through which we will offer up our lives for the sake of our gracious Emperor."[2]

To become military volunteers, Koreans had to be at least seventeen years of age and 160 centimeters tall, and to have undergone six months of preinduction training at a military camp operated by the government-general of Korea (shortened to four months in 1941). The minimum height requirement for Japanese military conscripts at *kōshu* level (rank A) was 155 centimeters as of 1934 (lowered to 152 centimeters in 1942), so the physique required of Korean volunteers was greater than that for Japanese conscripts. To inspire Koreans to join the Japanese military, the government-general of Korea carried out publicity campaigns, issued invitations, and applied covert pressure. During the six years when national conscription was in force in Japan, 303,394 Koreans volunteered, but only 5,330 actually underwent training in the Japanese army.[3]

Chae Won Yong joined the Seventy-seventh Infantry Regiment of the Thirtieth Army Division on December 8, 1941. After performing border control duties in Korea and Manchuria for two years, he was sent in 1944 to the island of Mindanao in the Philippines, where he fought against the U.S. Army and Filipino guerrillas and then fled to the hills, knowing nothing of Japan's surrender on August 15, 1945. Although technically a volunteer, Chae claims that he joined the army under pressure from his elementary school teacher.[4]

Korean Student Soldiers

On October 20, 1943 (the eighteenth year of the Shōwa era according to the Japanese calendar), when the Japanese military retreat was already beginning, a "decree temporarily employing special army volunteers"[5] was promulgated in Korea with immediate effect. Under this decree, men who had completed their secondary education and were currently studying at a place of learning in a program lasting two or more years—in other words, students at the tertiary level—became eligible to serve in the military.

Shin I Su, who entered the army under these terms, had become a student soldier while studying at a Japanese university, although at the time it was impossible for Koreans to join the Japanese army. He says that certain teachers at the university referred to Koreans as *yabanjin* (barbarians), and sometimes anger and distress at what he was hearing made him stop taking notes. Moreover, he found it difficult to rent lodgings and was subjected to discriminatory treatment. He enrolled as a student soldier because Koiso Kuniaki of the government-general of Korea had stated in a speech that the fate of Korea would be uncertain unless Koreans joined the military. He joined the Japanese military out of concern for his country, even if not quite shouting "banzai!" for His Majesty the emperor. There were 3,893 Korean student soldiers such as Shin.[6]

It has been said that these student soldiers were forcibly recruited, but their status was nevertheless that of volunteers, even if in name only. However, the Japanese War Ministry had already decided to extend conscription to Koreans and Taiwanese on the grounds that it would be difficult for the Japanese army to maintain its combat force without additional manpower. According to ministry projections, the number of Koreans and Taiwanese was expected to reach 200,000 by about 1946 and to climb to 400,000 thereafter.[7]

Korean Conscript Soldiers

On May 10, 1942, the Asahi newspaper carried the following report:

> Due to the ever-strengthening trend towards the incorporation of Korea as an Imperial Nation [referring to the complete assimilation of Korea by Japan under the rule of the emperor], and in response to the ardent loyalty of heart shown by Koreans, the Government has decided to extend military conscription to Korea; therefore it was decided in a meeting of the Cabinet on the 8th to proceed with various preparatory measures with a view to implementing this policy from 1944.[8]

Military conscription came into force in Korea on August 1, 1943 (under Law Number 4 of March 1, 1943), but it took the government-general of Korea more than one year to complete the preparations. The idea that the extension of military conscription to Korea was a response to an "ardent desire on the part of Koreans" was *tatemae*—a convenient fiction for legitimizing conduct—on the part of the government of Japan. In reality, the mobilization of Koreans was necessary to supplement Japan's inadequate combat forces and reduce Japanese fatalities. No matter how strongly the government-general promoted the policy through publicity campaigns and propaganda, many Koreans resisted the idea of joining the Japanese military. In the end, Koreans were mobilized through the administrative and police machinery of the government-general; the first conscription drive (lasting from April 1 to August 20, 1944) claimed a "success rate" of 94.5 percent.

However, significant numbers of young people had already been mobilized to work as *gunzoku* (civilian employees of the military) or recruited to go to Japan as laborers. The effect of conscription, therefore, was to absorb nearly all the young people on the peninsula who had remained outside the Japanese labor system. While conscription was in effect in 1944 and 1945, 110,000 young Koreans were forced to become soldiers, but these conscripts were of poorer quality than the volunteer soldiers who, through their education, understood the Japanese language and way of life and therefore could achieve "satisfactory" results in their military careers. A high percentage of Korean conscripts lacked proficiency in Japanese. Moreover, their physical condition was not as good, and they had experienced a sudden dislocation in their lives. Conscripts often performed poorly in training, and the military units they joined lacked cohesion. Many tried to desert, and the Japanese responded with brutal punishments, including beatings and summary executions. A lack of mutual understanding, or ethnic tensions, could easily cause incidents that constituted a breach of military discipline.

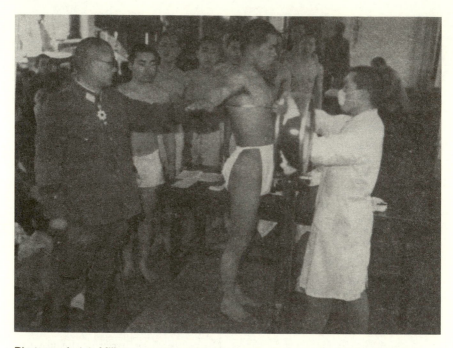

Photograph 4.1. Military recruits undergoing a physical examination in Chiyoda prefecture in Japan during the Pacific War. (Photograph courtesy of the *Mainichi Shimbun*.)

How many Koreans served in the Japanese army between 1938 and 1945? Figures published by the Support Bureau of the Ministry of Health, Welfare, and Labor, which took over from the Ministry of War and the Admiralty, show 116,294 soldiers and 126,047 civilian employees of the military, or a total of 242,341, and record 22,182 fatalities. These figures are based on the number of *Zaitaishōmeisho* (Certificates of Presence in the Armed Forces), attesting to military service, that were issued by the Ministry of Health, Welfare, and Labor. The certificate shows the posting and unit, date of enlistment, rank, domicile (registered address), name, and date of birth of a recruit.

Significant numbers of Koreans who became soldiers or civilian employees of the military are missing from these rosters. Among other things, it is unclear whether those drafted in the second phase of conscription, implemented just before Japan's surrender, are included in the published figures. For example, to obtain recruits for the Guandong Army, Koreans living near the Soviet–Manchurian border received draft cards on August 1, 1945, and enlisted on August 9. They were detained by forces of the Soviet Union in the wake of Japan's defeat, and it is unlikely that the War Ministry has records of their fate.[9]

According to a document issued for internal reference in 1949 by Japan's Investigative Agency for Public Safety, called "General Condition of Koreans Resident in Japan," 186,980 Koreans served in the army, and 22,299 in the navy. In addition there were 154,907 civilian employees of the army and navy, giving a total of 364,186.[10] These figures exceed those of the Ministry of Health and Welfare by 121,845. The difference is greatest in the case of the army, which had between 130,000 and 200,000 Korean troops and employed more than 120,000 civilians. In addition, although they were not formally members of the armed forces, military laborers (*gunpu*) worked for the Japanese army and navy. In other words, the number of Korean soldiers and civilian employees of the military who fought and worked alongside Japanese soldiers is much greater than the figures published by the Ministry of Health and Welfare indicate.

Koreans were stationed in every region occupied by Japanese forces, from northeastern China to Burma, New Guinea, and the islands of the Pacific, as were the women and girls forced to become "military comfort women." On the island of Biak, West Papua (Irian Jaya), Indonesia, there is a trench that local people call the "Japanese pit." I have visited the site twice. Five thousand Japanese soldiers are said to have died in this trench, but the memorial includes names that are clearly Korean.

Defeat and Withdrawal

Japan signed a formal surrender agreement on September 2, 1945. As members of the Japanese military, Korean servicemen gave up their arms, but Korean troops were demobilized and withdrawn separately from the Japanese. Immediately after Japan's surrender, on August 18, 1945, the War Ministry issued a set of "Detailed Regulations on the Main Points for Demobilization of the Imperial Armed Forces." Point 10 of this document states: "In accordance with the decision of demobilization officials, soldiers legally domiciled in Korea shall, until further notice, be placed outside the control of their respective units."

Korean soldiers were treated separately from their Japanese counterparts in order to be repatriated, although with Allied assistance Koreans returned home without major difficulties. However, owing to the confusion of defeat and the process of direct repatriation from the occupied territories, many Korean servicemen did not receive wages due them, or the money in their military postal savings accounts. In 1950 the Japanese government cleared debts payable to foreigners and others resident overseas. For the army, this procedure was carried out in Fukuoka Prefecture, and for the navy in the Demobilization Department at Kure. At the time, however, Japan had no diplomatic relations with South Korea, North Korea, or Taiwan, so it was impossible to settle debts or pay wages in these territories as was done in Japan. Such an arrangement had to await improved relations with the nation-states concerned. The Japan–South Korea Treaty that took effect on January 6, 1966, included an Agreement on Property and the Right of Claim and partially resolved this issue for Korean soldiers who returned to South Korea by handling the clearance of wartime wages, postal savings balances, and the like through the South Korean government.

Japan was prohibited from paying pensions to soldiers in the former occupied territories, an issue unrelated to the nationality of the soldier, whether Japanese or Korean. When the San Francisco Peace Treaty came into force on April 28, 1952, the Japanese government promulgated a Law for Support of the War Wounded and of the Bereaved Families of the War Dead[11] and began providing relief to soldiers wounded in war and to the families of those who had died. Koreans and Taiwanese who had served in the Japanese military were left out of this scheme on grounds that they were not Japanese nationals. The standard in determining eligibility for support payments was inclusion in the *Naichi-kōseki,* the Domestic Family Register. Since Koreans were recorded in the *Chōsen-kōseki,* they did not qualify.

The treatment of Korean soldiers who remained in Japan was complicated. Kim Jae Chan lost his right leg as a result of wounds and was hospitalized at the Military Hospital in Sagamihara in Kanagawa Prefecture. During the Allied occupation of Japan he received a pension designated for the war wounded, but after the peace treaty came into force and the occupation ended, the pension was discontinued on grounds that he was no longer a Japanese national. Kim attempted to negotiate with the Japanese authorities and was told that in order to continue receiving his war pension, he had to adopt Japanese nationality. He and his family did so in 1964, resolving the issue. However, wounded Korean former soldiers who did not become naturalized Japanese did not receive pensions.

In the 1990s, a movement began in South Korea to locate former soldiers, including those mobilized during the Pacific War period, and secure compensation for them. In 2001 the Japanese government awarded a meager 2 million yen (about US$16,650) on compassionate grounds, and a one-time payment of a further 2 million yen, to each qualified veteran who would claim it. It had taken ten years for Korea to obtain a ruling on compensation, and the amount eventually given was a paltry sum offered as a cash-in-hand payment.

Such was the treatment by the Japanese government of soldiers and of civilian employees of the military recruited from its colonial territories during the war. To wage war, the Japanese government took control of the lives and possessions of people throughout Asia. The number of Koreans and other Asians forcibly recruited as laborers or as soldiers remains unknown. The rosters of Korean soldiers have been given to the government of South Korea, but in Japan these same rosters are not available to the general public.[12]

There are still families in South Korea who have yet to receive notification from the Japanese government of the death of family members killed in action while serving in the Japanese armed forces. However, sixty years after the end of the war, substantial research is taking place concerning Koreans and other Asians mobilized in the war, and information on the subject is finally coming to light.

5

Korean Forced Labor in Japan's Wartime Empire

Naitou Hisako

In recent years, harsh questions have been raised as to Japan's war responsibility from an Asian perspective. As a nation, Japan has not really faced up to its past errors. However, little by little, protests voiced by people in Asia have changed the image that the Japanese have of their own country's history. The first Japanese-language work to provide a many-sided discussion of the issue of the forced labor of Koreans was Park Kyung Sik's *Chōsenjin Kyōseirenkō no Kiroku* (Records of the Forced Recruitment of Koreans), published in 1965. At the time, descriptions of the forced labor of Koreans and the issue of postwar compensation were being removed from Japanese history textbooks intended for middle and high school students. Now, although there are only a few lines describing Japan's wartime treatment of its then-colony Korea, at least the topic is mentioned.[1]

Outside the domain of school textbooks, the issue of forced labor by Koreans has been taken up as a theme by the Japanese media and in popular literature. In the latter category, Hahakigi Hōsei's *Mitabi no Kaikyō* (Three Trips Across the Strait), winner of the Yoshikawa Eiji Prize for Literature in 1993, stands out as an important work.[2] Readers of this novel are able to understand the mechanism of forced recruitment and to experience for themselves the weight of the suffering that the process inflicted on Korean people.[3]

At the beginning of *Mitabi no Kaikyō,* the main character, an elderly businessman named Ha Si Gun who lives in Pusan, Korea, receives a letter from an old friend in Japan who lives in northern Kyushu. The letter describes the condition of the coal mine where Ha Si Gun and other Koreans used to work. Coal can no longer be extracted from the mine, so it is to be closed down and redeveloped under a plan to attract businesses to the area. The letter prompts Ha Si Gun to cross the sea once again, to return to Japan after 45 years.

In the novel Ha Si Gun is the second son of a farming family in the province of Kyongsang-bukto. In October 1943, at the age of seventeen, he goes to Japan to work in place of his sick father, who has been assigned to labor duties there. He and his fellow labor recruits are taken to the port in a sealed, airless freight train, then bundled into the lowest hold of a ship. This is his first crossing of the Tsushima Strait, the body of water between the southern part of the Korean peninsula and the northern part of the Japanese island of Kyushu that gives the novel its title.

The official who recruits them in Korea says they will work in a shipyard, but once in Japan they are sent to a coal mine. In the miners' dormitory, five people occupy a room measuring three *tsubo* (less than ten square meters). There are only three bedrolls per room because, with some people working the day shift and others the night, there is no need to have one bedroll per person. The bedrolls are dirty, the straw tatami matting on the floor is extremely old and worn thin, and there are no ceiling boards. A three-meter-high fence rings the dormitory, which turns out to be a prison.

Although some wages are paid, life in the coal mine is extremely harsh. Gas leaks, cave-ins, and accidents caused by frantic driving of the coal trucks result in frequent deaths among Koreans and Japanese alike. However, Koreans—and only Koreans—also die by lynching. The men who carry out these macabre, mind-shaking killings are Japanese squad leaders and their Korean subordinates, who use rubber whips and batons on anyone who attempts to escape. They even castrate the leader of the Korean workers to inflict humiliation on him. In the mines they work closely with the guards and cooperate in the search for fugitives and in taking steps to prevent escape. Three basic countermeasures are employed to prevent and discourage workers from running away: the guards and members of the labor section who do the monitoring and patrolling are for the large part former policemen; there are guards patrolling in front of the railway stations, inside the stations, and on the trains; and any captured fugitive can expect severe punishment in the form of beatings and torture, possibly to the point of death.

After enduring these conditions for one year and two months, Ha Si Gun makes a desperate, and successful, bid to escape. Of the one hundred people who crossed with him from Korea, twenty or more have already perished in the coal mine. No temple receives their bodies, which are buried in the coal hill, and of course their relatives receive no death notification. After his escape, Ha Si Gun is rescued by a Korean businessman who manages a company in Japan. Working as a laborer handling cargo on the docks, he lives through Japan's defeat in the war, and then immediately uses the money he has saved working in the harbor to pay for a passage to Korea on a fishing vessel. This is his second crossing of the strait. Back in Korea, Ha Si Gun deliberately puts all things to do with Japan out of his mind. This changes, however, when he learns that the coal mine, which claimed the lives of so many of his companions, is to be obliterated. Feeling an obligation to make clear Japan's responsibility for the forced labor of Koreans, he crosses the strait a third time, returning to Japan after forty-five years. For him, the coal hill is an enormous grave for the Koreans who perished doing forced labor. He asks that something of the mine be allowed to remain, in some form or other, to commemorate those who died there, and to remind Japan of its war responsibility.

Mitabi no Kaikyō is a work of fiction, but it presents an accurate account of conditions during the war years. The author, Hahakigi Hōsei, considers the treatment of Korean forced laborers to be criminal behavior for which Japan as a nation should take responsibility. His novel is written from the point of view of one who raises the question of Japan's war responsibility through detailed historical testimony. With the passage of time, Japan's wartime behavior has faded into the past, and even though they might encounter the term "forced recruitment of Koreans" in the course of their school education, most Japanese find it difficult to grasp just what that phrase means. The importance of *Mitabi no Kaikyō* lies in the fact that it fully conveys the crime that was the forced labor of Koreans in general by describing the tragedy inflicted on one Korean. Familiarity with the human and historical detail conveyed in the book makes it easier to understand the forced recruitment of Koreans.

The System of Forced Recruitment of Koreans in Japan's Wartime Empire

Since the early 1990s a Committee of Inquiry into the Truth about Korean Forced Labor, consisting mainly of Koreans resident in Japan but including some Japanese, has been investigating the issue of Korean forced labor. The results are being collected for publication on a region-by-region basis.[4] However, it remains unclear to what extent those companies that used Korean forced labor kept records on the subject, and even now, more than fifty years after Japan's defeat, the whole truth about Korean forced labor has yet to emerge, and the subject remains contentious.

Those who seek to deny Japan's war responsibilities tend to take issue with the term "forced" in the expression "forced recruitment of Koreans." They insist that during the war Koreans came to Japan of their own free will and were not "forced" in the sense of being compelled to work. After the war, in making decisions on whether or not to award compensation, both government and industry in Japan gave the terms "forced" and "voluntary" a very narrow interpretation, and refused to acknowledge that compensation was due to Koreans who worked in Japan during the war.

Nonetheless, what lay behind emigration from Korea to Japan was the violence of colonial control. The term "forced recruitment" need not be restricted to kidnapping or abduction. There were many cases in which discriminatory treatment inside Korea forced Koreans to decide to cross over to Japan as workers. This can be described as forced recruitment by indirect means. Also, inside Korea, there was a rigorously enforced policy known as *kōminka kyōiku* (conversion to an imperial people through education); this involved education being conducted in the Japanese language and the forced adoption of Japanese-style names by Koreans. Koreans were educated to follow the Japanese "of their own free will," and people mentally harnessed in this fashion were unable to resist pressure to cooperate in the war effort.

Systematic forced recruitment of Koreans lasted from 1939 to 1945. From 1937 Japan had been engaged in all-out war with China and for this reason was experiencing a shortage of labor. As a matter of national policy, Japan sent Koreans and Chinese as workers to the Japanese home islands, to Sakhalin, and to the various southern territories. In April 1938 a Total Mobilization Law was promulgated, and in July 1939, national conscription came into force. Labor legislation provided a basis for mobilization plans in Japan and its colonies. The labor mobilization plan of 1939 allocated 1.1 million workers, including 85,000 Koreans. This was the beginning of the systematic forced recruitment of Korean labor.

The history of the forced recruitment of Koreans can be divided into three periods according to the method of recruitment: "recruitment through private hiring" from September 1939 to February 1942; "recruitment through official mediation" from March 1942 to August 1944; and "recruitment through national conscription" from September 1944 to August 1945.

"Recruitment through private hiring" was initiated by a note entitled Migration of Korean Laborers to the Home Territory, jointly signed by the Ministry of the Interior and the Ministry of Health and Welfare. Dated July 28, 1939, this note authorized the recruitment of Koreans as workers in such industries as construction and mining. From the middle of September 1939, agents representing Japanese companies were dispatched by the colonial government-general of Korea to various parts of the country, where they recruited workers on a private basis. The officially designated recruitment areas were Chungchong-namdo, Chungchong-bukto, Cholla-namdo, Chollabukto, Kyongsang-namdo, and Kyongsang-bukto. The harvest in Korea that year had been poor, and the first round of recruitment went well because many people living in rural areas were seeking work. However, demand for labor in munitions factories and mining was increasing in Korea as well as in Japan, and a local labor shortage started to develop. Furthermore, word spread about harsh conditions faced by Korean workers in Japan, and recruitment through private hiring became increasingly difficult.

In this first period, the government controlled the recruitment process, following the Key Points for Handling the Recruitment and Passage of Korean Laborers. Another regulation, Knowledge Concerning the Said Laborers after Passage to the Home Territories, stipulated that Korean workers were not free to change their place of work of their own accord. Thus the character of forced labor that would bind the Korean worker to a fixed workplace had already become apparent during the first period. With respect to wages, Knowledge Concerning Laborers after Passage to the Home Territories stipulated that Korean laborers should not spend their wages with the exception of small sums to cover living expenses. The details of this arrangement were left to individual employers. There were many cases where Korean laborers received only a small allowance and were forced to "save" the balance of their wages as a means of preventing their escape.

During the second period, from March 1942 to August 1944, there was "recruitment through official mediation," the type of forced recruitment depicted in *Mitabi no Kaikyō*. Under this arrangement, which was based on Key Points in the Introduction of Korean Laborers to the Home Territories, the Korean Labor Association, an auxiliary body of the government-general of Korea that acted as an official agency for workers, carried out recruitment. Public officials and the police reportedly entered the homes of farming families and sometimes used violence in the course of recruitment. However, even with these methods and the addition of the provinces of Kwangwondo and Hwanghaedo to the recruitment areas, only 70 to 80 percent of the designated number of people could be obtained. Accordingly, the age range for Korean laborers, officially set at between twenty and thirty-five years of age, was widened to include boys as young as thirteen and men of fifty or over. In *Mitabi no Kaikyō*, the seventeen-year-old protagonist takes the place of his father, who is about fifty.

The third period, which lasted from September 1944 to August 1945, involved "recruitment through national conscription" and was based on a system of conscription introduced in Korea in September 1944. This was forced recruitment in both name and deed and generated strong resistance. In 1944, during a ten-day period from October 16 to 25, conscription orders were issued throughout Korea, and not a single person complied. After police investigations, a total of 23,166 persons were conscripted, and ultimately each munitions plant in Japan received a contingent of 1,000 Korean workers. The same period saw a steep rise in the number of those escaping forced labor, and the escape rate in the coal mines of Kyushu is said to have reached some 80 to 90 percent.

Table 5.1

Number of Koreans Recruited by Force to Work in Japan, 1939–45 (by industry segment)

	Coal mining	Metals mining	Construc- tion	Dock labor (cargo handling and transportation)	Factory labor, other
1939	24,279	5,042	9,479	—	—
1940	35,441	8,069	9,898	—	1,546
1941	32,415	8,942	9,563	—	2,672
1942	78,660	9,240	18,130	—	15,290
1943	77,850	17,075	35,350	—	19,455
1944	108,350	30,900	64,827	23,820	151,850
1945	797	229	836	—	8,760
Total	357,792	79,497	148,083	23,820	199,573

Source: Yamada Shōji, "Chōsenjin Kyōserenkō" (Forced recruitment of Koreans) in *Kingendaishi no naka no Nihon to Chōsen* (Issues of recent history concerning Japan and Korea) (Tokyo: Tokyo Shoseki, 1991), p. 178.

The Treatment of Korean Laborers

Demand for labor routinely increases in a wartime economy, and Japan used Korean workers to overcome labor shortages. The principal industries that employed Korean workers were coal mining, construction, cargo handling, and transport around the docks. Table 5.1 shows statistics of the number of Koreans forcibly recruited to work in Japan.

Koreans endured harsh treatment at many work sites. The brutality toward workers in coal mines and munitions factories is verified by testimony from numerous sources, although for many years former labor conscripts were reluctant to speak about their experiences. The treatment of Korean laborers in the third period of "recruitment through conscription" can be seen from the example of Nakajima Aircraft's Handa Plant (Aichi Prefecture), described at the time as the most advanced manufacturing facility of its kind in East Asia.[5] In January 1945, some 1,000 Korean conscript laborers were sent to Nakajima Aircraft's Handa Plant. They were accommodated in a dormitory about two kilometers from the plant and worked from dawn till dusk under the eye of Japanese squad leaders. Parties of Korean laborers were sent to work at different factories inside the Handa Plant, sometimes sharing the same workplace as Japanese students of both sexes. Many of the Korean laborers were also young, and for this reason there was a certain amount of bonding. From the Korean conscript workers the Japanese female students learned an old Korean folk song about exile and imprisonment, the "Song of Ariran," and there were occasions when Japanese and Koreans would sing it together during break periods. After Japan's defeat, some of the female students even returned to Korea with the conscript workers. Yet open discrimination and mistreatment were rampant. The factory squad leaders often used Korean workers as an outlet for the frustration of the Japanese male students.

In May 1945 an incident occurred at Nakajima Aircraft's Handa Plant. About fifty Korean conscript workers started shouting "Give us rice; we're too hungry to work!," hitting their hammers on the bench-board at the same time. When the astonished squad leader started to beat two or three of these people, he was himself in turn beaten, and there was uproar in the factory. Finally, a party of the armed military police normally assigned to guard the Handa Plant suppressed the riot. Every Korean who had protested by refusing to work, every person in the row of fifty people, was cruelly beaten to death with baton blows and kicks from the squad leaders.

In August 1945, upon learning of Japan's defeat, the Korean factory conscripts chose a representative from among themselves who on several occasions approached the company to negotiate better conditions and a return home. Nakajima Aircraft's Funabashi Ryōhei, the head of the health and welfare staff at the dormitory, took charge of this difficult task. Through the Administrative Services Office of the Nagoya Railroad Company he arranged special trains for the transportation of the conscript workers. From the middle of September, chartered trains carried Koreans from the Handa Plant in Aichi Prefecture to the ports of Senzaki in Yamaguchi Prefecture and Hakata in Fukuoka Prefecture.

In the same period, a branch of the Korean union was formed at Chita in Aichi Prefecture, mainly by resident Koreans engaged in construction and engineering, and this organization sponsored farewell meetings for the Korean conscript workers. Near the site of Nakajima Aircraft's Handa Plant, what was said to be the first and last official interaction between resident Koreans and Korean conscript workers took place.

The Korean conscript workers from Nakajima Aircraft endured considerable hardship while returning to their homeland. Owing to a typhoon, trains en route to Yamaguchi Prefecture and Fukuoka Prefecture halted on the line. When the Koreans bound for Hakata finally arrived at the port, there was no ship to carry them, and they spent five uncomfortable nights in a warehouse before eventually departing. Because the company official Funabashi oversaw the safe return of the Korean conscripts working at Nakajima Aircraft's Handa Plant, repatriation to Korea was arranged relatively quickly.[6] However, few companies that had used Korean conscript labor provided help with repatriation, and many simply threw the Koreans out without settling back wages or other matters. Some of these conscript workers could not even pay the cost of transportation from the factory where they had worked to a port of embarkation and were unable to return home.

Another tragic episode in the repatriation of Korean conscript workers was the loss of the *Ukishima Maru* on August 24, 1945.[7] Fully loaded with Koreans who had been in the Shimokita peninsula of Aomori Prefecture, the ship was bound for Pusan, but it suddenly exploded and sank during a stop at Maizuru Bay in Kyoto Prefecture. The cause was never determined. Some say it was a suicide bombing ordered by military personnel on board; others, that the ship hit a U.S. mine. According to Japanese government figures, the *Ukishima Maru* incident cost 524 lives. However, the actual number of passengers, the number of fatalities, and the names of the deceased remain unknown. In the wake of Japan's defeat, the *Ukishima Maru* incident caused widespread fear among Koreans in Japan. Some were so afraid that they gave up altogether on the idea of returning home by ship.

The Koreans had been conscripted because they were Japanese subjects and had been forced to work under severe conditions. To conceal the fact of forced labor, workers were hastily dispatched home on board the *Ukishima Maru* in the aftermath of defeat. When the ship sank, Japanese fatalities on the *Ukishima Maru* were treated as deaths in combat and the bereaved families received pensions, but the Korean victims were ignored. In 1992, some eighty surviving passengers and relatives of those who died on the *Ukishima Maru* filed a lawsuit at the Kyoto District Court seeking an apology and compensation. In 2001 a judgment was handed down that recognized a breach in the duty to ensure safe repatriation and ordered that compensation amounting to 45 million yen be paid in compensation to a group of Korean survivors, although the demand for an official apology at the national level was rejected. However, in a stunning turnaround, the Osaka High Court reversed this judgment on May 30, 2003. The judge upheld the central government's position that under the Imperial Constitution the state was not responsible for compensation to individuals for damages incurred through the exercise of state power.

Awaiting Solutions

Koreans died in large numbers not only on the *Ukishima Maru* but also at places of work in Japan during the war. However, full compensation and an apology have yet to be given for those deceased Koreans sacrificed in the course of forced labor. The lack of detailed information concerning the *Ukishima Maru* incident is typical of the entire issue of the forced recruitment of Korean labor: the numbers of people involved is not known, no complete rosters exist, and there are substantial discrepancies in the statistics and estimates that are available. For example, to go by statistics in the "Inquiry into the Number of Koreans Involved in Japan's Mobilization" issued by the Administrative Services Bureau of Japan's Ministry of Finance in 1947, the

Table 5.2

Estimates of Total Numbers of Koreans Recruited by Force, 1939–45

1939	1940	1941	1942	1943	1944	1945	Total
53,120	59,398	67,098	119,851	128,350	286,432	10,622	724,871

Source: Higuchi Yūichi, *Nihon no Chōsen/Kankokujin* (Japan's [North Korea and South Korea–affiliated] Koreans) (Tokyo: Dōseisha, 2002).

Table 5.3

Maximum Number of Koreans Forcibly Recruited to Work in Japan

1939	1940	1941	1942	1943	1944	1945	Total
53,120	81,119	126,092	248,521	300,654	379,747	10,622	1,199,875

Source: Yamada Shōji, "Chōsenjin Kyōseirenkō" (Forced recruitment of Koreans), in *Kingendaishi no naka no Nihon to Chōsen* (Issues of recent history concerning Japan and Korea) (Tokyo: Tokyo Shoseki, 1991), p. 178.

number of Koreans recruited between 1939 and 1945 was 724,787.[8] Similarly, a history of resident Koreans in Japan published in 2002 places the number at 724,871.[9] (See Table 5.2.) Based on reports such as these, the figure normally cited for the number of Korean forced workers is about 700,000 people.[10] However, this figure is almost certainly too low, and some researchers claim that more than 1.5 million Koreans were forcibly recruited.[11] Based on the *Chōsen Keizai Tōkei Yōran* (Directory of Economic Statistics for Korea) and other sources, Yamada Shōji suggests a figure of 1.2 million people.[12] (See Table 5.3.) One reason for the discrepancy is that Koreans recruited and sent abroad as forced laborers sometimes had family members join them. From the first period of "recruitment through private hiring," both company officials and police officers encouraged the Koreans to bring their families to Japan to ensure a sufficient labor force. A contemporary police report on a group of 14,127 Korean laborers in Japan shows that 40,158 family members had joined them.[13]

This chapter has provided a preliminary overview of the forced recruitment of Koreans to work in Japan. Through national conscription and other means, Koreans were recruited as forced labor inside Korea, in Japan proper, and in other parts of the Japanese empire. There was also forced recruitment of women and girls to become "comfort women" for the military as well as female laborers.[14] The overall picture concerning these recruitment activities remains unclear. More than fifty years after Japan's defeat in the war, it is still not possible even to ascertain the numbers of people who were forcibly recruited, but it is certain that many Koreans who should have received compensation after the war did not.

Part V

Taiwan

6

Total War, Labor Drafts, and Colonial Administration

Wartime Mobilization in Taiwan, 1936–45

Hui-yu Caroline Ts'ai

Hung Huo-chao (b. 1917) was sent to Rabaul in the South Pacific in March 1943, and in 1944 lost the lower part of his left leg in an air raid. In 1975, he became involved in a compensation lawsuit against Japan that continued for the next seventeen years.[1] He said:

> This is an issue of basic human rights. Demanding war debts from the Japanese is to earn back Taiwanese dignity. What we demand is to be repaid with reimbursement equal to that of our Japanese counterparts. That is, we demand the same compensation as Japanese in order to earn back our face as Taiwanese.[2]

In an interview, Hung commented,

> We are not doing this only for money. Even if we get the money back, we are too old to spend it. The victims of the war have by and large perished from the earth. All we want is to demand justice and righteousness [from Japan], or we will die with a great grudge.[3]

Like other Taiwanese war veterans, Hung was demanding the same level of compensation received by Japanese veterans, something he and his Taiwanese comrades in arms had been denied. To understand this demand, it is necessary to know something about Taiwan's place in Japanese wartime mobilization.

Wartime Taiwan experienced three major types of labor mobilization covering industrial laborers, military laborers, and mass-mobilization laborers— a category that includes people mobilized through neighborhood organizations

101

Map 6.1 **Taiwan, 1941–45**

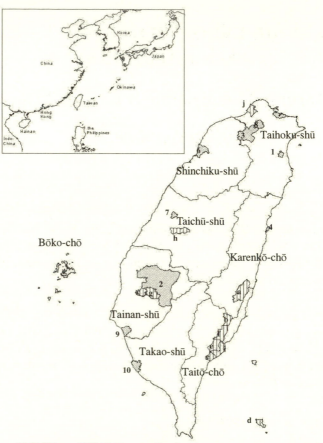

MAP: Taiwan, 1941-45 (places mentioned only)

Shū / Chō	Prefecture / Sub-prefecture	Shi / Gun		City / County	Gai / Shō / Sho		Town / Village /Off-Island
Bōko-chō	The Pescadores (Sub-pref.)	1	Gilan	Yi-lan	a	Gyokuri (shō)	Yu-li (village)
Karenkō-chō	Hua-lien-kang (Sub-pref.)	2	Kagi (gun)	Chia-yi (county)	b	Ikegami (shō)	Ch'ih-shang (village)
Shinchiku-shū	Hsinchu Prefecture	3	Kaisan (gun)	Hai-shan (county)	c	Kōbeki (shō)	Hou-pi (village)
Taichū-shū	Taichung Prefecture	4	Karenkō	Hua-lien-kang	d	Kōtōsho	Hung-t'ou-yu (off-island)
Taihoku-shū	Taipei Prefecture	5	Kirun	Keelung	e	Pinan (shō)	Pei-nan (village)
Tainan-shū	Tainan Prefecture	6	Shinchiku	Hsinchu	f	Shikano (shō)	Lu-yeh (village)
Taitō-chō	Taitung (Sub-pref.)	7	Taichū	Taichung	g	Shiragawa (shō)	Pai-ho (village)
Takao-shū	Kao-hsiung Prefecture	8	Taihoku	Taipei	h	Sōton (shō)	Ts'ao-t'un (village)
		9	Tainan	Tainan	i	Taitō (gai)	Taitung (town)
		10	Takao	Kao-hsiung	j	Tamsui (gai)	Tan-shui (town)

for youth corps (*seinendan*) and *hokō* (in Chinese, *baojia*) service. Recruitment of industrial laborers was limited, since the number of skilled workers was relatively small. They were recruited mainly to increase military-related industrial production in "the South"[4] and to facilitate industrial expansion in

Japan proper and in Taiwan. Military laborers, organizationally closely related to the youth corps and consisting primarily of unskilled workers, were part of an empirewide flow of labor used to meet strategic military requirements. Mass-mobilization laborers made up the largest—and the most hotly debated—category because of the implications their recruitment had for Japan's assimilation policy, although in an interesting paradox this kind of labor mobilization has often been dismissed as simply a variation on general practices for total war. The *hokō* system harnessed the labor of the entire population and is explored here partly through the memories of men who were *hokō* members in wartime Taiwan. This chapter examines major forms of labor recruitment and the disciplinary society of Taiwan at war and concludes with a brief consideration of the issues of governmentality,[5] subjectivity,[6] and the signification of an entangled identity shaped by Japanese colonial administration.

Dōka, Kyōka, and Kōminka

Japanese colonial rule involved a policy of assimilation (*dōka*), and the demand for workers—among other things—created a need to "educate and transform" (*kyōka*) the Taiwanese as part of that policy. This policy was intensified when war broke out between China and Japan in July 1937, becoming *kōminka*—Japanization or imperial subjectification. As Leo Ching explains in his book *Becoming Japanese:*

> If *dōka* had meant for the colonized "to become Japanese" (*nihonjin to naru*), *kōminka* now meant, "to become good Japanese" (*yoki nihonjin to naru*). More important, as the war escalated and the mobilization effort intensified, *kōminka* no longer meant for the colonized "to live as Japanese" (*nihonjin toshite ikiru*) but "to die as Japanese" (*nihonjin toshite shinu*). To die as Japanese in the name of the Emperor had become synonymous with being a "good" Japanese.[7]

Ching underscores the historical connection between *dōka* and *kōminka*, presenting *dōka* as a colonial project prior to 1937 and *kōminka* as a kind of colonial subjectification forcefully put into practice after 1937. *Kōminka*, he argues, "entailed for the colonized, as *dōka* did not, the 'interiorization' of an objective colonialism into a subjective struggle over, not between, colonial identities." The "onus of becoming Japanese" shifted from the colonial state to the colonial subjects. It is not a question of identity but "a matter of fate," not a process of becoming but "a state of being."[8]

Dōka was an assimilationist principle underlying Japanese colonial rule, and from the very beginning education served as the key channel for its transmission, with elementary schools (*kōgakkō*) set up specifically for the Taiwanese becoming a battleground for competing identities. Komagome Takeshi has argued that *dōka* policies as carried out in Japan's colonial empire can be further divided into two modes of assimilation: "national integration" (*kokka tōgō*) and "cultural integration" (*bunka tōgō*). In his formulation, "national integration" refers to legal and political institutions, such as "the extension of home rule" (*naichi enchō shugi*) versus colonialism, while "cultural integration" points to issues such as assimilation versus differentiation. These two modes of integration operated via built-in, mutually conflicting functions. Racial nationalism lay at the core of "national integration" and legitimated discrimination and separation of the colonized from the colonizer, while linguistic nationalism was central to "cultural integration," justifying oneness and assimilation of the colonized with the colonizer. Komagome argues that the Taiwanese came to be gradually excluded from imperial Japan's "national integration" while at the same time undergoing cultural integration.[9] Chen Peifeng has extended Komagome's argument regarding the built-in conflicts between the two *dōka* modes, metaphorically describing the relationship as an instance of "*dōshō imu*" (same bed, different dreams).[10]

However, the outbreak of war did not immediately bring about a transition from *dōka* to *kōminka*. As a movement, *kōminka* (1937–41) predated Imperial Subjects for Patriotic Service, or ISPS (*kōmin hōkō*, 1941–45),[11] which suggests a need to examine closely the evolution of assimilation policies in relation to wartime mobilization. Moral suasion (*kyōka*)—in Chen Wensong's words "struggling for the youth"—had been the key to Japan's nation building in the interwar period. In the 1920s the process took place against the background of an emerging nationalist movement.[12] As in Japan proper, the Japanese government appealed to individual Taiwanese by giving them a central role in a communal-regeneration movement, thus implicitly privileging them as the bearers of national culture.[13]

Subjectivity in Taiwan derived from the colonial administrative system, as mediated through local elites and other agents. The Movement for Reviving National Customs (*minpū sakkō undō*) in the mid-1930s marked the shift from moral suasion to general mobilization and made it possible for the colonial government to filter its influence down to the basic levels of society, the family, and the individual. An early hamlet revival association had appeared in Taiwan in 1932, and rural revitalization as a movement (*buraku shinkō undō*) in Taiwan got under way in 1934. With the launch of the Movement for Reviving National Customs in July 1936, hamlet revival units were set up in every township and village as the lowest level of the colonial administration. These hamlet revival units, in turn, were organized around the *hokō* system (households organized along the decimal system) or *ōaza* (subvillage geo-administrative units, or natural villages). According to the official definition, the "hamlet" also served as the "front line for national defense" and the "base for the operation of marching towards the South."[14] For the aborigines, to whom the *hokō* system generally did not apply, the youth corps served as the major channeling mechanism for wartime mobilization—first of labor and later also of soldiers.[15]

When the Sino–Japanese War broke out in July 1937, the Movement for Moral Suasion was quickly transformed into a Movement for National-Spirit Mobilization (*kokumin seishin sōdōin*), which began in Taiwan in September. On April 1, 1938, Japan passed a National Mobilization Law and applied the law to Taiwan and Korea on May 5. Under *dōka,* conscription had been an idea to be realized gradually, with labor requirements met by military employees and volunteers,[16] but *kōminka* entailed new kinds of labor mobilization in Taiwan.

Industrial Laborers and the Empirewide Labor Flow

Justin Adam Schneider has argued for a more positive treatment of colonial Taiwan as an active participant in imperial Japan's overseas expansion. While admitting that the concept of "subimperialism" when applied to wartime Taiwan has its own ambiguities in practice, Schneider maintains that it provides "a useful theoretical distinction between expansion driven by forces on the imperial periphery and action coordinated from the metropole." He contends that the *Taiwan takushoku kaisha* (Taiwan Development Corporation), as a national-policy company, was oriented toward a "developmental imperialism," especially after Pearl Harbor when there was "a new economic complementarity with South China and Southeast Asia in which the latter supplied raw materials for processing in Taiwan, rather than competing with Taiwan in the export of primary agricultural products to Japan."[17] The mobilization of industrial labor illustrates exactly this shift of the Government-General toward a new approach to development during the war. After 1937 the Government-General actively sought industrial expansion in heavy and chemical industries, but Taiwan largely remained an agricultural economy based on rice and sugar. The scale of wartime industrialization in Taiwan remained small, and so too did the number of industrial laborers.

Industrial labor mobilization began in 1936 in accordance with Governor Kobayashi Seizō's vision of an industrialized Taiwan based on agricultural processing and tied to South China and Southeast Asia. After the outbreak of the Sino–Japanese War, however, a Five-Year Plan to Expand Productivity based on manufacturing and designed to expand industrial capacity rapidly supplemented this scheme. A four-year plan was implemented instead—on

April 1, 1938—and in the following year this scheme was merged with the three-year plan of Japan proper.[18]

The Bureau for Military Supply (*gunjukyoku*, later renamed the Bureau for Resources, or *shigenkyoku*) had been set up within the cabinet at the time of the First World War[19] to carry out investigations and develop mobilization plans for Japan proper and for Japan's imperial possessions. During the interwar period the bureau dealt mainly with raw materials and fuel supplies, not manpower, and there were no labor drafts in the colonies. In September 1937, shortly after the July 7 Marco Polo Bridge Incident, the cabinet approved an Outline for National General Mobilization. The following month the Bureau for Resources was expanded into the Planning Institute (*kikakuin*) and became the center of operations for administering resources—including labor—in wartime Japan. Within the Planning Institute, the Committee for Labor Mobilization controlled labor matters, and beginning with the 1939 fiscal year drafted an annual plan of labor supply and demand to regulate both unskilled and skilled labor. In July 1939 the cabinet passed a set of rules for labor mobilization and ordered Japan's colonies and possessions to restructure labor administration along the same lines. In this way, an empirewide establishment for labor mobilization aimed at total war came into being. Beginning with the 1940 fiscal year, Taiwan's yearly labor plan had to be submitted to the Planning Institute for approval, thus completing the integration of Taiwan into the empire so far as labor affairs were concerned. The 1941 labor plan called for regional movement of workers within the empire and was Japan's first attempt to extend labor mobilization into the "Greater East Asian Co-prosperity Sphere" (*Dai-Tōa kyōeiken*).

After Japan expanded the scope of the Pacific War in December 1941, the annual labor plan was upgraded to an implementation plan for national mobilization, and the scope of mobilization quickly grew, extending to all "nationals," including students and women.[20] Both "labor mobilization" (prior to 1941) and "national mobilization" (after 1941) took place in Japan proper as well as throughout Japan's colonies. However, in areas under Japanese occupation, "labor mobilization" was preferred to "national mobilization," as in the recruitment of *rōmusha* (laborers), revealing Japan's official ideological preferences toward people in Southeast Asia.[21]

One key element of this expanded labor plan was the regional labor movement within the territories controlled by Japan. Prior to 1941, unskilled laborers from Taiwan were sent to Southeast Asia, while skilled laborers were dispatched to Manchuria and occupied China. After 1941, however, labor shortages began to surface in Taiwan, a problem that was partially solved by importing labor from Japan and by using Allied prisoners of war (POWs). As Kondō Masami has pointed out, Taiwan occupied a place distinct from that of Korea or Japan. Korea supplied physical labor, as illustrated by the use of Koreans in the coal mines of Japan proper and Karafuto (South Sakhalin). Japan poper supplied cadres for key industries and for military-related transportation and communication enterprises. For its part, Taiwan provided soldiers and semi-skilled laborers, the former generally assigned to Southeast Asia and the latter to Japan.[22]

Source material for research on the movement of labor in Japan's wartime empire is highly dispersed and far from complete. The plans for labor mobilization and national mobilization, however limited in scope, offer a glimpse at the way labor was moved from Taiwan to other regions in the early 1940s. The picture thus reconstructed shows that 4,000 laborers were sent to work in "enterprises in the South" in 1941. In 1942, the year the labor mobilization plan became a scheme for "national mobilization" (*kokumin dōin*), the number sent "outside Taiwan" reached 26,800, and in 1943 the figure was 8,482. The expression "outside Taiwan" referred not only to Southeast Asia but also to Japan proper. The target for the year was 107,400, and thus the laborers sent overseas constituted about one-fourth of the total number mobilized.[23] Those sent to Southeast Asia were mainly Taiwanese who had been drafted (*chōyō*). Many of those sent to Japan proper in 1943–44 ended up working at Japan's air bases on behalf of the navy (prewar Japan lacked a separate air force). They came to be known as "Taiwan boy laborers" (*Taiwan shōnenkō*) and reportedly totaled 8,419.[24]

Conscription was authorized under the Ordinance for Drafting Nationals (*kokumin chōyōrei*), which took effect in the colonies on October 1, 1939, and played a key role in wartime labor mobilization. Initially directed toward selected key industries, the ordinance was expanded and modified to apply to all Taiwanese society, in accordance with the changing situation. In effect, it gave Taiwanese the "right" to "participate" in imperial Japan's military service as Japanese "nationals," but stipulated that "drafting by requisition" (*chōyō*) should be secondary to "recruiting by solicitation" (*boshū*). It was mainly applied to labor sent to Southeast Asia. The Government-General recruited some laborers by "solicitation," though the line between this and conscription was a thin one.

Initially the Government-General of Taiwan abided by this rule, but in 1942 it decided that "recruiting by solicitation" was not viable and yielded to pressure from the army and the navy to accept what came to be known as "drafting by name-pointing" (*shimei chōyō*), whereby the military nominated desirable technical workers to work in key enterprises, such as mining or petroleum. When even this measure proved inadequate, the government turned to "labor requisition." The construction of the Port of Takao (Kao-hsiung) in southern Taiwan is illustrative of this policy change in labor mobilization. As various scholars have noted, the pattern of labor mobilization in Taiwan was repeated in Korea.[25] To supply industrial laborers, both male and female, on the radically expanded scale required for total war, the Government-General developed a plan to mobilize 61,700 workers in fiscal year 1940; 76,300 in 1941; 107,400 in 1942; and 92,990 in 1943—a total of 338,390. Assuming that labor supply in Taiwan before 1940 had been roughly in line with demand, this scheme—taken in conjunction with military and industrial projects—made labor shortages inevitable.

Meanwhile, the number of Chinese laborers in Taiwan, about 50,000 on the eve of the Sino–Japanese War, quickly dwindled to a negligible level after the war broke out because laborers rushed back to China and the Government-General banned the import of labor from China. When industrial labor shortages appeared in 1941, workers were brought in from outside the island. The planned supply of "overseas labor" was 3,500 in 1941; 8,000 in 1942; and 1,422 in 1943. These workers came mainly from southern China but also included some from Japan proper as well as POWs from Southeast Asia. However, efforts to import labor from Japan proper to work in Taiwan's key industries and transportation enterprises were, like similar attempts in Japan's other occupied areas, small in scale and largely unsuccessful. The POW workforce consisted mainly of American and British soldiers captured in the Philippines and Singapore. Their numbers were supposed to reach 6,000 in 1942, the only year for which numbers are available, but the actual figure was just 2,400.[26]

The demand for labor grew in Taiwan partly because of large-scale military projects, such as construction of a military port in Takao that came to be known as "strategic location F." "Recruiting by solicitation" alone could not match the sharply increased demand, and to ensure a constant supply of labor in Takao, the Government-General created an island-wide Taiwan Central Labor Association in October 1940. Meanwhile, two prefecture-level associations were set up in Takao and neighboring Tainan. Beginning with a single operation to supply labor for the navy, associations of this kind—with financial support from the Government-General starting in 1941—soon turned into an island-wide recruitment system. Local labor organizations also multiplied, operating through the administrative hierarchy and within established spatial boundaries.

By April 1941, when the ISPS movement was launched, Patriotic Service Units (*hōkōhan*) had already laid the groundwork. Launched in 1939 as a response to the Movement for National-Spirit Mobilization, Patriotic Service Units soon mushroomed in cities and counties. Also formed was an island-wide allied-prefecture association. By 1940, Patriotic Service Units had been turned into cell units. Significantly, Patriotic Service Units operated alongside the *kō* (ten to twenty households) structure of the *hokō*.[27]

Thus, even before the start of the ISPS in 1941, the *hokō* was stealthily being drawn into the establishment.

One activity of the Movement for National-Spirit Mobilization was "patriotic labor service" (*kinrō hōshi*). Each prefecture and subprefecture worked out its own operating rules. Taihoku Prefecture organized a Patriotic Labor Service Corps (*kinrō hōkokudan*) that was divided into three teams targeting schools, youth, and the general public. In Shinchiku (Hsin-chu) Prefecture, the corps was formed in July 1938 and included teams of married women, female youths, and the middle-aged, as well as workers in local government (*shi, gai,* or *shō*), companies, banks, and factories. At the base of the Shinchiku Patriotic Labor Service Corps were hamlet revival associations set up at the county level, and *chōkai* (neighborhood associations primarily but not exclusively for Japanese residents) in Shinchiku City. Women had their own Patriotic Labor Service Corps. Over half of the labor service corps functions were actually carried out by school teams and the youth corps.[28]

Another example was the Labor Association of Tainan Prefecture, set up on November 1, 1940. It took on a pyramid shape, organized along the same lines as the administrative hierarchy, as was typical in Japan's wartime empire. At the city (*shi*) or county (*gun*) level there were branches (*shikai*), and at the township (*gai*) or village (*shō*) level there were chapters (*bunkai*). Each allied *hokō* section set up a unit of the Patriotic Labor Service Corps, which brought issues relating to labor management in key industries under the supervision of the prefecture's labor association. The key to centralizing the mobilization of industrial labor in Taiwan was ISPS, a counterpart to the Imperial Rule Assistance Association (*Taisei yokusankai*) in Japan proper.

The ISPS began operating in April 1941, giving priority to training and war preparation in rear areas and to accelerating military-related production. In terms of training, the ISPS set up a number of institutes that generally incorporated the term "expanding to the South" (*takunan*), such as *Takunan nōgyō senshi kunrenjo* for agriculture and *Takunan kōgyō senshi kunrenjo* for industry. To increase production, the Government-General launched a Movement for Patriotic Service in Industry (MPSI; in Japanese, *Sangyō hōkō undō*) in September 1941 and required every mining and industrial plant that employed more than fifty laborers to set up MPSI corps units. By March 1943, the number of these units had reached a peak of 330, with 60,429 participants.

To streamline the labor administration further, the colonial government dissolved the Taiwan Central Labor Association on February 13, 1943, integrating it (now under the name *Taiwan sangyō hōkōkai*) into the umbrella organization of the ISPS. In December 1943 the Government-General set up a National Mobilization Department under the Bureau of Mining and Industry. Accordingly, each level of the administrative hierarchy had an office devoted to national mobilization.[29]

Military Laborers and Total War

Laborers drafted in wartime Taiwan received assignments throughout the empire, fluctuating in accordance with Japan's accelerated overseas expansion and eventual collapse. *Taiwan takushoku kaisha* (or *Taitaku),* for example, had 34 Taiwanese employees in 1939, but around 300 in 1943, more than one-third of them working overseas. Moreover, as Adam Schneider has cautioned, these figures underestimate the total number of Taiwanese employees, as some went overseas under the name of *yōin* (literally, the necessary personnel) or *genchi saiyō* (local hires), categories that do not appear in directories of employees.[30]

As soon as Japan expanded into Southeast Asia in the late 1930s, the Government-General of Taiwan began to dispatch support staff and laborers to the region in response to requests from military commands operating there. Regions within the sphere that received Taiwanese personnel included Indochina, Thailand, Malaya, eastern Indonesia, and Burma. One of the designated "areas of cooperation" was the supply of "personnel required by a military administration" *(gunsei yōin),* a category that consisted mainly of civilian staff with experience in administration, financial affairs, and sugar-related industries. The largest deployment was of Taiwanese military laborers *(kinrō yōin),* or employees on daily wages. Next were employees under contract *(koin* or *yatoi),* skilled workers between ages twenty-five and fifty, but this category was more Japanese than Taiwanese, as was the case with support staff.[31]

While military laborers were initially enlisted by the Taiwan Army in response to the outbreak of the Sino–Japanese War, the demand grew as Japan moved into Southeast Asia. As Kondō Masami has explained:

> At the request of the military, Taiwanese males between the age of 20 and 30 naturally became targets for recruitment. The five standards for selection listed by the Government-General were: (1) enthusiasm for public service; (2) an understanding of the Japanese language; (3) good behavior, with no bad habits; (4) physical health, with no diseases; (5) physical toughness, sufficient for normal labor. Each of five prefectures chose from lists prepared in cities, towns and villages. Thus, a Taiwan Special Patriotic Labor Service Corps, numbering 1,000, came into existence. A majority of the corps members were simply recruited and then sent to the battlefields.[32]

As mentioned above, the Government-General organized a labor bureau in October 1940 to handle enrollment of these "laboring soldiers," working through the schools to secure recruits. Along with Japanese soldiers and lo-cal coolies, they constituted one of three major elements at the battlefront. Their jobs ranged from transporting military supplies and constructing air-ports to growing vegetables and other mundane tasks. Taiwanese translators working for the army and the navy (*kaigun tsūben* and *rikugun tsūyaku*) formed a special category and were treated as lower-ranking officers. Thanks to their language and cultural affinities with China, Taiwanese translators were drafted for service in central China soon after the Sino–Japanese War broke out. More were sent to South China in late 1938, to Hainan Island (at the southern tip of mainland China) in early 1939, and after 1940 to all of occupied China. Although translation was their major job, Taiwanese trans-lators also helped in intelligence work, performed various assignments in military administration (such as road or military camp construction, POW trials, and propaganda work), and sometimes served as mediators between occupation authorities and local residents. The ambiguous role of Taiwan-ese translators often invited both suspicion from the Japanese military and bitter feelings from the Chinese residents, who described them as the "im-perial military" (*kōgun*) or "running dogs" (*zougou*). After the war, people seeking revenge beat more translators to death than any other category of Taiwanese laborers.

Police assistants (*junsaho*) were another special category. Police forces badly needed to be strengthened in occupied China after full-scale war broke out in 1937, and the first recorded dispatch of Taiwanese policemen took place on November 25 of that year. Taiwanese police assistants were later sent to Japanese-occupied Java and the Philippines, and especially to Hainan Island. The first two dispatches of policemen from Taiwan to Hainan Island in 1941, a total of 366 men, consisted mainly of Japanese police officers whose task was to "maintain social order." The rapid outflow of such a large police contingent from Taiwan forced prefecture and subprefecture govern-ments to recruit new members for their own police forces. When a labor request from the Hainan Navy Garrison Office came again in July 1942, the Government-General began to turn to Taiwanese with no prior police train-ing. Beginning in 1943, Taiwanese police assistants were assigned to fight-ing units, providing supplementary manpower for the navy.[33]

Taiwanese (as well as aboriginal) laborers were organized into various laboring corps specifically set up for them, because colonial people in Tai-wan could not serve in the imperial military until January 1945, when con-scription came into force. They were sent to work overseas as members of bodies such as the Taiwan Agricultural Volunteer Corps (*Taiwan nōgyō giyūdan*), Taiwan Special Patriotic Labor Service Corps (*Taiwan tokusetsu rōmu hōkōdan*), Taiwan Special Labor Corps (*Taiwan tokusetsu kinrōdan*),

Taiwan Special Agricultural Corps (*Taiwan tokusetsu nōgyōdan*), Taiwan Boy Laborers, Formosa Patriotic Volunteer Corps (*Takasago giyūtai*), Special Army Volunteers (*rikugun tokubetsu shiganhei*), and Special Navy Volunteers (*kaigun tokubetsu shiganhei*). Many young unmarried Taiwanese girls were also enlisted to serve as military assistant nurses, and some were forced to become "comfort women" (*ianfu*).[34]

As early as September 1937, when the main theater of battle in the Sino–Japanese War moved from northern to central China, the Taiwan army sent troops to help fight in the Shanghai area. One of the first units to go to China was a branch (*shitai*) of the Taiwan Defense Force, Shigefuji Chiaiki. On September 12, 4,300 soldiers departed from the Port of Kirun (Keelung), followed by another 1,200 the next day. There was no transport corps in the Taiwan army at that time, and 850 Taiwanese were drafted as military laborers (*gunpu*) to carry luggage, ammunition, and food supplies.[35] In April 1938, a group of Taiwanese was sent to central China to work as "military farmers" (*gunnōfu*) near Shanghai, Nanjing, Anqing, Wuchang, and Hankou. They were organized into the Taiwan Agricultural Volunteer Corps and mainly cultivated vegetables for the military. Starting in March 1939 agricultural instructors and instructor assistants were also sent to South China[36] and subsequently to Hainan Island and Southeast Asia as well, to improve agriculture in frontline areas.

A Taiwan Special Patriotic Labor Service Corps went to Indochina and the Philippines in October 1941 to assist with military-related work and agricultural production. Similar "special corps" made up of Taiwanese laborers were later sent to Malaya and Singapore to help collect source material and information, facilitate transportation, as well as maintain social order.[37] The corps targeted people between twenty and thirty years of age who had previously received training from the Patriotic Service Youth Corps (*gongyō hōkoku seinentai,* PSYC), an organization set up in 1940 in commemoration of Japan's "2,600th anniversary of nation-building." In 1943 there were eight district PSYC institutes, and the PSYC recruited selected trainees from the youth corps or among ex-military laborers. Training was relatively short, lasting from three to six months, but more than sufficient to pass on basic military skills and large doses of moral and spiritual uplift. "Graduates" of the training institute were allocated to local PSYC teams or became cadres of local youth corps units, or of the *Hokō* Able-bodied Corps (*hokō sōteidan*). The Able-bodied Corps was an integral part of the *hokō* system and followed the structure of the allied *hokō*. Because the main purpose of the Able-bodied Corps was to assist in police affairs and in times of "emergency," units were organized alongside—and directed by—the police boxes in their respective jurisdictions. In 1943, the Able-bodied Corps was replaced by an Air-Defense Corps (*keibōdan*), which also incorporated the Firefighting Corps (*shōbōgumi*) and the Air-Raid Defense Corps (*bōeidan*).

The "drafting" of comfort women from Taiwan began as early as November 1938, when "comfort houses" (*ianjo*) were set up in China in large numbers. The first recorded date available for instituting the system of "comfort houses" in China was 1932, around the time of the Shanghai Incident. In the aftermath of the Nanjing Massacre, the number of comfort houses increased sharply, starting in late 1937 and continuing into 1938.[38] Prior to July 1941, an estimated 2,268 permits were issued to personnel involved in the comfort business, covering their departure from Taiwan to China. Taiwanese accounted for 405 of these permits, less than the number of Japanese (1,182) or Koreans (681). A majority (2,139) was sent to southern China, but at a later date Taiwanese comfort women also went to Southeast Asia. While the total number of Taiwanese comfort women mobilized during the war remains difficult to reconstruct, one study puts the figure at no less than 1,000.[39] The issue of comfort women remains highly controversial, having been suppressed and "forgotten" for a generation.[40]

The need for increased medical care in both China and Southeast Asia after 1942 led the Government-General of Taiwan to turn to girls, unmarried and mostly between sixteen and twenty-five years of age, to serve in the military as assistant nurses, or in a few instances as qualified nurses (*kangofu*). A total of 900 Taiwanese girls were recruited between 1942 and 1944 to work for overseas army hospitals, mainly in Canton and Hong Kong but also in the Philippines.

By late 1941, more than 20,000 Taiwanese had enrolled in the war as military support laborers (staff included).[41] Military laborers could be obtained through requisitions or drafts (*chōhatsu* or *chōyō*). In practice there was little difference between voluntary recruitment and compulsory service, and supposedly benign recruitment exercises conducted by the military sometimes provoked violent resistance. Moreover, the status of military laborers was a constant source of dispute. While the Taiwan army headquarters proposed to treat military laborers as "military support staff" (*gunzoku*), until July 1943 a category that included all personnel not in a combat role, the central army headquarters continued to place them outside the military establishment. Military laborers did not even figure in the proverbial hierarchy: "military men, military horses, military dogs, and military support staff" (*gunjin, gunma, gunken, gunzoku*).[42]

Studies of modern Japan have long paid attention to conflicts over policy decisions with respect to Taiwan, and recent research has demonstrated the subtlety and complexity of the mechanisms involved.[43] For example, along with the well-known tensions between the army and the navy, and between advocates of the "movement towards the North" and the "movement towards the South," could be added conflicts between political parties, between the military and the civilian bureaucracy, and between the colonizer and the colonized. The attitude of the central headquarters of the army toward these laborers, as opposed to the more pragmatic approach suggested by the Taiwan Army headquarters, is an example of contentiousness between the metropole and the colonies during the period of mobilization for total war. Similar tensions arose later in disputes over the course of industrialization in Taiwan and the timing of the military conscription system to be applied to the Taiwanese as a whole.

The Government-General in Taiwan took steps to ensure that Taiwanese military laborers received the minimum pay guaranteed to day laborers. Rules for the Wartime Allowances of the Army (*chokurei* 133 of 1894) stipulated that laborers outside the ranks of military men and military support staff receive "appropriate payment in kind." By "appropriate" the colonial government meant the equivalent of the average wages paid for daily labor in the Taiwan market, which was far more than regular soldiers (*gunjin*) received (in 1943, about 1 yen per day compared with 6 yen per month).[44] Military laborers were "treated as daily laborers," although the terminology changed frequently, particularly after 1941. The Taiwanese remained at the bottom of the military structure until July 1943, when conscription was introduced. Then a revised rule for the army clearly stipulated that, while Taiwanese military laborers were "employees (*yōnin*) in terms of status," they were to be "treated as military support staff (*gunzoku*)."[45] Thus, Taiwanese military laborers were finally promoted to the rank of Japanese civilian military auxiliaries—just as the war situation was worsening.

The Pearl Harbor bombing produced a burst of "volunteer fever," and the situation of those who volunteered for military service changed drastically. The outbreak of the Pacific War in December 1941 was the turning point, and by January 1942 the number of volunteers had increased fourfold. By March, it was eighty-three times greater. The number of new "special volunteers for the Army" (*Taiwan rikugun tokubetsu shiganhei*) at each stage of recruitment in Taiwan was as follows: 5,041 by September 1941; 5,719 in late November 1941; 7,852 in late December 1941; 19,629 in January 1942; and 421,606 in March 1942. Systematic recruiting of Taiwanese volunteers for the army was instituted in April 1942, and by March 1943 the number of youths over seventeen years of age who had registered as candidates reached 600,000, a stunning figure given that the male population of Taiwanese youth between seventeen and thirty years of age was just 633,325 in January 1940.[46]

Taiwanese youth who volunteered to enlist in the army in 1942, 1943, and

Table 6.1

Taiwanese and Korean Army Volunteers

Year	Number of volunteers		Number accepted		Ratio of number accepted to number of volunteers	
	Taiwan	Korea	Taiwan	Korea	Taiwan	Korea
1938	—	2,946	—	406	—	1:7.3
1939	—	12,348	—	613	—	1:20.1
1940	—	84,443	—	3,060	—	1:27.6
1941	—	144,743	—	3,208	—	1:45.1
1942	425,961	254,273	1,020	4,077	1:417.6	1:62.4
1943	601,147	303,294	1,008	6,300	1:596.4	1:48.1
1944	759,276	—	2,497	—	1:304.1	—

Source: Kondō Masami, "I minzoku ni taisuru gunji dōin to kōminka seisaku: Taiwan no gunpu o chūshin nishite" (Military mobilization targeted at ethnically foreign peoples and imperial subjectification policies: The case of Taiwanese military laborers), *Taiwan kin-gendaishi kenkyū* (The research of modern/contemporary Taiwan) 6 (1988): 149–50.

1944 totaled 425,961; 601,147; and 759,276, respectively. Since the Training Center for Army Volunteers accepted only 1,020; 1,008; and 2,497 Taiwanese youths in these years, this meant that the application process was extremely competitive. The surprisingly strong response contrasts sharply with the situation in Korea, strategically Japan's most important colony, where the people were far less enthusiastic. (See Table 6.1.) During the period 1942–44, the Training Center for Army Volunteers accepted more than 5,500 applicants, including 1,300 aborigines. For the navy a system for recruiting volunteers (*Taiwan kaigun tokubetsu shiganhei*) was introduced in August 1943, and by July 1944, when the Training Center for Navy Volunteers was closed, more than 11,000 volunteers between the ages of sixteen and twenty-four had joined the navy.[47]

By October 1943, Japan's military posture had turned from offensive to defensive, and Japan began to construct a "Sphere of Absolute National Defense," with an eye to protecting Japan proper against an Allied attack. This plan involved constructing airports in the eastern part of the Indonesian archipelago, and 28,000 members of the Taiwan Special Labor Corps were dispatched to the New Guinea Islands, the New Britain Islands, and the Celebes in thirty rounds. A round of recruitment was organized by prefecture, averaging about 1,000 workers, and groups were sent at least from early 1943 through July 1944. In addition, there were two drafts of Taiwan Special Agricultural Corps, sent from Taihoku and Tainan Prefectures, respectively, and totaling approximately 2,000 workers.[48]

Beginning in March 1942, aborigines, too, marched off to war under the name of *Takasago teishin hōkokutai* (Formosa Volunteer Corps for Public Service), soon renamed *Takasago giyūtai* (Formosa Patriotic Volunteer Troop). In total, ten rounds of aborigines (including two for the navy) were mobilized between December 1941 and August 1945, a total of 4,500. The recruitment—as for the Han Taiwanese—was very competitive.

Again, from 1942, youngsters were mobilized for war. Boy laborers (*shōnenkō*), mostly between the ages of thirteen and eighteen, were sent to Japan between March 1943 and March 1944 in eight rounds. As in Japan proper, even students "departed for the front" (*gakuto shutsujin*). Student mobilization within the island began in October 1943, targeted at providing military training for college and high school students. Middle school students were organized into Taiwan Patriotic Service Students Corps (*Taiwan gakuto hōkōtai*). Students became a major source for industrial labor at the rear, particularly after the Outline for Mobilizing Students (*gakuto dōin yōkō*) came into force in March 1944. Virtually all students—both male and female—who had not done military service were now mobilized for labor, in accordance with their skills and physical strength.[49]

By March 1944, Taiwan had entered a stage of "decisive battles." The Ordinance for Drafting Nationals came into full force in July and was applicable not only to industrial and mining industries but also to the transportation, communications, and construction industries. This large-scale national mobilization went hand-in-hand with mass mobilization of labor, orchestrated through colonial administrative mechanisms. More than 400,000 Taiwanese, grouped by gender and age, were drafted to work in designated sites or joined in various mass organizations for labor. Women, for example, were organized into labor corps (*joshi kinrō teishintai*) when the ordinance came into force in August 1944, and more than 300,000 unmarried female youths were mobilized in this way. However, prior to July 1944, units of the Women's Patriotic Labor Service Corps (*joshi kinrō hōkokutai*) had already been organized as a provisional measure, and worked for a maximum of two months. Female members of the *teishintai* (volunteer corps) drafted by the new ordinance were to work for extended periods, sometimes lasting a year or more.[50]

In January 1945, when Japan was clearly losing the war, conscription was finally implemented in Taiwan. Of 45,726 who underwent physical examinations, 4,647 were ranked as A and 18,033 were ranked as B; that is, about half of them were physically fit for military service, and indeed the majority of those physically fit for military service ended up being taken into the military. These conscripts were virtually all assigned to the defense of Taiwan, as shipping them overseas had become all but impossible. In February, a newly created Taiwan Labor Corps for the Defense of the Fatherland (*Taiwan gokoku kinrōdan*) began to mobilize the masses in large numbers, amounting to 270,000–300,000 per day (not including labor mobilized as part of other organized groups). This completed the last stage of labor drafts in colonial Taiwan.[51]

According to an often-cited number based on official postwar Japanese statistics,[52] the military mobilized a total of 207,183 Taiwanese as laborers, and more than 92,000 of these conscripts remained in Taiwan. The Government-General estimated in late 1945 that the number of laborers mobilized after July 1937 and sent to work overseas (*tōgai e no kinrō dōin*) who "remained behind" (*kaigai zanryū*) after the war in "all places of the South" (*Nanpō kakuchi*) (apparently including China) was 92,748. The figure includes 5,870 skilled laborers and 8,419 workers sent to "arsenals in Japan proper" (*Nihon naichi heikishō*), which tallies with the number of Taiwan boy laborers.[53] The 1973 Japanese official estimate is clearly a very conservative number based on a survey carried out in the months shortly after Japan's surrender and thus reflects those who survived the war rather than all those originally mobilized to work overseas.

The number of military laborers sent overseas between 1937 and 1945 remains subject to debate. A classified document dated February 1, 1944, reported the results of a survey that showed a total of over 160,000 "Taiwanese residing outside the island." Of this number, about 100,000 military employees (*gun yōin*) were in "various places of the South," 15,000 military laborers (*gunzoku*) in Japan proper, and the rest in South China. The figure omits small groups in central and North China or in Manchuria.[54] Since estimates of deceased Taiwanese range from 30,304 to 146,000,[55] the total number mobilized overseas at the end of the war must have been well over 200,000.

Mass Mobilization of Labor

All initiatives for drafting labor—military laborers included—came to a virtual standstill after mid-1944, as Taiwan geared up for "decisive battle." From this time on, the Government-General by and large had to rely on mass labor, for which conscription was only one source. Mass mobilization was spatially structured and linked to the administrative hierarchy. In contrast to military and industrial mobilization, both more or less based on a relationship with the Japanese state as the biggest employer, mass mobilization was a national effort geared toward the "services of the public" (*hōkō*) in the "service of the state" (*hōkoku*). Two examples are the Youth Corps and the *hōkō* system.

The Youth Corps

The Youth Corps in prewar Japan, which was formed between the Sino–Japanese and Russo–Japanese Wars, was built alongside existing youth groups (*wakamono nakama* and the like) and developed into a local community organization.[56] A "trinity" in youth education—the youth corps, the military, and the local reservist system (*zaikō gunjinkai*)—acquired ideological underpinnings after the First World War. The idea was to build a mass organization following the boundaries of a spatially structured society. Tanaka Giichi (1864–1929), who organized the Youth Corps of Great Japan in 1917, employed the slogan "good people make good soldiers," which embodied a belief in local solidarity.[57] For the first time "youth" (*seinen*) became a catchword.[58]

Unlike Japan proper, however, colonial Taiwan had no similar tradition to build upon,[59] and the youth corps depended on support from local elites. It also relied heavily on the support and guidance of colonial authorities and was satirized as an "organization manufactured by the bureaucracy" (*kansei dantai*). The Taiwan Youth Corps began as an extension of "moral suasion" (*kyōka*) programs in the interwar years. The development of youth "organizations for moral suasion" (*kyōka dantai*) prior to 1926, a period Miyazaki Seiko associated with the Youth Association (*seinenkai*), varied from place to place, and groups were called by different names.[60] Wang Shih-ch'ing, for example, taking a town (Kaizan, or Hai-shan) near Taihoku (Taipei) City as a case study, identified four stages of development in the evolution of the moral-suasion movement in the interwar period: cultural assimilation (*dōfūkai*), 1914–25; prefecture-wide allied *dōfūkai*, 1925–31; allied associations of moral suasion (*kyōka rengōkai*), 1931–36; and hamlet revival associations (*buraku shinkōkai*), 1936–37.[61] The turning point came in 1926 when the Youth Corps, which was set up along the lines of the administrative hierarchy above the level of county (*gun*) and city (*shi*), became involved in social education. In 1930 the Youth Corps began to be standardized on an islandwide basis, following the district boundaries of primary schools. Members were divided by gender into *seinendan* for male youth and *joshi seinendan* for female youth, with both corps setting an age limit of twenty for members, calculated by Japanese (or Western) as opposed to Chinese counting.[62] In this way, *seinenkai* became an institutionalized *seinendan,* integrated a step further into the imperial state.[63]

As mentioned above, through the Movement for National-Spirit Mobilization the Youth Corps was linked to the *hokō* system and built into the ISPS establishment. The Youth Corps was organized in accordance with the "structured spatiality" of the *hokō*.

A youth corps unit (*bundan*) was usually based on one (but sometimes more than one) *aza* (a geo-administrative unit roughly equivalent to a *kō* of the *hokō*), or set up at the level of hamlet (a natural village or subvillage unit). Supporters' associations (*kōenkai*) were also organized into *hokō*-based alliances (*rengō hokō*), each formed by a cluster of *hokō* units under the jurisdiction of the nearest local police box, thus following the same spatial boundaries as police districts.[64] The youth corps used "hamlet assembly halls" (*buraku shūkaijo*) for their activities. It became compulsory, beginning with the Sino–Japanese War, for all youths—girls as well as boys—to join the youth corps, and from a base of 600 local youth corps groups with 25,000 members in the early 1930s, the organization expanded to 928 units with 420,110 members by 1942.[65]

Selected members of the youth corps received training through the Patriotic Service Youth Corps or became volunteer soldiers. The PSYC helped build large-scale projects (such as shrines and roads), and a few even went to Southeast Asia as military laborers. The Government-General set up the first PSYC in February 1940, and the five prefectures soon set up their own regional training centers. PSYC trainees were all around twenty years of age, carefully chosen from the localities and very limited in number—totaling only about 200 each round; in the case of Taihoku Prefecture, for example, 2 each were sent from every hamlet revival unit, most of them former military laborers or cadres of the youth corps. The goal was to provide military training to these chosen cadres in an intensive short-term program lasting two to three months, and then put them back to work as "local mainstays" (*chūken jinbutsu*). It was hoped that in this way the youngsters would provide "public services for the nation" in their home communities.[66] By 1943, the PSYC system was further institutionalized through the creation of two new programs. One was a Training Institute for Reforming Imperial Subjects (*kōmin renseijo*), which doled out "education as a discipline" to uneducated Taiwanese youth to prepare them for a military environment they would have to face. Another was a Youth School (*seinen gakkō*), successor to the Youth Training Institute (*seinen kunrenjo*) for young Japanese, which prepared educated Taiwanese youth for military service.

Publicity and peer pressure generated by "volunteer fever" no doubt contributed to wartime mobilization.[67] In contrast with the industrial labor draft, the recruitment of military laborers and the organization of local groups that mobilized labor underwent a shift from forced requisitioning to "volunteerism" (such as *shiganhei*). Appeals for participation in the war invoked patriotism, public service, and loyalty to the emperor as the embodiment of the nation. Although the Japanese were engaged in an aggressive war, volunteers were told they were fighting for "public good." The mass media also helped shape an image of loyal subjects in such a way that military labor became praiseworthy, hence the term "military laborers of glory" (*homere no gunpu*).

The success of the volunteer mobilization in Taiwan can also be attributed to "group volunteering." Shinchiku (Hsin-chu) Prefecture provides an example: the Department of Peace Preservation forced members of the Able-bodied Corps (*sōteidan,* affiliated with subdistrict allied *hokō* units but supervised by local police boxes) to "volunteer," after which administrative bureaus and public groups, from the city hall to associations in the prefecture, schools, and county and village governments, took steps to provide instruction. After the mayor urged public servants to "set an example," city employees began to "volunteer." The numerical increase in such "volunteers" derived precisely from such quasi-coercive mechanisms. Kondō Masami attributed this "group volunteering" to the "cooperation" of the schools, the police, and the *hokō.*[68]

The Hokō System

The *hokō* system provides an illustration of the issue of governmentality versus subjectivity.[69] Voluntarism—and, more broadly, Taiwanese loyalty to the Japanese emperor—was not simply a form of "false consciousness"; rather, the process of wartime mobilization translated bureaucratic rationality into governmentality, a phenomenon that raises questions about subjectivity and identity as well as political loyalty in general.

The Japanese used the *hokō* to secure labor from the early years of colonial rule. Although the *hokō* system originated in China, it was a central feature in Japan's colonial rule over Taiwan after 1895, providing an auxiliary organization that supported the police administration. It targeted the Han Taiwanese exclusively, organizing them in a hierarchy based on units of ten. Accordingly, *hokō* draftees were largely confined to Han Taiwanese, as the system excluded all foreigners (such as Koreans and Japanese) and most aborigines. Moreover, mass mobilization as such was based on the household rather than the individual as the basic unit in the mechanism responsible for mobilization, and as a consequence some individuals were drafted more than once. This is not to say that those outside the *hokō* necessarily weathered the war years any better than the Han Taiwanese, but the arrangement shows that race and ethnicity were significant during the war.

In principle, ten households formed a *kō,* and ten *kō,* a *ho,* although the actual units were multiplied many times over, and there were numerous variations.[70] Reorganized during wartime, the *hokō* system was given the added mission of prosecuting total war and constituted a distinct type of mass mobilization in Taiwan and throughout the empire. Thus over the half century of Japanese rule, the colonial government turned this millennium-old Chinese neighborhood organization of joint responsibility into a tool of colonial governmentality, with striking efficiency and success. I have dealt with the overall operation of the *hokō* system in detail elsewhere and will limit my discussion here to its role in wartime Taiwan's mass mobilization of labor. Suffice it to say that as a "social spatiality" endowed with a kind of subjectivity, the *hokō* was not only an organization for social control but also a local "self-rule" (*chihō jichi*) organization—however partial and controversial "self-rule" remained. Meanwhile, it was also a "colonial space" where spatial multiplicity along the boundaries of the administrative hierarchy was possible. As noted by John Noyes, "Here the discourse of colonization has an important role to play in the mythologization of the colonial landscape as an empty space. Colonial landscape is produced as one possible level of spatiality onto which desire may be mapped in the service of social production."[71]

Between 1993 and 1997, I conducted three major oral history projects on the *hokō* system, analyzing questionnaires completed by more than 3,000 informants and interviewing 300 elderly people.[72] In 1904 the number of *hokō* people mobilized by the *Kagi-chō*[73] to build roads reportedly reached more than 600,000 laborers or coolies (*jinpu*). The *hokō* performed a variety of tasks, including crime and plague prevention, construction and maintenance of highways and bridges, cultivating land, and increasing crops. In 1914, more than 55,000 *jinpu* were drafted to provide military transportation as part of a large-scale anti-aboriginal suppression action in eastern Taiwan. Also, the North–South Thoroughfare, completed in 1923 and more than 300 kilometers in length, was constructed with a significant input of labor drafted through the *hokō,* and often on lands donated by local residents.[74] Campaigns for "patriotic service" escalated after 1937. In western Taiwan, for instance, county governments in 1938 repeatedly commandeered *hokō* to plant roadside trees and forest belts, among other things, in the name of "labor service for public good (*hōkō*)." Similarly, *hokō* in the eastern part of Taiwan collected horse fodder and old pavement stones for military use.[75]

During the 1930s, the colonial government—in response to the Great Depression and increasing conflicts in China—mounted a Movement of Production Expansion in Taiwan. In 1933, for example, tens of thousands of *hokō* cultivated newly opened land, producing "products of national interest" such as rice, sugarcane, jute and castor-oil plants, and carried out reforestation along hills, water banks, and coastal areas. Figures indicate that during this year alone 1 million out of a total population of 5 million were drafted (although there were sometimes overlaps in counting).

When Taiwan entered the stage of "fighting decisive battles" (*kessen*) in

March 1944, Japan's central Headquarters for the defense of Taiwan gave priority to the air war. Airport expansion and construction work thus increased dramatically, and the *hokō* were summoned to provide labor. According to one estimate, there were sixty-five air-war-related sites by August 1945: twenty-four "air bases," twenty-seven "satellite airports," twelve "airport runways," and four "water-plane ports."[76] The number of military sites for air defense in an area as small as the island of Taiwan was impressive.

The following section draws on two pieces of oral testimony to examine the *hokō* system in connection with the entangled identity that came to mark Taiwanese. Ch'en Chin-shui of Yu-li (in southern Hua-lien) recalled vividly how his local oxcart association was mobilized to help construct military facilities near the city of Karenkō (Hua-lien-kang, in northern Hua-lien). Labor drafts there, he said, were routine during wartime and usually lasted around one month, but oxcart drafts lasted fifteen days plus time spent on the road. Ch'en recounted one unforgettable experience shortly before the end of the war when he and his fellow villagers were drafted to work on a makeshift airfield runway project in Taitō (T'ai-tung, a subprefecture to the south of Karenkō).[77] The oxcart troop consisted of up to eighty oxcarts and moved slowly. Air raids forced them to take cover frequently, making the journey a nightmare, and it took them more than three days to cover a distance of less than 80 kilometers. Moreover, they had to pay most of their own expenses (including hay for the oxen, although meals at the construction site were supplied by people living nearby). In another case, I interviewed the head of an allied *hokō* unit at Houpi (Kōbeki, in Tainan Prefecture). Lai Te-tai recalled leading eight *ho* units that worked for several months helping construct a nearby airport.[78] He rarely went home during this period but was still expected to fulfill other duties in his villages (such as handling pork rationing).

The surveys reveal that mass labor drafts in colonial Taiwan were considered onerous. However, when asked to compare the Japanese and the later Nationalist governments, some interviewees felt the Japanese were better. They preferred the *hokō* system to its postwar counterpart (*cun-li-lin*) because the heads of *hokō* units (*hosei*) during the Japanese period, whether elected or appointed, were on the whole well respected, competent, and incorruptible. More factors are involved in this analysis, but the issue lies beyond the scope of this chapter. Suffice it to say that labor drafts both entailed and were conditioned by governmentality and identity.

Conclusion

Let us return for a moment to the disabled war veteran Hung Huo-chao. From his childhood, he was instilled with the notion that he was an imperial subject of Japan. Recalling how his Japanese officers instructed him before he was sent to the war, he could not but curse the Japanese emperor for fooling him. And, thinking of what a tragic price he had paid—he was disabled—for defending Japan, he began to hate the Japanese for their abuses. In defining himself as a "Japanese national," or at least in identifying himself as a "son of the Emperor," Hung was talking about a postwar subjectivity empowered by colonial governmentality. To call Hung a Taiwanese victim of Japanese wartime indoctrination, therefore, is a reductive statement claiming that he tricked himself into believing what was not true. Instead, we see here how the past was both invoked and subverted through living memory.

Japan did not endorse "marching toward the South" (*nanshin*), as opposed to "marching toward the North" (*hokushin*), as national policy until 1936. In Taiwan, this policy was further elaborated three years later and embodied in a slogan: "Japanization, industrialization, and marching toward the South" (*kōminka, kōgyōka, nanshinka*). The year 1936 also brought the establishment of the Taiwan Development Corporation (*Taitaku*), a semiofficial "company for implementing state policy" (*kokusaku kaisha*). Industrial policy in Taiwan during the "Fifteen Years' War" (1931–45) aimed at quickly expanding products in response to military requests, and an increasing number of industrial laborers was accordingly requisitioned: from 60,000 in 1932; to 87,000 in 1937; to 137,000 in 1941; and thereafter 20,000 more every year.[79]

The Law of Air Raids came in force as early as November 1937, and soon Taiwan was to become a stepping-stone for Japan's "march toward the South." Labor drafts mobilized to support fighting first in China and later in Southeast Asia focused on agricultural assistance, with the Taitaku spearheading the invasion. The movement to convert Taiwanese into "loyal subjects of the emperor of Japan" began at this point. This movement quickly involved Taiwanese of all ranks in "patriotic service," and labor service became one way to show devotion to the nation. The fact that the war was waged against China—the origins of most Taiwanese or at least of their ancestors—complicated Japan's labor operations: logically Taiwanese had to be completely converted into Japanese before they could be deployed to the front. The military's suspicion of possible Taiwanese betrayal led to its decision primarily to mobilize military laborers. Volunteerism as illustrated in the conscription system thus reflected deliberate calculations in the political dilemma Taiwanese faced, and also an opportunistic response to the rules of the game through which Taiwanese reconciled a hard reality with a rising awareness of self-identity.

In late June 1941, the cabinet passed a resolution to enhance the role of Taiwan in Southeast Asia, thus pushing labor mobilization to a new peak. Meanwhile, Taiwan was given the mission of providing military supplies by stepping up military-related industrialization, of chemicals in particular, and by quickly expanding or constructing air bases. From a stepping-stone prior to 1941, Taiwan was now poised to become an "aircraft carrier" that would "never sink." Labor mobilization was quickly ramped up, in terms of both industrial and military drafts.

As a mode of wartime mobilization, however, labor drafts were a double-edged sword for the colonizers. To effectively mobilize labor, especially labor with some skills, the Government-General had to plan carefully and to arrange training; it did both remarkably well until the final stage of the war. The coordination programs with the military included, among other things, administrative supervision, surveys and investigations, maintenance of social order, mollifying the people with propaganda, medical care and plague prevention, communications and transportation, resource supply, finance, public undertakings, and industrial development. And it had to give the volunteers or draftees training to make sure that they had the discipline necessary to follow their instructions. Thus, the Government-General initiated many training programs and institutes as the war developed. While social education was at the center of the *kyōka* movement during the interwar years, in wartime physical training increasingly became the core program, targeted at "selfless patriotic service" (*messi hōkō*) and "drilling to become imperial subjects" (*kōmin rensei*). Institutionally, the Government-General did a good job of transplanting existing local organizations to the colonial administration, encouraging them to cross their boundaries by forming upper-level associations alongside the administrative hierarchy. It also shuffled the organized groups around by merging, creating, or integrating (or some combination of the three) them into an umbrella organization headed by the Governor-General. The role of colonial administrative initiatives illustrates the growing importance of colonial governmentality in this context. By 1945, therefore, Taiwan was not only a disciplined society—it was a disciplinary one.

To conclude, "volunteer fever" among the wartime generation of Taiwanese youths was as serious as any other authentic attempt on the part of the colonized to assimilate themselves to become Japanese, as the case of Hung Huo-chao shows. *Dōka, kyōka,* and *kōminka* were not simply concepts, policies, or slogans to be defined, dictated, or priced. They marked a historical stage in the development of colonial spatiality, a battleground for political contention, and a mechanism of modes of power. That is why in the case of labor mobilization, colonial governmentality could be controlled, manipulated, or subverted. This analytical approach applies to the theoretical framework of subjectivity as well. Any attempt to assess the Japanese colonial legacy in Taiwan has to take into consideration the translation, transmission, and transgression of the twin discourses of governmentality and subjectivity.

Total war served as a catalyst. In view of Japan's colonial vision of "gradualism" with regard to Taiwan, this catalyst might not have been indispensable to long-term changes in governmentality and subjectivity, but it was a key factor in the rapid change that in fact occurred. Timing, too, was decisive. Military mobilization for labor, as engineered by the Governor-General had a clearly identifiable pattern of development, with each stage corresponding to Japan's overall military condition in the war. The first stage, from July 1937 to December 1941, featured the dispatch of military laborers and military farmers to the China theater. The second stage, from Pearl Harbor through September 1944, was distinguished by the sending of army and navy volunteers to Southeast Asia. And the third and last stage, the final year, which came to be known as the period of "fortification" (*yōsaika*), was a period when the conscription system came to the fore. In an ironic twist, Japan's racial concern over the role of the Taiwanese in the China theater contrasted with its realistic calculations over the deployment of the Taiwanese in Southeast Asia. The conscription system also reveals this intriguing play of the changing conditions brought about by the war in Japan's policy-decision process.

Any serious comparative study of Taiwan needs to deal with the fact that the island was under Japanese colonial rule for fifty years. Fifty years amounts to two generations, or three stages of political shifts. The span of colonial rule in Taiwan is often neglected in comparative colonial studies, for example, in comparisons between Korea and Taiwan in terms of their pro- or anti-Japanese complex, or between nations of Southeast Asia and Taiwan in terms of postwar struggle for state building. The parallels are relevant to Taiwan but can also be misleading. Any attempt to contextualize Taiwan within the framework of the Japanese empire has to avoid reductionism. Labor drafts in wartime Taiwan should thus be treated with care. Collective narratives of the elders on the *hokō* as oral history should also be evaluated critically.

So far as wartime mobilization was concerned, labor drafts in the colonial context point to the problematic in theorizing a binary framework with "cultural integration" set against "national integration," as Komagome Takeshi has argued.[80] Taiwan's labor mobilization also highlights the difficulty of applying a Weberian framework in terms of "formal rationality" versus "substantial rationality."[81] On the whole, labor drafts for total war serve as a case study to illustrate how colonial subjectivity was both shaped and subverted in colonial Taiwan. Simply put, it was in the context of the changes brought about by total war that colonial subjectivity was asserted, redefined, and subverted. In this sense, labor drafts in wartime Taiwan confirmed the possibility of alternative mechanisms of power.

At the same time, in the case of labor mobilization, the representation of governmentality in colonial Taiwan was a function of colonial modernity. Thus, when the established order of Japanese colonial rule collapsed in 1945, the colonial subjectivity it had shaped was ironically turned into a cultural and political critique against the new regime—in the name of colonial modernity. Immediate postwar Taiwan witnessed this translation of colonial governmentality into postcolonial subjectivity. As such, colonial governmentality was objectified, mythologized as an embodiment of modernity.

Taiwan's contributions to the war came at a cost that must be measured in both the short and the long run. Taiwan played an important role in providing laborers for Southeast Asia and South China, and it served as a backup labor pool for Japan proper. Technical support staff was also sent from Taiwan to Manchuria and occupied China, while some Japanese laborers and POWs were moved to Taiwan. When preparations for total war drove Japan to mobilize colonies such as Taiwan, the Taiwanese masses were empowered for the first time to claim some kind of equality with the Japanese. In this way they became endowed with a certain degree of subjectivity, if only in the sense of equivalence in terms of obligations and death. It is in this sense that Japanese wartime labor drafts in Taiwan both defined and invoked the convertibility of colonial governmentality into subjectivity.

Part VI

Indonesia

7

"Economic Soldiers" in Java

Indonesian Laborers Mobilized for Agricultural Projects

Shigeru Sato

Japan's advance into Southeast Asia was driven by its desire to gain control over natural resources, oil in particular. In comparison with some other parts of the region, Java was not rich in strategic resources, but the island had another kind of resource in the form of manpower, a population of almost 50 million that comprised more than half of the people in Japanese-occupied Southeast Asia.[1] The Japanese needed workers for a wide range of projects and mobilized large numbers of Javanese laborers, called *rōmusha* in Japanese. Nearly 300,000 Javanese *rōmusha* were sent to other parts of Southeast Asia and the Pacific, where they experienced harsh conditions and a brutal work regime. More than half of them never made it back to Java.[2]

Despite the importance of this issue, many details remain unclear, and the subject is obscured by fallacies. One such fallacy is the tendency to associate the term "Javanese *rōmusha*" only with workers sent overseas. In fact, a majority of the forced laborers were put to work on the island of Java. Another misconception is that the *rōmusha* worked mostly on military projects. It is true that the Japanese drafted labor to construct military facilities, but the vast majority of *rōmusha* were mobilized for nonmilitary projects in agriculture or the textile industry, undertaken to feed and clothe the local population. The Japanese coined the term "economic soldiers" (*perajurit ekonomi* in Indonesian) or "worker-soldiers" (*perajurit pekerja*) for these drafted laborers to create a feeling that becoming *rōmusha* and toiling to increase production was a heroic action, comparable to military service. Their propaganda stressed that laborers, like soldiers, must devote themselves fully to supporting the ultimate aim of the war, described as the liberation of Asia from Western colonialism.

This chapter provides information on trends in labor mobilization in Java, with a particular focus on the agricultural campaign, considering its purposes, the reason for its failure, and its far-reaching consequences.

Why did the Japanese need so many "economic soldiers"? The answer lies in changed economic circumstances and Japan's idea of developing a pan-Asian "co-prosperity sphere." This expression was deceptive because Japan went to war to secure strategic resources, and without making preparations for building co-prosperity. The draft guidelines for the military administration in Southeast Asia, prepared in February and March 1941, reveal this lack of preparation by stating: "The primary aim shall be to obtain resources, and if possible, to enable the peoples on the occupied land to maintain a minimum standard of living."[3] As investigations into economic implications of the planned military venture progressed, it became clear that the secondary aim in the above statement, after the proviso "if possible," could not be achieved. Over the preceding century the economies of Southeast Asia had become increasingly enmeshed with world markets. Mass-produced goods had flowed into the region, and by the 1930s people depended on imports for clothing, medicines, construction materials, machinery, and other essential items. The region exported large quantities of a small number of specialized items, mainly primary products such as oil, tin, rubber, sugar, coffee, and tobacco. After cutting Southeast Asia off from the West, Japan did not have the capacity to supply needed manufactured goods, nor could it absorb Southeast Asian exports in quantities sufficient to sustain the economy of the region.

Incorporation of the Southern Regions into a co-prosperity sphere by dint of military force would inevitably disturb the local economies and day-to-day lives of the local people. Japan's initial planning simply disregarded this matter and left the local people to bear the full brunt of the economic slow-down. There was, however, a limit to what could be ignored, because economic chaos might foment anti-Japanese feeling and lead to widespread social unrest. Steps needed to be taken to avert this outcome.

In February 1942, well after the invasion was launched, the Japanese created the Council for Constructing Greater East Asia (Dai Tōa Kensetsu Shingi Kai). The plan initially was to develop an industrial zone centered on Japan and including Manchukuo and North China, with the remainder of the Japanese empire supplying raw materials and providing markets for industrial products. The occupied Southern Regions were, therefore, not to be industrialized. Soon, however, the Allied counteroffensive shattered the region's marine transportation, compelling Japan to alter this scheme. In June 1943, Tokyo authorities officially decided to start fostering certain industries in the occupied territories, with a view to achieving self-sufficiency in each of the smaller occupied units.[4]

The co-prosperity sphere thus became a constellation of small, economically isolated units, a change that required industrial restructuring and systematic relocation of labor within each region. In the process, the production efficiency of labor plummeted. Although much labor was mobilized for producing food and clothing for local use, those items became increasingly scarce. Nutritional deprivation among the poorer segments of society manifested itself as dysentery and hunger edema. Reported cases of dysentery in occupied Java doubled each year, from 1,257 in 1942 to 2,332 in 1943; to 5,801 in 1944; and to 6,859 in the period January–June 1945.[5] The number of starving patients brought in each month to the Semarang Central Hospital increased steadily from 70 (of whom 27 died) in November 1943 to 163 (of whom 109 died) in March 1944.[6] A severe drought in the middle of 1944 caused the situation to deteriorate even further, and people dying at the roadside from hunger and disease became a common sight.[7] The following account, taken from Pramoedya Ananta Toer's novel *The Fugitive,* written soon after the Japanese surrender, concerns the final stage of occupation.

> When you go to the city you see children sprawled lifeless at the side of the road. In front of the market and the stores, down beneath the bridge, on top of garbage heaps and in the gutters there are corpses. Nothing but corpses. The place is filled with the dead—children and the old people. And you know what they do? If they are going to die, before they take their final breath, they first gather a pile of teakwood or banana leaves that have been used to wrap food in. And they cover their bodies with those leaves and they die. It's like they know that in two hours they're going to die and that after they are dead no one is going to prepare them for burial. These are crazy times we're going through. And I don't know why it is. In all my life this is the first time I've seen anything like it. Corpses. Wherever you go, unattended corpses.[8]

The occupation deprived a large number of villagers of their livelihood, and the number of beggars increased both in the cities and in the countryside. In Pramoedya's novel, the village head who made the remark quoted above became wealthy by smuggling teak. Beggars swarmed to a circumcision rite for his son, and when the boy asked his mother why she didn't give them something, she replied, "These days, there are thousands of them around. They are like ants. And if you pay any attention at all . . ."[9]

Many of those who lost their livelihood in their villages migrated to the cities. According to one estimate, Jakarta's population grew by 42 percent (from 594,000 to 844,000) during the occupation.[10] The Japanese even rounded up homeless people in the cities, but most of them, particularly women, were found unfit for work due to poor nutrition and illness. These wretched people were given a modicum of food and medication and put to work as soon as possible.[11]

Phases of Labor Mobilization

The Japanese conducted "total mobilization" campaigns in various forms. At first the campaigns were little more than slogans, but in the latter part of the occupation the mobilization of labor caused extensive dislocation of population and created enormous hardships throughout the island. Japanese records show mobilization taking place in three phases. In the first the military administration employed workers to rehabilitate Java's infrastructure, for example, by rebuilding road and railroad bridges and harbor facilities destroyed by the Dutch scorched-earth strategy. This phase began immediately after the invasion and continued until the end of October 1943. The second phase, construction of airstrips and other military facilities, began in mid-August 1943, and the third, devoted to increasing production, soon followed, beginning in early October. (See Table 7.1.)[12]

Until late 1943 Java had a great deal of unemployment. The island was still feeling the effects of the Great Depression, and the outbreak of war in Europe and the Japanese invasion that soon followed exacerbated the problem by cutting off Java from its export markets. One of the first tasks for the Japanese local administrators in Java was, therefore, to create jobs for the unemployed.

The demand for labor in the first and the second phases was small compared with the numbers seeking work. In the third phase, however, the occupation authorities carried out a thoroughgoing "total mobilization" campaign, and many villages now had to deal with a shortage of workers rather than unemployment. The authorities soon realized that the simultaneous conduct of military and economic campaigns was unsustainable and suspended their military projects at the end of December to concentrate on the latter.[13]

The trend in labor mobilization is reflected in the monthly record of railroad passengers in Java throughout the war. (See Table 7.2.) Early in the occupation, the railroads in Java were already carrying more passengers than before the war. The numbers remained steady until July 1943, increased slightly when the defense projects began in August, rose further when the production-increase campaign began in October, but declined when the rehabilitation project ended at the close of the month. The production-increase campaign gradually intensified and reached its peak in September 1944, just before the onset of the rainy season when the Japanese were trying to complete many irrigation and drainage projects. After military projects stopped at the end of 1944, the passenger numbers again declined.

During the peak period, the railroads in Java were carrying 12 million more people per month, or 400,000 more people per day compared with 1942, and most of the additional passengers were *rōmusha*. This figure, how-

Table 7.1

Three Phases of Labor Mobilization

1942				1943				1944				1945		
3	6	9	12	3	6	9	12	3	6	9	12	3	6	9

rehabilitation

construction of airstrips

production increase

Source: "Kōkyō Shisetsu no Gaikyō" (Overview of Public Works) (BUZA NEFIS/CMI, encl. 3, 1776 and 2048).

Table 7.2

Number of Passengers Carried by Java's Railroad Lines

Month	1942	1943	1944	1945
4	—	5,943,263	13,922,644	10,492,392
5	—	6,538,115	14,541,944	10,740,299
6	6,666,432	7,930,809	14,978,350	11,227,510
7	6,640,491	7,964,197	16,684,671	11,617,551
8	6,869,711	8,789,708	15,396,350	
9	6,901,558	8,751,405	18,205,431	
10	8,576,366	11,395,118	18,103,717	
11	6,553,940	9,220,469	16,861,165	
12	7,311,392	10,767,716	15,891,540	
1	6,850,074	11,311,156	13,090,781	
2	6,212,748	11,656,992	9,783,125	
3	7,049,314	13,840,108	10,987,849	
Total	69,632,026	114,109,056	178,447,567	44,077,752
Average per month	6,963,203	9,509,088	14,870,630	11,019,438

Source: "The Survey of the Railway Affairs to be Succeeded," p. 48 (NIOD IC 012516).

ever, represents only a small fraction of the movement of forced labor, since railroads were used mostly for long-distance trips. The majority of *rōmusha* remained in their residencies and reached the work sites by walking.

This increase in railroad passengers was achieved in the face of a general deterioration of transportation in Java. The carrying capacity of the railroad fell owing to a range of problems, such as shortages of fuel and spare parts. The total daily average distance covered by all trains declined from 73,626 kilometers in April 1944 to 57,217 kilometers in July 1945. The distance covered by passenger trains decreased even more sharply, from 18,768 to 5,909 kilometers.[14] The increase in the movement of people involved using freight cars to carry passengers.

One document, apparently produced sometime in 1945, shows how goods trains and mixed trains were used for transporting people. The railroads in Java and Madura were divided into 115 sections. In one of them, between Merak and Cilegon in West Java, two goods trains operated a combined traction tonnage of 470, with two-thirds of this capacity designated for passengers and the remainder for freight. Taking Java and Madura as a whole, goods trains and mixed trains (excluding passenger trains) had a combined traction tonnage of approximately 136,000, at least 20 percent of which was used for passengers.[15]

Although the number of passengers nearly tripled, the amount of luggage carried decreased slightly during the occupation. This would indicate that most conscripted laborers carried few items with them. They were typically ordered by local authorities, such as village heads, to gather at certain places and were sent away immediately in fully packed freight wagons, sometimes without being allowed to prepare for the trip or even to let their families know they were leaving.

The large-scale mobilization of labor in the third phase required Java-wide coordination. The authorities set up a network of labor mobilization agencies called Rōmu Kyōkai (Labor Associations), put in place prior to the fiscal year that began in April 1944, and employers who needed laborers submitted requests to their local branch. To obtain *rōmusha* from other residencies, the Rōmu Kyōkai at the residency capitals sent requests to the central office in Jakarta, which coordinated the movement of labor throughout Java. Table 7.3 shows statistics for the first three months of the 1944 fiscal year, as compiled by local Rōmu Kyōkai offices.

The information in Table 7.3 covers only twelve of Java's nineteen residencies and principalities, and because many reports were prepared in early June they do not include people mobilized later in that month. Moreover, unlike demand, the supply of labor was difficult to record accurately. For example, at a site in Rumpin in Bogor residency, the employer requested 25,000 persons for unpaid labor service (*kinrō hōshi*). The job began on May 5, 1944, with 4,839 workers, and peaked on June 26 with 23,213. However, records for this work site show that new people arrived every day and others left, suggesting that the total number of individuals mobilized for the project was much larger than 25,000. Fourth, there was mobilization throughout Java that did not go through the Rōmu Kyōkai. The report from Kedu was submitted with a comment (handwritten in Japanese but apparently by an Indonesian official) that the exact labor situation within the residency could not be determined because many workers were being mobilized directly by the army. The Rōmu Kyōkai was supposed to deal with all *rōmusha* mobilization including that for military purposes, but the army often sent trucks to villages on twenty-four hours' notice and carried people away for their projects. In addition, there was a great deal of unrecorded, miscellaneous mobilization for a wide variety of tasks ranging from construction of air-raid shelters to compulsory cultivation of various crops.

The table shows that certain residencies, such as Jakarta and Bogor, generally met their requirements despite heavy demand. Mobilizing labor was apparently more difficult in residencies such as Bojonegoro and Surakarta, where the standard of living was low in the countryside. Cirebon did not meet demands for labor within the residency and received no requests from elsewhere, probably because of peasant riots in Indramayu regency between April and July 1944.

Table 7.3

Rōmusha Mobilization from Twelve Residencies, April–June 1944 (number of workers)

From	Within the Residency		To Other Residencies		Total	
	Demand	Supply	Demand	Supply	Demand	Supply
Jakarta	9,883	10,333	1,000	604	10,883	10,937
Bogor	28,580	27,187	1,000	777	29,580	27,964
Priangan	31,993	28,505	768	485	32,761	28,990
Cirebon	23,265	11,475	0	0	23,265	11,475
Semarang	4,199	3,920	9,467	7,566	13,666	11,486
Kedu	—	—	5,500	4,643	5,500	4,643
Surakarta	29,290	10,665	1,355	764	30,645	11,429
Yogyakarta	1,325	1,325	1,265	1,269	2,590	2,594
Bojonegoro	4,060	2,689	5,180	2,201	9,240	4,890
Malang	18,543	13,174	12,282	8,274	30,825	21,448
Madura	10,055	7,293	5,800	5,058	15,855	12,351
Besuki	0	0	1,800	1,283	1,800	1,283
Total	161,193	116,566	45,417	32,924	206,610	149,490
Achievement (percent)		72.3		72.5		72.4

Source: "Rōmu Kyōkai Reports," NIOD IC 005720-97.

Table 7.4

Rōmusha Mobilized from the City of Semarang, December 1943–October 1944 (number of workers)

Destination	Demand	Supply	Achievement (percent)
Outside Java	9,500	2,956	31.1
Other residencies	2,000	615	30.8
Within the residency	4,200	136	3.2
Within the city	1,000	885	88.5
Total	16,700	4,594	27.5

Source: "Rapport inzake werving en transport van Romusha's in de Residentie Semarang" [Report on recruitment and transportation of *rōmusha* in the residency of Semarang] BUZA NEFIS/CMI, encl. 3, 3535.

In the second half of 1944, a large-scale labor mobilization exercise coincided with a severe drought. Few Rōmu Kyōkai reports have been found for this period, but Table 7.4, which is based on information compiled in late 1944 by the Rōmu Kyōkai of the city of Semarang, shows how difficult labor mobilization became at the time. Semarang recruited labor by assigning quotas to kampong heads, by using employment agencies, and by sending vehicles around the city searching for workers. The rate of success was very low, and the report offers the following reasons for the poor results:

1. There was no more unemployment in the city;
2. Agriculture required that labor be retained within each village;
3. Farmers were afraid that their rice fields might be taken by others while they were away;
4. The wages (35 cents per day within Java and 50 cents outside Java) were too low;
5. Many employers in the city offered better wages;
6. The promised remittance of part of the wages to the families was irregular and insufficient; and
7. People were afraid of the medical checkup that workers received before being sent away (this requirement was eliminated after June 1944).

The Production-Increase Campaign

The Japanese gave the strongest possible publicity to agricultural projects and particularly to rice production, claiming they could double the rice output of Java in five years. According to Japanese propaganda, the campaign was important because Java was a key element of the co-prosperity sphere and also a major logistics base for Japan in the Southern Seas. However, there is reason to think that these explanations were a facade used to mask the real reason for the campaign. The demand for Java's food by the Japanese, whether within Java or elsewhere, was never large in comparison with Java's productive capacity. Moreover, the campaign proved counterproductive because it depleted village workforces, but the Japanese continued their efforts and even intensified them toward the end of occupation, under the same old catch phrase of "total mobilization for production increase."[16]

Morooka Masao, the Japanese official in charge of irrigation works throughout Java, left voluminous notebooks that cast much light on the agricultural campaign.[17] His records provide a reason for the campaign that the authorities never publicized: substantial areas in Java were taken out of food production and planted with fiber-yielding crops. Clothing and sacking had been imported prior to the occupation, and the war caused a shortage of these and other fiber-based products throughout the occupied areas. Cotton was by far the most important clothing material. The territories that made up the co-prosperity sphere produced about 10 percent of the world's cotton, mainly in northern China, while they consumed about 25 percent. After World War I, Japan became the largest exporter of cotton goods in the world, but Japan's textile industry relied almost entirely on raw cotton imported from British India and the United States. To maintain the same level of consumption without these imports, approximately 930,000 extra tons of cotton had to be produced within the co-prosperity sphere. Java had a small textile industry that Dutch authorities had promoted in the late 1930s, but it produced no more than 10 percent of local cloth requirements and required imported yarn to do that. Jute was another crucial fiber: before the war, gunnysacks, used to store and transport sugar, rice, and other products, had been imported from the Bengal region of India, which accounted for about 97 percent of the world's jute production, but supplies from this source were no longer available.[18] The problem demanded urgent attention, and authorities in Java developed a five-year plan early in 1942. (See Table 7.5.)

Before the war, Java imported approximately 60 million kilograms of cotton products annually. Even if the five-year plan met its targets, the amount of cotton Java would have produced was no more than 30 million kilograms in 1947. By 1943 garments and textiles had almost completely disappeared from the Javanese market. In the latter part of the occupation many people had no clothes to wear, and the existence of nearly naked people became a serious hindrance to the mobilization of labor and to many other social activities. School attendance dropped because a large proportion of children had no decent clothes to wear to school. Muslims could not go to mosque because it was improper to enter a holy place without being properly clothed,

Table 7.5

Five-Year Plan for Planting Fiber-Yielding Crops in Java, 1942–47 (in hectares)

	1942	1943	1944	1945	1946	1947
Cotton	(2,500)	30,000	50,000	90,000	150,000	180,000
Ramie	(150)	1,150	7,150	13,150	21,150	31,150
Roselle and jute	(6,000)	10,000	15,000	18,000	20,000	25,000
Total	(8,650)	41,150	72,150	121,150	191,150	236,150

Source: Gunseika Jawa Sangyō Sōkan [Conspectus of the Industries in Java under the Military Administration], (originally published in Java in 1944, repr. Tokyo: Ryūkeishosha, 1990), vol. 1, pp. 289–351.
Note: Figures for 1942 are results; figures for later years are projections.

and the requirement that corpses be wrapped in a white cloth for burial became difficult to fulfill.

Recognizing the severity of the problem, the Japanese increased the area to be planted with cotton in 1945 to 127,500 hectares and also advanced plans for planting ramie, another fiber-producing plant, setting a target of 31,150 hectares for 1945.[19] They also encouraged both farmers and nonfarmers to plant fiber-yielding plants in their house compounds, distributing seed and leaving the produce at the growers' disposal, hoping in this way to obtain a further 720,000 kilograms of cotton and 6 million kilograms of ramie.[20]

Not all agricultural projects were for the local economy. The Japanese also expanded castor-oil plant cultivation to extract lubricants for airplane engines and a kerosene substitute for the local population. According to one report, this crop was planted on 178,740 hectares in 1944, about 10 percent in irrigated fields and the rest in dry fields.[21]

During the first two years of the occupation, the impact on food production of cultivating nonedible crops was not serious because the area used remained small, and many sugar fields were being converted back to rice. Other land previously planted with export crops was also used for food crops such as maize and cassava.

From 1944, the area under nonedible crops became large enough to affect food production. To mitigate the negative impact, the Japanese attempted to expand agricultural land by reclaiming swamps and clearing forests, and to increase the area suitable for rice by constructing and extending irrigation canals. These initiatives, however, could not compensate for the losses due to the cultivation of nonedible crops.

The major rice-producing residencies of Besuki and Malang in East Java were most suitable for growing cotton. In these two residencies, plans called for cotton to take up 50,000 hectares in 1945, and between 1944 and 1945 the area under wet rice had to be reduced by 11,390 hectares, and production by 18,690 tons.[22] Ramie, roselle, and jute were planted mainly on dry fields. Consequently, cassava production had to be reduced by 5,890 hectares and 50,260 tons between 1944 and 1945, according to the plan drawn up in 1944.[23]

When the Japanese launched their production-increase campaign, the mass media reported extensively on projects designed to increase food production and published impressive figures about the land to be converted to rice fields and the expected increase in production. The stories seemed to suggest that greatly enhanced land areas with improved water control were going to be made available for food crops. The reality was very different. Despite the tremendous effort, and the conversion of export-crop fields to food-crop fields, the area available for food crops declined slowly but steadily owing

Table 7.6

Irrigation Works (results for 1944 and plans for 1945)

	Area (hectares)		Budget (guilders)	
	1944	1945	1944	1945
General Bureau (new)	40,220	40,037	950,200	1,140,000
Residencies (new)	10,790	20,730	451,200	1,502,100
Residencies (improvement)	128,000	98,729	4,071,200	4,805,300
Total	179,012	159,486	5,472,600	7,447,400

Source: "Study of Irrigation of Java/Madoera," BUZA NEFIS/CMI, encl. 3, 1776.

to increases in the areas planted with nonedible crops. According to a Japanese plan drawn sometime in 1943, some 3,799,000 hectares of land were planted with wet rice in 1943, and the area set aside for rice in 1945 was 83,000 hectares less.[24]

Irrigation Projects

One of the ways the Japanese attempted to prevent decreases in rice production was by improving water supplies to make double-cropping possible in many areas. They drew up increased budgets for extension and improvement of irrigation networks during the coming years. For more than a century the Dutch had constructed extensive modern irrigation works in Java, mainly for sugar estates. Between 1916 and the onset of the Great Depression in 1929, they spent about 7 million guilders annually on irrigation projects, after which they pruned the budget to between 1 and 3 million guilders.

In the first two years of the occupation, the Japanese made few changes to Dutch irrigation policies. The budget for the 1943 fiscal year was 2.27 million guilders (of which 1.26 million guilders was for maintenance and repair works and 650,000 guilders for alterations). However, plans for 1944 and 1945 called for substantial increases. The budgets for irrigation projects and the areas to be covered are shown in Table 7.6.

The General Bureau of Public Works in Jakarta carried out large projects in areas where preexisting technical canals for sugar estates needed to be connected to the nontechnical irrigation works for rice fields. Other works were the responsibility of each residency or principality. In addition to the above, the General Bureau received 2.5 million guilders for repair and maintenance of the existing systems for the 1945 fiscal year. In early 1945 large-scale land extension and improvement projects were under way at sixty-two locations in Java.

As far as the budget was concerned, the projects from 1944 onward looked like a return to the prerecession period, but actual expenditures were apparently larger than the scheduled budgets, and work was much more labor-intensive than in the Dutch era. To illustrate this point, I will examine one project in Yogyakarta and Surakarta conducted by the General Bureau. It involved construction of a main canal, 18,700 meters long with a 560-meter tunnel, and connecting the canal to existing nontechnical systems that extended for 19.5 kilometers in Yogyakarta and 12.5 kilometers in Surakarta. This would improve water control over an area of 8,359 hectares, providing an additional 9,644 tons of rice per annum, including rice from double-cropping, which would become possible on 3,000 hectares of land.[25]

In the original plan, the budget was set at 94,500 guilders (634,900 guilders for materials, 205,100 guilders for wages, 78,000 guilders for land purchase, and 26,500 guilders for administration). This budget was based on meticulous calculations. The cost for shifting soil was, for instance, calculated according to a scale that included ten grades, ranging from 23 to 80 cents per cubic meter depending upon the conditions of the ground. The lowest cost was based on an estimate that removing 1 cubic meter of soil would require 0.6 rōmusha at a wage of 35 cents per day and 0.02 foremen at a wage of 1 guilder. According to a newspaper article, the project involved moving nearly 1 million cubic meters of soil.[26] This volume of soil removal alone would have cost 230,000 guilders and required 602,000 man-days of labor, supposing that all the land used fell into the easiest category. The budget for wages was clearly insufficient, and the deficiency had to be met by local governments. The General Bureau requested principality governments to supply much of the labor and cover the associated costs on condition that the principalities would acquire the ownership of the completed system.

Work began on July 20, 1944, and was completed on July 5, 1945. According to the newspaper report on its completion, the project was initially thought to require 5 million man-days of labor. From September 1944, labor recruitment became difficult and the number of workers on the project declined. The General Bureau was determined to finish it before the onset of the rainy season, and toward the end work continued around the clock on a three-shift system, and even schoolchildren were mobilized. The project absorbed 2.72 million man-days (7,700 workers per day on average), including 210,000 man-days of unpaid labor service. The wages for 2.5 million adult males at the official rate would have amounted to 932,883 guilders, although the rates for women and children were lower. The newspaper reported that the entire project had cost 1.2 million guilders, but according to an official letter sent to Morooka Masao, the actual cost was 1.5 million guilders.[27] The expenditures exceeded the initial calculations, partly because authorities in Jakarta did not prepare an adequate budget, and the local governments were requested to cover part of the wages paid to the *rōmusha*. The Japanese also made systematic use of unpaid labor, *kinrō hō shi*. Across Java over 20 percent of unskilled temporary laborers mobilized by Japanese worked under *kinrō hō shi* terms.[28]

The irrigation projects absorbed a very large number of workers because shortages of equipment and materials made it necessary to use highly labor-intensive methods. The Japanese had commandeered most trucks and heavy machinery for military use. Soil had to be dug with simple tools such as mattocks and hoes, and carried away in baskets or with bare hands. As for construction materials, Portland cement and iron rods were unavailable, and substitute materials such as pulverized bricks, trass (volcanic rubble), and timber had to be used instead.[29]

In the Jatilawang and Wangon areas of Banyumas, the Japanese built irrigation canals that were 42 kilometers long. This project involved construction of tunnels at more than ninety places and all of them had to be built with timber, technically more difficult and more costly than using ferroconcrete, and the resulting structure was weaker. Most of all, it was more labor-intensive because it required cutting and transporting logs. Mobilizing labor was as difficult as elsewhere, and the project managers could obtain only around 3,000 workers per day, many fewer than were required. Nevertheless, they were determined to meet the scheduled date of completion and drove the workers extremely hard. To finish on time, they modified their construction plans and at certain places erected structures that were flimsier than originally planned.

In addition to the sixty-two irrigation projects, there were other irrigation-related works. In a dry area in Indramayu, for instance, the Japanese planned to build a hydroelectric power plant—needed because coal shortages made thermal plants difficult to operate—that would generate 10,000 kilowatts of electricity. At the same time, the water from the dam would irrigate 18,000 hectares of land, increasing rice production by 27,000 tons per annum.[30]

Consequences of the Agricultural Projects

The output of food in Java rapidly declined during the latter part of the occupation. Table 7.7 shows statistics for the four main food crops, as discovered and calculated by Pierre Van der Eng.

Both the harvested areas and total production of rice and cassava fell steadily. Maize declined too, recovering slightly in 1945. Sweet potatoes declined in the first two years but increased substantially in the next two years. The sharp falls in 1944 were to a large extent the result of a severe drought that caused vast areas to be left unplanted for want of water. The

Table 7.7

Production of Food Crops

	1941	1942	1943	1944	1945
Production (1000s of tons)					
Stalk paddy	8,993	8,302	8,122	6,870	6,470
Cassava	8,736	8,735	7,521	5,263	4,623
Maize	2,433	2,165	1,604	1,177	1,399
Sweet potatoes	1,475	1,312	1,084	1,486	2,288
Harvested areas (1000s of hectares)					
Paddy	4,101	4,026	4,132	3,572	3,203
Cassava	1,003	976	950	829	551
Maize	2,229	2,214	1,812	1,399	1,488
Sweet potatoes	205	189	180	259	350

Source: Pierre van der Eng, *Food Supply in Java during War and Decolonisation, 1940–1950* (Hull: University of Hull, Centre for South-East Asian Studies, 1994), Table A1, p. 73.

drought affected the 1944 harvest and the planting season that followed, causing poor results in 1945 as well. Sweet potato production increased because this crop did well in dry conditions.[31]

Beyond this natural mishap, however, there were complex reasons for the decline in the harvested area for rice:

1. Land suitable for food cultivation was planted with nonfood crops;
2. The new methods of rice cultivation that the Japanese introduced were not suited to conditions in Java;
3. Low official purchase prices of food crops and restrictions on the free market acted as disincentives for rice growers;
4. Labor mobilization reduced the availability of manpower in the villages;
5. The population of draught animals and the number of tools available for tillage declined;
6. Projects for expanding and improving agricultural fields were often not completed, and some remained unfinished at the time of the Japanese surrender;
7. Extensive deforestation aggravated flooding in the wet season and drought in the dry season;
8. Although new irrigation canals were being constructed, the existing canals often fell into disrepair; and
9. Some completed works deteriorated rapidly due to careless planning, the use of poor-quality construction materials, and flooding.

There is abundant documentary evidence for each of the above points, but I will deal here only with those directly related to labor.

In February 1946 the returning Dutch conducted a survey of the conditions in all thirty-one major irrigation systems in Central Java. They found that in certain areas irrigation canals had been extended and dry land converted into irrigated rice fields, while in others irrigated fields had been converted into dry fields. A number of projects were left unfinished, sometimes due to the Japanese surrender, and sometimes to shortages of labor, materials, and funding. Some projects had been launched hastily, without proper geological surveys, and were discontinued when they proved technically unfeasible.[32]

Flooding increased sharply after 1944 owing to extensive deforestation. The Japanese harvested much timber for irrigation and other construction works, for building wooden ships, and for firing steam locomotives. In pre-war Java, locomotives were fuelled mostly with imported coal, but coal supplies were limited during the occupation, and consumption of firewood for locomotives nearly quadrupled, to 90,000 tons per month in 1945.[33]

When existing irrigation canals were destroyed and the supply of water to the fields stopped, local government officials told farmers to fix the damage themselves and refused to fund the repairs. It is not that the Japanese completely ignored the maintenance of existing irrigation channels. As mentioned above, in 1945 they allocated 2.5 million guilders to the General Bureau of Public Works for maintenance of irrigation systems, but ineffective administration interfered with distribution of the funds.

Labor distribution was also inefficient. Many projects were unable to secure sufficient labor, but some work sites had too much. Those recruited included people doing essential work in the villages, and their mobilization disrupted food cultivation.[34] Moreover, mobilized laborers had to bring their tools with them, a practice that soon caused shortages of agricultural implements in the villages. Producing new tools was difficult owing to a shortage of scrap iron, and vast stretches of rice fields were left uncultivated in the latter part of the occupation. When poorly irrigated fields were planted with rice, a plant disease attacked and devastated the crop.[35]

Plantation crops grown in prewar Java had lost their markets, and the Japanese attempted to grow food crops on plantation lands, but a number of accounts, including Japanese official reports, reveal gross mismanagement of plantations by Japanese. On a tea estate in Central Java, for example, an order was issued on December 23, 1943, to plant 650 hectares of land with food crops, one-third with cassava and two-thirds with maize (corn). The tea plants were pruned down to 40–60 centimeters above the ground so that they could grow back later. The results were very poor; there was no well-thought-out plan or adequate preparation, no time given for preparing green manure, and the seed sent to the estate was of poor quality.

In mid-January 1944, the workers were ordered to plant cacao on 250 hectares but the Japanese kept the purchase price excessively low. The plantation employees therefore deliberately, and in subtle ways, slowed down the work. Almost nothing had been done by the end of March. Seed arrived from East Java, but 60 percent of it was unusable. As a result, only about 18 hectares were planted. In April or May the workers were ordered to plant ramie on 590 hectares. A Japanese supervisor arrived to direct the project and quickly revealed his sheer incompetence. When the seedlings arrived, the soil had not been prepared, and only 20 hectares could be planted. Moreover, while this estate had a cableway, it broke down and was not repaired (probably due to a lack of spare parts), so no produce could be sent off.[36]

The campaign to produce fiber was equally unsuccessful. The Japanese planned to send cotton seeds from Japan, but in 1943 the shipment arrived after the growing season was over. When the seeds were eventually sown, the germination rate was low and the plants that did appear suffered from shortages of water and were badly damaged by disease and insects. The importation of pesticides had stopped, and an alternative produced locally from volcanic sulfur proved ineffective. Insects kept ruining the crops, but even if cotton had been produced in abundance, there was no prospect of overcoming shortages of spinning and weaving equipment.[37]

As for ramie, another plant that produced fibers suitable for textiles, the production target for 1943 was 1,430 tons throughout Java, but actual production was no more than 270 tons.[38] The area under ramie in 1944 was 8,293 hectares. The production target was set at 670,000 tons, but this figure was unrealistic and was lowered to 367,000 tons; actual production was 268,967 tons (40 percent of the original target and 73 percent of the reduced one). The Japanese decided to press ahead with ramie production and brought the plan for 1947 forward to 1945. Well over 30,000 hectares were prepared for ramie as shortages of clothing became increasingly acute.[39]

The cultivation of jute, another fibrous plant, also failed, in this case because the daily period of sunshine in Java was not long enough. The Japanese, however, managed to overcome the shortage of sacking in the latter part of the occupation by turning to sisal, a very coarse fiber normally used for making ropes and brushes. Java produced large quantities of sisal before the war, most of it for export, and after the military administration carried out successful experiments making sisal sacks they were produced in large numbers. In early 1945 about 1 million tons of sugar was stored in jute gunnysacks. The Japanese apparently transferred this sugar to newly woven sisal sacks and converted the 6 million gunnysacks into 12 million pieces of makeshift clothing that were distributed to *rōmusha* and to many govern-ment employees.[40]

Japanese agricultural policies achieved some successes in rice produc-tion. After the Japanese surrender, the agricultural committee of the regency of Sidoarjo reported that the average annual production of rice in the re-gency—453,766 tons from 1937 to 1941—had increased to 634,794 tons during the occupation. The report explained that unlike the Dutch, the Japa-nese paid much attention to rice production. However, in 1946 Sidoarjo be-came a battlefield, with many villagers joining the war for independence. The workforce that remained in the villages was insufficient to carry out food cultivation, and irrigation water was not regulated properly. As a result, rice production fell to 360,958 tons in 1946.[41]

In short, not all Japanese projects were futile or counterproductive, but the negative effects far outweighed the positive. In particular, the produc-tion-increase campaign reduced the output of food in Java and caused great distress to the villagers mobilized for the campaign. Around the time of the Japanese surrender, each residency and principality submitted data on the pro-duction and delivery of rice and other food crops in 1945 up to the fourth of August.[42] These reports show calamitous economic conditions prevailing in most parts of the island. The residency of Banyumas, for example, reported that the area under cultivation decreased because the rising death rate had caused a manpower shortage. Moreover, there was insufficient seed rice, and a drought that began in May prevented cultivation of rice in the dry season.

Forced Laborers and Their Fates

The Japanese administration aimed at supplying the following food items per person per day to *rōmusha* involved in irrigation work: 400 grams of rice, 300 grams of other cereals such as tapioca and corn, 50 grams of meat or fish, 200 grams of vegetables, 30 grams of salt, 10 grams of sugar, 10 grams of spice such as chili, and 0.03 grams of cooking oil. The standard working period was eight hours per day, and those who did overtime work for more than three hours per day were to receive an extra 100 grams of rice.[43] In practice the diet of the *rōmusha* was far below this standard, and the situation worsened progressively after the drought struck in 1944. One reason lay in the Japanese failure to procure sufficient quantities of food. When large-scale labor mobilization began in late 1943, the administration also launched a campaign for delivery of rice to the government. The pri-mary objective was to maintain smooth distribution of rice for both civilian and military purposes by controlling the portion of Java's rice that was milled by machine, about 20 percent of the total crop. This campaign malfunctioned,

Table 7.8

Targets and Results of Rice Procurement (in tons)

	1941	1943	1944	1945
Target		1,995,000	2,086,400	1,732,000
Result	1,985,000	1,490,500	1,341,100	(875,669)

Sources: Shigeru Sato, *War, Nationalism and Peasants: Java under the Japanese Occupation 1942–1945* (Armonk: M.E. Sharpe, 1994), pp. 117, 122. The figure for 1945 was calculated at the end of July (BUZA NEFIS/CMI, encl. 3, 2350).

and in 1944 rice deliveries amounted to just 64 percent of the target. (See Table 7.8.)[44] Some of the food meant for work sites was also diverted by fraud and theft.

Conditions were so bad that many *rōmusha* ran away from their work sites or escaped en route to them. Work sites could be several hundred kilometers away from their villages, and because escapees usually had no money to buy food, some starved to death before reaching home.[45] Even when *rōmusha* were mobilized within their own residency, they often had to walk a considerable distance to the work site every day. In one such case villagers were promised 100 grams of rice a day, but on arrival were told they would receive the rice after they completed their assigned period of work, which was one week. They refused to remain under such conditions and returned to their homes the same morning, a walk of two hours.[46]

It would not be accurate to imagine that the Japanese could mobilize such a large workforce by coercion alone. The occupation impoverished people to such a degree that in order to survive many had to accept any work that became available. Obtaining food became increasingly difficult for the poorer elements of society as food production declined, and the black market caused prices of food to soar beyond the reach of the poor. Small farmers were among the hardest hit. Their crops could fetch good prices on the black market, but it was difficult for them to move rice out of the villages, and they had to rely on Chinese brokers. While these brokers did not dare to flout government regulations openly, they effectively lowered prices by the expedient of saying that they were not interested in buying the rice at the official price (for all sorts of reasons—excessive moisture, for example). There are reports of farmers bursting into tears and imploring the brokers to buy the grain, even at a price much lower than the official rate.[47] Farmers who succumbed to these tactics had to supplement their income and generally did so by becoming laborers.

In many villages the majority of the population was landless, and their situation could be even worse. They often had nothing to sell except their own labor. Before the war people in this position earned a living by working for landed villagers, or through cottage industries, petty trade, and so on. Their incomes soon became insufficient to purchase daily essentials, and they, too, had to become *rōmusha*.

All the drafted laborers, except *kinrō hō shi,* received wages, and during the course of the occupation the nominal wages for unskilled labor increased twofold. Employment opportunities for unskilled laborers rose dramatically, and cash income for the rural population increased very substantially. Commodities, however, were so scarce that price inflation outstripped the rise in income, and the value of the currency plummeted. Many people, including those with large amounts of cash in their hands, found it impossible to survive in their villages, causing a vast exodus to the cities, where people hoped to find some way to make a living.

The drought in 1944 exacerbated malnutrition among the rural population and lowered people's immunity to disease. During this difficult period, the mobilization of *rōmusha* reached its peak. Work sites were often in malarial swamps and forests, but while Java produced large amounts of quinine, which was used as antimalarial medicine, its distribution was inefficient. Dutch intelligence officers observed that "cases of malaria increased out of all proportion" and "hundreds of thousands of people" died during the period of drought alone.[48]

After the surrender, the Japanese authorities submitted to the Allied forces the following summary report concerning the welfare of the local inhabitants (cited in original English):

> Judging from the result of investigation of such physical and mental functions as constitution, bodily strength and willpower, it is impossible to say generally that the nutritional condition of inhabitants is favorable.
>
> Especially, chronic malaria, venereal disease and skin disease is spreading extraordinarily among lower villagers. Moreover the dietary custom of them is unscientific. As a result of these facts, the bodily strength of lower villagers is very weak and the labor capacity is also inferior. . . .
>
> The defects of nutrition, such as malnutrition and hunger [edema], are spreading extraordinarily in the Residency of Banjoemas and a certain part of the Residency of Pekalongan.[49]

From January 23 to February 3, 1946, the Netherlands Forces Intelligence Service (NEFIS) conducted an investigation into the general situation of the health and food supply among the local people in Sukabumi regency. A Dutch officer first interviewed the local police chief, who was generally cooperative, but when asked if the population in the district was obtaining adequate amounts of food and medical care, he looked embarrassed and said that the situation was quite normal, with no difficulties at all. The Dutch officer soon discovered that, contrary to the police chief's statement, starvation and disease were rife in the rural districts, and the hospitals were understaffed and badly stocked with medicine. British forces, operating an interim military administration, began providing the destitute with medical aid and some food, including one mess tin of rice per person per day. The number of people who came for the rice rapidly increased from 60–100 to 700–800 persons per day. The Dutch officer reported (cited in original English):

> Unfortunately all aid had to cease when the B[attalio]n returned to BUITENZORG. This was a very bitter disappointment to the destitutes who were by then coming in from distances as such as 20–30 miles. The gratitude expressed and the signs of a new hope among these people, showed, I think, that the assistance rendered was appreciated.
>
> Most cases treated were for tropical ulcer, malaria and dysentery, malnutrition is very marked indeed. Cases occurred of people dying whilst waiting for assistance near the Camp.[50]

Concluding Remarks

In August 1940 the Japanese authorities in Tokyo advanced the idea of a Greater East Asia Co-Prosperity Sphere. The primary aim was to put most of East and Southeast Asia under Japanese control and secure a direct supply of essential strategic resources. A corollary of this scheme was that fundamental economic and industrial restructuring had to take place if an economically self-sufficient bloc were to be constructed, but the Japanese plunged into war without any long-term workable plan to achieve co-prosperity. The occupation shattered prewar economic structures, with negative consequences that soon became apparent.

Many of the economic measures that the Japanese introduced in the occupied territories during the second half of occupation, such as labor mobilization and the forced delivery of rice, were intended to counter difficulties faced by local communities. Japanese propaganda in Java asserted that the campaigns were partly to support the Japanese war effort and partly to construct a New Java, but these statements were deceptive. The Japanese launched their production-increase campaign knowing that efforts to generate large quantities of import substitutes would undermine food production. The hasty measures they introduced were ineffective at best and often counterproductive, and despite the "total mobilization" of labor to produce clothing and food, the supply of these and other essentials shrank rapidly. Moreover, the "economic soldiers" mobilized for the campaigns suffered from overwork, hunger, and diseases, and many of them died. The Japanese invasion was, it is true, an opportunity for Indonesian nationalists to promote their cause, but the co-prosperity sphere was a co-misery sphere for the general populace of the occupied territories. In the process of constructing their co-prosperity sphere, the Japanese made many blunders, the greatest one being to start the war with no clear plan for carrying out their ambitious objectives.

As the Japanese empire crumbled under the Allied counteroffensive, the military administration in Java deteriorated unstoppably, with devastating consequences for the local people. By early 1945, it was clear that the military administration could not overcome the problems that the invasion had created. The Japanese were losing on the battlefield and also in the sphere of economic administration. Nevertheless, the Japanese authorities in Java did not contemplate capitulation. For the people of Java, it was a small redeeming aspect in the overall misfortune that the authorities in Tokyo decided to surrender before the military administration in Java saw any need to admit failure.

8

The Road to Hell

The Construction of a Railway Line in West Java during the Japanese Occupation

Harry A. Poeze

During their occupation of Southeast Asia (1942–45), the Japanese held troops captured in the occupied Dutch, French, and English colonies as prisoners of war. They also interned European civilians, removing the entire upper layer of colonial society.

Japan's military administrations used male internees as forced laborers, initially on small projects in the vicinity of the internment camps that were often near the detainees' original place of residence, or in the case of soldiers the place of surrender. Later the Japanese transported large numbers of prisoners of war and internees to distant locations, where they constructed roads, airfields, and defense works deemed necessary for the war effort. To relieve the shortage of laborers in Japan proper, internees also worked in mines and factories there. The working conditions were invariably bad, with insufficient food and poor health care.

The most extreme project, with respect to both the number of forced laborers used as well as the extent of the suffering, was the construction of the 415-kilometer Thailand–Burma railway,[1] but this was only one of a number of railway projects undertaken by the Japanese. Others included a line across the Kra Isthmus in southern Thailand, the Tondongkura railway in southwestern Sulawesi, a railway extending 220 kilometers across Sumatra, and a line in West Java.[2]

From Harry A. Poeze, "De weg naar de hel. De aanleg van een spoorlijn op West-Java tijdens de Japanse bezetting," in *Oorlogsdocumentatie '40–'45. Tweede jaarboek van het Rijksinstituut voor Oorlogsdocumentatie* (War documentation 1940-1945. Second yearbook of the State Institute for War Documentation)(Amsterdam, 1990), pp. 9–47. Published with permission of the Netherlands Institute for War Documentation.

Map 8.1 **West Java**

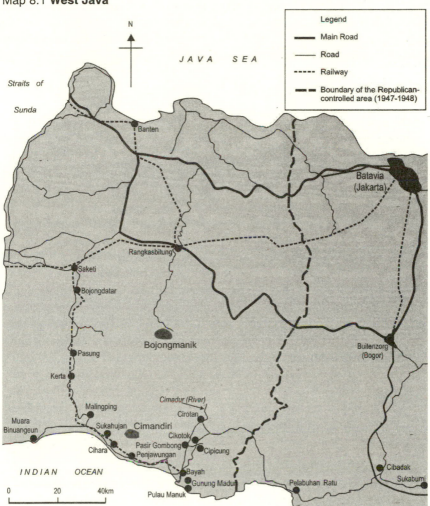

The latter, built between Saketi and Bayah in the inhospitable region of South Banten, carried brown coal from mines in Bayah to other parts of the island. European involvement in the construction was limited to a small number of Dutchmen who worked in supervisory or technical functions. *Rōmusha*—Javanese forced laborers—did the heavy work, and thousands of them died during the construction and maintenance of the railway. For them it was truly a "road to hell," as an Indonesian journalist called it in a news report published in 1947,[3] but the story of this railway line is little known. Few survivors recorded their experiences, and accounts of the occupation contain only occasional passing references to it. Telling this story is a gesture of remembrance for the nameless victims, but it also shows the way in which Japanese economic directives were carried out, and the Japanese approach to a large-scale project.

Pit Coal in Banten

In the nineteenth century the introduction of steamships, the construction of railways, and the expansion of the manufacturing industry increased the demand for coal in the Netherlands Indies. For strategic and commercial reasons the Dutch administration considered it of major importance not to be dependent on foreign sources, and played an active part in the search for coal reserves and in the actual mining process. The first state mine opened in 1849 in Southeast Borneo but met with little success. In 1866 important coal deposits were discovered in Sumatra's west coast residency, and in 1891 the government set up a company known as the Ombilin mines to work these deposits. This operation soon surpassed its smaller competitors.[4]

The search for workable deposits of coal on Java, the most important island of the Netherlands Indies, was a matter of great interest. In the course of a series of geological explorations across the island, Friedrich Junghuhn discovered the Bayah and Cimandiri coalfields in South Banten, and the samples he took turned out to be of good quality. Toward the end of the century the government mining service carried out a very detailed investigation of these coalfields, which were the only ones on Java rich enough for exploitation.[5]

Around 1900 there was some public discussion about the Banten coalfields in which strategic considerations figured strongly. The coal was tested in a government steamer with good results, and a correspondent named Ritter stated in the *Bataviaasch Nieuwsblad:*

> Before all else I have to get it off my chest that, no matter what kind of coal is found in those fields, the government really, truly has to exploit those fields.
>
> There is so much written pointing to the F.E. [Foreign Enemy], fortresses and other defense measures are readied, but what does this all mean if Java is without coal in times of war? Nothing at all, is it not? We cannot be dependent on the outside, we have to be able to shift for ourselves on Java no matter what the cost, and as long as no other coalfields are found, we must exploit these.

The writer then pleaded for the mining of these brown coal deposits near Bayah, arguing that a cableway could carry the ore from Bayah to Bogor.[6]

In 1901 the results of the government's investigations and probably the optimistic reports in the press moved a businessman named A.W.R. Kerkhoven to apply for a concession, and in 1903 he received a grant covering part of the area for a period of seventy-five years.[7] Kerkhoven must have concluded very quickly that exploitation was not worthwhile. The seams of coal were thin and too spread out and irregular to be able to compete with the Ombilin mines, the exploitation of which was then just getting under way using infra-structure constructed by the government at a very high cost. Banten lacked railway connections and port facilities,[8] and Kerkhoven could only hope that the government would decide to place strategic considerations ahead of eco-nomic concerns and provide similar assistance in West Banten.

During the First World War, locally produced coal had to supply local needs as far as possible, and the government conducted further exploration looking for coal deposits on Java, including a reinvestigation of the three Bantenese coalfields in 1915 and 1916. The investigation also included coal deposits at Bojongmanik, between Rangkasbitung and Java's south coast, but prospects there were even gloomier than for the Cimandiri and Bayah fields. The quality was poorer, and transport problems even more severe. Although Cimandiri coal was of somewhat better quality, it would require deep mining, far more than in the case of Bayah coal. The mining engineer K.G.J. Ziegler concluded an exhaustive report with this evaluation:

> The expenditure of a large amount of capital for the creation of opportunities for transportation of the coal to its markets, which would considerably increase the already high mining costs, is not justified. First the south of Banten will have to be mature for connection to the traffic system on other economic grounds; only then will the Eocene coal basins located there, the Bayah field and the Cimandiri field, probably be able to contribute in some way to the further development of the country; yet this contribution as well should not be rated too highly.[9]

Ziegler's report was published, and his research data stored in the archives of the Mining Service (*Dienst van het Mijnwezen*). Overall, estimates indicated that costs for coal from South Banten would be more than double those for coal taken from the Ombilin mines, and the exploitation of coal in South Banten seemed to have been written off permanently. Kerkhoven had by this time given up hope for a profitable operation and offered to sell his conces-sion to the government, but his offer was declined.

Gold and Silver Mining

Routine prospecting carried out in South Banten in 1924 indicated the pres-ence of significant quantities of gold and silver. Between 1924 and 1929 explorations in the mountainous and isolated region north of Bayah confirmed these results, and private prospectors began to arrive in the area. In 1928 southern Banten was officially reserved for government research. In 1931 the Mining Service produced an extensive report that contained all relevant data, including maps, providing anyone interested in applying for an exploitation license with sufficient details to gauge the profitability of such an enterprise.[10] The government estimated a minimum yield of gold and silver worth more than 5 million guilders, but the report emphasized that there were major infrastructure problems. Mining operations would require construction of a road either to Rangkasbitung or to Pelabuhan Ratu. From Rangkasbitung an unsurfaced road led to Malingping, near the coast, but it was usable only in the dry season. Bayah was accessible only by foot or on horseback. From Pelabuhan Ratu, 20 kilometers of road led westward to a tea and rubber plantation, but beyond this point there were only footpaths that meandered through the mountainous terrain, providing limited access to Cikotok, centrally located in the exploitation area, and to Bayah. The coast near Bayah did not possess a safe harbor, and rough seas made it hazardous to sail small craft in this area.

Because of the world economic crisis and the need to invest large sums in infrastructure and mining installations, some time passed before industry accepted the invitation of the government to develop gold and silver mines in the area. In May 1934 the Netherlands Indies Exploration Company (N.V. Exploratie Maatschappij Nederlandsch-Indië) and the Stannum Mining Company (N.V. Mijnbouw Maatschappij Stannum) jointly set up the South Bantam Mining Company (N.V. Mijnbouw Maatschappij Zuid-Bantam). The former company, founded in 1930, explored concession areas in the archipelago to assess the possibilities for mineral exploitation, and after locating a suitable location either handled mining operations itself or sold the rights to another company. The shares of the company were traded on the Amsterdam stock exchange.[11] Stannum was an offshoot of the Billiton Company (NV Billiton Maatschappij), founded in 1920 as a pure exploration company. Stannum began new projects and founded or took part in new companies, with the mother company covering any losses.[12]

The founding of the South Bantam Mining Company followed lengthy talks with the government of the Netherlands Indies that resulted in a tracing and exploitation contract in June 1935 for the core area already examined by the Mining Service, and a tracing contract in November 1935 for a larger area, in all covering some 400 square kilometers. The contracts, in accordance with the Netherlands Indies Mining Law, required the company to pay 25 percent of any profits to the government and an additional 250,000 guilders to compensate the government for exploration expenses.[13]

A renewed calculation of costs and expected gains produced encouraging results, and construction and development activities began in the second half of 1936. The company decided to build a road to the west, connecting the mine site with the company's base in the hills at Cikotok, where the head office, storehouses, workshop, laboratory, sick ward and houses were located. The 31-kilometer-long road was ready early in 1938. To meet its energy requirements the company constructed a hydroelectric station on the Cimadur River about 5 kilometers west of Cikotok at Pasir Gombong. Cikotok housed processing facilities to separate gold and silver from the ore that was brought in. Each ton of ore yielded about 9 grams of gold and 400 grams of silver, and the installation could handle 150 tons a day.

Roads were also constructed linking the mines to Cipicung and later, after promising indications had been discovered in the tracing area, to Cirotan (11 kilometers away). These roads, covering a total of 55 kilometers, were completed in 1938. In 1939 the other installations were also ready, including the hydroelectric station and the cableways that transported the ore from the mines to the processing facility. In this way the isolated region was opened within a short period time, at a cost of more than 3 million guilders, with funds raised through stock issues and bank loans. As of 1939 the South Bantam Mining Company employed about 50 Europeans, 120 Indonesian supervisors and 1,100 Indonesian workers. During the high point of the construction no less than 6,500 workers were engaged, and stockholder confidence was high.[14]

The company began operations on November 1, 1939, and from January 1940 the processing plant ran at full capacity; weekly and monthly bulletins provided information about production. Estimates prepared in late 1939 placed the ore reserves at 520,000 tons, and the value of the precious metals to be taken from the ore at 14 million guilders, figures that surpassed all previous estimates. However, the shadow of the world war already hung over these optimistic projections: German machinery ordered for the mines was not delivered, and operations at Cirotan had to be closed down because the company was unable to handle ore from this site.[15]

In 1940 the South Bantam Mining Company processed more than 61,000 tons of ore, which yielded 488 kilograms of gold and 25,500 kilograms of silver with a value of 1,566,000 guilders. This output made the mine the second largest gold producer (with 17.5 percent of the total production) and the largest silver producer (54.5 percent) in the Netherlands Indies. Other deposits were nearly all on Sumatra.[16] Details for 1941 are lacking, but between January 1941 and February 1942 the South Bantam Mining Company booked a profit of about half a million guilders.[17]

The Japanese Invasion

The occupation of Indonesia was an important part of the Japanese plan of conquest, for the oil and other natural resources of the archipelago were considered essential to the prosecution of the war. When Japan's lightning campaign reached its climax with the surrender of the Netherlands Indies army in March 1942, plans for economic exploitation were already in place. For certain strategic items these plans called for increased production and shipment of supplies to Japan; for others, the goal was sufficient production to meet local requirements. The Japanese considered the mining of nonessential minerals such as gold and silver unimportant as long as the war continued.

For purposes of the military administration, Japan separated the archipelago into Java, Sumatra, and the "Great East," and each division needed to be self-sufficient because shipping and production capacity elsewhere could not supply needed commodities or manufactured goods. Contact between the areas was difficult and generally discouraged or forbidden.[18] Before the war, Java imported about 700,000 tons of coal annually, mainly from Sumatra, but under the circumstances of the occupation it was impossible to bring Sumatran coal to Java. Japanese authorities on Java had to find a way to provide for the needs of the island, and particularly to operate train services, which were of great strategic importance. The Japanese were aware of the coal reserves in South Banten and envisaged mining this coal to meet local requirements. Shortly after the Dutch surrender, Japanese experts went to the office of the Mining Service in Bandung, where geological and engineering data had been assembled, and began preparing a report on the coal reserves in Bojongmanik, Cimandiri, and Bayah.[19] The working of the Banten coalfields had in principle already been assigned to Sumitomo, one of the large and powerful economic conglomerates that dominated the Japanese economy, with a production target of 300,000 tons by the end of 1943.[20] The role of Sumitomo in the actual exploitation of the Bayah mine was minimal; the Japanese army took care of the infrastructure, provided the workforce, and used the produce. It is unclear whether investments and loss or profit for Sumitomo were involved and, if so, what sums were involved.

In Cikotok the South Bantam Mining Company had prepared for war. European staff members were either mobilized as part of the regular forces or trained in Cikotok and admitted into the home guard. Soldiers from the Netherlands Indies military forces had been assigned to the area, and a secluded shelter was built for the women and children. A destruction brigade was ready to carry out a scorched-earth policy. When the Japanese landed on Java, a large part of the European personnel employed by the South Bantam Mining Company left for military service, and mining operations were shut down. An "emergency formation" under administrator Kriek protected the enterprise, and action had to be taken on a few occasions to maintain order and prevent robbery and looting. On March 5, 1942, destruction of mining equipment was carried out, albeit not on a large scale.

Shortly before the surrender, an English stay-behind party under the command of Laurens Van der Post reported to Kriek. Van der Post, who had only recently arrived in Java, had orders to assist with the evacuation of Allied soldiers and, if possible to set up a guerrilla resistance force in cooperation with the Dutch. He selected Banten's inhospitable south coast as a base and ended up in Cikotok, taking over the safe evacuation location prepared for the women and children, since it was no longer needed for its original purpose. British, Australian, and Dutch soldiers later joined him, and he was supplied with radio transmitters and an extensive arsenal of weapons. The group numbered about 100.[21]

On March 20 the first Japanese appeared at the gold and silver mines at Cikotok. Among them was a party of engineers traveling to Bayah to examine the situation there. Kriek thought it wise to leave and reported to his superiors in Batavia, who told him to negotiate with the Japanese about reopening the mine.[22] In May 1942 the Japanese authorities decided that the remaining workers should be used for maintenance work, and Kriek was told that he should return to the enterprise. The reason was that Japanese economic experts had decided to exploit the brown coal near Bayah and needed the South Bantam Mining Company with its substantial complement of personnel to support the mining of coal. Kriek resumed contact with the Van der Post group, but Van der Post himself had rather ingloriously surrendered in late April, and the last members of his group would become prisoners of war in August 1942.[23]

After the Japanese occupier had decided on the fate of the enterprise, the tense situation in Cikotok calmed down. The European staff could hardly keep the Indonesian workers in line anymore, and a workers organization was making extreme demands on the defeated colonial rulers. The Japanese army had a substantial military engineering unit in the area, but its task was to improve the footpath from Cikotok to Bayah as fast as possible to facilitate movement by automobile, and it did not intervene in labor matters.[24]

In July 1942 the first mine opened in Bayah, operating with the assistance of two Dutch engineers transferred from the South Bantam operation.[25] In the same month the Japanese fired all but about a hundred employees of the gold and silver mines. Twelve European staff members remained in service, all in supervisory or technical roles. A few weeks later, according to engineer J.M. Weehuizen, the general manager, "We were flooded by a horde of Japs (army), who didn't respect at all the arrangements their economic

Photograph 8.1. Lieut. Gen. Harada Kumashaki and his party during a visit to a coal mine in Bayah. *(Asia Raya,* 16 June 1944.)

experts had made with us. They immediately occupied a large part of our head office and the other workspaces and some of the European houses, and requisitioned for themselves all facilities and supplies of the company." Thousands of laborers soon arrived to construct a road from Cikotok to Bayah, and another one along the coast to Penjawungan, including a large wooden bridge over the Cimadur River at Bayah. Work also began on infrastructure for the mine and on extending the electricity supply from Cikotok to Bayah. When the latter job was completed, supplies of electricity to Cikotok were shut off and all the power generated by the hydroelectric station went to Bayah. Installations and stores at Cikotok that were useful for mining brown coal were confiscated. The Japanese efforts advanced efficiently: the Cikotok–Bayah road was soon passable, and Bayah had electricity. That was how matters stood when Kriek and Weehuizen were unexpectedly interned in Bogor (Buitenzorg) on November 24.[26]

The Cikotok enterprise remained under the management of a European solicitor and a Chinese-Indonesian mining engineer, but little gold and silver mining seems to have taken place, although according to information Weehuizen received while he was interned, the Japanese did mine lead and zinc at Cirotan.[27] There were, however, other developments. In June 1944 the commander of the Japanese army and senior administrator for Java, Lieutenant General Harada Kumashaki, made a visit to industrial sites in West

Java, and the report of his visit noted that he saw a mine and a processing installation for copper, a product of vital importance for warfare. His report gives the impression of considerable activity, with some copper being shipped to Japan.[28]

The Construction of a Railway Line

The decision to exploit the mine made it necessary to find a way to remove the ore.[29] The road between Bayah and the harbor at Pelabuhan Ratu, difficult at the best of times, was often impassable in the wet season and was not designed to carry heavy vehicles. In any case, trucks were in short supply, and it was illogical to use scarce and valuable gasoline to transport brown coal. The purpose of the Pelabuhan Ratu road was simply to open Bayah so that building and mining materials could be brought into the area, and the same was true of a road constructed from Bayah to the west that started in Malingping and joined the Bayah road at Penjawungan. The two roads also had military significance, since Banten's south coast was well suited for the infiltration of Allied spies and offered a favorable site for landing an invasion force. The Japanese knew very well that the Banten coast was vulnerable and had to be defended.[30]

July 1942 brought initial preparations for constructing a railway.[31] The first task was to survey the planned line, a job carried out by eight Japanese experts with the assistance of seven support staff (including three Dutchmen) selected from the staff of the railway companies on Java. With the assistance of a small number of Indonesian helpers and porters, they laid out a railway line 89.35 kilometers in length, with fifty-nine bridges and nine stations. The highest point of the line was 113 meters above sea level, and the lowest section, between Malingping and Bayah, 10 meters above sea level.[32]

Before the war a number of rail companies had operated in Java, including the State Railway (Staatsspoorwegen), the Netherlands Indies Railway Company (Nederlandsch-Indische Spoorwegmaatschappij), along with various smaller steam tram companies that served particular regions. Toward the end of 1942 the Japanese merged these companies into a single organization with its headquarters in Bandung.[33] The railway constructed between Saketi and Bayah used rails and ties taken from depots all across Java. Considering that the total length of the railway network on Java was 5,400 kilometers, it can be assumed that the construction of 90 kilometers of railway line could be done from the replacement reserve.

Early in 1943 the Japanese assigned experienced engineers, building experts, supervisors, and other specialist railway personnel originating from various places in Java to work on the Banten line. Because few Indonesians had the requisite training and skills, the Japanese were forced to use Dutch personnel, although this was contrary to the general policy of completely eliminating the Dutch presence and placing "full-blooded" Dutchmen in internment camps. The number involved can be estimated at twenty-five, with a similar number of Indonesians.

The first group of senior officials traveled by train to Saketi, accompanied by several hundred *rōmusha* from Central and East Java hired for an indefinite period to provide heavy labor in preparing the roadbed. A locally recruited workforce performed lighter tasks. The party went by truck from Saketi to Bojongdatar, a rubber plantation located 10 kilometers south of Saketi, where the *rōmusha* were housed in long, wooden sheds. A month later there was a large-scale move to Malingping, a point midway along the line where project headquarters were situated.[34]

For construction purposes the route was split into sectors, apparently about ten in number, each with a workforce given the task of completing the assigned section in a year. Work teams consisted of a few Dutch or Indonesian experts, a Japanese supervisor, and about a thousand *rōmusha*. Separate teams handled bridge construction.[35] One of the overseers, a man named Tjakradipura, who was responsible for the *rōmusha* on part of the Saketi–Malingping sector, later said in an interview that he considered the workload and the treatment acceptable, and made no mention of cruelties. Only 3 members of his team of 1,000 workers died.[36] However, his report conflicts with testimony from other sources, including a statement by the Indo-Dutchman R. Sadhinoch who, under a Japanese chief, handled personnel matters. He visited all teams along the whole planned line of track in the course of his work, and told a colleague about

> the ruthless occupier, who fagged us out and allowed us not a single free day and was guilty of the death daily of dozens of romusha, who were made to do slave labor, received very bad and insufficient food and almost no medical treatment. Those weakened romusha had practically no resistance to disease, and countless numbers fell victim to malaria. The Japanese did not care what happened to them, after all there was a new supply of romushas every week.[37]

He wrote in some detail about the poor health of the workforce:

> Malnutrition (hunger oedema), malaria, tropical ulcers (ulcus tropicus)—in which a large part of the patient's bone was visible—but also snakebites were the causes, and terribly decimated a considerable number of the romusha. Nowhere on Java have I encountered so many poisonous snakes

as in South Bantam. It was so bad that the population after dusk didn't dare go out on the street. If at night one urgently had to leave home then they went out with at least four men, waving torches and loudly shouting, which chased the snakes from the streets. There was no serum present against these snakebites and those who were bitten by a poisonous snake hence were doomed to die.

The medical care for all the personnel, including the romusha, along the Saketi-Bayah route consisted of two Indonesian doctors . . . plus a "mantri"—a male nurse. The stock of medicines mainly consisted of aspirin, quinine, and dressings. In Malingping a provisional "sickbay" was constructed, a shack put together from wood and bamboo in which twenty "baleh-baleh" [bamboo sleeping benches] were placed, and upon those a "tikar" [a sleeping mat of woven reeds]. This number of "beds" was obviously insufficient and only the very seriously ill, most of them suffering from blackwater fever [malaria in an advanced stage] were hospitalized there. Because of the lack of the necessary medicines these patients had practically no chance of survival.[38]

Sutawinangun published an account of the railway construction in the Indonesian weekly *Siasat* in 1953. He said that workers were recruited under false pretexts, with many fine words about "efforts for the fatherland" and promises of rewards and favorable working conditions.[39]

But after they had reached their designated location their hopes for a happy existence instantly vanished when they saw the romusha who had arrived earlier, men who had the task of carrying heavy loads and were as emaciated as skeletons. The causes for this lay in a shortage of food and a lack of medical care. Their bodies were no longer clothed with textiles, but with trousers and shirts made from bags, and even these were often already torn, and only poorly mended because there was no tailor. What's more, thread could not be bought in the little shops, and even twine to replace thread was hard to obtain. Gruesome indeed. Day and night there was heavy work, with no consideration for the scorching sun, the heavy rain, or the hard wind that ravaged the laborers; all that because they were afraid of the word "*bagero*" that the Japanese spat at them, or of their own countrymen who felt themselves to be boss. The power of mind and body, which gradually grew less, was forced to an even greater effort, to the last drop of energy. Amongst the thousands of neglected and emaciated people, not a few dropped dead and lay in the middle of the field in the heat of the sun, or next to a heap of earth they had dug out themselves. Others died on the banks of a river, of thirst, whilst they crawled towards it in search of water, breathing their last before they could quench their thirst. Still others died while resting under a tree, when their illnesses reached a crisis. All of this had become commonplace, nobody was disturbed by it, took any notice of it, or mourned about it. Everybody just looked out for his own welfare, which possibly in turn would also be at risk tomorrow or the day after tomorrow. Quite a few bodies lay unnoticed, and were only found after the flesh had been completely eaten by animals. Very gruesome indeed. They were buried just anywhere, not in a particular place.[40]

Haji Moh. Mukhandar, born and raised in Bayah, provided Islamic funerals for deceased *rōmusha* and later described what he had seen during the construction:

Without human feeling the supervisors beat the workers when they saw them slack off in their work, or when they couldn't proceed because of exhaustion. The workers ate the remains of food, for which they fought, while the Japanese entertained themselves by throwing sand or water at them, laughing their heads off as if at a funny play. . . . Anything that was edible served as food. Leaves, and tubers, some of which only appeared edible and turned out to be lethal. Also the drinking of water from *sawah* [rice fields] or drains was not unusual in those days. This suffering every day claimed human lives in the whole area of the railway in construction. Some workers were shot because they tried to run away, but far more died because of cruel tortures and unbearable suffering.[41]

Tan Malaka also wrote of his experiences. In June 1943 he traveled to Bayah, where he had been assigned to work at the mine.[42]

The construction of the Saketi-Bayah road devoured the energy and lives of thousands of unpaid romusha. There were no provisions made for the housing, feeding, or health of the romusha, who were forced to work in a previously uninhabitable area infested with malarial mosquitoes. As a result of the hard work, lack of food and medicines, and the ever-present Japanese whip, the romusha fell like rice stalks before a scythe.

The local people told me that the name "Saketi," which means one hundred thousand, had now been fulfilled. They said there was a prophecy that the 150 kilometers separating Saketi and Bayah would one day be spanned by an iron road traversed by an iron horse and that this road would require a sacrifice of no less than a *saketi* of human victims. So now the prophecy had come true.

I was unable to verify whether in fact the construction of the Saketi-Bayah railway had taken the lives of one hundred thousand romusha. Neither could I find out whether this prophecy had been known before its construction. I heard from all sides, however, that the loss of life during the construction had been truly horrifying, and the tremendous physical and spiritual destruction that I witnessed in my first year at Bayah made me feel that the sacrifice mentioned in the prophecy may well have been levied.

About five or six kilometers from Bayah, along the coast, was a place called Pulau Manuk, which was feared by everyone, for few were the romusha who emerged from that place uninfected by fatal diseases such as ulcerated boils, dysentery, and malaria. The romusha were provided with insufficient food, very few medicines, and an inadequate nursing staff; practically no care at all was given to the sick and dying. Every day along the road from Pulau Manuk to Bayah one could see romusha covered with festering lesions struggling to reach a marketplace or an empty building where they could stretch themselves out to await death. In all the towns along the road from Saketi to Jakarta the markets, roadsides, and empty yards were filled with living corpses. Sometimes in the Bayah area up to ten corpses were buried in a single grave, because of official indifference and the lack of grave diggers. In the rainy season corpses were piled into graves half filled with water.[43]

Groups of volunteers recruited from the *seinendan*, or youth corps, worked alongside the *rōmusha* and suffered the same fate.

The Seinendan who came from Pekalongan and Kedu arrived marching in formation and singing, with flags flying. They wore clean clothes and carried suitcases. But after their term of service expired—a month later—they returned home in smaller numbers than when they arrived; their clothes were in rags; their suitcases sold; and their bodies were skin and bone, wracked with malaria, ulcers, and dysentery.[44]

Sutawinangun estimated that more than 15,000 workers died.[45] Another source said that construction claimed 50,000 victims, and another 20,000 perished in the Bayah mines, making the number of victims nearly as great as the number of railway ties.[46] Other sources suggest that 40 percent of the workers died,[47] putting the number of victims at 35,000.[48] Two eyewitness accounts cite 60,000 and 42,000 deaths.[49] Tan Malaka wrote that of 15,000 workers in Bayah, 4,000 to 5,000 died every month.[50] An ex-*rōmusha* from Central Java who was sent to Bayah in 1943 said that only 5 or 6 of his group of 33 survived to the end of the war. They had been promised that they needed to work for only a hundred days but had no opportunity to return home.[51] The total number of victims cannot be ascertained, but the extent of the suffering seems limitless.

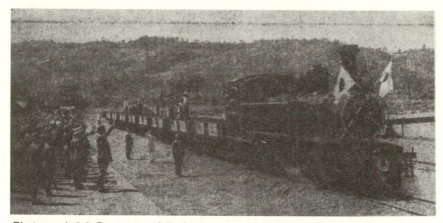

Photograph 8.2. Departure of the inaugural train on the new Bayah railway. (*Asia Raya,* 6 April 1944.)

The railway line was completed in March 1944, and a festive opening took place on April 1. High authorities came to Saketi for the ceremony. At 12:40 the first train departed, loaded with freight. News reports announced that a railway line, a main road, and a telegraph line had been completed. An electricity station had also been built, so that all conditions for exploitation of minerals had been met. A Javanese region had been opened.[52] The published reports were vague about the location of the railway line to avoid providing the enemy with any vital information. However, although the Netherlands Forces Intelligence Service (NEFIS) in Australia acquired very little data about developments on Java generally, it managed to publish a report describing construction of the railway and giving a detailed account of the coal deposits in Bayah.[53]

After the railway was officially opened, teams of *rōmusha* remained along the line to provide maintenance, although this work was less demanding than what had come before.[54] The majority of these *rōmusha* came from densely populated areas in Central and East Java. Most signed on for three months, but some for four, six, or eight months.[55] Detailed figures covering the period April–June 1944 are available for eleven of Java's twenty residencies, and they give an indication of the total size of *rōmusha* shipments and of the numbers sent to work at the railway and mine. Six of the eleven residencies, mainly in Central and East Java, supplied *rōmusha* to Bayah and Saketi. In all they exported 17,500 *rōmusha* during this period, and 5,000 going to Bayah, half the number demanded by the Japanese. These figures, for a three-month period and covering just half of Java, emphasize the considerable claim that the railway and mine laid on the *rōmusha,* and show the importance the Japanese attached to this enterprise.[56]

Photograph 8.3. Opening of an addition to the railway line. (*Djawa Baroe.*)

Resistance against Construction of the Railway

After the Japanese victory, the European population on Java had little opportunity to engage in resistance activities. Lack of support from the local people, who adopted a hostile or at best indifferent stance toward their former colonial rulers, made effective organization and action extremely difficult, and the police apparatus, which had functioned very efficiently during the colonial period, now served the Japanese with equal effect. The former masters were watched as minutely as their colonial subjects had been in the past.

The Japanese almost immediately limited the freedom of movement of the European population, and took control of the news media. Contact with the Allied side was impossible, and little information was received from external sources. Radios were modified to limit reception and then sealed, and the Japanese controlled the local release of information. News that contained details the enemy might use to his advantage—and many things fell under this category—was either not released or presented in very vague terms. In these circumstances it is hardly surprising that countless rumors circulated and sometimes grew to fabulous proportions. In particular rumors about Allied landings and victories in the archipelago, and about resistance movements and infiltration, circulated widely, and are reported as established fact in countless diaries and reports from this period.

As large-scale internment of the European population proceeded, the likelihood of resistance from that quarter steadily diminished. Soon only a small group of experts whose services were needed for the provision of essential economic services remained outside the camps. A special armlet worn at all times proclaimed them to be "Nippon workers," and they were closely watched and strictly supervised. In the transportation and communications sector, the knowledge and experience of the Dutch and Indo-Europeans was indispensable to keeping the railways running, and in this sector Indonesianization took place slowly.[57]

In setting up a resistance movement, railway employees had the great advantage of being part of a network of people that extended across Java. Bolstered by the general expectation that the Allies would soon chase out Japan, and with naive amateurism, a group of them formed an illegal organization that undertook the transport and storage of weapons, disseminated information, and carried out sabotage. The structure of this resistance movement was far too open, and too many people knew what was being done. The Japanese military police, the Kempeitai, on several occasions rounded up portions of the organization. More than two hundred railway workers were arrested in these crackdowns.[58]

The Dutchmen sent to Banten for the construction of the railway were probably aware of the resistance network set up by their colleagues. One of those involved was Sadhinoch, who was housed in Malingping with an Indonesian named Diponegoro, a head supervisor for the state railway who had been based at Purwokerto and was now charged with supervision of the Malingping–Bayah section. Diponegoro, who was around forty-five years of age, was a Javanese aristocrat, and considering his job clearly must have received a good education. He also wielded substantial personal authority over other Javanese. Sadhinoch and Diponegoro, who were already casual acquaintances, soon developed a close relationship. Exceptionally for an Indo-European, Sadhinoch sympathized with the radical nationalist movement, and with communism, distinct political positions but often conflated by the Dutch. When he discovered their spiritual kinship, Diponegoro told Sadhinoch that he was leader of the Partai Komunis Indonesia (PKI) in Purwokerto and was also active in party activities in Banten.[59]

The PKI had been banned in the Netherlands Indies after the uprising of 1926–27. The Dutch had been highly apprehensive of a communist resurgence, sometimes to the point of paranoia, and a revival in 1935–36 quickly resulted in the arrest and banishment of key figures. Of the newly formed core only one man, Pamoedji, remained free, and he cautiously proceeded to form a number of communist cells and recruit a limited number of cadre members. The latter had to hide their involvement and could not openly distribute propaganda, organize, or carry out political action.

The Dutch tolerated one leftist party, Gerindo, which united leftist nationalists, communists, social democrats, and leftist radicals. Although their knowledge of Marxist doctrine was limited, many Gerindo members felt attracted to communism, and this along with the fact that Gerindo had adopted an unconditional antifascist position, openly citing Japan as an example, made the Japanese deeply suspicious of the organization.

Soon after the occupation began the Japanese disbanded all political parties. Gerindo's networks, however, continued to exist and to some extent provided a foundation for clandestine organizations. These groupings had a strong local character, and their names varied according to location or region. The PKI, which was accustomed to operating as an underground organization, attempted to coordinate these scattered groups. Its initial goals were modest: cadre formation, anti-Japanese propaganda, and the maintenance of an organizational structure.

Opposing the PKI stood the Kempeitai, which like the Netherlands Indies government saw communism as its most dangerous enemy, and hunted down alleged communists with just as much effort and even more ruthless consequences. The intelligence apparatus for the most part now consisted of Indonesians who rendered service to the Japanese. Several thousand Indonesians were arrested on suspicion of being involved in PKI activity, and many—including Pamoedji—were put to death.[60]

Diponegoro is not mentioned in any of the few written sources that deal with wartime communist activities, apart from the information provided by Sadhinoch. His prewar place of residence was the Central Javanese city of Purwokerto, which is not inconsistent with PKI involvement. The PKI had its center in Surabaya and branches in other cities in East and Central Java.

Diponegoro's initiatives are notable for his efforts to enroll Indo-Europeans in his resistance network. Other communist organizers seemed to consider that the physical absence of Europeans made such cooperation impossible, although it was consistent with the political line of the PKI (and before 1942 Gerindo), which subordinated the struggle for national independence to the struggle against aggressive fascism. The communists sought to cooperate with the Europeans against fascism, and a man with the intellectual background of Diponegoro, as sketched by Sadhinoch, might well have adopted this line in contrast to the populist-nationalist approach that generally characterized the wartime PKI. Diponegoro cautiously approached others about setting up a resistance group. Sabotage of the railway construction was an obvious tactic, for both the communists and the anti-Japanese Dutch railway technicians. In June 1943 Diponegoro arranged a meeting involving eight Dutchmen and Indonesians to work out a plan of action. Those present were Sadhinoch, building expert Barkey, section supervisor R. Brouwer, engine driver Brugman, head supervisor C. Dijckhoff, section supervisor E.A. Schweichler, and principal clerk J.A.P. Sumual. Sadhinoch, whose job required him to travel the entire route of the railway, was appointed liaison officer. Diponegoro formulated the goals of the group:

1. Collect blueprints of stations and bridges;
2. Collect and stockpile explosives for blowing up strategic objects;
3. Delay and disrupt construction of the railway;
4. Prepare to receive, care for, and accompany any Allied spies put ashore by submarine between Muarabinuangeun and Cihara; and
5. Appoint persons who could fill the power vacuum that would arise when the Japanese had to retreat from South Banten.

Diponegoro claimed that he had received word from Australia about an imminent landing of Allied agents, but this is unlikely to have been true. He was probably trying to impress the group, basing his statement on the prevailing widespread rumors. According to Sadhinoch, the PKI used employees of the mail service to carry messages.

Diponegoro's group appeared to have the resources they needed to carry out the proposed program, and they assembled blueprints and hid a few hundred kilograms of explosives near the coast. The group raised money by claiming payment for bills twice and putting more workers on the wage sheet than were actually present.

In December 1943 the group blew up a bridge pillar to delay construction of the railway line, although the Japanese command blamed the damage on flooding. After this success some group members seem to have become careless and loose-tongued. In May 1944 Diponegoro, Sadhinoch, and Schweichler discussed what was happening. They suspected betrayal, and Sadhinoch noticed that he was being followed. In early June Diponegoro gave the order to break off all contact among group members, and a few days later he disappeared. On June 15, 1944, the Kempeitai arrested the seven remaining conspirators along with three Dutchmen who were not part of the group. All were taken to the prison at Serang, where the Kempeitai subjected them to torture until the war ended in August 1945. Sadhinoch was asked about his relationship to Diponegoro, whom the Japanese seemed to consider an important communist leader, and about his role in subversive activity. Members of the group were considered "special prisoners" and kept in complete isolation. Even prison personnel were not supposed to talk to them, and they received no medical care and little food. Brugman died in May

1945 from injuries received at the hands of the Japanese, and Sumual was paralyzed on one side owing to brain damage. One guard, a former class-mate of Sadhinoch, told him in early August that they had all been sentenced to death and were to be executed on September 6, 1945. The Japanese sur-render saved their lives, but they were marked forever by the experience.[61] Diponegoro vanished without a trace. After the war Sadhinoch tried to locate his mentor, but without success.[62]

Accounts of the resistance during the Japanese period list many names but do not mention Diponegoro.[63] The name was not an alias because he had been employed under that name by the railway in Purwokerto. Was he an agent provocateur? It seems very improbable. His experience as a political organizer was too great, and if he had been, why was the group allowed to remain active for a year? The Kempeitai responded ruthlessly to the slightest indication of disloyalty. The group was isolated and could not be used as bait to discover information about resistance activity elsewhere. Moreover, why were three innocent people arrested? And why was the group not executed shortly afterward? From a Japanese point of view their activities were seri-ous enough for that. The reason can only lie in a Japanese desire to wring information from the arrested persons about Diponegoro and their own resis-tance activities.

Diponegoro's life, like that of so many convinced anti-Japanese commu-nists and radical nationalists, may have come to an anonymous end because of the Japanese. Or it is possible that a natural death denied him a further role in history.

The Mining Enterprise

The mining of brown coal in Bayah started in July 1942.[64] Production de-tails are not known, although Tan Malaka mentions a daily output of 100 tons.[65] According to a postwar Japanese report the railway system in Java transported 24,000 tons in 1942; 71,000 tons in 1943; 72,000 tons in 1944; and 25,000 tons in the first half of 1945. Monthly totals gradually rose from 3,000 tons to a peak of 8,600 tons in August 1943. Prior to the opening of the Bayah railway in April 1944, the monthly average was 7,000 tons, but the figure subsequently decreased to between 3,000 and 4,000 tons per month in 1945.[66] It is reasonable to assume that starting in 1943, when existing sup-plies had been consumed, the figures closely approximate the output of the Bayah mines and reflect production levels there. The decrease following the opening of the railway line is strange and was probably the consequence of the limited reserves of brown coal and the exhaustion of human and material resources. The Bayah mining operation was modest at best; in 1939 coal production in the Netherlands Indies totaled 1,781,000 tons, while production at Bayah never came close to the target figure of 300,000 tons.

Considerable amounts of brown coal must have been brought out of Banten by road before the opening of the railway line, possibly moving along sections of the roadbed that had been prepared in advance. Bayah had more than a thousand automobiles,[67] and both Saketi and Sukabumi, where there were existing railway lines, could be reached by road. Considering the state of the roads and the probable destination of the coal, Saketi seems the most obvious transshipment point, but cargoes nevertheless went to Sukabumi and Cibadak.[68] After the opening of the Bayah railway, its daily capacity of 300 tons (and 194 passengers) was more than sufficient to handle the output of the mines.[69]

Bayah coal was mined at Gunung Madur and Cimang.[70] There were about twenty shafts in all, some of them as deep as 140 meters, and they employed more than a hundred miners. Narrow-gauge railway lines, the longest measuring 8 kilometers, linked these sites with Bayah, where the coal was transferred to other transport.[71] Initially the Bayah works employed around 20,000 people in the mines, on transport, on construction work, and in the administration, but by August 1945 the number had fallen to about half that. Tan Malaka briefly summarized the mining operations:

> In all but a few places deep mining was necessary to get at the coal. The coal seam was usually only a meter wide, the veins were not particularly long, and the coal extracted from them was very soft. In addition, the machinery was antiquated and the labor force was weak because of the lack of food and training. Finally, the organization of both production and administration was extremely unsatisfactory.[72]

As far as the mine is concerned, especially in the later period there was mention of a regular relief of the *rōmusha* after their term of three months. Those who managed to survive went home in very poor condition. A collection of human wrecks, they traveled with an escort of mine personnel in separate railway carriages to spare other passengers the sight and stench of the *rōmusha,* many of whom were afflicted with suppurating tropical ulcers.[73]

In the latter part of the occupation there was talk of improving the living conditions of the *rōmusha* by providing more facilities at the mine and by paying attention to hygiene and medical care. Credit for this initiative belongs to Tan Malaka, who had been appointed head of the office responsible for *rōmusha* affairs, and a number of young kindred spirits. However, given the heavy work, the unhealthy surroundings, the shortage of medicines, and the very parsimonious rations, little could be done.

The group around Tan Malaka consisted of a few colleagues and a number of youthful soldiers who had volunteered for the elite PETA corps (Sukarela Tentara Pembela Tanah Air, Volunteer Army for the Defense of the Fatherland), which recruited educated, nationalist-minded Indonesians. In early 1943 a PETA company that numbered 120 men was stationed in Bayah to protect the coast. In addition auxiliary soldiers, *heiho,* were used around Bayah. This isolated region was thus flooded with mine employees, *rōmusha,* and young soldiers, and the original population felt threatened by this situation. Absorbed as they were in the daily struggle for survival, they, like the mine staff, cared little for the fate of the *rōmusha.* It took a man of the stature of Tan Malaka to attempt to relieve their suffering, and his appeal to nationalist and humanitarian feelings produced some results, although relations between the local population and the newcomers remained tense.[74]

The strongest *rōmusha* worked in the mines, receiving 1 guilder and 400 grams of rice a day. The others were used as woodcutters, ground workers, or porters for 40 cents and 250 grams of rice a day. A public kitchen set up in Bayah in 1944 provided a breakfast of sweet potatoes or glutinous rice with coffee and a lunch and dinner of rice, vegetables, and a bit of salted fish for about a thousand *rōmusha* each day at a price of 10 cents per person. The rice ration was then 300 grams a day, but by 1945 it had dropped to 250 grams.[75] An announcement shortly before the Japanese surrender said that the ration would be reduced to 200 grams a day, and an allocation of 100 grams of rice a day for women and children would be eliminated entirely. By this time the general food situation had become so bad that rationing applied not only to *rōmusha* but also to mine employees and the original inhabitants of the region, and the announcement caused widespread discontent. *Rōmusha* ran away, and in Gunung Madur people planned to go on strike. The surrender took place before the anticipated harsh response from the Japanese.[76] For the *rōmusha,* and for the entire population of Java, the food situation had worsened dramatically during the occupation. Famine reigned across the island, causing the deaths of an estimated 2 million people.

Other sources provide additional information on food in Banten. A colleague of Tan Malaka mentions a daily ration of 300 grams of rice, sometimes with tapioca.[77] One *rōmusha* remembers servings of rice, tapioca, salt fish, and sugar. He supplemented this with coconuts and even managed to sell a portion of his food.[78] Sutawinangun mentions a ration of 150 grams of rice and a few grams of salted fish.[79] As far as clothing was concerned, *rōmusha* received a pair of short trousers and a shirt once every six months. Textiles had become extremely scarce, and most sold these goods to villagers, clothing themselves in sacks or in sheets of latex.[80]

In 1944 a hospital was set up in Cikaret, between Gunung Madur and Bayah, where sick and dying *rōmusha* gathered. The building was a simple structure made of bamboo, but it could accommodate 700 *rōmusha* in clean surroundings, and offered safe drinking water, a pharmacy, and a few male nurses. In Bayah itself there was a small hospital under the management of two Chinese doctors.[81] Medicines were in short supply, and only quinine was readily available. Malaria was endemic and tropical ulcers a constant danger.[82]

The changes introduced during the occupation reshaped Bayah. Tan Malaka wrote: "In a few years time the small, remote and unknown kampong, called Bayah, as a result of the coal supply around it, had become a town, an administrative center, complete with workshops, a railway station and an electric station."[83] The population had in those few years increased to four or five times its prewar size.[84]

The Japanese considered Bayah's mine a large and prestigious enterprise. The visit by Java's highest administrator, Lieutenant General Harada, and other dignitaries in June 1944 shows the importance attached to the project. Harada arrived on June 5 and after a welcoming ceremony spent the night in Bayah. The next day he visited two of the mines and even went inside carrying a lamp. He talked with workers from high to low, showing great interest. An accompanying report about this "war industry" presents a heroic picture of the "gigantic task, the struggle of man against nature" and the opening of "impenetrable, secluded jungle" where thousands of workers "black from the coal and dedicated to the cause of war and the motherland" did their jobs under Japanese guidance. A careful reading of this account shows some veiled criticism as well. The workers had left their families and villages behind and now lived an extremely parsimonious existence housed in sheds. Everybody felt sorry for them. The evening market, the polyclinic, and the regular movie and theatrical performances could not make up for that.[85]

Sukarno and Mohammed Hatta, who cooperated with the occupier, also visited Bayah, where they made what were in those days obligatory speeches of praise.[86] Sukarno later recalled his visit: "With reporters, photographers, the Gunseikan—Commander-in-Chief—civil authorities and I made trips to Banten, the western tip of Java, to inspect pitiable skeletons slaving on the home front down deep in the coal and gold mines. It was terrible."[87]

After the Occupation

The sudden Japanese surrender on August 15, 1945, and the Indonesian proclamation of independence two days later came as a surprise to Bayah. As the news spread, mine employees and PETA members took control of the area.

The Japanese feared Indonesian revenge, but they were quietly shipped off to a rendezvous point to await the arrival of the Allied soldiers. The *rōmusha,* as far as they were able, started to return home. The food situation quickly improved, but hunger edema claimed many more victims.[88]

From Jakarta a prominent representative of the militant youth who had given an important impulse to the proclamation of independence came to Bayah to promote the formation of battle groups and a representative body.[89]

The mine continued to operate, now under Indonesian management. On October 2, 1945, it was nationalized and, as the Bayah State Coalmine, placed under the authority of the Republic Office for Coal Mines. The Republic, like the Japanese, needed coal to keep the railways operating, and supplies from Sumatra seemed unattainable for the foreseeable future. On December 1, 1945, the mine was put under the Department of Transport in Yogyakarta, showing its great importance to the railways. The new management considered a daily production of 400 tons possible, provided workers and materials were available. It mainly lacked the former. Most of the *rōmusha* had left and the thinly populated surroundings of Bayah could not supply sufficient manpower. In the chaotic conditions that prevailed at the time, it was impossible to obtain workers elsewhere.[90] Widespread unrest in Banten in the final months of 1945 was a further impediment to restoring production. A coalition of orthodox Muslim leaders, communists, and grassroots leaders, entirely made up of local people and characteristic of the region, turned against the central government and chased away government representatives and the police.[91] Power in Bayah fell into the hands of radical and militant communists, but the central Republican authorities violently suppressed this social revolution in December 1945.[92]

During 1946 the mine began to produce coal once again, with a reported output of 50 tons a month—a low and probably incorrect figure.[93] The railway also continued to function. In May 1947 a report on Banten stated,

> The "road to hell" is now very busy. The train is always packed, but the whole construction is Japanese style and is not so durable. The same is true of the pit coalmine of Gunung Madur, set up as a war enterprise that, however hard it might be, had to yield production in short time. According to our informant the mine construction can only be used for three years.[94]

After the First Police Action (July–August 1947), in which Dutch troops occupied a large part of Java, the Republic was pushed back to Central Java. The Dutch did not occupy the Bayah region, but the Republic could no longer reach the area by land, and a naval blockade made contact by sea intermittent and risky. Banten was completely thrown onto its own resources. The train and probably the mine as well continued to function but faced many difficulties.[95] In 1948 the train journey from Rangkasbitung to Bayah took half a day, with an old wood-fired locomotive serving the route.[96] In Bayah itself decay set in.

> The forests where companies and buildings had been constructed, and which became just as busy as the city, gradually grew quiet again as in the past, before there had ever been humans there. In the Japanese days the town was busy, there was abundant electric lighting, and everywhere, as in a dream, sounded the sweet sound of radios. With the surrender of Japan all these structures deteriorated, and eventually disappeared entirely, becoming level with the ground, and the area returned to its former condition, the jungle.[97]

To honor the memory of the *rōmusha* who perished at Bayah a monument was erected at the station in 1946 or 1947,[98] near the entrance to the village from the direction of Malingping. Its height was 3 meters and the sides measured 1.5 meters. A list of victims, with tens of thousands of names, was placed in a cavity at the front of the structure. The list disappeared during the Second Police Action in December 1948 and was never recovered. However, a memorial service continued to be held every year on May 1. The monument eventually decayed because of lack of maintenance, and an agreement in 1952 that the government would take over that responsibility was ineffective because of infighting among the government services. In 1980 the monument was gone, although the spot where it stood could still be identified.[99]

In contrast with the decay at Bayah, Cikotok recovered when gold mining resumed there. In 1948 the whole enterprise was again operating, with mining in Cirotan and transport of the ore by cableway to the processing installation in Pasir Gombong, with energy supplied by the electric station. Gold was of far greater importance to the Republic than coal or copper. The Republic needed foreign currency to purchase military and other supplies. A rigorous Dutch blockade prevented the export of most goods, but it was possible to smuggle out small quantities of valuable commodities such as gold, cinchona, opium, and vanilla by boat or by plane. The mine, which produced about 10 kilograms of gold monthly, was an invaluable source of foreign exchange and made the Cikotok area a high priority; the Republic stationed able personnel and a sizable garrison force there.[100]

In the early morning of December 23, 1948, Dutch troops entered Banten, and that evening the Grenadiers Combat Group of the Seven December Division occupied Cikotok. By moving quickly the Dutch managed to prevent Indonesian forces from blowing up the heavily mined complex. Bayah was occupied the following day, and Dutch army units reached Saketi on

December 26, and Malingping on December 27. There was hardly any resistance, and the main obstacle to the Dutch advance was the extremely bad condition of the roads. However, the Dutch subsequently faced intense guerrilla activity, a kind of warfare for which the terrain was very well suited. Transport and supply caused major problems for the Dutch, and contact with a number of stations, such as Malingping, was possible only by air.[101]

The occupation gave the South Bantam Mining Company a long-sought-after chance to attempt to restore mining operations in the area. The prospects seemed good. In his first report after the occupation of Cikotok, the commanding officer wrote that the situation there was "favorable." "The various offices, houses, gudangs [warehouses] and work floors have been mined in many locations. We are making good progress with clearing these away. The electric station at Pasir Gombong is completely undamaged."[102]

The fighting delayed repairs, but in the following months the road to Pelabuhan Ratu was restored, and travel along it was reasonably safe. The Cikotok–Bayah route was also firmly in the hands of the Dutch troops. The occupation of Cikotok and Bayah was considered important for economic reasons, but the Dutch had no interest at all in exploiting pit coal. Shipping coal would in any case have been impossible. Dutch troops could use the Bayah–Saketi route only during daylight hours and under heavy escort, and the railway was not operating. Bayah was of interest to the Dutch because the Japanese had built up the mine using machinery and installations taken from private companies and government agencies, who now sent representatives to conduct inventories and arrange for the return of their property. When Dutch forces abruptly vacated Bayah and Cikotok in October 1949 and transferred the area to the Republican army on the basis of military agreements that anticipated the final political settlement, five representatives of electricity companies, agricultural firms, and trading companies also left. Only the Indonesian representative of the Netherlands Indies Management Institute (*Nederlands-Indische Beheers Instituut*), a government agency founded in 1940 that was responsible for the management of properties whose owners were absent or unknown, remained behind. During this exodus, Bayah's transformer disappeared and the lights went out again—this time for more than thirty years. The head administrator for the South Bantam Mining Company remained at his station and kept the enterprise running with the aid of a Republican garrison force,[103] but the firm stopped operations after Indonesia became independent, and its mining assets were liquidated in 1951.[104] A private European investor seems then to have attempted to run the mine, but with poor results. In the 1960s the Indonesian government took over the enterprise and it remains in operation today as the state company Logam Mulia (Precious Metals).[105]

The Indonesian authorities could not immediately reopen the railway line. Darul Islam forces became active in the area in the second half of 1949, seeking to establish a Muslim state, and militant communist armed groups were also in the vicinity, fighting against the Indonesian federal government. They were suppressed only with great effort.[106]

By 1951 access to Bayah by road had become extremely difficult. In January of that year, train service resumed briefly to ship machinery out of Bayah. Trains operated daily at first, but the service was soon reduced to once a week, and then stopped altogether, to the regret of the people and government of South Banten.[107]

The Indonesian railways formed a commission in November 1951 to study the possibility of reopening the line. Its conclusions were negative. There were no concentrations of population along the route that could provide passengers, and the demand for freight service was small. Nine stations had been completely destroyed, eighty-five bridges had to be rebuilt, and the track and roadbed needed repair along the entire route. These costs could never have been recovered by returns from the line, and the report suggested the much cheaper alternative of improving roads in the region. An inevitable demolition process started, and valuable items were removed for use elsewhere by the railways, or taken by people living in the surrounding area.[108] The rail line gradually disappeared, and in 1980 only the foundations of bridge pillars remained along the coast, although in Bayah traces of railway track and raised transshipment platforms were still discernible.

All buildings from the period of Japanese occupation have disappeared from Bayah. The bamboo structures disintegrated shortly after they were abandoned. Demolition and conversion of land to rice cultivation soon followed. Sutawinangun concluded his account on this melancholy note:

> This applies also to the coal shafts, where in the past romusha walked to and fro, in and out the shaft, without awareness of day or night, until they eventually collapsed. Gradually the shafts became closed off by landslides and big rocks, and by heavy rains, because of which they now sometimes flood from an indeterminate direction. They look like caves, overgrown and sealed off by large and small trees on landslides of earth and stones, and where furthermore evil spirits hide. Nobody now still dares to come near or enter there, because they are filled with vipers and beautiful striped panthers.[109]

9

The *Heiho* during the
Japanese Occupation of Indonesia

Kaori Maekawa

During the Pacific War large numbers of young men from the Indonesian archipelago served alongside Japanese soldiers as *heiho* (auxiliary soldiers) in the Japanese army and navy. Technically civilian employees of the military, the *heiho* supplied labor for the Southern Army (Nanpō Sōgun) in its effort to sustain the Asia–Pacific War. They served in many areas, including Java, the Lesser Sunda Islands, Borneo Sumatra, Sulawesi, Malaya, Thailand, Burma, Indochina, East and West New Guinea, and the Bismarck and Solomon Islands along the Australian front.[1]

In contrast with Pembela Tanah Air (PETA), the Japanese-sponsored local military body whose members became the nucleus of Indonesia's national army and played an important role in the struggle for independence, the *heiho* have received scant attention; if they are remembered at all, it is usually as members of an auxiliary organization that performed miscellaneous services for the Japanese army and navy.[2] However, the *heiho* constituted the largest military body created by the Japanese during the occupation in Indonesia. Members received regular military training, and after the Japanese surrender participated in the struggle for independence at the local level.[3]

This chapter explains the origin and development of the Japanese *heiho* system in the occupied southern areas and especially in the Netherlands East Indies (NEI) during the Asia–Pacific War, when serious manpower shortages forced the Japanese to depend on local recruitment to augment manpower recruited from Japan proper. The *heiho* system was intended to provide a provisional military body that could be developed into an independent indigenous force for the defense of Southeast Asia. The topic will be examined by looking at the *heiho* system in the context of military mobilization practices in Japanese colonies generally, and then reviewing the use made of *heiho* in Indonesia. Generally speaking, the *heiho* was a military labor group serving as part of the Japanese army and navy, although it drew on professional soldiers who had served in military bodies in the prewar NEI, and some of its

members had regular Japanese military training and more combat experience than the personnel in PETA. A consideration of the role of the *heiho*
within the Japanese military establishment provides an opportunity to examine to what degree the Japanese maintained links with military personnel
from the colonial period, and the way Japan planned to utilize indigenous
personnel to bring the Co-prosperity Sphere into being.

Manpower in the Co-prosperity Sphere

By early 1942, the shortage of manpower in Japan proper had given rise to
competition between the army and navy for human resources throughout the
Japanese empire.[4] As a result of the prolonged Sino–Japanese War and the
extension of the conflict to Southeast Asia, as many as 7 million men had
been mobilized to serve in the Japanese army, a figure that exceeded the
number considered sustainable given the concurrent need for manpower to
serve in defense industries and to produce consumer goods in Japan. In January 1942, the Army Ministry prepared a manpower study that suggested dealing with this issue by mobilizing "non-Japanese" to reinforce the Japanese
army. The authors of this document wrote: "In consideration of difficulties in
sustaining the level of forces, and the sacrifices we have to make, it is not the
time for debate but for urgent measures to utilize people in the colonies to
build troop strength."[5] They contended that a serious decline in the population in Japan would result if conscription was enforced only for Japanese
and would leave Japan with insufficient manpower to sustain the Co-prosperity
Sphere if the Pacific War was successful.

Limited mobilization of non-Japanese had already taken place in the
recruitment of auxiliary policemen—the Kenpei-ho (auxiliary military
police) in Korea and Taiwan after 1919, and the Ken-ho (auxiliary police) in Manchuria after 1937. In addition, a special volunteer system
introduced in colonial Korea in 1938, just after the outbreak of the Sino–
Japanese War, and in Taiwan in April 1942, recruited local people as auxiliary troops assisting the Japanese army and navy. Such arrangements
not only helped overcome manpower shortages in the military but also
fulfilled Japan's intention of granting full military membership to non-
Japanese territories in the Japanese empire. In principle, Taiwanese and
Koreans were regarded as Japanese, and the Koreans had undergone forced
assimilation through modifications to their education system, prohibition
of the use of the mother tongue, and adoption of Japanese-style names.
When the Sino–Japanese War broke out, an extended debate was taking
place concerning military conscription in Korea and Taiwan, and in May
1942 the cabinet decided to introduce conscription in Korea. This became

official policy in March 1943, but the program was not implemented until the following year.

There were significant differences between forced assimilation in Taiwan and Korea, and the policies Japan followed in other occupied territories. In Indonesia, for example, military mobilization did not reflect a move toward assimilation but was dictated by Japan's needs for additional manpower to prosecute the war. People were asked to cooperate with Japan in order to build Asia Raya Timur (Indonesian for "Greater East Asia") and strengthen the defense of the Indonesian homeland against the Allies.

The Origin and Expansion of the *Heiho* in Indonesia

A discussion of the *heiho* during the Japanese military occupation of Indonesia must begin with an explanation of the situation of indigenous troops during the Dutch colonial period, their internment after the Japanese conquest, and their later incorporation into the Imperial Japanese Army. The colonial government maintained three military forces in the Indies: the Royal Netherlands Indies Army (Koninklijk Nederlands-Indisch Leger, KNIL), the Police Forces (Marechausee) and the Royal Navy (Koninklijk Marine). These forces maintained *ruste en orde* (law and order) in Java and were used to conquer and control local rulers in the Outer Islands. The Javanese made up the greater part of the colonial army, but their dedication to the Dutch cause was always suspect. In the latter part of the colonial period, Christian Ambonese and Menadonese emerged as strong supporters of the colonial regime and gained a particular reputation for loyalty. Accordingly, they received preferential treatment when compared with other ethnic groups, and the colonial government began employing men from these areas as soldiers and lower-level bureaucrats. (See Table 9.1.)

After achieving overwhelming military success in British Malaya, culminating with the surrender of Singapore on February 15, 1942, Japan invaded the Netherlands East Indies, hoping to utilize the natural and human resources of the archipelago to resolve the deadlocked Sino–Japanese War and build the Greater East Asia Co-prosperity Sphere. Dutch military forces were too weak to mount an effective defense, and the colonial government surrendered on March 8, 1942. The capture of strategic points in the southern region had occurred at a pace that exceeded expectations, and Japanese military authorities calculated that the Allied forces would not be able to counterattack until after 1943.[6] The General Staff Office judged that it would be possible during this interval to defend the seas around the Malay Peninsula and Java with the First and Second Fleets of the Japanese navy, freeing the army for operations elsewhere. The military's "Tactical Guidelines for 1942" called

Table 9.1

Membership of the KNIL by Ethnic Group, 1930 (in percent)

	KNIL	Population
Javanese	50.5	47
Menadonese	20.4	0.5
Ambonese	16.1	0.4
Sundanese	7.2	14.5
Timorese	4.3	1.5
Malay	0.7	1.6
Madura	0.4	7.3
Bugis	0.3	2.6
Acehnese	0.25	1.4

Source: KNIL statistics in 1935 compiled by Sanbō Honbu (General Staff Office), "Ran'in Gun no Soshitsu oyobi Nōryoku ni kansuru Kentō" (The Investigations regarding the nature and ability of the KNIL), August 31, 1941, Military Archival Library, NIDS, Tokyo; Census in 1930, Taiwan Sōtokufu Gaijibu ed., *Nanyō Nenkan*, vol.2 (South Seas' Year-Book, vol.2) (Taihoku: Nanyō Kyōkai Taiwanshibu, 1943), pp. 424-427.

for the redeployment of some troops from the Southern Army to China and Manchuria, and an "army reformation" program (Gun'yō Sasshin)—pending since the outbreak of the Sino–Japanese War—accordingly reduced the army strength in the southern area and revised the order of battle of the Japanese army in China.[7] Other troops from the Southern Army had already been deployed for cleanup operations in areas such as the Lesser Sunda Islands and Dutch New Guinea, and the garrison left behind in Java and Sumatra was reduced in strength to around one-fourth of its original size. In March 1942, the initial landing force attacking Java had included 55,000 men, but the size of the garrison on Java was 15,000, comprising 8,000 soldiers in operational units and a further 7,000 troops performing various services at military bases.[8] This garrison force had to maintain order, deal with the enormous numbers of prisoners of war (POWs) and internees that had fallen into Japanese hands after the Dutch surrender, and prepare for an Allied counterattack. To meet the anticipated need for manpower to carry out these tasks, military authorities in Tokyo authorized the use of local personnel as auxiliary troops in occupied areas, and the recruitment of local youths to fill vacancies in Japanese military units.[9] It was impossible to anticipate what the response would be, but given the reduced strength of Japanese forces in the southern areas as a result of the army reformation, mobilization of human resources in occupied territories was a necessity.

Shortly before the outbreak of hostilities, the First Research Section in Japan's General Staff Office had examined the idea of using indigenous troops to restore order in occupied territories. The Section's "Blueprint for

Enforcement of Military Administration in Dutch East Indies" stated, "The [Japanese] Army will support the utilization of local troops or police who surrendered to Japan in order to clean up the remaining enemy forces, if necessary," and suggested organizing local surrendered soldiers into units for this purpose.[10] In November 1941 the general headquarters of the Southern Army unveiled a more detailed set of plans. The "General" section of this document stated, "The Army shall guide existing police or indigenous troops for the maintenance of order under the support and the instruction of the Japanese force," while the part concerning the Netherlands East Indies specified, "We shall guide the security guards to be reorganized with indigenous military units to take over the Japanese task of maintenance of order."[11] The idea of using local people in these capacities became part of the major policy documents for the military administration of the occupied southern territories, namely the "Principles Governing the Administration of Occupied Southern Areas" and the "Principles for Administering Occupied Southern Areas in Accordance with Southern Operations" approved by the liaison conference between the imperial headquarters and the government in November 1941.[12]

The Army Ministry also gave active consideration to reinforcing the Japanese army through large-scale military mobilization in occupied territories. A document entitled "A Study of Japan's Human Resources in the Greater East Asian War," issued in January 1942, stressed the importance of "conserving troop strength" and noted that "measures like the utilization of indigenous military personnel within the Co-prosperity Sphere are such an essential condition for carrying out the Reformation of the Japanese Army that it is necessary to accelerate these studies."[13] In March 1942 Japan held around 93,000 POWs from the Dutch Colonial Army, mainly from the KNIL but including militia personnel mobilized after the war began.[14] It was too costly to feed and house such a large number of detainees, and in that month the 16th Army, which was responsible for Java, ordered the release of all captives interned in POW camps "except for Chinese, Indians, Ambonese and Menadonese, along with the members of white race." The instruction added that after their release, local troops could be used "on behalf of the Japanese police, if necessary."[15]

The decision not to free Ambonese and Menadonese prisoners can be traced to a series of intelligence studies conducted on the KNIL in August 1941 by the Japanese General Staff Office, which called attention to the strong links between these groups and the Dutch:

> While cadres of the Dutch Colonial Army are regarded as being loyal to their country, Eurasian personnel are inferior, and in the case of indigenous personnel, the extent of loyalty toward their country is uncertain.

Christian Menadonese and Ambonese as a whole, however, have strong loyalty to the Dutch Colonial Government, due to their receiving material benefits from the colonial authorities.[16]

Accordingly, Ambonese and Menadonese were kept in detention for fear that they might participate in anti-Japanese activities or cause instability.[17]

In April, Colonel Nishiura Susumu, at the time chief of the Military Affairs Bureau in the Army Ministry, suggested incorporating indigenous troops into the Japanese army.[18] He argued that such an arrangement would make it possible to "improve them gradually, and lead to the creation of an independent force which would defend Greater East Asia in the future." Legal obstacles could be overcome by treating such personnel as civilian employees of the army, on the model of the auxiliary military police in Korea, Taiwan, and Manchuria.[19] The Army Ministry, already embroiled in the army reformation program, supported this suggestion.

On July 29, 1942, the chief of the General Staff of the Army Department within general headquarters approved the use of indigenous troops to augment Japanese forces in the southern area. The Army Ministry issued a set of guidelines on September 23, 1942, and this marked the formal beginning of the *heiho* system, although recruitment had already begun among former POWs.[20] On February 27, 1943, imperial headquarters informed the Southern Army that it would be unable to fulfill manpower requests because of a dearth of manpower in Japan proper and a lack of transport to bring recruits to the South.[21] On April 22, 1943, the headquarters of the Southern Army drafted a regulation to put the *heiho* guidelines into effect, marking the start of systematic, large-scale military mobilization of young men in occupied southern territories.[22]

To summarize, the formative stage of the *heiho* early in the occupation proceeded as follows. Military authorities in Tokyo considered the possibility of using local soldiers to augment Japanese forces in the occupied territories at an early date. The idea gained added impetus from two sources: (1) a preoccupation among military authorities in Tokyo with army reform, a scheme that dated from before the outbreak of war and eventually gave rise to Colonel Nishiura's proposals for recruitment of indigenous troops, and (2) pragmatic decisions on the part of local army units in occupied territories seeking to overcome manpower shortages and to find satisfactory ways of dealing with the enormous pool of POWs that fell into their hands. The convergence of these lines of thinking led to the recruitment of large numbers of *heiho* to replenish Japanese forces. The enlistment of local troops served three purposes. First, it was an important measure for overcoming difficulties caused by insufficient numbers of Japanese soldiers. Second, it

Table 9.2

Looted Armaments in Java, March 1942

Airplanes	117
Artillery pieces	940
Heavy and light machine guns	4,228
Rifles, pistols	80,778
Antiaircraft searchlights	5,153
Ammunition	1,728,585
Live machine-gun and rifle cartridges	89,071,820
Bombs	36,000
Automobiles, tanks, armored vehicles, and the like	1,059
Motorcars	9,500

Source: Bōeichō Bōeikensyūsho Senshishitsu (NIDS), ed., *Senshisōsho 3: Ran'in Kōryaku Sakusen* (War history series 3: Netherlands East Indies Operation) (Tokyo: Asagumo Shinbunsha, 1967), pp. 593–94.

represented a major attempt to win former soldiers over to Japan's side and nullify any possible threat they might pose to the new regime. Finally, the arrangement gave the Japanese access to large quantities of captured weapons. (See Table 9.2.)

Heiho Recruitment

Heiho recruitment passed through three distinct stages: (1) From the beginning of the occupation in early 1942 until the regulations were issued in April 1943, recruiting activities concentrated on prisoners of war, who had at least minimal prior military experience. These recruits, who served with the army, can be described as "incipient *heiho*." (2) Beginning around May 1943, when Japanese forces were withdrawing from the central part of the Solomon Islands and strengthening their defenses in the Lesser Sundas, the focus shifted to unemployed young men without military experience. Recruitment was systematic but voluntary, and those who enlisted during this period also served with the army. (3) Around March 1944, with the military situation deteriorating in the eastern archipelago, forced recruitment began to take place on a large scale. Many of the *heiho* enrolled during this period served in the eastern archipelago, some under the army but others with the navy. The following sections will examine each of these phases in greater detail.

Incipient Heiho

In the early stages of the occupation, manpower was mainly mobilized from among indigenous members of the KNIL and the Marechaussee being held in POW camps. Jurisdiction over Java lay with the 16th Army, and its 2nd and 48th Divisions were responsible for the defense of the island. However, when the Allied counterattack began in August 1942 around Guadalcanal, the Japanese army altered the deployment of its forces to strengthen the eastern part of the Indonesian archipelago against a possible Allied attack from northern Australia, and began constructing airfields and strong points to protect supply lines in this area.[23] The 48th Division was placed under a newly organized 19th Army created to defend the Timor zone and the Lesser Sundas, while the 2nd Division moved from Java to the Solomon Islands under the 17th Army.[24] To handle defensive arrangements in Java, the Southern Army created new 13th and 14th Independent Garrison Units, which consisted of just eight battalions along with an infantry regiment. These units required additional personnel to man military installations and keep watch for air raids and submarines.[25] Moreover, expansion of the battle zone to include the Solomon Islands, the Bismarck archipelago (17th Army), and East New Guinea (18th Army) led to the creation of an Eighth Area Army in November 1942. The most urgent issue in this period was to man supply lines within the enlarged battle zone.

Ambonese and Menadonese now began to be "released" from POW camps and, after swearing an oath of loyalty to Japan, were inducted into the Japanese military as *heiho* and transferred to the eastern front, mainly to Rabaul, Bougainville, and New Guinea but also to Aru, the Kei and Tanimbar Islands, and the southern Moluccas.[26] They continued to wear KNIL uniforms but were rarely permitted to bear arms and generally provided labor.[27] One Ambonese, a former member of the KNIL, offered the following explanation of his situation:

> I was interned in Darmo Camp in Surabaya with my comrades, and signed a document written in Japanese. . . . The day after, I received a bayonet, personal belongings and one pair of boots. . . . After that, part of us were sent to Surabaya, New Guinea, Biak island and other areas. As I was ignorant, I thought I had only become a POW. But I heard, much later, that we had become *heiho*.[28]

Realistically there was no alternative, because anyone who refused induction faced the prospect of torture or even execution. Therefore, most Ambonese and Menadonese POWs ended up becoming *heiho*.[29]

The Japanese authorities in Java also began trying to attract recruits among the former Javanese, Sundanese, Madurese and Timorese POWs who had been released and sent back to their villages.[30] Official announcements sought "Indonesian males with military experience or military training,"[31] and some ex-POWs volunteered their services to get work, or were called up for service through village headmen.[32] Most of these recruits, sometimes together with ex-KNIL Ambonese and Menadonese, were transported to Manokwari, Sarmi, Noemfor, and Biak Islands in western New Guinea, or to islands in the northern Moluccas such as Halmahera.[33]

Systematic Recruitment

Around May 1943 the 16th and 25th Armies in Java and Sumatra began systematic large-scale recruitment of *heiho*, and mobilization efforts now shifted away from former soldiers and toward single men above sixteen years of age who had no prior military experience. Plans called for training 800 *heiho* as cadres and making each of them responsible for 10 subordinates, giving a total strength of 8,000 men—equivalent to the existing strength of the Japanese garrison force in Java.[34] According to the *heiho* guidelines, recruits had to be in good health, between the ages of eighteen to thirty years with no criminal record, and single. They also needed to demonstrate a positive attitude.[35] Most were local youths recommended by village headmen or mayors, officials at the lowest level of the military administration. Some enlisted because they had "an aspiration to become cadre of *heiho* units," but many simply received an "order from the village head to go."[36] Training camps opened in Magelang and Cimahi on August 5, 1943, and the period of instruction was two months. The initial batch of personnel was subsequently sent to a camp established in Bogor in October 1943 and became the nucleus of the PETA force rather than *heiho*.

After September 1943 large-scale recruitment began in earnest. Prospective recruits were expected to have studied the Japanese language for more than half a year, and to pass character tests and a quiz in simple mathematics as well as a physical examination.[37] At this stage most recruits had relatively high educational qualifications, having finished a three-year course at the village school (*sekolah desa*/Volksschool) and often the following two-year course at the continuation school (*sekolah samboengan*/Vervolgschool) as well. Education bureau heads in the various states, municipalities, and territories that made up the Military Administration Department recommended candidates for selection,[38] but the main avenue for recruitment was through the *seinendan*, youth organizations the Japanese had created to mold young people to meet the needs of the military authorities and eliminate nationalist tendencies.[39] One ex-*heiho* stated in an interrogation report that the *seinendan* seemed to operate as if its members were destined to become *heiho*.[40]

Japanese sources assert that many applicants volunteered spontaneously in the early phases of recruitment among the general population. Newspapers published accounts claiming that "youths eagerly took examinations in response to the reports regarding the recruitment of Heiho," and Lieutenant General Inada Masazumi stated, "The Heiho enjoys popularity in Java, and considerate youths all volunteered."[41] Assuming that such reports are true, there appear to be three possible explanations for this interest in serving with the Japanese army. One is that the Japanese issued propaganda appealing to the recruits' self-esteem and offered a degree of protection to their families, who received a *sakura* emblem to display at their entrance gate as a sign of their loyalty and devotion.[42] Second, enlistment provided a guaranteed livelihood, with salaries more than twice those paid to people mobilized as forced laborers (*rōmusha*); and finally, those who became *heiho* avoided the possibility of becoming *rōmusha*.[43] One former *heiho* testified, the "there was no option other than to be Heiho or to be *rōmusha*, and I determined to be Heiho. For my being scapegoat, no one was mobilized as *rōmusha* from my family."[44] It should be said, however, that many recruits apparently did not realize that becoming a *heiho* might mean being sent to distant places, or that they could find themselves engaged in combat.

Large-scale *heiho* recruitment was successful for a time, but as the selection of troops for PETA got under way throughout Java, applications for service as *heiho* decreased sharply, since PETA was an Indonesian force with an Islamic character, and its members served in Java close to their home villages.[45] The decline occurred as the tide of the war was going against Japan, and led the military to turn to forced recruitment.

Forcible Enrollment and the Recruitment of Naval Heiho

On March 16, 1944, about one year after promulgation of the army's *heiho* regulations, the Japanese navy introduced the *heiho* system into areas under naval administration.[46] New regulations allowed both the army and the navy to recruit and employ *heiho* throughout Indonesia, and the services worked in cooperation with each other.[47] Since several divisions from the 16th and 25th Armies had been deployed to areas under naval administration in the eastern archipelago for operations, it was rational to replenish manpower there. Moreover, it was both difficult and risky to shift manpower from distant areas, and this was an additional reason to mobilize local people. The army recruited candidates in the navy-administered area at Menado in August, and in Java during October 1944 and March 1945. The navy staged major *heiho* recruitment exercises in May and November 1944, drawing recruits from areas under naval administration and also from Java.[48] During this period the military authorities imposed quotas for recruitment of *heiho* and created registers listing individuals eligible for service, who had to undergo physical checkups and other examinations every half year as a preliminary to enrollment in the Naval *Heiho* Training School.[49] As before, the *seinendan* was a major source of recruits.

Army and navy *heiho* regulations stated that if detachments were transferred from the operational area of one army to another, existing *heiho* were to be discharged and replaced by members recruited in the new region.[50] However, it was impractical to discharge *heiho* in the midst of an ongoing operation, and these provisions were not carried out.

The Numbers Recruited to Be *Heiho*

Heiho were sent to destinations across Indonesia and as far afield as Burma, the Philippines, Thailand, and French Indochina. It is difficult to determine the exact numbers involved, for many were killed and others deserted at the time of the Allied landing. However, it is possible to develop some reasonable estimates by referring to the operational histories of individual military units. (See Table 9.3.)

The figures in Table 9.3 indicate that number of *heiho* who served in the Indonesian archipelago was much larger than the figure normally cited, which is around 25,000.[51] The Chief of the general staff of the Southern Army, Shimizu Noritsune, informed Tokyo on September 4, 1943: "The total number of members of the armed forces in the Southern Army is three hundred thousand and military employees number thirty thousand. Heiho are now fifty thousand so far, and we are making every effort to increase the number."[52] This figure was for the Southern Army as a whole, and includes Burmese and Malayan *heiho*. Given the date of this statement, it probably refers to incipient *heiho*, that is, former POWs.

A statement prepared by the headquarters of the 16th Army indicated that in August 1945 the number of *heiho* was 24,873 in Java, 2,504 in Timor, and around 15,000 in the eastern region (the Solomon Islands, Manokwari, Halmahera, and New Guinea) and other areas such as Sumatra, Malaya, Thailand, French Indochina, and Burma.[53] However, these figures refer only to *heiho* under the command of the 16th Army, and to get a fuller picture it is necessary to include the numbers assigned to other armies.

The 17th Army, the 18th Army, and the military units under the 8th Area Army also included substantial numbers of Indonesian *heiho*—1,263 as far as can be determined from individual unit histories—who served in Special Installation units (Tokusetsu Butai) responsible for airfield construction and transportation.[54] (See Table 9.4.) These men ultimately became combatants when Allied forces reached New Guinea.[55] Based on these figures, the number of army *heiho* adds up to more than 63,037 men, and there appear to have

Table 9.3

Heiho Attached to Japanese Military Units

Unit	Number of heiho
25th Army in Sumatra	8,915
Seventh Area Army and 9th Air Division (excluding Java)	2,782
46th Division in Malaya and the Timor zone*	3,500
48th Division in the Timor zone*	3,000
5th Division (in the vicinity of Seram, Aru, Kei, and Tanimbar islands)†	5,544
35th Division (Manokwari, Sorong, Noemfor)†	4,385
36th Division (mainly in western New Guinea, especially Sarmi, Hollandia, Biak)†	3,322
32nd Division in Halmahera†	3,640
The Allied Asiatic personnel under the Eighth Area Army (mainly in western New Guinea, Solomon islands)	8,800
Total	43,887

Sources: Headquarters of the General Staff in Indonesia, "Order of Battle—GYUGUN and HEIHOs—SUMATRA," AL5/21233/G; NEFIS Interrogation Report AI2/4789/G., AI2/5998/G., AI2/6379/G., AI2/8947/G., AI2/9103/G., AI2/9156/G., AI2/10448/G., AI2/11010/G., AI2/11054/G., AI2/11057/G., AI2/15609/G., AI2/15788/G., AI2/17801/G., CADMvD, The Hague; AWM54 573A/2/1, AWM54 1010/9/1, Australian War Memorial, Canberra; Daiichi Fukuin Kyoku (First Demobilization Bureau), "Indoneshia Hōmen Butai Ryakureki" (Brief history of military units in Indonesia); "Seibu Nyūginia Hōmen Butai Ryakureki" (Brief history of military units in western New Guinea); "Yuki 36 Shidan Senshi" (The war history of 36 Division), unpublished document written in 1946, p. 71, Military Archival Library, NIDS, Tokyo; Bōeichō Bōeikensyūsho Senshishitsu (NIDS) ed., *Gōhoku Hōmen Rikugun Sakusen* (The army's operation in northern Australia), p. 660; Oda Jun'nosuke, *Harumahera Kamotushō* (The history of Halmahera supply depot) (Tokyo: Shinjusha, 1986), p. 118; Harumahera Kai, *Harumahera Senki* (The war history of Halmahera) (Tokyo: Harumahera Kai, 1976), pp. 81, 192.

Notes: *With the dissolution of the Second Area Army in June 1945, the 46th and 48th Divisions fell under the Seventh Area Army and the 16th Army.

†These divisions were under direct control of the Second Area Army.

Table 9.4

Asian Personnel under the Eighth Area Army

	Indian	Indonesian	Malay	Chinese
Wewak, Hollandia	3,027	—	10	—
Rabaul	2,684	1,181	—	1,397
Bougainville	278	82	—	80
New Ireland	—	—	—	61
Total	5,989	1,263	10	1,538

Sources: Rikugun Shō (Army Ministry), "Dai 8 Hōmen Gun Hensei Jin'in Hyō" (The battle order of the Eighth Area Army), Military Archival Library, NIDS, Tokyo; Chaen Yoshio, *BC Kyū Senpan Gōgun Rabauru Hōtei Shiryō* (Documents on BC Class Rabaul Australian war tribunal) (Tokyo: Fuji Shuppan, 1990), p. 144; AWM54 1010/3/1—3/12, Australian War Memorial, Canberra; MP742/1 336/1/1205, National Archives of Australia, Victoria branch, Melbourne.

been a further 20,000 to 30,000 naval *heiho*, although this number cannot be confirmed because the relevant documents were burned at the time of the Japanese surrender.[56] This information is consistent with data from the Forum Pusat Komunikasi, an ex-*heiho* organization that by 1995 had registered the names of 72,257 former *heiho*.[57] Thus there were probably about twice as many *heiho* as there were members of PETA, which had a strength of around 36,000 (Table 9.5).

Experiences of the *Heiho*

Training and Discipline

Heiho recruits received military training at army or navy *heiho* training schools before being formally integrated into military units. Schools were located on Java at Surabaya, Jakarta, Malang, Semarang, Jatigare, Bandung, and Sukabumi, and in Sumatra at Tanjung Melawang, Medan, and Belawan. There were naval *heiho* schools in Sulawesi at Makassar and Menado, in the Lesser Sundas at Singaraja, and on Borneo at Banjarmasin and Tarakan. Most of these sites were previously military barracks or other KNIL installations.[58]

Recruits were supposed to spend six months undergoing training similar to that given to Japanese infantry soldiers.[59] At Magelang and Cimahi, trainees received instruction in military skills such as drill in squad and platoon formations, sentry activity, scouting, throwing of hand grenades, and attacking at close quarters with tanks. They also had subject studies and Japanese-language instruction.[60] The emphasis throughout the training course was on military discipline and what it meant to be a soldier. However, it is questionable to what extent ordinary *heiho* training schools taught recruits how to handle arms. *Heiho* did not receive combat training until 1944, which suggests that they were originally expected to perform duties in the rear.[61] Moreover, the period of training was frequently shortened in connection with an emphasis on achieving rapid increases in troop numbers.[62] For example, Javanese attached to the 11th Special Land Duty Company (Tokusetsu Rikujō Kinmu Dai Jōuichi Chūtai) trained for just four months in Bandung, and those with the 34th Company for three months in Sumatra.[63] The 27th Special Automobile Service Company received just one month of practical training, and a Javanese recruited in 1943 was sent to Surabaya immediately after enrollment to help construct an air-raid shelter.[64] The early *heiho* recruits who were released POWs often served with antiaircraft batteries or other military installations and carried looted weapons that they already knew how to use; thus it was unnecessary to train them in the same way as infantry soldiers.[65] *Heiho* trained in the last stage of the war did learn how to handle arms and were equipped with machine guns, rifles, and other weapons: "Each

Table 9.5

Number of *Heiho* Personnel at the Time of Japan's Capitulation

Area	Number of *heiho*
Singapore, Malaya	4,063 (1)
Java	24,875 (2)
Sumatra	11,697 (3)
Lesser Sunda Islands	4,338 (1)
Halmahera, Maluku (Seram, Ambon, Aru, Kei Tanimbar)	9,194 (4)
Western New Guinea	7,607 (5)
East New Guinea, Solomon, Bismarck Archipelago	1,263 (6)

Sources: (1) The Headquarters of the 16th Army Java, "Explanation regarding all kinds of armed bodies," Nishijima Collection, Waseda University; Rikugun shō (Army Ministry), "Dai 7 Hōmen Gun Hensei Jin'in Hyō" (The Battle Order of the Seventh Area Army), "Dai 8 Hōmen Gun Hensei Jin'in Hyō"(The Battle Order of the Eighth Area Army), Military Archival Library, NIDS, Tokyo; NEFIS Interrogation Report, CADMvD, The Hague.

(2) The Headquarters of the 16th Army Java, "Explanation regarding all kinds of armed bodies," Nishijima Collection, Waseda University.

(3) "Order of Battle-Gyugun and HEIHOs Sumatra," CADMvD, The Hague.

(4) AWM54 573A/2/1 Australian War Memorial, Canberra; NEFIS Interrogation Report, CADMvD, The Hague; Daiichi Fukuin Kyoku (The First Repatriation Bureau), "Indonesia Hōmen Butai Ryakureki" (Brief Record of Military Units in the Area of Indonesia), Military Archival Library, NIDS, Tokyo.

(5) Daiichi Fukuin Kyoku, "Seibu Nyuginia Hōmen Butai Ryakureki"(Brief Record of Military Units in the Area of Western New Guinea), Military Archival Library, NIDS, Tokyo; AWM54 1010/9/1 Australian War Memorial, Canberra; NEFIS Interrogation Report, CADMvD, The Hague.

(6) Rikugun Shō (Army Ministry), "Dai 8 Hōmen Gun Hensei Jin'in Hyō" (The Battle Order of the Eighth Area Army), Military Archival Library, NIDS, Tokyo; AWM54 1010/3-1-3/12, Australian War Memorial, Canberra; MP742/1 336/1/1205 Australian National Archives, Victoria branch, Melbourne.

Note: The number of Western New Guinea shown at the time of formation of unit, excluding numbers sent to Thailand and Burma, and Navy *heiho*.

Heiho was provided with a rifle and a bayonet and other weapons and ammunition were to be supplied . . . on the same level as Japanese soldiers."[66]

Duties

Military forces operating in the occupied southern territories urgently needed labor for transportation, logistics, and construction work such as building airfields, particularly in eastern Indonesia, which formed part of Japan's defensive perimeter. On the whole, early *heiho* provided auxiliary services, acting as "air-defense troops, tank troops, transportation troops, and in the Navy as marine sweeping forces and the marine troops at the base commands."[67] They were an extremely welcome addition since they took the place of Japanese soldiers who were needed for other tasks. Within the army,

Table 9.6

Proportion of Indonesian *Heiho* in Tokusetsu Butai (Special Installation Units) (percentage)

Company	Proportion of *heiho*
Special Automobile Service Company	46.9
Special Land Duty Company	89.8
Special Construction Service Company	88.7
Special Water Duty Company	88.5
Special Marine Transport Company	84.2
Special Installation Infantry Company	85.4

Sources: Daiichi Fukuin Kyoku (The First Repatriation Bureau), *Indonesia Hōmen Butai Ryakureki* (Brief record of military units, area of Indonesia); *Seibu Nyūginia Hōmen Butai Ryakureki* (Brief record of military units, area of western New Guinea); *Tobu Nyūginia Hōmen Butai Ryakureki* (Brief record of military units, area of eastern New Guinea); Rikugun Shō Chōsei (Army Ministry), *Dai 7 Hōmen Gun Hensei Jin'in Hyō* (The battle order of the Seventh Area Army); *Dai 8 Hōmen Gun Hensei Jin'in Hyō* (The battle order of the Eighth Area Army), Military Archival Library, NIDS, Tokyo; Morimoto Takeshi, *Jawa Bōei Giyūgun Shi* (History of the PETA Army) (Tokyo, Ryukei Shosha, 1992), pp. 623–33.

a great number of *heiho* were attached to Special Installation Units created in accordance with operational requirements.[68] These units were supply corps under the direct control of the 7th or 8th Area Armies or army headquarters in those regions and were not attached to the infantry regiments. Higher echelons arranged the use of these *heiho* units as needed. In many Tokusetsu Butai companies, about 20 percent of the officers and men were Japanese, and the remaining 80 percent *heiho*. (See Table 9.6.) Most of these units were dispatched to frontline locations, such as New Guinea, the Solomon Islands, the Bismarck Islands, Rabaul, and Bougainville, where they built airfields alongside Taiwanese, Chinese and Indonesian *rōmusha,* and Malayan and Indian ex-military laborers. Their duties also included ferrying supplies to battle sites and operating transport facilities in rear areas, serving as guards for POW camps, doing garrison duty at various military installations, and serving in the infantry. Owing to Allied attacks on Japanese transports, large numbers of *heiho* perished before reaching their destinations,[69] and others died subsequently as a result of air raids, desperate food shortages, or tropical diseases. In this they shared the experiences of the Japanese soldiers.

Following creation of the Ultimate Defense Area in September 1943,[70] the 16th Army in Java was required to perform dual tasks, operating a supply base for the Southern Army and preparing for an Allied attack. Meanwhile, to protect Java, the 13th and 14th Garrisons were reorganized into the 27th and the 28th Independent Mixed Brigades; the former was based at Bandung and made responsible for West Java, the latter at Surabaya with responsibility for Central and East Java. These brigades included considerable numbers of *heiho*,[71] and operational units within these brigades were on average 20 percent *heiho*.[72]

The Treatment of Heiho

Heiho duties and conditions of service were almost the same as those of Japanese soldiers. They received military ranks, entering service at the level of private second class, and in principle *heiho* moved through seven ranks in the same way as Japanese soldiers, earning promotion by performing distinguished deeds or after completing a certain term of service. Army *heiho* were eligible to become first-class squad leaders, and naval *heiho* could become naval first-class leaders. However, it seems to have been impossible to achieve these higher ranks during the three and a half years of the occupation, and the former *heiho* I have met held the rank of private first class or at most superior private. *Heiho* gained promotion through hard work and obedience, although some members received promotions as a reward for treacherous conduct toward their comrades.[73] Both army and navy *heiho* had an obligation to salute all Japanese, whether soldiers or civilians. Former *heiho* state that there were distinctions between themselves and the Japanese with respect to salaries, accommodations, and meals, although the situation varied according to the social background of those concerned. The *heiho* also apparently suffered a certain amount of maltreatment.[74] Japanese soldiers sometimes seem to have behaved arrogantly toward them, and NEFIS interrogation reports contain many references to physical assaults as punishment for infractions of military discipline. Superior officers repeatedly hit *heiho* on the face and shouted loudly at them, treating them in the same way they did Japanese soldiers. For Muslims, striking someone on the head was extremely rude and a religious taboo, and former *heiho* frequently complain about this behavior.

For many youths from rural villages, the training camps provided a first experience of military training and discipline. Being in military life and also in a different culture left them bewildered, but apart from the fact that they were struck regularly, they found the food and the level of medical treatment to be adequate. Some military units made special provisions showing respect for the social customs of *heiho* as regards meals or worship, but in units where *heiho* served alongside Japanese soldiers such arrangements were rare. Trainees were required to bow in the direction of the imperial palace and recite the imperial mandate, without exception,[75] and Muslim *heiho* considered it a grave insult to be forced to bow facing the imperial palace rather than in the direction of Mecca.

Salaries paid to *heiho* were much lower than the amounts prescribed. While in barracks they received one-third of their salaries, with another one-third sent to their families at home and the balance automatically deducted as a pension fund contribution and held in the postal savings system. An ex-KNIL soldier from Menado said that single men received 30 guilders and married men 35 guilders per month. After one month of actual work, his group received six months' wages as a lump-sum payment in advance, but following their transfer to the Outer Islands they received no further pay. This informant had heard that a volunteer *heiho* worker from Padang received 65 guilders per month (390 guilders in a lump sum for six months).[76] According to the regulations, the minimum pay for second-class *heiho* was 30 guilders per month,[77] but newly enrolled *heiho* who were not married received only 18 to 20 guilders. One informant also said that ex-KNIL personnel were paid 35 cents a day while those recruited from the civilian population were paid more than 1 guilder per day.[78] It is clear that actual pay was generally around one-third of the amount originally promised, and that civilian volunteers received more than ex-POWs. Very few *heiho* ever received the sums they contributed to the postal savings scheme.

Reports concerning meals vary from person to person. Most *heiho* came from Java and were accustomed to eating rice as their staple food, and those from food-deficit areas were pleasantly surprised to receive three meals a day, even though their food was inferior to that eaten by Japanese soldiers. Where the Japanese received meals of rice, the *heiho* sometimes got rice porridge or bread with soy paste, a diet poorer than that served in POW camps. Moreover, many *heiho* were sent to areas where food was in short supply and suffered from malnutrition, with some starving to death, especially in New Guinea. There are accounts of *heiho* driven by hunger to steal military provisions, and then being executed following court-martial proceedings for infringements of military discipline. The ill treatment of *heiho* resulted in war-crimes prosecutions after the war of some of the Japanese soldiers involved.

Conclusion

Heiho recruitment during the occupation period in Indonesia was part of an extensive process of mobilization of manpower throughout the Greater East Asia Co-prosperity Sphere during the period of Japanese military expansion. These auxiliary soldiers were made responsible for the defense of various regions in order to supplement Japanese forces, which were spread over a wide area. Japan had anticipated the need for additional personnel, not only for military administration but to provide troops in rear areas and on the battlefield, and had expected to undertake military mobilization in occupied territories. Following the victorious invasion of the Dutch East Indies in the first phase of the Pacific War, the Japanese military had to establish indigenous military bodies that could help defend the Co-prosperity Sphere against Allied counterattacks and consolidate Japanese control over the occupied areas. The *heiho* system in Indonesia was a prototype of a larger plan to create local military bodies to defend the entire Co-prosperity Sphere. The establishment of PETA in Java and Bali and the Giyūgun volunteer army in Sumatra were a second step in this process, even though these bodies were created as a result of Japanese losses and required political compromises with the local population to secure their cooperation. The Japanese military authorities intended to integrate the *heiho* with the Giyūgun Sumatra and PETA as a single indigenous military body in occupied NEI, but this was never done.[79] Following Japan's surrender, many ex-*heiho* became Republican freedom fighters in Java or Sumatra during the revolutionary period, while others joined the KNIL and supported federalism and regionalism.

10

Indonesian *Rōmusha* and Coolies under Naval Administration

The Eastern Archipelago, 1942–45

Remco Raben

The aspect of the Japanese occupation that dominates the private and collective memories of the people of Indonesia, apart from a dearth of consumer goods and pervasive hunger, is the forcible recruitment of coolie laborers. Tens of thousands of these workers, who were known as *rōmusha,* died of malnutrition, of disease, and of maltreatment. Most were buried in unmarked graves far from home, with no record of their deaths and no notice sent to their waiting families.

This war experience has found its way into several expressions of collective memory, including the diorama at the base of the National Monument in Jakarta, and feature films such as *Badja membara* (1961) and *Rōmusha* (1973). However, the wartime employment of Indonesian laborers received only limited attention from academic researchers until the 1990s, when two Japanese historians, Aiko Kurasawa and Shigeru Sato, each published research showing that systematic mass recruitment and relocation of Javanese laborers outside of Java was part of Japan's overall labor policy.[1] Even larger numbers of "volunteers" worked within Java constructing roads, tunnels, canals, and railways, or filling jobs in agriculture and industry. Very few Javanese, it seems, escaped the labor drafts. According to Sato, as many as 10 million men—almost the entire "mobilizable" element in a population of 50 million—were employed for shorter or longer periods during these three and a half years.[2] The exact number of people sent out of Java cannot be determined, but several postwar reports mention a credible figure of 300,000.[3]

Translation of Remco Raben, "Arbeid voor Groot-Azië. Indonesische koelies in de Buitengewesten, 1942–1945," (Labor for Great Asia: Indonesian coolies in the Outer Islands, 1942–1945), in *Oorlogsdocumentatie '40–'45: Negende jaarboek van het Rijksinstituut voor Oorlogsdocumentatie* (Amsterdam: Walburg Pers for the Rijksinstituut voor Oorlogsdocumentatie, 1998), pp. 81–111. Published with permission of the Netherlands Institute for War Documentation.

While some information is now available concerning the recruitment of Javanese *rōmusha,* the situation in the rest of the archipelago remains little known. The discussion that follows examines the labor situation in the eastern part of the Indonesian archipelago, a region administered by the Japanese navy, by looking at the Celebes (Sulawesi), the Moluccas (Maluku), New Guinea (Irian), and Borneo (Kalimantan), paying attention both to local recruitment and to the use of Javanese *rōmusha* in these areas.[4] It will become evident that Japanese labor drafts caused great hardship and much loss of life, and that the different types of labor mobilization complemented each other.

The Japanese administration based its economic policies on guidelines formulated by the cabinet in Tokyo prior to the attack on the Netherlands East Indies. The first requirement was to consolidate Japan's military conquests and to bring the war to a successful end. Raw materials and manpower had to be placed at Japan's disposal as quickly and efficiently as possible to achieve the rapid rehabilitation of vital industries, and the oil and mineral resources of Sumatra, Kalimantan, and Sulawesi were particularly important to the Japanese war effort. In May 1942 the Association for the Study of the Economy in the Southern Areas (Nanpō Keizai Konwakai) prepared a study emphasizing that economic efforts should concentrate on the resources of the so-called Outer Islands, using labor from Java for the purpose.[5] This plan was inspired by prewar practice, when labor-intensive enterprises in the Outer Islands relied very heavily on imported manpower from Java, but wartime arrangements in the archipelago were not to be a simple copying of Dutch colonial practice. In economic and administrative terms, the Japanese regime broke with Dutch rule by dividing the archipelago into three separate regions under different military commands. These administrative units had explicit orders to promote autarky within their territories, a policy that also applied to each subdistrict or island. Consequently, the conquered territories had to meet the needs of the Japanese forces based there, as well as those of their own people. One of the originators of this economic policy, Colonel Ishii Akiho, acknowledged after the war that the policy inevitably involved deprivation for the local people.[6]

The military administration became the largest employer of Indonesian labor, and when the fighting turned sharply in favor of the Allies in 1943, forcing Japanese armies in the southwest Pacific onto the defensive, the military buildup intensified, creating an ever-larger demand for manpower. During the final year and a half of Japanese military administration, labor recruitment reached levels that caused serious disruption to Indonesian society.

The Mobilization of Labor

The exact scale of labor mobilization across the archipelago cannot be determined, but it is possible to get some idea of the situation from interrogation reports and eyewitness accounts collected by the Netherlands Eastern Forces Intelligence Service (NEFIS) during and immediately after the war. Informants fell into Allied hands in various ways, with most of them picked up from boats in the Java or Flores Sea by Allied submarines or amphibious aircraft. Sometimes vessels were torpedoed, but many bewildered fishermen and sailors simply saw a submarine surface next to their boats and found themselves taken captive to be brought to Australia for questioning about conditions in Japanese-controlled territory.

The interrogation reports make it clear that there was widespread and systematic recruitment of labor, and that the process involved coercion. Most laborers worked near their place of residence and for limited periods of time. However, large industrial facilities and military construction projects needed many more workers than could be recruited locally, and in such cases the Japanese mobilized labor from other parts of the archipelago. Imported labor went to industrial centers, mines, and shipyards on Kalimantan and Sulawesi, and to airstrips and other military facilities further east in the archipelago, in Nusa Tenggara and Maluku, and on Irian.

In the beginning, labor recruitment followed the administrative geography of the Outer Islands. Every *minseibu* (administrative districts in areas under naval administration) was expected to provide for its own labor requirements, and coolies were sent to other *minseibu* only in exceptional circumstances. Local Japanese administrators and officers usually organized the recruitment, and each village had to supply a certain quota of laborers; on Java the requirement was often some twenty to thirty, in the Outer Islands less. The method of recruitment was left to the headmen, but the Japanese pressured them to meet their quotas. With the intensification of construction projects, labor began to be drawn from peripheral areas into strategically and economically important centers, but because the deployment was mostly of a local or regional nature, much of this process has remained hidden from view. Still later in the war, the need for manpower became acute as airstrips were constructed or repaired, ship construction was stepped up, and food shortages became increasingly serious. Consequently, labor recruitment was speeded up, with the authorities resorting to harsher methods and transporting laborers over larger distances.

Roughly speaking there were three kinds of labor: *sukarela,* or "voluntary" work, often done on a rotating basis for short terms of a week or ten days in return for a piece of cotton cloth; coolie labor for wages; and unpaid short-term labor in the guise of preexisting communal obligations based on the Dutch system of *herendienst*—a tax in the form of labor that normally required a few days of service each month.[7] For instance, on August 27, 1943, the Japanese authorities on Banda issued a rule regarding labor obligations, or *pekerjaan rodi,* literally a "labor order," a term used previously in connection with the *herendiensten.*[8]

On Java an extensive administrative apparatus supported labor mobilization, utilizing bodies such as the Romu Kyokai, the Badan Pembantoe Peradjoerit Pekerdja (BP3), and the Barisan Pekerdja Soekarela, along with organizations that recruited *heiho* (auxiliary soldiers) and members of the youth militia (*seinendan*). An extensive registration exercise facilitated recruitment. On the Outer Islands the recruitment apparatus was simpler, and distinctions among various kinds of labor service less sharply drawn, but there too recruitment had strong bureaucratic support in areas that the Dutch had administered under direct rule. Village heads in Banjarmasin, for instance, kept registers of laborers, who worked without pay for a month at a time in rice storehouses, on road projects, and at the Maluka airfield.[9] All men between seventeen and forty years of age not working in essential industries had to join the (*tenaga*) *sukarela, heiho,* or *gotong royong* (the latter a Chinese labor corps mainly used to grow vegetables).[10] In Balikpapan, all men between eighteen and thirty years of age were drafted for *heiho* service.[11]

In many areas and particularly in remote parts of the Outer Islands, the Dutch had utilized a form of indirect rule that left considerable power in local hands, and Japanese control over these places was similarly weak, with little in the way of the organizations for training and mobilization found in more populous areas. For example, on several islands in the southern Moluccas—such as Damar, Teun, Nila, and Serua—there was initially no permanent Japanese occupation, only occasional visits by boats carrying military patrols. In such places village heads regularly failed to supply the numbers demanded, much to the annoyance of the Japanese navy authorities.[12] During August 1943 the Japanese summoned the headmen of the Damar Islands, called "regents," to Banda and told them to remove all Dutch flags and royal portraits, and to supply laborers. Back in their villages the regents ignored the Japanese orders. Several months later, in November, five Ambonese policemen visited Damar and exhorted the regents to deliver their quota of laborers swiftly, but still little was done. In May 1944 a Japanese detachment arrived on a motorboat to fetch coolies, but bombs from a Dutch airplane destroyed the ship. The Japanese authorities then lost patience: one month later 200 men landed on Damar and raided the island. Many inhabitants fled into the interior, and their villages were plundered. One headman, the regent of Kehli, was captured by the Japanese. A second expedition followed in July, during which the entire population of Kehli was caned.[13]

The case of the Damar Islands shows how widely the net of mobilization was cast and that even people living in remote places eventually could not escape the attentions of the military administration. The conclusion seems to be justified that a system of total mobilization existed in the area under navy administration, although recruitment in the Outer Islands was less systematic and consistent than on Java; the distances were much greater, the local circumstances diverse, and the nature and intensity of the Japanese occupation different from island to island. It is impossible to present a comprehensive account of labor recruitment in the Outer Islands, but by utilizing intelligence reports and other data on certain areas, it is possible to develop at least an impressionistic portrait of the situation in the eastern archipelago.

Menado

Labor recruitment was extremely intensive in the Menado district, the northern part of Sulawesi, which included Minahasa and two small archipelagos north of Menado—the Sangihe and Talaud Islands. It was a strategic area for air defenses, and a number of mines and shipyards operated along the coast. It had long been the practice for coolies to come to Menado from the less affluent Sangihe and Talaud island groups, and these places remained an important source of manpower under Japanese rule, when recruitment became harsher.[14] Many islands in the Sangihe archipelago did not have a Japanese garrison force, but all became subject to press-gang parties.[15] Labor was also required for local duties on the islands themselves. Some laborers worked near their homes, as in the village of Lengeneng on Greater Sangihe, which in late 1944 had to supply 10 men daily to work in the Japanese warehouses for wages of 25 cents per day. Eventually recruitment activities reached even remote places, such as the tiny island of Tahulandang in the Sangihe group, where the Japanese forced 500 coolies to leave their homes in March 1945 to work at the shipyards in Menado and elsewhere in Sulawesi.[16]

Menado's shipyards required large numbers of laborers, and many Sangiheese were deployed there, especially at Bitung and Inobonto, where several thousand coolies worked building wooden ships. Large areas of forest were cut in Bitung to provide timber for these vessels.[17] In 1943 there were 3,000 Sangiheese in the Bitung yards, and a further 600 at other locations, including Inobonto, where as of February 1944 a workforce of 3,000 coolies serviced the wharves.[18] Elsewhere on Sulawesi, shipbuilding facilities operated in Pomelaa and Kendari, and at Pare Pare on the west coast, where 3,000 coolies built twelve 170-ton ships per month.[19]

Some labor took the form of *herendienst*. On Siau (Sangihe) every man eighteen years of age and older had to register with the Japanese administration and work for two days each month. Some were selected for full-time service and in most cases were taken to the shipyards in Bitung and Inobonto, nominally for a period of six months.[20] In the neighboring Talaud Islands the Japanese required almost all men between twelve and sixty years of age on Karakalong and Salebabu to join the *soekarela* or *seinendan*. *Soekarela* built roads and houses, and served as porters, earning 20 cents per day; *seinendan* members—the youngest—worked one day per week, without pay. With so much time and energy consumed by Japanese projects, living conditions deteriorated swiftly, and food became scarce.[21]

Around Likupang, at the northern tip of Menado, every boy and girl between twelve and twenty years of age was registered as a member of the *seinendan*. They received military training and had to work daily tending vegetable gardens and digging trenches, building shelters, and constructing roads. In October 1944 *seinendan* enrollment was about 3,000. Workers on projects could return home in the evening, although those who came from greater distances were accommodated in former Chinese shops. Many adults from this region joined the *soekarela* and performed similar tasks.[22] One eyewitness account described membership of the *soekarela* as voluntary for men between seven and sixty years of age, and for women between ten and fifty, but in practice, although the word *soekarela* means "volunteer," labor service was compulsory.[23] The confusion in nomenclature is understandable: Japanese propaganda called every contribution to the public cause "voluntary."

The Moluccas (Maluku)

The pattern of mobilization and employment in Menado was repeated further to the east in the Moluccas. There was hardly any industry or mining in this region, but central Maluku had many airfields and needed large numbers of laborers at Tantui, Halong, Laha, and Liang (on Ambon and Hitu), Pelau (on Haruku), Amahai, Makariki, and Ruta (on Seram). The Japanese started recruitment for military projects in the Moluccas at an early date: by 1942 a workforce composed entirely of Ambonese from surrounding villages was already beginning to enlarge an airfield at Laha on Hitu.[24] Workers were recruited by force. For example, a boat captain from Serua, who had sailed to Ambon to sell fruit, was seized by the Japanese and sent to Laha. While working at the landing strip he received two rice meals per day but no money, and no clothing or cigarettes. He toiled daily from 7 A.M. until 4:30 P.M., with only 15 minutes' rest. After a year he escaped.[25]

Work at most sites was completed during the first half of 1944, but the airfields soon came under attack by Allied bombers and needed ongoing maintenance. In 1943 laborers from Ambon, Haruku, and Saparua—the most densely populated islands—were enlarging an old airfield at Amahei on the island of Seram. Allied bombers regularly attacked the site, and a raid on December 23, 1943, killed 300 laborers. Within a month a new draft of coolies arrived to repair the damage.[26] By this time, labor quotas had been imposed on all village heads. Each village had to supply dozens of coolies, with new shifts relieving the previous workforce. The pressure on the Ambonese population was particularly great, not only because the Japanese built a large number of airfields in the area, but also because the Japanese military force based there, some 25,000 strong, required large amounts of locally produced food. The Japanese administration ordered new rice fields and sago gardens to be laid out, for example, on Hoamoal, and recruited Ambonese to do the work.[27] As supply lines were increasingly disrupted, the Japanese intensified cultivation on Seram and other islands and moved inhabitants of Ambon to these locations to clear jungle for farmland.[28] In 1944, the Japanese abandoned repair work at damaged airstrips in Ambon and redirected the labor force involved in this work to food production.[29]

The North Moluccan islands of Ternate, Tidore, and Halmaheira were also strategic points in the Japanese defense perimeter, and thousands of local coolies worked on projects there. Local sources of labor soon proved to be inadequate, and starting in November 1943 about 600 forced laborers from Sangihe were brought to Kau, on Halmaheira, where they constructed an airfield for wages of 25 cents per day.[30] In February 1945, 500 forced laborers from Halmaheira and Sangihe were on Tidore, building an airfield. Food was scarce and on Halmaheira coolies planted vegetables to sustain themselves, but the Japanese often looted their gardens. Many laborers had only loincloths to wear.[31]

In the South Moluccas the Kai Islands were not occupied until July 1942, but construction work at five airfields started that same year, with laborers drawn from Little and Great Kai and the surrounding islands. The mechanisms of recruitment were similar to those in other areas: village heads were ordered to supply young men, who registered in the village square and sometimes left immediately for construction sites, traveling by boat or on foot. Building projects were staffed entirely by local laborers forcibly recruited from a total population of just 45,000 people. The selection process was arbitrary, with some men drafted repeatedly. One resident of Little Kai recalled:

> During the years [of the occupation] we had to labor frequently for the Japanese at the airfields. . . . The Japanese came and told the *orang kaya* [important men] of our village that they needed a certain number of men to

work at a particular place. The specified number of men from the village actually left to work. But we were often beaten. . . . Frequently we had to work day and night. . . . There was hardly any food. Many Kaiese died, also from diseases such as malaria. . . . After a while we fled back home, but later we had again to work somewhere else. I worked at several airfields.[32]

A resident of Great Kai, who worked for three or four months on at least two airstrips on Little Kai, said later:

We had to toil very hard: we had to dig, to haul stones and more of this work. . . . We slept in shacks. When you got ill, you were left to your own devices. . . . The Japanese did not concern themselves about you. Eventually a few of us escaped, back to Ohoiwirin. We were at the end of our tethers, entirely exhausted. But other men from Ohoiwirin were forced to work for the Japanese. So actually we worked in shifts.[33]

The labor drafts left only a small number of people to plant crops at home, and resulted in serious food shortages.[34] On Babar and Leti, nearby island groups, agricultural output decreased dramatically because of the demands for forced labor.[35]

Labor gangs from other islands often supplemented local manpower. Hundreds of Ambonese and Menadonese *heiho* (auxiliary soldiers) helped local workers construct airfields and roads on the Tanimbar Islands. By October 1943 nearly all men from Tanimbar had been forced to become laborers, either on the islands or elsewhere, leaving women and children to cultivate the gardens. Many villages were abandoned as large numbers fled to the interior, and this was the reason the Japanese introduced *heiho* to provide manpower.[36]

New Guinea (Irian)

New Guinea (Irian), on the eastern periphery of the Japanese territory, lay near the battlefront and had extensive mineral resources, making it a crucial place for the Japanese. However, the island was largely uncultivated and lacked infrastructure, and the local population was too small to provide the labor demanded by Japanese officials. Large numbers of workers were brought in from neighboring islands, along with *heiho* from Java, to construct airfields and do agricultural work.[37] Both the import and local recruitment of laborers started early. Jefman Island, just west of New Guinea, had an important airbase built entirely by forced laborers from surrounding islands—in particular Peniki—who did the job without machinery.[38] The coolies slept on their boats

Photograph 10.1. Laborers building a light tramway in New Guinea (July 1943).
(Reproduced courtesy of the *Mainichi Shimbun*.)

and received 10 guilders per month (about 35 cents per day) along with one cup of rice daily, for which they had to pay.[39] At Manokwari, on the main island of New Guinea, 2,000 inhabitants from local villages were forced to work for 25 cents per day.[40] In June 1944 the Japanese sent 400 people from Manokwari into the mountains to grow sago, and by November half of them were dead from dysentery, beriberi, and starvation.[41] Elsewhere, on the tiny island of Wakde on the north coast of New Guinea, just west of Hollandia, 1,200 Papuans built an airfield, subsisting on rations of sago porridge and under constant threat from Allied air raids.[42]

The Japanese scoured the adjacent islands to obtain laborers for New Guinea. Men from the small island group Aju, north of Manokwari, were forced to work in Sorong, on New Guinea, and a March 1944 report indicated that some 500 coolies had died there of illness and starvation.[43] The original population of Sorong had also been mobilized, and those not sent to the airfields had to perform other duties. The Japanese subdivided the area into districts and assigned each district a specific task, such as delivering building materials to work sites. Village heads along the coast recruited Papuan coolies in the interior. Labor service officially lasted three months, but in practice release depended on finding a substitute. This became increasingly difficult as inhabitants fled to other islands to escape being pressed into service.[44]

Borneo (Kalimantan)

The oil wells, mines, and industries of Kalimantan required large concentrations of labor. The island was a vital source of oil and minerals, and meeting labor demands of the government and the companies that had taken over management of the enterprises became a crucial issue. A Japanese report written in 1946 summarized the dilemma:

> The exploitation of Borneo was totally dependent on manpower since the beginning of our military rule. We encountered the greatest difficulties because of an enormous lack of laborers. . . . There was no good prospect for production, because the great need for food cultivation made it impossible to transfer agricultural laborers to factories and workshops.[45]

Local Dayaks provided much of the labor for the vegetable gardens that mushroomed in and around most coastal towns, and for the mines, although there were also some Chinese laborers.[46] In this respect Japanese policies deviated from the practices under the Dutch regime, when companies were very reluctant to recruit local people as laborers.[47] Gold mines remained closed during the occupation, but the Japanese restored production in the diamond and mercury mines. About 3,000 laborers worked in the diamond mines of Pantek, near Ngabang, in western Kalimantan, where digging resumed in July 1944. Other mines in Kalimantan employed smaller workforces, ranging from a few hundred to as many as 1,000 coolies. Digging methods were primitive and the work was hard. Reports and eyewitness accounts tell the usual story of illness, rough accommodations, bad health care, and the disappearance of sick coolies.

Smaller numbers of local laborers were employed by power stations, such as the one at Teluk Bayur, in northeastern Kalimantan, and by the shipyards of Banjarmasin, on the south coast, where in February 1945 1,000 coolies recruited from neighboring villages worked in the dockyards of the Konan Kayon Company, 600 in the adjacent Nomura shipyard, and another 1,000 in the docks of the Borneo Shushin.[48] Several thousand more laborers worked for Japanese shipyards, timber companies, and mines in Balikpapan and Pontianak, and Dayaks and Banjarese were also employed in the oil fields.[49]

Kalimantan's oil was vital to the Japanese war effort and was one of the main targets of the Japanese attack on the Dutch East Indies. One important center of oil production was the island of Tarakan, which lay close to the north coast of Kalimantan. The Dutch destroyed oil wells and refineries as part of a scorched-earth policy, but the Japanese restored these facilities and resumed production, although postwar reports indicate that there was a great deal of improvisation, and wartime production of oil barely reached 30 percent of prewar levels. Around 500 to 600 coolies were recruited by force in Balikpapan and Surabaya to work for the oil industry in Tarakan, along with large numbers of local villagers.[50]

A small number of eyewitness reports attest to the existence of forced recruitment in the interior of Kalimantan. In the village Dadahup, north of Banjarmasin, men who did not deliver enough rice to the Japanese were forced into labor; they numbered 100 men out of a total 500 in the village. They were promised wages of 2 guilders a day but received only 60 cents along with food.[51] In West Kalimantan (Pontianak), where fewer large companies operated, forced laborers worked at airfields for pay, almost like a regular job, but, "Even when they were gravely ill, they were forced to work, and when they tried to escape, they were mistreated. Many died from malaria."[52]

Javanese *Rōmusha* in the Outer Islands

Early in the war, the Japanese made Java the most important source of manpower for the exploitation of Indonesia. Java had provided labor for the large industries and plantations in the other islands since the late nineteenth century. Demographic pressure made Java very suitable for this role: in 1942, the population of the island was about 50 million, and that of the other islands combined only 20 million. However, Java was not the only source of manpower used by the Japanese in Indonesia.[53] The Javanese *rōmusha*, like Allied prisoners of war sent to Flores, the Moluccas, Sumatra, and Siam, only supplemented labor recruited locally, and large transports of workers only took place when local mobilization fell short.

The mobilization of Javanese labor was complicated by the administrative fragmentation of the archipelago under Japanese rule, and required coordination among different military units and administrations. In July 1943, talks took place in Makassar between the navy and representatives of the 16th Army, which administered Java, to arrange for the supply and payment of coolies from Java who were to be employed in the navy areas. Then, in October, the heads of departments of labor throughout the southern regions assembled in Singapore to establish procedures for sending coolies from Java to other parts of Southeast Asia.[54]

By this time some Javanese coolies were already in the Outer Islands. In August or September 1942, the Japanese brought 200 Javanese carpenters, drivers, and masons—all apparently skilled craftsmen—to Babo, on New Guinea. They were jobless people from Surabaya and had been told that they would be employed in the oil fields at Balikpapan, on Borneo. To their dismay they ended up at the far end of the archipelago.[55] Eyewitness reports suggest that such deceit was common.

In addition to this early coolie recruitment, the Japanese sent large numbers of *heiho*, drawn from prisoner-of-war-camps on Java, to Nusa Tenggara, Maluku, and New Guinea. These were Indonesians who had served in the Dutch army, and they were released specifically to be enrolled as *heiho*. A number of witnesses reported late in 1944 that 3,080 *heiho* from Surabaya, Malang, and Bandung had landed in Manokwari between November 1943 and February 1944, joining around a thousand coolies from Surabaya.[56] Some 700 of these workers were dead within a year, the result of harsh working conditions and malnutrition.[57]

With the war turning against the Japanese, labor needs became more pressing and recruitment was speeded up. There is no certainty about the numbers of Javanese laborers sent away from their island during the occupation. K.A. de Weerd reported a number of 270,000 to the International Military Tribunal in Tokyo,[58] a conservative estimate, while a Japanese report of 1946 mentioned a total of 294,000, broken down as in Table 10.1.[59] The figures include *heiho* sent out from Java. According to these statistics, more than three quarters of the coolies—some 225,100—went to the Outer Islands, principally to Sumatra but also to South Sulawesi and South Kalimantan, while another 69,000 were sent to locations outside the former Netherlands

Table 10.1

Japanese Figures for Javanese Laborers Sent to Work Outside of Java

Destination	Number of workers
Sumatra	120,000
Malaya	31,000
Thailand and Burma	6,100
North Borneo	31,700
South Borneo	48,700
Celebes and Sunda islands	32,400
Ambon	5,500
Timor and Halmaheira	5,800
New Guinea	12,700
Indochina	200
Total	294,100

Source: Netherlands Institute for War Documentation, IC 005.709.

East Indies, in particular to Singapore, British Borneo, and the Thailand–Burma railway. One report, written seven months after the war, mentions 120,000 Javanese coolies in Sumatra, 11,800 in Kalimantan, 18,000 in South Sulawesi, and "several thousand" in Seram, Halmaheira, and New Guinea as of March 1946—a considerably smaller number than the earlier survey indicated, but possibly excluding the *heiho*.[60]

From postwar reports concerning the laborers found in different parts of the archipelago, it is apparent that the *rōmusha* transports were not confined to the Javanese. Allied administrators counted at least 4,200 Sangiheese employed outside their islands, as well as 7,500 Menadonese.[61] Likewise, about 6,000 workers were sent from Bali to other islands, and another 4,000 from Lombok, along with numerous Madurese and Sumatrans.[62] All shared the fate of the thousands of coolies from Java.

Working and living conditions for laborers varied greatly. In many cases the laborers received between 25 and 60 cents per day, about the same as prewar coolie wages, but the comparison is misleading because prices of food and most other products had increased as much as tenfold compared to prewar levels.[63] Moreover, it was common practice to make deductions from laborers' wages for daily meals or rations, and in many cases the wages promised were not paid at all.[64] The quality of life for people who had jobs deteriorated dramatically compared to the already poor situation under the Dutch labor regime.

Coolies forced to labor far from their homes and for long periods of time suffered most from the bad and scanty food, harsh punishments, and poor medical care. Many eyewitness accounts speak of inferior accommodations, minimal clothing, and severe hunger at the work sites, especially among transported coolies and convict laborers. Of 18,000 Javanese counted in South Sulawesi in November 1945, nearly half were described as being in a "deplorable" state.[65] Because coolies working locally often cultivated gardens and returned home periodically, their physical condition was generally better than that of the Javanese, who were deployed permanently and lived in labor camps with inadequate facilities. Rianta, a *rōmusha* from Indramayu, was employed with 1,000 other Javanese at Kendari, on Sulawesi, and found conditions there bearable; there was sufficient food and the regimen was fairly pliant despite frequent aggression on the part of Japanese overseers. During the first six months, only 8 men died. He was then moved to Pomelaa with 200 other men to build an airstrip, and 40 members of the group died within a year.[66] In Manokwari (Irian), at least 2 men died each day in a workforce of 1,200 coolies; altogether there were more than 300 deaths between December 1943 and April 1944. Of the survivors, 150 were sent to Numfor, and 50 of them were dead by July.[67] On Muna, the island adjacent to Butung, 1,500 Javanese *rōmusha* began work at an airstrip in late 1943. Locked inside the camp, they could not supplement their meager rations, and within a year 500 had died.[68]

These fragmentary data suggest that the death rate in Javanese coolie communities was as high as 35 percent, and probably even higher at some sites. The true mortality rate of the coolies cannot be determined. Henk Hovinga, drawing on a survey prepared by the Red Cross in June 1946, calculates that 77,000 *rōmusha* died.[69] This figure is based on the number of Javanese who found "shelter" with NEBUDORI (the Netherlands Bureau for Documentation and Repatriation of Indonesians), but unknown numbers of coolies remained in the areas where they were employed, or still roamed around, seeking food or trying to reach Java on their own.

Conclusion: Forced Labor and the Greater East-Asian Co-prosperity Sphere

Information about Japan's mobilization of labor is fragmentary but allows for the conclusion that voluntary employment, forced labor, and intensive recruitment for Japanese projects—the distinction is never altogether clear—were as frequent in large parts of the Outer Islands as they were on Java. With the exception of a few major projects such as the Pekanbaru railway in Sumatra and the Tondongkura railway and mines in southwestern Sulawesi, the numbers of Javanese *rōmusha* lagged far behind the number of coolies recruited locally or those transported from other places in the Outer Islands. The Javanese coolies only supplemented local labor.

Japan's labor policies in Indonesia were not unique. In most occupied areas the Japanese mobilized laborers to carry out military construction projects and to grow food or other needed crops.[70] The Japanese viewed the Indonesian population as a major resource and placed disproportionate pressure on the archipelago to provide manpower for the Japanese war effort. Indonesia's location near the front lines of the Japanese expansion necessitated a huge buildup of military infrastructure, and Indonesian mineral reserves and industries were important to the Japanese war economy. Within the archipelago, the population was distributed unevenly, and much of it was far removed from the places where labor was needed. The practice of employing *rōmusha* far from their home districts and undertaking large-scale relocations of workers made labor mobilization in the archipelago extremely disruptive. The years of Japanese rule in Indonesia are primarily remembered as a time of massive enslavement and hardship—at least outside of the nationalist and upper-class discourses that see the occupation as a preparatory stage for independence and even as a period of resistance against foreign occupation.

The total mobilization of the population of Java and the Outer Islands was one of the cornerstones of Japan's economic policy in the Indonesian archipelago. The Japanese subjected Indonesians to a fusillade of propaganda intended to arouse in them a spirit of self-sacrifice and total commitment to the Greater East Asian Co-prosperity Sphere. Film, radio, journals, and pamphlets summoned the Indonesians to work for the Greater East Asian cause. Toward the end of 1944 a set of guidelines for the mobilization of *rōmusha* (*Garis-garis besar tentang pengerahan rōmusha*)—stated:

> In order to achieve a swift victory, we expect every inhabitant to put their power at our disposal, voluntarily and with all conviction. The old, wrong spirit of the laborers should be discarded. . . . The spirit of willingness and zest for work should be roused and concentrated in every resident.[71]

Whether the slogans had any effect cannot be ascertained, but increasing pressure did little to inspire enthusiasm among the people of the archipelago. The cooperation of local headmen was decisive for the success of mobilization, and in remote areas raids by Japanese patrol boats played a major part. But mobilization did not depend solely on physical force or deceit. Three other considerations were equally important. One was large-scale unemployment caused by the closure of companies and the collapse of exports, which forced workers to take any job that was available. A second was the long tradition of fulfilling communal obligations traditionally owed to a lord by working for the Dutch administration. Finally, many generations of workers from Java had found employment in Sumatra and Borneo, and the *rōmusha* followed in their wake. However, in the latter part of the occupation, the flow of workers dwindled as horrifying reports spread about conditions at the work sites, and the Japanese turned increasingly to deceit, coercion, and abduction to obtain manpower.

Unquestionably, the Japanese coupled harshness with a strong idealism. The principle of absolute obedience and devotion to the construction of Greater East Asia evoked incomprehension from the Indonesians, which understandably caused frustration on the part of Japanese administrators. However, ideological principles played little part in the daily practice of labor recruitment and utilization. Strategic considerations, feelings of superiority, and especially the pressure of war had a much stronger effect on the actions of local Japanese authorities than vague notions of a Greater East Asia. Okada Fumihide, the *minseifu sokan,* or chief civil administrator of the naval area, wrote that Japanese entering the archipelago initially viewed the indigenous people with sympathy and saw them as capable workers, but within a short time became disillusioned by their lethargy and started to think they were of low intelligence.[72]

Japan's massive mobilization of manpower disrupted life in much of Indonesia. Large numbers of people were withdrawn from agriculture and fishing, causing food shortages in areas of intensive mobilization. Where recruitment was most intrusive, entire communities were crippled.

In the Indonesian archipelago, co-prosperity was little more than a propaganda slogan. In the formulation of war aims and the creation of the Greater East Asia Co-prosperity Sphere, Japanese interests were always paramount, and the idea of co-prosperity included a hierarchical relationship between prosperous industrialized Japan and the underdeveloped areas at the periphery of its sphere of influence.[73] Moreover, plans developed by the cabinet in December 1941, in the aftermath of Pearl Harbor, shifted Japan's priorities: economic policy in the occupied territories had to concentrate primarily on the supply of materials needed to continue the war; the implementation of co-prosperity came second.[74] During the conquest and occupation of the "southern regions," an initial loss of life and reduced prosperity was something to be borne in the spirit of self-sacrifice by "liberated" peoples.[75] Prime Minister Tōjō Hideki had spoken in January 1942 about elevating regions "whose progress of culture and civilization had been strongly impeded by the ruthless exploitation" of the Western colonial powers.[76] The Japanese alternative proved to be much harsher.

11

End of a Forgotten Drama

The Reception and Repatriation of *Rōmusha* after the Japanese Capitulation

Henk Hovinga

Rōmusha and the End of the War

Millions of people lost their lives in the Second World War. The suffering and death of Europeans, Americans, and Australians is minutely recorded in hundreds of books. The world film archives are full of historical material that gives a poignant portrayal of their struggle and demise. All but forgotten, however, is the drama of millions of Javanese slaves the Japanese occupation forces recruited in the years 1942 to 1945 to work under inhumane conditions for the Japanese war machine. Some 300,000 of these forced laborers were sent outside Java, and three quarters of them perished.

The Japanese called them *rōmusha,* which means no more than simply worker, or, in the terminology of the colonial era, coolie. In the tropical heat the *rōmusha* built railroads, roads, ports and bunkers, extending to the farthest islands of the South Pacific occupied by Japan. They worked in the coal mines of Bayah, on Java, and built railroads on Sumatra and in Burma. They constructed airfields in British Borneo, the Malay Peninsula, the Moluccas, the Andaman Islands, and Cambodia. They chopped roads through the jungle of the Celebes, labored in the bauxite mines of the Riau archipelago, and hacked tunnels and storage facilities out of solid rock in Borneo and at Bukittingi (Fort de Kock) on Sumatra.

The number of *rōmusha* who perished as a result of the privations they experienced cannot be determined accurately. The Japanese kept flawed ad-

This chapter is a translation of Henk Hovinga, "Einde van een vergeten drama. Opvang en repatriëring van romusha na de Japanse capitulatie," in *Tussen banzai en bersiap: De afwikkeling van de Tweede Wereldoorlog in Nederlands-Indië,* ed. Elly Touwen-Bouwsma and Petra Groen (The Hague: Sdu Uitgevers, 1996), pp. 73–94. Published with permission of the Netherlands Institute for War Documentation.

ministrative records, and many of these records were burnt after the capitulation. Based on surviving Japanese documents, eyewitness accounts, and the reports drawn up shortly after the Japanese capitulation by the Netherlands Bureau for Documentation and Repatriation of Indonesians (NEBUDORI), Netherlands Indies Red Cross (NIRK), Netherlands Indies Civil Administration (NICA), and the Netherlands Eastern Forces Intelligence Service (NEFIS), a global estimate can be made, however, of the total number of Indonesian laborers who perished. The list (according to the locations where the deaths occurred) is as follows: Sumatra, 97,000; Singapore and Malaya, 19,000; British Borneo, 27,000; Dutch Borneo, 11,000; South Celebes, 8,000; New Guinea, 11,850; Moluccas, Sunda Islands, and Timor, 23,800; Siam, 5,000; Riau, 1,000; Andamans, 600; Cambodia, 150; for a total number of 204,400. To that must be added 90,000 Javanese who died in the residency of Bantam on the western end of Java. This list does not include the victims who perished during or after their transport to Hong Kong, Japan, Guadalcanal, and an unknown number of smaller islands. No data is available for these places. Also excluded are local coolies on Borneo, Celebes, Sumatra, and New Guinea who were put to work on their own islands and certainly suffered as much as the workers who were shipped overseas. The survivors went home after the capitulation, and the uncounted dead namelessly remained behind. It is therefore probable that considerably more than 300,000 Indonesians died in *rōmusha* service. In fact the Japanese crime toward their fellow Asians was much greater. In this study I have limited myself to the fate of the Indonesian workers who originated from the former Netherlands Indies, but the Japanese also conscripted Chinese, Malays, and Tamils in Singapore and the former British Malaya (presently Malaysia) on a large scale. Most of these people had to work on the Thailand–Burma railway, together with similarly recruited Burmese and Thai workers. In all probably 190,000 *rōmusha* originating from British territories worked on the railway. Postwar reports and eyewitness statements concerning the Thailand–Burma railway indicate a mortality of 80,000 to 100,000 Asian laborers. Together with the deceased *rōmusha* from the Netherlands Indies, the total death toll in Southeast Asia then comes to approximately 400,000. A handful of official and academic papers have been written about these forgotten dead, but not a single book records their fate.

Around 4 million people from the agrarian areas of Java worked as *rōmusha* under the Japanese for shorter or longer periods of time.[1] Originally they served more or less voluntarily, attracted by promises of high wages and good food and by assurances that their families would be well cared for, promises that proved false.[2] But by 1943 the number of volunteers fell sharply when it became clear to everyone that most *rōmusha* received insufficient food and no medical attention, and labored until they dropped.

Table 11.1

Rōmusha Employed Outside of Java: Number of Survivors

Within the Indies (excluding Java)	
New Guinea	850
Timor	850
Ambon	1,000
Ternate	2,300
South Celebes	10,000
Balikpapan	4,000
Banjarmasin	10,000
Sumatra	23,000
Subtotal	52,000
Outside the Indies	
Singapore	8,500
Kuala Lumpur	1,750
Penang	1,750
Bangkok	300
Tamuang (Thailand)	4,700
Phnom Penh (Cambodia)	600
Andaman isles	600
British Borneo	5,000
Riau	2,000
Subtotal	25,000
Total (excluding Java)	77,000

In the meantime the fortunes of war had turned against the Japanese. The Japanese war machine had to be strengthened at any cost. Nominally, *rōmusha* service remained voluntary. In reality hundreds of thousands of new slaves were seized in movie theaters and at the market and carried off, pressed into service through violence, intimidation, and threats of punishment.[3] Most of them—men and women—were put to work on Java. Those *rōmusha* who constructed irrigation works for a few weeks in their own districts could consider themselves fortunate, although some of these people died at their work sites. Of those sent from East Java, Madura, or Bali to the railroad and the coal mines of Banten in West Java, few would ever see their *kampung* and *desa** again.

Yet the worst tragedy befell those sent to work outside Java—to the other islands of the archipelago, including New Guinea, or to Malaya, Singapore, Thailand, Burma, British Borneo, Indochina, and Hong Kong. Cautious estimates, based on limited sources, suggest that probably upward of 300,000 Javanese coolies were shipped to locations outside Java in tightly packed ships without sufficient drinking water or adequate sanitary facilities. Hundreds of people died on these transports without ever seeing their destination. Of the 300,000 *rōmusha* taken abroad, only about 77,000 survived—a mortality rate of 74.3 percent.[4] (See Table 11.1)

*Kampung: hamlet; *desa*: village.

Fine Japanese slogans about the establishment of a "Greater East Asian Co-prosperity Sphere" under the leadership of Tokyo, within which the subjugated territories would later get independence, were good propaganda for Japanese rulers and nationalist leaders alike. The reality was that Japan needed the resources of Indonesia to fight the war—first and foremost raw materials such as oil, bauxite, wood, nickel, and rice—but also manpower.[5] Even before the capitulation of the Royal Netherlands Indies Army (Koninklijk Nederlands-Indisch Leger, or KNIL) on March 8, 1942, Japan had identified Java as a place with nearly inexhaustible reserves of human labor upon which it could draw freely to fight the war. With raw materials, what had been used was no longer available and had to be replenished. This dictum applied just as much to people as to oil, and it was cheaper, faster, and more efficient to secure new slaves than to nurse sick or dying workers. And the workers died by the thousands—from exhaustion, malnutrition, malaria, beriberi, and tropical ulcers. The same ailments plagued the white civilians and military prisoners of war in the internment camps, but there was one difference. In the camps for white workers there were always a few doctors who did what they could in primitive sickbays, using the scant medication available. In most *rōmusha* camps, however, there was no medical care at all. Those who became ill and could no longer work generally died. In Japanese terms this was not inhumane. Individuals did not matter. The only thing that mattered was the work that people got through—and, of course, the question of how quickly replacements could be delivered.

When the Japanese occupied the whole archipelago in 1942, few people believed that the war would last more than a few months. The Japanese capitulation took place only three and a half years later, and then it came as a surprise to the Dutch optimists of old. The former administrators had philosophized in the camps over the reconstruction of "our Indies" after the war, but nobody had the capacity to make concrete plans or to undertake preparatory measures.[6] The same applied to the Allied armies. They had their hands full with the final decisive battle.

Japan's capitulation on August 15, 1945, came so suddenly that there were—except in areas reconquered earlier—no Allied troops to take over authority from the Japanese. It was a liberation without liberators. The local forced laborers were released, but the white prisoners had to stay in the camps. The greater part of South and Southeast Asia in those days was suffering from destruction, chaos, and human misery. On Java a terrible famine reigned.[7] The civilian food supply had collapsed because of the forced requisitioning of rice and a shortage of men to work the paddy fields as result of excessive recruitment of *rōmusha*. Countless families were submerged in deepest poverty because of the absence of a breadwinner. Medication and textiles were hardly to be found. With all the misery that the white population endured in the internment camps, it is too often forgotten that on Java alone the war claimed a toll of more than 2 million lives.[8]

In Singapore, when the internment camps of Changi were opened and the first emaciated ex-prisoners of war went out on the streets after August 15, 1945, they found a totally impoverished city. Walking cadavers stumbled along the roads—bald, suffering from scabies and tropical ulcers, and wrapped in gunnysacks or wearing only loincloths. These were Javanese who, left to their fate by the Japanese, had emerged from the *rōmusha* camps in search of food. There were corpses in the streets, and conditions were even worse in the camps themselves. The dead lay everywhere, in piles or simply strewn about. And among them, in an unbearable stench, were people who lacked the strength to stand up and go into the town.

A team of a few dozen prisoners of war, mostly Dutch, whose condition was only slightly better, immediately began relieving the most pressing needs. The dead were buried and the sick assembled and cared for as much as possible.[9] In the absence of even the beginnings of a real relief organization, the emaciated ex-prisoners of war started improving the horrific sanitary conditions. Lacking building materials, they used palm leaves and garbage to patch up the biggest holes in the roofs of the *rōmusha* barracks, which were leaking badly. Gutters were dug in the *rōmusha* camps to carry away the human excrement that lay scattered all over. The water supply was provisionally repaired.

The first British troops landed in Singapore only on September 5, 1945, three weeks after the Japanese capitulation. Ten days later, on September 15, the British Military Administration (Malaya) (BMA) began operations in Singapore. A special bureau for refugees and displaced persons, the R&DP Branch, became responsible for the *rōmusha*, and the early Dutch helpers started to cooperate with this body. A so-called sweeping party was formed, made up of one Dutchman and two Englishmen. At night they cruised through the decrepit city by car, searching for wandering Javanese. Those they located were assembled for the time being in the newly cleansed camps, or taken to the Nee Soon hospital. Only when the *rōmusha* were concentrated could medical attention and an organized food supply be provided.[10]

In Singapore and elsewhere the Japanese hardly showed themselves. They simply left their former forced laborers to their fate. In remote places they did not even mention, or at least not until much later, that Japan had surrendered. In some camps along the Thailand–Burma railway they said that Japan and the Allies had reached an agreement and were now friends again. "But," they added, "the Europeans are only concerned with their own fate. They won't lift a finger for you."[11] In this way they sowed distrust. Arising from this situation, and partly under the influence of news stories that slowly seeped in about the declaration of an independent Indonesian republic, the initial reception and care of *rōmusha* were sabotaged and delayed by political agitation in the weeks that followed.

Everywhere in the liberated territories the British military started providing first aid, but their own subjects took precedence. In PakanBaru the British ex-prisoners of war were given medical care and repatriated first.[12] Weeks later came the turn of the Dutch and then—insofar as means sufficed—the Javanese. Some had already formed gangs by then to try to stay alive through crime.

Registering and assembling the emaciated and wandering former forced laborers were the first requirement. The Japanese did nothing about that. They were mainly worried about their own fate. And further, they hid behind the stipulation in the armistice agreement that they must maintain the status quo while awaiting the arrival of the Allied troops. Even at this point most Japanese did not feel responsible for the fate of their former slaves, although there were a few exceptions. There is a story, for example, about a Japanese citizen who at his own expense rented a boat and transported 100 *rōmusha* from Palembang to Batavia.

The reception, care, and repatriation of the *rōmusha* thus became a matter for the Allies. But they had a problem in that the Japanese kept no records of the workers they had recruited, or at least none that were adequate. And insofar as there had been records, these were in many cases burned by the Japanese shortly after their capitulation.[13]

In November 1945 the Dutch Indies government established the Netherlands Bureau for Documentation and Repatriation of Indonesians (NEBUDORI). This organization concerned itself mainly with the rehabilitation and repatriation of the Javanese—Dutch subjects who had been taken to distant places outside the borders of the Dutch Indies. NEBUDORI was active in Singapore, Malaya, Siam (Thailand), Burma, and British Borneo. Later, at the request of the local residents, it was also charged with the care of 2,000 *rōmusha* employed in the bauxite mines in the Riau archipelago who were near starvation.[14]

Other areas of Indonesia, such as Java and Sumatra, did not fall under the jurisdiction of NEBUDORI. There the local residents, with assistance from the Netherlands Indies Civil Administration (NICA) and the organization for the Recovery of Allied Prisoners of War and Internees (RAPWI), tried to help tens of thousands of starving *rōmusha* find food and work, and space on a ship for their repatriation. For the reception of *rōmusha* left behind in Borneo and the Great East (including the Celebes, the Moluccas, and New Guinea), a central bureau for repatriation of Javanese and other Indonesians was established in Makassar in May 1946. More will be said on this subject later.[15]

Help for *Rōmusha* Outside the Indonesian Archipelago

The headquarters of NEBUDORI were set up in Singapore under the directorship of Dr. H.J. Friedericy, who would later gain a reputation as a writer through his short novel *The Last General* and other titles. NEBUDORI was an organ of the Netherlands Indies government, but the headquarters was located on British territory and most of the places where NEBUDORI had to recover and repatriate Javanese coolies were under British control. That meant that NEBUDORI was heavily dependent on the British military authorities. Before the Dutch bureau was founded, the reception of the *rōmusha*, as well as their nutrition, housing, clothing, and transport, was completely in British hands. Even though the volunteer helpers were nearly all Dutch ex-prisoners of war, the camps fell under British management. Friedericy had to use all his diplomatic talents to obtain a degree of freedom of movement for his organization. For example, he could not get authorization to buy and distribute food independently because the food supply was entirely controlled by the British. Furthermore there were constant problems with the staffing. The Dutch ex-prisoners of war who provided some relief in the initial weeks were too weak to continue with this work and had to be replaced. But requests for fresh, qualified personnel from Java went unanswered.[16] NEBUDORI camps each housed between 1,500 and 2,000 Javanese, and some had only a single Dutch camp commander assisted by one medic. The NEBUDORI organization, which initially operated with just 125 volunteers, gradually shriveled up as more and more personnel returned to Java or the Netherlands. At the same time, registration work kept expanding as laborers were located in more far-flung locations, from the Andamans, in the Bay of Bengal, to Guadalcanal, in the Solomon Islands.

Singapore became the transit point for all Indonesian repatriates, and the six camps there could house 8,500 *rōmusha*. In December 1945 NEBUDORI started registration by means of a card system. But there, too, problems arose. Many Javanese knew their name and that of the *desa* they came from, but not the name of the subdistrict, district, or regency. Every camp inhabitant received an aluminum badge with an embossed number that corresponded to his registration card. But some ran away, reported again at another camp, and obtained a new badge. Others sold their badge, or paid to obtain one with a lower number in the hope of faster repatriation. Sometimes it seemed as if that simple badge was worth a boat trip to Java.[17] But that was far from being the case. For the moment there were no ships available for transport to Java. First, the Europeans and their allies had to get home.

Final responsibility for the six Singapore camps rested with the BMA. The camps consisted of wooden barracks that had roofs made from palm leaves (*atap*), each with room for 50 to 150 persons. The British provided food and medication, while the Dutch handled camp organization. NEBUDORI was confronted with an increasing number of holdups of camp inhabitants. Gangs formed that made whole areas unsafe. Friedericy reported that, "a small amount of pocket money and an adequate supply of smokers' requisites would greatly reduce the problems, including that of the many thefts in the camps."[18]

But he got nothing. And when Dutch camp commanders managed to lay hands on some clothing from Japanese stocks and handed it out, the trousers and shirts disappeared within twenty-four hours, sold on the black market of Singapore.[19] Later the British tried again, but this clothing, too, vanished. Thereafter, the authorities no longer handed out clothing until just before the moment of repatriation. The number of holdups and thefts gradually diminished as more and more camp inhabitants found jobs with Chinese contractors in Singapore and in the harbor. They could now buy cloth and cigarettes with their own money, although the British held back 30 cents from their daily pay for food and housing in the camps.

Although thefts diminished, new problems appeared. The longer repatriation was delayed, the more political unrest grew in the camps in Singapore, Sumatra, and Thailand. On Java, Sukarno and Hatta had proclaimed the independent Republic of Indonesia on August 17, 1945. The Dutch did not take the red and white revolution seriously and sneered at what they saw as "extremist elements." The British, on the other hand, were cautious. They had strict orders not to interfere in the political dispute between the Netherlands and the new republic.

Chinese communists and Indonesian Republicans launched an intense propaganda campaign against all things Dutch, and the British turned a deaf ear to Dutch requests to take steps against this activity. They also watched passively when Indonesian nationalists set up their own Republican reception camp in Pasir Panjang in Singapore. A few hundred Javanese moved to this new facility, but the housing and food supply were so poor that many later wanted to return to a Dutch facility. However, the "defectors," as the Dutch saw them, were turned away. They would have to find their own way back to Java. Only a few people with serious illnesses, who "recanted," were restored to grace and taken back by the Dutch camp command. With regard to this matter, too, the British military authorities looked the other way.[20]

Republican activists succeeded in infiltrating the camps. They organized strikes among the Javanese who worked in the camps and tried to raise money for the Republican cause. Some *rōmusha* wholeheartedly supported the infiltrators, and others succumbed to intimidation. A plan to storm a depot that held food supplies leaked out and was thwarted.[21] When things threatened to get out of hand completely, the British took action. Political propaganda within the camps was forbidden and activists were arrested. The British intelligence service passed on data concerning suspicious persons to NEFIS, who then, together with the BMA, conducted an investigation and took appropriate measures.[22] The political unrest, which was strongest in the last three months of 1945, resulted in the creation of a camp guard, with armed sentries and "loyal" unarmed members taking part in a newly organized native camp police force.[23]

As a counterweight to the communist and Republican propaganda, NEBUDORI produced a magazine called *Pelita Djawa di Tanah Asing* (The Light of Java in Foreign Lands), which was distributed in the Javanese camps. This little magazine was filled with news about Java and about world events, but the most important element, of course, was pro-Dutch propaganda. *Pelita Djawa* appeared for the first time on December 12, 1945. Eight more issues followed. Friedericy took great pains to get more pro-Dutch literature into the camps, but succeeded only sporadically, partly as a result of open or secret obstruction by Republican sympathizers.

In the meantime the British military command had become impatient with political unrest. In September and October 1945 there was serious bloodshed in East Java during the battle for Surabaya, in which a British general, A.W.S. Mallaby, was killed.[24] The British Military Administration gave NEBUDORI an ultimatum that the six camps in Singapore had to be vacated by July 1, 1946. The Dutch Indies government agreed to cooperate but pointed out that a lack of shipping space was delaying repatriation. The English questioned whether there were other reasons for the delay. They suspected the Dutch of deliberately delaying repatriation of the Javanese, fearing that returnees would join the Republican forces. That had already happened with returned *heiho,* the Indonesian auxiliary soldiers of the Japanese.[25] In any case, on April 30, 1946, the first 500 departed for Batavia on board the British ship *Ekma.*[26] On May 3 a second load of 560 Javanese left, and by the end of June all the camps in Singapore had been vacated. They remained operational for a time because additional repatriates from Kuala Lumpur, Penang, Bangkok, and Riau were returned to Java via Singapore.

In Malaya, NEBUDORI did not start to collect and register wandering *rōmusha* until March 1946. Although these laborers were initially in very bad shape, their condition improved rapidly as they began to find jobs. The crime rate was considerable and theft a daily occurrence, but there was little political agitation.

Apart from the Javanese, there were also Chinese, Malay, and Tamil forced laborers in Malaya. In all, 3,500 people were assembled in the big Sungei Besi camp in Kuala Lumpur and in smaller camps on Penang in the north. A single camp set up on the Combe Hill estate, owned by a Chinese million-aire, eventually replaced these smaller camps, and all Javanese were concentrated there.[27] The BMA managed the camps in Malaya, which were under the direct command of two British officers. In October 1945 a Dutch camp staff and a physician arrived. They established good relations with the English and enjoyed considerably more freedom of action than their colleagues in Singapore. In June 1946 most Javanese returned home in two transports, the *Maetsuycker* and the *Klipfontein.* Some 200 ex-*rōmusha* opted to remain behind, some in south Thailand. They had found work, married local women, and started families.

Although NEBUDORI was active mainly in areas outside the Netherlands Indies, it also operated in the Riau archipelago. There, close to Kijang on the island of Bintang, about 2,000 *rōmusha* lived in thoroughly miserable conditions.[28] They barely had clothes on their backs and survived on little more than a handful of rice a day. The Japanese had brought those slaves to Riau to extract bauxite, the raw material for aluminum. During the Japanese occupation 1.4 million tons of bauxite ore were sent to Japan, around 70 percent of what the Japanese aviation industry needed. When a NEBUDORI delegation arrived on Bintang, it discovered four horrific *rōmusha* camps. One, called the "schoolboys camp," was populated by boys between twelve and eighteen years of age who had been recruited under the promise that they would be sent to Japan and become engineers. To explain why they were made to drag baskets of bauxite-bearing earth in Riau, they were told that every future engineer had to start out like this.[29] The *rōmusha* of Bintang returned to Java at the end of July 1946 on the *Maetsuycker.*

When the people in Riau were on the point of repatriation, NEBUDORI received a message reporting that 600 *rōmusha* were stranded in the Andaman Islands, close to Burma. They wanted to return to Java, but not on a Dutch ship. The Netherlands was at war with the Indonesian Republic, and they did not believe that the Dutch would actually take them back to Java. NEBUDORI flew two of the group's leaders to Batavia, where the Indonesian Red Cross told them they had nothing to fear. Eventually they came to believe this, but the group remained adamant in their refusal to be brought back on a Dutch ship. Friedericy then deleted these people from his list of displaced Indonesians.[30] The Javanese stayed where they were, and there they and their descendants presumably remain to this day.

In British Borneo the *rōmusha* worked on roads and airfields under dreadful conditions.[31] It was well over a year after the Japanese capitulation before NEBUDORI received the first reports about their existence. According to the Japanese, nearly 32,000 *rōmusha* had been taken to British Borneo. NEBUDORI registered only 5,000 survivors, working in Brunei and

Sarawak.[32] This would indicate a mortality of more than 84 percent. The survivors were liberated before the Japanese capitulation, and they recovered quickly thanks to food, clothing, and medication provided by Australian troops. When NEBUDORI representatives began the registration process in British Borneo, they discovered that many had found local jobs and were—by *rōmusha* standards—fairly well off. There is no mention of anti-Dutch feeling, but in the end just 1,000 men decided to return to Java.[33] They left for Surabaya in October 1946 on board the *Klipfontein*. Upwards of 3,500 men voluntarily remained behind.

Although Japan was already aware by the end of 1943 that it could not win the war, as late as January 1945 around 750 forcibly-recruited *rōmusha* were shipped to Cambodia, where they helped build a military airfield 45 kilometers north of Phnom Penh. As elsewhere, conditions were extremely bad, and 20 percent died within seven months. When a NEBUDORI delegation under Friedericy arrived at the end of 1945, the situation had—with the exception of housing—already improved considerably. The British RAPWI organization had provided food and medication, and the Japanese had handed out clothing. A Dutch camp command made up of ex-prisoners of war ordered the Japanese to build new housing close to Phnom Penh, and this was done. A French physician took charge of medical assistance, but the British retained responsibility for the food supply and finances. In contrast with other areas, the Javanese *rōmusha* here had good relations with the local population after they moved into their new accommodations, although there were occasional fights, mainly over Cambodian women. A few chose to remain behind when the group was repatriated in June 1946.[34]

Of all the areas where the organization worked, the camps along the Thailand–Burma railway caused the greatest problems for NEBUDORI.[35] As in Singapore, the records begin to mention serious problems arising from political agitation around the end of 1945. The large distances involved made the problems worse. The railroad line was about 415 kilometers long, and for much of this distance passed through inhospitable jungle. Dutch military volunteers under the command of Captain J.S. Krom, along with a party of British officers, started as early as September to scout the area and map concentrations of railroad coolies. At that time the camps were still under the command of the Japanese. Unfortunately for the Allies, immediately after the capitulation the Japanese burned most of the administrative paperwork.[36] The exact numbers of *rōmusha* and their whereabouts were therefore largely a matter of guesswork. Probably there had been—in addition to more than 60,000 Allied prisoners of war—about 200,000 coolies used for the construction and maintenance of the railroad.[37] Most were Chinese, Malays, and Tamils from Malaya, along with Burmese and Thais, but there were also around 10,000 Javanese. As of June 1946, NEBUDORI had registered only 5,000 Indonesian survivors. This figure suggests that overall half of the Javanese had died, but witnesses said that in the interior sectors of the railroad the mortality rate was as high as 80 or 90 percent. Nobody has exact data.[38]

Health conditions were very poor. Probably 70 percent of the *rōmusha* should have been hospitalized, but facilities were not available.[39] There was also little medicine and few doctors. Medicine and food were brought in by the British at Rangoon and then dropped by parachute for the camps alongside the track. Conditions were best among the Javanese technical railroad personnel, people the Japanese found hard to replace. These educated Javanese had received better medical care, sometimes even in small Japanese hospitals rather than the shabby barracks used for sick coolies. Those who suffered most were the real track coolies, most of them Tamils from Malaya.

The process of withdrawing the *rōmusha* proceeded slowly because the railroad had to remain in operation to move prisoners of war and others out of the area, and to bring in supplies of food and other necessities for those who remained behind.[40] Everybody connected with the functioning of the railroad thus remained in service. The others were concentrated in a few camps of bamboo barracks in the area of Tamuang. These so-called displaced persons fell under the Civil Administrative Service of the British military command. Financing and nutrition were not centrally managed, and the quality of the camps differed. This caused tension among the camp inhabitants. The situation was chaotic and was made worse because the track coolies were of many different nationalities. After the peace treaty between Thailand and Great Britain was signed in 1946, the British troops and military organizations departed. Friedericy arranged matters so that the care of the Indonesian *rōmusha* in Thailand was placed in the hands of the Dutch Mission in Bangkok on July 1, 1946. The leaders of this effort were Colonel Haverkorn van Rijsewijk and Major Piets. When the British were gone, the Dutch physician Renes set up a small hospital camp for the Javanese in the Tamuang area.[41]

The guards at the Tamuang camps consisted of armed Japanese and un-armed ex–forced laborers. Holdups were a daily occurrence.[42] Even after the inhabitants were transferred to Bangkok, the crime rate remained high. There was also growing political activity. For example, 230 Javanese and Sumatrans working at a sawmill in Bangkok refused to be registered, wanting nothing to do with the Dutch.[43] The long wait for repatriation ships and the fact that there was almost no work outside the camps intensified the political unrest. On August 17, 1946, some 1,500 Indonesians, who had been transferred to the New Life camp in Bangkok, celebrated the first anniversary of the Republic of Indonesia by hoisting the red and white flag.[44] The Javanese made no secret of their intentions to fight for the republic as soon as they reached home. Repatriation, via Bangkok and Singapore, commenced only in August 1946, and the last group left in November.

In the same month NEBUDORI ceased operations.[45] The service had by then brought 15,624 people back to Java.[46] Most returned via Tanjung Priok, the port of Batavia, where a reception camp had been set up for 2,000 men. Those wishing to go to Republican territory were housed in a camp situated on Kramat No. 73 in the capital. From there they were transferred to the Indonesian Red Cross (PMI), which provided further transport.

The PMI was also actively engaged in the repatriation of the Javanese. There is, however, no mention whatsoever of coordination of their work with the efforts of NEBUDORI, RAPWI, NICA, and the local residents. According to NEFIS estimates, the Indonesian Red Cross had by March 1946 brought about 3,600 ex–forced laborers from Sumatra to Pasar Ikan in Batavia, using chartered boats. These people originated from the areas around Palembang and Lampung on South Sumatra. Captain R. Ijzerman of NEBUDORI made contact on one occasion with PMI headquarters in the capital.[47] There he heard that this Republican organization provided the ex-coolies with food, clothing, pocket money, and cigarettes. But the Republicans, like NEBUDORI, complained that the returning Javanese sold the clothes again on the black market at Pasar Atom, the present Pasar Baru, where just after the war a lively trade flourished in everything that was forbidden. That included stolen gold and jewelry, arms, ammunition, uniforms, gasoline, and all sorts of matériel taken from Japanese and Allied supply depots. The ex-coolies sold their Red Cross clothing for exorbitantly high prices to Europeans newly returned from the camps.

As mentioned above, NEBUDORI was first and foremost charged with the registration and return of Javanese located outside the Dutch Indies. Of the 25,000 people repatriated, NEBUDORI handled more than 60 percent.[48] However, a much larger group of *rōmusha* needed assistance in the Outer Provinces of the Indies. They numbered around 52,000.[49]

Help for *Rōmusha* within the Archipelago

In Makassar (South Celebes) in May 1946, NICA set up a Central Bureau for Repatriation of Javanese and Other Indonesians (CEBREJA). This body dealt mainly with *rōmusha* in the Dutch part of Borneo, in the Celebes, and in the rest of the eastern archipelago—an area that included New Guinea, the Moluccas, and other islands up to and including Timor. The head was Otto Albert Gobius (b. 1898 in Buitenzorg), an official of the Indies administration who was attached to the Dutch government in London in 1941. After the Japanese capitulation, Gobius returned to his country of origin as a civil servant and was assigned to NICA in Makassar. Together with his assistant, Hehanussa, Gobius was assigned rooms in the governor's office, where NICA was also located.

In fact, CEBREJA was part of the NICA organization. Such at least was the recollection of M. Kasim Yahya in 1995, when at the age of seventy-seven he was working in the "Rotterdam" fortress in Makassar trying to save a historical library filled with rare Dutch books facing a near certain demise. Just after the war, Kasim Yahya worked in the NICA building, located on the Gouverneurslaan. He recalled Gobius as a skillful but quite authoritarian organizer who spoke Javanese fluently and communicated easily with the Javanese *rōmusha*.

On the initiative of Gobius, a first reception barracks was set up alongside the Malimonganweg (presently Jalan Tarakan) for wandering *rōmusha*. Shortly thereafter five more barracks arose, forming the so-called Mariso camp, more or less at the site where the nautical college now stands. The people initially housed there were more dead than alive. According to Yahya:

> Many died alongside the road of hunger and exhaustion. Those who still lived were just like moving skeletons. They ate all they could get their hands on, even if it were only rotting food waste. Most came on foot from Tondongkura, where they had been made to work in the coalmine. That is in the mountains, 11 km east of Pangkajene. And Pangkajene is 60 km north of Makassar on the west coast of Celebes' southern peninsula. The Javanese had also constructed a railroad from Makassar to the coalmines of Tondongkura.

Kasim Yahya remembers that construction of the railroad began in 1943. As happened nearly everywhere else, the *rōmusha* labored until they dropped. The only thing that mattered was completing the railroad as quickly as possible. The Japanese war industry and Japanese warships needed coal. That was more important than the suffering of the people, more important even than the atrocious quality of the railroad track. According to Kasim Yahya, the line was extremely dangerous. On several spans the rails rested only on piled up wooden blocks. There had been no cement to construct bridge pillars in the rocky riverbeds. Derailments during the transport of coal to Makassar were a daily occurrence. But there were sufficient *rōmusha* to repair the track and to manually lift the carriages back on the tracks. Immediately after the Japanese capitulation NICA demolished this hazardous rail line. The workers who handled the job were the same *rōmusha* who had survived the construction of the track, or an existence as mine workers in Tondongkura. Only this time they were treated well and given decent food and wages by the NICA. Even the *rōmusha* who worked in the harbor of Makassar benefited, earning a bowl of rice with some salt fish in return for loading the ships that carried the railroad materials to Surabaya.

Like Friedericy, Gobius set up a registration system and issued aluminum badges carrying numbers that corresponded to two registration cards recording personal data.[50] When a laborer departed, one card was taken by the escort of the repatriation transport and handed to the authority taking care of reception on Java. For those who wanted to go to Republican territory, that was the Indonesian Red Cross. The other copy was for the central administration in Makassar. Only registered *rōmusha* from Borneo and the Great East could claim free transport. In this it did not matter whether they were pro-Dutch or supporters of the new republic.

Nobody was forcibly put on the boat. Anyone who did not want to return, perhaps because he had found a job or a wife in his new living surroundings, was free to stay. But those who remained could not claim assistance. For the majority, who did want to return, the wait for transport was a long one.

Registration of laborers and assembling them in camps remained the first concern of CEBREJA. The bureau also made efforts to find jobs for those who were waiting. This arrangement worked fairly well. During 1946, thousands of *rōmusha* were put to work on Borneo and in the eastern archipelago on behalf of the government services—in the forestry department, in the agriculture and mining industries, and with the Royal Dutch Navy. Others earned a living as dockworkers, got jobs as furniture makers or tinkers, or sold food and homemade cigarettes. The wages paid for work in government service varied from place to place. In the South Celebes, an unskilled laborer on average received 90 cents a day. A skilled worker (*tukang*) received 1 to 2 guilders, but an overseer did not receive more than 1.5 guilders. The Mariso camp in Makassar withheld 45 cents per day to pay for food.

CEBREJA tried to make life for those waiting in the camps as bearable as possible, given the extremely limited means available. Humanitarian considerations ranked first, but of course politics also played a part. A bureau such as CEBREJA, supported financially by NICA (which meant the Netherlands Indies government), was in the first place interested in caring for the victims of the Japanese as well as possible. Republican propaganda was countered by distribution of Malay-language newspapers and magazines that were not outspokenly anti-Dutch. The government intelligence service even organized radio broadcasts in Makassar through which the former forced laborers could greet their families on Java.[51] Performances of *ludruk* (folk theater) and *wayang* (puppet theater) were held in the camps. Camp canteens sold coffee, tea, and cigarettes at cost, not an unnecessary luxury since on the free market a cup of coffee with sugar cost a quarter of a guilder—in the southern Celebes more than a quarter of the lowest daily wage. In South Borneo the price of coffee was even higher. For the seriously ill, hospitals with hundreds of beds were set up at Makassar and also at Banjarmasin, on Borneo. Dutch and Indonesian physicians provided medical care.

The lucky ones, who after a long wait finally got on the boat for Java, were given medical examinations before departure and vaccinated against smallpox, typhoid, and cholera. Married men with families on Java went first, but most simply had to wait.

Java was not the final destination for all repatriates. During 1946 CEBREJA also sent home several hundred people who were originally from Bali, Lombok, Flores, and Timor.

The Japanese had brought some 18,000 slaves to the South Celebes, of whom 10,000 remained alive in November 1945, a mortality rate of 45 percent; 8,000 of those who did survive were in very bad condition.[52] During the first months after the Japanese capitulation, the starving survivors roamed around searching for food and stealing whatever they could find. A so-called Palace Report of the government intelligence service dated May 29, 1946, stated:

> they were simply left to their fate and wandered around everywhere in the hope of managing to get a bite of food somewhere. They however were strangers in this land, and could not find shelter or even a small plate of rice anywhere. Many suffered from hunger oedema, avitaminosis and other diseases. Some simply lay down on the side of the road, to—perhaps with a last thought to wife and children in their desa—die alone.[53]

These miserable beings could expect nothing from the local population. In Palopo the mood was openly hostile, following the lead of the local administration.[54]

The chaotic way the Japanese moved people from here to there is apparent from the fact that—while the Japanese sent labor to the Celebes—a group of 3,500 men awaiting transport in the Moluccas at the end of 1945[55] included around 1,000 people who had been taken away from the Celebes to labor elsewhere.[56] Similarly, among 8,000 people on the waiting list in Dutch Borneo (Banjarmasin) at the end of 1945 there were 540 from Menado, in the northern Celebes.

The working and living conditions of the unfortunate laborers brought to Manokwari, in New Guinea, were particularly tragic. According to Japanese accounts they numbered 12,700.[57] The Red Cross could find only 850 people after the war. However, the few survivors were liberated earlier than their fellow sufferers in the other parts of Southeast Asia, for on April 22, 1944, the Americans landed in New Guinea and General Douglas MacArthur set up his temporary headquarters in Hollandia. The CEBREJA leader, Gobius, wrote in the magazine *Uitzicht* of October 30, 1946:

> After the liberation of Hollandia, I repeatedly had occasion to meet with newly liberated Javanese. In general they were in a very neglected state. A loincloth and some rags usually was their only possession. Practically all suffered from scabies and malaria; very many, however, also had dysentery, hookworm disease or other tropical illnesses. The medical NICA units worked miracles with the initially very primitive aids they had at their disposal. Much actual help was provided by the finely equipped medical division of the American army. After several weeks the strongest Javanese reported for work as servants in the NICA camps, as apprentice medics in the hospitals, or in some cases as supervisors. Gradually, too, workers came forward to work in the supply, technical and the liaison offices, or to load and unload ships and airplanes. It did not take much effort to convince the romusha who were still hiding in the forests that the Japanese regime had permanently been destroyed and that they could report safely with the Americans and NICA. Many enrolled as guides for NICA and supplied the advancing Americans with very valuable intelligence. A large number also joined units of the KNIL or the Royal [Dutch] Navy after a period of training in Australia or Merauke.[58]

The drama that took place on Sumatra was unimaginable. Of 120,000 Javanese *rōmusha* brought to Medan, Pakan Baru, Padang, Bukittingi, and Palembang, according to NEFIS barely 23,000 remained alive in 1945.[59] The mortality exceeded 80 percent. In the area around Pakan Baru, where *rōmusha* and Allied—mostly Dutch—prisoners of war had to build a 220-kilometer railroad track through swamp and forest,[60] the responsibility for the first reception and registration of laborers rested with the British military authorities. The former resident, W.H. Coert, reported that after the capitulation hundreds of Javanese, practically naked and covered with scabies, were wandering around near Logas, midway along the railroad track.[61] The prisoners of war were already enjoying all sorts of snacks dropped into the camps by parachute. The medic A. De Boer, who was the last person transferred to Pakan Baru, could not stand to see how hundreds of coolies crowded against each other and begged for food on the other side of the barbed wire of the prisoner of war camp.

> Each was in an even worse state than the one before. Many pushed into the camp and the camp police had trouble to gently keep those folks away

from the immediate surroundings of the newly freed prisoners of war. Every time I ate a tasty Dutch Rusk, removed the silver paper from a chocolate bar or had something delicious to polish off, I got a feeling of melancholy because of what I saw around me: exhausted Indonesians, often dying alongside the track.[62]

In November 1945 more than 3,000 coolies, begging for food, had gathered around the prisoner of war camps 1 and 2 near Pakan Baru. The British, under the command of Major P. Langley, placed them in shabby coolie camps. Medic De Boer volunteered to work there and found "hundreds of dead bodies and human remains" in old barracks. Immediately after the capitulation the local population was extremely friendly to the liberated prisoners of war. According to De Boer: "Chickens and cattle were brought to us and the ex-prisoners of war were invited everywhere. There were frequent parties, and each house proudly flew a small, Dutch flag. Hundreds visited the ex-prisoners of war in their camp. Several Sumatrans let themselves be treated by our doctors with the medication dropped for us."

Within a few weeks the mood had changed from elation to distrust and hatred. After Major Langley and resident Coert gathered the first 3,000 *rōmusha* in old coolie camps at PakanBaru, De Boer observed:

> The republic becomes disagreeable. Kidnapping of Javanese who have been in contact with us occurs daily. Republican Infiltration becomes more audacious. They started with terror. Demonstrations of Indonesians, armed with spears, knives and firearms of any sort, increased daily. It even went so far that the so-called Mountbatten hotel, where the English officers were stationed, was attacked one evening in October. The extremists disarmed the English. After a strong protest from the Allies, the weapons were returned. The English commander, Major Langley, was of the opinion that the Dutch should be evacuated as soon as possible, and this was done. The Javanese *rōmusha* then were left to the care of the Japanese because we ourselves were not capable of protecting these people.

The ex–prisoner of war W.P. Gerharz reported on Republican agitation in Pakan Baru after the Japanese capitulation:

> Gradually several thousand emaciated Javanese coolies who had worked on the railroad tottered alongside the track to PakanBaroe. The Indonesian administration had taken a few measures, but the majority still turned to the Dutch for help. . . . Unhappily the extremist elements in Pekan Baroe

naturally observed this Dutch treatment of Javanese coolies. The leaders were continuously threatened and incidents took place. Unexpectedly a serious brawl broke out in the small *pasar* [market] that had been opened just outside of the camps for the benefit of the coolies and where red-and-white propagandists had snuck in unnoticed. The situation gradually became very tense and made it necessary to protect this group of Indonesians, who had put themselves under Dutch authority.[63]

After the abolition of the Pakan Baru camps and the departure of the last prisoners of war on November 24, 1945, Coert also went to Padang. He had to leave the remaining *rōmusha* of the PakanBaru railroad in Republican territory in the hands of the Japanese military assisted by Indonesians. The Japanese promised to take good care of the Javanese and in fact did so, at least during the first few weeks. But in December 1945 a few *rōmusha* reached Padang and reported that nearly all had left Pakan Baru because, in return for hard labor for the Japanese, they got only some rice and *ubi* (tapioca or sweet potato) leaves to eat. Contrary to what the Japanese had promised Coert on his departure, the Javanese got no supplementary food—no meat, vegetables, or sugar. The people who had run away from Pakan Baru now hung around places such as Bukittingi, Taluk, Kelapa Sawit, and Nilem searching for something to eat.[64]

In the meantime, Coert worked in Padang, along with Major Langley and a Japanese interpreter, on the registration of *rōmusha* who were still roaming around. His bureau, the Javanese Coolie Concentration Sumatra, was under the supervision of the British military headquarters in Padang. In fact the opportunities for registration were very limited. The English did not authorize travel outside the protective cordons around Medan, Padang, and Palembang. Elsewhere the Republic was active. The British required the Japanese to report every ten days on the condition of the 20,000 coolies for whom they and their (Republican) Indonesian helpers were responsible. Nearly 3,000 of the *rōmusha* were ill, according to the Japanese. Tropical ulcers and malaria topped the list, which did not even include malnutrition and dysentery. In reality the condition of their ex–forced laborers was much worse than the Japanese wanted people to know.[65]

Elsewhere in Sumatra the situation was also very bad. In Medan, plans for the reception, registration, and care of *rōmusha* came to nothing because of Republican obstruction. On the Helvetia estate, measures were taken to receive 2,000 men in a newly set-up camp. But that facility was never used because the Republicans opposed the presence of a Dutch physician. Other attempts also failed. At the request of RAPWI, the English tried to work with

T.M. Hassan, the Republican governor of Sumatra. He promised to cooperate but did nothing. Attempts at reception and registration also failed in Palembang, although the condition of the coolies roaming around there was very poor. The English refused to cooperate with Coert and his men, considering it too dangerous for the Dutch to work in the camps.[66]

On Java, where the majority of *rōmusha* had worked, the Japanese did nothing to help their former slaves return home. They were left to their fate, without money or any means of transport. *Rōmusha* who worked on projects near their homes usually managed to get back on their own,[67] but a large number of *rōmusha* had been taken to a sparsely populated and underdeveloped part of the residency of Banten at the western end of West Java.[68] There they worked under the most terrible conditions on the Gembor airfield at Serang, on the road and railroad from Saketi to Bayah, and in the Bayah coal mines. Many of those forced laborers came from far away—Madura, Bali, Lombok, and East Java. In November 1944 about 100,000 *rōmusha* were working in the Banten area, but at the time of the capitulation only about 10,000 of them remained alive, a mortality rate of 90 percent.[69]

A solid organization to receive the emaciated survivors and help them return was nonexistent on Java. The war to liberate the Indonesian Republic from Dutch rule was at hand. The island was the scene of hunger, chaos, and armed struggle. The only existing relief organization was the Badan Pembantu Prajurit Pekerja (Relief Organization for Work Soldiers), the BP3, set up by the Japanese military administration in August 1944 at the insistence of the nationalist leaders. Mohammad Hatta in particular was seriously concerned about the fate of the *rōmusha*.[70] News about the miserable conditions under which they worked and lived, and the countless deaths, had by then already permeated everywhere. The Japanese formally supported the work of BP3 but only made funds available in a limited way. They mainly used the BP3 action program as propaganda to show off their treatment of those they still referred to as volunteer workers. The BP3 could not provide relief to the *rōmusha* in their work areas. A few local exceptions aside, the BP3 also could do little or nothing for the families the workers left behind.[71]

After the Japanese capitulation, BP3 opened offices in several places, but it had little to offer. Here and there they gave the *rōmusha* notes that asked bus and truck drivers to transport them for free. Sometimes the *rōmusha* could also ride the train for free, if the *pemuda* (youth) forced railroad personnel to agree. But even then the workers faced the problem of how to reach a particular station and how to get from that station to their own *desa*. In fact there was only one option: to walk. But that is exactly what most could no longer do. Tan Malaka, who was a supervisor in the Bayah coal mines, wrote:

"They walked alongside the roads like living corpses, and lay down beside the road, at the markets, in empty buildings and movie theatres to wait for death. Rats feasted on the fly-covered corpses."[72]

In the first months after the capitulation the station at Tanah Abang in Jakarta, where trains from Banten arrived, was full of ragged and filthy *rōmusha* who wound up stranded there, without the strength to go any further. Some died at the railroad stations. Alongside the roads from Banten to the east, charity groups ran soup kitchens, where the tottering *rōmusha* could get a cup of *bubur* (rice porridge). Some also received food from *pemuda*, who were busy defending the Republic.

One of the former BP3 workers in Bandung was Suparna Sastra Diredja. In a comment on the war history written by Dr. L. de Jong, Diredja wrote:

> In the months between August and December '45 I saw with my own eyes hundreds of corpses and graves alongside the road when I drove from Bandung to Jakarta via Bogor or Purwakarta by jeep. Some people got to Semarang after months of walking, but died before they could reach their kampungs in East Java. On all main roads to the west you could see groups of emaciated people, from a few dozens to a few hundreds. People who no longer had the strength to walk. People without hair on their heads who seemed to be made merely out of skin and bones. Walking skeletons whose ribs you could count and whose only clothing consisted of a loincloth. Some fell down and died on the shoulder of the road. And he who examined the pouch or bag of such a dead person, even if only to find the name and kampung, usually found nothing at all. Or at the most a crumb of gaplek (dried cassava).[73]

Conclusion

Between May 1946 and April 1947, a total of seventy-seven ships brought more than 52,000 *rōmusha* back to Indonesia. The last official transport took place in July 1947, nearly two years after the Japanese capitulation.[74] The efforts of the British to repatriate their subjects, mainly Tamils, Chinese, Malays, and Burmese, to their countries of origin, have been left out of consideration in this study.

What happened to those not officially repatriated is anyone's guess. The Indonesian Red Cross brought a few thousand back to Java by local sailing boats. Possibly, in the course of time, several thousand more managed to return to their native soil on their own. It is certain, however, that many thousands of the former slaves from Java never returned. They simply got lost and were never found, or were forgotten and left behind, voluntarily or involuntarily. Those who survived, or their descendants, continue to live in Borneo, Sumatra, Halmaheira, and the former New Guinea. They founded families on desolate islands such as Guadalcanal or in the Andaman archipelago, or in Indochina or elsewhere.

In the spring of 1995 an elderly couple from Vietnam arrived at the Sukarno–Hatta airfield in Jakarta. The woman was part of an official delegation. At her special request, she was accompanied by her husband, an ex-*rōmusha* who had remained in Saigon in 1945. Half a century had passed since he had set foot in the land of his birth.

Part VII

Malaya

12

Labor in the Malay Peninsula and Singapore under Japanese Occupation

Paul H. Kratoska

The Japanese invasion of Malaya caused sudden and widespread unemployment. Estates and mines, cut off from their overseas markets, reduced production or stopped operations altogether, throwing their own laborers out of work along with people employed in the many industries that serviced the export sector. In the first year of the occupation there were few opportunities to find jobs, and many people sold personal belongings to get money to live on. In 1943, however, the Japanese began recruiting workers for military construction projects, and by 1944 the country was experiencing labor shortages. The Japanese responded by creating new channels to recruit labor. They also forced male workers out of nonessential occupations, drew women into the workforce, and mobilized the population to provide labor on a part-time basis.

Japanese Attitudes toward Malayan Workers

The Japanese generally blamed the hardships of the occupation on British policies, but they also complained that people in Malaya did not work hard enough and needed to adopt a new spirit of enterprise. A visiting parliamentarian commented late in 1942 that the people of Japan "understand that the Malayan people had eked a bare existence easily under the British and the hot climate of the country tended to make the people lazy." He expressed a hope that things would change.[1] In the state of Perak, responding to a suggestion by the governor that it would be difficult to increase rice cultivation because the Malays did not like to work hard, a Malay District Officer explained that, "what he has done is to get the people together in different places and talk to them, explaining the position and telling them to get to work. He said threats have even been used that if they do not plant their land they will be arrested and put in the lock-up without food for 3 days. He said that that is the way to make these people work."[2]

Early in 1943, on the first anniversary of the "Re-birth" of Pahang, the governor of that state announced that it was necessary to cultivate "an industrious spirit" among residents of the state. "As the land is fertile and full of agricultural products, it has brought about a state of 'easy-life' among the people with a deficiency in the spirit of toil for their own food. . . . We must wipe out people who only eat and do no work."[3]

Newspaper editorials also extolled the dignity of manual labor:

> The ideal of the Nippon Government is that every worker, no matter what his occupation may be, should have his small plot of land, which he should cultivate with his own hands and bathe with his own sweat, for to every Nippon-zin [Japanese] there is no happiness so sweet as the happiness that comes with achievement. Peasants seek happiness in the mire of their padi fields and find it in the growing grain and the fruits of the harvest. Workers who have their little plots of land can seek the same happiness by laboring in their spare time, and find the same happiness of achievement in the vegetables or fruit produced by the earth as a reward for their toil.[4]

Unemployment

Although unemployment was widespread in the early months of the occupation, the Japanese were reluctant to acknowledge that able-bodied workers could not find jobs. According to the Labor Department in Selangor, a "majority of those who registered as unemployed were persons who had lost interest for work on estates and mines and those who through a declining state of health had drifted to a life of vagrancy."[5] The administration in Perak claimed that coconut plantations and oil palm estates, tea plantations, and even rubber estates were reporting labor shortages, and a newspaper report written in October 1942 suggested that there was no lack of work in Perak, just a need to redistribute labor. Yet unemployment was so widespread in the state that the government carried out a program of public works to alleviate distress.[6]

Estate Laborers

The Japanese provided rice to laborers on rubber and oil palm estates for doing maintenance work. In principle, those on enemy estates were to receive a "full ration" of rice until the end of April and "Government rations" after that, but it was difficult to arrange transport, and estates in remote areas did not receive their allocations.

In May of 1942 a syndicate of eighteen Japanese rubber companies operating as the Singapore Rubber Association (Syonan Gomu Kumiai) took control of the rubber industry. The association allowed laborers to work for ten to fifteen days a month, paying wages that were slightly below prewar levels.[7] The Japanese military administration strongly encouraged the laborers to spend the rest of their time growing food. Before the occupation more than 60 percent of the rice consumed in Malaya had been imported, but these supplies had largely come to a stop because no shipping was available. A Japanese official told plantation workers in Selangor that the population was not self-supporting with regard to food production because of the British policy of "mean exploitation," and that Japan's policy of providing facilities to grow food crops demonstrated its regard for the welfare and prosperity of the people. Estate laborers had a "golden opportunity" to become self-sufficient and would have themselves to blame for their suffering if they did not seize this opportunity and "show themselves industrious." To drive home the point, the speaker concluded, "Laborers who do not avail themselves of this facility will not be given any work on Estates; nor have they a claim to be supplied with rice to maintain themselves in laziness and indolence."[8]

The Singapore Rubber Association failed to make money, and in April 1943 the government cut back on estate work. Large numbers of people were left without any way to earn a living, and the following November the labor inspector for Kelantan reported:

> A major portion of the unemployed laborers, Indians and Chinese, are almost starving . . . and some of these have slowly drifted into towns and are maintaining themselves by begging on the streets[,] and diseases are taking a heavy toll on them due to absence of medical aid.[9]

By the end of the war the number of people living on "enemy" estates in Malaya had fallen by nearly 50 percent, from 380,000 in May 1942 to 190,200. The active estate workforce (men, women, and children) amounted to 69,800 laborers, and some 27,700 of these were simply growing food.[10]

There was a high incidence of malaria among estate laborers during the occupation. In Selangor, for example, deaths from malaria increased tenfold, from 0.7 per thousand in 1939 to 7.2 per thousand in 1942,[11] and more than 80 percent of the malaria cases occurred on estates. The British administration had dealt with the disease by draining mosquito breeding sites or applying antimalarial oil, a mixture of crude oil and kerosene, to destroy mosquito larvae. During the occupation, many estates discontinued antimalarial measures, and local government agencies halted regular treatment of breeding areas because they could not obtain sufficient quantities of antimalarial oil. The Ulu Langat Sanitary Board, for example, normally used 450 gallons of oil per month, but during 1942 it was allocated just one-third that amount and adopted a policy of monitoring breeding areas and applying oil only when large numbers of larvae were found.[12] By October 1942 the Rubber Department had begun supplying oil extracted from rubber as a substitute for the antimalarial oil used before the war, and this provided some relief, but supplies were irregular.[13] In towns and near military camps, officials attempted to deal with the problem through improved drainage, but little could be done on estates and in rural areas.

White-Collar Workers

Educated people faced unemployment owing to the closure of schools, reductions in staffing levels in government departments, and a loss of clerical positions owing to the sharp decline in foreign trade. In August 1942 there were some 3,800 clerks and teachers looking for jobs in Singapore, and a similar number in Kuala Lumpur.[14] In October 1942 the Welfare Department in Singapore compiled a register of 9,433 people seeking work, most of them skilled laborers, clerks, or teachers.[15] The anticipated arrival of additional Japanese businesses promised to create jobs for office workers, but for many people in this category the occupation was a time of great hardship.

The Japanese had little sympathy for the educated unemployed. The governor of Perak said in late 1942:

> I would advise all these educated people who are jobless to go back to the land, where there is every prospect in growing foodstuffs and in rearing cattle and poultry. It is a most pitiable thing in this country that those "educated" people dislike manual labor. This state of mentality is most repugnant to our Nippon Seisin—Nipponese Fundamental Thought. We will have nothing to do with these people.[16]

In the same vein, an officer with the Fisheries Department urged educated young men to discard the false pride that made them look down on fishing, and use their trained minds to develop improved methods of catching fish. "Under the New Order the honest laborer was just as good as any pen-pusher."[17]

Farmers

Because Malaya was a food-deficit area before the war, the wartime military administration placed a strong emphasis on cultivation of food crops. Officials pressed farmers to grow root crops such as sweet potatoes and tapioca along with rice, and required them to plant vegetables on the land around their houses, raise chickens and ducks, and spend long hours tending their rice fields. In the 1970s, Malay farmers in the Krian irrigation area recalled having to spend the entire day in their fields, even when they had no work to do, because Taiwanese overseers stationed in the district would abuse them if they went home.[18]

People living in urban areas faced similar pressure to plant vegetables on vacant land, or to move out of the city and grow food on unused land in rural areas. Living conditions in the cities were sufficiently poor that substantial numbers of people followed this advice, but they had no experience of farming and found it difficult to survive. In 1943 the administration began creating agricultural settlements intended to absorb a large proportion of the urban population. Around 40 percent of the population of Singapore was scheduled for relocation, primarily to a Chinese settlement called New Syonan, which was located at Endau in northeastern Johor, or to Fuji Village, a Roman Catholic settlement in the state of Negri Sembilan. Overall, the Japanese set up more than thirty resettlement sites for Chinese residents in various parts of Malaya.[19]

Labor for Military Construction Projects

The Japanese recruited large numbers of Malayan workers for construction projects, both within Malaya and in neighboring territories. In March 1943, for example, the Japanese advertised for laborers to build an airfield in Borneo, and in April 1944 to work on a Trans-Sumatran railway. They also recruited some 20,000 Malayan laborers to construct a railway line across the Isthmus of Kra, in southern Thailand. Within Malaya the Japanese needed workers to construct airfields, develop irrigation facilities, and prepare defensive works.[20] For one project near Kuala Pilah, in Negri Sembilan, the authorities summoned 3,000 men from surrounding areas, ordering them to bring their own tools and cooking utensils. To get water for drinking and bathing, they dug wells and collected rainwater.[21]

Conditions at the work sites were extremely harsh, and many laborers died of malnutrition and disease. Malaria was a particular problem around construction sites, where mosquitoes bred in holes dug as part of earthworks and in wells dug by the laborers. On one project that employed around 2,500 laborers in 1942 and 1943 to build a landing field at Port Swettenham, the state Medical Department reported that three to four workers died of malaria or malnutrition each day.[22]

The largest Japanese project was the Thailand–Burma railway, a branch line that linked the rail networks of the two countries. Work began in November 1942, and the original plan called for the job to be completed by the end of 1943. Japanese forces in Burma needed the line urgently, and in February 1943 Japanese authorities in Tokyo advanced the date for completion to August. This schedule could not be met, and the line eventually opened on October 25, 1943.

Nearly 62,000 European prisoners of war were sent to Burma and Thailand to work as forced laborers on the project, and 12,399 of them died there. Around the middle of 1943, the Japanese began recruiting large numbers of Asian workers to speed up construction work, the majority of them from Malaya and Burma, but some from Java, Thailand, and French Indochina as well. Japanese sources placed the number of Asian workers at 182,496 and acknowledged 42,214 deaths. However, they also reported that 92,220 Asian laborers deserted, and in view of the fact that many of these workers left the camps to escape from a cholera epidemic, it is certain that a substantial number did not survive.[23] One Allied estimate places the size of the Asian workforce as high as 269,948 and the number of deaths at 72,996 (27 percent), but the figures are unreliable, particularly for Burma.[24]

British sources place the number of workers sent from Malaya to the Thailand–Burma railway at 78,204.[25] State labor offices in Malaya began recruiting labor for the railway project in July 1943, operating through district offices, the Public Works Department, rubber estates, mining companies, military contractors, the Indian Independence League, and the Oversea Chinese Association.[26] The administration told workers that their period of service would be short and they would be able to return home when it was finished. Dependents of workers who went to Thailand were to receive an allowance of 15 Malayan dollars per month, plus a gratuity of 120 dollars and a certificate of service if a laborer died, but the allowance stopped if a laborer absconded.[27] Most of these promises were not fulfilled. In December 1943 the District Officer for Kulim complained that dependents of 3,000 Indians who had left for Thailand six months earlier had yet to receive a letter or news of any kind, and not a single person had returned. Moreover, the promised allowances seem not to have been paid regularly.[28]

After the railway was completed, the line required considerable upkeep owing to destruction caused by Allied bombing and flood damage. Many of the surviving prisoners of war were moved elsewhere, but Asian laborers remained in camps along the railway line to perform maintenance work, and in February 1944 the Japanese were trying to recruit additional workers.[29] Following the Japanese surrender, the Allies prepared assembly points for systematic repatriation of laborers, but some workers simply left the camps and attempted to reach home on their own.[30]

Training Programs

The Japanese needed people with job specialties that were not widely available in the Malayan workforce, so they set up programs to teach these skills. An institute to train seamen began operations in February 1943, and training was also offered in techniques to build, salvage, and repair ships. In April 1944 a Syonan Industrial School began to train technicians, offering a range of courses that included auto mechanics and methods of producing flour. Farmers and fishermen also received instruction, learning "Nipponese methods" for pursuing their craft.[31]

Labor Shortages and Tightening Labor Control

In 1943 the Japanese set up labor offices in Singapore and the peninsula, and created registers that were used to help unemployed workers find jobs.[32] In August of that year, the labor offices were brought under a Central Labor Control Committee and regional labor control committees, and in September a committee was formed to allocate manpower. In 1944 officials in Singapore and in the states of the peninsula required all laborers to register, and made an attempt to control labor through the use of Employees' Identity Books (*Romu Tetyo*), but the rules were widely ignored.[33]

In the last two years of the occupation, labor became increasingly scarce in Malaya. Much of the country's surplus labor had been absorbed by Japanese projects, and reports of very poor conditions at work sites made people reluctant to respond to recruitment efforts. Although wages rose—in 1943 estates paid workers 1 dollar per day with free food and lodging, but by 1945 the rate was 20 dollars per day with food and lodging—inflation had devalued the currency to such an extent that even a twentyfold increase in wages was not attractive. In the state of Kedah, for example, a standard measure of rice cost 18 cents before the war, 6 dollars in August 1944, and 24 dollars in February 1945, and the price of a coconut rose from 2 cents to 2 dollars and 30 cents over the same period.[34]

In towns and cities, the Japanese sprang "traps" in which they blocked off streets or the entrances to cinema halls and checked the papers of all those caught inside, allowing men with employment papers to go but taking others away to become laborers.[35] Similarly, men found sitting around in coffee shops were liable to be seized and put to work on construction projects.

In December 1943 the Japanese began enrolling the people of Malaya in organizations that provided supplementary labor. The most important was a labor service corps, the *seicho*, which had branches throughout the country. For every 250 inhabitants, 20 men had to become *seicho* members. They generally worked in their spare time at locations near their homes, but in some cases they were mobilized for longer periods.[36]

In the same month, the Japanese administration in Perak formed an organization called the Kinrohoshitai, which worked to increase food production and improve the image of manual labor. Members helped grow food but also worked on military construction projects. Some projects were large—an airfield at Ipoh required 1,000 workers each day, and construction of "protecting sheds" along the railway in the Krian District involved more than 4,000 workers. Food was difficult to procure, and one scheme that was to send workers to a project site for a week at a time had to be abandoned in favor of an arrangement where workers returned home each evening and furnished their own food. The governor rejected a suggestion that participants be given an extra ration of rice in the same way as members of the *seicho*, pointing out that the Kinrohoshitai had been created precisely because rice was in short supply.[37]

Many projects required labor on a short-term basis. In December 1943 villages in Province Wellesley had to supply 20 workers for every 250 residents to erect a fortification along the waterfront near the town of Butterworth, using the trunks of coconut trees. In Perak, villagers were routinely called upon to repair roads and drains, and on one occasion a number of men had to go to Pondok Tanjong to erect a structure to protect the railway tracks there. According to Haji Mubi bin Che Long, the job was not difficult, but he had to walk 15 miles to reach the work site.[38] In Kelantan the Japanese routinely ordered village headmen to provide laborers, normally 20 men at a time, to dig ditches, build fortifications and military camps, make roads, and cut the jungle. The working day lasted from eight in the morning until four in the afternoon, and laborers received 1 dollar per day but had to supply their own food.[39] At Sungei Aceh, in the state of Perak, families were called upon to weave fifty containers for bottles, each 1 foot long and 4 inches wide, from a kind of sedge normally used to make sleeping mats. They never learned what purpose these containers served. People living in Kedah were ordered to make bottle cases out of grass, for which they received 2 dollars per hundred initially, and later 1 dollar per hundred. An adult could complete between fifteen and twenty pieces per day. They also produced rope, rice bags, and mats from the same materials, and for similar rates of pay. Reported production in the first eight months of 1943 amounted to more than 21,000 kilograms of rope, 31,000 rice bags, nearly 1.7 million bottle cases, and 78,500 mats.[40]

Women in the Workforce

At the start of the occupation the Japanese showed little interest in female labor, possibly because of the high levels of male unemployment. In Selangor, for example, the administration issued a circular announcing that all female government employees were to be terminated with one month's notice, and that any woman wishing to rejoin government service had to apply to the chief Japanese officer for the department concerned.[41] A newspaper article that appeared in October 1943 stating that the Allies were using women to handle technical work in airplanes nicely illustrates the negative attitude toward women in the workforce. The *Syonan Shimbun* commented: "The inter-mixed divisions in the front line will surely appear to be demoralized."[42]

In October of 1942 the governor of Perak complained that, while some "women folk" took part in agricultural work or other kinds of production, "to my regret by far a greater part of them are merely sitting down idle, wasting away their time doing nothing but a little bit of domestic works."

> Fair sex, no doubt, are weaker than men and physically unable to bear very heavy works. However, there are domestic handicrafts of very light nature, such as spinning and weaving. The material thereof are obtainable in abundance in this country from banana trees and others, and also from rami, which will be extensively cultivated in future. Not only will these handy works increase the income of a family, but will also relieve the monotony of the daily routine of life. Especially at the time of the present shortage of clothing this will contribute greatly to the stabilization of the livelihood of the people.[43]

The district officer for Krian questioned whether women had time for additional work.

> The women of the two principal races, to wit, the Malays and the Chinese, were engaged in the flourishing industries of food production, the former in the cultivation of rice and the latter in the rearing of poultry and pigs and the curing and salting of fish. They were very fully engaged, but were happy and contented and giving of their best. Such being the situation in his district, he said the prospects of employing female laborers in the spinning and weaving industry were practically nil.[44]

The governor replied that his aim was "to introduce some working ideas among those ladies who had a lot of spare time for work of this kind" and said his criticisms were not directed at "those who were already engaged in work of one kind or another."

> His Excellency the Governor said the intention was to put female labor to the weaving and spinning industry besides their present work. Spinning, His Excellency pointed out, is so easy that even a child could do it. In this connection His Excellency informed the meeting that an order had been

placed in Thailand for 1,000 hand looms and instructed the District Officers to inform the lady folks in their districts accordingly. . . . His Excel-
lency further said that Malay women had very nimble fingers and so they
must be very good at this kind of work.[45]

By 1943 the Japanese were paying greater attention to the potential contribution of women to the workforce. In July the *Syonan Shimbun* published
a story about two "pretty" Malay girls who had made history by braving
public opinion to work in government offices. The story explained that most
Malay girls employed in this way came from prosperous families and were
not working because they needed money but because they wished to help the
Japanese administration.[46] In the same month the governor of Perak said that
greater attention should be given to the education of women, both in schools
and in informal settings. "If we know how to cultivate the mental faculties
and raise the virtue of motherhood, that is also education." He called for the
creation of women's associations, "where women can exchange their opinions
in connection with the understanding of our war objects,"[47] and when Malay
women at Batu Gajah did form such an organization the newspaper greeted the
move with lavish praise. Speaking at the group's inaugural meeting, the governor said, "Malai women had been backward but now they as much as men
have an equally important part to play. Intelligent and wise womanhood begets
intelligent and wise children." Japanese women, he added, had already made
great progress "and now are a shining example to the world."[48]

In an interview after he visited Japan in December 1943, Ishak bin Haji
Muhammad, editor of the *Berita Malai* newspaper, praised the way women
were replacing men in many jobs; the story was headlined "Nippon Women
Are Diligent, Energetic, Women of Malai Should Follow Suit. . . ."[49] Ishak
said that Malay women should follow the example of Japanese women and
replace traditional dress with loose *mompe* trousers, which the *Syonan
Shimbun* newspaper later described as "more practical and less cumbersome
than the sarong for real wartime work."[50] Also in December 1943 the head of
the Propaganda Department for Penang complained that "in Syonan and other
places in Malai, there are a good number of idlers, especially the women
who have been notably lacking in spirit of service."[51] In 1944 the newspapers published additional positive stories about women as workers. One article advised Malay women to "discard unnecessary customs such as
prohibiting them from mixing with the men" and work in "production plants,
offices, etc. instead of remaining at home."[52]

In February the Japanese created a Women's Employment Bureau in
Singapore, and in connection with a program to encourage men to concentrate on war-related work, the head of the General Affairs Department in

Pahang told district officers that "in order to increase to the utmost limits necessary labor, all light easy and unimportant jobs done hitherto by males shall, in future, as far as possible be taken over by females." Women were to become messengers and do menial tasks in government offices and for private firms, and work as laborers in handwork industries, as cooks and "boys" in private households, and as street sweepers. Men were to devote themselves to "cultivation of foodstuffs, munitions industry and other manual labor."[53]

In 1944 the government began a propaganda campaign that asserted that it was unpatriotic for women to remain at home and emphasized that the administration was creating acceptable working conditions for women. Newspapers published letters from women saying how much they enjoyed their jobs, and a February 1944 radio broadcast from Singapore stated:

> Malai women now realize that their role in total warfare is as important as men. For the first time in the history of Malai, Malai women have boldly come forward to contribute their share toward the achievement of final victory. Today Malai women are working in government and commercial offices as clerks, interpreters and telephone operators. They are also working in [military] stores, factories and other establishments engaged in war production.[54]

Japan's Domei news agency reported in April that women were working as bank clerks, telephone operators, interpreters, and sales girls, and also in agriculture, freeing men for "heavier, more important and more responsible tasks."[55] The campaign continued into 1945. A discussion that took place in Batu Gajah in January concluded:

> Women's responsibilities in the war are varied. There are some of our women folk who are busily engaged in agriculture but there are others who have much leisure and are sitting idle. Opportunities are ever open for them to take up light home industries such as weaving and spinning—materials being in abundance in this country—fibre from banana, pineapple and even bark of trees. At this time of shortage of clothing, this will contribute greatly to the stabilization of the livelihood of the people.[56]

At the end of 1944 the administration took steps to obtain additional labor for war-related activities by forcing men to leave jobs that were declared nonessential or could be handled by women. A Change of Trade Ordinance required men between the ages of fifteen and forty to give up jobs that did not contribute to the war effort in favor of food cultivation, war-related production, or the manufacture of essential items such as soap and paper. The goal was to close 60 percent of all shops to free labor for war production. Among the jobs men could no longer hold were the following: porters, waiters, information clerks, janitors, launderers, touts, guides, salesmen, clerks, itinerant peddlers, hawkers, telephone operators, ticket collectors, and elevator operators. Exceptions were made for those who were crippled or lame, those working at sea, and those who fell into other special categories.[57] The law threatened the survival of many businesses, but Chinese shopkeepers were offered the alternative of making a substantial donation to the Overseas Chinese Association, and large sums of money were apparently collected in this way, although records are lacking.[58]

Enforcement of the Change of Trade Ordinance further increased the importance of female workers, who took over some of the jobs vacated by male workers. It also seems to have generated rumors that women were to be forced to work, a suggestion the *Syonan Shimbun* took pains to rebut:

> The authorities wish it to be clearly understood, however, that they are not compelling women to work or putting into effect any ordinance for mobilization of female labor power. The authorities respect the many religious and racial customs prevailing in this city and they will not compel women to work unless they voluntarily wish to do so.[59]

Conclusion

Farmers and workers had a difficult time during the Japanese occupation, but their experiences depended on the attitude of local Japanese officials. Indians living in the southern part of Province Wellesley said that the Japanese stationed there were good men who were willing to give and take and did not make unreasonable demands, although some people from the area were recruited to go to Thailand to work on the railway there.[60] For most workers the occupation brought increasing hardship, as an already poor element of the population attempted to cope with shortages and rising prices. Suffering from malaria and deficiency diseases, and unfamiliar with vegetable cultivation, large numbers of people accustomed to life in the cities or on rubber estates struggled to produce enough food to keep themselves alive and healthy. Many did not succeed, and the end of the occupation found workers in Malaya malnourished and suffering from deficiency diseases, while the physical growth of their children was severely stunted.[61]

13

Malayan Labor on the Thailand–Burma Railway

Nakahara Michiko

Endless streams of wretched Coolies from Malaya are plodding their slippery way to the jungle road. Those who speak English frequently have sad words to say about the recruiting methods of Nipponese used to secure their services. A powerful factor seems to be starvation in Malaya since the rice ration is reduced from the normal 8 katis a week to 3. These poor wretches are dying up here in countless thousands. A number of Nipponese soldiers have also passed through recently, plodding resolutely through the mud in single file.[1]

When the Imperial Japanese Army landed on the east coast of the Malay Peninsula early on December 8, 1941, the Fifteen-Year War begun in 1931 entered its final stage. During the ensuing six months, Japanese forces achieved a series of swift victories, seizing all of Southeast Asia and extending their control into the South Pacific. However, the imperial navy suffered a decisive defeat in June 1942 at the Battle of Midway and lost control of the seas. Air and surface transportation quickly deteriorated, and by the fall of 1942 surface transportation between Malaya and Burma, where the Japanese faced Allied forces in India, became a serious problem.[2]

Rangoon fell to Japanese forces on March 8, 1942, and a Japanese military administration took control of the country on June 4. The only effective link between Burma and the rest of Southeast Asia was by sea; there was no railroad, and not even a proper road, between Burma and Thailand, and the existing transportation system proved inadequate for Japanese needs. According to the report "The Situation after Independence in Burma,"

As for maritime transportation, attacks by enemy airplanes and submarines had made transportation by large ship between Malaya and Burma almost impossible by the autumn of 1943. 'Ant transportation' by sailing vessels and small wooden ships is being carried out along the coast and difficult inland rivers. It is impossible to meet urgent Burmese civilian demands by such transportation.[3]

The defeat at Midway immediately affected the maritime supply route to Burma via Singapore, and to prevent Japanese forces from being entirely cut off, the Japanese high command undertook construction of a rail link connecting existing track in Burma and Thailand. According to Lieutenant Colonel Hiroike Toshio, a member of the railway general staff, the plan for a Burma–Thailand railway was first conceived on October 18, 1941, when he was discussing operation plans with Lieutenant General Hattori in his cabin on board the *Konan-maru* on the South China Sea, the night before landing at Haiphong. The idea seemed almost impossible: to build a 415-kilometer railway in fourteen months through a rugged, trackless, and pestilence-ridden tract of jungle known for having one of the highest average rainfalls in the world during the rainy season.

The Southern Army unofficially began preparations even before it received formal orders to build a Thailand–Burma railroad in June 1942.[4] Construction work began with sending laborers to camps along the planned route to clear jungle, erect sleeping huts, build roads, and prepare construction materials and food. A Japanese construction force with a total of 13,000 men, including the Fifth and Ninth Railway Regiments, was assigned to the project. In the early days of the construction period, the railway regiments enlisted local labor, Siamese on the eastern stretch, Burmese on the western. When the supply of local workers proved insufficient, prisoners of war (POWs) were transferred from Malaya and the Dutch Indies. In February 1943, the Southern Army brought forward the original completion date by four months, which meant that the railway was to be finished by the end of August 1943. The Southern Field Railway Headquarters ordered the Japanese Twenty-ninth Army in Malaya to enlist coolies, and the workforce was driven much harder than before. As the summer advanced it became clear that the revised schedule could not be met. The reasons were as follows:

1. *Transportation:* Demands for road transport increased daily. As construction gradually pushed farther into the mountains and jungle away from the bases, the problem of bringing up materials and supplies became critical. The road, which was constructed parallel to the track, was rendered impassable in many places by the monsoon rains. For some time after the monsoon started, the rivers did not rise sufficiently for river transport.

Table 13.1

Statement of Thailand–Burma Railway Employees, End of September 1945

	Number employed	Died	Employed at present	Deserted	Repatriated
Malays no. 1 batch	70,000	28,928	5,600	22,964	2,508
Malays no. 2 batch	2,300	439	51	351	1,459
Coolies' families	2,100	107	85	124	1,784
Specialist coolies	727	12	35	215	465
Malayan Railways works employees	1,057	77	125	423	432
Malayan electrical works employees	166	16	12	45	93
Malayan employees	839	31	16	220	572
Dressers	660	10	365	141	144
Temporary dressers	53	3	10	39	1
Overseers	214	10	70	104	30
Post office employees	88	1	87	—	—
Total	78,204	29,634	6,456	24,626	17,488

Source: "Statement of Burma–Siam Railway Employees as at end of September 1945," document IY, translated from an original Japanese document, WO 325/57 D.

2. *Labor:* Notwithstanding the inflow of replacements and reinforcements, the labor potential had been drastically lowered by the high incidence of disease among POWs and coolies alike.[5]

Finally, the date of completion was changed to October 31.

Malayan Labor on the Railway

The Thailand–Burma railway was one of the largest construction projects carried out by the imperial army during the Japanese occupation of Southeast Asia. The Japanese mobilized a huge labor force to construct the railway, consisting of 62,000 prisoners of war and an estimated 200,000 Asian laborers recruited from Thailand, Burma, Malaya, French Indochina, and the Indonesian archipelago. The death toll among laborers was very high.[6]

Table 13.1 shows the number of Asian laborers employed and the death rate according to a Japanese source. Overall, according to the table, out of 73,027 people sent from Malaya to work on the railway, 23,944 workers (33 percent) had been repatriated or were still employed at the end of the war. A total of 29,634 (37 percent) were reported dead, and 24,626 (31.5 percent) had deserted. Given that the peak of desertion occurred during the period when cholera was spreading along the railway and laborers fled in fear in all

Table 13.2

Allied Estimates of Asian Laborers Employed on the Thailand–Burma Railroad

	Total employed	Repatriated	Estimated deaths (minimum)	Percentage of deaths
Malayans	78,204	6,456	40,000	51
Javanese	7,508	—	3,000	40
Chinese (from Siam)	5,200	1,300	1,000	20
Indochinese	200	120	25	12.5
Burmese	91,384	13,540	30,000	30
Total	182,496	21,446	74,025	41

Source: "Report on Coolie Camp Conditions on the Burma-Siam Railway during the Period November 1943 to August 1945," p. 75, in WO 325/56.

directions through the jungle, it is likely that many of those listed as having deserted also perished. Thus it is highly probable that the death rate was much higher than these figures suggest. It should also be noted that the Japanese who prepared these figures were, at the time of compilation, aware that they would face trial as war criminals.

Table 13.2 shows a calculation prepared by the Allies after the war concerning the number of Asian laborers employed on the railroad. Figures for Burma are particularly suspect, because many Burmese deserted before reaching the work camps. These statistics show a death rate of 51 percent for laborers from Malaya, but my interviews suggest it must have been higher. The table does not take deserters into account, and based on these figures nearly 32,000 people are not accounted for. Among the 124 Malayans I interviewed, only one person believed that as many as half of those who deserted returned safely.

In addition to coolie laborers, a number of government employees from Malaya were sent to Thailand. They came from a variety of departments, including the Malayan railway, electricity, telecommunications, water, post office, and hospitals. In Thailand they worked in their specialty. For example, Samydurai Anthony worked in the post office in Sentul, Kuala Lumpur. He was sent to Thailand to open a post office in Kanchanaburi in October 1942. According to him, there were four post offices along the Thailand–Burma railway, in Kanchanaburi (Thailand), Kinsaiyok (Burma), Tamajo (Burma), and Aparon (Burma). There were four people working at each of these post offices, which carried on regular post office business to cater to the increasing number of soldiers working along the railway. Also, laborers who did not have anywhere to keep their money deposited it in post office savings accounts.[7]

Labor Recruitment

For the first year, Japanese soldiers and POWs were the main labor force for the railway project. However, in the spring of 1943 the field railway head-quarters of the Southern Army ordered the Twenty-ninth Army in Malaya to recruit additional workers. The Twenty-ninth Army passed the task along to the military government, the Gunseikanbu. In March advertisements began to appear in Malayan newspapers for coolies to work in Thailand. The stated duration of the contract was normally three months, after which workers would be returned to their homes. They would receive free rail travel, hous-ing, food, and medical services, and would be paid 1 dollar per day, with an advance of 10 dollars on signing the contract.[8]

In Singapore the head of the Welfare Department, Shinozaki Mamoru, was in charge of recruitment.[9] "There was a strong demand for these coolies from the Railway Construction Units," he said, and the orders he received were "peremptory." Singapore opened a labor office under Shinozaki's di-rection. "Seventy thousand were enlisted and sent to Siam in 1943, but only two or three thousand could be sent in 1944 and 1945. . . ." Officers of South-ern Field Railway Headquarters pressed him very hard to provide more coo-lies, and Shinozaki met the allotted quotas "through contractors and through advertising in papers, or the sending of circular letters to all communities." The officially stated period of employment was six months, for wages about three times those prevailing in Singapore. Shinozaki also offered the job to beggars and homeless people collected in a police roundup. According to Shinozaki, the early groups of laborers were all volunteers, attracted by the high wages.[10]

L. Sanjiwi was one of the laborers who applied to work in Thailand. In an interview he explained that he was working at Puchong Estate, in Selangor, and heard about a job in Thailand that paid well. In March 1943 he applied voluntarily through the estate office, together with 25 other laborers from the same estate, including his father. They were taken from the plantation by truck to Kuala Lumpur, where they found many other Tamil laborers. He received registration number 236 and his father 237. They were given 10 dollars and slept in an open field. The next morning an official from the labor office came and gave them advice about living in Thailand, telling them, for example, to drink only boiled water, and to burn wood to kill mosquitoes. They were sent to Kanchanaburi by freight train, and from there they walked, with three Japanese soldiers escorting about 700 laborers. Each laborer car-ried a sack of rice on his back and walked through the jungle for seven days. Along the way they saw many dead bodies, abandoned and covered with flies. His father returned to Malaya in 1944, and he himself escaped from the

Photograph 13.1. Ronsi, Burma. c. 1943. Native laborers working on a bridge on the Burma–Thailand railway. Ronsi is approximately sixty kilometers south of Thanbyuzayat, or 354 kilometers north of Nong Pladuk (also known as Non Pladuk). (Courtesy of the Australian War Memorial [Negative Number P00406.036].)

No.	Nama Cooly	Kampong	Nama waris yang hampir sekali dan perabitan-nya	Kampong	Wang Pendahuluan	Tanda tangan
43	Mat Yusoff b.H.Senik	Daerah Bt.Awang T.Tinggi	Limah bte. Ismail - isteri	Tebing Tinggi	10. 00	
44	Ag.Besar b.Koter	Daerah Semerak S. Petai	Eshah bt. Ag.Kechik -	Sungai Petai	10. 00	
45	Hamat b.Beh	G.Lalang	Membunga bt. Ismail -	Gong Lalang	10. 00	
46	Deris bin Awang	Kg.Lembah	Wan Minah bt. W.Harun - Isteri	Kg. Lembah	10. 00	
47	Ag.Mat b.Salim	Cherang Ruku	Mek bt. Mahmood - "	Cherang Ruku	10. 00	
48	Dermaan bin Kundor	"	Kundor bin Jamal - Bapa'	"	10. 00	
49	Che Ngah b.Che Kar	"	Zainab bt. Mat Ali - Isteri	"	10. 00	
50	Hamzah b.Daud	Raja Dagang	Minah bt. Mat Hassan - "	Raja Dagang	10. 00	
51	Mohamed bin Botok	Ch. Ruku	W.Ismail bin W.Salleh-Penggawa	Ch. Ruku	10. 00	
52	Hamat bin Jusoh	Kuala Semerak	Mek Senik bin Ag.Besar - Ibu	K. Semerak	10. 00	
53	Ag.Besar b.Sakmah	"	Membunga bt. Senik - Isteri	"	10. 00	

Photograph 13.2. List of laborers sent to work on the Thailand–Burma railway from the Pasir Puteh District in the Malaysian State of Kelantan. (Pasir Puteh [Kelantan] file 176/2603 [1943] Malaysian National Archives.)

labor camp when British bombing started. One day after he arrived in Takrin, in Thailand, a siren wailed and many white soldiers appeared. One of them was making a speech in front of many soldiers. The white soldiers were drinking *samsu* (alcohol) and shouting, "[The] monkey has surrendered." Sanjiwi was sent back to Penang by ship with about 10,000 other laborers. The English officer in charge of the laborers from Malaya was Major Bangs. When he arrived home, he received 5 dollars at the labor office.[11]

Workers did not return home after the promised "three or four months," and it did not take long for terrible rumors to spread about the "good jobs in Thailand." Lieutenant Colonel Sugiyama Akira, who was in charge of the Labor Department, considered the inability of the enlistment scheme to supply fresh workers a major failing. "At first, we planned to change the laborers every two or three months. If such a change had been carried out smoothly and we had a fresh supply of laborers all the time, management and maintenance of the line would have been far easier."[12]

The workforce included substantial numbers of women and children. Ikeda Shoichiro sometimes heard the officer in charge of construction complaining about the number of old men, women, and children registered as laborers, and he realized that the recruitment officials in Malaya had used this means to make up the numbers, which otherwise would have fallen short of assigned targets.[13] Of a list of 175 laborers based on files of an ex-railway coolies association in Kelantan, 43.4 percent were children or young people between twelve and nineteen years of age.[14] Similarly, among 104 people I interviewed, 40 percent were children between ten and eighteen years of age. Mohsa bin Jusoh was twelve years old and had been taking care of his mother. One night the village head came to his house accompanied by a Japanese soldier and ordered him to go to Thailand.[15] Daud bin Abdullah worked on a rubber estate. One day, Japanese soldiers came to collect laborers, and the office clerk chose Daud. He was 12 years old and an only child, so his parents decided to go with him. Both died in Thailand.[16]

The "Summary of Examination" produced in connections with war crimes interrogations of Yamamoto Kimio, a captain with the Fourth Special Railway Headquarters, who was imprisoned at Bangkwang Jail in Bangkok, includes the following comment about the wages paid coolies from Malaya and Java:

> The women and children received a little less. This came into effect in about November 1944. For long term service, for those who were on the BURMA–SIAM railway from March 31st 1944, a special allowance was paid. From March 1945 these coolies were paid 5 ticals a month. The women received 4 ticals a month. Children from 12–16 received 3 ticals. Children under 12 received 2 ticals.

Yamamoto's statement shows that there were enough children working on the railway for the Japanese to create special regulations for their pay.

Forced Labor

Faced with a shortage of job applicants, the Gunseikanbu was soon obliged to use a strict quota system to obtain the 100,000 laborers demanded by the Southern Army. As a first step, officials ordered each plantation and district to supply a certain number of laborers. Plantations were the easiest targets. Among 76 people from various plantations I interviewed, 2 voluntarily joined a group of people sent to Thailand from their plantations, 29 were ordered or forced to go to Thailand by *kerani* (estate clerks), supervisors, or officers from the Labor Department, 3 accompanied their families, and 41 were forced to go by Japanese soldiers who came to the plantations. The *kerani,* often accompanied by Japanese soldiers and local police officers, went from house to house to select laborers, promising that they could return home after three months. Japanese soldiers also carried out raids on plantations, seizing workers and loading them onto trucks. One night Devarayan s/o Hookan, for example, was sleeping outside his house. A noise awakened him around two o'clock in the morning, and he found that Japanese soldiers had surrounded the living quarters on the plantation. Many young people ran away, but he was caught by soldiers and loaded onto a truck. A total of 26 people from the plantation were sent to Thailand from Kuala Lumpur.[17]

Major General Fujimura Masuzo summarized the labor problem of the military administration in Malaya as follows:

> In July 1943 we were ordered to supply 100,000 laborers to accelerate the construction of the Burma–Siam Railway. To supply 100,000 laborers at that time, we had to take workers away from the delivery of important defense resources which Japanese companies had started here. We explained the situation to the Southern Army and begged them to reconsider. But owing to repeated orders from them we were compelled to recruit laborers forcibly. As a result we regrettably gained a bad reputation.[18]

Recruitment of labor by force involved press gang methods. Free motion picture shows were advertised, and when the theater was full the doors were locked and all adult males seized and placed on trains bound north.[19] The Japanese also collected laborers in similar fashion from streets, houses, shops, and amusement parks: a group of 18 Chinese people that I interviewed in Johor in 1991 were all taken in this way. Many people were kidnapped and taken to Burma or Thailand without even being allowed to bid farewell to their families.

Mooniandy Ramasamy was one of those kidnapped:

> I was working on Kuala Selangor Estate. One day I was walking along the road toward Bukit Rotan near my house. A Japanese military lorry stopped, and the soldiers said something to me in Japanese. I could not understand them. The soldiers forced me to get into the lorry. There were already thirty other people there. I was wearing only a pair of shorts and sandals. I begged them to let me go home to put on a proper shirt and pick up a blanket. The Japanese soldiers did not allow me to go home; instead they sent me directly to Kuala Lumpur and loaded me onto a freight train for Siam. There we started by cutting dense jungle. The Japanese did not give me a proper shirt or blanket for seven months. I had to work in the jungle and sleep on the bamboo floor in a hut, half naked and without any blanket.[20]

Haji Mohamad Yusoff bin Yassin, aged 16, was walking along Jalan Besar in Seremban when a Japanese truck suddenly stopped and soldiers forced him to get into the vehicle. There were about 10 people in the lorry. They took him to the railway station and he was sent directly to Thailand in a boxcar. After a year he escaped from the camp. Walking barefoot through the jungle, stopping and working in villages along the way, he eventually reached home.[21]

Asian Laborers Working on the Railway

Robert Hardie, who worked on the Thailand–Burma railway as a POW, mentioned Asian coolies in his diary, written in Takanun, Thailand.

> A lot of Tamil, Chinese and Malay laborers from Malaya have been brought up forcibly to work on the railway. They were told that they were going to Alor Star in northern Malaya; that conditions would be good—light work, good food and good quarters. Once on the trains, however, they were kept under guard and brought right up to Siam and marched in droves up to the camps on the river. There must be many thousands of these unfortunates all along the railway course. There is a big camp a few kilometres below here, and another two or three kilometres up. We hear of the frightful casualties from cholera and other diseases among these people, and of the brutality with which they are treated by the Japanese. People who have been near these camps speak with bated breath of the state of affairs—corpses rotting unburied in the jungle, almost complete lack of sanitation, a frightful stench, overcrowding, swarms of flies. There is no medical attention in these camps, and the wretched natives are of course unable to organize communal sanitation. (July 3, 1943)[22]

After a long trip in boxcars to Banpong, laborers walked about 1 mile from the station to the first staging camp, where they underwent a medical check. Ikeda Shoichiro was in charge of medical inspections for laborers at Banpong, and he and other Japanese officers based at a quarantine station in a Buddhist temple used to give laborers several different vaccinations, including one against cholera, and to examine their feces. Detailed lists of laborers were kept, recording their names, domiciles, and guarantors, and the names of persons who would receive payment if the laborers died. Every man got a registration number, but women and children often went unrecorded.

The workers then started a long trip into the jungle to working camps. Accommodation in the camps was poor: the huts had bamboo floors and thatched roofs, and all were overcrowded, with the occupants sleeping in spaces less than two feet wide. The roof provided little protection against the rain. During the rainy season the huts became a filthy morass.

The railway regiment failed to provide enough hospitals, doctors, and medicine. A report on Tamil laborers' conditions mentioned that there were only two hospitals in Kanchanaburi, the largest construction site town. In the larger hospital there were about 4,000 patients, with four or five doctors (Indians and Malays) and 40 to 50 hospital attendants. The other hospital had 3,000 patients and only one or two Japanese doctors who did nothing to assist the poorly trained staff. The patients were suffering from malaria, dysentery, beriberi, wounds received in accidents while working on the line, and tropical ulcers, and they complained that neither clothing nor medicine was provided. The food in the hospital, consisting of rice, vegetables, and a small quantity of fish, could at best be described as barely sufficient. There were many complaints that the water supply, even for drinking, was inadequate. For months no water was available for washing purposes.

If the conditions and medical treatment were poor in the hospital, things were worse in the camps, where medication for laborers was almost nonexistent.[23] The following quotation is from Lieutenant Colonel Sugiyama:

> In February 1943, during the most important period when alterations to the various plans were to be made in accordance with the shortened opening date of the railway, the commandant, Major General Shimoda went missing due to a plane mishap [he was later confirmed as dead]. And although his successor, Major General Takasaki, possessed much experience in railway affairs and was also a man of action, he was taken ill soon after his arrival to his post and was unable to devote his whole ability in his work. [He later died in Malaya.] These events no doubt, had much influence on the labor service. Moreover, the same could be said of the absence of a

certain capable sanitation unit commander at this important period, because of a plane accident. He had been newly appointed to take up and control sanitation affairs during the construction, especially in providing full measures against the spread of epidemic.[24]

In May 1943 cholera broke out along the line in Burma. According to the report of regimental headquarters of the Ninth Railway Regiment, there were major outbreaks in Thailand, at Takanun in the latter part of May 1943, and at the Malay labor camp at 125 kilometers in early June 1943, but the disease spread to other camps along the line. The fear of cholera caused panic among POWs, laborers, and even Japanese army personnel.[25] The laborers in the area were so terrified that both healthy and infected workers fled the camps. The fear spread to newly arrived laborers, who deserted on their way to the work sites. The epidemic began at the onset of the monsoon season, and the long spells of rain added to the misery.[26]

Those infected with cholera were isolated from the camps and abandoned with little or no medical treatment; they were simply left to die. It is impossible to know how many perished, but there are estimates of the death toll. One source says there were about 10,000 deaths,[27] while the Japanese medical authorities of the Ninth Railway Regiment estimated 6,800 dead.[28] Rarjana s/o Kyobolo recalls that many laborers died in his camp, known as Nieke. The Australian POWs dug huge holes to be used as mass graves. Every morning dead bodies were tossed into the hole and covered with a little soil. The next morning those who had died in the night were thrown in and covered. This continued until the hole was full of bodies. Then they closed the grave, but the covering of soil was very thin, however, and limbs sometimes stuck out.[29]

Kawase Hiromichi was part of an investigation team sent by the Gunseikanbu in Rangoon, Burma, to travel along the railway and assess the prospects for completing the whole line by the end of August 1943. Conditions were miserable in the laborers' camps he saw. Some huts had no roofing despite the heavy rain, as there was a shortage of roofing material.[30]

> I entered Thailand via Rangoon and Thanbyuzayat to investigate conditions in the camps and the progress of construction. My first impression was of the ghastly rain, and that the Japanese who were working there did not have any knowledge about the rainy season. Among the laborers including the POWs and coolies only 10 to 15 percent of them could work. The rest were sick. Cholera and plague had spread but there was no medicine. We sent a report to the Southern Army Headquarters saying it was impossible to complete the construction by the end of August.[31]

The problems in the coolie camps were not an inevitable consequence of the environment. Their conditions seem to have been much worse than those in the POW camps, where workers remained subject to the prisoners' own internal military structure, with their own organization and discipline. In addition, the POWs had their own medical officers. All these elements were lacking in the coolie camps occupied by Asian laborers. A group of 214 so-called overseers in principle had some jurisdiction over the camps, but military officers had authority to submit formal complaints, or negotiate to improve conditions, and the overseers did not. The Asian laborers' ignorance of hygiene served to accelerate the spread of disease, especially when the epidemics started, and they had to depend entirely on the poor facilities of the Japanese railway regiment when they required medical attention.

The quantity and quality of food provided varied from place to place. Amar Singh investigated Tamil labor camp conditions in July 1944 in his capacity as secretary of the Social Welfare and Public Health Department of the Indian Independence League's headquarters in Bangkok. He was accompanied by Dr. P.K. Poduval, Swamy Kalasam, Narain, and three Japanese, a Captain Terajima attached to the Hikari Kikan and two journalists.[32] He found that rations in Kanchanaburi approximated the standards set by the labor office, but in the interior the situation was very different, with workers getting small portions of rice, very poor vegetables, and no fish.

According to a 1943 report by P.V. Maegarry, there were about 3,000 laborers, including Tamils, Eurasians, and Malays, in Tonchang camp. Their diet was "rice and vegetable water—morning and evening." The sick received no food and no pay.[33] In the coolie camp at kilometer 228 in Thailand, coolies ate "poor quality rice and small amounts of vegetables (such as dried spinach and potatoes)."[34] A report by U Aung Hin contains a short description of food in the coolie camps during the construction of the railway. He wrote, "the food the coolies were given consisted mainly of rice supplemented by a few vegetables, cooking oil, meat or dried fish. Sometimes only rice and vegetables were available and many reports came in of the quantity supplied being far short of that required."[35] Many people I interviewed complained about the quantity and quality of food. A few Tamil laborers said there was a lot of rice and others said the rice they ate in Thailand was better quality than the rice they had eaten in Malaya. Simmasalam told me that meals supplied by the Japanese army were basically a kind of rice and vegetable soup. They had enough rice and sometimes dry fish. He spent all his money buying fried noodles and tobacco.[36] The camps far away from the town usually suffered food shortages, especially during the rainy season. When and if Asian laborers received their wages, they often spent the money on additional food bought from Thai peddlers, such as bananas, noodles,

Table 13.3

Ninth Railway Regiment: Reported Diets Provided to Railway Laborers

Ingredient	Quantity according to Ninth Railway Regiment report (grams)	Quantity according to 1944 specifications (grams)
Polished rice/Main foods	800	550
Meat	150	50
Fresh rations/Vegetables	500	400
Salt	30	20
Sugar	5	20
Cooking oil/Fats	0.07	25
Spices/Seasoning	5	20
Tea	3	5

Source: "Labor Condition and Coolie Medical Treatment in Burma under the Ninth Railway Regiment in Post-Construction Period" (submitted by the Ninth Railway Regiment), WO325/57, Document N.

fried rice, eggs, peanuts, palm sugar, *samsu* (alcohol), tobacco, opium, and cakes. In comparison with the POWs, the rate of survival of the Asian laborers was generally much lower. The survival rate was better for some Tamil laborers who formed groups of 20–25 people, often all from the same plantation. In such cases, the members of the group knew each other and were able to work together. One group managed to stay together through the whole construction period. They assigned one person to act as cook, and enjoyed relatively decent Indian-style food. They also learned how to treat tropical ulcers. As a result, 25 of the 27 people survived to return to the plantation in Malaya. This sort of organization and discipline was necessary to survive.

The figures reported by the Ninth Railway Regiment to the Allied powers who investigated them after the war are shown in Table 13.3, along with a second set of figures, which may be closer to reality, that appear in a Japanese document dated September 1, 1944, entitled "Notification for Agreement Concerning Treatment of POWs Detached for Labor."

The railway regiment had plans to provide proper rations for laborers, but faced many obstacles. In the early stages of construction, poor transportation caused the food supply to deteriorate. Camps were spread along the route of the railway, and it was often difficult to obtain supplies, particularly during the rainy seasons when roads flooded and bridges were washed away. An Allied report adds, "It is also certain that many Japanese gunzoku (civilian employees) made quite a good deal of money on the sale of whatever supplies they could lay their hands on. These things are common knowledge but it is very difficult again to make specific charges against individuals."[37]

The End of the War

The Thailand–Burma railway was completed on October 25, 1943, when the two lengths of track, which started from Nong Pladok in Thailand and Thanbyuzayat in Burma, were finally joined together at Konkuita. The construction period, calculated from the beginning of the official surveys, lasted almost 470 days. The railway immediately became the target of air raids by the Allies, but Japanese engineers used Asian and POW laborers to repair track and rebuild bridges with incredible speed. The line transported large numbers of people, including Japanese soldiers, Indian National Army soldiers in the Imphal campaign in Burma, and the Japanese military sex slaves. Bill Bangs, one of the POWs in Nong Pladuk Camp, saw them. "A train with Japanese 'comfort girls' on the way to Burma stayed the night in Nong Pladuk and they went to the water pipes and bathed naked. The wire fence overlooking the water pipes was soon crowded with British other ranks [enlisted men] who had never seen anything like this."[38]

Asian laborers learned of the end of the war in various ways. Dato Abu Kassim bin Haji Mohamad heard the news in Kin Sayok. He saw a Japanese captain crying and soldiers wildly slashing the trunks of banana trees in grief.[39] Kannu knew the war had ended when the POWs came out of their camps and made a noisy commotion. Airplanes flew overhead and dropped food and medicine. "White men took it all, however, and gave the laborers nothing."[40] Sitaram s/o Johan found out about the Japanese surrender when Japanese soldiers burned all the papers in the camp.[41] Devanayagam s/o Perumal heard the news from white soldiers. He said Japanese soldiers in the camp were drinking, singing, and crying.[42] Seenivasan s/o Kuppan said that right after the war Indian soldiers descended by parachute and asked many questions about labor conditions along the railway and other matters, in Tamil. Japanese officers apologized to the laborers.[43] Sunnasamy s/o Ganapathy was told one day by a Japanese officer that he did not need to work. Then two Indian soldiers and two white men arrived by train. They told the laborers that Japan had surrendered but warned them not to attack the Japanese.[44] Subramaniam s/o Sinnakannoo heard of Japan's surrender from Japanese officers. That night the soldiers cooked white rice and vegetable curry for the Tamil laborers. He felt something very special had happened.[45]

When the Japanese soldiers were disbanded and interned in the POW camps, repatriation of the laborers became the responsibility of the British Military Administration. Immediately after the war, Noel Ross, who was in the Malayan Civil Service (MCS), along with another MCS officer who

was in Chinese affairs and a Tamil-speaking officer from the Labor Department, accompanied Lieutenant Colonel James of the Selangor Battalion of
the Federated Malay States Volunteer Force and a doctor to see what could
be done to help the Malay, Chinese, and Indian laborers who had been
forced by the Japanese to work on the railway.[46] Subramaniam s/o
Sinnakannoo reported that the day after he heard of the Japanese surrender, British officers arrived at the camp. The Japanese were still there, and
they looked quite sad. The British officers asked the laborers whether they
had any complaints. Many laborers told them about the very irregular payments they received. Subramaniam s/o Sinnakannoo personally had a hard
time when he returned to Malaya because his parents and brothers reproached him for not sending them any money, although the Japanese had
not paid him the wages he was due.[47] British officers who could speak
Malay, Chinese, and Tamil asked the Asian laborers many questions about
Japanese atrocities, cruelty, and their experiences, and some of the laborers completed questionnaires. Gradually they were sent from various camps
along the railway to Bangkok.

In September 1945, the British Military Administration was set up in
Malaya to handle the transition to civilian rule. All of the MCS officers
who were in Malaya at the fall of Singapore had been interned, and upon
their release many of them were repatriated to the United Kingdom. Because there were not enough MCS officers, Bangs, a Kelantan rubber planter
before the war, volunteered to work as a repatriation officer, helping RAPWI
(the organization for Recovery of Allied Prisoners of War and Internees)
return laborers to Malaya and to the Netherlands East Indies. He had employed many Malays on his plantation before the war and could speak the
language, and he now began to assemble Malays and people from Sumatra
who had drifted to Bangkok. Bangs remained in Thailand until May 1946,
when he took the boat carrying the last remaining Malays, Indians, Chinese, and Sumatrans to Singapore and Penang.[48]

The British Military Administration (BMA) in Malaya reported in January 1946 that two ships had begun the task of bringing displaced Malayans
home from the Kanburi area, and that 2,000 persons had returned during
January. The BMA planned to increase that figure to 3,500 per month.[49]
When the Asian laborers were sent back to Singapore or Penang, some of
them received money, usually between 10 and 50 dollars, and some rice,
sugar, blankets, or shirts, but many laborers received nothing at all. Possibly they did not register with RAPWI, or returned to Malaya on their own,
or were repatriated before the Japanese surrender or after the last boat left
Bangkok. Some workers did not return to Malaya, opting to spend the rest
of their lives in Thailand.

Conclusion

From its inception, the construction plan for the Thailand–Burma railway was almost impossible to realize, in terms of finance, the time necessary for completion, labor force, medical facilities, food, clothing, transportation, and all other aspects. The order was issued at the imperial headquarters in Tokyo, where nobody had sufficient knowledge of conditions in the jungles of Thailand. In the Japanese army, orders were absolute and unquestioned, deriving their authority from the emperor, who was the sovereign and supreme commander of the armed forces. Once an order was issued, Japanese soldiers sought to carry it out irrespective of the cost. After the war, the Japanese soldiers and Korean prison guards involved in the construction of the Thailand–Burma railway were accused of inhuman and cruel treatment of Asian laborers and POWs: eighteen of them were executed, and thirty-three sentenced to life or long-term imprisonment. This contrasts sharply with the Tokyo war crimes trial, where seven people were sentenced to death to take responsibility for the whole war. The emperor was never put on trial.

The tragedy of the Thailand–Burma railway was caused by general indifference in the Japanese army to logistics, and a fanatic spiritualism and racial prejudice against other Asians. Those responsible for the railway did not have time to make detailed plans concerning individual laborers' working hours, quantity of work, food supply, materials for accommodation, medical support, wages, welfare, and so on. They treated laborers cruelly and irrationally, much as they themselves were treated in the Japanese army. After the war, Japanese soldiers were held individually responsible, but it was, in many cases, beyond their individual power and ability to act differently.

Today 12,043 Allied soldiers are buried in cemeteries in Kanchanaburi, Thailand. The gravestones seem to stretch on forever. However, there are no cemeteries, and no individual gravestones, for the Asian laborers who died building the railway. They were buried if they were fortunate, or else abandoned in the jungle, or thrown into the river or into a common grave. In 1988, the site of a mass grave was found in Kanchanaburi by accident, and the bones of more than 700 bodies were excavated. Villagers said it was a burial site used for the Asian railway construction laborers.

Part VIII

Philippines

14

Labor Usage and Mobilization during the Japanese Occupation of the Philippines, 1942–45

Ricardo T. Jose

Throughout the territories they occupied during World War II, the Japanese mobilized large numbers of workers for military-related projects carried out by army and navy units in the field and by Japanese development companies. In the Philippines their preferred approach was to make Filipinos in the Executive Commission (1942–43) and then in the new Philippine Republic (1943–44) responsible for labor recruitment. Before the war, Philippine labor had become powerful and well organized, with active trade unions and a strong awareness of labor rights, but Japan's labor policies sharply curtailed workers' rights, and for this reason were met with suspicion if not outright opposition. The government of the Philippine Republic, under President Jose P. Laurel, tried to ensure that workers were treated well and received acceptable rates of pay, but despite having given nominal sovereignty to the Philippines, the Japanese frequently ignored these efforts. As Allied forces pushed toward the Philippines, Japanese demands for labor increased sharply, but few Filipinos responded to recruitment efforts because it was known that working conditions were very poor and the Japanese often did not live up to their promises. In the end the Japanese resorted to forced labor to obtain the manpower they needed.

Philippine Labor before World War II

Philippine labor conditions in the immediate prewar years varied greatly, depending on the type of work and place of employment. Labor unions had been organized during the American colonial administration, and these organizations worked to achieve better wages, regular working hours, a greater percentage of crops, and other benefits. They also fought against unfair treatment of laborers, union busting, and indiscriminate layoffs. Through strikes and protests the labor movement made some gains, securing improvements in working conditions and raising wages in certain types of jobs. When the Philippine Commonwealth Government was inaugurated in 1935, President Manuel L. Quezon pledged to protect labor and to provide fair regulations to guide the relationship between labor and capital. These provisions, he said, together with "solicitous regard" by the government for the well-being of the poor, would be the key to economic and social balance in the Philippines, which in turn would guarantee domestic peace and stability.[1]

The Commonwealth Government followed up on these promises by embarking on a social justice program to improve labor conditions and balance the needs of labor and capital. New laws set a minimum wage of 1 peso per day, fixed a standard eight-hour working day with overtime pay, and established the Court of Industrial Relations to adjudicate disputes between organized labor and management. To oversee labor affairs, the Department of Labor was organized under a secretary who held a cabinet-level appointment. The department sought to ease unemployment, mediate between labor and management, and ensure the safety of workers. However, strikes and demonstrations escalated during the Commonwealth era; in 1940 there were more than twenty major strikes in Manila, and at least eight more in 1941. In rural areas, there was also considerable dissatisfaction. The Commonwealth set up agricultural banks for peasant farmers, and encouraged cooperatives, but in matters such as land ownership and sharecropping arrangements, change was slow to come, and there was considerable unrest in the provinces.[2]

With the outbreak of the Sino–Japanese War in 1937, followed two years later by war in Europe, the Philippines began to experience economic difficulties as ships were diverted to war zones and demand for Philippine products declined in some markets. President Quezon sought emergency powers to deal with these developments, and the National Assembly granted his request. Among other things, these powers allowed the president to require all able-bodied citizens who had no useful occupation to engage in farming or in other productive activities, to take over farmlands, to control labor and transportation, and to prohibit strikes, commandeer ships, and requisition any public service or enterprise.[3] Critics charged Quezon with creating a dictatorship, to which he responded that what was being implemented, for a limited period, was constitutional authoritarianism.

However, Quezon hesitated to use the powers he had been given, and the situation continued to deteriorate. Legal restrictions on the international movement of commodities disrupted trade, and the shortage of cargo vessels limited the movement of crops and other products within the archipelago and left a significant volume of Philippine export goods rotting in storage. A number of public and private construction projects had to be stopped because building materials were unavailable, and the freezing of Japanese assets by the United States in July 1941 stopped exports of iron ore to Japan. Unemployment rose in affected areas, and life became harder for people in the countryside. Mobilization of the army and an increase in defense construction works absorbed some of the jobless but did not solve the unemployment problem.[4]

In April 1941 Quezon created the Civilian Emergency Administration (CEA) "to safeguard the integrity of the Philippines and to insure the tranquility of its inhabitants." The CEA was an interagency organization created to overcome bureaucratic obstacles to the Philippine effort to become self-sufficient and otherwise to deal with difficulties arising from the war. Its responsibilities included evacuating civilians, stockpiling food, increasing food production, and mobilizing industries to achieve self-sufficiency. Although the CEA's goals were broad and far-reaching, progress was slow and the country remained on a peacetime footing even as the threat of war became more real. Military and civilian plans were neither coordinated nor integrated, leading to confusion when war did break out.[5]

The CEA created the Labor Coordination Office, which mobilized laborers to plant gardens and carry out defense-related construction. The Secretary of Labor, Leon Guinto, became the CEA's labor administrator, and he enlisted labor leader Faustino Aguilar to organize battalions of workers and deal with the related administration. These units were formed in Manila, Rizal, Bulacan, Tarlac, Cavite, Laguna, and Pampanga in connection with defense projects.[6]

In October 1941 a delegation from the National Commission of Labor, a nongovernmental umbrella organization acting on the behalf of organized labor and peasantry in the Philippines, conferred with General Douglas MacArthur, commander of military forces in the Philippines, seeking to clarify the role that workers would play in the event of war. The representatives of labor and the peasantry made a solemn pledge to rally under the banner of the democracies and give the United States and the Philippine armed forces all possible assistance in case of a war against the Axis powers. However, coordination between the CEA and the military was poor,[7] and when war broke out on December 8, 1941, the inadequacy of the government's labor mobilization arrangements was all too evident. Quezon used his emergency powers to order the CEA food administrator to take over farmlands, and to require unemployed but able-bodied persons to engage in farming and other productive activities to prevent a shortage of food. With the war already under way, the food administrator had to draw up rules and regulations to carry out Quezon's orders. Labor and farmer battalions organized under the Labor Coordination Office tried to harvest rice and other crops abandoned by their owners, and to plant short-term crops on idle land. However, they found it difficult to obtain tools, and ran into bureaucratic obstacles, for example, in trying to obtain authorization to plant crops on playgrounds and other city land. Before the work could progress very far, Japanese forces landed in the Philippines.[8] With the coming of the Japanese, President Quezon and key members of his administration moved to Corregidor, and the president later evacuated to the United States to serve as head of a government in exile. The CEA ceased operations, and its labor mobilization plans were abandoned.

Labor under the Japanese Military Administration, 1942–43

Japanese forces entered Manila on January 2, 1942, and immediately set up the Japanese Military Administration (JMA). Largely operating through existing administrative structures, the JMA had three immediate objectives: restoring peace, acquiring resources needed for Japan's war effort, and achieving self-sufficiency for the army in the occupied territories.[9] Labor mobilization was essential for all of these goals, but the new administration did not have a department of labor, and a number of departments— including General Affairs, Interior, Industry, and Public Works—became involved in labor affairs.

In January 1942 the JMA ordered the immediate reopening of match, rope, and cement factories, coconut oil refineries, and other stores and factories that could provide employment and ensure the supply of basic commodities to meet the needs of the Japanese military and local residents.[10] As the Japanese consolidated their power, and particularly after organized military resistance ended in May 1942, they began putting into place longer-range economic plans to reorient the Philippine economy in line with the Greater East Asia Co-prosperity Sphere, a grandiose but ill-conceived plan to unite all of Asia in a single economic unit, to which the Philippines contribution was to be cotton, abaca, copper, manganese, and the like. However, short-term needs were rice, wooden ships, and alternative fuels for the Japanese and Filipinos, especially since Japanese shipping was insufficient to tie the sphere together. Some rice was imported from Thailand, and some cotton looms were brought in, but hardly any other imports appear to have reached the Philippines. Accordingly, Philippine agriculture was directed toward achieving self-sufficiency in food, as opposed to the prewar colonial policy of emphasizing export products such as sugar, and a massive nationwide food production campaign was launched in May 1942. The United States had been the major purchaser of Philippine sugar, and the loss of this market left the sugar industry with excess capacity. Japan's agricultural program called for planting unused sugar land with food crops, or with cotton, another strategic commodity in short supply. Some of the sugar that continued to be produced was to be used to make industrial products, such as alcohol and butanol. Abaca would continue to be grown in Mindanao, and coconuts harvested for coconut oil and other purposes. Mines yielding ores directly needed by the Japanese war industry—such as copper, chromium and manganese—continued to operate, and the ore was sent to Japan, but other facilities, such as the gold mines in northern Luzon, were shut down and the machinery transferred to the functioning mines. The Philippine fishing industry was to be developed under Japanese tutelage. The Japanese considered the industrial situation in the Philippines very poor and overly dependent on the United States. The country's limited machine industry and shipbuilding facilities were to be expanded under Japanese control, but needed munitions and chemical facilities were completely lacking. The Japanese planned to reconstruct the country's light industries, and took over the operation of all major facilities (machine industry, alcohol, cotton spinning mills, newspaper printing, oil refineries, and the like). In late 1942, a program was launched to build wooden ships suitable for interisland transport.[11]

Recruitment of Labor

The JMA acquired Filipino labor in two ways. The first, used for jobs of strategic importance, was direct hiring by the army, which ran some extraction and manufacturing operations itself, or by private Japanese companies operating in the Philippines. Direct recruitment took place in connection with mines, factories producing war-related materials, shipyards, and army-managed farms growing cotton or the new *horai* rice from Taiwan.

The second approach was to send requests for labor through the Philippine Executive Commission (EC), established by the JMA on January 23, 1942, to handle routine administration and assist the JMA in various ways. The head of the commission, Jorge B. Vargas, was bluntly told that his task was to maintain peace and order, control and regulate the movement of goods out of and into Greater Manila, arrange for the surrender of all firearms and ammunition, carry out relief activities, and secure access to labor, materials, and other resources as well as various installations and facilities needed by the Japanese. He also had to help bring Japanese directors and experts in administration into government departments. The Japanese, for their part, promised to recognize the status and authority of Filipino officials, protect life and property, guarantee freedom of worship, and recognize "existing laws and orders, as well as customs and usages, excepting those incompatible with the new situation."[12]

The EC, like the JMA, had no specific office for labor affairs, which were subsumed under the Bureau of Public Welfare, itself part of the Department of Education, Health and Public Welfare headed by Claro M. Recto. The Director of Public Welfare was Hilario Lara.[13] Operating through the EC, the JMA created two institutions to facilitate labor mobilization. One was a system of district and neighborhood associations used in Japan proper and throughout its colonial empire. These associations handled the rationing of food and basic commodities, provided a way to check on anti-Japanese activity, and later became a channel for recruiting labor. The second institution was the Kapisanan sa Paglilingkod sa Bagong Pilipinas (Kalibapi, the Association for Service for the New Philippines), a nationwide organization modeled on the Imperial Rule Assistance Association (*Taisei Yokusankai*) that provided crowds of people to attend pro-Japanese rallies, and later was used to recruit forced labor.[14]

During the battles of 1941–42, combat units hired any laborers they could find to repair roads and bridges needed for military operations. The EC handled labor recruitment for other projects, working through local government and the Department of Public Works and Communications. It mobilized Filipino workers to reconstruct roads and bridges, repair railroads and communications facilities, salvage ships, and so on. The JMA funded these operations, but workers often had to bring their own food, bedding, and tools.[15]

One major source of labor was prisoners of war (POWs) captured after the surrender of the U.S.–Philippine defense forces in 1942. The release of Filipino POWs began in July 1942, and after their release many POWs faced a difficult situation because jobs were scarce and many were far from home and had no family support. The Bureau of Public Welfare of the EC and civic agencies such as the YMCA cared for as many of the former POWs as their resources would allow, and placed ads in the newspapers seeking work for them.[16]

An agricultural reservation in Los Baños became a recuperation camp and farm for some POWs, and others were pressed into service in mining and other strategic industries. For example, when the Taiheiyo Kogyo (Pacific Mining Company) was unsuccessful in its efforts to recruit laborers for a manganese mine in Bani, Camarines Sur, its managers petitioned the JMA for Filipino POW labor, and were allowed to go to a POW camp and select the men they needed. Other mines also used POW labor.[17]

Labor Control

The JMA issued rules governing wages, hours, and working conditions, and set up associations to enforce these regulations and facilitate control. Rules setting minimum wages and maximum working hours were suspended, and a system of forced savings was put into effect, effectively reducing laborers' take-home pay. The pension system was abolished. The minimum pay for those in government service was set at 300 pesos a year (lower than before the war), later increased to 360 pesos a year for employees who were the sole supporter of a family. No minimum rates were set for nongovernment labor, although the Japanese recommended 80 centavos as the basic daily wage for unskilled workers. There was, however, a maximum rate. The suspension of the law limiting maximum working hours meant that workers could be made to complete longer workdays without receiving overtime pay, and with the unions abolished the laborers had no effective recourse. The JMA later introduced wage differentials for government employees, and suggested that private companies in Manila pay fair wages and bonuses to increase productivity, but these suggestions had little effect.[18]

The JMA created various associations for labor according to trade. For example, rice and cotton growers, mine operators, fishermen, seamen, retailers, and makers of matches and oils were all organized in this way. Skilled workers such as ship carpenters had to register with the JMA, as did all labor contractors, who also had to join an association approved by the JMA. In September 1943, the Central Labor Association (*Chūō Rōmu Kumiai*) was set up to "reorganize, adjust, supply, and control labor for war requirements and other industrial activity." All Japanese and Filipino laborers were "enjoined to affiliate with the association for the realization of this order."[19]

The Japanese army and navy secured indirect control of existing industrial plants by entrusting their management to Japanese firms, with the JMA giving directions concerning products to be manufactured and their disposition as well as the employee lists and salary schedules. Monthly reports on labor, expenses, and production had to be submitted to the JMA. Among the businesses taken over were major companies owned by the government before the war, such as the National Abaca and Other Fibers Corporation and the National Development Company.[20]

Reorientation of Labor through Educational Institutions

Inculcating a love of labor became a major goal of the school system, and was one of six basic educational principles promoted by the JMA. Aside from strengthening practical training in schools, the Japanese established specialized schools and institutes to retrain and reorient workers in both the government and private sectors. For example, the Government Employees Training Institute inaugurated in October 1942 was designed to "rejuvenate the employees spiritually, morally and physically" and instill in them the spirit of reconstruction of the new Philippines as a member of the Greater East Asia Co-prosperity Sphere. Classes continued through 1943.[21]

The Kalibapi opened a Worker's Institute in May 1943. In addition to vocational training, the institute offered courses in Japanese, the Filipino national language, Asian and Filipino culture, and other subjects intended to help students imbibe "traditional Oriental values" and become more loyal and efficient workers. The course lasted for one month, and by October a total of 1,533 persons had gone through the program, but its impact cannot be determined.[22]

Other schools and training institutes included an agricultural high school established in Manila in December 1942, and the Philippine Mariners' Training Institute inaugurated in September 1943 to train crews to man the wooden ships being built. Free instruction was offered to train mechanics to work in Japanese companies, and even POWs received special instruction in various trades.[23]

Unemployment

At the start of the occupation, there was serious unemployment in urban areas of the Philippines. The downsizing of the government, along with the closure of banks and companies owned by American and other hostile aliens, and of many schools, left large numbers of people without work, and the release of POWs swelled the labor force even further. In rural areas the occupation brought a deterioration of peace and order as well as growing unemployment, and people from the provinces migrated to the cities for safety and the lure of easy money only to find themselves without jobs. Manila developed a large "floating population" without stable jobs or fixed residences.[24]

Unemployment was recognized as a problem by the JMA as early as February 1942, when it ordered the EC to create the Employment Office for Greater Manila, which created a registry of unemployed workers.[25] In October the JMA set up the Government Civilian Liaison Office to help place those seeking work. Headed by a long-time Japanese resident of Manila, the office was able to find jobs for laborers but could do little to assist people in the professions or other white-collar workers.[26]

The JMA held a number of conferences to discuss this issue. One stop-gap measure was not to use machines in reconstruction work, in order to create more jobs. However, both the JMA and the EC recognized that more lasting solutions had to be found, since large numbers of unemployed workers would hamper the return of normalcy. Vargas suggested expanding public works projects, reopening more offices and factories, encouraging home industries, and bringing machines from Japan to manufacture goods for local use and for export.[27]

In January 1943, the EC, with JMA approval, created the Bureau of Employment under the Commissioner of the Interior. The bureau was meant to promote the "physical, material, and spiritual improvement of the working classes of the Philippines," and to remove any conflicts between laborers and employers by acting as an arbitrator between the two sides.[28] Emiliano Tria Tirona, appointed Director of Employment soon after the bureau was created, had a wide range of duties, among them monitoring the numbers of laborers (employed and unemployed) in the various provinces, taking steps to secure the safety and health of laborers, helping laborers secure employment and just compensation, and trying to control the movement of laborers to avoid overcrowding in some provinces and depletion of the workforce in others. Local governments carried out the policies of the bureau with the assistance of labor administrators, who prepared registers of workers and inspected workplaces to ensure safe working conditions and fair wages.[29]

Vargas also created the Advisory Board of Labor in March 1943 in recognition of "the important role labor plays in the social and economic rehabilitation of the Philippines," and the complexity of problems relating to labor and unemployment. This body was to study the labor situation and recommend to the Commissioner of the Interior, who had administrative supervision over the Bureau of Employment, ways and means of solving labor and unemployment problems.[30]

An editorial in the Japanese-controlled English newspaper the *Tribune* explained in March 1943 that before the war there had been efforts to make labor a factor in political affairs. The Japanese approach, it said, would "invigorate the Filipino workingman, inculcate in him the dignity of manual work, and make the nation virile and strong. . . . The resurgence of Philippine labor as a vital factor in the national economic scheme is foreseen as the eventual result of the constructive and sound policies adopted by the Japanese Military Administration with regard to labor affairs."[31] Japanese commentators on Philippine affairs before the war had looked with disfavor on the role of the labor unions, and the JMA dissolved all unions and political parties within one year of the start of the occupation. In place of a confrontational relationship between labor and management, the Japanese said they would raise the status of manual laborers to that of white-collar workers and professionals.[32]

One observer noted that attempts by the Bureau of Employment and the Japanese to make Filipinos appreciate labor failed. Those efforts "did not encourage even the hungry to love manual labor, for they saw nothing in manual labor that would improve their standard of living: the more they worked, the less they ate. The result was undernourishment and malnutrition and death from various diseases."[33]

Relief Efforts

The Bureau of Public Welfare had the task of providing relief to the unemployed, as well as to abandoned wives and children, the indigent, and people
adversely affected by the war. Prior to the creation of the Bureau of Employment, it also handled the duties of the prewar Department of Labor
relating to claims for compensation, and cared for released POWs who had
no families in Manila. The bureau conducted vocational training programs
in an effort to help the people help themselves rather than depend on outright relief.[34]

Labor Conditions

The Japanese-controlled media published glowing reports on labor programs
and working conditions. Cultivators found happiness in their work and considered the farm a "farmer's paradise." Those on Japanese-administered farms
were taught modern methods under iron discipline, as in Japan. Farmers benefited from the controlled economy, and laborers appreciated their higher
position in society. By June 1942, the development and acquisition of raw
materials was so satisfactory that army requirements were almost fulfilled,
and the army was becoming self-supporting according to plan.[35]

What the reports and media did not say was that some programs did not
proceed smoothly. Efforts to grow cotton and *horai* rice failed; neither crop
thrived in the Philippine climate, and farmers—deliberately or otherwise—
did not tend them effectively. Farmers who were compelled to plant these
crops suffered severe losses for which they received no compensation.[36]

Moreover, in the absence of a minimum wage, many laborers received as
little as 40 centavos a day, and some Japanese companies paid just 30 centavos.
Government salaries were effectively cut twice in 1943. Work hours were
long, and there was little extra pay. Food, when provided, was meager. Although many factories reopened, much of their output went to Japan or was
earmarked for Japanese military use. Filipino needs were secondary, and
consumer goods were in short supply.[37] It was hard to buy basic commodities, and particularly in the later stages of the occupation Filipinos accepted
the lower wages offered by Japanese firms because they were supplemented
by issues of rice, lard, matches, and cigarettes. One writer observed, "it was
not long before the workers in the cities and towns were glad to work for a
bowl of rice or a mess of camotes [sweet potatoes]."[38]

In some areas, workers were threatened with punishment if they
did not work for the Japanese. For example, Japanese soldiers forced
residents of Polillo Island to work for the Polillo Plywood Lumber Mills.

Anyone who refused was blacklisted and placed on a wanted list. Some fled the island to escape.[39]

Labor under the Japanese-Sponsored Republic of the Philippines, 1943–44

In an effort to generate greater Filipino support, the Japanese government under Prime Minister Tōjō Hideki promised the Philippines "the honor of independence" if Filipinos cooperated more sincerely with Japan. The offer aroused Filipino suspicions, but Tōjō pushed ahead with his plan and the JMA organized a special commission of top Filipino leaders and intellectuals to frame a constitution for a Japanese-sponsored republic. Drafted under close Japanese scrutiny, the constitution was completed in September, and formal independence ceremonies took place on October 14, 1943. The nationalist political leader Jose P. Laurel was chosen to be president.

The Constitution of 1943 contained provisions on labor similar to those in the prewar constitution, including a stipulation that citizens had a duty to render personal military or civil service. It also stated that the state would protect workers, particularly women and minors, and would mediate in disputes between labor and capital in industry and agriculture.[40] Whether these provisions could be enforced while the Japanese remained in the Philippines was open to question.

Laurel's Goals and Limitations

In his inauguration speech, Laurel highlighted the importance of labor, particularly for the production of food and basic necessities, and said his administration would work to ensure that all Filipinos enjoyed the minimum requirements of civilized life. Once this had been achieved, it would proceed to develop heavy industry in the country. "The common denominator," he said, "is hard work." He also stressed the need to achieve social justice: "The slogan should no longer be live and let live, but live and help live, so that the government may bring about the happiness and well-being, if not of all, at least of the greatest number."[41]

Laurel's government was circumscribed by a pact of alliance with Japan signed on the same day the Philippine flag first flew alone. The pact decreed perpetual friendly relations with Japan along with cooperation on political, economic, and military matters in the successful prosecution of Japan's war. The attached terms of understanding were more explicit: "The Philippines will afford all kinds of facilities for the military actions to be undertaken by Japan," and "the Philippines and Japan will closely cooperate with each other to safeguard the territorial integrity and independence of the Philippines."[42]

The wording of the pact caused concern to many Filipinos, who thought it meant the Philippines would join the war on Japan's side and that conscription would be imposed. Rumors to this effect became so prevalent that Laurel issued a clarification stating that the pact was defensive and did not entail a declaration of war. He also gave assurances that no Filipino soldier would be called upon to fight for Japan in the Philippines or elsewhere, except as part of defensive actions.[43] However, the Japanese put intense pressure on Laurel to declare war against the United States and its allies, and on September 21, 1944, after U.S. planes bombed Manila for the first time since 1942, Laurel could stall no further. He declared martial law and announced the existence of a state of war with the United States, but steadfastly stood by his pledge not to allow military conscription.[44]

The Philippine Republic also had to accept a secret agreement laying down basic principles and policies for the relationship between Japan and the Philippines. This allowed Japan to maintain military establishments in the Philippines, to continue to manage the associations it had created in 1942, and to control transport, communications, mines, shipyards, and factories producing war materials.[45]

Laurel thus began his presidency hobbled by Japanese-imposed conditions. With regard to labor, three matters required immediate attention: securing relief for the poor and unemployed, mobilizing workers for food production, and addressing Japanese demands for additional labor to work on war-related projects.

The EC had been organized as a tool to implement Japanese policies, but Laurel reorganized the government to make it serve the interests of the Filipino people. He retained the Labor Advisory Board and its officials, but reorganized the departments of the EC and made them into ministries. A new Ministry of Health, Labor and Public Welfare became responsible for labor issues, and a Bureau of Labor within this ministry replaced the Bureau of Employment. Placing labor and public welfare in the same ministry would ideally generate more comprehensive plans, and the country was divided into labor districts under a special administrator who worked in coordination with local governments to provide a more systematic approach to labor problems. The districts were North Luzon, South Luzon, Western Visayas, Eastern Visayas, and Mindanao and Sulu. Emiliano Tria Tirona, who had headed the EC's Bureau of Employment, became head of the ministry, and Juan L. Lanting was named Director of Labor. Tirona, Lanting, and other government officials who studied labor issues considered that problems arose in connection with the uneven distribution of population, the seasonal character of farming, the tendency of the provincial population to move to the city, and increases in the numbers of new graduates of schools and colleges who could not find work.[46]

Relief Efforts

When Laurel took office, providing assistance to the unemployed, the poor, invalids, widows, and war orphans was an immediate problem, and the second act passed by the republic's national assembly appropriated 2 million pesos for relief work through the Bureau of Public Welfare. At the same time, the bureau attempted to find work for those who were indigent so that they would not be dependent on handouts.[47]

Conditions in Manila worsened in 1944 as inflation rose to unprecedented heights and the population swelled with people from neighboring provinces. As the food situation deteriorated, the Laurel government set up community kitchens to give free rice to the unemployed.[48] The government also took steps to depopulate Manila, encouraging people to return to their provinces, and providing them with transportation. Some government offices moved out of Manila, and the number of employees kept in the capital was cut to an irreducible minimum.[49] The Laurel government planned some agricultural settlements but these did not materialize. The central point was to depopulate the city in the quickest way at the least expense to the government. It was felt that those in Manila could go to relatives in the nearby provinces, but not everyone had this option. The Japanese looked with disfavor on the depopulation plan because it would reduce the number of laborers available for military construction projects and the movement of supplies. Moreover, it was difficult to implement the scheme because of shortages of gasoline and spare parts, and insufficient transport. The Japanese military controlled most functioning vehicles and stocks of gasoline. This was just one point where Japanese needs competed with the wishes of the Laurel administration.[50]

Laurel tried to alleviate the plight of government employees by raising salaries as much as possible and granting bonuses. The mayor of Manila, Leon Guinto, increased the daily wage of workers in Manila to 2.40 pesos a day, and in mid-1944 to 3.50 pesos a day. While these measures looked good on paper, they could not cope with the skyrocketing prices of food and basic commodities.[51]

Labor for Food Production

One cause of inflation was a severe shortage of food and other basic commodities. In November 1943, a typhoon brought heavy rains that flooded Manila and nearby provinces, destroying crops and killing livestock. The losses had a serious effect on the Filipino population, and because the Japanese military also depended on locally produced food, more food had to be produced. Laurel's government extended credit to farmers, offered training, encouraged the organization of cooperative societies, and declared November 19 Farmers Day to give due recognition and respect to cultivators.[52] These measures accomplished little, and in February 1944 the National Assembly granted Laurel emergency powers to deal with the crisis. These powers, like those granted Quezon before the war, included the authority to mobilize labor for farming or other necessary services.[53]

In the same month, Laurel used his new powers to order the recruitment of all able-bodied persons between the ages of sixteen and sixty for civilian emergency service in food production. The order called for compulsory service without pay for one day a week, and people who were unemployed could be required to serve longer. The Ministry of Agriculture and Natural Resources oversaw the program and, through local government and district and neighborhood associations, compiled lists of all those subject to being called to serve. Beyond this, seeds had to be obtained, farm lots identified and listed, and tools provided. It was a massive task but could, if all went well, overcome the food crisis. Half of the Philippines population was affected, and in addition to providing a strong boost to efforts to increase food production, the measure was viewed as a social equalizer.[54]

The order was issued in February 1944, but it was not implemented until May. Laurel called on all inhabitants of the Philippines to devote "as much time as they could spare" on productive manual labor on Labor Day, which was set for May 6,[55] and on that day Filipinos, together with Chinese, Japanese, Indians, and other residents turned out to plant food crops, led by Laurel himself. The government issued a "Laborer's Decalogue" emphasizing love of work, striving for efficiency, and living within one's means. Prizes were offered to the best farmers, and an essay contest on labor was launched. The *Tribune* reported enthusiastically on the celebrations, saying they showed that the oligarchy was gone, and that only one class of Filipino existed.[56] However, people could redeem the obligation to work by providing a substitute worker or by paying 5 pesos per day, and the well-off thus escaped manual labor.

The first full day for compulsory labor to grow food was set for May 14, after a census had been conducted and places chosen for gardens. Neighborhood associations were used to ensure participation, and the *Tribune* editorialized: "Anything compulsory becomes voluntary to those who are willing to make the necessary contribution."[57] In Manila some 300,000 people turned out for work, a large number but less than the 420,000 expected. Many of those who came had no tools, and there were none available to give them. Moreover, volunteers were not assured of obtaining any of the food they grew: some of it was earmarked for neighborhood associations, some was destined for the government, and some it was said would go to the Japanese.

Not all volunteers were assigned to food cultivation work; some built air-raid shelters or helped with Japanese military construction. All in all, the occasion was less than a complete success, and there are no reports of further mass mobilization exercises by the government.[58]

Labor for Japanese Defensive Works

As fighting approached the Philippines, the Japanese constructed airfields, air–raid shelters and defensive works on a massive scale. The Japanese military required ever-larger numbers of laborers, as well as mechanics and technicians for their airplanes and wooden ships. To attract recruits for its training programs, the JMA offered free schooling and guaranteed employment, along with free transportation; meals, housing, and daily necessities at reasonable prices; competitive wages; and various benefits. Workers could apply directly to Japanese firms or to the armed forces, or they could submit applications through the Bureau of Labor, but the response was poor.[59]

To deal with the situation, the Japanese proposed to use the same methods as in the days of the JMA and the EC to recruit labor directly in parallel with recruitment carried out through Philippine government channels. Direct hiring overrode the constitution, as the government was unable to regulate terms and conditions, but the scale of the Japanese requests was becoming so large that the Bureau of Labor could not cope with the situation, and Japanese pressure on the government was growing stronger.[60] In an effort to strike a balance between Japanese needs and Filipino rights, Laurel created the Labor Recruitment Agency (LRA) in April 1944 under the Ministry of Health, Labor and Public Welfare, following a plan submitted by Tirona. The LRA would attempt to meet Japan's labor requirements as part of the terms of the pact of alliance, despite knowing that this labor would be used for military purposes, by assigning quotas to local governments and neighborhood associations. The LRA would ensure that laborers recruited under the scheme were paid and treated well, and that working conditions were satisfactory.[61]

Pablo Manlapit was appointed Field Executive Officer of the LRA in May and immediately began recruiting workers for the Japanese. The Japanese were very pleased, and the Japanese army, navy, and development companies all submitted requests. Filipinos were expected to be happy, too—people who were unemployed would be given jobs with regular wages and food rations, along with free transportation and board, and could see their families once a week. Whenever possible, the LRA would place a worker in his own province, and transfers to another province could be done only with the consent of the worker, who would receive extra compensation. Local governments would carry out actual recruitment, and the Advisory Board on Labor, created in 1943, would assist the LRA.[62] In Manila, Mayor Guinto created a municipal committee to carry out recruitment on behalf of the LRA, and various provinces formed similar bodies to set quotas for district and neighborhood associations. Manlapit, Guinto, Tirona, and other officials personally appealed for greater participation from the Filipino people. The Japanese-controlled media quickly reported success, claiming that thousands of workers had answered the call, and were satisfied with the good treatment, wages, and benefits given them.[63]

In reality the LRA was unable to satisfy Japanese demands. The Japanese army and navy wanted more than 80,000 workers immediately, a difficult target even in peacetime, and made harder in wartime by a lack of accurate labor statistics, inadequate transportation, and poor communications.[64] But the central problem lay in the reluctance of Filipinos to respond to the Japanese appeal. First, many of the jobs involved work on airfields and defensive works, which would only aid the Japanese in fighting against the United States, and prolong the war and occupation.[65] Moreover, working conditions were known to be poor: past promises of adequate wages, food, and good treatment had often not been fulfilled, and the Japanese subjected workers to corporal punishment for not working hard enough or failing to understand orders. When the Japanese were unable to find persons responsible for minor or perceived infractions, they sometimes punished innocent parties. At one point, laborers in the San Miguel Brewery threatened to strike when one of them was falsely accused and maltreated by the Japanese. Conditions became so serious that one of the resolutions adopted in the First Annual Visayan Convention, in April 1944, was that no Filipino should be subjected to corporal punishment while in the employ of companies of whatever nationality.[66] Workers also feared that they would be forced to go to distant places or even overseas, as had happened in the past. For example, a group of laborers from Tayabas (now Quezon) that was supposed to be brought to Manila was sent instead to Davao, on the south coast of Mindanao. In Tarlac, 20 men were recruited and taken to Davao, and only 5 returned. In Leyte when a group of men was forced to board a ship, several jumped overboard and were drowned. It was not uncommon for laborers to die en route to or at their places of work, without their families knowing where they were or what had happened to them. The end result was that few Filipinos wanted to work for the Japanese. They hid from the recruiting officials or escaped to the mountains. If forced to work, some fled, risking death in the process.[67]

The seriousness of the labor shortage resulted in the mobilization of Japanese civilians in the Philippines for war work. Many Japanese residents worked for the army, but more were needed—for intelligence, for munitions plants, and for the construction of military installations. Relatively unimportant

Japanese enterprises in Manila, such as restaurants, barbershops, and stores selling miscellaneous goods, were scaled down or closed, and some factories that were having difficulty operating for want of fuel and raw materials were forced to halt operations. The Japanese who formerly worked for these enterprises were assigned to food production, manufacturing, and other war-related activities.[68]

After Laurel declared martial law in September 1944, the pressure to provide Filipino labor to support Japanese forces grew still more intense. The Japanese threatened to introduce direct conscription, and prepared a draft proclamation that would allow them to do so. Faced with this threat, Laurel urged his officials to work harder to recruit laborers, and Teofilo Sison, who was named Inspector General of Martial Law and bore the responsibility of dealing with the Japanese, sent telegrams to the military governors instructing them to supply labor as needed by the Japanese. The LRA fell into disuse.[69] Japanese army and navy representatives increased the pressure by accusing Laurel of failing to carry out the Pact of Alliance, and he responded by issuing an order on November 2, 1944, that authorized military governors to require males from eighteen to fifty years of age to do forced labor. Laurel and his cabinet hoped that this concession would allow the government to continue to protect the welfare of Filipino workers and fend off Japanese demands for military conscription. At the very least, the order gained him some time, as details had to be worked out and it seemed possible that by the time the administrative mechanisms were in place the situation would have changed.[70]

By the time the order was issued, American forces had already landed on Leyte and air raids over Manila were becoming commonplace. The Japanese were desperate for workers, and they threatened anyone who refused service with severe penalties, including years of imprisonment or even death.[71] Even before the conscription order was issued, Japanese forces in the provinces had begun using neighborhood associations to recruit forced labor, including women and children, to construct airfields, tunnels, and fortifications, and to repair damage caused by air raids. Sometimes workers were present when attacks took place, and considerable numbers were killed or wounded.[72] Finally, impatient with the slowness of the neighborhood associations, Japanese soldiers began to pull people off the streets at bayonet point, and the government's attempt to maintain control of the process collapsed.[73]

With the return of the Americans to the Philippines, the archipelago became a battleground for the second time. Agriculture was disrupted, and factories along with industrial infrastructure were destroyed. The returning Philippine Commonwealth government restored prewar laws in territories that were freed from Japanese rule, but was in no position to develop and execute detailed policies regarding labor. The U.S. Army became the number one postwar employer of Filipinos and required no major recruitment effort, as many were out of work and actively sought jobs with the U.S. Army.

After the war, Laurel, Sison, and Tirona faced trial for collaborating with the Japanese. Among the counts against them were charges relating to their roles in the recruitment of labor for Japanese military projects. Sison was convicted, but the cases against Laurel and Tirona dragged on until President Manuel Roxas decreed a general amnesty for cases of political collaboration.[74]

Summary and Conclusion

The Philippines developed plans for the mobilization of labor shortly before the war, but these schemes had not been fully implemented when the Japanese seized control. The Japanese needed labor to achieve self-sufficiency in the Philippines in food and other basic goods, to extract strategic natural resources for the war effort, to supply the needs of Japanese military forces in the country, and to reconstruct roads and other infrastructure damaged during the fighting. Full employment also promised to help in the restoration of law and order. The Japanese military administration, either through direct hiring or through the Philippine Executive Commission, attempted to meet the Japanese-controlled economy's needs but was unable to employ all those who had been displaced by the war.

With the proclamation of independence in 1943, the government of President Laurel took over the task of mobilizing and distributing Filipino labor. The administration also had to provide relief for the large numbers who were out of work, and tried to help them find jobs. Labor was needed to grow food, and the Japanese required additional workers for defensive works, but Filipinos were reluctant to work for the Japanese because of maltreatment and the failure of the Japanese to meet their obligations. Labor quotas assigned by the Japanese were never met, and Japanese pressure led Laurel to issue an order sanctioning compulsory labor in late 1944. This too proved ineffective, and the Japanese turned to forcible direct recruitment until the war ended.

Part IX

Vietnam

15

Working for the Japanese

Working for Vietnamese Independence, 1941–45

Trần Mỹ-Vân

Japanese military expansion in Indochina began prior to the general assault on Southeast Asia and the Pacific in December 1941, and Vietnam served as a staging ground and supply base for troops advancing into other parts of the region. Until March 1945, the Japanese allowed the French administration to continue handling the affairs of the colony. This arrangement benefited the Japanese, who did not have to create a civil administration, but it complicated the situation of non-communist Vietnamese nationalists, who had looked to Japan to help them win independence from the French.

Although Vietnam was not formally occupied until just five months before Japan surrendered, the Japanese were a potent presence in the country, and they mobilized labor and other forms of support. They were not in a position to create patriotic associations for this purpose as they did in other Southeast Asian territories, so they worked through local groups, in particular the Cao Đài and the Hòa Hảo, two religious-cum-political organizations that supported Vietnamese independence and were at odds with the French.

In return for protection from French repression, and in the hope of gaining rewards later on, local nationalists provided assistance to the Japanese in the form of intelligence about local affairs, and labor for Japanese construction projects. This chapter looks at Vietnamese–Japanese relations during the war years, focusing on the Cao Đài and the Hòa Hảo, which cooperated with the Japanese in Cochin China, notably in the provision of labor services. Both groups adopted pro-Japanese positions in the belief that the Japanese would ultimately remove the French and establish an independent Vietnam under the dissident Prince Cường Để (1882–1951), who was living in exile in Japan.

The Vietnamese had wanted independence ever since the French began to place the country under colonial rule following a series of piecemeal and successful military actions in the second half of the nineteenth century. The rise of Japan at the turn of the century, following victory in the Russo–Japanese War, aroused great interest among Vietnamese nationalists, and some of them began to look to Japan for guidance and inspiration. A Travel East movement sent a number of young Vietnamese to Japan, following the lead of a renowned revolutionary, Phan Bội Châu (1868–1940). Prince Cường Để, a direct descendant of Crown Prince Cảnh, the eldest son of the founder of the Nguyễn dynasty, provided a focal point for opponents of French rule. The prince nurtured hopes that Vietnam could win back its independence with Japanese help, but the nationalists' faith in the Japanese proved to be misplaced. After Japan signed an agreement with France in July 1907 designed to enhance commercial relationships between the two countries, Châu and Cường Để were forced to leave the country.

By a twist of fate, Prince Cường Để made his way back to Japan in 1915, after roaming many parts of the world seeking alternative alliances without success. The prince's decision to lead a life of exile in Japan, interspersed with a few trips overseas, reignited the idea of Vietnamese resistance with assistance from Japan. One reason was that Prince Cường Để was seen to be supported by influential people in Japan who had Pan-Asian aspirations, among them Inukai Tsuyoshi (known as Inukai Ki) and General Matsui Iwane. Accordingly, those Vietnamese nationalists who continued to regard Cường Để as their symbol of continuing resistance and an expression of nationalism again saw an opportunity for Japan to help Vietnam.

The Cao Đài and the Hòa Hảo: Their Religious and Nationalist Aspirations

The Cao Đài religion came into existence in 1926 among a small group of local functionaries who were disillusioned with their situation and had become involved in spiritualism. Aside from their religious beliefs, which are essentially syncretic, the Cao Đài were anti-French and ardently patriotic. This posture became intense in the late 1930s, especially after the emergence of the Tây Ninh group within the Cao Đài. This group was under the astute and effective leadership of the so-called Cao Đài pope, His Holiness Phạm Công Tắc (1890–1959), who had a power base in Tây Ninh, and steadily expanded the Cao Đài religious and political network both within Vietnam and overseas. Tắc affirmed Cao Đài prophecies about an imminent world war, Japanese occupation of French Indochina, the liberation of Vietnam, and the return of Prince Cường Để. Not surprisingly, he got into trouble with the French authorities, who considered his pro-Japanese inclinations dangerous and in July 1941 exiled him to Madagascar.[1] However, Cao Đài political activities continued under the leadership of Trần Quang Vinh (1897–1975), who masterminded collaboration with the Japanese "to save religion and life" after receiving a directive from the Cao Đài deity "to look out for a venture" (October 28, 1942).[2] The expansion of Japanese power after their entry into Cochin China in July 1941 followed a series of successful military and commercial deals with the Vichy French authorities and appeared to be the opportunity he sought.[3]

The Hòa Hảo came to the notice of the French authorities only in 1939, when the founder and leader of Hòa Hảo Buddhism, Huỳnh Phú Sổ (1920–47), began to attract a large following. Sổ's growing reputation was partly attributable to his frequently quoted prophecy that French rule would end in 1939, a prognostication that nearly proved correct, given France's disastrous defeat at the hands of the Germans in that year. Sổ began to seek national salvation and freedom from French colonialism, and the Japanese came to his rescue when he was under threat of being taken out of the country by the French. In October 1942 Sổ moved to Saigon to live under Japanese protection. Under his leadership, the Hòa Hảo enlarged their base in western Cochin China (Miền Tây), the rice granary of the South and a region of much concern to the Japanese, who needed rice to sustain their war operations.[4]

During the Pacific War, both the Cao Đài and the Hòa Hảo were in contact with Japanese personnel in Indochina. Many of the latter were involved in commercial and cultural activities, but they also took an interest in politics. One of the most important Japanese was Matsushita Mitsuhiro, the director of Dainan Koshi, who acted as an intermediary for the Vietnamese nationalists in their dealings with the Japanese and with Prince Cường Đề.[5]

To the dismay of the nationalists, instead of removing the French, the Japanese in collusion with the Vichy administration allowed the French administrative, police, and security services to remain in place. This action derived from Japan's aim to maintain order and to secure Indochinese resources. Using the French administration was the cheapest and easiest way to administer Vietnam.[6] It minimized the size of the garrison force the Japanese maintained there and gave them access to supplies needed elsewhere in Southeast Asia. In May 1941 the French authorities in Indochina had already agreed to supply all of Indochina's surplus rice, rubber, and materials to Japan in exchange for Japanese manufactured goods, although few such goods ever materialized. Indochina, like Thailand, fell under the Foreign Ministry in Tokyo, and there was a sizable Japanese diplomatic mission headed by an ambassador alongside the military garrison force. These arrangements continued until the Japanese staged a *coup de force* on March 9, 1945.

Labor for the Japanese

On the political front, the conduct of the Japanese in Indochina called into question the sincerity of their slogans promoting "Asia for the Asians" or "Liberation of Asia from Western Colonialism." On the economic front, as the war persisted, the Japanese with their increasing demands proved to be merciless exploiters. The Vietnamese found themselves under two masters, the French and the Japanese—in the words of a Vietnamese saying, the country was like "a neck with two yokes." The Cao Đài undertook a range of activities in support of the Japanese under the leadership of Trần Quang Vinh. A Vietnamese interpreter named Lương Văn Tưởng introduced Vinh to the Kempeitai (Japanese military police), and he struck a deal with the Japanese after three days of negotiations at the Kempeitei headquarters. His first secret meeting with two Japanese officers, named Kimura and Mochizuki, took place on November 18, 1942, with Tưởng acting as interpreter. Under the agreement they reached, the Cao Đài would assist the Japanese in return for protection from French repression.[7]

Tưởng occupied a house at 4 MacMahon Street, opposite Kempeitai headquarters, and Vinh together with other Cao Đài dignitaries moved there to have ready access to the Japanese. In January 1943, Vinh and twelve other Cao Đài leaders again met the two Japanese officers, who told them that the Japanese had not come to Vietnam to exploit the country but to liberate it from the West, and that the government in Tokyo supported Cường Để and his Vietnam Restoration League. The Japanese said they wished to enter into close collaboration with local political groups, and acknowledged the popularity of the Cao Đài and the recognition they received from the people. In this atmosphere the Cao Đài decided to offer the Japanese further assistance by recruiting volunteers to support the Japanese military. Vinh recorded the satisfaction that both sides shared with regard to the principle of collaboration, and the Cao Đài endorsed Trần Quang Vinh as their representative to deal with the Japanese.[8] This marked the beginning of the real involvement of the Cao Đài with the Japanese.[9]

The spiritual leader of the Hòa Hảo also collaborated with the Japanese, but the situation of the Hòa Hảo was slightly different. Most Hòa Hảo members were farmers, but many had abandoned their rice fields in the face of the conflict. From a "protected" base in Saigon, virtually next door to that of the Cao Đài, Huỳnh Phú Sổ sent out numerous messages calling on his people to serve the country by restoring cultivation. He also told young people they should learn Japanese. His associates distributed his messages by word of mouth or through multiple copies taken to the Hòa Hảo provinces. Many Hòa Hảo responded and returned to the fields, while some worked directly for the Japanese. Sổ was skeptical about Japanese intentions, but he believed they would eventually strike a blow against the French.

The Hòa Hảo understood the importance of rice and other foodstuff for Japanese operations. The export of Vietnamese rice to Japan decreased sharply in 1944 due to the loss of shipping, but the Japanese still demanded large quantities, with the burden falling on the shoulders of farmers in the South. The Japanese bought all surplus rice, paying for it according to the unfavorable official rate of exchange. Inflation skyrocketed as the French printed more paper money, and the Japanese settled their deficit in trade with Indochinese authorities by setting up "special yen credits."[10] The peasants found it difficult to store rice, and rice prices soared owing to shortages and stockpiling by the Japanese, as well as speculative buying by French and Chinese merchants.[11] The shortages were compounded by French and Japanese demands that rice fields be planted with corn, jute, and cotton, in some cases before the rice crop was ready for harvest.[12]

By 1944 Allied bombing had driven many workers to seek safety in the countryside, making recruitment of workers difficult. The Cao Đài volunteered to supply laborers to overcome this problem, and in the Saigon area the Japanese became heavily reliant on the Cao Đài for their workforce. Trần Quang Vinh acted as a labor contractor, calling upon Cao Đài youth to offer their services, and many young people heeded the call, heading to the cities to help the Japanese. Most were assigned to repair or construct boats in shipyards around Saigon, particularly in the Nichinan Shosen commercial shipyard near Rạch Ông Bridge, in Chợ Lớn district. A charity organization located within the Cao Đài temples, the Phước Thiện, looked after the families the workers left behind. The Cao Đài managed the work sites with minimal Japanese interference, and there was little of the brutality that characterized Japanese projects elsewhere in Southeast Asia. Workers who contracted malaria were treated with quinine that Vinh obtained from the Japanese, and those who became seriously ill were sent home. However, the pressure to meet Japanese demands for boats was very intense, causing stress among the workers.

Allied attacks had caused severe shipping losses, and in Vietnam as elsewhere the Japanese attempted to overcome the problem by constructing wooden boats. The Cao Đài first built five such vessels, then ten, and ultimately twenty. Mitsui and Company provided the materials, and the Japanese army paid 200,000 to 350,000 piasters per finished vessel.[13] Most Cao Đài lived and worked in the shipyards. Being vegetarians, they ate simple food with lots of vegetables, rice, and seeds. Any extra money they earned was channeled back to their families or to their temples. As additional workers arrived, more rows of huts were erected and named after the home provinces or districts of the men who stayed in them. By late 1944 there were more than 3,000 laborers, enough to be organized into work regiments. These groupings were set up in such a way as to support the religious hierarchy. The construction of a vessel was assigned to a team from a particular province, and the religious leader of the province took charge of that project. The finished boat was named for the group that built it. Within the shipyards, twenty provinces were represented. Many high Cao Đài dignitaries visited to raise the morale of the workers, and according to Vinh, they had to shave their beards and don workers' outfits instead of their usual religious garb to avoid French detection. Vinh often visited the shipyards to keep workers informed of events and maintain appearances, and he later commented on his own difficulties and unhappiness arising from the behavior of the Japanese. However, collaboration with the Japanese was the only option open to the Cao Đài, who otherwise faced French repression.

The Japanese demand for labor intensified from mid-1943, as noted by the province chief of Gia Định, a man named Schneider, who described "a new phenomenon" in a note to the director of labor (July 7, 1943) regarding the recruitment of workers for Japanese firms in the timber industry. He claimed that the Japanese lured labor from rubber plantations with offers of higher pay, and that on at least one occasion a Japanese truck went to a public works area and took away thirty coolies. When a foreman took a group of coolies to a Japanese installation, he became head of the group and received 3 piasters a day, while coolies received only 1.20 piasters daily.[14] During times of pressure, the workers received more, especially those with skills. For instance, the daily pay of a carpenter, blacksmith, or bricklayer could reach 2 or even 3 piasters. If a worker signed a two-year contract, he received additional benefits, including two sets of work clothes upon starting on the job, a monthly allowance of 8 piasters for his wife and 6 piasters for each child, and two boxes of matches. The drain on the workforce forced local landowners to increase wages. Around Gò Vấp (near Saigon and Chợ Lớn), for instance, landowners offered from 1.20 to 1.50 piasters daily, as compared with only .60 piasters prior to the arrival of the Japanese.[15] In accordance with the spirit of collaboration (hiệp tác), many Cao Đài were willing to work for the Japanese, and the Cao Đài maintained that they did not seek high pay despite great demand for their labor.

Vinh regarded intelligence work as the most effective and beneficial service to the Japanese. A number of Cao Đài followers were planted in French offices, residences, and military installations around Saigon–Chợ Lớn, and they mapped out French activities, including details of car license plates and their routes and destinations. Vinh considered the Cao Đài intelligence service a major factor contributing to the success of the Japanese coup de force on March 9, 1945.

As late as November 1944, pro-Japanese nationalists regarded the stationing of further Japanese troops in Vietnam in a positive light because of their desperate wish to see the Japanese remove the French. However, famine conditions had already begun to appear in northern and central Vietnam, a development for which the Japanese were partly to blame.[16] Disruption of the transport system and bombing made it hard to carry rice from the South to the food-deficit areas of the North, but increasing Japanese demands for more resources and more food were also responsible. Although committed to working for the Japanese, the Cao Đài laborers became increasingly restless, to the point that they began to question Trần Quang Vinh's leadership. Vinh himself faced a dilemma in that the more he associated with the Japanese military authorities and diplomats, the more he ran the risk of displeasing the Kempeitai. In his opinion the Kempeitai wanted to keep control of the Cao Đài, and on a few occasions they severely reproached him, threatening at one point to withdraw their protection and take back the Cao Đài central headquarters. On this occasion Vinh complained to higher Japanese authorities within army headquarters, and the Kempeitai officer concerned was transferred.

There was some friction arising from competition to finish vessels and pressures caused by living in a confined area. The merits or otherwise of working for the Japanese at times led to heated debates. Generally speaking the workers felt let down by the Japanese, who had failed to remove the French. When air raids began, the workers' morale and energy were further sapped. Because shipyards and ports were easy targets for attack, they felt very vulnerable. Visits by dignitaries to uplift workers' spirits became even more frequent, and arrangements were made to ensure that workers had access to at least one senior figure at all times.

A few months after Cao Đài workers began to assemble in the shipyards, Vinh launched a military venture that reportedly originated in an instruction from Cường Để. Two semimilitary groups, Nội Ứng Nghĩa Binh (the Interior Righteous Army) and Cận Vệ Quân (Body Guard), were organized among the shipyard workers with a total membership of 3,240 persons.[17] In the daytime they continued to work as usual, but at night they practiced martial arts and received combat training. They were greatly disappointed that they could not show off their prowess to the Japanese, who were primarily concerned that the French not become aware of these activities. On one occasion there was an opportunity for the Cao Đài workers to demonstrate their skills to senior Japanese officers, including the commander-in-chief of the army, but the workers' enthusiasm was dashed when they were made to line up in their tiny huts, armed only with sharp bamboo sticks. They could not stage a public spectacle or even make noise for fear of attracting the attention of the French.[18]

The Hòa Hảo also had a paramilitary unit, the Bảo An (Protectors of Peace), created in 1944 with Sổ's blessing. Like the Cao Đài workers, members practiced martial arts and the handling of weapons that consisted mainly of sharpened bamboo. Some male members joined the Black Dragon Society and the Brave Soldiers group while waiting for an opportunity to strike against their enemies.

Cao Đài and Hòa Hảo activities were reinforced by positive support from Cường Để and from the Japanese. August 1944 brought the establishment of a provisional government led by Prince Cường Để. The four key members of this provisional government were Ngô Đình Diệm, Nguyễn Xuân Chữ, Lê Toàn, and Cường Để's General Secretary Vũ Đình Duy. The group held meetings at the Japanese army headquarters and received some assistance from Colonel Hayashi Hidezumi of the military police and other Japanese officials, and from Matsushita, who had been assigned by the army to be the head of the Cao Đài "service troops."[19] These activities are the most concrete indication of links involving the Japanese Indochina Station Army (later reorganized as the 38th Army under the command of Lieutenant General Tsuchihashi), Prince Cường Để, and nationalist elements within Vietnam.

As the time to strike the French drew near, up to 20,000 Cao Đài volunteered to back up Japanese forces, including more than 3,000 workers in the shipyards. Trần Quang Vinh also provided Matsushita with 20,000 piasters intended to speed up the Japanese strike against the French. Colonel Hayashi was reportedly touched by the sincerity of the Cao Đài but refused to take that money, returning it to Matsushita.[20]

According to Nguyễn Ngọc Hòa, "We kept on waiting desperately for the opportunity, which was seen to be so very ripe already. Unity within the Cao Đài groups was collapsing. We began losing all faith and trust in the Japanese." When the Lunar New Year came—the year of the rooster (1945)—people recalled an old prophecy of Trạng Trình: "In the year of the Rooster peace would come again" (*Thân dậu niên lai kiến thái bình*). This gave people a feeling of optimism. The Cao Đài counted "not just days and nights but minutes to pluck the ripe fruit." They had weapons prepared—spears, sharp bamboo sticks, short knives, and long swords—and stocks of dry food—rice cake, roasted rice, salt, and sesame seeds—as well as sauces. Inside the Nichinan shipyard and the main Cao Đài headquarters, hundreds of sewing machines were producing soldiers' uniforms. Hòa, who was selected as a member of the An-Nam Yasa Butai, an information/intelligence special unit attached to the Japanese military, had an opportunity to try the uniform on. It included a white beret, shorts, sandals, and a short-sleeved white shirt. The sleeves bore an embroidered emblem consisting of Chinese characters and a white band with the red rising sun on it, with the word *An* (Peace) at its middle. Hòa vividly remembered his venerable elder leaders nodding their heads in approval of the outfit.[21]

On March 1, 1945, Hòa visited Japanese army headquarters, picking up news from the interpreters and translators there to pass on to his superiors. The next day a group of Cao Đài leaders went together to the shipyards to calm their workers' nerves. On March 3 and 4, Hòa was sent to the Japanese embassy to collect more information. On the fifth, back at army headquarters, he learned of their urgent need for more interpreters at an advanced level. Rushing back to Cao Đài headquarters, Hòa collected names to provide to the Japanese. Early on the evening of March 8, the workers at the shipyards received word that the long-awaited moment had finally arrived. Two trucks dropped off their uniforms, and they were asked to put them on quickly. In unison they knelt down to pray to their God. At this moment Trần Quang Vinh became their inspiration again, as he had resolutely pursued his mission. The workers turned soldiers wondered what would happen next but were told just to await orders. Everyone bowed and waited. Very soon, in small groups, they were directed to climb onto covered trucks. They lay down while the trucks sped toward various targets.[22]

The March Coup and Independence under the Japanese Masters

The Japanese *coup de force* on March 9, 1945, was accomplished with little disruption or bloodshed.[23] Two days earlier Vinh had accompanied a Japanese five-star general in his jeep to make a full round of inspection at strategic points in the Saigon and Chợ Lớn areas. On the night of the coup, the Japanese entrusted the Cao Đài with all sorts of tasks. In the cities they scaled high fences surrounding French buildings to seize French personnel, tying them up with cords and guarding them. The Cao Đài also guarded buildings, streets, and strategic areas to maintain peace and order immediately after the coup. Some 2,500 Cao Đài took part, less than the 3,000 that had been anticipated. The whole operation progressed smoothly, and very few people were injured, in part because the Cao Đài considered it against their religion to hurt the French.

In the provinces the Cao Đài also helped Japanese forces remove French authorities. Nguyễn Ngọc Hòa and his Cao Đài brother Nguyễn Hữu An, for instance, were assigned to a Japanese platoon sent to occupy Tân An Province on the morning of March 10. They called out through a loudspeaker for the French and their Vietnamese soldiers at their main barracks to surrender to the Japanese army. Later the head of the team, First Lieutenant Tachibana, with Hòa as interpreter, interrogated the French chief judge, who had disguised himself as a peasant to escape but was spotted because his "fair skin showed through." After that they took over the plantations owned by the French. [24] All in all, the Cao Đài were the main Vietnamese group working with the Japanese to put an end to eighty years of French rule. They made their mark on history with great pride. Their headquarters filled with Vietnamese nationalists celebrating the news, and most of them expected Prince Cường Để to come back to lead an independent Vietnam. In this, however, they were to be greatly disappointed.

Having seized power from the French, the Japanese simply became another colonial master. They occupied all senior positions, and on March 30, 1945, General Tsuchihashi declared that a great misunderstanding existed on the subject of independence in Indochina. "The independence of the Empire of Annam and that of Cambodia have been proclaimed. However, Cochin China was not only under military control, it was under Japanese military control." The most unexpected outcome was the retention of Emperor Bảo Đại and the formation of a government headed by Trần Trọng Kim, without the participation of pro–Cường Để nationalists (April 1945). The Japanese, especially the military, were primarily concerned with stability and the continuity of supplies as the Pacific War turned against them, and they sacrificed Cường Để for their own benefit. It is said that Mrs. Song Thu, a woman greatly admired by the Japanese on account of her dedicated work and commitment to Vietnamese independence, wept uncontrollably upon hearing that General Tsuchihashi, now governor-general of Indochina, had refused to let Cường Để enter the country.[25] The leader of the Hòa Hảo also felt betrayed. He set up a committee to demand immediate and full independence to Vietnam, but could do nothing apart from making comments about Japanese imperialism and pseudo-independence.

The Japanese seemed more concerned about the French than about their Vietnamese supporters. Following a complaint lodged by Frenchmen who had suffered at the hands of the Hòa Hảo, Minoda ordered the arrest of the organization's military strongman, the Bảo An leader Trần Van Soái. When Emperor Bảo Đại alerted Ambassador Yokoyama to rough treatment of French residents at the hands of the Kempeitai, Yokoyama also responded (April 25, 1945), urging his people to make a distinction between French policies and French individuals. The latter, he said, "have contributed to the success of mankind. We have to treat these people in the spirit of Great East Asia. When a bird wounded by arrow, suffers at the hand of the hunter, no one has the heart to kill it. According to the bushido code, there is nothing more despicable than torturing the weak who have no weapon to defend themselves."[26]

The French were even given a chance to return to work. Part of the commander-in-chief's decree read:

All French public servants and technicians who desire to continue to work with the new government should get back to their respective offices. Those public servants and technicians that agree to work, will receive salary as before. The same goes for those who work for private companies."[27]

Many French officials accepted the offer, and the Vietnamese complained bitterly that nothing had changed. They felt that the Japanese had allowed the French to pursue "a very smart strategy." While the French could no longer play the political game, "having to bow down and bury their heads at their desks under the new rulers," they were still in control of the administration, ready to get their own back whenever the demise of the Japanese came.[28] The Japanese seemed to believe that the French were better workers than local people, an attitude that incensed the Vietnamese. "That really stank," Nguyễn Ngọc Hòa remarked.

Trần Kỳ Nam, a journalist from Điễn Tín, later wrote, "The governor of Cochinchina, Minoda Fujio was just like Pages, no more no less," referring to Pierre Pages, a former French governor remembered for his toughness and his hostility to the Cao Đài. Nam accompanied Governor Minoda on a familiarization trip to the southern provinces, where Minoda's speech to the province chiefs, village notables, and local residents who gathered to welcome him stressed his wish to see the early restoration of peace and order. Minoda urged everybody to remain calm, to carry out their duties, and to obey and listen only to those officers appointed by the Japanese authorities. He warned, "in governing the country only the government in power can make decisions, no political party can. Whoever disobeys the order, will be punished severely."[29] The new governor's message was clear, and people realized he meant what he said. Minoda's decision to get tough derived from multiple problems that he was confronting. The euphoria created by independence had seemed to get out of hand. In addition, there were expectations, especially from those who were pro-Japanese, that local people would fill some high positions vacated by French officers. Minoda reportedly had become aware that some Vietnamese had given themselves titles and that others were lobbying for them.

At the same time the Japanese were urging Vietnamese employees to work harder. A memo from the head office of one Japanese governor (April 28, 1945) to all offices stated: "During the past period too many public servants asked for leave of absence, virtually every body! In today's atmosphere public servants should maximize their work to be good examples for the public, and make their contribution in this difficult time, especially after this country was relieved." Japanese observation about lax work habits on the part of the Vietnamese made their way into another memo, dated July 9, 1945, which received wide distribution:

Too many groups, many people get together in private conversation, mutter-
ing endlessly in their offices or along the corridors. The worst thing is that
some public servants even organize gambling in their places of work. . . .

Is the delay in paper works and communication of documents due to
negligent management or due to the could not care less attitude of public
servants or their lack of discipline aiming to disturb the administration?[30]

The period from the March 9 coup to the official surrender of the Japanese in mid-August 1945 shaped the subsequent history of Vietnam. The
Cao Đài and Hòa Hảo could only watch helplessly as events unfolded. All
their hard work seemed wasted. The unpopularity of the Japanese during this
short period, aggravated by famine in the north and severe Japanese exploitation of Vietnamese resources, destroyed any remaining faith among their
nationalist supporters. The steady decline of the Japanese-backed Bảo Đại–
Trần Trọng Kim government in Huế worsened the national political situation. The Việt Minh took advantage of the growing discontent to expand
their revolutionary activities. The Cao Đài's only hope was to bring Cường
Để back home to salvage the worsening situation. Together with other pro
Cường Để and pro-Japanese nationalists, Vinh spent much of July and August at the Japanese headquarters, pressing hard for Cường Để's early return. Finally it seemed he might come back to be Bảo Đại's supreme adviser,
and the Cao Đài erected arches, banners, and viewing stands to welcome
him. In the end, however, the Japanese, on the verge of defeat, did not follow
through, claiming there was no airplane available to bring Cường Để home.

The leader of the Hòa Hảo was given the task of improving the food situation in the post-coup period. The Japanese felt that Sổ's earlier messages
had caused people to abandon farming. Huỳnh Phú Sổ took the opportunity
to meet with his followers after many months away. He left Saigon on June
20, 1945 for a two-month trip, under the banner "Encouraging Farming Production" (Khuyến Nông). Accompanied by several close associates and two
Japanese, Sổ visited eleven southern provinces, stopping at 107 locations
and delivering an average of two speeches each day.[31] It is hard to determine
the success of Japan's Khuyến Nông program in terms of rice production
and the provision of rice to the needy as demanded by the Japanese authorities. It came late and was a difficult venture, given the ongoing Allied bombing. The Japanese expressed disappointment with Sổ and questioned his
sincerity, based on reports that while Sổ was on tour his associates sent out a
secret message to devotees that said, "When Đức Thầy says 'white' he means
'black' and when he orders 'black' you take it as 'white.'"[32] It appeared that
the Hòa Hảo leader, while obliged to obey Japanese instructions, used covert
messages to convey his wish that he did not want his people to cater to the

Japanese in light of their exploitative behavior. This helps explain why, on August 3, 1945, Governor Minoda declared that the "Hòa Hảo sect is not officially recognized, it is simply tolerated."[33] Like many other nationalists, Số strongly questioned Japan's policy of granting full independence to Vietnam while keeping Cochin China under Japanese control. He also predicted their impending defeat, commenting in 1944, "The Japanese cannot finish eating a rooster." This remark was both pointed and prescient, given that the infamous famine happened in 1945, the lunar year of the rooster, and that the Japanese surrender came later in the same year.

Conclusion

During their military occupation, the Japanese exploited Indochina while keeping French administration in place—a "parasitic colonization" that forced the Vietnamese to live under two masters.[34] Many people were dislocated, with some moving to the cities to work in Japanese installations and others escaping to the countryside to avoid bombing. The leaders of the Cao Đài and Hòa Hảo, in pursuit of independence, were directly or indirectly trapped into the recruitment of labor for the Japanese. Their belated independence was incomplete and very brief, and their ultimate goal was not achieved. Moreover, after the Japanese defeat, the Cao Đài and the Hòa Hảo, as loyal supporters of the Japanese, faced retribution from others.

It is not known how many of the Cao Đài and Hòa Hảo members were actively involved in the making of Japan's Indochina empire. Nor is it known how many of them perished as a direct or indirect result of the war. Huỳnh Phú Số, Trần Quang Vinh, and many more pro–Cường Để, non-communist nationalists ultimately met their deaths as a consequence of their political activities. This was very much related to their patriotism and to their collaboration with or reliance on Japan during the wartime occupation.

Part X

Memory and Reconciliation

16

The Origin and Development of Military Sexual Slavery in Imperial Japan

Chin-Sung Chung

This chapter discusses the origin of Japan's military sexual slavery in Asia between 1930 and 1945, the social structures that formed its background, the reasons the issue was suppressed for fifty years, how it has been and continues to be brought to light, and the responses and possible resolutions offered by the Korean and Japanese governments. Even though military sexual slavery involved a fundamental disregard for women, it has been alternatively concealed and unveiled according to changes in the balance of power among the countries involved. The problem of military sexual slavery intertwines with issues of nation, gender, class, and state, and academic discussions have often focused on one or more of these matters. The present chapter offers an overview of these issues, along with a lexicon with which to discuss them and to move further toward their resolution. It is, however, a preliminary account, since investigations of the subject are far from complete.

The Problem of Terminology

The expression "military sexual slavery," used to describe imperial Japan's forced prostitution mobilizations in the Asian territories of its colonial expansion, is still not universally accepted. Most commonly, it is confused with some variation on the term *chōngsindae* (voluntary corps; in Japanese, *teishintai*).[1] According to historical evidence, it referred to both men and women who were mobilized for a variety of activities including reportage, medicine, and manual labor during the 1940s. The Women's Voluntary Labor Corps and the Women's Voluntary Corps (for the most part, the names were used interchangeably) mobilized women to work in munitions factories in both Japan and Korea beginning in the early 1940s. These bodies gained legal status with the promulgation of the Order for the Women's Voluntary Corps for Labor in August 1944,[2] but the vision of a Women's Voluntary Corps outlined in 1944 specified qualifications that were not relevant to Korean women. Most Korean women were mobilized instead by *ganassen* (governmental guidance) and a free application system.[3] Unlike those of its Japanese counterpart, the boundaries of the Korean Women's Voluntary Corps remained unclear, allowing mobilization under its name for various purposes, including military sexual slavery.

The evidence that the Women's Voluntary Corps was used for the mobilization of military sex slaves is clear. Some testimony states that Korean women were transferred as military sex slaves for Japanese troops in Manchuria as part of an organization known as the Wartime Special Voluntary Corps.[4] Yoshida Seiji, a chief in the Department of Labor Mobilization at the Patriotic Association for Labor of Yamaguchi Prefecture, testified that he had engaged in the forcible transfer of Korean women to Cheju Island in 1943 as part of a "Women's Voluntary Corps for the Comforting of the Imperial Army."[5] Several women, appealing to the Korean government for support, testified that they had been taken from elementary schools to become military sex slaves in war areas under the name of the Women's Voluntary Corps.

Most Koreans who lived through the colonial period think of the Women's Voluntary Corps and military sexual slavery as one and the same. The term "comfort women" (*ianfu* in Japanese) appeared frequently in army records of the 1930s, but Koreans recall other expressions such as "draft of unmarried women," "service corps," and Women's Voluntary Corps, which they believe referred to forced laborers or sex slaves. The extent to which this belief is true is difficult to determine, as written records from the 1930s, even those in progovernment newspapers, are scanty at best.[6] In short, "Women's Voluntary Corps" was legally defined terminology, but "military sex slaves" was not. The extent to which the Women's Voluntary Corps was used for the mobilization of sex slaves has yet to be determined.

A further problem with terminology arises with the term "comfort women," another expression that never had official status. It began to be used in the 1930s, along with words such as "barmaid" (*shakufu*), "women in the drinking business" (*shūgyōfu*), "courtesan" (*gijo*), or "other professional women" (*tokushu fujo*), all of which refer to prostitutes. In Japan the term "war comfort women" was widely used, and the Imperial Japanese Army had "military comfort stations." Both Japanese and Koreans point out the inappropriateness of the term "women participating in war" (*jagun*), which refers to women who follow the army voluntarily, such as war reporters or nurses.[7] International women's organizations initially used the expression "forced war comfort women,"[8] which resembled the term "military comfort women" (*gunwianbu*) used by the media during the 1940s,[9] but later opted for "military sexual slavery by Japan." It has been argued that referring to the women concerned as comfort women obscures their real situation. Yoshimi Yoshiaki describes them as "war slaves,"[10] while Kang Man-gil prefers "sex slave."[11] The Korean Council for Women Drafted for Military Sexual Slavery by Japan (hereafter the Korean Council) and the Korean Research Institute of the Women Drafted for Military Sexual Slavery by Japan (hereafter the Research Institute) used the expression "Japanese military sexual slavery" (*ilbongunwianbu*), and the South Korean government followed this usage when it adopted the law to provide financial support to the victims in the same year.[12] The United Nations has followed the Korean Council in referring to "Japanese military sexual slavery," and I use this terminology in the discussion that follows.

Background of Military Brothels and the Mobilization of Colonized Women

Prostitution, militarization, and the military are linked throughout the world; however, the Japanese army's systematic, well-planned, and inhumane implementation of the military sexual slavery policy brought the military exploitation of women to new levels. In this section, I will illuminate the sociohistorical factors that enabled military sexual slavery to take place.

After the Meiji Restoration in 1868, the Meiji government revitalized and strengthened the existing emperor system, by which the emperor had absolute power.[13] Expanded public education indoctrinated the Japanese public with the ideology of national submission to the emperor, and the government's policy of economic development employed this national ideological framework to impose economic and social strictures on the people. The Japanese emperor system can be characterized as a family-state system, in which the ordinary citizens were constitutionally incorporated into the state as members of a family headed by the emperor. Discrimination against women and an imperialist colonialist mentality were two products of this system. Based on an earlier legal and social conception of the family—the *ie* of the Edo period, in which wives were legally the private property of their husbands and allowed no action on their own—the Meiji civil code and the Meiji constitution defined wives as the legal property of husbands and therefore limited their legal rights.[14] The Meiji licensed prostitution system, too, borrowed heavily from its Tokugawa predecessor, which featured regulated public prostitution, including heaviest recruitment from the lower classes, to maintain middle- and upper-class women's desexualized roles under the *ie* system by providing an outlet for male sexual desire. With Japanese imperialism this class-based mobilization of women into licensed prostitution under the family-state extended into its colonies, including Korea and Taiwan.[15]

As Japan's militaristic regime carried its imperialist incursions into Manchuria in 1931 and China in 1937, the Japanese government enforced a series of domestic policies including economic controls and labor and military mobilization to support imperialist activity. By the end of the war, more than 7 million Japanese men had been mobilized as soldiers, and more than 13 million citizens mobilized for labor.[16] And yet these numbers never seemed sufficient, giving rise to the perceived necessity to mobilize Koreans and Chinese. Women's spirit, labor, and bodies were mobilized for the war effort. The government inspired Japanese women to show their loyalty by bearing sons to dedicate to the emperor. There was also an emphasis on motherhood and loyalty to the state. Books were published with titles such as *Mother of Japan, Mother of the Military State, Mother of Patriotism, Asia-Building Mother, Praising Mother,* and the like, and the Greater Japan Wornen's Association (*Dai Nippon Fujin Kai*) emphasized the importance of child rearing for the production of loyal subjects. However, the government mobilized lower-class and colonized women to labor for the war machine in fields, factories, and particularly in brothels.[17]

When Japan opened to the West in 1854, the country was in an early stage of capitalism compared to Europe. Colonial exploitation was Japan's major means of accumulating capital. In Korea, Japan's mercantilist colonial economic policies included imposing Japanese monetary standards on the country; pursuing immigration policies favoring civilian colonization that deprived Koreans of their land on a massive scale; making Korean farmers produce only rice; requiring all industrial goods to be imported from Japan; and expropriating prime agricultural land for immigrant Japanese farmers—all of which rapidly devastated the native Korean economy.[18] The majority of the Korean population fell into poverty. Especially after 1931, the Japanese forced many Korean farmers to migrate to Manchuria in an apparent effort to disperse the nation.[19] Some 48 percent of the rural population suffered starvation, and 13 percent of the urban population lived in abject poverty.[20]

In addition, since Korea was the first stepping-stone in Japan's advancement onto the Asian continent, Korea was treated from the beginning with a strong policy of cultural and political assimilation with Japan.[21] The 1938 Japan–Korea One Body Policy (*naisen ittai*) suppressed Korean language and customs, tried to bring the ideology of the emperor system to Koreans, and (in 1939) required the Japanization of all Korean surnames. The Japanese General Mobilization Order of 1938 extended these imperialist assimilation policies, mobilizing Koreans for labor, military service, and sexual services. The Korean League for Mobilization of National Power (hereafter the Korean League), founded in 1940, implemented mobilization policies on behalf of Japan. The Korean League consisted of governmental and civil organizations, including schools, and it controlled the entire Korean population through groups comprising ten households each. The league mobilized more than 360,000 Koreans as soldiers, 240,000 as military personnel, and 2 million more as laborers.[22] Many Koreans were sent to dangerous military areas even when Japanese defeat was predicted.[23] They worked in hazardous conditions,[24] and women serving as battlefield sex slaves often became sterile. It appeared as if the Japanese military was driving Koreans to national extinction. Koreans lived under the surveillance of the military police and the coercion of the Korean League, and mobilization of manpower was all too prevalent. It is not difficult to imagine how desperately poor women or their families, economically disempowered, culturally oppressed, and subject to intense regulation in daily life, might easily be mobilized into prostitution by alluring dreams of employment.

The Development of Military Sexual Slavery

Military brothels built by the Japanese army date back to 1905, but their establishment near encampments of Japanese soldiers dates from about 1937, when the Japanese government and army became more deeply involved in enforcing wartime colonial policy.

Soldiers' diaries from the 1905 Russo–Japanese War confirm that the Japanese army built brothels for the troops during that conflict. They contain entries such as "most of the women at the army brothel were Chinese" or "the fees at the army-authorized brothels were very expensive."[25] However, the army does not appear to have systematically created brothels in its first forays abroad. Diaries recovered from the Japanese Siberian Expedition of 1918–22 record only that many soldiers caught venereal diseases, a fact insufficient in itself to prove the existence of army brothels.[26]

In 1932, during the Shanghai War, Lieutenant Okamura, the chief of staff of the Shanghai Detachment, asked the governor of Nagasaki Prefecture to send military comfort women for the troops. Okamura later said he was pleased to see that soldiers' rapes of Chinese women decreased after the arrival of women from Japan.[27] He also stated that he had gotten the idea from the Japanese navy, which was stationed in the same area—evidence that the navy had established overseas military brothels prior to 1932.[28] Another record shows that the Japanese army and navy in Shanghai established military brothels at the beginning of 1932.[29] By 1934, there were already fourteen navy brothels in Shanghai that limited access to military personnel, and prostitutes at these brothels were required to undergo regular medical examinations administered by military doctors.[30]

Not all brothels in Japanese-occupied territories were army-run, however. Records from 1933 show that the Japanese army in Manchuria performed regular checks of the sanitary conditions in brothels and prostitutes' health to prevent venereal diseases among soldiers.[31] These brothels do not appear to have been built and run by the army, but they may have served as prototypes for military brothels established systematically by the army in later years.

The Establishment of a Systematic Policy by the Japanese Government, 1937

It was not until late in 1937 that the Japanese government created an official brothel policy and began to establish brothels systematically in areas where soldiers were stationed. The Japanese occupation of Nanjing was under way, and civilian rape emerged as a serious problem.[32] The war between Japan and China had lasted longer than anticipated; thus, the Japanese government began to mobilize human resources in Japan and in the colonies too. Mobilization of military sex slaves thus occurred in the wider context of war efforts throughout the country and the occupied territories. Many army records concerning military brothels after 1937 have recently been uncovered. In December 1937, a chief of Japanese troops dispatched to central China was directed to build military brothels in Nanjing, and a chief of the Tenth Troop ordered military police to build brothels in Huzhou.[33] Beginning in March 1938 direct orders from the Japanese Ministry of the Army appear in the records. The Department of Military Affairs, a subgroup of the Ministry of the Army, sent orders to the commanders of troops in North and central China to exercise caution in selecting people to mobilize women for military brothels.[34] At an April 1938 meeting of the Ministry of the Army, the Ministry of the Navy, and the Ministry of Foreign Affairs, the decision was made for the army or the navy to manage military brothels directly, without interference from local consulates.[35] The Bureau of Education of the Ministry of the Army ordered the thorough preparation of sanitary equipment destined for military brothels and a ban on soldiers going to prostitutes other than those at the military brothels.[36]

By July 1941, the Japanese army had begun preparing for war against the United States, Great Britain, and the Netherlands. As a result of its experiences in China, the military planned to establish brothels for the use of soldiers in Malaya, Singapore, Indonesia, and the Philippines.[37] When the Japanese army in Manchuria planned special training sessions to prepare for war against Russia, the army requested 20,000 women for army brothels from the Korean colonial government, and 8,000 women were actually mobilized for that purpose.[38]

As Japan began to occupy larger areas after August 1942, the Ministry of the Army began to systematize its policy for establishing military brothels throughout Japanese-occupied territories. A chief in the Department of Rewards at the Office of Personnel in the Ministry of the Army said that he had wanted to put 100 military brothels in North China, 140 in central China, 40 in South China, 100 in South Asia, 10 in the South Sea Islands, and 10 in Sakhalin, for a total of 400 military brothels.[39] The Ministry of the Army also regularly sent condoms to military brothels and supported them financially.[40]

The Role of Other Organizations in the Japanese and Colonial Governments

Along with the Ministry of the Army, the Ministries of Foreign Affairs and the Home Office also helped carry out policies of military brothels. While these brothels were controlled directly by the Ministries of the Army and the Navy, the Ministry of Foreign Affairs investigated the situations of Japanese citizens and colonized peoples abroad, intervened in immigration matters, and ultimately controlled the consulates. The Ministry of Internal Affairs encouraged women and brothel managers to go abroad and controlled the mobilization of women.[41]

Contemporary records show that the colonial government, too, was aware from 1938 onward that Korean women and brothel owners were being transferred to China.[42] As mentioned previously, the Korean government sent 8,000 Korean women to the Japanese army in Manchuria in 1941. Another record contains a report by the chief of police in the Korean colonial government detailing shipments of Korean women and brothel owners to China.[43] As of December 1994, 167 victims had been reported to the Korean government, and 51 of them (32 percent) testified that they had been recruited by policemen, local officials, or other members of the colonial government. Some testified that they had been mobilized as members of the Women's Voluntary Corps, only to become military sex slaves.

The Taiwanese colonial government, too, was involved in carrying out military sex slave policy; however, its role appears to have been to evaluate traveling women and brothel managers. It was also actively involved in establishing military brothels in the South Sea Islands.[44]

Characteristics of Military Brothels

With very few exceptions, military brothels were created exclusively for soldiers and kept separate from the public prostitution system. Soldiers were allowed to frequent only military brothels, and regular checkups on prostitutes' health by military doctors guarded against diseases being transferred to soldiers.

The army handled all administrative details, including the transfer of women, and it both established and managed a number of brothels, although others were established by the army and then handed over to civilian management, or else established and operated by civilians with army permission. Some brothels were built after their civilian managers applied for permission to do so, and some were preexisting public brothels redesignated for military use. Many preexisting brothels in remote areas were also temporarily limited to military use for the duration of the troops' stay in their area.

Although there were many different brothel establishment and management styles, they fit into a pattern. In the early stages, brothels were established and run by the army with increasing civilian investment. In later years, the army resumed direct control over military brothels, but brothel management descended into chaos toward the end of the war.

When the Japanese military first began systematic implementation of the brothel system in China, most brothels were under direct military control. One record from January 1938 describes "two comfort facilities: one was managed by the supply base and the other by the military unit."[45] A record from April 1938 states that "military brothels are to be managed and controlled directly by the Army or the Navy."[46] The mobilization of women at this time seems to have occurred mainly in Korea, with some mobilization in Japan. Many sources say that the majority of women were Koreans, while the mobilization of Chinese women occurred only when unavoidable.[47] As one military record from April 1939 notes, "There were cases when local women were used because of the difficulties in the establishment of a brothel."[48]

After a short period of direct army control, civilians began to participate in the brothel system on a large scale. References to "persons who went to China to open army brothels" appear often in documents written after late 1939.[49] Civilians appear to have participated from the early stages in the brothel system in southern Asia and the South Sea Islands as well. Civilians often applied to the army to run military brothels, and in such cases the army would provide buildings and other extensive assistance.[50] At this time, the mobilization of women occurred primarily in Korea.

As time passed, military brothels extended across a greater geographical area, and women were sent further from home, as in the case of Korean women who were mobilized for Manchurian brothels in July 1941. Some women, either part or all of the population of one brothel, were temporarily dispatched to remote locations that were without brothels for the troops stationed there.[51]

Control of many brothels had passed to civilians in the early 1940s; however, as civilians began to have difficulties acquiring materials and human resources, the military reestablished direct control over military brothels. This happened, for example, in Indonesia in late 1943 and in Okinawa in 1944,[52] and the change meant more coercion in the mobilization process, and more women taken from the immediate areas of occupation as well as from Korea. At this time, some Dutch women were also mobilized in Indonesia.

Toward the end of the war, military brothels became highly disorganized. The army continued to establish military brothels in Japan; however, in southern Asia brothels began to depend on civilians as it became increasingly difficult for the army to transfer Korean women to the area.

The Mobilization of Military Sex Slaves

As previously mentioned, the majority of women in brothels were Korean or Japanese, or from the local population of occupied areas. Pioneering works on the subject by Aso Tetsuo and Senda Kakō show that Koreans made up 80 to 90 percent of all women in brothels, and soldiers as well as victims have testified that the majority of women in southern Asian and the South Sea Islands brothels were Korean.[53] Army records of the results of women's health tests show that 30 percent of women in brothels in China were Chinese. One may suspect that the remaining 70 percent were Korean.[54] Much evidence exists to show that local women in occupied areas were mobilized, but their numbers are not known.

Whether the nationality of women in brothels was important to brothel owners or not remains an issue. According to some testimony, Japanese women were used for officers, Korean women for ordinary soldiers, and Chinese women for military employees.[55] Other records show, however, that officers and soldiers shared the same women, and that the only difference was that officers were assigned women at different times.[56] We can, however, assume that the women's treatment varied according to their nationality at some brothels.

Under Japanese regulations, prostitutes were to be at least eighteen years old in Japan and seventeen years old in Korea.[57] Some documents specify age limits, but the majority of army brothel regulations give no age limits,[58] and victims were reported to the Korean government as ranging from eleven to twenty-four years old at the time of transfer. The majority of women taken were between fourteen and nineteen years of age, thus demonstrating a Japanese preference for women under twenty, but young women of other ages were also used. The majority of Korean women taken for military sexual slavery were from the rural lower classes, possibly to minimize any social unrest occurring as a result of the mobilization.

The method by which women were mobilized is one of the most controversial points of dispute between Japan and the Asian countries victimized. The Japanese government has acknowledged that the majority of women were taken against their will by means of deception or force, but it has yet to confront the fact that the government was the main culprit in their mobilization.[59] No written records describing the mobilization process remain, but testimony of the women themselves and of those involved in their transfer describe mobilization as occurring through false offers of good jobs and by means of force exerted by police, army, and government officials. The army provided transportation even when civilians were transferring women, and as all civilians needed an official pass to leave the country and travel abroad, the government's involvement in women's mobilization and transportation is clear.[60]

Procedures Followed by Military Brothels

The majority of military brothels had their own regulations specifying time schedules, fees, regular medical checkups, and sanitary conditions; however, the regulations varied little from brothel to brothel. All regulations were to be strictly observed, but according to many testimonies, that was not always the case.[61]

One of the most important regulations determined the amount of time allotted to each rank of soldier and the days allotted to each unit in instances where several units shared one brothel.[62] Many victims testified that time regulations according to rank were roughly observed, as so many soldiers would come at the same time and could stay for only a few minutes. Fees, too, were determined by regulations and were primarily paid with tickets sold to the troops prior to their visit.[63] Women in the brothels received little or none of the brothel's profits. In some cases, when the women were given the tickets, they submitted the tickets directly to the brothel managers without cash reimbursement.

Regular medical checkups for venereal disease were another important part of the brothel system. Women were required to have weekly, monthly, or bimonthly checkups, and some records of these examinations have been discovered in the years since the war.[64] The Japanese government provided the brothels with condoms and emphasized the importance of sanitary conditions, but despite these efforts, venereal diseases were common among brothel women. Diseased women were injected with the highly potent "Number 606" medication, probably the mercury-based antibiotic Salvarsan, and women with serious diseases were prohibited from returning to the brothels after their conditions were discovered, although where they were sent is unclear.

Alcohol and violence were prohibited by brothel regulations, but these regulations were not strictly followed. There is much testimony telling of cruelty or violence toward women perpetrated by soldiers or brothel managers.

The Army's Postwar Treatment of Women and Women's Lives Back Home

At the conclusion of the war, the Japanese army did not repatriate the women it had mobilized for brothels in war areas. Both soldiers and victims testify that the Japanese army forced women to commit suicide, killed them by putting them in caves or submarines, or deserted them at the brothels.[65] Many victims describe how one day the soldiers simply stopped coming. Some then returned home on their own with great difficulty, while others stayed at U.S. military camps, or were repatriated with the help of the United States.

For nearly fifty years after the war ended, military sexual slavery remained entirely outside public knowledge. The Japanese government planned and executed its policies of military sexual slavery in secret and destroyed the vast majority of relevant documents after Japan's defeat.[66] For decades those documents that remained were inaccessible to the public.

The most fundamental factors of Japan's avoidance of its war responsibilities should be examined in a broader historical perspective, considering among other things U.S. postwar policy toward Japan. The United States intended to use Japan as a bulwark against the spread of communism in Asia and thus helped with Japan's recovery and capitalization after the war. The U.S.-led Allied countries were very generous toward Japan when punishing its war criminals and calling for an indemnity for its Asian victims. In return, the United States acquired information that Japan had developed through live human experimentation at Army Unit 731 in Manchuria, and used the military sex slaves after the war in Okinawa.[67]

Other Allied countries did not seriously concern themselves with Japanese war crimes against Asians either, unless they involved direct losses to those countries, and this discriminatory attitude extended to military sexual slavery. There was not a single case of punishment of any of the people responsible for the military sexual slavery of Asian women. However, in the Batavia Trial in 1948 thirteen Japanese soldiers were punished, and three executed, for mobilizing Dutch women for sexual slavery in Indonesia.[68]

The Japanese perception of themselves as war victims is another factor hindering their admission of war responsibility. Most Japanese, from high-echelon government officials to progressive intellectuals, view themselves

Photograph 16.1. This photograph appears in the US National Archives with the caption "Four Jap girls taken by Troops of Chinese 8th Army at village on Sung Shan Mill on the Burma Road when Jap soldiers were killed or driven from village. Chinese soldiers guarding girls. 3 Sept. 1944. Photog: Pvt. Hatfield." In fact they were Korean, and the woman on the right, Ms. Pak Yong Sim, has met with researchers working on the issue of the use of comfort women by Japanese soldiers. The pictures on the opposite page show Ms. Pak in the year 2000. (U.S. National Archives 111-SC-230147.)

not as offenders but as victims. The Japanese government and civil movement organizers have been concerned only with Japanese victims, not with other Asians. For example, the Japanese government only removed Japanese from Sakhalin Island and left behind the Koreans who had been forcibly transferred to work there before Japan's defeat. The Japanese A-bomb victims' organization, which is considered to be the symbol of the antiwar movement, has demanded that the government admit war responsibility toward the Japanese victims, without even considering the Korean victims who returned to Korea after the war.[69] By 1990 the Japanese government had paid as much as 30 trillion 60 million yen to Japanese war victims, and continues to spend 1.9 trillion yen annually on the Japanese victims. In comparison, Japan has spent only 1 trillion yen on all the non-Japanese Asian victims.[70]

Most Asian countries were former colonies, and were both weak and economically impoverished. This situation contributed to their failure to pursue Japan's war responsibility. China gave up the demand. Korea, the Philippines, and Indonesia resolved the compensation issue by accepting small sums of money combined with loans and technological training. In addition, these Asian governments suppressed the voices of their own people lest they disturb Japan and stop the flow of economic assistance from Japan.

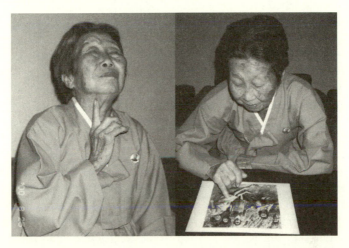

Photograph 16.2. Photographs of Pak Yong Sim taken in August 2000, in Pyongyang, North Korea, by Ms. Nishino Rumiko. In the picture on the left Ms. Pak is pointing at a scar on her neck. She received the injury when she resisted a Japanese soldier at the comfort station in Nanking, and the soldier threatened her with a long sword. She struggled stubbornly and was cut. She bled heavily and a doctor had to be called to dress the wound. In the picture on the right she is pointing to herself in a copy of the photograph reproduced on p. 314. Ms. Pak told researchers that the baby she was carrying when the picture was taken was stillborn, and she was never able to conceive again. She does not know what happened to the other women in the photograph, and says she does not have a clear recollection of the circumstances when the picture was taken. (Photographs courtesy of Ms. Nishino Rumiko.)

Furthermore, patriarchy in these countries silenced both victims and the soldiers who used the military brothels. We have even seen how the Korean victims of forced labor were reluctant to identify themselves for fear that they would be linked to military sexual slavery. Class often plays a role here. Since military sexual slavery is considered a form of prostitution, albeit forced, women of the middle and upper classes have not wanted to concern themselves with the issue. In short, the victims of military sexual slavery have suffered not only national exploitation but also sexism and class discrimination. Thus the problem of military sexual slavery long remained buried.

Military Sexual Slavery, the Problems that Ensued, and a Social Movement

Public disclosure of military sexual slavery was not initiated by a government or by historians. The process began with an exchange between one civilian, Yun Chŏng-ok, who had not forgotten her wartime experience of barely escaping mobilization in the Women's Voluntary Corps, and a Korean Church Women's Federation group protesting Japanese sex tours to Korea in the 1980s. The linkage between sexual slavery and sex tourism was further developed by the vibrant *minjung* (people's) movement, which undertook a critical examination of Korean history. Public disclosure was thus indebted to the development of a social movement in South Korea.

After meeting Yun Chŏng-ok, the churchwomen realized that contemporary sexual exploitation of Korean women by Japanese had deep historical roots. In February 1988, the group visited the remains of several brothels, and in April they held a symposium to report their findings. In May 1990, the Korean Church Women's Federation, together with other women's organizations, issued a statement demanding that South Korean President Roh Tae Woo raise the issue of military sexual slavery during his state visit to Japan.

The issue began to receive public attention in Japan during the following month, when Motooka Shoji, a member of the Socialist Party and of the Upper House of the Diet, called upon the Japanese government to investigate military sexual slavery. At the time, the Japanese government denied any responsibility, a position that angered the Korean women's groups and created the impetus for further activism. In July 1990 the Korean Research Group of Women Drafted for Military Sex Slavery by Japan was formed, followed in November by formation of the Korean Council for Women Drafted for Military Sexual Slavery by Japan to serve as an umbrella group for Korean women's organizations. Encouraged by the attention given to this issue, the first military sexual slavery victims came forward in August 1991. Archival research carried out in that year in the United States and in Japan located documents that supported this accusation, and women began calling a victim hotline that the Korean Council set up in September 1991, as well as a Japanese Hotline for Military Comfort Women, created in January 1992. The Japanese government published two reports—on July 6, 1992 and on August 4, 1993—but historians and civil organizations continue to uncover additional documents.

Since these first steps, the social movement in Korea has centered around the Korean Council, with additional action by the Korean Association of the Families of Pacific War Victims, an organization created in the early 1970s for the families of those killed in forced labor and military service. The primary function of both organizations is victim support: the Korean Council organizes financial aid, connects victims with foreign organizations, and provides counseling. The Buddhist Human Rights Association, a member organization of the Korean Council, runs shelters for victims and arranges some financial support.[71] The Korean Council also launched a series of demonstrations, held every Wednesday at the Japanese Embassy in Seoul, to express its desire to bring Japanese war responsibility to light and to garner public support. Ongoing Wednesday demonstrations began on January 8, 1992.

In addition to support services, the movement's more political activity is the investigation and uncovering of hitherto concealed and distorted historical information on military sexual slavery. Working in conjunction with the Korean Research Institute, the Korean Council publishes victim testimonies, including a collection of statements by Korean victims living in China that were gathered on a fact-finding mission in 1993.[72] The Korean Council has issued calls for the Japanese government to reveal the contents of government documents and has held joint symposia with Japanese research groups. It also maintains its own research groups, including the Committee for Research and Investigation and the Committee for Legal Problems, set up in 1994 by recruiting lawyers, historians, and scholars of international law. Documents and archival materials, including photographs and victims' personal letters, will be kept in a memorial library.

Korean and other victims want the Japanese government to acknowledge its war crimes, apologize to its victims, provide compensation, and punish those responsible for military sexual slavery, actions that will validate the honor of the women concerned. To this end, Korean organizations are forming international alliances with women's and victims' groups in other Asian countries and with women's human rights organizations worldwide. Along with its main office in Seoul, the Korean Council also has a branch office in Pusan and cooperative organizations of Korean Americans in New York, Minnesota, Washington, D.C., Germany, and Canada.

Compensation for Victims and the Search for Justice

One of the ultimate goals of the military sexual slavery movement is to make the Japanese government pay monetary compensation to victims and punish those responsible. The Korean Council has asked lawyers and scholars of international law to find legal grounds for demanding compensation and determining appropriate amounts.

In December 1991 the Korean Association of Families of the Pacific War Victims brought incidents of forced labor and the draft to the attention of the Tokyo District Court, and it is currently increasing the number of victims included in that claim. One victim has also sued in her own right.[73] The Pusan branch of the Korean Council raised the same issues in Yamaguchi Prefecture at the Shimonoseki District Court on December 25, 1992. Because not one suit heard before a Japanese court has thus far been successful, the Korean Council has also brought the issue of military sexual slavery to international forums for justice, including the United Nations, the Permanent Court of Arbitration, and the International Labor Organization (ILO). A group of scholars and activists brought this issue to the U.S. courts in 2000, and lawsuits have continued in the United States until the present.

In February 1994 the Korean Council submitted a bill of indictment to the Tokyo District Prosecutor's Office, but this bill was rejected without a clear explanation.[74] The Korean Council then began calling for new legislation to provide compensation to the victims, rather than trying to rely on existing Japanese law. Public pressure arising from legal suits in Japan and internationally has provided support for such a change.[75]

Despite a shortage of resources, the movement has mustered considerable support within Korea and has also managed to win international backing. Its most important international interaction has been at the United Nations. The United Nations became involved in 1992, when a representative of the Korean Council visited New York to submit an appeal to the secretary-general. The Korean Council then made an intervention at the Sub-Commission on the Promotion and Protection of Human Rights (hereafter the Sub-Commission) under the aegis of the World Council of Churches in Geneva in 1992.[76] The Sub-Commission resolved in 1993 to nominate a Special Rapporteur to carry out an in-depth investigation of systematic rape, sexual slavery, and slavery-like practices during armed conflicts, an appointment that was approved by the Commission on Human Rights (UNCHR, the Sub-Commission's parent body) in 1994. This was a result of efforts by the Korean Council and other Asian women's and civil organizations to link Japanese military sexual slavery with the victimization of women in other armed conflicts and placed the issue in the international arena as part of the general subject of women's experiences during armed conflicts, although some groups in Korea and China felt there were problems with this approach because other instances did not occur in the context of colonialism. The Sub-Commission produced a series of reports on the issue, the most important one (dated 1998) prepared by the Special Rapporteur, Ms. Gay McDougall. The report spelled out the Japanese government's legal responsibility to pay compensation, and also the legal liabilities of individual criminals. In 2000 the Sub-Commission passed a resolution calling upon the High Commissioner for Human Rights to submit a yearly report on the issue, dealing with systematic rape, sexual slavery, and slavery-like practices during armed conflict.[77] The Korean Council also proposed initiatives at the Vienna World Conference for Women in August 1995.[78] In cooperation with other Korean organizations and Asian nations, the council's aim is to make Japan clear its name internationally of past crimes before taking a seat as a permanent member of the UN Security Council. To this end, it submitted a counterreport criticizing the Japanese government's 1993 report to the UN on whether Japan had kept the International Covenant on Civil and Political Rights, eliciting a response from the Japanese government that military sexual slavery had occurred before the covenant became binding.[79]

On the occasion of the fifty-second anniversary of its founding, the UNCHR adopted a resolution on the prevention of violence against women. It also accepted the Special Rapporteur on Violence Against Women, Radhika

Coomaraswamy.[80] Fifty-eight international human rights organizations and women's organizations formed an international alliance to support Coomaraswamy's report on sexual slavery in wartime, which recommended that the Japanese government acknowledge its war crimes, reveal the whole truth, issue an official apology, punish criminals, and pay legal reparations. Another important international arena where Japanese military sexual slavery has been discussed is the ILO. The Korean labor unions in cooperation with the Korean Council and with Japanese labor unions have submitted appeals to the ILO Committee of Experts on the Application of Conventions and Recommendations (hereafter the Experts Committee) to review the case of Japanese military sexual slavery as a violation of the Forced Labor Convention (ILO Convention 29 of 1995). The Experts Committee published reports that the Japanese government should take appropriate measures toward the victims demands as expressed many times since 1996. The Korean Council and Korean and Japanese labor unions continue to submit appeals to the Experts Committee, and make efforts for this issue to be selected as one of the important individual cases that are to be intensively discussed at the Committee on the Application of Standards, a part of the International Labor Conference.[81]

Military sexual slavery activism has been strong in other international forums as well. Activists participated in the Asian Solidarity Forum on Military Sex Slavery by Japan, a forum of women's organizations that met in August 1992 in Seoul. Representatives of the Philippines, Taiwan, Hong Kong, Thailand, Japan, and Korea participated in both this and subsequent forums in 1993 in Tokyo and in 1995 in Seoul. The International Commission of Jurists (ICJ) formed an investigative group that traveled to South Korea, North Korea, Japan, and the Philippines before publishing a report in 1994 that concluded that individual rights to claims remained the main issue, as it was during negotiations for the Korea–Japan treat in 1965. It advised the Japanese government to provide appropriate compensation to victims.[82]

All these efforts by Asian women's organizations led to the establishment in the year 2000 of the Women's International War Crimes Tribunal for the Trial of Japan's Military Sexual Slavery. This was a people's tribunal based upon the model of International War Crimes Tribunal on Vietnam, as established by European intellectuals in 1967. The tribunal was organized with five judges, including currently practicing judges and law professors, as well as ten prosecutor teams from Japan and victimized countries such as Korea, China, the Philippines, Indonesia, Taiwan, Malaysia, East Timor, and the Netherlands. One point worthy of note was that both South and North Korea worked as a unified team for the prosecution.

The judges ruled that the Japanese government had a legal responsibility to provide compensation, and found that ten individuals, including Emperor Hirohito, had been guilty of crimes against humanity. Even though it was a people's tribunal, the rulings have been tried as legal precedents.

The Korean Government Responses and Public Opinion

When military sexual slavery first attracted public attention, the Korean government supported the issue and formally raised it with Japanese prime minister Miyazawa during his January 1992 visit to Korea. Miyazawa replied that the Japanese government apologized, and would undertake self-reflection and not repeat past mistakes. The Korean government fully accepted this response.[83] In July 1992 a Korean Ministry of Foreign Affairs task force on the problem of military sexual slavery published a report entitled "The Interim Report on the Investigation of the Problem of Military Sex Slavery." Since then, however, the Korean government has shown ambivalence, helping victims and supporting the activities of civil organizations but not treating the matter as a pending question in Korean–Japanese relations. Domestically, the Korean government supports the Korean Council's activities at the UN and gives information to civil organizations. A law requiring the government to provide financial assistance to victims was passed in May 1993, and 158 victims eventually received government financial support under this legislation.[84] The Korean government also gave a special President's Award to Yun Chŏng-ok, who first raised the matter in 1993.

Although the Korean government took steps to support military sexual slavery victims within the country, it proved unwilling to disturb relations with Japan by pursuing the questions of Japan's responsibilities to victims. In March 1993 the Korean government told the Japanese government it would make no monetary claims for compensation, and it raised no official objections to the proposed Japanese Asia Women's Fund—a fund for compensation of victims financed entirely by donations from private individuals and corporations. Bilateral talks between Japan and Korea have focused on economic cooperation and on security issues concerning North Korea.

Korean society overall also demonstrates an ambiguous combination of support for victims and disregard for military sexual slavery as an issue. Many organizations offer services to victims; for example, Chungang Hospital, a large general hospital run by Hyundai Corporation, the largest business conglomerate in Korea, provides full medical services for all the military sexual slavery victims. After an initial boom in media coverage of military sexual slavery, however, many Koreans, like their government, seemed to find issues such as economic cooperation more pressing, and media attention declined.

The Japanese Government Response

In the beginning, the Japanese government strongly denied any governmental responsibility for military sexual slavery.[85] With the gradual uncovering of evidence, the government changed its attitude, but it still disclaimed any legal responsibility. Initial changes in the Japanese government's stance began with the discovery of relevant Japanese army records in the United States in November 1991, and with the worldwide attention given to the active campaigning of Korean civil organizations. Katō Kōichi, director of the Japanese Cabinet Secretariat, directed six government departments—the police, the Office of Defense, and the Ministries of Foreign Affairs, Education, Welfare, and Labor—to investigate potentially relevant documents immediately prior to Prime Minister Miyazawa's January 1992 visit to Korea. This exercise led to Miyazawa's apology in Korea on January 17, 1992, and recognition of government involvement in issues surrounding military sexual slavery by the Japanese Diet on January 29, 1992.

Apologies notwithstanding, the Japanese government refused to define military sexual slavery as a criminal offense or acknowledge any legal responsibility for the practice. On February 26, 1992, the Minister of Foreign Affairs, Watanabe Michio, stated that "the problems concerning military sexual slavery are those of humanism and politics rather than law," and a spokesperson for the Ministry of Foreign Affairs' Asia Department said in a public statement that as far as international law was concerned the problems of military sexual slavery were fully resolved.[86] On July 6, 1992, the Japanese government published a report based on government records that acknowledged government involvement in military sexual slavery but did not admit that force had been used in recruiting women for this purpose. The government then supplemented its own findings with Korean publications and victim testimonies, and issued a second report on August 4, 1993, that admitted that forced mobilization had occurred but asserted that it had been implemented and carried out not by government officials but by civilians. Prime Minister Hosokawa also acknowledged on August 10, 1993, that the Japanese army had invaded other parts of Asia during the Second World War.

Such changes in the government's position were strongly attacked by conservative commentators who, ignoring recent evidence, reiterated the government's official position during the winter of 1993–94. In May 1994 Minister of Legal Affairs Nagano Shigeto described the Second World War as a war of liberation in which Japan freed Asian countries from their colonial situation. He described the military sexual slavery system as an extension of public prostitution and not all bad.

Given both UN and ICJ calls for proper compensation, Prime Minister Murayama announced in August 1994 the creation of a "Plan of Exchange for Peace and Friendship." He described this measure as a solution to military sexual slavery, which, he said, had hurt the dignity and honor of women. Under the plan, direct government compensation would be replaced by the creation of an institute for investigation, research, and exchange among Asian countries, thus shifting responsibility for compensation to the Japanese people. The Japanese government also hinted at an institution along the lines of the later Asian Women's Fund, stating that it wished to explore options for the broader participation of the people. The prevailing government position was summed up in a December 1994 statement from the governing Liberal Democratic Party's subcommission on the problem of military sexual slavery:

> The Japanese government has responded sincerely from the perspectives of international law and foreign relations through the San Francisco Treaty, peace treaties between the countries involved, and other treaties to the problems of compensation for foreign labor, the draft, and the problem of military sexual slavery. However, from a humanistic point of view, we will encourage the broader participation of the people to raise funds and distribute them to victims. The government will cooperate with this activity.[87]

In the face of strong opposition from civil servants and labor unions, the Japanese government began to plan for the welfare, including medical care, of Pacific War victims. Government representatives attended a meeting of individuals interested in establishing an Asia Women's Fund in June 1995. Among the promoters were progressive intellets, who had long been active participants in the movement on behalf of Korean residents in Japan and Koreans who had remained behind on Sakhalin. With this step the Japanese government attempted to deal with the problems left behind by military sexual slavery. Japan appears to have decided that to become a world power it needed to resolve the issues arising from military sexual slavery that had so seriously damaged its international reputation. Civil organizations in the victimized countries of Asia, however, criticized this "civil fund," describing it as a way of avoiding acceptance of government responsibility, of denying Japan's war crimes, and of creating the pretence but not the substance of government generosity. Victims in Korea, the Philippines, Taiwan, and other countries refused to accept what they saw as comfort money, saying that they sought to restore honor, not recover money, and that their objective would not be accomplished by financial compensation and condolences but rather by

Japan's admission of its crimes.[88] Some of the poorer victims have been allowed to receive money from the Asia Women's Fund, but the result has been to create divisions among the victims.

Public Opinion in Japan

The Japanese government's somewhat paradoxical action in creating an Asia Women's Fund, a move that disregarded five years of effort on the part of Asian civil organizations, can be explained in part as a reflection of conservative public opinion in Japan. Although many Japanese scholars, lawyers, and organizations have participated in the military sexual slavery movement, they have not been able to overcome the prevailing apathy of mainstream Japanese society.

The Japanese War Responsibility Data Center, Uri Women's Network, Japanese Christian Women's Cooperation Society, and other organizations that work in cooperation with the Korean Council agree with the council in most areas, but they somewhat express subtly different positions. For example, the Korean Council sees Japan's policies of suppressing Korean customs, language, and spirit, forcing Koreans to adopt Japanese names, and mobilizing Koreans as military sex slaves—often in dangerous locales—as a policy of national extinction, but the Japanese organizations see these measures as part of an effort to quench nationalistic spirit but not the nation itself.[89] Also, many Japanese who have worked with the Korean Council oppose its demand that those responsible be punished, claiming that such people are already very old or have died.

Many Japanese organizations working on the military sexual slavery issue, such as the Korean Council, believe that the solution to the problem of military sexual slavery is to correct concealed and distorted history, to establish military sexual slavery as indisputably a war crime and a crime against humanity, to make the Japanese government compensate victims, and to punish those responsible. However, others only emphasize that victims from other Asian countries must be compensated together with those from Japan, and any concept they may have of the injustice of colonialism and war, and of military sexual slavery as a crime, is less clearly articulated.[90]

Japanese society has been hostile to the military sexual slavery movement, and generally ignorant about the issue involved apart from what they read in school textbooks. Some middle school history textbooks glorify Japan's occupation of Asian countries and disregard war crimes, including military sex slavery. Moreover, journals and newspapers in Japan have published articles insisting that for Koreans the issue was resolved by the Korea–Japan treat of 1965, and for other nationalities by treaties with the countries concerned. These articles have urged the government not to respond to victims' claims or to pressure from the UN, the ICJ, or other international organizations.[91] They assert that other countries raise the issue of military sexual slavery as a maneuver to extract economic assistance from Japan, and that South Korean groups have also used the issue to get closer to North Korea by positing a common problem.[92] Some articles have praised military sexual slavery for having prevented large-scale rape of civilian women and births out of wedlock by providing a means of satisfying and controlling men's sexual needs, and have lauded government-enforced medical checkups for women in the brothels.[93] Disregarding clear evidence to the contrary, they argue that there was no forced mobilization and that poverty drove many Korean families to sell daughters to brothel keepers. They argue that Koreans have persisted with the story of forced mobilization to avoid the international humiliation of admitting what went on during Korea's colonial period.[94]

Conservative Japanese commentators are unhappy that military sexual slavery has become an international issue involving the United Nations. They insist that for the UN to pay attention to military sexual slavery at the expense of other human rights abuses in Western nations is an instance of racial discrimination against Japan, and they call for Japan to submit its own reports to counter Korea's efforts to brainwash the UN, the ILO, and other international forums.[95] Right-wing groups strongly criticize the Japanese government whenever it admits a mistake or offers an apology in connection with this issue. They argue that the Japanese government should not take such steps, and they regularly publicize the names of government representatives who do so, describing them as dangerous people who damage Japanese interests.[96] Along with its attention toward Japanese organizations, Japanese conservative opinion also disparages other Asian peoples, and especially Koreans, saying that for all their criticism, Asian nations remain dependent on Japan, and threatening negative consequences if they continue to raise the issue of military sexual slavery.[97]

Conclusion

Military sexual slavery involved a fundamental disregard for the rights of women. It was an instance of violence perpetrated by a strong imperialist nation against the populations of weaker nations and by the state against civilians. It was also an example of class discrimination, as the majority of women involved were from the lower classes. Its violence was heightened by wartime conditions. The uneven power relations among nations, based on specific configurations of gender, nation, state, class, and a wartime setting, have determined the process by which military sexual slavery has been disclosed as well as state and public reactions to its disclosure.

Military sexual slavery, created and concealed under the cloak of uneven power relations among nations, has become one of the most important social issues in postwar Korea, and as such has benefited from changes in focus from labor and class interests to more humanitarian, value-oriented concerns as well as to an increased interest in women's issues. Similarly, new social movements have helped generate interest in military sexual slavery as a social issue in Japan, and the Korean government's involvement has brought the issue to the attention of the Japanese government. Most of all, however, the rise in prominence of the women's movement in Korea has helped to make women's voices heard against patriarchy-enforced silence, leading to disclosure of the problem, and creating solidarity with women's organizations worldwide.

Nevertheless, a solution to the problem of military sexual slavery remains distant. Japan's power in the international arena, its still undeveloped conceptions of human rights, a dearth of international bodies committed to maintaining human rights, and the comparative weakness of social movements in Asian countries have all impeded efforts to resolve the issue. Japanese lobbying has effectively countered attempts to deal with the matter through the United Nations, and the sheer number of important women's issues that must be addressed has diluted the intensity of many Korean women's organizations that were once strongly committed to resolving the military sexual slavery issue. Yet military sexual slavery can only be further addressed as women's power grows, democracy takes stronger root in many societies, Asian countries gain power in foreign relations and internal equality among their populations, and the world settles into peace.

17

History, Memory, Compensation, and Reconciliation

The Abuse of Labor along the Thailand–Burma Railway

E. Bruce Reynolds

Other than the fall of Singapore and the extensive warfare in the Philippines and Burma, no aspect of World War II in Southeast Asia is as well known in the West as the construction of the Thailand–Burma railway. The sufferings of Allied prisoners of war (POWs) who labored under the Japanese on the "Death Railway" have been described in numerous memoirs and were depicted—although inaccurately—in David Lean's award-winning film *Bridge on the River Kwai,* based on Pierre Boulle's novel.[1] The focus on the POWs, however, has drawn attention away from the fact that the Japanese brought material and labor from across mainland and island Southeast Asia to build the railway.[2] This chapter looks at the role of the host countries in the railroad project, further describes the conditions faced by the Asian laborers, and examines the varied retrospective views and attitudes of former participants. It concludes with comment on the ongoing campaigns by the laborers and other victims of Japanese aggression to obtain apologies and compensation, as well as the efforts by other survivors to effect reconciliation.

The Japanese Southern Army conceived the Thailand–Burma railway and pushed it through to completion, but it became an international project. Japan's Korean colony provided guards and overseers for the camps, and the host countries were—albeit under Japanese pressure—actively involved in the construction, while the workforce included not only POWs from Britain, Australia, the Netherlands and the United States, but also laborers recruited from across Southeast Asia.

The Japanese army viewed completion of the railway as an absolute military necessity because in successfully invading Burma via the Thai border town of Mae Sot in 1942, their forces had traversed a tortuous mountain track that motor vehicles could negotiate only in the dry season. Recognizing that supply ships would face attacks from Allied submarines and aircraft along the sea lanes to Rangoon, the Japanese army command considered a dependable land supply route essential to the defense of Burma.[3]

The idea of connecting Thailand and Burma by rail did not originate with the Japanese army. G.A. Hicks, chief engineer of colonial Burma's railways, noted in a 1934 speech:

> As long ago as 1905 investigations were made into a connection with Siam [Thailand]. Two routes, one at Three Pagodas Pass and one at Amya Pass have after investigation been turned down . . . as they pass through very difficult and unproductive country. The one which has achieved more attention is via Moulmein, Ye, Tavoy, and Mergui, thence eastward across the Mawduang Pass to the Siamese railway station of Prachuab Kirikhan.[4]

Japanese army engineers favored the Three Pagodas Pass route. Not only was it the shortest and most direct path between Bangkok and Rangoon, but the envisioned right-of-way along the Kwae Noi River would require no tunnels and less large-scale bridging than the alternatives. Undeterred by the fact that British engineers had judged this route too difficult, the Japanese, buoyed by a sense of invincibility engendered by their early war victories, saw the project as a suitable challenge to their ingenuity and willpower.[5]

The difficulties of the terrain and the can-do attitude of the Japanese engineers were emphasized in a contemporary Japanese press account. The article's colorful description of a region inhabited only by loathsome creatures such as inch-long ants, "leeches as long and thick as one's index finger that drop from overhanging branches like hail upon any warm blooded animal, including man," and a "monstrous lizard bigger than the average Japanese" was accompanied by the engineers' prediction that they could complete the line within a year. They outlined "plans for constructing large barracks to house laborers, and fully equipped hospitals" as the rails advanced into the jungle.[6]

These projections proved overly optimistic in every respect. First, the effort to gather the necessary construction materials from all over the region consumed much time. The famous eleven-span iron bridge over the Mae Klong (Kwae Yai) River at Kanchanaburi came from Java. The Japanese expropriated steel rails from Java, Malaya, and Indochina. Second, construction began before the route was fully surveyed, leading to unpleasant surprises such as unanticipated rock barriers that, in the absence of adequate heavy equipment, had to be laboriously removed with dynamite, simple tools, and bare hands. This forced the Japanese to muster an ever-larger polyglot army of workers from across Southeast Asia.[7] Finally, the Japanese army's failure to provide adequate logistical support for this force created a massive human tragedy.

The fact that Tokyo and the Japanese Southern Army—which had direct command responsibility for the project—made decisions with little regard for the actual circumstances along the line contributed greatly to this manmade disaster. For example, despite disruption of construction by severe flooding during October 1942, higher authorities sought in January 1943 to advance the target date for completion to the end of May 1943. The engineers on the scene eventually convinced their superiors that such a schedule was impossible, but were ordered nonetheless to press ahead with utmost speed. Their frenzied effort to complete the line, coupled with an early onset of the rainy season in April 1943 and a cholera epidemic, intensified the misery of the laborers and caused the death toll to spiral upward. A 1943 British intelligence report claimed 85 deaths in 24 hours at one Australian POW camp and the disposal of the corpses of 161 Indian laborers in a single mass burial. The British report estimated that "not more than one-fifth of the work force is fit for work" and noted that the Japanese failure to provide adequate food and medicine hardly seemed logical given their desire for a Herculean effort to complete the railway line.[8]

From the beginning, the Japanese had expected Thailand and Burma to play major roles in the railway construction, but the Thai, proud of their nation's status as the lone independent state in Southeast Asia and resentful of the intrusion of Japanese forces into their country in December 1941, were less-than-enthusiastic participants. Since its inception in the 1890s, Thailand's national railway system had been viewed as a means of promoting national security. While foreign experts had helped plan and construct the railway, the Thai government had ensured that no foreign power would control the completed lines.[9] In keeping with this policy, the Bangkok government initially suggested that the Japanese supply the materials for the line and let the Thai do the job. Thai engineers, however, anticipated that it would take several years to complete the line, so there was no possibility the Japanese army would agree.

Alarmed by reports that the army intended to build the line whether Thailand liked it or not, Japanese ambassador Tsubokami Teiji warned the Foreign Ministry in July 1942 that such unilateral action could do irreparable damage to bilateral relations.[10] However, the unequal nature of the Thai–Japanese alliance and the determined stance of the Japanese army left the Thai government little scope for resistance. On September 16, 1942, Premier Phibun Songkhram signed an agreement with Japanese military attaché Major

General Moriya Seiji that promised to provide accommodations for construction units, land for the right-of-way, railroad ties (sleepers), wooden poles, lumber, cement, and sand. Thailand also agreed to contribute engineers and laborers, and to assist the Japanese army in obtaining trucks, boats, and work elephants. The Japanese army would direct the construction and operate the completed line.[11]

For the main body of the labor force, the Japanese turned to the Allied prisoners they had captured in seizing control of Southeast Asia. As noted above, the travails of the British, Australian, Dutch, and American POWs who labored on the railway are well known, making it unnecessary to retell their story in detail here. In short, the Geneva Conventions forbade employing prisoners of war on military projects, but the Japanese—who had not ratified the conventions and whose own soldiers were told that suicide was preferable to capture in battle—simply ignored this prohibition. A directive to POW camp commanders in June 1942 warned that prisoners could not be permitted to live freely as idlers, so their "labor and technical skills should be fully utilized for the replenishment of production, and contribution rendered toward the prosecution of the Greater East Asia War for which no effort ought to be spared." Of the roughly 60,000 POWs employed on the Thailand–Burma railway, more than 12,000 died, most succumbing to disease after being weakened by undernourishment and physical hardship.[12]

While their numbers are harder to pinpoint, far more Asians than POWs eventually labored and died along the railroad line. Estimates of their numbers (including residents of Thailand and Burma) range from 200,000 to 300,000. One Dutch officer concluded that their ranks included 80,000 workers from Malaya (resident Indians and Chinese as well as Malays), 45,000 from the East Indies, and 10,000 from Indochina.[13] The multiethnic nature of the workforce is indicated clearly in a precise breakdown Colonel Hiroike Toshio provided for two Asian labor units under the Ninth Railway Regiment in Thailand. One of them he listed as 67 percent Malay, 25 percent Chinese, 2.3 percent Thai; the other as 88.1 percent Indian, 4.5 percent Malay, 3.4 percent Chinese, 2.3 percent Thai, and 1.7 percent Vietnamese.[14] Estimates of deaths among these laborers run as high as 100,000, although no one knows for sure. In November 1945 the British estimated the number of laborers from Malaya at 75,000, nearly half of whom (32,000) died in service, while another 16,000 escaped to unknown fates.[15]

Despite Japanese wartime propaganda about Asian solidarity, the Asian workers, lacking the trained leadership and the military structure that enabled the POWs to maintain a degree of order and discipline in their camps, faced even worse circumstances than the European captives.[16] POWs were well aware of this reality, and many commented on the sad plight of these

Asian laborers. For example, in April 1943 Australian colonel Edward "Weary" Dunlop described the passage by his camp of 400 Tamils who had been hired on the false promise of being sent to work in northern Malaya:

> It was a sad sight to see these poor wretches trudging their way up the deep slushy mud of our road guarded by armed N[ipponse] troops—a wonderful tribute to the new order in South-east Asia. A few spoke English and pathetically asked when the British were coming back to Malaya. It is reported that they spent the night in the English area next door in the open and wet. Just another of those dreary, homeless mass migrations of war along a road of sickness and death.[17]

Three months later, Dunlop wrote:

> Endless streams of wretched coolies from Malaya are plodding their slippery way up the jungle road. Those who speak English frequently have sad words to say about the recruiting methods the Nipponese used to secure their services. A powerful factor seems to be starvation in Malaya since the rice ration is reduced from the normal 8 katis a week to 3. Those poor wretches are dying up here in countless thousands.[18]

British POW Arthur Lane, who worked in various capacities along the railroad from the fall of 1942, vividly described the horrible circumstances the Indian workers faced. En route upriver by barge in mid-1943, his party stopped at a Tamil camp called Rin Tin, 132 kilometers above Kanchanaburi. He found it packed with "emaciated men and women, some with children clutching their hands." He added:

> The sight was enough to cause a fit man to throw up. There were men with great ulcers chewing away their arms and legs, others totally blind being led by others practically unable to support themselves, let alone assist others. Women suffering from ulcers and palagra [pellagra], mostly in a state of undress, which didn't matter, they had lost all resemblance to women and their bones showed through in [the] same places as the men.

An Australian corporal remarked to Lane, "most if not all of them will be dead in the next few days."[19]

After a stint at a camp near the Burma border, the Japanese sent Lane with a small work party to Brenkassi (elsewhere rendered as Branokassi), 150 kilometers upriver from Kanchanaburi, to dispose of the bodies of Tamils felled by cholera. Lane wrote:

Once disease struck the natives it left the Japs with a very embarrassing situation, not only were they unable to feed them they were in no way able to help them combat the dreaded cholera. So in order to hide their embarrassment, they took to the barges and left the poor souls to die. It was some time before the natives realised that they had been abandoned, they had no boats, no food and no means of purchasing any. The possibility of them being able to obtain food from the local people was a non-starter, consequently they started to die. This was just what the Japs wanted, the sooner they all died the sooner the Japs could have them totally disposed of.[20]

Lane estimated that in ten days his 15-man crew buried approximately 2,000 rotting corpses in seven large pits. They "found nothing of a personal nature, no rings or brooches, no wallets or purses. It was as if [the laborers] had never been there." A Japanese officer praised the POWs for their efforts in completing the gruesome task and rewarded them with two days' rest.[21]

A rare published account by one of the Asian laborers appeared in the *Japan Times* in 1991. Soong Yit Koi, a Chinese from Malaya, told a reporter that a Japanese officer had approached him in a Seremban park in August 1942 and sought to enlist him for a 1–4 month stint as a civilian employee. Afraid to refuse, Soong was sent with nearly 800 other Chinese, Indians, and Malays to Thailand, where he worked from dawn to dusk, day after day. "Before the completion of the railroad in October 1943," he recalled, "we had almost nothing to eat because there was no transportation to supply food." Subsequently he was employed at such tasks as cutting wood used as locomotive fuel. Soong claimed that only 49 members of his group remained alive at the end of the war.[22]

Japan's allies played an active role in providing laborers for the project. The Thai government took primary responsibility in providing workers for the first and least difficult segment of the line, the portion that crossed the plain between the junction with Thailand's southern railway at Nong Pladuk and Kanchanaburi. Maintaining a Thai labor force soon became problematic, though, as these workers had the advantage of being able to abscond with relative ease when conditions became unpleasant. Also, news of disease and adverse working conditions spread rapidly within Thailand, making further recruitment difficult.[23]

Bloody clashes between Thai civilians and policemen and Japanese soldiers in December 1942 at Ban Pong, near the point where the Thailand–Burma railway joined Thailand's southern line, further soured the feelings of Thai laborers and officials toward the railway project. This clash, which left several Japanese soldiers dead, developed after a Japanese sentry slapped a Buddhist monk. Ill will lingered afterward on both sides. Reflecting this,

Japanese railroad officer Colonel Hiroike noted that while it could not be denied that Thailand had made major contributions to the project, "from the beginning to end the Thai were criticized and no one had a good thing to say about them."[24]

Nonetheless, faced with orders to rush the project to completion, the Japanese were forced to seek Premier Phibun's assistance in coping with a shortage of labor in early 1943. Phibun firmly resisted any additional effort to recruit Thai laborers, claiming that this would disrupt vital agricultural production. Instead, the Thai government joined the Japanese authorities in pressing the Chinese chamber of commerce to recruit Chinese laborers, a significant number of them recently displaced from Northern Thailand as a consequence of Phibun's order that all noncitizens must evacuate that region. The Japanese were willing to accept this alternative because they considered Chinese workers more diligent and reliable than their Thai counterparts.[25]

On March 28, 1943, representatives of the Japanese railway unit in charge of the project summoned the leaders of the Chinese Chamber of Commerce to request that it provide 10,000 Chinese laborers, including skilled workers, at 2.7 to 3.5 baht per day, substantial wages at the time. The leaders of the Chinese community, which remained very vulnerable to Japanese and Thai government pressures at this stage of the war, agreed to set up a committee and formulate a plan.[26]

Japanese ambassador Tsubokami reported in mid-May that the quota had been met, despite his own initial doubts and "enemy propaganda and rumors which are even now rampant." No doubt the most problematic "rumors" concerned the cholera epidemic that wrought havoc in the work camps along the railroad and even reached Bangkok in late June. This disruptive factor meant that still more workers would be needed in order to meet the target date for completing the line.[27]

The Japanese appealed to the Thai government, which again dumped responsibility in the lap of the Chamber of Commerce. A 19-man committee headed by the chamber's Chairman Ch'en Shou-ming (Tan Siew-men) conducted a new recruitment campaign. By mid-August more than 2,000 additional workers had been dispatched and efforts were under way to double the 500,000 baht raised earlier in the Chinese community to support the project.[28]

According to later Japanese reports, the Chamber of Commerce raised a total of 1.2 million baht and signed up 16,000 laborers before the railway was completed in October 1943. Yet a year later the Japanese army was seeking additional laborers—5,000 by the end of 1944—to maintain and improve the line. A further 1,800 workers were needed in January 1945. The Chinese chamber of commerce reportedly agreed to raise 800,000 baht to fund the recruitment effort.[29]

In addition to assisting with labor recruitment, the Thai government was forced by bilateral agreements to lend the Japanese local currency to cover military-related expenditures in Thailand, including the railway construction. A loan agreement covering such expenditures for the last six months of 1942 apportioned 4 million out of a total budget of 40.5 million baht for railway construction.[30] For the first six months of 1943 the Thai agreed to provide 18 million baht in loans, including 8 million for the Thailand–Burma railway.[31] Barely had the ink dried on this pact when Tokyo, determined to hasten the pace of construction, notified Bangkok that an additional 13 million baht would be required, 10 million of it earmarked specifically for the railway.[32] The loan agreement for the second half of 1943 totaled 87.4 million baht, with 10 million budgeted for the Thailand–Burma railway and another 15 million for a second rail line, across the narrow Kra Isthmus.[33] In the end, supplements brought this military loan budget up to 143 million baht. A whopping 275 million baht loan request for the first half of 1944 included 50 million for maintenance and upgrading of the completed Thailand–Burma railway, plus another 20 million for the Kra Isthmus line.[34]

In Burma, the Japanese induced their puppet regime to recruit laborers for the portion of the line that advanced toward the Thai border from the town of Thanbyuzayat. The Japanese in Rangoon characterized the building of the railway as part of an effort to break down a British-enforced isolation of Burma from neighboring Thailand. This explanation conveniently ignored the fact that the Burmese and Thai previously had been the bitterest of enemies, and that the latter had good reason to welcome a British-imposed end to a series of Burmese invasions. Still, Burmese leader Ba Maw and his colleagues responded enthusiastically to the Japanese appeal, assembling what they came to call the "Sweat Army" (*Chwe-tat*). Ba Maw later reflected:

> We were so carried away by the very thought of such a doorway being opened towards the east and the rich promises it held out to the Burmese that I am afraid we didn't think enough of some of the hard realities; for example of the prodigious difficulties we would meet when actually raising and caring for a vast labor force to be employed in a totally new form of manual labor for the Burmese, in one of the wildest and most pestilential jungles in Burma.[35]

Estimates of the number of Burmese who labored on the railway vary. Ba Maw claimed 65,000, while a Burmese official told a Dutch officer after the war that 90,000 were involved.[36] Although the Burmese government recruited these workers through levies supervised by local officials—who by Ba Maw's own admission often misused their authority to punish their enemies or obtain bribes—many Burmese took up the task with patriotic fervor. Colonel Hiroike rated the Burmese as the most cooperative supporters of the project, but the price paid was tragically high. Ba Maw acknowledged that after the first phase of construction "more than half the laborers had disappeared, having either fled or been killed off like flies by black-water fever, the deadliest form of malaria, and other jungle camp epidemics." Still, the Burmese leader credited the Japanese command with good intentions, noting that working conditions did gradually improve. He rationalized that the worst incidents, where Burmese were driven "like slaves," occurred in out-of-the-way camps run by "war-brutalized men."[37]

In Malaya, the Japanese-backed Indian independence movement also cooperated in the effort to mobilize labor. Its recruiters emphasized the importance of the railway to the liberation of India and employed the deceptive slogan "Let's go to Thai-nadu!"—a term that meant "the Motherland" (India) to Tamils.[38]

Such Indian participation in labor mobilization evoked bitter comments in the memoir of journalist M. Siviram, himself a publicist for the independence movement. In his recollection of a rail journey from Bangkok to Singapore in early 1943, Siviram vividly described the state of poverty and desperation that played a major part in convincing Tamils to join the railway labor units:

> One sight that struck me as the most unpleasant novelty in Malaya, where I had lived before, was the crowd of semistarved Indian children in loincloths, gathered at every railway station, begging for alms. It was a pathetic sight—these children with their lifeless eyes, sunken cheeks, stomach bulging out like balloons, and arms and legs that were merely dry sticks. They sang Japanese songs to rouse the sympathy of the Japanese officers in the military compartment and begged for alms in all languages— English, Japanese, Hindustani, Tamil, Malay, and Chinese. And how eagerly those hungry urchins jumped at everything that was thrown out the window—a lump of rice or a bit of fish from the officers' mess tins, or an over-ripe banana from their lunch basket. What terrible poverty and destitution that sight represented! And that in Malaya, where Indians were never seen begging along the railway line.[39]

Siviram went on to describe the Tamils he saw aboard the "dozens" of northward-bound military trains:

> Each wagon carried a couple of hundred of these people. Men, women, and children were huddled together in the sweltering heat of the goods

wagons, while the younger fellows perched themselves precariously atop the wagons to gain a breath of fresh air while getting roasted in the process. These people had been recruited for labor from the rubber plantations in Malaya, either by force directly employed by the Japanese or through the treachery of some Indian hirelings of the Japanese. The sight of these unfortunate people, crowding rice depots at the railway stations, was indeed heart-rending—a jostling bunch of humanity in hunger and distress, shouted at, cursed and slapped by everyone.[40]

Ram Singh Rawal, like Siviram an active member of the Indian independence movement in Thailand, joined in condemning Indian colleagues in Malaya for their involvement in labor recruitment. Rawal charged them with partial responsibility for the fact that innocent workers fell into "cruel and devilish hands" and were forced to labor under conditions "not only horrible, but also hell-like." The few who survived disease, he added, became "disabled and invalids as a result of malnutrition, beating, jungle-sickness, cancers and so on."[41]

After the war, the Allies sought revenge against the Japanese and their Korean subordinates who had abused European POWs but made no effort to assign blame for the recruitment of Asian laborers, or to mete out punishment for their mistreatment. Political considerations eventually forced the British to abandon plans to prosecute such rebellious colonial subjects as Ba Maw and the leaders of the Indian independence movement, but in any case the recruitment of their fellow Asians to work for Japanese was hardly viewed as the worst of their sins in British eyes.

As an independent state with an internationally recognized government when the war began, Thailand's status was different. But while the British showed considerable eagerness to exact revenge on the Thai for their support of the Japanese invasions of Malaya and Burma and their declaration of war in January 1942, they seemed little inclined to blame them for the sufferings of the POWs—much less those of the Asian labor force—during the construction of the Thailand–Burma railway. This attitude probably to some extent reflected the fact that by war's end most Allied POWs had come to view the Thai as benefactors because some residents along the railway had taken personal risks to provide assistance and had provided shelter for the few POWs who managed to escape. One very grateful escapee, Richard A. Brown, a British private, told an interviewer in 1945:

I have nothing but admiration for the Thai people. They are very kind and their hospitality is great. And I can honestly say they are quite the finest race of people I have ever met. How anyone could ever wish to fight these people I don't know. The nation that would declare war on Thailand must be insane.[42]

While the thinly stretched British South East Asia Command made a major effort to rescue Allied POWs as quickly as possible at the end of the war, assistance to displaced Asian laborers received no such priority. Some individuals, however, did take up the task. One of them was Major Andrew Gilchrist, before and after the war a British diplomat, who led a POW rescue team into peninsular Thailand at the end of August 1945 on behalf of Force 136, the Asian branch of the Special Operations Executive (SOE). When Gilchrist found that all the European prisoners had been moved elsewhere, he arranged for the removal of 100 Indian POWs, then sought to assist the thousands of Tamil and Malayan laborers encamped near Chumphon. Most of the laborers had worked on the Kra Isthmus railway project, but others were survivors from the Thailand–Burma railway who were straggling southward.

An Office of Strategic Services (OSS) team that arrived at the beginning of September assisted Gilchrist and described the situation:

> The Malay camps visited were in dense jungle, surrounded in all cases by trees and heavy vegetation. They were living in small bashas, sleeping on the bare ground for the most part. The bashas were poorly lighted, very poorly ventilated, and in swampy terrain. The rain every day made these places subject to millions of insects, much malaria and pneumonia. The food these people were eating was rejected food that the Jap would not touch. It consisted wholly of rotten, worm infested rice, with outside purchases on the part of the Malays impossible because the Japs had paid them in money that could not be spent locally.[43]

The plight of these British colonial subjects horrified Gilchrist. He described a "hospital" he inspected in one of the camps:

> It was nothing but a ghastly charnel house; a series of small rotting huts in heavy jungle with thirty serious cases and a few corpses huddled together on filthy wooden floors. The smell was intolerable; the commonest diseases were tropical ulcers, and dysentery—many people had *four* diseases ulcers, dysentery, beri-beri, and malaria. . . . The only medicine on view was a kind of weak red disinfectant. . . . Food consisted of rice and vegetable soup, in the most meagre quantities. Sanitary arrangements were non-existent, and all the patients were indescribably filthy and verminous.[44]

"The Japanese attitude was not so much one of obstruction as of total incomprehension," Gilchrist continued; "they could not understand why anyone took so much interest in those miserable creatures." A Japanese doctor and the local commander blamed a lack of medicine and equipment for the sad state of the ill laborers, but Gilchrist found this an unacceptable excuse for the lack of sanitation and basic provisions. He concluded that when workers fell ill "the Japanese system had been to push them out into the jungle to die."[45]

Even though a British army medical team arrived on September 10, 25 more laborers died over the next seven weeks, mostly from dysentery, malnutrition, and pneumonia. The medical team's leader, Capt. R.H. Heptinstall, reported:

> After my first visit to the coolie camps, it was obvious that some considerable improvements in their living conditions had to be made. Several camps were condemned, and new ones constructed by Japanese labor, whilst others were improved. Japanese supervision of camp hygiene had been deplorable, and no attempt had been made to arrange for latrine accommodation, and washing and cooking facilities. Every single camp was overcrowded, and the coolies scantily clothed. Their diet, however, was adequate, but whether this had been so for the previous three years was very questionable. The poor physical state of many coolies would suggest that improved diet was recent.[46]

Despite the local efforts of the army medical team to manage the situation, Gilchrist found the overall British response to the laborers' plight most unsatisfactory. In a report to his superior, Gilchrist angrily criticized a South East Asia Command order to the Japanese that they, not the British, were to bear responsibility for the maintenance of these Malay and Indian laborers. Noting a report that the Swiss Red Cross had taken up the task of aiding the survivors along the Thailand–Burma railway, Gilchrist wrote:

> These coolies are the unfortunate people who we were unable to defend in the face of the Japanese in 1941/42; they were all British subjects and were employed in Malaya (many of them being brought from India for this purpose) for the benefit of British interests.
>
> It appears to me that the person or persons who issued the order I have mentioned have little or no idea of the responsibilities that an empire carries with it, and I shall be grateful if you will take an opportunity of bringing this to the notice of any higher authorities who are likely to be interested.[47]

It is not clear what, if any, impact Gilchrist's complaint had, but he was not alone in his disapproval of the British command's lack of concern for its suffering colonial subjects. Several British officers of the Federated Malay

States Volunteer Force, who had been POWs along the Thailand–Burma railway themselves, took personal responsibility for looking after the unfortunate Asian laborers, traveling along the line to collect survivors and organize relief camps. One later commented: "We should never be able to look any Malayan in the face again if we do not see that those stranded in Siam are safely collected and finally repatriated."[48]

In late November 1945 the British military administration in Malaya sent a mission headed by Yap Pheng Geck, head of the Chinese section of the Citizen's Advice Bureau, to investigate the situation in Thailand. It reported that more than 24,000 Malayan residents, including "a few hundred women and children," had been accounted for in the relief camps. This figure included 17,703 Indians, 4,085 Chinese, and 2,538 Malays. Javanese survivors numbered 4,711.[49] The mission found that surrendered Japanese had been put to work building huts and doing necessary heavy work in the camps, while the recuperating laborers were paid for "lighter camp duties." Yap described the accommodations as "the best that can be supplied under the circumstances," adding that ample food and adequate medical treatment were available. The survivors, he said, were "actually better off than they might be in Malaya," where rice and other commodities were in short supply. Special facilities had been established to enable the survivors to communicate by letter with relatives in Malaya, and a repatriation program aimed at returning 1,000 to 1,500 persons per month by sea and rail had been formulated.[50]

Not all of the survivors entered these camps, however. Understandably wary of military authority, some attempted to reach home on their own. W. Stanley Moss, an SOE officer who set up residence in the British consulate in the southern coastal town of Songkhla in the wake of the Japanese surrender, noted a continual flow of "refugees and other lost souls of all nationalities seeking repatriation."[51]

Other stranded laborers decided to remain in Thailand. One Javanese stayed in rural Kanchanaburi Province, adopted a Thai name, and did not return to his native island for fifty-three years. The man, Boontum Wandee, made headlines when he revisited the village of his birth in 1995.[52]

Those POWs and Asian laborers who did not survive the war had received a symbolic gesture on March 12, 1944, when the Japanese army dedicated a monument in their honor. Colonel Dunlop, one of 40 POWs in attendance, described the two-hour ceremony at length in his diary. He found the monument "impressive,"[53] but the Japanese gesture angered other POWs. A Dutch officer spoke for his immediate group—and probably the majority of POWs—in saying that when they saw the monument after the war, "the cynicism of the Japanese in commemorating those whom they had driven, mercilessly and callously to their deaths struck us full force."[54] Some former POWs are said to have defaced the memorial by throwing rocks at it.[55]

At the end of the war the remains of POWs buried along the Thailand–Burma railway were disinterred and either returned to their homelands or reburied in one of three well-maintained military cemeteries, but the mass graves of Asian victims remained unmarked and ignored.[56] When construction workers accidentally uncovered one such grave in Kanchanaburi Province in 1990, a local resident told a journalist:

> Every morning the Indians dug a hole in this area to bury the dead bodies in the evening. Some days, two or three bodies were buried, some days more than five. This happened throughout the period of the railway construction.

Another said that many more such gravesites surely existed elsewhere along the "Death Railway."[57]

Although Japanese veterans associated with the railway who have written memoirs say little about the treatment of Asian workers, they have commonly attributed the severe handling of the POWs to a lack of supplies and equipment and the necessity of following orders. To illustrate the precedence accorded to military priorities over human considerations, a Japanese officer recalled that when he had once asked that ill POWs be given some time off, a superior had responded: "The work cannot be delayed even a single day. We must complete our assigned task. We have to keep working, even if the prisoners are reduced to the last man."[58]

A hierarchical worldview facilitated Japanese rationalization of the harsh treatment they meted out to members of the labor force. Japanese soldiers had been indoctrinated to view surrender as dishonorable, and they scorned enemies who had capitulated. An example of their callous attitude toward the POWs is recorded in the memoir of Byōdō Tsūshō, a government civilian employee who visited a railroad construction site. A Japanese noncommissioned officer (NCO) remarked to him, "Human beings certainly cling to life. Even though cholera is epidemic here and they get sick, they cling to life." Byōdō commented, "He said it nonchalantly as if he were waiting for them to die."[59]

Asian laborers were looked down upon for a different reason. The Japanese saw themselves as the natural leaders of East Asia, so it seemed only appropriate that other Asians on the lower rungs of the regional ladder should be willing to sacrifice, even to the extent of giving their lives, to achieve the goals of winning a "sacred" war and establishing East Asian co-prosperity.

Further, as Australian POW Kenneth Harrison has noted, inhumane treatment was often meted out because the POWs and Asian laborers were at the end of a chain of brutality in the Japanese army. Harrison, one former POW from the Death Railway who made a serious effort to understand his tormenters, wrote:

> We fiercely resented the Japanese habit of punishing by blows and beatings, but it did not seem quite so bad when we realized that corporal punishment was normal throughout the I[mperial] J[apanese] A[rmy]. It was quite normal for officers to beat up N.C.O.s with fists, sticks, or swords, and for N.C.O.s to beat up privates. It was not uncommon for the unlucky recipients to be left unconscious after such treatment. Unfortunately for us, the poor little one-star recruit had only one group he could beat up, and it was a fact that many beatings we received happened only because some battered Jap wanted to restore "face" by belting a few prisoners of war.

The Koreans, who ranked below the lowliest Japanese and were constant victims of discrimination and physical punishment themselves, were particularly prone to taking out their frustrations on the POWs.[60] An escaped POW reflected a common attitude toward the Korean guards when he reported in mid-1945:

> These people are absolutely insane. They delight in punishing the prisoners, and are always looking for any excuse to beat a man up. Words cannot describe these people; I cannot emphasize sufficiently to what extent these Koreans will go in punishing a prisoner. They are absolutely rotten to the core.[61]

American Flying Tiger pilot Charles Mott, who was captured very early in the war and survived the railway ordeal, offered a surprisingly nuanced analysis of Japanese brutality. He theorized that "original orders from Japan were made out on a civilized basis" but "flagrant and brutal abuses occurred in jungle working groups where brutality, incapacity and disinclination of the Japanese officers and NCOs made them possible." He saw the humiliating treatment accorded POWs as "part of a campaign to exalt the Nipponese by degrading comparison," adding:

> Psychologically the Jap is so constituted that he works himself up into a tremendous rage which must find expression in some brutal act. As in any people, the decent are in the majority. However, the difference lies in the fact that the Japs permit the sadists and barbarians among themselves uncurbed expression.[62]

Some Japanese have offered a straightforward social Darwinian explanation of why the POWs and the Asians working on the railway suffered much higher death rates than Japanese soldiers. As Gavan Daws noted in his 1994 book, *Prisoners of the Japanese,* they argue that the laborers, as inferior beings lacking in spirit, were less able to endure hardships. Byōdō hewed to this line, attributing the POW's susceptibility to disease to the "luxurious conditions" that they had previously enjoyed in Singapore.[63] But while Harrison indicated that at one remote camp his captors were "just as hungry as we were,"[64] and one Japanese officer stationed near the Burmese–Thai border described frogs, snakes, and lizards as "normal provisions,"[65] there is little doubt that Japanese soldiers fared better than their captives and hirelings. Moreover, not a few of the POWs and laborers were already sick or severely weakened when they reached their work sites.

Some Allied POWs have been willing to accept efforts by their former enemies to effect reconciliation. Dunlop, for example, in 1991 agreed to meet an old tormentor, Yi Hak-nae, a former Korean camp guard who spent eleven years in Sugamo Prison for mistreating Australian POWs in the Hintok Camp. Some of Dunlop's comrades criticized him for accepting Yi's apologies and an engraved watch, but the Australian doctor chose to interpret the Korean's gesture as an example of "the little bit of good in every man."[66] In a similar vein, 10 former British POWs have formed the Burma Campaign Fellowship Group to promote reconciliation. "There is no question that hatred destroys the hater rather than the hated," one of them, Dudley Cave, has declared. Cave was among a few former POWs who participated with Japanese veterans in a joint ceremony at Kanchanaburi on the fiftieth anniversary of the end of the war.[67]

Most ex-POWs, however, remain embittered. Some, who scheduled a separate fiftieth anniversary commemoration several days later, were quoted as saying that if any Japanese appeared they would be thrown into the river.[68] "Hate for the Japanese continues to eat away at most former Allied POWs like a cancer," wrote Micool Brooke, a journalist who has interviewed a number of them in recent years. He added, "Many . . . have cited the needless deaths of their comrades for their undying hate for the Japanese. Many are driven to make pilgrimages to the graves of their friends, as their sorrow for the dead grows every day that they live."[69]

One such unreconciled veteran of the railway construction, Charles Peall, stated:

> People who go back and shake hands with Japanese guards on the River Kwai [Kwae] appall me. We can't forgive and we can't forget. It is with us 24 hours a day. The word "reconciliation" is taboo until such time as the Japanese apologise for what happened and recompense the prisoners of war, and then we will think about it again.[70]

Like the POWs, some surviving Asian laborers have sought to obtain an apology and compensation from the Japanese. For example, some 300 Malayan Chinese petitioned the Japanese government in 1991. Tokyo replied, however, that the 1967 war settlement with Malaysia, which provided no compensation for individual victims, had closed the matter.[71]

Koreans who served as guards on the railway have also joined the clamor for redress. Convicted war criminal Yi, who ran a taxi company in Tokyo after his release, sought an apology from the Japanese government. Yi, who said he was pressured into joining the imperial army and merely followed orders, complained, "Japanese war criminals were treated well after the war; they received pensions and qualified for financial assistance, but we Koreans were excluded because of our nationality."[72]

Tokyo has been able to hold to its refusal to compensate any victims of the Thailand–Burma railway project because none of the groups involved has succeeded in turning its grievance into an international political issue to the extent that the former "comfort women" have in recent years. Criticism over Japanese abuse of the "comfort women"—many of whom have alleged that they were tricked or forced into becoming military prostitutes—became sufficiently intense that Tokyo could not ignore it. In order to avoid setting a precedent of direct governmental compensation payments that would encourage renewed claims by other war victims, the Japanese government established a private fund to provide aid to the former "comfort women." This has not resolved the issue, though, as donations have failed to meet expectations, and the victims have refused to accept this type of settlement.[73]

On the Japanese side, only a few former participants have adopted a forthrightly apologetic stance in regard to the mistreatment of the POWs and Asians who labored on the Thailand–Burma railway. Best known among them is Nagase Takashi, a former army interpreter, who has sought tirelessly, and with some success, to promote reconciliation. Takase's 1993 meeting with a long-embittered British officer, Eric Lomax—in whose interrogation and torture Nagase had been involved—is detailed in Lomax's 1995 memoir.[74] Similarly, Australian Trevor Dakin surmounted his bitter hatred of the Japanese to accept Nagase's apology and participate with him in a wreath-laying ceremony at the POW cemetery in Kanchanaburi in 1994.[75]

As mentioned previously, though, other ex-POWs continue to spurn such approaches. Arthur Lane has accused those who have buried the hatchet with the Japanese of "betraying their mates." He told journalist Peter Eng, "Give me a Japanese veteran now and I'll kill him. There's no way to apologize. Even if the Japanese crawled on their hands and knees that wouldn't change anything. They're all vermin. Only two (atomic) bombs were dropped. That's not enough."[76]

On the other side of the coin, many Japanese disapprove of Nagase's attempts at reconciliation. While his actions in establishing a Buddhist temple at Kanchanaburi and setting up the River Kwai Peace Foundation have received favorable publicity abroad, Nagase told journalist Brooke: "Most of the Burma–Siam Railway's veterans hate me. Not all of them share my desire to atone for wrongdoings in the past." Complaining that he had been labeled a traitor by fellow veterans, obstructed by his government, and ignored by the Japanese media, Nagase concluded, "Sadly, I don't think many Japanese support my work."[77] In another interview with the *Japan Times*, Nagase revealed that even among those Japanese veterans who had agreed to accompany him on trips to Kanchanaburi, "very few have shed tears or displayed deep emotion."[78]

In fact, some Japanese participants continue to view the construction of the Thailand–Burma railway as a glorious achievement. This sense of pride lay behind a veteran organization's purchase from the Thai government of a locomotive used on the railway for display at the Yasukuni Shrine in Tokyo.[79] It is also reflected in a volume published by the Japanese Association in Thailand, which attributed the line's completion to "magnificent technique and excellent army engineering," and described it as a "monumental work unparalleled in world history."[80] In a similar vein, a former Southern Army staff officer hailed "the fortitude and indomitable spirit of the construction units."[81] Even Lieutenant General Nakamura Aketo, who as commander of the Thailand Garrison Army earned a reputation among the Thai as an unusually humane Japanese officer, lauded the "enthusiasm and extraordinary administration" of Lieutenant General Ishida Hidekuma, the man who presided over the deadly rush to complete the railway, and who was executed as a war criminal as a consequence of his efforts.[82]

In extensive comments on the Thailand–Burma railway project in his memoir, Nakamura did not deny the suffering that accompanied the construction—he wrote of "sacrifice and overwork surpassing human strength" and acknowledged that "not a few POWs who were used as laborers succumbed to overwork and undernourishment and several thousand died due to the prevalence of cholera"—but he ignored the extent to which Japanese inattention to the health of the laborers contributed to the death toll. Instead he portrayed the cholera epidemic that spread down the line from April to July 1943 as an unfortunate natural force that the enemy unfairly turned against the Japanese: "the fact that it was largely POW and Malayan workers among the more than 5,000 people who died gave suitable 'inhumane treatment of POWs' propaganda materials to the enemy side and the result was that after the war many people were sacrificed as so-called 'war criminals.'"[83]

Nakamura is not alone in accusing the Allies of exaggerating the hardships faced by the POWs. A similar suggestion came recently from Nishino Junjirō, a junior-rank diplomat in the Japanese Embassy in Bangkok during the war and subsequently a prominent businessman in Thailand. "Japanese soldiers didn't torture POWs much," Nishino told *Bangkok Post* reporter Pravit Rojanaphruk. "Many died from malaria and diarrhoea. Even Japanese soldiers died from those diseases. The Japanese troops were not really cruel."[84] For his part, Byōdō suggested that the Allies made a big fuss about war crimes because they were humiliated by the fact that the Japanese were able to complete a railroad project that the British had declined even to attempt.[85]

Other former Japanese soldiers have sought to balance the scales by emphasizing the abuses they suffered as POWs after the end of the war. Those who were subjected to years of hard labor in the Soviet Union obviously have a strong basis for complaint,[86] but some soldiers detained in Southeast Asia have spoken out, too. Aida Yūji, who fell into Allied hands in Burma, emphasized British efforts to humiliate the surrendered Japanese in a book that became a best-seller in Japan in the 1960s and was subsequently translated into English.[87] In a similar vein, Oba Sadao, who spent nearly two years in British-run camps on Java, has recently complained that he and his fellow POWs were forced to do heavy, often dangerous, work while receiving only half the Japanese wartime ration of 3,200 to 3,600 calories daily. In an interview with a Tokyo newspaper, Oba charged that the Japanese were "deliberately detained by the British and Dutch as an unpaid workforce to cover critical labor shortages" in violation of the promise of prompt repatriation contained in the Potsdam Declaration.[88]

Clearly, the fact that so many surviving victims continue to nurture deep-seated hatreds and the perpetrators cling to rationalizations that justify the unjustifiable, prospects for general reconciliation are dim indeed. Neither formal apology nor financial compensation seem likely to have much effect on the attitudes of the former, while the latter cannot realistically be expected to assume personal responsibility for acts that reflected the spirit of orders from above and were encouraged by the internal dynamics of their army units. The fact that Japan is, after all, a group-oriented society, makes such action all the less likely and encourages the ostracism of guilt-driven individuals like Nagase. Further, the opportunistic timing and thinly veiled political considerations behind some of the recent campaigns for apologies and compensation make it even less likely that they will achieve any truly positive result.

For example, it is certainly no coincidence that such campaigns were renewed and intensified at the height of Japan's postwar prosperity in the 1980s. Daws described the situation from the perspective of the former POWs:

> By the 1980s [the Japanese] were all over Asia again, and not only that, they were invading America; there were Toyotas and Hondas everywhere. The Japanese were *the* world economic superpower; they had the old Allied powers bowing like prisoners.
>
> To the old POWs it looked as if Japan owned the future.

Daws added that the American ex-POWs deeply resented the American government's decision to give each Japanese American interned during the war a 20,000-dollar compensation payment.[89]

Until the 1980s both Western and Asian governments had found it expedient to downplay Japan's wartime offenses, but the end of the Cold War and Japan's reemergence as an economic power changed the situation. As George Hicks pointed out in *Japan's War Memories,* the Chinese government led the way in 1982 when it suddenly made an issue of the alleged watering down of war coverage in government-monitored Japanese history textbooks to hit back at Japan for initiating higher-level contacts with Taiwan.[90] Recognizing that it had found a convenient means to put Tokyo on the defensive, the Beijing government also began to make an issue of the Rape of Nanking for the first time.[91] Certainly China and other Asian countries have ample grounds for complaint about Japan's past behavior, but the way in which they have employed the issue suggests that the cynical pursuit of political advantage often has outweighed moral outrage as a motivating factor.[92]

This makes it easier to sympathize to some extent with the situation of the Japanese government. Each one of a series of apologetic statements by successive prime ministers and Emperor Akihito has been criticized as lacking adequate sincerity, and there is little prospect that any new statement that Japanese politicians and bureaucrats could agree on would be received any more favorably. Also, it is undeniably true that Tokyo's acknowledgment of the compensation claims of any one group of war victims would encourage a flurry of new demands by others, or even by descendants of dead victims. Japanese officials, including those inclined to acknowledge the nation's past mistakes, must ask: "Where will it all end?"

It also should be pointed out that as a consequence of Japan's rise to the heights of postwar prosperity there has been a tendency to lose sight of the fact that the Japanese did not escape punishment for their aggressive acts. In addition to sustaining 2 million military and civilian war dead, Japan lost its hard-won empire, and its cities were laid waste by Allied bombing. Its urban masses were destitute and on the brink of starvation when more than six years of American occupation began in 1945. Further, seven Class A war crimes suspects were convicted and hanged, 920 lower-ranking war criminals were executed, and more than 3,000 men served time in prison for war crimes.[93] Many guilty individuals escaped punishment, but this was inevitable under the circumstances. While the Japanese benefited from American Cold War policies that led to the abandonment of the purge of prewar political leaders, supported the rehabilitation of the nation's economy, and discouraged reparations claims from other Allies, Japan still had to negotiate war settlements with the various Asian nations. Ultimately those states decided not to press for compensation for individual victims of Japanese aggression, and they used the war settlements they did receive for other purposes.[94]

It is not clear that continuing to press Japan for apologies and compensation will produce any positive result in terms of international amity. Truly meaningful apologies must reflect heartfelt sentiment and be made by those responsible for the misdeeds to those who were victimized. But most surviving Japanese veterans seem disinclined to apologize, and some victims seem uninterested in such a gesture, while many others would question its sincerity. Despite the example set by their German counterparts, Japanese companies have refused to compensate Asian and POW slave laborers. Even if the Japanese government unexpectedly stepped in to create a compensation program, however, it would be criticized as inadequate in amount or scope, no matter how generous it might be. In any case, it would do nothing for the majority of the victims, who are long since deceased.

On another matter, it is easy to agree with the statement of Australian Charlie Warden, a former POW laborer on the Thailand–Burma railway, that young Japanese "should be taught their history so they know better and are not so ignorant of their war crimes,"[95] although the young Japanese would surely point out that such crimes were not exactly "theirs." Even if they are insufficiently aware of their nation's war crimes, though, the younger generation in Japan display attitudes that are far removed from those of their parents, much less those of their grandparents or great-grandparents. Despite periodic muscle flexing by the Japanese right wing, there is no indication that a significant percentage of Japanese youth is inclined to support anything akin to 1930s militarism. Nor is there anything that suggests a Japanese army might again rampage through Asia. And by the end of the twentieth century, a decade-long crisis had made "Japan Incorporated" seem a considerably less fearsome economic juggernaut than it appeared to be in the 1980s.

Certainly it would be a positive development if all nations provided their youth with accurate and balanced history textbooks, but nationalistic history texts are hardly unique to Japan. How many of the foreign government officials who have complained about the "whitewashed" nature of Japanese textbooks were truly in a position to cast stones? Do not the Chinese, for example, reside in a glass house in this regard?[96] For that matter, have Americans been eager to engage in the type of historical self-reflection that they urge on the Japanese? The negative public response and political pressure that forced the modification of the *Enola Gay* exhibit at the Smithsonian Institution in Washington, D.C. in 1995 suggest not.[97] Such episodes give Japanese officials and historical revisionists a convenient excuse to dismiss foreign critics as hypocrites.

That the Japanese mistreated the Allied POWs and Asians who labored along the Thailand–Burma railway—and wantonly killed and abused many other Asians and Europeans during conflicts between 1931 and 1945—is amply documented. Apologists who attempt to deny the obvious, or portray Japan's self-serving expansionist policies as motivated primarily by a desire to "liberate" other Asians, deserve the denunciations they receive. The Japanese—and all other peoples—need to examine the deeds of their forefathers in a balanced and critical fashion, and then encourage their children to do the same. As Richard von Weizsäcker has warned, "Anyone who closes his eyes to the past is blind to the present. Whoever refuses to remember the inhumanity is prone to the risk of new infection."[98]

Still, remembrance of past evils is a double-edged sword. Obsession with past wrongs can make it difficult, if not impossible, to move beyond and transcend them. Benjamin Barber, who points out that "a certain amount of studied historical absentmindedness" may be necessary to make reconciliation between previously hostile groups possible, appropriately warns that "Injuries too well remembered cannot heal."[99]

Notes

Introduction

1. *Syonan: Singapore under the Japanese: A Catalogue of Oral History Interviews* (Singapore: Oral History Department, 1986).

2. P.J. Suwarno, *Romusa—Daerah Istimewa Yogyakarta* (*Rōmusha*: Yogyakarta Special Region) (Yogyakarta: Penerbitan Universitas Sanata Dharma, 1999).

3. Lin Yone Thit Lwin, *Yodaya-Myanma Miyhta-lan Kodwe Chwaydat Hmattan* (Rangoon: Duwun Sarpay, 1968). Excerpts from this book are included in Paul H. Kratoska, ed., *The Thailand-Burma Railway, 1942–1946: Documents and Selected Writings* (London: Routledge, 2005).

4. See, for example, Ikehata Setsuho and Ricardo Trota Jose, eds., *The Philippines under Japan: Occupation Policy and Reaction* (Quezon City: Ateneo de Manila University Press, 1999), and Forum for Research Materials on the Japanese Occupation of Indonesia, *Bibliography on Japanese Occupation of Indonesia* (Tokyo: Ryukei Shyosha, 1996).

5. Information in this section is from a paper entitled "Pioneer and Labour in South East Asia Command: A Survey of the Service," War Office (WO) 203/2192, in the British National Archives (Public Record Office).

Chapter 1

1. Jerome B. Cohen, *Japan's Economy in War and Reconstruction* (Minneapolis: University of Minnesota Press, 1949), pp. 271–72.

2. Ibid., p. 275.

3. Japan's mobilization of labor was of particular interest to Allied intelligence. As one analyst with America's Office of Strategic Services explained, the "selection, timing, and stringency of the manpower controls provide at least a rough indicator of the strain that the Japanese economy is undergoing in maintaining its front line effectives and highlight some of the bottlenecks on the home front." Office of Strategic Services (OSS), Research and Analysis Branch (R&A), no. 1987, "Manpower Mobilization Measures in Japan" (December 1944) (henceforth "MMMJ"), p. 1. Additional information is found in OSS R&A Assemblage 45, "Manpower in Japan and Occupied Areas," extracts from shortwave Radio Tokyo and affiliated stations from December 1941 to July 15, 1944 (henceforth "MJOA").

4. Cohen, *Japan's Economy,* pp. 271–352.

5. Ministry of Economic Warfare, Survey of Economic Developments in the Far East in the Six Months ending 31st December 1944, no. 1 of 1945, p. 16, in Foreign Office (FO) 837/386, in the Public Record Office, London.

6. "MJOA," English-language radio broadcast from Manila, February 16, 1943, OSS Assemblage 45 (compiled August 26, 1944), p. 310.

7. Japanese-language broadcasts, September 21, 1943, and April 24, 1994, "MJOA," p. 215.

8. "MMMJ," pp. 4–5.

9. Cohen, *Japan's Economy*, pp. 287–88.

10. Japanese Monograph 167, Malaya Operations Record, 29th Army, Jan. 1944–Aug. 1945 (based on information provided by Lt.-Gen. Fujimura Masuzo and Lt.-Gen. Kawahara Naokazu, both former Chiefs of Staff of the 29th Army), pp. 8–10, 20; *Syonan Shimbun*, January 4, Syowa 19 [1944].

11. *Syonan Shimbun*, December 9, 2003.

12. See chapter 9 in this volume.

13. Tokyo, Japanese-language broadcast, March 1, 1944, "MJOA," p. 216.

14. Tokyo, Japanese home broadcast, December 8, 1943, "MJOA," p. 243.

15. Tokyo, Japanese home broadcast, April 24, 1944, and Japanese overseas broadcast, May 16, 1944, "MJOA," p. 276.

16. Article 4, National General Mobilization Law.

17. Cohen, *Japan's Economy*, p. 318.

18. "MMMJ," p. 6.

19. Cohen, *Japan's Economy*, pp. 277–82.

20. "MMMJ," p. 10; Cohen, *Japan's Economy*, p. 281.

21. Cohen, *Japan's Economy*, p. 274.

22. Ibid., p. 281.

23. Tokyo English-language broadcast, March 29, 1943, and Tokyo Japanese-language home broadcast, December 28, 1943, "MJOA," p. 239.

24. Manila, Spanish-language broadcast, May 17, 1943, "MJOA," p. 302.

25. Cohen, *Japan's Economy*, pp. 282–85, 327.

26. "MJOA."

27. Cohen, *Japan's Economy*, pp.274–75, 301–4.

28. A.J. de la Mare, "A Report on Japanese Agriculture under War-time Conditions, with special reference to the Food Supply," encl. in Craigie to Halifax, February 8, 1940, FO371/24735, F946/222/23, The National Archives (Public Records Office).

29. For examples, see Paul H. Kratoska, ed., *Food Supplies and the Japanese Occupation in South-East Asia* (Houndmills: Macmillan; New York: St Martin's Press, 1998), pp. 74–75, 170, 179, 210–11.

30. "MJOA," p. 270.

31. Tokyo English-language broadcast, April 4, 1944, "MJOA," p. 271. The reference is probably to the Sundanese people of West Java but could also refer to residents of the Lesser Sundas.

32. Cohen, *Japan's Economy*, p. 272.

33. de la Mare, "A Report on Japanese Agriculture under War-time Conditions.

34. "MMMJ," p. 11, and Far East Weekly Intelligence Summary No. 56 for week ending February 4, 1944.

35. "MMMJ," p. 11.

36. Tokyo, Japanese overseas broadcast, September 22, 1943, "MJOA," p. 33.

37. Ibid.

38. "MMMJ," pp. 11–12.

39. Cohen, *Japan's Economy*, p. 315.

40. "MMMJ," pp. 11–13; Cohen, *Japan's Economy,* pp. 272–73.

41. See chapter 13 in this volume.

42. Tokyo, English-language broadcasts, July 15, 1944, and July 7, 1944, "MJOA," pp. 289, 307.

43. Cohen, *Japan's Economy,* pp. 323–24.

44. Batavia, English-language broadcast, June 10, 1944, and Singapore, Japanese-language broadcast, June 11, 1944, "MJOA," p. 267.

45. "MJOA," pp. 268, 282, 289, 306–7.

46. Cohen, *Japan's Economy,* pp. 300–301, 324–25.

47. L. De Jong, *Het Koninkrijk der Nederlanden in de Tweede Wereldoorlog* (The Kingdom of the Netherlands in the Second World War), vol. 11B, *Nederlands-Indië* (Netherlands Indies), part 2 (The Hague: Staatsuitgeverij, 1985), p. 517.

48. Regarding the Sumatra railway, see Henk Hovinga, *Eindstation Pakan Baroe 1944–1945: Dodenspoorweg door het oerwoud* (Destination Pakan Baroe 1944–1945: Death railway in the Jungle) (Amsterdam: Buijten and Schipperheijn, 1996): and H. Neumann and E. van Witsen, *De Sumatra Spoorweg: Documentatie* (Middelie: Studio Pietes Mulier, 1985). Concerning the West Banten railway, see chapter 8 in this volume.

49. "MJOA," p. 253.

Chapter 2

1. This is a theme both of Ju Zhifen's chapter on North Chinese workers and Manchukuo (chapter 3 in this volume) and Matsumura Takao, Xie Xueshi, and Eda Kenji's *Mantetsu Rōdōshi no Kenkyū* (Studies on the Labor History of the South Manchuria Railway) (Tokyo: Nihon Keizai Hyōronsha, 2002).

2. Manshū Shimizu Gumi, *Manshū Shiten Nenkan* (Yearbook of the Shimizu Manchuria Office), quoted in Manshū Shimizu kai, ed., *Kōya* (Spacious Fields) (Tokyo: privately published, 1980), p. 144.

3. Kang Chao, *The Economic Development of Manchuria: The Rise of a Frontier Economy* (Ann Arbor: University of Michigan, Center for Chinese Studies, 1982), pp. 14–17, 32–33. According to Chao, construction activity measured in millions of 1934 Manchukuo yuan was 115.5 in 1929, increased to 143.6 in 1934, fell to 113.8 in 1936, then rose to 238.3 in 1939, and dropped to 153.8 in 1941. By 1941 agriculture accounted for less than 30 percent of GDP.

4. Construction employment figures through 1937 are from Kenchiku Gakkai Shinkyō Shibu, ed., *Manshū Kenchiku Gaisetsu* (Manchurian Construction Survey), hereafter abbreviated as *MKG* (Shinkyō: Manshū Jijō Annaisho, 1940), pp. 186–87. The 1940 Manchukuo census recorded a population of 44,596,000, with almost 21 million employed (74 percent in agriculture). To have almost half the population employed is a relatively large proportion, but 58 percent of the population was between sixteen and sixty years of age—largely because of the substantial migration of young people—and this was also a comparatively large proportion. The census also included in its labor force count some youths under fifteen, and almost 420,000 women engaged in household work, but probably undercounted women and children engaged in agriculture. Population statistics for 1939 recorded the labor force in agriculture, husbandry, and forestry as 23.5 percent. Wang I-shou, "Chinese Migration and Population Change in Manchuria" (University of Minnesota Diss., pp. 122, 125–27, 145, 185–88, 198–200. Chao estimates construction employment at 487,000 in 1939 and 518,000

in June 1941. This includes 286,515 employees of construction firms and an estimated 232,077 construction workers unaffiliated with a construction firm. In addition, about 40,000 were employed in manufacturing building materials in 1938. Chao, *Economic Development*, pp. 35–37, 89.

5. Chao, *Economic Development*, pp. 8–9; Wang, *Migration*, pp. 45–50, 100–101, 143–46; Thomas R. Gottschang, "Migration from North China to Manchuria: An Economic History, 1891–1942" (Ph.D. diss., University of Michigan, 1982), pp. 1–2, 44, 94–106, 138–48.

6. *MKG*, p. 438.

7. Kubota Hiroshi, "Manshū Shihai to Rōdō Mondai—Kōzan, Kōwan Niyaku, Doboku Kenchiku Rōdō ni Okeru Shokuminchiteki Sakushu ni Tsuite" (Control of Manchuria and the Labor Problem: On the Colonial Exploitation of Mining, Harbor Loading, and Construction Labor), in Kojima Reiitsu, ed., *Nihon Teikokushugi to Higashi Ajia* (Japanese Imperialism and East Asia) (Tokyo: Ajia Keizai Kenkyūjō, 1979), p. 324, note 2. *MKG*, pp. 437–38. The SMR set up technical schools in Manchuria in 1909 and 1911 and added a construction trades section to the second in 1918. Oka Hiromichi, "Manshū ni Okeru Kōgyō Kyoiku no Shinkō," (The Promotion of Industrial Education in Manchuria) *Manshu Kenchiku Zasshi* 15, 3 (March 1935): 113–15.

8. Japanese researchers and those in the construction industry referred to it as both the *batou* system (*batō seido*) and the coolie-boss system (*kūrī gashira seido*). See Minami Manshū Tetsudō Kabushiki Kaisha, Keizai chōsakai, *Manshū no Kūrī* (The Manchurian Coolie) (Dairen: Minami Manshū Kabushiki Kaisha, 1934), p. 36; *MKG*, p. 213.

9. *Sakakiya Senjirō Nikki* (The Diary of Senjirō Sakakiya) (Tokyo: Sakakiya Senjirō Nikki Kankōsha, 1970), pp. 368–72.

10. This description of the *batou* system in Manchuria is drawn from *MKG*, pp. 217–19; Matsu'ura Suke, "Manshū ni Okeru Kenchiku Rōdōsha ni Tsuite" (On Construction Labor in Manchuria), *Kenchiku Zasshi 51*, 631 (October 1937): 1207–13; Kubota, "Manshū Shihai," pp. 315–16; Minami Manshū Tetsudō Kabushiki Kaisha, *Manshū no Kūrī*, pp. 35–39; and *The Orient Year Book, 1942* (Tokyo: Asia Statistics, 1942), pp. 717–18. Makino Masaoto, author of the *MKG*'s labor section, held several concurrent government positions, including capital (Shinkyō) police architectural section chief, and Capital Construction Bureau engineer. Matsu'ura Suke was in the Shinkyō office of Ōmori gumi, a major construction firm in Manchuria. Zhang Shengzhen cites Sakakiya's *batou*, the Cui brothers, as developing a particularly strong network by cultivating ties among relatives in villages in the construction recruiting areas along the Hebei–Shandong border: "Doboku Kenchiku" (Construction), in Matsumura, Xie, and Eda, *Mantetsu Rōdōshi no Kenkyū*, pp. 218–19.

11. *MKG*, pp. 220–21; Matsu'ura, "Rōdōsha," pp. 1208–9.

12. *MKG*, pp. 213, 217; Kubota, "Manshū Shihai," p. 315. Describing the *batou* system as an "oyakata system and therefore feudal" recalled the socioeconomic relationships between lord and warrior-retainer, master and apprentice, and village stem and branch families of pre-1868 Japan. The *kobun* or *kokata*, the one "who played the role of child," often had labor or other service obligations to the *oyakata* or *oyabun*, the "one who plays the role of parent," who in turn had protective obligations. Thomas C. Smith, *The Agrarian Origins of Modern Japan* (Stanford, CA: Stanford University Press, 1959), pp. 24–35, 133–37. For *oyakata* in the pre- and early postwar Japanese construction industry, see John W. Bennett and Iwao Ishino, *Paternalism in*

the Japanese Economy: Anthropological Studies of Oyabun-Kobun Patterns (Minneapolis: University of Minnesota Press, 1963).

13. Minami Manshū Tetsudō Kabushiki Kaisha, *Manshū no Kūrī*, pp. 37–38; Eda Kenji, "Shū" (Conclusion), in Matsumura, Xie, and Eda, *Mantetsu Rōdōshi no Kenkyū*, pp. 496–98. Zhang Shengzhen, "Doboku Kenchiku," p. 218, says that for SMR railway construction, firms contracted with *batou* to carry out earthmoving projects and controlled workers directly (relying on *batou* for management) for laying rail, bridge building, and signal work, sometimes combining these two methods.

14. Detailed descriptions of Wada's methodology may be found in Minami Manshū Tetsudō Kabushiki Kaisha. Sōmubu. Shinsa Yakushitsu Jimu Nōritsuhan, "Jūji-in no Kan-i Tekizai Kanbetsu Hō: Chūgoku Jūji-in no Saiyō to Kansōgaku" (A Simple Method to Distinguish Properly Qualified Employees: Physiognomy and Recruitment of Chinese Employees), *Manshu Gijutsu Kyōukaishi* 11, 59 (1934): 19–41; and Wada Toshio, "Tekisei Kensa no Jōshikiteki Shudan to Shite no 'Kansōgaku,'" (Physiognomy as a Commonsense Means of Aptitude Testing), *Manshu Gijutsu Kyōukaishi* 11, 66 (1934): 473–97. The SMR continued to publish Wada's research on this topic as late as 1940.

15. "Jūji-in no Kan-i Tekizai Kanbetsu Hō," pp. 23–28.

16. Ibid., pp. 30–34; *MKG*, p. 205; Gottschang, "Migration from North China," pp. 101, 108. The "carpenter producing areas," the main recruiting area for construction workers, were in southeastern Hebei near the Shandong border in Yanshan and Changzhou counties. Secondary areas were nearby in Shandong.

17. For instance, the *Sakakiya Nikki*, January 16, 1939, p. 1093, in the context of "coolie transport and control," discusses domestic coolies (*kokunai kūrī*) and gives the total number of coolies (*kūrī sōinsū*) from outside Manchukuo (calling them both foreign workers—*kokugai rōdōsha* and foreign coolies—*kokugai kūrī*) as a million (the approximate number of North Chinese migrants into Manchukuo).

18. Minami Manshū Tetsudō Kabushiki Kaisha, *Manshū no Kūrī*'s discussion of the "meaning of kūrī," including etymological implications, and types of coolies is on pp. 25–29 and 32–35. For Japanese and Chinese terms glossed as coolie or taken as closely related by Japanese concerned with construction labor management in Manchukuo, see Minami Manshū Tetsudō Kabushiki Kaisha, *Manshū no Kūrī*, p. 25; *MKG*, pp. 438–39, 712; and Matsu'ura, "Rōdōsha," p. 1207.

19. Tanabe Heikaku, "Ryojun Bakugeki Enshū Kengaku no Shokan Narabi ni Manshū Kenchiku Kai no Kinkyō" (Impressions of Observations of Bombing Practice at Port Arthur and Recent Architectural Activity in Manchuria), *Kenchiku Zasshi* 47, 567 (February 1933): 270–71; *MKG*, pp. 211, 213–14. According to the *MKG*, Chinese carpenter, mason, and plasterer wages in Manchukuo in September 1939 averaged about 1.75 yen per day.

20. *MKG*, pp. 205–6; Matsu'ura, "Rōdōsha," pp. 1207, 1209–11. Zhang Shengzhen, "Doboku Kenchiku," in Matsumura, Xie, and Eda, *Mantetsu Rōdōshi no Kenkyū*, pp. 236–38, describes very difficult working and living conditions of railway construction workers in open country in northern Manchuria (including large and vicious insects capable of killing cows or horses), remote from basic facilities such as clinics to treat all-too-common illnesses and injuries. Conditions successively deteriorated with the 1937 intensification of fighting with China, increased hostility with the Soviet Union, and the outbreak of the Pacific War. Construction extended into November and December, and work injuries and deaths increased.

21. *MKG*, p. 206; Matsu'ura, "Rōdōsha," pp. 1207, 1209.

22. Manchukuo State Council, *An Outline of the Manchukuo Empire* (Dairen: Manchuria Daily News, 1939), 22, p. 7; *MKG*, pp. 183, 207–208. The absorption of Chinese into Manchu extended to language. The *Manchurian Construction Survey* also contains a Japanese-Chinese construction glossary entitled *Nichi-Man jutsugo*, or Japanese-Manchurian Terminology. Ethnic management included attempts to understand ethnic variations in efficiency. For such research, see *Manshū Doboku Kenchikugyō Kyōkai Gaiyō* (n.p., n.d., but published between December 1940 and 1943), p. 29.

23. Kubota, "Manshū Shihai," pp. 314–15; *MKG* (Manshū Doboku Kenchikugyō Kyōkai), which I am rendering as Manchuria Construction Association, was translated variously, including "Manchuria Public Works and Building Construction Association," in "New Building Law Announced," *Manchuria* 5, 4 (June 1, 1940): 262–63; "Manchurian Public Work Contractor's Association," *Manchuria Daily News,* special issue, July 20, 1940; and "Manchuria Civil Engineering and Architectural Association," *Manchuria* (January 1, 1938): 31.

24. Sakakiya cites a July 1932 attack on railroad construction by 250 "bandits," in which three *batou* were kidnapped and many Chinese workers wounded. *Sakakiya Nikki,* pp. 903, 920; Gottschang, "Migration from North China," p. 94.

25. Manshūkokushi hensan kankokai, *Manshūkokushi: Kaku Ron* (The History of Manchukuo, vol. 2, Detailed Studies) (Tokyo: 1971), pp. 1154–55; Okabe Makio, *Manshūkoku* (Manchukuo) (Tokyo: Sanseido, 1978), pp. 131–32; *Manchukuo Year Book: 1942* (Manchukuo Year Book Company, 1942), p. 632. When Osaka mayor Seki Hajime visited Manchuria, he was told it was a "bottomless bag" through which Japanese investment poured into the hands of workers returning to North China. *Seki Hajime Nikki* (The Diary of Seki Hajime) (Tokyo: Tokyo Daigaku Shuppankai, 1986), entry for August 13, 1933, p. 910.

26. *Sakakiya Nikki,* pp. 911–12, "Administration of Labour Affairs in Manchoukuo," *Manchuria* 6 (July 1941): 200; *Manchukuo Yearbook: 1942,* p. 641; *Manshūkokushi,* p. 1155.

27. *Sakakiya Nikki,* pp. 923, 932, 942; Kubota, "Manshū Shihai," p. 315; *Manshūkokushi,* p. 1155.

28. Gottschang, "Migration from North China," p. 101; Okabe, *Manshūkoku,* p. 132; Hiroshi Iwai, "Administration of Labor Affairs in Manchoukuo," *Manchuria* 5, 3 (April 1940): 113. Datong (Great East) Company was also called Datong Kungsu, Daito Koshi, and Daito Kungssu.

29. *Manshūkokushi,* pp. 1155–56; Anonymous, "Administration of Labour Affairs in Manchukuo," *Manchuria* 6 (July 1941): 200. The articles of incorporation of the Datong Company and the texts of the March 9 and March 21 laws, along with sample identity cards, are found in Minami Manshū Tetsudō Kabushiki Kaisha, Keizai Chōsakai, *Manshū Rōdō Tōsei Hōsaku* (Manchurian Labor Control Policies), vol. 2 (Dairen: Keizai Chōsakai, 1935), pp. 234–49. For construction industry pressure for labor immigration, see the lead editorial, "Rōryoku Mondai to Nichi-Man-Shi Teikei no Yōbō" (The Labor Problem and the Call for Partnership between Japan, Manchukuo, and China), in *Manshū Kenchiku Zasshi* 15, 5 (May 1935): 238.

30. Louise Young, "Colonizing Manchuria: The Making of an Imperial Myth," in Stephen Vlastos, ed., *Mirror of Modernity: The Invention of Tradition in Modern Japan* (Berkeley: University of California Press, 1998), pp. 95–109.

31. Minami Manshū Tetsudō Kabushiki Kaisha, Keizai Chōsakai, *Manshū Rōdō Tōsei Hōsaku,* vol. 2, pp. 614–18.

32. Ibid., pp. 617–18. The "Agreement to Supply Japanese Labor," on pp. 582–86, specified that the lowest standard daily wages at Shinkyō for carpenters and plasterers were to range from 2.5 to 3.5 yen, depending on skill; for laborers (*nimpu*), from 1.5 to 2.0 yen. The wages could be negotiated up or down if the work site was north or south of Shinkyō. According to the Manchuria Association of Architecture, in May 1934 daily wages for Chinese plasterers ranged from 1.25 to 2.3 yen and averaged 1.8 yen, while wages for laborers (*nimpu*) ranged from 0.6 to 0.85 yen, averaging 0.7 yen. This information is consistent with research on wages in Dairen by the MCA, which reported 1934 Japanese and Chinese plasterers' daily wages at 3.5 and 1.6 yen, respectively, and 1934 Japanese and Chinese *nimpu* wages at 2.0 and 0.65 yen. The negotiated agreement followed the existing wage structure in Manchuria, where wages for Japanese were often twice those for Chinese. On the other hand, Home Ministry research on wages at the end of 1935 reported that Osaka plasterers received 2.8 yen daily, compared with a national average of 2.33 yen; and Osaka *nimpu* day laborers were paid 1.5 yen, against a national average of 1.33 yen, so the agreed wages compared favorably with Japanese wages. *MKG,* pp. 206–8, 212. The agreement also provided advantageous working conditions compared to those of Chinese workers. Overtime was to be granted for more than ten hours of work, the employers' ability to arbitrarily move workers to another work site without negotiation was restricted, and the workers were not given the same tasks as Chinese laborers.

33. *Manshū Rōdō Tōsei Hōsaku,* vol. 2, pp. 617–33. Half of the Osaka *Nichi-Man Rōmu Kyōkai*'s 1935 budget was to be provided by the national government.

34. The 1935 quota is close to the number of immigration papers issued by the Datong Company (444,540) but somewhat less than Gottschang's adjusted estimate of 491,798 actual immigrants. Gottschang, "Migration from North China," p. 101; *Manchukuo Year Book: 1942,* p. 633; *Sakakiya Nikki,* p. 1005.

35. Gottschang, "Migration from North China," p. 101; Ramon Myers, "Creating a Modern Enclave Economy: The Economic Integration of Japan, Manchuria, and North China, 1932–1945," in Peter Duus *et al.,* eds., *The Japanese Wartime Empire, 1931–1945* (Princeton, NJ: Princeton University Press, 1996), pp. 148–59; Bureau of Information, Manchoukuo State Council, ed., *An Outline of the Manchoukuo Empire* (Dairen: Manchuria Daily News), pp. 138–45; *Manchoukuo Year Book: 1942,* pp. 405–18, 632. The Five-Year Plan projected doubled coal production, tripled electricity generation (with new hydroelectric plants of 590,000 kilowatts capacity), and iron production at more than nine times 1936 levels. Infrastructure improvements included 2,500 kilometers of new rail line, 13,000 kilometers of new roads, and improvement of existing roads and bridges. Increased Japanese immigration was intended to be primarily agricultural and so avoid the labor competition that Japanese workers faced. The *Manchoukuo Year Book: 1942,* p. 408: "As regards competition from cheaper native labor, the Japanese farmers have yet to meet with any inconvenience and in fact, the lower standard of living of the Manchurians would seem to be advantageous as long as it lasts, since the Japanese farmer at present is more in the position of an employer than otherwise in his relations with native laborers."

36. "Gunju Chohatsu hō" (Military Supplies Requisition Law), *Manshū Seifu Kōhō* (hereafter abbreviated as *MSK*), May 13, 1937.

37. "Sōdōinhō" (National Mobilization Law), *MSK,* February 26, 1938. See Articles 1, 21, 23–25.

38. "Bōeihō" (Defense Law), *MSK,* March 10, 1938; "Bōei i-inkai Kanri" (Defense Commission Supervision), *MSK,* April 20, 1939.

39. *Sakakiya Nikki,* p. 1041; *Manchuria* (January 1, 1938), p. 31; *Manshūkokushi,* pp. 1160–65; *MSK,* Imperial Ordinance 456, December 14, 1937, established the organization. Half the capital came from the Manchukuo government, 15 percent from the SMR, 15 percent from the Datong Company, 7.5 percent from the MCA, and smaller amounts from mining, industrial, and labor supply companies. The Guandong Army supplied no capital. Manshū Rōkō Kyōkai was also translated as Manchuria Laborer's Association and as Manchoukuo Labor and Industrial Foundation.

40. *Manshūkokushi,* p. 1060; "Administration of Labour Affairs in Manchoukuo," pp. 198–99; Iwai, "Administration of Labor Affairs in Manchoukuo," pp. 110–11.

41. *Manshūkokushi,* p. 1061–62; *Manchoukuo Year Book, 1942,* pp. 632–34; Okabe, *Manshūkoku,* p. 134; Zheng, "Doboku Kenchiku," p. 221.

42. *Manshūkokushi,* p. 1062; *Sakakiya Nikki,* p. 1101. One example was an agreement on April 28, 1939, among 240 companies to contain wages by banning labor competition and raiding among firms.

43. Myers, "Modern Enclave Economy," p. 155; Ramon H. Myers, "Japanese Economic Development of Manchuria, 1932–1945" (Univeristy of Washington diss., 1959), pp. 192–93.

44. Gottschang points out that there are few comparative wage and cost-of-living studies for Manchuria and North China in the early twentieth century but cites two SMR studies that show disparities. One, from 1940, shows that Manchurian construction workers and miners spent 46 percent of their income for minimum food requirements while Qingdao porters and mill workers spent almost 60 percent. The other, by Toiku Shirō of the SMR North China Research Office, indicated that both wages and wages divided by living expenses were higher in Manchuria. Manchukuo construction workers earned 1.66 times those in Tianjin. Gottschang, "Migration from North China," pp. 94–95, 132–36, 221–49. Toiku Shirō, "Hokushi ni Okeru Tai Man Rōdō Chikara Kyōkyū no Kinkyō" (The Recent Situation in North China of the Labor Power Supply for Manchuria), *Mantetsu Chōsa Geppō* 21, 1 (January 1941): 178–87, has ratios comparing daily wages in Northeast and North China for four different types of construction workers: *doken* (presumably including general construction workers) 1.66 yen; scaffold workers 1.96 yen; masons 1.69 yen; carpenters or sawyers 1.52 yen.

45. *Sakakiya Nikki,* pp. 1044, 1070, 1082–83, 1086–88.

46. Ibid., pp. 1089, 1093–94. Quotas were set at 48,250 workers for Okura gumi, 15,400 for Sakakiya gumi, 14,800 for Omori gumi, and 14,000 for Shimizu gumi, and ranged down to 6500 for other major firms.

47. Doihara had been a longtime Guandong Army staff officer and played a key part in planning the seizure of Manchuria and in its control and development (including the transport of China's best-known immigrant, Puyi, from Tianjin to become Manchoukuo's chief executive and, later, emperor). His presence along with that of other officers with Guandong Army backgrounds led Sakakiya to hope for North China army cooperation, but any sympathy for Manchukuo proved secondary to the needs of the North Chinese occupation.

48. *Sakakiya Nikki,* pp. 1094–96.

49. Ibid., p. 1096. Kubota, "Manshū Shihai," p. 324, cites the SMR's 1940 *Shina Keizai Nempō,* p. 247, estimation that 70.7 percent of 1939 North Chinese construction worker migrants were recruited in groups.

50. *Sakakiya Nikki,* pp. 1096–97.

51. Ibid., pp. 1097–1101; Kubota, "Manshū Shihai" pp. 316–18.

52. *Manshūkokushi*, p. 161; *Manchoukuo Year Book: 1942*, p. 641; *Sakakakiya Nikki*, pp. 1116–17.

53. *Sakakiya Nikki*, pp. 1118, 1154; *Manchoukuo Year Book: 1942*, pp. 272–73, 642–44.

54. *Sakakiya Nikki*, pp. 1154–55, 1167. *Manshūkokushi*, p. 1173, also argues that North China's high wages and inflation depressed migration to Manchukuo. The *Orient Year Book, 1942*, pp. 721–22, saw rapid food cost increases as the engine of wage increases.

55. Toiku, "Hokushi ni Okeru Tai Man Rōdō Chikara Kyōkyū no Kinkyō," p. 186; *China Weekly Review 97* (June 14, 1941): 54 (which even before the currency controls reported that emigration to the Northeast was slowing drastically); Takafusa Nakamura, "The Yen Bloc, 1931–1941," in Peter Duus, Ramon Myers, and Mark R. Peattie, eds., *The Japanese Informal Empire in China, 1895–1937* (Princeton, NJ: Princeton University Press, 1989), pp. 174–81; Higuchi, "Nyū-ri Man Rōdōsha no Keitei Kin Oyobi so Kingaku" (Money Carried and Remitted by Workers Entering and Leaving Manchuria), *Mantetsu Chōsa Geppō* 21, 2 (February 1941), 205–14; Gottschang, "Migration from North China," p. 97; *Manshūkokushi*, p. 1173. Coal miners were exempt from remittance restrictions.

56. *Manchoukuo Year Book: 1942*, pp. 637–38; Manshū doboku kenchikugyō kyōkai, ed., *Manshū Doboku Kenchikugyō Kyōkai Gaiyō* (Outline of the Manchuria Construction Association), n.p., n.d. pp. 36–57; Anonymous, "Manshūkoku no Doken Tōsei to Doken Kyōkai no Shin Hossoku" (Manchukuo's Construction Controls and the New Launching of the Manchuria Construction Association), *Manshū no Gijutsu* 17, 135 (1940): 264–66; *Manchuria* (June 1, 1940), pp. 262–63; Myers, "Modern Enclave Economy," pp. 164–69; *MSK*, May 23, 1940; *Sakakiya Nikki*, pp. 1106, 1133–34. The former MCA, which continued to operate in Dairen, was renamed the Kantōshū Doboku Kenchiku Gyōkai (Guandong Construction Association), with membership available only to companies without offices in Manchukuo.

57. Manshū doboku kenchikugyō kyōkai, ed., *Manshū Doboku Kenchikugyō Kyōkai Gaiyō*, pp 27-8, 47.

58. *Manchuria* (May 1, 1940), p. 213 (December 1, 1940), p. 601.

59. The regulations appear in *Manshū Kenchiku Zasshi* 21, 1 (January 1941): 35–37. A summary appears in *Manchuria* (December 1, 1940), p. 601. *Manshūkokushi*, p. 1167; *MSK*, January 20, 1941, 2042–2318; *Sakakiya Nikki*, p. 1125.

60. *Manchoukuo Year Book: 1942*, pp. 635–37; *Manshūkokushi*, pp. 1166–67; *Manchuria* (May 1, 1940), p. 213, (December 1, 1940), p. 601; *Orient Year Book, 1942*, p. 724.

61. *Sakakiya Nikki*, pp. 1124, 1149; Myers, *Japanese Economic Development of Manchuria*, p. 185.

62. *Manshūkokushi*, p. 1168; *Manchuria 4*, 8 (April 15, 1939): 1124–25.

63. *Manchukuo Year Book: 1942*, pp. 337–358; *Manshūkokushi*, pp. 1167–68, 1177–78.

64. Okabe, *Manshūkoku*, pp. 136–38; *Manshūkokushi*, pp. 1169–70, 1175; *MSK*, February 9, 1942, pp. 2223–89.

65. *Manshūkokushi*, pp. 1170–71, 1173; Myers, *Japanese Economic Development of Manchuria*, p. 196; Okabe, *Manshūkoku*, pp. 142–44.

66. *Sakakiya Nikki*, pp. 1156–61. Sakakiya was pleased enough with his performance to note than an opposing officer had called him the "Hitler of the construction world."

67. *Sakakiya Nikki*, pp. 1165–67; *Orient Year Book, 1942*, p. 721.

68. *Sakakiya Nikki*, pp. 1182, 1185, 1205–6, 1208–13.

69. Yukawa Hiroshi, "Manshūkoku ni Okeru Kenchiku Rōdōsha ni Oite" (Construction Workers in Manchukuo), *Kenchiku to Shakai* 25, 12 (December 1942): 9. Yukawa was an official in the architecture section of the Osaka Prefectural Police Department.

70. Yukawa, "Manshūkoku," pp. 9–10.

71. Ibid., pp. 11–12.

72. Manshū dengyōshi kai, ed., *Manshū Dengyō Shi*, (History of the Electrical Generation Industry in Manchuria) (Tokyo: Manshū dengyōshi kai, 1976), p. 584; *Sakakiya Nikki*, p. 1044; *MKG*, pp. 206–9.

73. *Sakakiya Nikki*, pp. 1205–6. Between 1936 and 1939, only 12–16 percent of immigrants were women or children.

Chapter 3

Author's note: In 1999 I carried out research on the North China Labor Association, an organization used by the Japanese to secure labor. The study investigated the way this body was structured and raised questions about its nature and how decisions were made, but the archival materials used for that article said very little about the laborers themselves, or about the underlying authority that directed the Japanese system of exploitation. The present study takes up these issues. It first appeared in a Chinese-language publication entitled *Kang ri zhan zheng yan jiu* (Journal of Studies of China's Resistance War against Japan) (Summer–Autumn 2001): 113–39. In the first issue of the same journal (1993), I published an article entitled "A Preliminary Study of Japanese Use of Forced Civilian Labor in China During the Second World War" that described Japan's wartime use of forced labor in China. The months that followed brought new discoveries and the collation of additional information based on further research using materials from the national archives. These efforts have shed further light on the arguments, problems, and quantification of this subject, providing a better understanding and a fuller statement of the evidence. The present chapter offers an account of these findings.

Editor's note: This chapter was translated by Ms. Chang Yueh Siang, at the time a graduate student in the Department of History at the National University of Singapore. Mika Toyota and Geoff Wade of the university's Asian Research Institute provided advice on terminology.

1. Chuan Jing Zheng Jiu, "The Direction of North China Labor Policy" (appendix, "The Mission of the North China Labor Association") [in Japanese], printed in the North China Labor Association's *North China Laborers' Times* 1 (November 1942): 14.

2. North China Research Institute, "A Summary of North China Economy and Matters Pertaining to the Mining Industry and Labor after the China Incident" [in Japanese], October 1943, p. 278 (from a copy in the Library of the School of Modern History Library, Chinese Academy of Social Sciences).

3. Office of War History, Japanese Defense Agency, *The Battle to Pacify North China*, vol. 1 [in Japanese], trans. Tianjin Group of Official Translators (Tianjin: Tianjin People's Publisher), 1982, p. 187.

4. *Editor's note:* Meng Jiang (Japanese Mōkyō) consisted of parts of Inner Mongolia along with the northern portion of Shanxi and the southern part of Chahar Province. These areas were amalgamated into a federation in November 1937 after

being overrun by Japan's Guandong Army. See *Kodansha Encyclopedia of Japan,* vol. 7 (Tokyo: Kodansha, 1983), p. 201.

5. Asian Development Board, North China Department of Communications, "A Summary of the North China Labor Question" (December 1940), pp. 220–24. North China Research Institute, "A Summary of the Post-Confrontation North China Economy and Matters Pertaining to the Mining Industry and Labor," pp. 277–78.

6. Prosper Asia Bureau, North China Department of Communications, "Summary of the North China Labor Question," pp. 223–24, 236–37.

7. Ibid.

8. Office of War History, *Battle to Pacify North China,* vol. 2, pp. 33–34.

9. North China Research Institute, "Summary of the North China Economy," p. 277.

10. Prosper Asia Bureau, North China Department of Communications, "Summary of the North China Labor Question," pp. 369–402.

11. North China Research Institute, "Summary of the North China Economy," p. 289.

12. Ibid., p. 282.

13. Places with Committees for the Regulation of Labor Matters included Beijing, Tianjin, Tsingdao, Bao Ding, Jinan, Taiyuan, Kaifeng, Xuzhou, Shan Hai Guan, Tang Shan, Tang Gu, Shi Men, and Yang Quan. See North China Research Institute, "Summary of the North China Economy," pp. 282–88. The Tianjin chapter, which appears to have been typical, had eighteen committee members, including eight representatives from the Army and Special Operations Units; one representative each from the Japanese Vanguards, the embassy, the police, the New People's Association, the Labor Association, and the Headquarters for Development; and four from the city council. Thus it may be seen that the Japanese army, police, vanguards, and special operations unit dominated the committees.

14. North China Research Institute, "Summary of the North China Economy," p. 282.

15. *North China Labor Association Book of Facts,* in The Second Chinese National History Archives (hereafter, Second Chinese Archives), Nanjing, China.

16. For details, see Ju Zhifen, "A Preliminary Study of the Numbers in the Forced Conscription of Labor in China," *Kang ri zhan zheng yan jiu,* 2001, no. 1, pp. 148–168.

17. "Minutes of the First Convention of North China, Manchurian and Mongolian Labor Affairs," December 12–13, 1941, Tianjin Archives, 218–1282, pp. 23–25.

18. Ibid., p. 22.

19. Excluding the area where North China Industries are concentrated, such as Yidong and Jinhai railway lines in the Tianjin area and Qingzhou railway line in the Jinan area.

20. North China Research Institute, "Summary of the North China Economy," pp. 233–35.

21. Ju Zhifen, trans., "The Japanese System of Labor in North China," from Ando Tetsuo, "North China Development Annual," Japan East Asian New Paper (Tianjin Branch), December 1944; reprinted in *Information for Modern History,* vol. 98 (2000): 109–10.

22. I discuss this system in detail in "A Study of the Numbers Controversy in the Japanese Labor System in North China," *Republican Archives* 4 (1999): 65–66; for Beijing archives J14-1-83 and J14-1-7, see ibid., 1–2, 10–13.

23. Research Institute for the Question of China, "China Research Financial Paper" (in Japanese), May 11, 1941, no. 138, pp. 46–47 (published every ten days). "Treaty of the Guandong Army and North China Military Regarding the Migration of Laborers into Manchuria" (in Japanese), April 5, 1941, Fushun Coal Mines Archives, 01-14-1-355, pp. 37–41.

24. Chen Ping, *The Thousand Mile No-Man's Land* (Beijing: CCP History Publishing House, 1992), pp. 89–90. North China Labor Association Department of Planning, "Survey Concerning the Four Counties along the Jidong [East Hebei] Railway Lines" (in Japanese), April 1943, Second Chinese Archive, document 2057-105, pp. 16–17.

25. Office of War History, *Battle to Pacify North China*, vol. 1, pp. 70, 233.

26. "Report of the Minutes of the Meeting to Discuss Labor Policies for Manchuria, Held by the North China Transport Police Department (Overseeing the Lines along the Villages of Care)" (in Japanese), Fushun Coal Mines Archives, Labor/1941/355, quoted in Su Chong Min et al., *Blood and Tears of the Laborer* (Beijing: Great Chinese Encyclopedia Publishing House, 1995), pp. 290–92.

27. As quoted in "Agreement of the Tianjin Special Municipality and the North China Transport Company, Regarding the 6,000 Men Supplied from the 'Villages of Care' to Manchuria in 1943 (with Appendixes), and the Agreement and Annexes of the Tianjin Special Municipality with the North China Transport Company, Regarding the 2,000 Men Supplied from the 'Villages of Care' to the Manchuria Railway Company in 1944," Tianjian Archives.

28. Wang Wei, "The Enemy's Plunder and Destruction of the Food, Labor and Land in the North China Occupied Territories," *Jin Cha Ji Daily*, March 9, 1943.

29. North China Research Institute, "Summary of the North China Economy," p. 222. See also North China Labor Association, "Consolidation of Data from the Various Chapters of the North China Labor Association," *North China Labor Times* (November 1942–December 1943), sections 1–3.

30. Ibid.

31. Ando Tatsuo, "Inauguration Speech," *North China Labor Times* 3 (December 25, 1943), p. 17.

32. Correspondence and appendixes regarding Wang Jing Wei's foreign ministry's appeal for the return of laborers belonging to the Shanghai Steamship Carpentry Union, January 1945, Document J2061–1627, Second Chinese Archives.

33. Documents regarding the Wang government's collaboration with the Sino–Japanese Labor Association to provide 1,500 laborers and their appeal for mediation, November 7, 1944, Document J2003-2-82, Second Chinese Archives.

34. "A Summary of the North China Labor Problem," p. 325, Table 192. The industries included transport, electricity, construction, coal mining, steel production, gold production, weaving, cotton spinning, and alum production. This table was drawn according to the Asian Development Board's Designated Committee of the North China Development Plan, Sixth Division (Labor). Committee members provided the numbers for each industry, based on the Manchurian Railway's North China Economic Survey and on the survey of the Asian Development Board, and thus I believe the information is fairly reliable.

35. North China Development Company, Planning Division, "Summary of North China Labor Affairs," June 1941, Liaoning Archives, p. 41, Table 29; this table has been simplified here.

36. North China Research Institute, "Summary of the North China Economy," pp. 226–27.

37. Ibid.

38. Second Chinese Archives, Nanjing, China. Document 2005-1-1627, pp. 1–42.

39. I suggested a figure for the number of laborers conscripted for the Japanese military engineering works in "A Preliminary Study" but did not discuss the matter in detail.

40. North China Development Company Planning Division's June 1941 edition of "Summary of North China Labor Affairs," Liaoning Archives, pp. 39–40, Table 28.

41. Manchurian Railway Authorities, "The Problem of Labor in Manchoukuo and the Movement of North China Labor into Manchuria in 1942," Ji Lin Institute of Social Sciences, Manchurian Railway Archives, DM566, p. 80.

42. Office of War History, *Battle to Pacify North China,* vol. 1, pp. 190, 215, 150.

43. Ibid.

44. Nie Rong Zhen, "The Enemy's Five Attempts to Subjugate North China and Their Failure," *Shanxi-Hebei Times,* December 8, 1942.

45. Ji Zhao Bin, Li Shao Wei, and North China committee concerning Japanese forced conscription, correspondence, Document 2005-1501, Second Chinese Archives.

46. In my earlier article, "A Preliminary Study," I estimated that 400,000 workers were conscripted for Japanese military engineering works. The figure is discussed here in greater detail.

47. From July 1938 the Japanese army based in Mongolia came under the direction of the North China Army.

48. Committee for Mongolian–Tibet Labor Matters, "Guide to Administration of Labor," July 10, 1939, printed in North China Development Company, Planning Division, "Summary of North China Labor Affairs," pp. 140–41. Committee for Mongolian–Tibet Labor Matters, "Agreement Regarding the Distribution of North China Laborers," July 1939, printed in "A Summary of the North China Labor Problem," p. 237.

49. Autonomous Mongolian government, "Guide to Administration of Labor," August 5, 1940, printed in "A Summary of the North China Labor Problem," pp. 245–47.

50. Research Institute for the Question of China, "The Importance of the Da Tong Coal Mines during the War" (in Japanese), *China Research Financial Paper,* nos. 224, 225 (October 11, 1943): 336–37.

51. North China Research Institute's report of October 1943 and the Japanese *China Research Financial Paper.* See ibid., p. 336, and North China Research Institute, "Summary of the North China Economy," p. 220.

52. According to a report written at the end of 1940 by the NCCD's Office of Laborers' Affairs, called "Labor Requirements in the First Year of the Three-Year Plan for the Development of Mongolian–Tibetan Industries."

53. "A Summary of the North China Labor Problem," pp. 238, 239.

54. According to data from a formal survey carried out by the North China Labor Association.

55. Projected figures for 1940 to 1942 taken from North China Research Institute, "Summary of the North China Economy," from a table depicting the results of the survey of the North China Labor Association, p. 218. The actual figures are quoted from North China Development Company's Office of Labor Affairs' report of November 1942, "The Outward Mobility of North China Laborers," which presents the results of the North China Labor Association's survey on Table 16, p. 35. Document 2024–2–401, Second Chinese Archives, Nanjing, China.

56. Minutes of the Third Convention of North China, Manchurian, Mongolian, and Central China Labor.

57. Minutes of the First East Asia Convention for Labor Matters.

58. This calculation is the basis of the figure of 400,000 men suggested by the author in "A Preliminary Study."

Chapter 4

1. Shina Jihen, *Daitōa Sensōkan Rikugun Dōin Gaishi* (Outline of the history of army mobilization in the China Incident and Great East Asia War), edited with a new introduction by Oe Shinobu (Tokyo: Fuji Shuppan, 1988).

2. *Shahin-shūhō,* July 13, 1943.

3. Higuchi Yuichi, *Senjika Chōsenjin no Minshū to Chōhei* (The Korean people during wartime and conscription) (Tokyo: Sōwasha, 2001), p. 14.

4. Utsumi Aiko, *Chōsenjin "Kōgun" Heishi-tachi no Sensō* (The Korean 'imperial army' soldier's war) (Tokyo: Iwanami Shoten, 1991), pp. 7–15.

5. Japanese War Ministry Directive 48.

6. This information is based on interviews with Shin I Su conducted in Tokyo in August 1982. See also *Hohei Zensho* (Infantry compendium) (Tokyo: Buyodo, 1940).

7. Japan's Ministry of War, *Daitōa-sensō ni Tomonau Waga Jinteki Kokuryoku no Kentō* (Consideration of our human strength as a nation regarding the Great East Asia War) (1942; reissued, Tokyo: Fuji Shuppan, 1987).

8. *Asahi Shinbun,* May 10, 1942.

9. This information is based on interviews with two former soldiers in the Japanese army, Lee Byong-kye and Won Bong-je, who were enrolled in the Kanto army in August 1945. Following Japan's surrender, they were interned and forced to work in the Soviet Union.

10. Regional Public Security Investigation Bureau, *Zai Nihon Chōsenjin no Gaikyo* (General Condition of Koreans Resident in Japan). This document is available in the National Diet Library, Tokyo, Japan.

11. Enacted on April 30, 1952, and made effective retrospectively from April 1 of that year, this law provided relief to those wounded in the war and to the bereaved families of those who died.

12. In Japan it is necessary to go through an attorney to request permission to view the *Zaitaishōmeisho* (Certificate of Military Service) or *Shibōshōmeisho* (Certificate of Death in Battle), which are maintained by the War Victims' Relief Bureau in the Ministry of Health and Welfare.

Chapter 5

Author's note: I would like to thank Miyamoto Masaaki for help with the content of this article, and Shaun Allen for assistance with the translation.

1. There are now a great number of publications dealing with the issue of the forced recruitment of Koreans. For a bibliography in Japanese, see "Reference about the Forced Recruitment of Koreans" by Yang Tae Ho, in *Chōsenjin Kyōseirenkō Ronbunshūsei* (Essays on the forced recruitment of Koreans), ed. Park Kyung Sik and Yamada Shōji, which includes a section of some thirty pages cataloging literature, essays, and articles on the forced recruitment of Koreans. The following works may be regarded as essential reading:

Hayashi Eidai, *Kesareta Chōsenjin Kyōseirenkō no Kiroku* (Erased records of Korean forced recruitment) (Tokyo: Akashi Shoten, 1989).

Hayashi Eidai, *Seisan-sarenai Shōwa Chōsenjin Kyōseirenkō no Kiroku* (Unresolved questions of the Showa era: Records of Korean forced labor) (Tokyo: Iwanami Shoten, 1990).

"Hyaku-man-nin no Shinsetaryon" (Editing committee compilation), in *Hyaku-man-nin no Shinsetaryon* (Life stories of one million people) (Tokyo: Tōhō Publications, 1999).

Kim San Chong, ed., *Shōgen Chōsenjin Renkō* (Testimony to Korean forced labor) (Tokyo: Shinjinbutsu-ōraisha, 1975).

Ozawa Yūsaku, *Kindai Minshū no Kiroku*, vol. 10, *Zainichi-Chōsenjin* (Records of the modern people, vol. 10, Korean residents of Japan) (Tokyo: Shinjinbutsu-ōraisha, 1978).

Park Kyung Sik, ed., *Zainichi-Chōsenjin-kankei Shiryō-shūsei* (Compilation of materials on Korean residents in Japan), vols. 4 and 5 (Tokyo: San-Ichi Books, 1976).

Park Kyung Sik, ed., *Chōsenjin Mondai Shiryō-sōsho* (Materials on the Korean question series), vols. 1 and 2 (Tokyo: San-Ichi Books, 1981–82).

Park Kyung Sik, *Chōsenjin Kyōseirenkō no Kiroku* (Records of Korean forced labor) (Tokyo: Miraisha, 1965).

Yang Tae Ho, ed., *Chōsenjin Kyōseirenkō Ronbun Shūsei* (Essays on the forced recruitment of Koreans) (Tokyo: Akashi Shoten, 1993).

2. Hahakigi Hōsei, *Mitabi no Kaikyō* (Three trips across the strait) (Tokyo: Shinchōsha, 1992). Hahakigi (b. 1947) was born in Fukuoka Prefecture. In addition to being a novelist, he is a practicing psychiatrist whose work on contemporary health care issues such as surrogate motherhood has received high praise. When he began *Mitabi no Kaikyō,* he had already produced work on the theme of Japan's war responsibility. In 1997, he won the Shibata Renzaburō Prize for his novel *Tōbō* (Escape), in which the protagonist, a military policeman in Hong Kong, confronts the prospect of military defeat.

3. Sekikawa Nastuo, "An interpretation of *Mitabi no Kaikyō,*" in *Mitabi no Kaikyō* (Three trips across the strait) (Tokyo: Shinchōsha, 1992). Three years after its initial publication, the book appeared in paperback (Tokyo: Shinchōsha, 1995), and by September 2001 the paperback version was in its eighteenth printing. A film based on the book was the first Japanese production to be shot in Korea after 1945.

4. The results of the investigation undertaken by the Committee of Inquiry into the Truth about Korean Forced Labor are contained in *Chōsenjin Kyōseirenkō Chōsa no Kiroku* (Records of the investigation into the forced recruitment of Koreans) (Tokyo: Kashiwa Publications, 1992). The records currently available are for the Shikoku, Osaka, Hyōgo, Chūbu/Tōkai, and Kantō areas.

5. See Satō Akio, "Nakajima Hikōki Handa Seisakusho no Chōsenjin-chōyōkō" (Korean conscript labor at Nakajima Aircraft's Handa Plant) (compilation recording the Handa air raids and the war), in *Handa Kūshū no Kiroku* (Records of the Handa air raids) (Aichi: Handa Kūshū to Sensō wo Kiroku-suru kai [The society for records of the Handa air raids and war], 1985).

6. Wakimoto Hisashi (b. 1920) served as a pastor in Fukuoka Prefecture for many years. Conscripted for wartime labor service under the Labor Mobilization Order for Religious Teachers, Wakimoto worked from July 1944 to October 1945 as dormitory inspector at the accommodations for the Korean conscript workers at Shōwa Electrical Engineering in Kawasaki, Kanagawa Prefecture. He recounts his

experiences in *Chōsenjin Kyōseirenkō to Watashi* (The forced recruitment of Koreans and I) (Kobe: Kobe Student Youth Center Publications Department, 1994). In this work, while taking upon himself his share of responsibility for the war, he nonetheless asks harsh questions about the war responsibility of the Japanese Christian community in general. However, there were very few officials who shared Wakimoto's and Funabashi's sense of anguish or responsibility for the forced recruitment of Koreans.

7. The following literature deals with the *Ukishima Maru* incident: Kim Chang Jon, *Ukishima Maru Pusan-kō e Mukawazu* (The *Ukishima Maru* does not sail for Pusan) (Tokyo: Kōdansha, 1984); Committee for the Execution of Mourning for the Martyrs of the *Ukishima Maru*, *Ukishima Maru Jiken no Kiroku* (Records of the *Ukishima Maru* incident) (compilation) (Kyoto: Kamogawa Publishing, 1989); *Kikan Sai* (Sai quarterly) 41 (2001) (published by the Osaka Education and Research Center for International Understanding).

8. The figures are in the *Historical Investigations Regarding the Activities of Japanese Nationals Overseas,* 11 vols., Korea, Formosa (Taiwan), China (Manchuria), Southeast Asia, the West. The board of investigations reportedly carried out this research concerning the finances of Japanese nationals overseas in 1946. From 1949 to 1950, the Administrative Services Bureau of Japan's Ministry of Finance examined them, but these investigations were not published, and the ministry has disclaimed any responsibility for "historical investigation" regarding the activities of Japanese nationals overseas. Nonetheless, these are the earliest and most detailed studies of Japanese activities overseas in Japan's wartime empire.

9. Higuchi Yūichi, *Nihon no Chōsen/Kankokujin* (Japan's [North Korea- and South Korea–affiliated] Koreans) (Tokyo: Dōseisha, 2002), p. 125.

10. Yamada Shōji, "Chōsenjin Kyōseirenkō" (Forced recruitment of Koreans), in *Kingendaishi no naka no Nihon to Chōsen* (Issues of recent history concerning Japan and Korea) (Tokyo: Tokyo Shoseki, 1991), p. 178.

11. See Kum Byeong Dong, "Nihon Teikokushugi no Chōsen-dōhō Kyōseirenkō to Gyakutai no Jittai" (Concerning the actual conditions of forced recruitment and abuse of Korean compatriots under Japanese imperialism), *Gekkan Chōsen Shiryō* (Korean resources monthly), August 1974.

12. Yamada, "Chōsenjin Kyōseirenkō" (Forced recruitment of Koreans), p. 178.

13. *Tokkō Geppō* (Monthly report of the thought control police), February 1944.

14. Yamada Shōji, a historian who for over half a century has been conducting research in connection with Koreans living in Japan, is currently the most energetic researcher looking at wartime forced labor by Koreans. Yamada is also cooperating in efforts to implement judicial rulings on the settlement of outstanding matters such as the payment of unpaid wages owed to Korean workers and has been trying to make clear Japan's war responsibility both through practical activities and through research. In an article entitled "Chōsenjoshi Kinrō-teishintai" (Formation of Korean female labor "volunteer" parties), published in *Zainichi-Chōsenjin-shi Kenkyū* (Historical research on Korean residents of Japan) 31 (2001), Yamada discusses in detail the circumstances in which Korean women were sent to work in Japan, pointing out the role that schools played as recruitment windows. It is important to note the different systems that applied to the recruitment of men and women.

Chapter 6

Author's note: I would like to express my gratitude to my colleague Peter Zarrow for his editorial help and comments on this and earlier versions of this chapter. I also want to thank Dr. Paul H. Kratoska, editor of this book, for his editorial work and suggestions to refine the chapter, Professor R. Bin Wong for his critical comments, and Wang Lu-hua for his assistance in drawing the map (Taiwan, 1941–45). In this chapter, "Taiwan" is used in preference to "Formosa" to refer to the islands (including the Pescadores, in the Taiwan Straits) under Japanese rule (1895–1945), as Taiwan was a term often employed by the Japanese during the colonial period. Partly, however, it is because Formosa or "beautiful island"—a term attributed to the Portuguese when they spotted this island in 1544—became a highly politicized term in postwar Taiwan, conveying an image of the Taiwan independence movement. I use the *Hanyu pinyin* romanization system for Chinese-text translation, except for personal and place names currently used in Taiwan.

1. Hung Huo-chao, "Hong Huozhao xiansheng fangwen jilu" (Hong Huozhao interview) in *Zouguo liangge shidai de ren: Taiji Ribenbing* (The lives and times of Taiwanese veterans), Oral History Series 1, ed. Hui-yu Caroline Ts'ai and Wu Ling-ch'ing (Taipei: Preparatory Office, Institute of Taiwan History, Academia Sinica, 1997), pp. 211–44. Strictly speaking, most Taiwanese overseas military draftees were not "soldiers" (*gunshi*), but military laborers (*gunpu*) or staff (*gunzoku*). A commonly heard general term in Chinese is "Taiji Ribenbing," and thus the English term "Taiwanese veterans."

2. Hung Huo-chao, quoted by Lin Chao-chen in "Taiji Ribenbing, quanyi shui wenwen" (Taiwanese veterans of the Japanese military—Who cares about their rights?), *Zhongguo shibao* (China times), June 6, 1994, 17.

3. Hung Huo-chao, interview with the author, T'ao-tun,Taichung, Taiwan, May 20, 1995.

4. In Japanese, *Nanpō* (the South) or *Nanpōken* (the Sphere of the South) is generally taken to mean today's Southeast Asia (largely a post–World War II term); in Chinese, the term is *Nanyang* (South Seas). As a historical term, it refers to the regions under Japanese military occupation in the early 1940s. See Milton Osborne, *Southeast Asia: An Illustrated Introductory History* (1979; repr. Sydney: Allen & Unwin, 1990), pp. 1–15; Shimizu Hajime, "Southeast Asia as a Regional Concept in Modern Japan." In *Locating Southeast Asia: Geographical Knowledge and Politics of Space*, ed. Paul H. Kratoska, Remco Raben, and Hank Schulte Nordholt (Singapore: Singapore University Press, 2005) pp. 82–112.

5. "Governmentality," referring to "techniques of government," is a neologism created by Michel Foucault. See his "Governmentality," in *The Foucault Effect: Studies in Governmentality,* ed. Graham Burchell, Colin Gordon, and Peter Miller (Chicago: University of Chicago Press, 1991), pp. 87–104.

6. For the "subjectivity" (or *shutaisei*) discourse in Japan, see Victor J. Koschmann, "The Debate on Subjectivity in Postwar Japan: Foundations of Modernism as a Political Critique," *Pacific Affairs* 54, no. 4 (Winter 1981): 609–31.

7. Leo T.S. Ching, *Becoming "Japanese"* (Berkeley: University of California Press, 2001), p. 97.

8. Ibid., pp. 95–97, 117–18.

9. Komagome Takeshi, *Shokuminchi teikoku Nihon no bunka tōgō* (Cultural integration in the colonies of imperial Japan) (Tokyo: Iwanami Bookstore, 1996), p. 74.

10. Chen Peifeng, *"Dōka" no dōshō imu* (Assimilation: Same bed, different dreams) (Tokyo: Sangensha, 2001).

11. Nakai Jun, "Hōmin hōkō undō no shinten" (The development of the movement of imperial subjects for public services), in *Taiwan keizai nenpō, 1944* (Taiwan yearly news, 1944) (Taihoku: Taiwan Shuppan Bunka Kabushiki Kaisha, 1945; Taipei: Nant'ien, 1996), vol. 4, pp. 251–310. Citations refer to the 1996 edition. For a recent study, see Lin Lan-fang, "Riju moqi Taiwan 'huangmin fenggong' yundong (1941–1945)" (The movement of "ISPS" in the last years of Taiwan under Japanese occupation, 1941–1945) (paper presented to the Third Conference on Wartime Nation-building and Taiwan Retrocession [Kangzhan jianguo ji Taiwan guangfu: Zhonghua minguo zhuanti di sanjie taolunhui], October 19–21, 1995). Lin's argument for periodization, however, was based on Nakai's.

12. Chen Wensong, "Seinen no sōdatsu: 1920 nendai shokuminchi Taiwan ni okeru seinen kyōka undō—bunkyōkyoku no setsuritsu o chūshin nishite" (Struggling for the youth: The movement of youth education in colonial Taiwan during the 1920s, with emphasis on the cultural education bureaus) (master's thesis, Department of General Cultural Studies [Sōgō Bunka Kenkyūka], Tokyo University, 2000).

13. The Japanese-language literature on the communal-regeneration movement is very rich. For discussions in English, see Sandra Wilson, "Bureaucrats and Villages in Japan: *Shimin* and the Crisis of the Early 1930s," *Social Science Japan Journal 1*, no. 1 (1998): 121–40, and Kerry Smith, *A Time of Crisis: Japan, the Great Depression, and Rural Revitalization* (Cambridge, MA: Harvard University Asia Center, 2001).

14. Hui-yu Caroline Ts'ai, "1930 niandai Taiwan jiceng xingzheng de kongjian jiegou fenxi: yi 'nongshi shixing zuhe' weili" (A spatial analysis of basic administrative units, Taiwan in the 1930s: The case of "agricultural implementation associations"), *Taiwanshi yanjiu* (Taiwan historical research) 5, no. 2 (December 1998): 55–100.

15. Ch'en Ying, "Cong 'buluomin' dao 'guomin': Riju shiqi Gaosha Qingniantuan de jiaoyu xingge" (From the "hamlet people" to the "national people": The educational characteristics of the aboriginal youth corps during the period of Japanese occupation) (M.A. thesis, Institute of Social Anthropology, Ch'ing-hua University, Taiwan, 1998), pp. 64–65.

16. Kondō Masami, "I minzoku ni taisuru gunji dōin to kōminka seisaku: Taiwan no gunpu o chūshin nishite" (Military mobilization targeted at ethnically foreign peoples and imperial subjectification policies: The case of Taiwanese military laborers), *Taiwan kin-gendaishi kenkyū* (The research of modern/contemporary Taiwan) 6 (1988): 163.

17. See Justin Adam Schneider, "The Business Empire: The Taiwan Development Corporation and Japanese Imperialism in Taiwan, 1936–1946" (Ph.D. diss., Harvard University, 1998), pp. 338, 342. "Subimperialism" here refers to "imperialism driven by forces on the periphery of an empire rather than in the metropole," and "developmental imperialism" refers to "an economic variant of this larger phenomenon of subimperialism" (p. 5). Schneider also suggests that "a historiographical tendency to see early prewar Taiwan as a nation-state in the making" has led to the treatment of Taiwan as "a passive colony" (p. 8).

18. Kondō Masami, "Taiwan no rōmu dōin" (Labor mobilization in Taiwan), in *Kindai Nihon no rekishiteki isō: kokka, minzoku, bunka* (The historical phase of modern

Japan: State, nation, culture), ed. Ōhama Tetsuya (Tokyo: Tōshui Bookstore, 1999), p. 166; Mukōyama Hiroo, *Nihon tōchika ni okeru Taiwan minzuku undō-shi* (The history of the nationalist movement in Taiwan under Japanese rule) (Tokyo: Chūō Keizai Kenkyūjo, 1987), p. 476.

19. See Roger Chickering and Stig Förster, eds., *Great War, Total War: Combat and Mobilization on the Western Front, 1914–1918* (Washington, DC: German Historical Institute, 2000).

20. See, for example, Hayashi Eidai, *Taiwan no Yamato tamashii* (The Yamato soul of Taiwan) (Osaka: Tōhō Shuppan, 2000); Yang Ya-hui, "Zhanshi tizhi xia de Taiwan funyu (1937–1945): Riben zhimin zhengfu de jiaohua yu dongyuan" (Taiwanese women under the wartime establishment, 1937–1945: Moral suasion and mobilization of the Japanese colonial government) (master's thesis, Ch'ing-hua University, 1994).

21. Kondō, "Taiwan no rōmu dōin" (Labor mobilization in Taiwan), pp. 159–63. See also Yamaguchi Ichio, "Taiwan ni okeru rōmu dōin" (Labor mobilization in Taiwan), in *Taiwan keizai nenpō, 1942* (The annual journal of Taiwan economy, 1942) (Tokyo: Kokusai Nihon Kyōkai, 1942; Taipei: Nan-t'ien Book Co., 1996), ed. the publisher (Taiwan Keizai Nenpō Kankōkai), vol. 2 of 4, pp. 141–68.

22. All these labor movements were greatly reduced in size after Japan had clearly lost control of the seas in 1943. Kondō, "Taiwan no rōmu dōin" (Labor mobilization in Taiwan), p. 186.

23. Ibid., pp. 178–79; Kondō Masami, *Sōryokusen to Taiwan: Nihon shokuminchi hōkai no kenkyū* (Total war and Taiwan: A study on the collapse of Japan's colonies) (Tokyo: Tōshui Bookstore, 1996), pp. 370–71.

24. Kondō, "Taiwan no rōmu dōin" (Labor mobilization in Taiwan), p. 181. In the wake of the fall of the "iron curtain" and in commemoration of the fiftieth anniversary of the end of World War II, the decade of the 1990s witnessed a surge of literature on the war years. Publication in the form of memoirs and photograph collections was a major genre of the books produced, and work on Taiwan boy laborers is no exception.

25. Ibid., pp. 181–82, 186.

26. Ibid., pp. 182–84. Information on these categories of labor is fragmentary, and they require further study.

27. Cheng Li-ling, "Zhanshi tizhi xia de Taiwan shehui (1937–1945): zhian, shehui jiaohua, junshi dongyuan" (Taiwan society under wartime establishment (1937–1945): Peace preservation, social suasion, wartime mobilization) (master's thesis, Ch'ing-hua University, Taiwan, 1994), pp. 50–51.

28. Ibid., pp. 62–63.

29. Taiwan Sōtokufu, ed., *Taiwan tōchi gaiyō* (An outline of the rule of Taiwan) (Taihoku: Taiwan Sōtokufu, 1945), pp. 75–77; see also Kondō, "Taiwan no rōmu dōin" (Labor mobilization in Taiwan), pp. 163, 166, 171–75.

30. Schneider, "The Business Empire," p. 277.

31. Taiwan Sōtokufu Gaijibu, *Nanpō kyōryoku yōin teiyō* (The outline for the personnel required in cooperation with the south)) (Taihoku: Taiwan Sōtokufu Gaijibu, 1943), pp. 103–19. See also Lee Kuo-sheng, "Zhanzheng yu Taiwanren: zhimin zhengfu dui Taiwan de junshi renli dongyuan (1937–1945)" (War and the Taiwanese: The military labor mobilization of the colonial government in Taiwan) (master's thesis, Taiwan University, 1997), pp. 99–104. A few Taiwanese also served as *shokutaku* (skilled part-time government employees with experience).

32. Kondō, "I minzoku ni taisuru gunji dōin to kōminka seisaku" (Military mobilization targeted at ethnically foreign peoples and imperial subjectification policies), p. 157.

33. Lee, "Zhanzheng yu Taiwanren" (War and the Taiwanese), pp. 104–16.

34. In the past decade, the growth of studies in Taiwan of wartime mobilization has been impressive, and oral history and biographies are particularly rich sources. For references, see Ts'ai and Wu, eds., *Zouguo liangge shidai de ren: Taiji Ribenbing* (The lives and times of Taiwanese veterans); Cheng Li-ling, ed., *Taiwanren Ribenbing de zhanzheng jingyan* (War experiences of Taiwanese-Japanese veterans) (Taipei: Taipei County Cultural Center, 1995); P'an Kuo-cheng, ed., *Tennō heika no akachan: Xinzhuren, Ribenbing, zhanzheng jingyan* (The children of the Japanese emperor: People from Hsin-chu county, Japanese soldiers, and war experiences) (Hsin-chu: Hsin-chu City Cultural Center, 1997); T'ang Hsi-yung and Ch'en Yi-ju, eds., *Taibeishi Taiji Ribing chafang zhuanji* (A special issue on Taiwanese-Japanese veterans, Taipei City) (Taipei: Taipei Historical Records Bureau, 2001); Lin Hui-yu, ed., *Yilan qilao tan Rizhi xia de junshi yu jiaoyu* (The military and education under Japanese rule: The oral history of Yilan) (Yilan: Yilan County Cultural Center, 1996).

35. Military labor of this kind was a significant feature of the first stage of labor mobilization, but by November 1940, the Taiwan army had set up a combat corps (*shidan*), the Forty-eighth Division, that handled many of these tasks. The role of Taiwanese *gunpu* was accordingly reduced.

36. "Military farmers" were sent to central China to help with agricultural work because fighting had devastated most of this area. South China suffered less war damage, and only agricultural instructors were sent there. See Ichibagase Yoshio, "Taiwan nōgyō giyūdan no sakkon" (Taiwan agricultural volunteer corps of these days), *Taiwan Nōkaihō* (Taiwan agricultural association news) 1, 5 (May 1939): 51–62. Nine rounds of agricultural instructors went to South China, mainly to the Canton area.

37. At least six rounds of the Taiwan Special Corps of Patriotic Labor Service can be identified so far, but the actual number cannot be ascertained.

38. See Lee, "Zhanzheng yu Taiwanren" (War and the Taiwanese), p. 175.

39. Ibid., pp. 117–26, 199–211.

40. The term commonly used by the Allies to refer to comfort women was "comfort girls." See George Hicks, *The Comfort Women—Sex Slaves of the Japanese Imperial Forces* (Australia: Allen & Unwin, 1995), p. 2. Recent debates over Kobayashi Yoshinori's political comic book, *Taiwanron* (On Taiwan), trans. Lai Ch'ing-sung and Hsiao Chih-ch'iang (Taipei: Qianwei, 2001), and its sequel are only a single recent and provocative case. For a good sourcebook in Japanese, see Yoshimi Yoshiaki, *Jūgun ianfu shiryōshū* (The collection of historical documents on military comfort women) (Tokyo: Ōtsuki Bookstore, 1992). For a survey in Chinese, see *Taiwan diqu weianfu fangcha gean fenxi baogao* (An analytical report on comfort women in Taiwan: A survey on case studies), edited and published by Taibeishi Funyu Houyuan Shehui Fuli Shiye Jijinhui (The Foundation for Supporting the Affairs of Women's Social Welfare) (Taipei, 1993).

41. Zaidan Hōjin Gunjin Kaikan Shuppanbu, ed., *Riku-kaigun gunji nenkan, 1942* (The military yearbook of the army and the navy, 1942) (Tokyo: Nihon Tosho Sentā, 1989), p. 308.

42. Kondō, "I minzoku ni taisuru gunji dōin to kōminka seisaku" (Military mobilization targeted at ethnically foreign peoples and imperial subjectification policies),

pp. 128–29. Some sources even add "military pigeons" (*gunkō*) ahead of *gunzoku, gunjin, gunma, gunken, gunkō,* and *gunzoku.* See Lee, "Zhanzheng yu Taiwanren" (War and the Taiwanese), p. 66.

43. Good introductions to wartime mobilization in Taiwan include Kondō, *Sōryokusen to Taiwan* (Total war and Taiwan), and Lin Chi-wen, *Riben ju-Tai moqi (1930–1945) zhanzheng dongyuan tixi zhi yanjiu* (A study on the system of wartime mobilization in the last phase of Japanese occupation in Taiwan, 1930–1945) (Taipei: Daoxiang, 1996).

44. Interviews with Taiwanese sent overseas as Japanese military laborers reveal that they received from two to three, and some even said four, times their normal pay compared with their wages in Taiwan. See, for example, interview with Huang Yu-tuan in Lee, "Zhanzheng yu Taiwanren" (War and the Taiwanese), p. 121; and interviews with Kao Ts'ung-yi, Ch'en Ch'un-liang, Hung Huo-zhao, and Liu Ying-hui in Ts'ai and Wu, *Zuoguo liangge shidai de ren: Taiji Ribenbing* (The lives and times of Taiwanese veterans), pp. 218, 281, 342, 377–8.

45. Kondō, "I minzoku ni taisuru gunji dōin to kōminka seisaku" (Military mobilization targeted at ethnically foreign peoples and imperial subjectification policies), pp. 129–30.

46. Ibid., pp. 149–50.

47. Taiwan Sōtokufu, *Taiwan tōchi gaiyō* (An outline of the rule of Taiwan), pp. 71–72. See also Lee, "Zhanzheng yu Taiwanren" (War and the Taiwanese), p. 141.

48. Kondō, "I minzoku ni taisuru gunji dōin to kōminka seisaku" (Military mobilization targeted at ethnically foreign peoples and imperial subjectification policies), p. 162. Kondō carefully explains that these were the only identifiable figures and that the actual number could be much higher. Lee Kuo-sheng points out, however, that the first dispatch of the Taiwan Special Labor Corps was earlier than May 1943, although the actual date remains unknown. See Lee, "Zhanzheng yu Taiwanren" (War and the Taiwanese), p. 93.

49. Lee, "Zhanzheng yu Taiwanren" (War and the Taiwanese), pp. 82–90, 127–33, 166–69.

50. Yang Ya-hui, "Zhanshi tizhi xia de Taiwan funyu (1937–1945)" (Taiwanese women under the wartime establishment, 1937–1945), p. 74.

51. Taiwan Sōtokufu, *Taiwan tōchi gaiyō* (An outline of the rule of Taiwan), pp. 72–73. See also Lee, "Zhanzheng yu Taiwanren" (War and the Taiwanese), pp. 41–47.

52. The figures were issued by Kōseishō (Ministry of Public Welfare), Japan, on April 14, 1973. This statistic concerns the estimates of deceased Taiwanese labor draftees, which in turn are key to the reparation movement in postwar Taiwan. For the development of this movement, see Hui-yu Caroline Ts'ai, "Taiwan minjian dui-Ri suopei yundong chutan: 'Panduola zhi xiang'" (The postwar compensation movement in Taiwan: A "Pandora's box"), *Taiwanshi yanjiu* (Taiwan historical research) 3, 1 (June 1996): 173–228; see p. 174 for the Kōseishō citation.

53. Taiwan Sōtokufu, *Taiwan tōchi gaiyō* (An outline of the rule of Taiwan), p. 75. Judging from the context here, "the South" would have included China, rather than Southeast Asia, although not extending to Japan.

54. "Tōgai zaijū hondōjin shirabe, 1944/2/1" (The survey of the Taiwanese residing overseas, February 1, 1944), in *Senjiki shokuminchi tōchi shiryō* (Data sources on wartime colonial rule), vol. 4 of 7, ed. Mizuno Naoki (Kashiwa Shobō Kabushiki Kaisha, 1998), p. 148.

55. The number 30,304 refers to those being worshipped at the Yasukuni Shrine. See the 1973 Kōseishō figures in ibid. The higher figure, derived from a private source in Chinese, is reported in Chung Chien, *Taiwan hangkong juezhan* (Fighting decisive air battles in Taiwan) (Taipei: Maitian, 1996), p. 289. It is based on 53,300 reported as dead and an additional 92,700 as missing. It is not clear how Chung derived his numbers and how he defined "dead" and "missing," but it seems likely that there is some overlap between these two categories. Chung's book is entertaining and informative, but he does not provide citations for his sources. Other sources in Chinese also suggest that more than 200,000 Taiwanese were mobilized to work overseas, but this number may have included civilians (and their households) going abroad for reasons other than labor drafts. For a discussion of the number of Taiwanese mobilized overseas for the war, see T'ang Hsi-yung, "Taimin canyu junwu zhi jingguo jiqi yingxiang: cong Rizhi dao zhanhou chugi" (The process and influences of the Taiwanese who served in the military: From the period of Japanese rule to the immediate postwar years), in *Taibeishi Taiji Ribing chafang zhuanji* (A special issue on Taiwanese-Japanese veterans, Taipei City), ed. T'ang and Ch'en, pp. 32–35. See also Lee, "Zhanzheng yu Taiwanren" (War and the Taiwanese), p. 224.

56. Sheldon Garon, "Women's Groups and the Japanese State: Contending Approaches to Political Integration, 1890–1945," *Journal of Japanese Studies 19*, no. 1 (Winter 1993): 5–41. For recent research in Japanese, see Watanabe Yōko, *Kindai Nihon joshi shakai kyōikushi: shojokai no zenkoku soshikika to shidō shisō* (The history of social education for females in modern Japan: The national organization and guiding thought of spinsters' associations) (Tokyo: Akaishi Bookstore, 1997); Miyazaki Seiko, "Shokuminchi-ki Taiwan ni okeru josei no Ei-jen-si ni kan suru ichi kōsatsu: Taihokushū A-gai no shojokai no jirei" (A case study on the role of the female as an agency in colonial Taiwan: An example of a spinsters' association in town A of Taihoku Prefecture), *Jen-dā kenkyū* (Gender studies) 6 (June 2003): 85–108.

57. For reference, see Richard J. Smethurst, *A Social Basis for Prewar Japanese Militarism: The Army and the Rural Community* (Berkeley: University of California Press, 1974).

58. Chen, "Seinen no sōdatsu" (Struggling for the youth), pp. 20–22; Miyazaki Seiko, "Taiwan ni okeru kō-Nichi undō no shutai keisei to 'seinen' kainen: 1920–1924 nen o chūshin ni" (The formation of the core and the concept of 'the youth' in Taiwan's anti-Japanese movement: With the focus on the years 1920–1924), *Gendai Taiwan kenkyū* (The study of modern Taiwan) 21 (2001): 104–23.

59. One exception was Taiwan's aborigines (except for the Ataiyals and the Yamis), who had their own traditions of age groups and/or assembly houses, a circumstance that helped Japanese plans to mobilize youth through the youth corps. See Ch'en, "Cong 'buluomin' dao 'guomin'" (From the "hamlet people" to the "national people), esp. chaps. 3 and 4. See also Sung Hsiu-huan, "Nihon tōchi ka no seinendan seisaku to Taiwan genjūmin—Ami zoku o chūshin toshite" (The policy of the youth corps and the aborigines of Taiwan under Japanese rule), in *Shokuminchi Jinruigaku no tembō* (Perspectives on colonial anthropology), ed. Nakao Katsumi (Tokyo: Fūkyōsha, 2000), pp. 123–69.

60. Miyazaki Seiko, "Shokuminchi jidai no Taiwan ni okeru seinenkai no seiritsu katei (1910–1926)—Hokubu Taiwan A gai no jirei o chūshin ni" (The process of the establishment of the youth association in Taiwan during the colonial period, 1910–26: A case study of town A in north Taiwan), in *Nihon no kyōiku shigakukaikyo* (The historical study of education in Japan) 46 (October 2003): 163–81.

61. Wang Shih-ch'ing, "Huangminhua yundong qian de Taiwan shehui shenghuo gaishan yundong" (The movement for reforming the social life of Taiwan prior to the movement of Japanization), *Si yu yan* (Think and talk) 29, 4 (December 1991): 5–63.

62. Tani Teruhiro, "Nihon tōchi ka Taiwan no seinendan" (The youth corps in Taiwan under Japanese rule), *Tsuruga ronsō* (Tsuruga collections of treaties) 8 (1993): 44–45.

63. Miyazaki Seiko, "Seinenkai kara seinendan e no tenkan: Taihokushū A-gai no baai (1926–1934 nen)" (The transformation from the youth association to the youth corps: The case study of town A in Taihoku Prefecture, 1926–1934), *Nihon Taiwan gakuhōpō* (Journal of Taiwan studies in Japan) 5 (May 2003): 21–41. Japanese and Western age calculations are based on elapsed calendar years, starting at birth with zero. Chinese reckoning is based on the number of lunar years in which a person has been alive, starting at birth with one.

64. For the relationship between hamlet revival units and *hokō* units, see Ts'ai, "1930 niandai Taiwan jiceng xingzheng de kongjian jiegou fenxi" (A spatial analysis of basic administrative units, Taiwan in the 1930s), pp. 55–100.

65. Kondō, "I minzoku ni taisuru gunji dōin to kōminka seisaku" (Military mobilization targeted at ethnically foreign peoples and imperial subjectification policies), pp. 144–45.

66. Tani, "Nihon tōchi ka Taiwan no seinendan" (The youth corps in Taiwan under Japanese rule), pp. 52–53.

67. Chou Wan-yao, "Ribenren zai-Tai junshi dongyuan yu Taiwanren de haiwai canzhan jingyan, 1937–1945" (Japan's military mobilization and the Taiwanese overseas war experiences, 1937–1945), *Taiwanshi yanjiu* (Taiwan historical research) 2, 1 (June 1995): 91–102.

68. Kondō, "I minzoku ni taisuru gunji dōin to kōminka seisaku" (Military mobilization targeted at ethnically foreign peoples and imperial subjectification policies), pp. 148–52.

69. Yao Jen-tuo, "Renshi Taiwan: zhishi, quanli, yu Riben zai Tai zhi zhimin zhilixing" (Understanding Taiwan: Knowledge, power, and colonial governmentality in Taiwan under Japanese rule), *Taiwan shehui yanjiu jikan* (Taiwan: A radical quarterly in social studies) 42 (June 2001): 119–82. For details, see his doctoral dissertation, "Governing the Colonized: Governmentality in the Japanese Colonisation of Taiwan, 1895–1945" (Ph.D. diss., Department of Sociology, University of Essex, 2002). Yao's research is perhaps the only serious attempt so far to use Foucault's theorization of governmentality to assess Japanese colonial rule in Taiwan, but his work concerns mainly the first half (1895–1920) of Japanese rule in Taiwan, thus leaving interwar and wartime Taiwan little touched.

70. For an overview of the evolutionary structure and functions of the *hokō* system, see Hui-yu Caroline Ts'ai, "The *Hokō* System in Taiwan, 1895–1945: Structure and Functions," *Zhongxing Daxue Wenshi Xuebao* (Chung-hsing journal of history) 23 (March 1993): 127–48. For the policing role of the *hokō*, see Ch'ing-ch'ih Ch'en, "Police and Community Systems in the Empire," in *The Japanese Colonial Empire, 1895–1945*, ed. Ramon H. Myers and Mark R. Peattie (Princeton, NJ: Princeton University Press, 1984), pp. 213–39. Unless otherwise noted, my discussion of *hokō* mobilization is based on material detailed in these sources. See Hui-yu Caroline Ts'ai, "One Kind of Control: The *Hokō* System in Taiwan under Japanese Rule, 1895–1945" (Ph.D. diss., Columbia University, 1990).

71. "Spatiality" here refers to "colonial space," as defined by John Noyes, or the "metaphysical construction of space" and the "production of space." As a "social spatiality," argues Noyes, it allows "subjectivity to be understood as a socially activated representation." See his *Colonial Space: Spatiality in the Discourse of German South West Africa, 1884–1915* (Chur, Switzerland: Harwood Academic Publishers, 1992), pp. 7, 11.

72. Hui-yu Caroline Ts'ai, "Japanese Rule in Taiwan as Oral History: Findings of Hokō Questionnaire Surveys, 1992–1993," *Xingda Lishi Xuebao* (Chung-hsing journal of history) 4 (May 1994): 121–44. The findings appeared in a series of articles and books dealing with the *hokō* system, the *gaishō* (town and village) administration, and veterans. See Hui-yu Caroline Ts'ai: (1) "Baozheng, baojia shuji, jiezhuang yichang—koushu lishi" (Baojia headmen, Baojia secretaries, and township offices—Oral history), *Shilian zazhi* (Journal of historical association) 23 (November 1993): 23–40; (2) *Taiwan fengwu* (Taiwan local studies) 44, 2 (June 1994): 69–111; (3) *Taiwan fengwu* (Taiwan local studies) 45, 4 (December 1995): 83–106; (4) *Taiwanshi yanjiu* (Taiwan historical research) 2, 2 (December 1995): 187–214; (5) *Taiwan fengwu* (Taiwan local studies) 47, 4 (December 1997): 69–112; as well as her book *Zouguo liangge shidai de ren: Taiji Ribenbing* and *Rizhi shidai Taiwan de jiezhuang xingzheng* (Township administration in Taiwan under Japanese rule), Taichung County Oral History Series, (Feng-yuan: Taichung County Cultural Center, 1997).

73. Chia-yi, a subprefecture; after 1920, a *gun* or county of Tainan-*shū*.

74. Washisu Atsushiya, *Taiwan keisatsu yonjūnen shiwa* (Notes on the forty years' history of the police in Taiwan) ([Taihoku?], 1938), p. 250. See also Cheng, "Zhanshi tizhi xia de Taiwan shehui (1937–1945)," (Taiwan society under wartime establishment (1937–1945), p. 26. *Jinpu* refers to the counting of coolies and thus may have inflated the actual figure of *hokō* residents mobilized in this way.

75. Hui-yu Caroline Ts'ai, "The 'Social Service Movement' (*shakai hōshi undō*) in Taiwan, 1932–1945: The *Hokō* System for Wartime Mobilization," *Zhongxing Daxue Wenshi Xuebao* (Journal of the college of liberal arts, national Taiwan Chung-hsing university) 24 (July 1994): 87–103.

76. Chung, *Taiwan hangkong juezhan* (Fighting decisive air battles in Taiwan), pp. 57, 140.

77. The only "air base" in the Taitō Subprefecture at that time was located in Pinan (or Pei-nan), the site of today's Taitung Feng-nien Airport. The other two places were "airport runways"; one was Shikano (Lu-yeh), today's Ch'ih-Shang, and another was on today's off-island, Lan-yu. Thus, it is possible that the air enforcement Ch'en worked for was Shikano. See Table 7 in Chung, *Taiwan hangkong juezhan* (Fighting decisive air battles in Taiwan), p. 60.

78. The nearest "satellite airport" to Kōbeki (or Ho-pi) was Shiragawa (or Pai-ho), Tainan Prefecture, although it is not certain whether the airport Lai mentioned in his oral history was exactly this. See Table 8 in Chung, *Taiwan hangkong juezhan* (Fighting decisive air battles in Taiwan), p. 61.

79. Taiwan Sōtokufu, *Taiwan tōchi gaiyō* (An outline of the rule of Taiwan), p. 73.

80. Discussed earlier in connection with Komagome's *Shokuminchi teikoku Nihon no bunka tōgō* (Cultural integration in the colonies of imperial Japan).

81. "Formal rationality" here is used to contrast with "substantive rationality." For discussion of the two terms, see Richard Colignon and Mark Covaleski, "A Weberian Framework in the Study of Accounting," *Accounting, Organizations and Society* 16, 2 (1991): 141–57.

Chapter 7

Author's note: Much of the information cited in this chapter derives from the Netherlands Forces Intelligence Service/Centrale Militaire Inlichtingendienst collections at the Netherlands Ministry of Foreign Affairs (abbreviated as BUZA NEFIS/CMI) and the archives of the Algemene Secretarie te Batavia at the National Archive (NA ASB) in The Hague, and the Indonesian Collection at the Netherlands Institute for War Documentation (NIOD IC) in Amsterdam. The Research School of Pacific and Asian Studies, the Australian National University, and the International Institute for Asian Studies, Leiden, sponsored my research in the Netherlands in 1995 and 1996–97. I would like to express my gratitude to the above institutions and their staff for making my research possible and pleasant.

1. Excluding Thailand, which remained independent, and French Indochina, officially administered by the French until March 9, 1945.

2. For the number of expatriated Javanese *rōmusha*, see "The number of native labourers sent out from Java," IC 005709; for work conditions and Japanese brutality, see Shigeru Sato, "Forced Labour Mobilization in Java during the Second World War," *Slavery & Abolition: A Journal of Slave and Post-Slave Studies*, 24, 2 (August 2003), 97–110; for *rōmusha* repatriation, see Shigeru Sato, *War, Nationalism and Peasants: Java under the Japanese Occupation 1942–1945* (Armonk: M.E. Sharpe, 1994), pp. 155–61, and chapter 11 by Henk Hovinga in this volume.

3. Iwatake Teruhiko, *Nanpō Gunsei Ronshū* (Essays on the military administration in the southern regions) (Tokyo: Gannandō, 1989), p. 24.

4. The document making this change in official policy was adopted on June 12, 1943, at the Imperial Headquarters-Government Liaison Conference. See "Nanpō Kō Chiiki Keizai Taisaku Yōkō" (Outline of the economic policies with regard to Ko areas), *Nansei Hōmen Rikugun Sakusen—Marēe, Ran'in no Kōbō* (Tokyo: Asagumo Shinbunsha, 1976), pp. 110–12.

5. "Personnel," NIOD IC 01229-35. This observed trend is more significant than the numbers indicate because unreported cases were, beyond any doubt, many times larger.

6. Boentaran Martoatmodjo's article "Pemandangan Singkat Perihal Kesehatan dan Makanan Rakjat dll" (Brief Overview of the People's Health and Food, etc.). In *Berita Ketabiban: Madjallah dari Djawa Izi Hōkō Kai* (Medical news: Journal of the Java Medical Service Association) (Jakarta: Djawa Izi Hōkō Kai, 1944), pp. 4, 5, 6, pp. 43–52, BUZA NEFIS/CMI, encl. 3, 2475. The article was based on Boentaran's ongoing research, and the rise in the incidence of starvation was clearly not a mere seasonal fluctuation.

7. According to one estimate, the total population of Java increased from 48,792,000 to 49,926,000 between 1941 and 1943, but then declined to 49,199,000. See Pierre van der Eng, *Food Supply in Java during War and Decolonisation, 1940–1950* (Hull: University of Hull, Centre for South-East Asian Studies, 1994), pp. 74–76. This estimate is important, but it is based largely on unreliable statistics cited in E. de Vries, "Vital Statistics under Japanese Rule," *Economic Review of Indonesia* 1 (January 1947): 18–19. Unrealistic figures cited as normal birth and death rates are one indication of the problems with the figures in de Vries's article. I thank the late Wim F. Wertheim for pointing this out and for sending me his article, "The Forty Percent Test: A Useful Demographic Tool," *Ekonomi dan Keuangan Indonesia* (Economy and finance in Indonesia) 8, 3 (March 1955): 162–88.

8. Pramoedya Ananta Toer, *The Fugitive*, trans. Willem Samuel (Harmondsworth: Penguin Books, 1990), p. 33.

9. Pramoedya, *The Fugitive*, p. 13.

10. H.M.S. Cumberland, "Provisional Proposals for Reoccupation of Batavia without Immediate Occupation of the Rest of Java," September 22, 1945, NIOD IC 005309.

11. *Jawa Shinbun* (Java daily), February 6, 1945.

12. "Kōkyō Shisetsu no Gaikyō" (Outline of the public works), BUZA NEFIS/CMI, encl. 3, 1776 and 2048. In the second phase the Japanese opened new airstrips at sixteen locations in Java and Madura, while converting some existing strips into vegetable fields. They also constructed other facilities, such as coastal fortifications at strategic locations.

13. NIOD IC 012412 and BUZA NEFIS/CMI, encl. 3, 1776. In principle the Japanese military suspended all the construction of coastal fortifications and airstrips at the end of 1944, but this did not mean they abandoned their defense effort altogether. Toward the end of the year they started building a large fortress in Mt. Malabar, south of Bandung, which was designed to entrench the entire Japanese population in Java in preparation for a full-scale invasion by the Allies. This effort intensified after Major General Mabuchi arrived from the New Guinea battlefront in mid-March 1945.

14. "The Survey of the Railway Affairs to Be Succeeded," NIOD IC 012513-17, pp. 45–9.

15. "Diagram Showing Sectional Transport Capacity of Java Railways System," NIOD IC 012243.

16. For the final intensification of the campaign, see the daily newspapers *Asia Raya* (Greater Asia) and *Jawashinbun* (Java daily) of July 1, 1945.

17. BUZA NEFIS/CMI, encl. 3, 1776. His notebooks contain a wide range of information on subjects such as the prewar state of agriculture in Java, blueprints for new irrigation and drainage works, budgets, labor, construction reports, and newspaper clippings. They are approximately 1,000 pages long, including insertions; there is no pagination.

18. For more information, see my chapter "Japanization in Indonesia Re-Examined: The Problem of Self-Sufficiency in Indonesia," in *Imperial Japan and National Identities in Asia, 1895–1945*, ed. Li Narangoa and Robert Cribb (London: RoutledgeCurzon, 2003), pp. 270–95.

19. *Jawashinbun*, March 30, 1944.

20. *Jawashinbun*, January 11, 1945.

21. *Gunseika Jawa Sangyōo Sōkan* (Conspectus of the industries in Java under the military adminstration), vol. 1, pp. 400–8.

22. A complete list of areas and production figures of major crops in each residency in 1944 and the plan for 1945 is available as a booklet, *Shōwa 20 Nendo Jūyō Nōosakumotsu Seisan Keikaku* (Production plan for important agricultural products in 1945) (Jakarta: Jawa Gunseikanbu, 1944), BUZA NEFIS/CMI, encl. 3, 1776.

23. Ibid.; and *Gunseika Jawa Sangyō Sōkan*, vol. 1, p. 106.

24. BUZA NEFIS/CMI, encl. 3, 1776.

25. "Gunsei Yōsuiro Kairyō Kōji Gaiyōsho" (Outline of the irrigation canal improvement project by the military administration), BUZA NEFIS/CMI, encl. 3, 1776.

26. "Study of Irrigation of Java/Madoora," BUZA NEFIS/CMI, encl. 3, 1776.

27. BUZA NEFIS/CMI, encl. 3, 1776. The letter was from the secretary-general of Yogyakarta, the sultan of Yogyakarta, and the *susuhunan* of Surakarta.

28. Mori Fumio, "Gunsei Shubo" (Notes on military administration), in *Gunsei Shiryō*

(Historical materials on the military administration), no. 90, Defence Agency, Tokyo.

29. A similar situation prevailed in many other fields of work. The railroads in Java annually used 29,000 tons of steel and iron in the prewar years. During the war, no more than 1,000 tons of secondhand steel and iron were available. No cement was available in 1945, so 3,000 tons of a cement substitute was requested. NIOD IC 101250 and 012500.

30. A report from the Japanese to the Allied forces, BUZA NEFIS/CMI, encl. 3, 1776.

31. "Jawa ni okeru Shokuryō Jijō Gaikyō" (Outline of the food situation in Java), BUZA NEFIS/CMI, encl. 3, 2060, and *Jawashinbun,* January 11, 1945.

32. Report from the NEFIS branch office in Semarang to the director of NEFIS in Jakarta, May 5, 1946, BUZA NEFIS/CMI, encl. 3, 1817.

33. NIOD IC 012500. For information on coal in occupied Java, see chapter 8 by Harry A. Poeze in this volume.

34. "Kaoem Tani dengan Barisan Soeka Rela" (Farmers in the voluntary labor service front), NIOD IC 032286-87.

35. BUZA NEFIS/CMI, vol. 1, 1775 and 1780. The disease was known as *omo mentek.*

36. "Eenige Algemeene Gegevens over de Landbouw en Veestapel gedurende Japansche Bezetting, Maart 1942–September 1945" (General data on agriculture and livestock during the Japanese occupation, March 1942–September 1945) BUZA NEFIS/CMI, vol. 1, 1780. This is an eyewitness account by a Dutchman or a Dutch Eurasian who continued working as a plantation administrator throughout the occupation period. Most Dutch people were put in concentration camps but a few thousand remained outside and worked under the Japanese.

37. For more details, see my article, "Japanization in Indonesia Re-Examined."

38. P.M. Prillwitz, "The Estate Agriculture during the Japanese Occupation," *Economic Review of Indonesia* 1 (January 1947): 17.

39. "Jawa Saibaikigyō no Gaikyō to 19 Nendo Jisseki" (Outline of the agricultural estates in Java and the results in 1944), July 20, 1945, BUZA NEFIS/CMI, encl. 3, 2058.

40. BUZA NEFIS/CMI, vol. 1, 1761. In fact, the Dutch foresaw the problem of sacking supply and conducted this experiment soon after war broke out in Europe. At the end of July 1945, there were stocks of 1 million 40-kilogram and 3 million 100-kilogram bags. See *Gunseika Jawa Sangyō Sōkan,* vol. 1, pp. 321–27; "Jawa ni okeru Shokuryo Jijo Gaiyo" (Outline of the food situation in Java), BUZA NEFIS/CMI, encl. 3, 2060; and *Kana Jawashinbun* (Java daily in Kana), February 3, 1945.

41. "Pedoman Tentang Daja Oepaja oentoek Menambah Hatsil Pertanian Daerah Sidoandjo" (Guidelines for the effort to increase agricultural production in the district Sidoarjo). BUZA NEFIS/CMI, encl. 3, 3145.

42. "Keadaan Tanaman di Djawa pada Tahoen 1945" (Crop conditions in Java in 1945), ARA SBS 5656.

43. BUZA NEFIS/CMI, encl. 3, 1776.

44. The trend of rice delivery was also reflected in railroad statistics. The total amount of rice transported by rail in the first three months of the main harvesting season, April, May, and June, was 183,142 tons in 1943; 137,840 tons in 1944; and 108,455 tons in 1945. "The Survey of the Railway Affairs to Be Succeeded," NIOD IC 012510-13.

45. NIOD IC 037296.

46. NIOD IC 031773.

47. "Pemandangan Oemoem Keadaan Sekarang" (General observation of the present situation), NIOD IC 040158.

48. NEFIS Interrogation Report, BUZA NEFIS/CMI, vol. 1, 44, and "Oorlogsschade" (War damage), NIOD IC 006477.

49. "Personnel," NIOD IC 012221.

50. "Report on the General Situation Regarding the Health of the Inhabitants of Soekabumi Area," February 19, 1946, p. 3, ARA ASB 3371.

Chapter 8

1. For accounts of the Burma railway, see H.L. Leffelaar and E. van Witsen, *Werkers aan de Birmaspoorweg* (Workers on the Burma railway) (Franeker: T. Wever, 1982), and Clifford Kinvig, *River Kwai Railway: The Story of the Burma-Siam Railway* (London: Brassey's, 1992).

2. In 1976 Henk Hovinga published *Dodenspoorweg door het oerwoud* (Death railway through the jungle) (Franeker: T. Wever) about this project. A third expanded version of this book appeared in 1982 under the title *Eindstation Pakan Baroe 1944–1945: Dodenspoorweg door het oerwoud* (Destination Pakan Baroe, 1944–1945: Death railway through the jungle) (Amsterdam: Franeker, 1982). For additional information, see H. Neumann and E. van Witsen, *De Sumatra Spoorweg* [. . .] (Middelie, 1985).

3. Soedjati, S.A., "Siasat mengoendjoengi Banten (Siasat visits Banten)," *Siasat* 1, no. 20 (May 17, 1947): 12.

4. Alex L. ter Braake, *Mining in the Netherlands East Indies* (New York, 1944), pp. 59–62.

5. R.D.M. Verbeek and R. Fennema, *Geologische beschrijving van Java en Madoera* (Geological description of Java and Madura), vol. 2 (Amsterdam, 1896), pp. 782–84.

6. This letter to the editor appeared under the heading "Een kabelbaan naar de Bajah-kolenvelden" (A cableway to the Bayah coalfields), *De Indische Mercuur* 23 (December 4, 1900): 884–85.

7. "De Javasteenkool voor het front" (Java coal for the front), *De Indische Mercuur* 24 (August 13, 1901): 623–24; N. Wing Easton, "Kolen" (Coal), in *Encyclopaedie van Nederlandsch-Indië*, 2nd ed., vol. 3 ('s-Gravenhage-Leiden, 1919), p. 407.

8. "Java-steenkolen" (Java coal), *De Indische Gids* 25, no. 1 (1903): 917–18.

9. K.G.J. Ziegler, "Verslag over de uitkomsten van mijnbouwkundig-geologische onderzoekingen in Zuid-Bantam (Report on the results of minerolgical and geological investigations in South Banten), *Jaarboek van het Mijnwezen in Nederlandsch Oost-Indië* 47 (1918), Verhandelingen, part 1, pp. 41–123.

10. "Verslag van het onderzoek naar het voorkomen van ertsafzettingen in Zuid-Bantam" (Report on the presence of ore deposits in South Banten), *Verslagen en Mededelingen betreffende Indische delfstoffen en hare toepassingen* 20 (1931): 1–75.

11. N.V. Exploratie Maatschappij Nederlandsch-Indië, annual reports, 1933–1938 (Batavia, 1934–1939). Reports for years after 1938 have not been located.

12. A.F. Kamp, *De standvastige tinnen soldaat, 1860–1960/N.V. Billiton Maatschappij* (The steadfast tin soldier, 1860-1960: The Billiton Company) ('s-Gravenhage, 1960), pp. 249–53.

13. Contract draft agreement in *Staatsblad van Nederlandsch-Indië 1935* (Gazetteer of the Dutch Indies, 1935), no. 63.

14. N.V. Mijnbouw Maatschappij 'Zuid-Bantam,' annual reports, 1936–1938 (Batavia, 1937–1939).

15. Information derived from *De Indische Mercuur* 62 (August 9, 1939): 459; 63 (February 7, 1940): 58; 63 (March 27, 1940): 131; 63 (April 24, 1940): 184; 63 (May 1, 1940): 195; 63 (May 8, 1940): 210.

16. R.W. van Bemmelen, *The Geology of Indonesia*, vol. 2, *Economic Geology* (The Hague, 1949), p. 133; Ter Braake, *Mining*, pp. 55–58.

17. David W.N. Kriek, *Speciale missie nr. 43 in Bantam (Java)* (Special mission no. 43 in Banten, Java) (Amsterdam, n.d.), p. 5.

18. See M.A. Aziz, *Japan's Colonialism and Indonesia* (The Hague, 1955), pp. 99–120, 182–93; John O. Sutter, *Indonesianisasi: Politics in a Changing Economy, 1940–1945*, vol. 1, *The Indonesian Economy at the Close of the Dutch Period and under the Japanese* (Ithaca, NY: Cornell University Press, 1959), pp. 138–45; L. de Jong, *Het Koninkrijk der Nederlanden in de Tweede Wereldoorlog* (The Kingdom of the Netherlands during the Second World War), vol. 11A (Leiden, 1984), pp. 714–16.

19. Van Bemmelen, *Geology*, pp. 66–69. Prospecting for coal was also carried out in Sukabumi and Rembang, but the results were negative. Sutter (*Indonesianisasi*, p. 163) is wrong in stating that the search for pit coal on Java began only when the supply by ship from Sumatra was no longer possible.

20. *Japanese Military Administration in Indonesia* (Washington: United States Joint Publications Research Service, 1963), pp. 295–97; Tan Malaka, *Dari pendjara ke pendjara* (From jail to jail), pt. 2 (Djogjakarta, 1948), p. 148; De Jong, *Het Koninkrijk der Nederlanden in de Tweede Wereldoorlog*, vol. 11B, p. 513.

21. Kriek, *Speciale missie*, pp. 4–7, 22–40; "When an Inner Voice Spoke," *World War II Investigator 1–9* (1988): 7–17.

22. Kriek, *Speciale missie*, p. 50; J.M. Weehuizen, "Het beheer van het bedrijf der N.V. Mijnbouw Maatschappij 'Zuid Bantam' vanaf het begin der Japansche bezetting tot 24 November 1942" (The management of the South Banten Mining Company from the beginnning of the Japanese occupation till November 24, 1942) (typed report, March 1946, in the Kriek collection), p. 1.

23. Kriek, *Speciale missie*, pp. 60–61. Concerning Van der Post, see Kriek, passim, and "When an Inner Voice Spoke," 7–17; De Jong, *Het Koninkrijk der Nederlanden in de Tweede Wereldoorlog* (Leiden, 1988), vol. 11A, p. 424, and vol. 13, pp. 165–66.

24. Weehuizen, "Beheer 'Zuid Bantam,'" pp. 2–3; Kriek, *Speciale missie*, p. 63.

25. *Asia Raya*, April 6, 1944 (*Asia Raya* was the only daily newspaper in Jakarta). D.W.N. Kriek, interview with the author, Amsterdam, January 16, 1989.

26. Weehuizen, "Beheer 'Zuid Bantam,'" pp. 1–7; Kriek, *Speciale missie*, pp. 68, 71, 75. *Asia Raya*, August 19, 21, and 22, and September 17, 1942, published short reports on the sending of workers to the Cikotok gold mines. It appears that they were used in road construction and to open the mine. In *Asia Raya*, December 17, 1942, there is mention of construction of roads from Malingping and Cikotok to Bayah. There is no reference to pit coal mining.

27. Weehuizen, "Beheer 'Zuid Bantam,'" pp. 3, 5. An overview of the economy of Java prepared by the Japanese military command in 1944 mentions that mining in Cikotok had resumed under the management of the Mitsui conglomerate. Lead and zinc were mined, with labor supplied by around 1,200 *rōmusha*. See Aiko Kurasawa, "Mobilization and Control: A Study of Social Change in Rural Java, 1942–1945" (Ph.D. diss., Cornell University, 1988), p. 214.

28. *Asia Raya*, June 10, 1944 (articles on pp. 1 and 2). The report mentions tin, but this is a mistake. Although for security reasons the report does not mention place names, Harada clearly visited Pasir Gombong and Cirotan. See Van Bemmelen,

Geology, pp. 155–56. The ore of Cirotan contained gold, silver, copper, lead, and zinc. These last three could be mined economically only as by-products of gold and silver, but Japan used other standards to assess viability. At full processing capacity the maximum daily yield of copper was only about 200 kilograms.

29. *Asia Raya,* April 6, 1944.

30. T.Sk. Sutawinangun, "Tjerita Bajah: 'Tugu Romusha' memperingati keganasan Djepang" (The story of Bayah: The rōmusha monument memorializes Japan's cruelty), *Siasat* 7, no. 314 (June 14, 1953): 14; *Asia Raya,* December 17, 1942; D.W.N. Kriek, interview with the author, Amsterdam, January 16, 1989.

31. Tb. Sutawinangun, "Bajah serba pajah" (Bayah—all in trouble), *Siasat* 5, no. 240 (January 18, 1951): 14, gives a date of October 1942. After the conclusion of the whole line in March 1944, reports appeared that placed the beginning of the construction in February (*Asia Raya,* April 6, 1944) and April 1943 (*Djawa Baroe,* April 15, 1944, p. 11). Japan's success in completing such an extensive work in just one year was mentioned with pride.

32. Letter from R. Sadhinoch, dated Schiedam, November 24, 1989; "The Survey of the Railway Affairs to Be Succeeded," Nederlands Instituut voor Oorlogsdocumentatie, Indische Collectie (NIOD IC) 12467-12554, pp. 56 ff. The survey was prepared by Japanese officials after their capitulation on orders from the Allied authorities.

33. R. Sadhinoch, report no. 1 (1987). Sadhinoch (b. 1920), an Indo-Dutchman, worked with the service personnel matters of the division of construction and bridges in the Bandung headquarters. Sadhinoch remembers that the line was intended for the shipping of gold ore from Cikotok. His memory is faulty here, or else the Japanese railway management withheld information concerning their intention to mine brown coal.

34. Sadhinoch, report no. 1; Sadhinoch letter, November 24, 1989; R. Sadhinoch, interview with the author, Schiedam, July 13, 1989.

35. Tjakradipura, interview with the author, Jakarta, October 30, 1980; Sadhinoch, report no. 1. Tjakradipura belonged to the staff of one of the construction teams between Saketi and Malingping and was responsible for a section 6–7 kilometers long near Pasung.

36. Tjakradipura, interview with the author, Jakarta, October 30, 1980. It is difficult to account for Tjakradipura's statement, unless he wanted to give a favorable picture of his own involvement in an inhumane undertaking. His group did have the advantage of working on an early stage of the project, when material conditions were still bearable, and in an area that was not malarial.

37. Sadhinoch, report no. 1.

38. Sadhinoch letter, April 16, 1990.

39. At first the *rōmusha* were volunteers, but as people became aware of the poor working conditions, there was an ever-greater use of force in the recruitment process. Each residency had to supply a specified number of *rōmusha,* an obligation that was passed along to lower administrative units. The actual recruitment took place in villages and towns and often involved coercion, arbitrariness, and bribery; de Jong, *Het Koninkrijk der Nederlanden in de Tweede Wereldoorlog,* vol. 11B, pp. 530–38. The recruitment of *rōmusha* for the construction of railway lines and mining work did not deviate from the general picture.

40. Sutawinangun, "Tjerita Bajah," p. 14.

41. "Kakek Emok Mukandar yg mengurus mayat romusha" (Old Emok Mukandar who took care of the romusha corpses), *Angkatan Bersenjata,* July 12, 1979.

42. Before he was banished by the Dutch government in 1922, Tan Malaka was a prominent leader of the Communist party. In exile he continued to play an important role in the communist movement, until he broke with it in 1927. His own illegal radical-nationalist party was rounded up by the government. Tan Malaka then moved to China and Singapore and for a time had virtually no contact with Indonesia. He returned in 1942 under an alias. After a period of time in Jakarta, where the Japanese were suspicious of him, he thought he had found a safe and secluded refuge in Bayah, where he lived under the name Iljas Hussein. He was hired as a mining supervisor after responding to an appeal in Jakarta for mining employees. For additional details concerning Tan Malaka, see Harry A. Poeze, *Tan Malaka, strijder voor Indonesië's vrijheid, Levensloop 1897–1945* (The life of Tan Malaka, fighter for Indonesia's freedom, from 1897 till 1945) ('s-Gravenhage, 1976).

43. Tan Malaka, *Dari pendjara ke pendjara,* pp. 147–48. Elsewhere (p. 156) he writes that thousands of emaciated *rōmusha,* who had fled, were wandering between Bayah and their place of residence; most of them died of disease and hunger. English passages are from Tan Malaka, *From Jail to Jail,* trans. Helen Jarvis (Athens: Ohio University Center for International Studies, 1991), pp. 156–57.

44. Tan Malaka, *Dari pendjara ke pendjara,* p. 157. Translation from Jarvis, *From Jail to Jail,* p. 167.

45. Sutawinangun, "Tjerita Bajah," p. 14.

46. Sutawinangun, "Bajah serba pajah," p. 14.

47. Soedjati, "Siasat mengoendjoengi Banten," p. 12.

48. Kriek, *Speciale missie,* p. 19.

49. Haji Moh. Mukhander, interview with the author, Bayah, September 22, 1980; A.L. Tobing, interview with the author, Bayah, September 21, 1980.

50. Tan Malaka, *Dari pendjara ke pendjara,* pp. 159–60.

51. Abdulkadir Djaelani, interview with the author, Pulau Manuk, September 21, 1980.

52. *Djawa Baroe* 9 (April 15, 1944), 11; *Asia Raya,* April 6, 1944.

53. "Additional Report on Coalfields and a New Railway Built by the Japanese in West Java," NEFIS report, August 10, 1944, NIOD IC 60895.

54. Sadhinoch, interview with the author, July 13, 1989. According to Sadhinoch, even at the time of his arrest in June 1944 the whole railway line was not yet in use over its total length.

55. Letter from the Republican Office for the Bayah mine in Jogjakarta, December 8, 1945, NIOD IC 5605. Tan Malaka, *Dari pendjara ke pendjara,* pp. 156, 157.

56. These figures have been extracted from the original overview in NIOD IC 5723-5797.

57. See, for instance, I.J. Brugmans, ed., *Nederlandsch-Indië onder Japanse bezetting; Gegevens en documenten over de jaren 1942–1945* (The Dutch Indies under Japanese occupation. Data and documents for the years 1942–1945) (Franeker, 1960), pp. 279–80.

58. R. de Bruin, "Het Indisch verzet" (The Indies resistance), *Moesson* 32, no. 5 (October 1, 1987): 14–15; de Jong, *Het Koninkrijk der Nederlanden in de Tweede Wereldoorlog,* vol. 11B, pp. 341, 455–56.

59. Sadhinoch, Reports 1 and 2 (1989).

60. Harry A. Poeze, "The PKI-Muda," *Kabar Seberang* 13–14 (1985): 157–76. Very little is known of the history of communism during the Japanese occupation, but a few personal memoirs have been preserved and published. See Anton Lucas,

ed., *Local Opposition and Underground Resistance to the Japanese in Java* (Clayton, Vic: Centre of Southeast Asian Studies, Manash University, 1986). This volume mainly concerns the course of events in some East Javanese cities, but Lucas (pp. 25, 58) mentions that a regional network existed in Banten and that in 1943 the Japanese arrested thirteen PKI members there. Another source mentions a Bantenese resistance group that maintained contact with resistance elements elsewhere but had most of its members arrested in 1944. See Michael C. Williams, "Banten: Rice Debts Will be Repaid with Rice, Blood Debts with Blood," in *Regional Dynamics of the Indonesian Revolution: Unity from Diversity,* ed. Audrey R. Kahin (Honolulu: University of Hawaii Press, 1985), pp. 54–81. Sidik Kertapati, in *Sekitar Proklamasi 17 Augustus 1945* (About the Proclamation [of Independence] of August 17, 1945) (Djakarta, 1964), pp. 25–30, mentions groups active in West Java. Tan Malaka had no involvement with them.

61. Sadhinoch, reports 1 and 2; Sadhinoch letters, Schiedam, July 17 and August 22, 1989; Sadhinoch, interview with the author, July 13, 1989. Schweichler confirms Sadhinoch's accounts of the events. In a notarized statement, Sumual said that Sadhinoch and the others were involved in political action against the Japanese occupier. One of the three arrested persons, who was not a member of the group, was released in April 1945, so the statement that all arrested persons were sentenced to death is not entirely correct. Procesverbaal verhoor A.W. Geisler door Regeeringsbureau tot Opsporing van Oorlogsmisdadigers, NIOD, IC 18678, January 16, 1946. In Sadhinoch, report no. 2, he mentions being told that in Serang his fellow prisoners included a Singapore Arab who was set ashore in South Banten, and that the man died as a result of torture. No confirmation for this can be found. The man might have been an agent recruited in Mecca from among pilgrims stranded there or, more likely, an innocent victim of Japanese suspicion. De Jong, in *Het Koninkrijk der Nederlanden in de Tweede Wereldoorlog,* vol. 11C, pp. 173–286, provides an overview of the work of the Allied intelligence services.

62. Sadhinoch, interview with the author, July 13, 1989.

63. Kertapati, *Sekitar proklamasi,* pp. 25–30.

64. *Asia Raya,* April 6, 1944.

65. Tan Malaka, *Rentjana ekonomi* (Economic plan) (Soerakarta, 1946), pp. 8–9. Tan Malaka (in *Dari pendjara ke pendjara,* pp. 148–49) errs when he speaks of 100 tons a month.

66. Survey of the railway affairs, NIOD, IC 12467-12554, pp. 42–45.

67. A.L. Tobing, interview with the author, September 22, 1980.

68. Sadhinoch letter, April 16, 1990.

69. Communications and transportation, NIOD, IC 12239-12322. This concerns a report that was drawn up after the Japanese surrender by Japanese agencies for Allied authorities.

70. Tan Malaka, *Dari pendjara ke pendjara,* p. 149, also mentions Cihara, situated along the railway line 15 kilometers from Bayah, in the Cimandiri field. Either Tan Malaka is mistaken and another name should be read for Cihara, or else exploitation of Cimandiri coal was involved. No other source mentions exploitation of the Cimandiri field, which suggests that Tan Malaka may be wrong.

71. A.L. Tobing, interview with the author, September 22, 1980.

72. Tan Malaka, *Dari pendjara ke pendjara,* p. 149. Translation from Jarvis, *From Jail to Jail,* p. 158.

73. Ibid., pp. 165–67.

74. Djajarukmantara, interview with the author, Jakarta, September 26, 1980. Djajarukmantara was commander of the PETA unit in Bajah. Tan Malaka, *Dari pendjara ke pendjara,* p. 161–62.

75. Tan Malaka, *Dari pendjara ke pendjara,* pp. 155, 167, 179–81.

76. De Jong, *Het Koninkrijk der Nederlanden in de Tweede Wereldoorlog,* vol. 11B, pp. 571–72.

77. A.L. Tobing, interview with the author, Bajah, September 22, 1980.

78. Abdulkadir Djaelani, interview with the author, September 21, 1980.

79. Sutawinangun, "Tjerita Bajah," p. 14.

80. Abdulkadir Djaelani, interview with the author, September 21, 1980.

81. Tan Malaka, *Dari pendjara ke pendjara,* p. 168.

82. Abdulkadir Djaelani, interview with the author, September 21, 1980.

83. Tan Malaka, *Dari pendjara ke pendjara,* p. 172.

84. Djajarukmantara, interview with the author, September 26, 1980.

85. *Asia Raya,* June 10, 1944, 1, 2.

86. Tan Malaka, *Dari pendjara ke pendjara,* pp. 162–64, gives an account of the visit that probably took place in August 1944. A press report is missing, but there are two references to a visit in *Asia Raya* (August 4, 1944, and May 14, 1945).

87. Cindy Adams, *Sukarno: An Autobiography* (Indianapolis, IN: Bobbs-Merrill, 1965), p. 192.

88. Sutiwinangun, "Tjerita Bajah," p. 15. Tan Malaka had no role anymore in these events. He had left in early August for Jakarta. Tan Malaka, *Dari pendjara ke pendjara,* p. 183.

89. A.L. Tobing, interview with the author, September 22, 1980.

90. Summarized from four letters by Republican authorities concerning the Bayah mines, October–December 1945, NIOD IC 5605.

91. Williams, "Banten," pp. 54–81.

92. A.L. Tobing, interview with the author, September 22, 1980; Tjakradipura, interview with the author, October 30, 1980.

93. A.H. Nasution, *Sekitar perang kemerdekaan Indonesia,* vol. 5, *Agresi Militer Belanda I* (About the Indonesian War of Independence, vol. 5, The First Dutch Agression) (Bandung, 1978), p. 446.

94. Soedjati, "Siasat mengoendjoengi Banten," p. 12.

95. Nasution, *Sekitar perang kemerdekaan,* p. 8; *Pemberontakan PKI 1948* (The PKI [Communist Party of Indonesia] insurrection in 1948) (Bandung, 1979), p. 155.

96. Matia Madjiah, *Kisah seorang dokter gerilya dalam revolusi kemerdekaan di Banten* (Impressions of a guerrilla doctor during the revolution of independence in Banten) (Jakarta, 1986), pp. 149–50. The author traveled this route as a conscript in the Republican army.

97. Sutawinangun, "Tjerita Bajah," p. 15.

98. Tobing (interview with the author, September 22, 1980) states that he took the initiative to erect a memorial in 1946, at the instigation of Tan Malaka. An earlier request from Tan Malaka to the Japanese mine management to create a memorial had been refused. Sutawinangun, "Tjerita Bajah," p. 15. Nasution, *Sekitar perang kemerdekaan,* vol. 8, p. 156, mentions an inaugural ceremony on August 17, 1948.

99. Sutawinangun, "Tjerita Bajah," p. 15; personal observation.

100. Matia Madjiah, *Kisah seorang dokter,* pp. 151–54. The first time that gold was transported by plane, some 20 kilograms on October 1, 1948, the plane crashed in bad weather over Sumatra. *Sejarah operasi penerbangan Indonesia periode 1945–1950*

(The history of the Indonesian air operations during from 1945 till 1949) (Jakarta, 1980), pp. 80–81.

101. *Herinneringsalbum 1e Infanterie Brigadegroep C Divisie "7 December,"* vol. 4 (March 1, 1948), *Demobilisatie* (Memorial album 1st Infantry C Brigade 7 December Division) (Leiden, n.d.), pp. 23–28, 52–54; Alfred van Sprang, *Wij werden geroepen: De geschiedenis van de 7 December Divisie C* (We were called, the history of the 7 December Division C) ('s-Gravenhage, 1949), pp. 187–203; Nasution, *Sekitar perang kemerdekaan,* vol. 10; *Perang gerilya semesta II* (Total guerrilla war, II) (Bandung, 1979), pp. 191–211.

102. Van Sprang, *Wij werden geroepen,* p. 197.

103. Letters from Ir. L.L.J. van Loenen, Cikotok, to the director of the South Bantam Mining Company in Jakarta, October 20 and November 12, 1949, in the Kriek archive.

104. Kamp, *De standvastige tinnen soldaat,* p. 253.

105. Kriek, interview with the author, November 16, 1989.

106. Van Sprang, *Wij werden geroepen,* p. 209; Van Loenen letter, October 20, 1949; Williams, *Banten,* pp. 75–76.

107. Sutawinangun, "Bajah serba pajah," pp. 14–15.

108. S.J., "Saketi-Bajah memang pajah (Saketi-Bajah is indeed a difficult journey)," *Siasat* 6, no. 258 (April 6, 1952): 7.

109. Sutawinangun, "Tjerita Bajah," p. 15.

Chapter 9

1. Headquarters of the 16th Army in Java, "Explanations Regarding All Kinds of Armed Bodies," staff paper by the operations sections of the headquarters of the 16th Army, Java, and preserved in the Nishijima Collection, Institute of Asia-Pacific Studies, Waseda University, Tokyo.

2. Regarding PETA, see Benedict Anderson, *Java in a Time of Revolution: Occupation and Resistance, 1944–1946* (Ithaca, NY: Cornell University Press, 1972); George MacTurnan Kahin, *Nationalism and Revolution in Indonesia* (Ithaca, NY: Cornell University Press, 1952); Nugroho Notosusanto, *The PETA Army during the Japanese Occupation of Indonesia* (Tokyo: Waseda University Press, 1979); Aiko Shiraishi, "Jawa Bōei Giyūgun no Setsuritsu"(The establishment of the Java Volunteer Forces) *Tōnan Azia Rekishi to Bunka* 4 (November 1974): 3–39; Akira Nagazumi, *Pemberontakan Indonesia pada Masa Pendudukan Jepang* (Jakarta: Yayasan Obor, 1988), p. ix. One reason for the neglect of the subject of *heiho* by foreign scholars is that few are able to read the relevant documents, most of which are in Japanese.

3. Concerning regional history during the independence struggle, see Audrey Kahin, ed., *Regional Dynamics of the Indonesian Revolution: Unity from Diversity* (Honolulu: University of Hawaii Press, 1985).

4. Bōeichō Bōeikensyūsho Senshishitsu (Military History Department, National Institute for Defense Studies, hereafter: NIDS), ed., *Senshisōsho 99: Rikugun Gun Senbi* (War history series 99: The army's preparation for war) (Tokyo: Asagumo Shinbunsha, 1979), pp. 352–53.

5. Rikugunshō Heibika (Army Ministry, Department of Armaments), "Daitōa Sensō ni Tomonau Waga Jinteki Kokuryoku no Kentō" (A study of Japan's human resources in the Greater East Asian War), January 20, 1942, reprinted in Takasaki Ryuji, ed., *Jūgonen Sensō Gokuhi Shiryōshū,* vol. 1 (Tokyo: Fuji Shuppan, 1987), p. 18.

6. Bōeichō Bōeikensyūsho Senshishitsu (NIDS), ed., *Senshisōsho 92: Nansei Hōmen Rikugun Sakusen* (War history series 92: The Army's operation in Southwest Area) (Tokyo: Asagumo Shinbunsha, 1976), p.44.

7. Bōeichō Bōeikensyūsho Senshishitsu (NIDS), ed., *Senshisōsho 99: Rikugun Gun Senbi* (Tokyo: Asagumo Shinbunsha, 1979), pp.340-53.

8. Unpublished manuscript by 16th Army Operational Staff Officer Miyamoto Shizuo, private collection.

9. Although the optimum arrangement was to secure new recruits from Japan proper, this was impracticable. In an effort to overcome such difficulties, the government amended the Military Draft Bill on February 18, 1942, to increase the rate of enlistment by suspending the student privilege of temporary exemption from conscription and by conscripting soldiers from colonized Taiwan and Korea. Kato Yoko, *Chōhei Sei to Kindai Nihon 1868–1945* (The conscription system and modern Japan, 1868–1945) (Tokyo: Yoshikawa Kobunkan, 1996), pp. 240–41.

10. "Ranryō Higashi Indo ni okeru Gunsei Shikō Yōryō" (A blueprint for enforcement of military administration in Dutch East Indies), March 31, 1941, was prepared by Lieutenant Colonel Nishimura. Japanese military authorities began making plans for the military administration of the southern areas in February 1941 after the First Research Section (Sanbō Honbu Daiichibu Kenkyū Han) was attached to the General Staff Office. The Section had drafted fifteen reports by the end of March. Nishimura pointed out in an interview that they started this research concerning occupation policies without any materials, and that the General Staff Office took a leading role in this research, with no reference to the army or navy. However, he indicated that there was cooperation with *Taiwan gun* (Japanese army in Taiwan) and *Nanpō Kyōkai* (Southern Association). Goto Ken'ichi, *Nihon Senryoki Indoneshia Kenkyu* (Tokyo: Ryukei Shosha, 1989), p. 21.

11. Nanpōgun Sōshireibu (General Headquarters of the Southern Army), "Dai Jūisshō Nanpōgun Gunsei Shikō Keikaku An" (Chapter 11: Draft outline for implementation of military administration in the South), November 3, 1941, the Military Archival Library, NIDS, Tokyo. This document was divided into two sections, the first containing general plans for military administration over occupied territories, and the second dealing with occupied areas individually.

12. The liaison conference between the imperial headquarters and the government, "Nanpō Senryōchi Gyōsei Jisshi Yōryō" (Principles of the execution of administration in the occupied southern areas), November 20, 1941, and "Nanpo Sakusen ni tomonau Senryochi Gyosei Jisshi Yoryo" (Principles for administering occupied southern areas in accordance with southern operations), November 25, 1941.

13. Rikugunshō Heibika (Army, Ministry, Department of Armaments), "Daitōa Sensō ni tomonau Waga Jinteki Kokuryoku no Kentō" (A study of Japan's human resources in the Greater East Asian War), p. 22.

14. The breakdown of POWs captured in Java as of March 25, 1942, was as follows: Dutch (including militia) 66,219; Australian 4,890; British 10,626; U.S. 883. Bōeichō Bōeikensyūsho Senshishitsu (NIDS), ed., *Senshisōsho 3: Ran'in Kōryaku Sakusen* (War history series 3: Netherlands East Indies Operation) (Tokyo: Asagumo Shinbunsha, 1967), pp. 593–94.

15. The 16th Army, "Furyo Shūyō Yō" (An order concerning interned captives), March 25, 1942, Military Archival Library, NIDS, Tokyo.

16. Sanbō Honbu (General Staff Office), "Ran'in Gun Jō 2 Gō: Ran'in Gun no Soshitsu oyobi Nōryoku ni kansuru Kentō" (The second report: Investigations regard-

ing the nature and ability of the KNIL), August 31, 1941, Military Archival Library, NIDS, Tokyo. The document appears to be part of a group of intelligence studies containing valuable information about the General Staff Office's view of the KNIL and its former members, but the rest of the series apparently has not survived.

17. I.J. Brugmans, *Nederlandsch-Indië onder Japanse Bezetting: Gegevens en Documenten over de Jaren 1942–1945* (Franeker: T. Wever, 1960), pp. 522–23; NEFIS interrogation report, AI2/6173/G., Centraal Archieven Depot, Ministerie van Defensie (hereafter: CADMvD), The Hague.

18. No official record survives concerning Nishiura's proposal. He had been a member of the Military Affairs Bureau since 1931 and became its head in April 1942. It was during a year spent at the French Staff College (1935–36) that the idea occurred to him of using foreign troops to defend occupied areas. Colonel Nishiura said in an interview that General Lyautey's idea of using Moroccan soldiers within French forces, and their activities in the Battle of the Marne in World War I, deeply impressed him and provided the inspiration for introducing *heiho* into the Japanese army. He assigned Major Kaizaki, a member of the Military Affairs Bureau, to further this scheme in the occupied Dutch East Indies. Nihon Kindai Shi Kenkyū Kai, ed., *Nishiura Susumu shi Danwa Sokkiroku* (Tokyo: Tokyo University Press, 1968), pp. 378–79; Nugroho Notosusanto, *The PETA Army*, pp. 76–77; Ōta Hiroki, "Rikugun Nanpō Senryōchi no Heiho Seido (Jō)" (Regulations on Heiho in army's occupied southern area), *Seiji Keizai Shigaku*, no. 328 (1975): 15.

19. Nihon Kindai Shi Kenkyū Kai, *Nishiura Susumu shi Danwa Sokkiroku*, pp. 378–79.

20. The code name for this program was "Tairikushi 1196." "Heiho Kitei" (Heiho guideline), Riku-Amitsu, no. 3636, September 23, 1942.

21. Nampō Gun (Southern Army), "Nampō Gun Heibi Zōkyō ni Kansuru Iken" (Requirement for empowerment of Southern Army), February 21, 1943; Bōeichō Bōeikensyūsho Senshishitsu (NIDS), ed., *Nansei Hōmen Rikugun Sakusen* (Tokyo: Asagumo Shinbunsha, 1976), p. 95.

22. "Heiho Kitei Shikō Saisoku" (Regulation for carrying out *heiho* guidelines) was dated April 22, 1943.

23. Bōeichō Bōeikensyūsho Senshishitsu (NIDS), ed., *Nansei Hōmen Rikugun Sakusen*, p. 95; *Rikugun Gun Senbi*, pp. 360–61.

24. Bōeichō Bōeikensyūsho Senshishitsu (NIDS), ed., *Senshisōsho 23: Gōhoku Hōmen Rikugun Sakusen* (War history series 23: The army's operation in northern Australia) (Tokyo: Asagumo Shinbunsha, 1969), pp. 62-63; *Senshisōsho 63: Daihon'ei Rikugunbu*, vol. 5 (War history series 63: The army division of the imperial headquarters, vol. 5) (Tokyo: Asagumo Shinbunsha, 1973), pp. 339–42.

25. Takeshi Morimoto, *Jawa Bōei Giyūgun Shi* (History of PETA Army) (Tokyo: Ryukei Shosha, 1992), pp. 53–54.

26. NEFIS interrogation report, AI2/9374/G. In this interrogation, Ambonese and Menadonese soldiers stated that they were transferred from POW camps directly to *heiho* units. The first *heiho* unit, established as the 1st Special Land Duty Company in Rabaul, consisted of 200 British Indian Army personnel and 26 ex-KNIL Menadonese along with 10 Japanese officers and ordinary soldiers. The British Indian Army personnel were men who had refused to join the Indian National Army in Singapore and Malaya. The 1st to the 6th Special Land Duty Companies and the 16th to 20th Special Sea Duty Companies traveled to the Solomon and Bismarck islands and to East New Guinea between February and October 1943. Most of these units were composed of a

mix of POWs, including KNIL and British Indian Army personnel. Kaori Maekawa, "Ajiajin Heihi to BC-kyu Senpan Saiban: Taiheiyō Sensō Makki ni okeru Nyūginia Sensen to Indonesia Heiho" (Asiatic prisoners of war and the BC class war tribunal: Indonesian Heiho in New Guinea during Second World War), *Jōchi Ajia Gaku* (Sophia Journal of Asian Studies) *19* (2001): 87-107.

27. Former platoon captain of the Special Land Duty Company in Ceram, interview with the author, December 1995, Takasaki, Japan.

28. Brugmans, *Nederlandsch-Indië onder Japanse Bezetting,* pp. 522–23.

29. Maekawa, "Asiatic Prisoners of War," pp. 89–92. L. de Jong, *Het Koninkrijk der Nederlanden in de Tweede Wereldoorlog Deel II b, Nederlands-Indië II* tweede helft (Leiden: Martinus Nijhoff, 1985), pp. 604–8. Jacob Zwaan, *Nederlands-Indië 1940–1946: Japans Intermezzo, 9 maart 1942–15 augustus 1945* (The Hague: Omniboek, 1985), p. 255. There are many reports of POWs being beaten for refusing to serve as *heiho,* especially among the Ambonese and Menadonese. See, for example, NEFIS Interrogation Report, AI2/51/51/G., AI2/5998/G, CADMvD.

30. NEFIS interrogation report, AI2/6173/G., AI2/6272/G., AI2/7521/G., AI2/8487/ G., AI2/8581/G., AI2/8582/G., CADMvD, nos. 366–378, 404–407, 410–417. These ex-KNIL soldiers were mainly Javanese and were released from internment between March and May 1942.

31. The Surabaya office of Jawa Gunsei Kanbu (Java Military Administration Headquarters) issued calls for ex-personnel who had military experience on August 1, 1942, and January 2, 1943; *Kan Po,* nos. 1 and 13 (repr., Tokyo: Ryukei Shosha, 1989).

32. "An informant states that every village head in Java had received a written order from the Japanese Administration, to the effect that every ex-soldier, originally released by the Japanese, had to report for duties in Heiho." NEFIS interrogation report, AI2/6379/G., AI2/6676/G., CADMvD.

33. Maekawa, "Asiatic Prisoners of War," pp. 93–98. NEFIS interrogation report, AI2/5998/G., AI2/6272/G., AI2/7250/G., AI2/8779/G., AI2/9103/G., AI2/9156/G., AI2/ 9415/G., AI2/10252/G.

34. Morimoto, *Jawa Bōei Giyūgun Shi,* p. 54.

35. Headquarters of the Southern Army, "Regulations for Carrying Out Heiho Guidelines," article 1. Two supplemental regulations clarified recruitment procedures. The first, Riku-Amitsu no. 3452 (June 9, 1943), notified the Southern Army of the practice of "temporary placement of employees as Heiho." By "employees" the regulation meant indigenous troops among the ex-POWs who were forced to become *heiho.* The second regulation was Riku-Amitsu no. 4414 (July 16, 1943). See "Heiho ni kansuru Ken" (Matters concerning *heiho*), issued by the Imperial General Headquarters Army Department.

36. Morimoto, *Jawa Bōei Giyūgun Shi,* p. 56.

37. Article 6 in the Headquarters of Southern Army, "Regulations for Carrying Out Heiho Guidelines."

38. Kishi Koichi, Nishijima Shigetada, *et al., Indonesia ni okeru Nihon Gunsei no Kenkyū* (A study of the Japanese occupation in Indonesia) (Tokyo: Ōkuma Kinen Shakai Kagaku Kenkyūsho), Waseda University Press, 1959), p. 192.

39. Since *seinendan* activities were carried out at the members' own expense, members were selected from elements that were relatively well off and could afford the cost and time. Aiko Kurasawa, *Nihon Senryō ka no Jawa Nōson no Henyō* (Transformation of Javanese rural society under Japanese rule) (Tokyo: Soshisha, 1992), p. 315.

40. Ibid., 313, 317.

41. Bōeichō Bōeikensyūsho Senshishitsu (NIDS), ed., *Nansei Hōmen Rikugun Sakusen,* p. 168; Jawa Gunsei Kanbu, *Jawa Nenkan Kigen 2604 nen* (Java yearbook) (Jakarta: Jawa Shinbun Sha, 1944; repr., Tokyo: Biburio sha, 1973), p. 52.

42. *Celebes Shinbun,* June 10, 1944.

43. Kurasawa, *Jawa Nōson no Henyō,* p. 205. According to Kurasawa, ordinary *rōmusha* received 40–50 cents per day while *heiho* got at least 30 guilders per month.

44. NEFIS interrogation report, AI2/7853/G., AI2/6379/G., CADMvD.

45. Nugroho Notosusanto, *Pemberontakan Tentara Peta Blitar Melawan Djepang, 14 Pebuari 1945* (Djakarta: Departemen Pertahanan Keamanan, Lembaga Sedjarah Hankam, 1968), p. 11.

46. See Kaigunshō (Navy Ministry), "Kaigun Heiho Kisoku" (Regulations concerning naval *heiho*), code-name Tatsu 73, March 16, 1944, and "Kaigun Heiho Kisoku Shikō ni kansuru Ken" (Enforcement of naval *heiho* regulations), code-name Kanbōjin 349.

47. Article 9 in "Regulations Concerning Naval Heiho," and articles 1 and 2 in "Enforcement of Naval Heiho Regulations."

48. Java Shimbunsha, *Djawa Baroe,* no. 23 (repr., Tokyo: Ryukei Shosha, 1992), p. 21. Java Gunseikanbu (Java Military Administration Headquarters), *Kan Po,* no. 44, (repr., Tokyo: Ryukei Shosha, 1989). The first announcement of naval *heiho* recruitment appeared in the *Celebes Shinbun* of Makassar on May 6, 1944, and concerned southern Sulawesi. In South Borneo a similar announcement appeared on May 31, 1944. Advertisements appeared over a period of one month. The preliminary examination of potential recruits took place on June 29 and 30 at sixteen locations in Sulawesi, with a second and final examination in July. Candidates entered Kaigun Heiho Gakkō (Naval Heiho Training School) at Singaraja on August 6, and at Makassar on August 8, 1944.

49. In Makassar a general order required all male inhabitants between eighteen and twenty-three years of age to report at the Minseibu office for enlistment in *heiho* by July 1, 1944. NEFIS interrogation report, AI2/7655/G., CADMvD.

50. Articles 8 and 9 in "Regulations for Carrying Out Heiho Guidelines," and article 4 in "Enforcement of Naval Heiho Regulations."

51. See, for example, Benda et al., *Japanese Military Administration in Indonesia: Selected Documents,* p. 192.

52. For Shimizu's estimate of the number of *heiho,* see Bōeichō Bōeikensyūsho Senshishitsu (NIDS), ed., *Nansei Hōmen Rikugun Sakusen,* p. 169.

53. Headquarters of the 16th Army, Java, "Explanations Regarding All Kinds of Armed Bodies," p. 4.

54. In Japanese the word "tokusetsu" refers to "temporary installations by request according to the military situation." See Bōeichō Bōeikenkyūsho Senshishitsu (NIDS), ed., *Senshisōshō 102: Rikukaigun Nenpyō* (War history series 102: Chronology of the army and the navy: Military terms and words) (Tokyo: Asagumo Shinbunsha, 1980), p. 374.

55. Compiled from interviews with ex-*heiho.*

56. Compilation of NEFIS interrogation report, AI2/7213/G., CADMvD.

57. This figure is close to the 70,000 suggested by Jacob Zwaan in his *Nederlands-Indië 1940–1946,* p. 87. It is unclear whether this figure is meant to be the total aggregate figure, or the number as of August 1945.

58. NEFIS interrogation report, AI2/9374/G., CADMvD.

59. Training materials were found in the *Guntai Kyoiku Rei* (Volume of Military Education) and *Guntai Kyoiku Rei Bessatsu* (Separate Volume of Military Education). See Article 10 in "Regulations for Carrying Out Heiho Guidelines."

60. NEFIS interrogation report, AI2/5917/G., CADMvD. Morimoto, *Jawa Bōei Giyūgun Shi,* p. 56.

61. George S. Kanahele, "The Japanese Occupation of Indonesia: Prelude to Independence" (Ph.D. diss., Cornell University, 1967), p. 119.

62. Daiichi Fukuin Kyoku (First Demobilization Bureau), "Indoneshia Hōmen Butai Ryakureki" (Brief history of military units in Indonesia), pp.281, 279, 541-42, Military Archival Library, NIDS, Tokyo.

63. Ibid., p. 281. The 11th Company was transported to West Timor, 34th Company engaged in guard in Halmahera. These units consisted of Javanese, Sundanese, Padang, and Batak ex-KNIL personnel. NEFIS interrogation report, AI2/17801/G., CADMvD.

64. First Mobilization Bureau, "Indoneshia Hōmen Butai Ruakureki," p. 279; Brugmans, *Nederlansch-Indië onder Japanse Bezetting,* pp. 523–24.

65. Zwaan, *Nederlands-Indië 1940–1946,* p. 247; Morimoto, *Jawa Bōei Giyūgun Shi,* p. 53.

66. Headquarters of the 16th Army, Java, "Explanations Regarding All Kinds of Armed Bodics," p. 4.

67. Kishi Kōichi et al., *Nihon Gunsei no Kenkyū,* p. 192.

68. Special installations companies maintained and supported the supply lines for the Japanese army and navy, handling loading and transportation, construction of airfields and barracks. The Japanese military historically looked down on these activities, which was a weakness in their military tactics. Bōeichō Bōeikenkyūsho Senshishitsu (NIDS), ed., *Rikukaigun Nenpyō* (Tokyo: Asagumo Shinbunsha, 1980), p. 374.

69. Zwaan reports that many *heiho* lost their lives when *Tango Maru* was torpedoed by the American submarine *Racher.* See Zwaan, *Nederlands Indië 1940-1946,* p. 264.

70. To restore its position on the Pacific front, Imperial Headquarters decided on September 30 1943, to retreat to the line of defense for the Ultimate Defense Area (Zettai Kokuō Ken), which included the Chishima islands, Ogasawara Island, the South Sea islands, western New Guinea, the Lesser Sunda islands, and Burma. Imoto Kumao, *Daitōa Sensō Sakusen Nisshi* (Tokyo: Fuyo Shuppan, 1998), pp. 482–85.

71. *Heiho* recruited after formal establishment of the regulations generally remained in Java, while "incipient *heiho*" were frequently dispatched to places outside Java.

72. Daiichi Fukuin Kyoku (First Demobilization Bureau), "Jawa Sakusen Kiroku Dai 16 Gun" (The16th Army operational record in Java), Military Archival Library, NIDS, p. 7.

73. NEFIS interrogation report, AI2/6379/G., CADMvD.

74. There are many references to these points in NEFIS interrogation reports and interviews with ex-*heiho.*

75. NEFIS interrogation report, AI2/6461/G., CADMvD.

76. NEFIS interrogation report, AI2/4789/G., CADMvD. In NEFIS interrogation report, AI2/6379/G., CADMvD, an informant states that for married men pay was as follows:

> Private second class (one star): 35.00 guilders per month
> Private first class (two stars): 40.00 guilders per month

Superior private (three stars): 45.00 guilders per month
Lance corporal (one yellow stripe): 50.00 guilders per month

77. A salary table for army *heiho* was attached to the "Regulation for Carrying Out Heiho Guidelines."
78. NEFIS interrogation report, AI2/12991/G., CADMvD.
79. In Sumatra "the HEIHOs and GYUGUN were being reorganized into a unified body, and the title of this body was to be GYUHEI." HQ 26 Indian Division weekly intelligence summary 8, 1945, Hoofdkwartier van de Generale Staf van het Leger in Indonesië, CADMvD, The Hague. Regarding Java, 16th Army Operational Staff Officer Miyamoto Shizuo wrote, "PETA, which lacks anti-aircraft, transportation units and so on, in case it forms an Independent Army, will be strengthened with appropriate Heiho personnel." Miyamoto Shizuo, *Jawa Shūsen Shoriki* (A record of the disposition of the end of the war in Java) (Tokyo: Jawa Shūsen Shoriki Kankōkai, 1973), p. 29.

Chapter 10

1. Aiko Kurasawa, "Mobilization and Control: A Study of Social Change in Rural Java, 1942–1945" (Ph.D. diss., Cornell University, 1988), published in Indonesian as *Mobilisasi dan kontrol: Studi tentang perubahan sosial di pedesaan Jawa, 1942–1945* (Jakarta: Grasindo, 1993), and in Japanese as *Nihon Senryoka no Jawa Noson no Henyo* (Tokyo: Soshisha, 1992); Shigeru Sato, *War, Nationalism and Peasants: Java under the Japanese Occupation, 1942–1945* (St. Leonards: Allen and Unwin, 1994). For earlier, if sketchy, accounts of Javanese *rōmusha*, see L. de Jong, *The Collapse of a Colonial Society: The Dutch in Indonesia during the Second World War* (Leiden: KITLV Press, 2002), pp. 242–51, a translation of chs. 5–10 of volume 11B of *Het Koninkrijk der Nederlanden in de Tweede Wereldoorlog* ('s-Gravenhage: Staatsuitgeverij, 1985); Theodore Friend, *The Blue-Eyed Enemy: Japan against the West in Java and Luzon, 1942–1945* (Princeton, NJ: Princeton University Press, 1988), pp. 162–66. For detailed studies of *rōmusha* employment on Java, see P.J. Suwarno, *Romusa Daerah Istimewa Yogyakarta* (Yogyakarta: Penerbitan Universitas Sanata Dharma, 1999), and Harry A. Poeze, "De weg naar de hel: De aanleg van een spoorlijn op West-Java tijdens de Japanse bezetting," in *Oorlogsdocumentatie '40-'45: Tweede jaarboek van het Rijksinstituut voor Oorlogsdocumentatie* (Amsterdam and Zutpen: Walburg Pers, 1990), pp. 9–47. A translation of the latter article is included in this volume as chapter 8.
2. Sato, *War, Nationalism and Peasants,* p. 158.
3. Kurasawa, *Mobilisasi dan Kontrol,* p. 175, relies on a Japanese postwar statement that the figure was 270,000.
4. For a personal impression of the Japanese administration in the navy areas, see Okada Fumihide, "Civil Administration in Celebes, 1942–1944," in *The Japanese Experience in Indonesia: Selected Memoirs of 1942–1945,* ed. Anthony Reid and Oki Akira (Athens: Ohio University, 1986), pp. 127–58.
5. Kurasawa, *Mobilisasi dan Kontrol,* p. 124; "Outline of Economic Policies for the Southern Areas" (December 1941), in *Japanese Military Administration in Indonesia: Selected Documents,* ed. Harry J. Benda, James K. Irikura, and Koichi Kishi (New Haven: Yale University Southeast Asia Studies, 1965), pp. 17–25, esp. pp. 17–18; W.G. Beasley, *Japanese Imperialism, 1894–1945* (Oxford: Clarendon Press, 1987), pp. 243–46.

6. Goto Ken'ichi, "Modern Japan and Indonesia: The Dynamics and Legacy of Wartime Rule," in *Japan, Indonesia and the War: Myths and Realities,* ed. Peter Post and Elly Touwen-Bouwsma (Leiden: KITLV Press, 1997), pp. 14–30, esp. p. 25. The article is reprinted as part of a collection of essays by Goto Ken'ichi: *Tensions of Empire: Japan and Southeast Asia in the Colonial and Post-Colonial World* (Athens: Ohio University Press; Singapore: Singapore University Press, 2003).

7. This was the situation, for example, on Selayar. See Netherlands Institute for War Documentation, Amsterdam, Indische Collectie (hereafter IC), 060.880, Netherlands Eastern Forces Intelligence Service (hereafter NEFIS) AI2/5020/G., interrogation report 102, July 24, 1944, p. 7; Archive of the Ministry of Foreign Affairs, The Hague (hereafter BUZA), NEFIS Archive, CMI 44, AI2/3796/G., interrogation report, May 31, 1944, pp. 3–4.

8. IC 060.873, NEFIS AHI/1345/G., translation and description of documents from native administrative units (Banda Neira), p. 2.

9. IC 061.059, NEFIS AI2/9761/G., interrogation report 751, December 31, 1944, pp. 2, 6.

10. IC 061.053, NEFIS AI2/9760/G., interrogation report 708, December 31, 1944, p. 7; the Chinese corps is called *Kantongrojong* in the source, possibly an error for *gotong royong* (organization for mutual help), which also existed on Java. See Sato, *War, Nationalism and Peasants,* p. 74.

11. IC 061.221, NEFIS AI2/15632/G., interrogation report 1900–1906, June 21, 1945, p. 5.

12. BUZA NEFIS/CMI 199, AI2/511/ZG., interrogation report, January 27, 1944, p. 4; BUZA NEFIS/CMI 44, AI2/2131/Z.G., n.d., p. 3, for a raid in Serua, Nila, and Teun in January 1944. For recruitment on Nila, see IC 060.914, NEFIS AI2/5768/G., interrogation report 219/226, August 17, 1944, pp. 4–5.

13. BUZA NEFIS/CMI 201, YC/14849/G., report of Captain Bartlema on the Damar Islands, May 31 /June 2, 1945, pp. 1–2.

14. G.C.W.C. Tergast, "Schets van den landbouw op de Sangihe-en Talaud-eilanden," *Landbouw. Landbouwkundig tijdschrift voor Nederlandsch-Indië* 11, no. 4 (1935–36): 125–44, esp. 128.

15. BUZA NEFIS/CMI 64, terrain study 83, Menado, September 11, 1944, p. 64.

16. IC 061.198, NEFIS AI2/14097/G., interrogation report 1636 and 1668–1694, May 15, 1945, pp. 4, 6; IC 061.191, NEFIS AI2/13829/G., interrogation report 1709–1762, May 30, 1945, p. 7.

17. IC 060.973, NEFIS AI2/7655/G., interrogation report 184 III, October 18, 1944, p. 3; IC 061.215, NEFIS AI2/15192/G., interrogation report 1855–1896, June 13, 1945, p. 5, mentions that large numbers of coolies were working in the five shipyards of Bitung in September 1943.

18. BUZA, NEFIS/CMI 45, FY5274-4, report on the location of shipyards, etc., August 4, 1944.

19. IC 061.187, NEFIS AI2/13828/G., interrogation report 1247–1248, May 2, 1945, p. 7.

20. IC 060.973, NEFIS AI2/7655/G., interrogation report 184 III, October 18, 1944, p. 4.

21. IC 061.177, NEFIS AI2/13198/G., interrogation report, April 14, 1945, p. 6.

22. IC 061.129, NEFIS AI2/11815/G., interrogation report 1071, March 3, 1945, p. 5.

23. IC 061.173, NEFIS AI2/12991/G., interrogation report 1358, April 9, 1945, pp. 8–9.

24. Richard Chauvel, *Nationalists, Soldiers and Separatists: The Ambonese Islands from Colonialism to Revolt, 1880–1950* (Leiden: KITLV Press, 1990), p. 178.

25. IC 060.846, NEFIS AI2/2131/Z.G., interrogation report, April 12, 1944, pp. 8–9.

26. IC 061.108, NEFIS AI2/11055/G., interrogation report 1069, February 7, 1945, pp. 4, 6.

27. Chauvel, *Nationalists, Soldiers and Separatists,* p. 178.

28. De Jong, *The Collapse of a Colonial Society,* p. 237.

29. For the phases of these labor tasks, see Netherlands Institute for War Documentation, unpublished report by C.J.F. Stuldreher, "Rapport van onderzoek betr. de dwangarbeid van burgers op het eiland Ambon, de Uliassers en de zuidwestkust van Ceram tijdens de Japanse mil. bezetting in de jaren 1942–1945" (n.d.), esp. pp. 61–62.

30. IC 061.215, NEFIS AI2/15192/G., interrogation report 1855–1896, June 13, 1945, p. 6.

31. IC 061.192, NEFIS AI2/13874/G., interrogation report 1785–1806, May 4, 1945, pp. 4–5.

32. Xaf Lasomer, "Chaos betul: een ware chaos. De Kei-eilanden in de Tweede Wereldoorlog (1942–1945)," *Timbang* 16 (1992): 59–65, esp. 63 (oom Ngamelubun).

33. Lasomer, "Chaos betul," 64–65 (oom Ohoioeloen); see also R. de Bruin, "De Kei-eilanden onder Japanse bezetting" (research report, Rijksinstituut voor Oorlogsdocumentatie; Amsterdam 1978), IC 082.036, pp. 4–5.

34. E. Melis and Hans Toonen, eds., *Verzet contra de Japanse bezetting van Nederlands-Indië in de Tweede Wereldoorlog: De geuzen van het Indisch verzet 1942–1945* (Bussum: Comité Ancol, 1996), pp. 174–75.

35. IC 061.208, NEFIS AI2/14854/G., interrogation report 1807–1838 and 1840–1847, June 4, 1945, pp. 3–4.

36. R. de Bruin, "De Japanse bezettingstrijd op de Aroe-, Kei- en Tanimbar-eilanden" (unpublished report, Rijksinstituut voor Oorlogsdocumentatie; Diemen, 1988), IC 082.041; see also BUZA NEFIS/CMI 44, AI2/560/Z.G., interrogation report, n.d., p. 2; IC 061.120, NEFIS AI2/11214/G., interrogation report 1074 (C. Hattu), February 12, 1945, pp. 3, 6–7; IC 061.124, NEFIS AI2/11414/G., interrogation report 1246 (J.M. Sumual), February 20, 1945, p. 5; IC 061.240, NEFIS 4152/RAM8/G., interrogation report 2026 III, 2028 III, 2033 III, and 2034 III, September 12, 1945, p. 5; IC 061.105, NEFIS AI2/11054/G., interrogation report 1006–1011, February 7, 1945, p. 7.

37. Navy Ministry Secretariat, "Principles Governing Military Administration in New Guinea," 1942, in Benda *et al., Japanese Military Administration,* pp. 214–18.

38. BUZA NEFIS/CMI 44, AI2/4301/G., interrogation report, July 1, 1944, p. 8.

39. BUZA NEFIS/CMI 44, AI2/3045/Z.G., interrogation report, May 9, 1944, pp. 1–5.

40. IC 060.843, NEFIS AI2/2279/Z.G., interrogation report, April 15, 1944, p. 5.

41. IC 061.111, NEFIS AI2/11057/G., interrogation report 1131–1195, February 7, 1945, p. 4.

42. IC 060.910, NEFIS AI1/5685/G., report of H.C. Brouwer, August 12, 1944, p. 11.

43. Cited in IC 061.104, NEFIS AI2/11053/G., interrogation report 624 II of J. van der Wyck, February 7, 1945, p. 6.

44. BUZA NEFIS/CMI 44, AI2/4301/G., interrogation report, July 1, 1944, p. 8; IC 060.977, NEFIS AI2/7744/G., interrogation report 447, October 23, 1944, pp. 4–5.

45. IC 060.839, NEFIS AF3/34358/-, April 27, 1946, "Overzicht van het Burgerlijk Bestuur van Borneo," p. 7.

46. BUZA NEFIS/CMI 1761, Geologie en mijnbuw in West-Borneo, February 18, 1946, pp. 12–15.

47. Thomas Lindblad, "Koelies in Kalimantan. Sociale segregatie en economische expansie (1900–1930)" in *Onderscheid en minderheid. Sociaal-historische opstellen over discriminatie en vooroordeel aangeboden aan professor Dik van Arkel,* ed. Herman Diederiks and Chris Quispel (Hilversum: Verloren, 1987), pp. 303–14, esp. p. 306.

48. IC 061.221, NEFIS interrogation report 1900–1906, June 21, 1945, pp. 5, 10–11.

49. IC 061.221, NEFIS AI2/15632/G., interrogation report 1900–1906, June 21, 1945, pp. 8, 11; IC 061.053, NEFIS AI2/9760/G., interrogation report 708, December 31, 1944, p. 12.

50. IC 061.207, NEFIS interrogation report 1931/T, June 4, 1945.

51. IC 061.187, NEFIS AI2/13828/G., interrogation report 1247–1248, May 2, 1945, pp. 10, 12.

52. IC 061.037, NEFIS AI2/9269/G., interrogation report 661–669, December 12, 1944, p. 11.

53. Cf. Nicholas Tarling, *A Sudden Rampage: The Japanese Occupation of Southeast Asia, 1941–1945* (London: Hurst, 2001), p. 230.

54. Kurasawa, *Mobilisasi dan Kontrol,* pp. 125–26; Sato, *War, Nationalism and Peasants,* p. 156.

55. IC 060.843, NEFIS AI2/2279/Z.G., interrogation report, April 15, 1944, p. 5.

56. IC 061.031, NEFIS AI2/9103/G., interrogation report 489, 490, 498, 500–501, 504, 539–540, 542–543, 547, December 4, 1944, p. 3.

57. IC 060.992, NEFIS AI2/7914/G., interrogation report 408 (Slamet bin Tjodoel), October 28, 1944, p.3; the bad living conditions are confirmed by IC 061.159, NEFIS AI2/12457/G., interrogation report 1130, March 23, 1945, p. 8.

58. Sato, *War, Nationalism and Peasants,* p. 159.

59. IC 005.709, "The Number of Native Laborers Sent out from Java."

60. BUZA NEFIS/CMI 1761, HA1/26267/-, Letter from S.W. Tromp (head Economisch-Technische Afd.) to Thesaurier-Generaal W. Alons, March 27, 1946.

61. IC 005.713-005.714, Letter from O.A. Gobius (Conica) to the Director BB (internal administration), May 25, 1946.

62. Njoman S. Pendit, *Bali berdjuang* (Den Pasar: Jajasan Kebaktian Pedjuang Daerah Bali, 1954), p. 13–14; Geoffrey Robinson, *The Dark Side of Paradise: Political Violence in Bali* (Ithaca: Cornell University Press, 1995), p. 80; *Japanese Military Administration in Indonesia* (Washington, 1963) (translation of *Indonesia ni okeru Nihon gunsei no Kenkyu* [Tokyo, 1959]), p. 321.

63. Ellen Leenarts, "Coolie Wages in Western Enterprises in the Outer Islands, 1919–1938," in *Coolie Labor in Colonial Indonesia: A Study of Labor Relations in the Outer Islands, c. 1900–1940,* ed. Vincent J.H. Houben and J. Thomas Lindblad (Wiesbaden: Harrassowitz, 1999), pp. 131–55, esp. pp. 133, 155.

64. Suwarno, *Romusa Daerah Istimewa Yogyakarta,* pp. 52–58.

65. IC 005.612, "Sitreps van R.N.I.A. L.O. Morotai," November 3, 1945.

66. IC 005.686-005.687, testimony of Rianta, August 23, 1946.

67. IC 005.622, NEFIS AI2/8046/G., November 4, 1944, pp. 1–2; also in IC 060.996.

68. IC 005.669–005.671, testimony of Amat Nawi, August 16, 1946.

69. Henk Hovinga, "Einde van een vergeten drama. Opvang en repatriëring van romusha na de Japanse capitulatie," in *Tussen banzai en bersiap: De afwikkeling van de Tweede Wereldoorlog in Nederlands-Indië,* ed. Elly Touwen-Bouwsma and Petra Groen (The Hague: Sdu Uitgevers, 1996), pp. 73–94, esp. p. 74. A translation of this article appears as chapter 11 in this volume. The survey can be found in IC 005.717, message Aneta, June 26, 1946.

70. Mark R. Peattie, *Nan'yō: The Rise and Fall of the Japanese in Micronesia, 1885–1945* (Honolulu: University of Hawaii Press, 1988), pp. 82–83; Paul H. Kratoska, *The Japanese Occupation of Malaya: A Social and Economic History* (London: Hurst, 1998), pp. 181–89; Bob Reece, *Masa Jepun: Sarawak under the Japanese, 1941–1945* (Kuching: Sarawak Literary Society, 1998), pp. 149–50.

71. *Garis-garis besar tentang pengerahan romusha* (H n.p., Naimabu Romukyoku [c. 1942] (translated in *Nederlandsch-Indië onder Japanse bezetting: Gegevens en documenten over de jaren 1942–1945,* ed. I.J. Brugmans *et al.* (Franeker, 1960), pp. 500–502.

72. Okada, "Civil Administration," p. 155.

73. See, for example, Beasley, *Japanese Imperialism,* p. 233.

74. Muhammad Abdul Aziz, *Japan's Colonialism and Indonesia* ('s-Gravenhage: Martinus Nijhoff, 1955), p. 183; "Outline of Economic Policies for the Southern Areas, Adopted at the Conference of Ministers Concerned, December 12, 1941," in Benda et al., *Japanese Military Administration,* pp. 17–18.

75. "Principles Governing the Administration of Occupied Southern Areas, Adopted at the Liaison Conference between Imperial Headquarters and the Government, November 20, 1941," in Benda *et al., Japanese Military Administration,* p. 2.

76. "Tojo on the Greater East Asia Co-Prosperity Sphere," in *Japan's Greater East Asia Co-Prosperity Sphere in World War II: Selected Readings and Documents,* ed. Joyce C. Lebra (Kuala Lumpur: Oxford University Press, 1975), p. 79.

Chapter 11

1. Aiko Kurasawa, "Mobilization and Control: A Study of Social Change in Rural Java, 1942–1945" (Ph.D. diss., Cornell University, 1988), p. 259.

2. L. de Jong, *Het Koninkrijk der Nederlanden in de Tweede Wereldoorlog* (The Kingdom of the Netherlands in the Second World War), vol. 11B (The Hague: Staatsuitgeverij, 1985), p. 515.

3. Kurasawa, "Mobilization and Control," pp. 235, 237, 244.

4. Rapport Nederlandsch-Indisch Roode Kruis, June 26, 1946, Netherlands Institute for War Documentation Indies Collection (IC) 040582.

5. Kurasawa, "Mobilization and Control," p. 220.

6. Henk Hovinga, *Eindstation Pakan Baroe, 1944–1945* (Franeker, 1982), p. 135.

7. Kurasawa, "Mobilization and Control," p. 273.

8. De Jong, *Het Koninkrijk der Nederlanded in de Tweede Wereldoorlog,* vol. 11B, p. 558.

9. A.C. Lijsen, "Overzicht van de Javanenorganisatie in Zuid-Oost Asië," Singapore, 1946, p. 9, IC 040582.

10. "Kort overzicht betreffende de Javanenkampen in Z.O. Asië," July 1946, pp. 1, 2, NIOD IC 005577-005586.

11. J.S. Krom, "Javaansche arbeiders in Siam en Burma," September 21, 1945, p. 1, IC 005431.

12. Hovinga, *Eindstation Pakan Baroe,* p. 274.

13. Krom, "Javaansche arbeiders"; Hovinga, *Eindstation Pakan Baroe,* p. 280; "Aftermath of co-prosperity, Indonesian slave labor for Nippon and what became of it," NIOD IC 056367.

14. NIOD IC 040582.

15. O.A. Gobius, "De Japansche romousha-politiek," *Uitzicht 1* (1946–39): 5, IC 040582.

16. Lijsen, "Overzicht Javanenorganisatie," 1946, pp. 5, 6, NIOD IC 040582.

17. Ibid., p. 3.

18. H.J. Friedericy, "Kort verslag van de zoogenaamde 'displaced Indonesiërs' in Zuid-Oost Asië," p. 16, IC 005539-005576, 005555.

19. Lijsen, "Overzichte Javanenorganisatie," 1946, p. 3, IC 040582.

20. Ibid., p. 2. Friedericy, "Kort verslag van de 'displaced Indonesiërs,'" pp. 30, 31, NIOD IC 005569-005570.

21. Lijsen, "Overzicht Javanenorganisatie," 1946, II, IC 040582.

22. Friedericy, "Kort verslag van de 'displaced Indonesiërs,'" p. 31, IC 005570.

23. "Kort overzicht betreffende de Javanenkampen," p. 3, IC 005579.

24. C.L.M. Penders and U. Sundhausen, *Abdul Haris Nasution: A Political Biography* (St. Lucia: Queensland University Press, 1985), p. 21.

25. Kurasawa, "Mobilization and Control," pp. 269, 270.

26. Lijsen, "Overzicht Javanenorganisatie," 1946, II, IC 040582.

27. Ibid., 12–14. Kort overzicht betreffende de Javanenkampen, 5–8, IC 005581-005584.

28. Lijsen, Overzicht Javanenorganisatie, 1946, pp. 18, 19, NIOD IC 040582.

29. Ibid., p. 18.

30. Ibid., p. 19.

31. Ibid., pp. 1, 20.

32. Ibid., p. 19; "Rapport Nederlands-Indisch Roode Kruis," IC 005717.

33. Lijsen, "Overzicht Javanenorganisatie," 1946, p. 19, IC 040582.

34. Ibid., pp. 16, 17. J.D. De Ropock, "Verslag betreffende de opsporing van door het Japanse leger naar Indochina weggevoerde Javaansche koelies," November 9, 1945, NIOD IC 005587-005592, 005587.

35. Krom, "Javaansche arbeiders," pp. 1–5, IC 005431-005435; Friedericy, "Kort verslag van de 'displaced Indonesiërs,'" pp. 6–9, IC 005545–005548; Lijsen, "Overzicht Javanenorganisatie," 1946, pp. 14–16, IC 040582.

36. K.A. Warmenhoven, "Maatregelen getroffen voor romusha uit Siam, S.A.," p. 5, NIOD IC 005530-005535. Warmenhoven states on page 3 of his report that the Javanese fared better on the Thailand–Burma railway than the Tamils from Malaya. The station personnel and the technicians who were responsible for the locomotives consisted for the main part of Javanese who had done the same work on Java. They were thus hard to replace: "Their medical treatment was better. They had clinics alongside the line, which, although insufficient, offered better treatment than that given the track coolies. They were usually hospitalized in Japanese and non-coolie hospitals. The losses then were smaller." Nonetheless, about half of the 10,000 Javanese working on the railroad died. Probably no more than 20 percent of the Tamils, Chinese, Thai, and Burmese survived. Cholera claimed many victims, especially in the rainy season.

37. L.H. Leffelaar and E. Van Witsen, *Werkers aan de Burma-spoorweg* (Franeker: T. Wever, 1982), p. 375.

38. Ibid., p. 376; de Jong, *Het Koninkrijk der Nederlanden in de Tweede Wereldoorlog,* vol. 11-b, p. 223.

39. Lijsen, "Overzicht Javanenorganisatie," 1946, p. 21, IC 040582.

40. Warmenhoven, "Maatregelen getroffen voor romusha," p. 4, IC 005533.

41. Friedericy, "Kort verslag van de 'displaced Indonesiërs,'" pp. 24–26, IC 005563-005566.

42. Lijsen, "Overzicht Javanenorganisatie," 1946, p. 16, IC 040582.

43. Ibid., p. 15.

44. Ibid., p. 16.

45. Ibid., p. 27.

46. Ibid.

47. R. IJzerman, "Rapport aan NEFIS over verwaarloosde koelies op Sumatra," January 28, 1946, p. 4, IC 005589-005601.

48. Lijsen, "Overzicht Javanenorganisatie," 1946, p. 27, IC 040582.

49. "Rapport Nederlands-Indisch Roode Kruis," IC 005717.

50. Gobius, "Japansche romousha-politiek," p. 5, IC 008528.

51. Ibid, IC 008566.

52. S.W. Tromp, "NEFIS Report Concerning the Number of Romusha's outside Java," March 7, 1946, p. 2.

53. "Regeerings Voolichtingsdienst," Paleisrapport, May 29, 1946, p. 2, IC 005487.

54. "Rapport Morotai," November 3, 1945, IC 005612.

55. "Rapport Nederlands-Indisch Roode Kruis," IC 005717.

56. R. Soeria Santosa, AMACAB report concerning the Romusha, early 1946, IC 005707.

57. Japans rapport, "The Numbers of Native Labourers Who Were Sent out from Java," IC 005709.

58. Gobius, "Japansche romousha-politiek," *Uitzicht,* p. 5, IC 008528.

59. De Jong, *Het Koninkrijk der Nederlanded in de Tweede Wereldoorlog,* vol. 11B, p. 523.

60. Hovinga, *Eindstation Pakan Baroe.*

61. W.H. Coert, "Coolie Situation in Pakan Baroe, September–November 1945," December 2, 1945, IC 048070.

62. A. De Boer, "Rapport Pakan Baroe [1945], I," IC 0022694.

63. "Verslag Ikol Gerharz Pakan Baroe," p. 6, Coll. NI 45-50, 043-D/14.

64. De Boer, "Rapport Pakan Baroe," pp. 1, 2, IC 002694-2695.

65. IJzerman, "Rapport aan NEFIS," pp. 1, 2, IC 005598-5599.

66. Ibid., pp. 3, 4, IC 005600-005601.

67. Suparna Sastra Deredja, "Rapport over romusha" (unpublished manuscript in the collection of the Netherlands Institute for War Documentation), p. 45.

68. Kurasawa, "Mobilization and Control," pp. 213, 214.

69. De Jong, *Het Koninkrijk der Nederlanded in de Tweede Wereldoorlog,* vol. 11B, p. 520; Tan Malaka, *Dari pendjara ka pendjara,* part 2 (Yogyakarta, 1948), p. 149. See also chapter 8 by Harry A. Poeze in this volume.

70. Shigeru Sato, *War, Nationalism and Peasants: Java under the Japanese Occupation* (St. Leonards, NSW: Asian Studies Association of Australia in Association with Allen & Unwin, 1994).

71. Ibid., p. 251.

72. Tan Malaka, *Dari pendjara ka pendjara,* pp. 159, 160.

73. Diredja, "Rapport romusha," pp. 47, 48.

74. Kurasawa, "Mobilization and Control," p. 270.

Chapter 12

For a fuller account of the war years in Malaya, see Paul H. Kratoska, *The Japanese Occupation of Malaya* (London: C. Hurst, 1998). Archival materials are held by the National Archives of Malaysia unless otherwise indicated.

1. Statement by J. Yokoyama, member of the Upper House of the Imperial Diet, during a visit to Malaya. Reported in the *Syonan Times,* October 20, 2602 [1942].

2. Minutes, Meeting of District Officers, July 6 and 7, 2602, Batu Gajah, 69/2602. The speaker was the District Officer for Krian, Raja Haji Ahmad.

3. Speech of the Governor on the Occasion of the Meeting on Re-Birth of Pahang, District Office Temerloh 300/2602.

4. "Happiness Through Labor," *Syonan Times,* October 18, 2602.

5. Annual Report, Selangor Kosei Kyoku, 2602, Selangor Kanbo, 59/2603.

6. District Office Kuala Kangsar, 168/2602; *Syonan Times,* October 29, 2602.

7. K. Iguchi, Controller of Rubber, Negri Sembilan, "Instructions to Enemy-Owned Rubber Estate Administrators," June 1, 2602, originally in State Forest Office Negri Sembilan (Rubber) 34/2602 but found in Negri Sembilan Secretariat 641/1945; Chief Officer, Rubber Dept, Annual Report for 2602, Sel Kan 111/2603 [1943].

8. Annual Report, Selangor Rubber Department, 2602, Selangor Kanbo, 111/2603.

9. Labour Inspector, Kelantan, "Report on the Conditions of the Labour Force in the State of Kelantan Before and After the Hostilities," November 3, 1943, Pejabat Menteri Kelantan 13/2486 [1943].

10. Summary of Economic Intelligence, no. 130, British Military Administration, DEPT/18/7.

11. "Report of the Selangor Medical Dept for the Years 1941–1946," RC Sel 296/1947.

12. Annual Report, Ulu Langat, 2602, Selangor Kanbo, 33/2603.

13. Annual Report, Ulu Selangor Sanitary Board, 2602, Selangor Kanbo, 108/2603.

14. Halinah Bamadhaj, "The Impact of the Japanese Occupation on Malay Society and Politics (1941–1945)" (M.A thesis, University of Auckland, 1975), p. 137, citing Selangor Kanbo, 60/2602 and 123/2602; Yoji Akashi, "Education and Indoctrination Policy in Malaya and Singapore under the Japanese Rule, 1942–45," *Malaysian Journal of Education 13* (December 1976): 9.

15. *Syonan Times,* October 8, 2602.

16. Minutes, Meeting of District Officers, November 5, 2602, Batu Gajah, 69/2602.

17. *Syonan Times,* October 14, 2602.

18. Author's personal discussions with rice farmers during the 1970s.

19. See Kratoska, *Japanese Occupation of Malaya,* pp. 277–83, and Hara Fujio, "The Japanese Occupation of Malaya and the Chinese Community," in *Malaya and Singapore during the Japanese Occupation,* ed. Paul H. Kratoska (Singapore: Journal of Southeast Asian Studies, 1995).

20. S.O.I. (Irrigation) (P. McNee), to Senior Civil Affairs Officer Selangor, November 6, 1945, Selangor Civil Affairs 331/1945; interview with Maimunah Naim, in Norhayati Maarup, "Sejarah Perkembangan Penanaman Padi di Skim Pengairan

Tanjung Karang pada Tahun 1930–1950-an," (History of the development of rice cultivation in the Tanjung Karang Irrigation Scheme, 1930-1950s), course paper written at Universiti Sains Malaysia and provided to the author by Dr. Abu Talib Ahmad.

21. Aripin b Othman, "Suatu Tinjauan Teoritis: Kehidupan Buruh (Paksa) Pembinaan Lapangan Terbang Zaman Jepun di Kuala Pilah, N. Sembilan" (A theoretical observation: the lives of forced laborers building the airfield at Kuala Pilah, Negri Sembilan, during the Japanese occupation), course paper written at Universiti Sains Malaysia and provided to the author by Dr. Abu Talib Ahmad.

22. Report of the Selangor Medical Dept for the Years 1941–1946, Resident Commissioner Selangor 296/1947.

23. "Report on Coolie Camp Conditions on the Burma-Siam Railway during the Period November 1943 to August 1945," p. 75, War Office (WO) 325/56.

24. These figures appear in FO 371/112291, minute by B.R. Pearn, August 4, 1954, and copy of a minute sent to the War Office by B.R. Pearn, July 13, 1954.

25. Ibid., and C.C. Brett, "Burma-Siam Railway," p. 25, WO 203/6325.

26. S. Woodburn Kirby, *History of the Second World War: The War Against Japan* (London: HMSO, 1957–69), vol. 2, pp. 427–28. Workers were also recruited in Burma.

27. N.A. Appan for Controller of Labour, Perak, to District Office Kinta, July 17, 2603 [1943], Batu Gajah 101/2603.

28. District Officer, Kulim to Under Secy Kerajaan Kedah, 27.12.2486/29.12.1362 [December 27, 1943], District Officer, Kulim to Under Secy Saiburi (Kedah) Govt, 8 Muharram 1363/4 Moreka Khom 2487 [January 4, 1944], Setiausaha Kerajaan (SUK) Kedah, 4/2487.

29. Correspondence between District Officer, Klang, the president of the Klang branch of the Indian Independence League, and the chairman of the Klang branch of the Oversea Chinese Association, Klang, 193/2603.

30. Concerning repatriation of workers, see chapter 11, by Henk Hovinga, and chapter 13, by Michiko Nakahara, in this volume.

31. Office of Strategic Services Research and Analysis Branch Assemblage 45, "Manpower in Japan and Occupied Areas," extracts from short wave Radio Tokyo and affiliated stations from December 1941 to July 15, 1944, vol. 2 (MJOA), pp. 241–43.

32. Rodo Jimu Kyoku Cho, Pahang, to DO, Temerloh, November 21, 2604 [1944], Temerloh, 73/2604.

33. Broadcast from Tokyo in Japanese, December 28, 1943, "Fortnightly Intelligence Report," Far Eastern Bureau, British Ministry of Information, no. 2, January 16–31, 1944, Colonial Office (CO) 273/673/50744/7; English-language broadcast, March 28, 1943, Office of Strategic Services (OSS) R&A Assemblage no. 45, "Manpower in Japan and Occupied Areas," vol. 2, pt. 3, August 26, 1944; "Malaya under the Japanese," US National Archives and Records Administration (NARA) Record Group (RG) 226 128585; DO Ulu Langat to President Selangor Chinese Oversea Association, November 28, 2604, Ulu Langat, 139/2604.

34. District Office Kota Star, Annual Report for 2487, 22.2.2488 [February 28, 1945], Kedah Secretariat, 208/2488.

35. OSS SN:P ZM-8934 Fr Det. 404 at APO 432, February 1945, NARA RG226 E136 F647.

36. "Malaya under the Japanese," NARA RG226 128585; English-language

broadcast, December 23, 1943, January 17, 1944, April 1, 1944, OSS R&A, "Manpower in Japan and Occupied Areas." Plans for the Penang Labor Service Corps called for 23,000 members. *Syonan Shimbun,* January 19, 2604.

37. Minutes, Conference of District Officers, October 4, 2604, Pejabat Tanah (Land Office), Larut, 161/2602.

38. Rozita bt Nordin, "Pentadbiran Tradisional Peringkat Daerah di Zaman Pendudukan Jepun di Tanah Melayu 1942–45," unpublished course paper from Universiti Sains Malaysia, n.d.

39. Adnan bin Ibrahim, "Pendudukan Jepun dan Keadaan Sosio-Ekonomi di Negeri Kelantan," unpublished course paper from Universiti Sains Malaysia, n.d., p. 7.

40. Siti Zubaidah bte Kassim, "Pengalaman penduduk Sungai Acheh yang bekerja sebagai Jikeidan Jepun" (The experiences of residents of Sungai Acheh who served as Japanese Jikeidan"]; District Agriculture Officer, memorandum, n.d., SUK Kedah 40/2486.

41. Selangor Kanbo Circular 16 of 2602, October 13, 2602, Selangor Kanbo 19/2602.

42. *Syonan Shimbun,* October 6, 2603.

43. Minutes, Conference of District Officers, October 4, 2604, Pejabat Tanah (Land Office), Larut, 161/2602.

44. Ibid.

45. Ibid.

46. *Syonan Shimbun,* July 29, 2603.

47. *Perak Times,* July 24, 2603.

48. Ibid., August 7, 2603; see also August 11, 2603.

49. *Syonan Shimbun,* December 15, 2603.

50. *Syonan Shimbun,* February 19, 2690; Ishak's comments appear in the *Syonan Shimbun* of December 15, 2603.

51. *Penang Shimbun,* December 17, 2603.

52. This appeal came from Che Aminah, daughter of the Chief Editor of the *Berita Malai* newspaper in Singapore, Abdul Rahim Kajai. *Syonan Shimbun,* January 15, 2604.

53. Pahang Syu Somubucho to District Officer Temerloh, "Introduction and Usage of Female Labor," February 12, 2604, Temerloh, 73/2604. See also *Syonan Shimbun,* February 21, 2604.

54. Singapore English-language broadcast, February 20, 1944, MJOA, p. 241.

55. Domei English-language broadcast, April 27, 1944, "Fortnightly Intelligence Report," Far Eastern Bureau, British Ministry of Information, no. 8, April 16–30, 1944, CO 273/673/50744/7.

56. Minutes, Penghulus' Conference, January 16, 2605 [1945], Batu Gajah, 11/2604.

57. "Malaya under the Japanese," NARA RG226 128585.

58. Minutes, Penghulus' Conference, January 16, 2605 [1945], Batu Gajah, 11/2604; Lau and Barry, "A Brief Review of Chinese Affairs," British Military Administration ADM/8/1, Malaysian National Archives; "Malaya under the Japanese," NARA RG226 128585.

59. *Syonan Shimbun,* February 12, 2605; the original was set entirely in capital letters.

60. Ramesh a/l Nagayah, untitled course paper, Universiti Sains Malaysia, n.d.

61. For sources, see Kratoska, *Japanese Occupation of Malaya,* pp. 320–21.

Chapter 13

1. E.E. Dunlop, *The War Diaries of Weary Dunlop* (New York: Viking Books, 1986), p. 264.

2. *Biruma no Dokuritsu Oyobi Dokoritsugo no Jōkyō* (The situation after independence in Burma), pp. 20–21, vol. 9, Nishijima Collection, Waseda University, Tokyo.

3. *Biruma no Dokuritsugo no Jōkyō* (Situation after independence in Burma), (Draft) History Section, 5: Transportation, pp. 20–21, Nishijima Collection AG 16.

4. Hiroike Toshio, *Taimen Tetsudo* (The Burma–Thailand railway) (Yomiuri Shinbunsha, 1971), pp. 40–53. *Daitōa Junkan Tetsudo Kensetsu Hosaku* and *Tairiku Tetsudo Kensetsu Hosaku,* in *Daitōa Junkan Tetsudo Kankei Shorui,* ed. Harada Katsumasa (Fujishuppansha, 1988), also discuss planning of the Burma–Thailand railway.

5. SEATIC no. 246, p. 8.

6. WO 325/56 VII: Coolie Mortality, p. 68. This and other War Office files are held by the British Public Record Office.

7. Samydurai Anthony (b. 1914), interview with the author, December 26, 1996, Kuala Lumpur.

8. "Treatment of and Mortality among the Coolie Labor Force Used in Construction and Maintenance of Thai–Burma Railway," Australian War Memorial (henceforth AWM) 54, 554/9/1, Appendix (B), p. 1.

9. "Information on the Enlistment of Malayan Coolies by the Japanese Military Government Obtained from Shinozaki Mamoru," Documents Illustrating Report on Coolie Camp Conditions on the Burma Siam Railway during the Period November 1943 to August 1945, WO 325/57, XC11323, Document J; and Shinozaki Mamoru, *Shonan—My Story* (Singapore: Times Books International, 1982), pp. 68–71.

10. WO 325/57, XC11323, Document J, Shinozaki.

11. I. Sanjiwi (b. 1925), interview with the author, August 12, 1991, Kuala Lumpur.

12. WO 325/56, p. 12.

13. Ikeda Shoichiro, *Pagoda no oka ni zashite* (Sitting on the hill of pagodas) (Ebine: Ikeda Shoichiro, 1989), pp. 118–20.

14. Mat Zin bin Mat Kib, "Persatuan Bekas Buruh Paksa dan Keluarga Buruh Jalan Keretapi Maut Siam–Burma 1942–1946 Persekutuan Melayu, 1958–1973: Satu Tinjauan Sejarah Perkembangannya" (Honors thesis, Universiti Sains Malaysia, 1988).

15. Mohsa bin Jusoh (b. 1931), interview with the author, March 17, 1993, Kuala Kerai, Kelantan.

16. Daud bin Abdullah, interview with the author, March 17, 1993, Kaula Krai, Kelantan.

17. Devarayan s/o Hookan (b. 1922), interview with the author, August 21, 1991, Raja Muda Estate, Kuala Slangor.

18. Lieutenant General Fujimura Masuzo and Lieutenant General Kawahara Naokazu, *Malai gunsei gaiyou* (Outline of military administration in Malaya), August 1945, in *Shiryōshū Nanpo no gunsei* (Documents: Military administration in Nanpō Shinonomesha, 1985), pt. 8, no. 6, pp. 494–95. For an English version, see the Japanese monographs held by the U.S. Army Center of Military History, no. 167.

19. "Treatment and Mortality among Coolie Labor Forces Used in Construction and Maintenance of Thai–Burma Railway," AWM 54: 554/9/1, Appendix (B).

20. Mooniandy Ramasamy (b. 1924), interview with the author, July 17, 1991, Bukit Nanas, Seremban.

21. Haji Mohamad Yusoff bin Yassin, (b. 1926) interview with the author, March 17, 1993, Kata Baru, Kelantan.

22. Robert Hardie, *Burma–Siam Railway: The Secret Diary of Dr. Hardie 1942–45* (London: Imperial War Museum, 1983), p. 104.

23. Reports on medical conditions in "coolie camps" can be found in the following documents: "Report on Coolie Camp Conditions on the Burma–Siam Railway, VI, Medical Conditions," W0325/56, pp. 52–63, "Coolie Mortality," pp. 68–74; SEATIC No. 246, Part IV, pp. 15–19 (2. Coolie Camps; 3. Health; 7. Mortality; 9. Burial of Dead); "Report of 9th Regt. H.Q. on Labor Conditions and Coolie Medical Treatment in Burma in Post-Construction Period," W0325/57, N-7.

24. "An Observation on the Enforcement of the Second Half of the Construction Period and Its Relations to Labor," W0325/57, Document 1.

25. W0325/57, Document M1, p. 7.

26. W0325/57, Document M2, p. 10.

27. *Tooi kiteki* (Steam whistle in the distance: Record of construction of the Burma–Thailand railway) (Asao-sha, 1978), p. 419.

28. "The Japanese are apt to make the figures as small as possible, so small as to be incredible. The medical authorities of the 9 R1y Regt., for instance, give an estimate of 6,800 cases. The coolies, on the other hand, give huge figures, and if one adds up their figures more coolies appear to have died during the cholera epidemic than there were ever on the line," WO/325/56, p. 60.

29. Barjana s/o Koybolo (b. 1927), interview with the author, August 3, 1991, Kuala Lumpur.

30. "Shelter: Attap-roof houses were used, which were quite sufficient against the monsoon." Comments submitted by the Ninth Railway Regiment, W0325/57, Document NI.

31. Kawata Hiromichi, interview with the author, October 1991, Tokyo.

32. "Summary of Examination of Amar Singh," WO 325/57, Document Y.

33. "Tonchan Spring Camp Cooly Camp, 1943," AWM 54: 554/9/1.

34. "Coolie Camp: 228 Kilo Peg Thailand," AWM 54: 554/9/1.

35. Appendix I extracts from official reports of "F" Force and from report by U Aung Hin, SEATIC No. 246, pp. 39–58.

36. Simmasalam (b. 1930), interview with the author, August 21, 1991, Teluk Intan, Perak, Malaysia.

37. W0325/56, p. 47.

38. *Kelantan Planters' Association Year Book for 1986,* p. 104. A Japanese army comfort house was opened in Banpong in the middle of July 1942. *Tooi kiteki,* p. 408.

39. Dato' Abu Kassim bin Haji Mobamad, interview with the author, August 11, 1991, Kuala Lumpur.

40. Kannu (b. 1922), interview with the author, August 12, 1991, Kuala Lumpur.

41. Sitaram s/o Johan (b. 1921), interview with the author, August 13, 1991, Kuala Lumpur.

42. Devanayagam s/o Perumal (b. 1925), interview with the author, August 16, 1991, Midland Estate, Klang, Selangor.

43. Seenivasan s/o Kuppan (b. 1929), interview with the author, August 16, 1991, Midland Estate, Klang, Selangor.

44. Sunnasamy s/o Ganapathy (b. 1922), interview with the author, August 18, 1992, Seremban, Negri Sembilan.

45. Subramaniam s/o Sinnakannoo (b. 1925), interview with the author, August 30, 1991, United Plantation.

46. Kelantan Planters' Association, *Year Book 1983*, p. 177.

47. Subramaniam s/o Sinnakannoo, interview; A.J. Stockwell, ed., *British Documents on the End of Empire,* ser. B, vol. 3, Malaya, pt. L, p. 177.

48. Kelantan Planters' Association, *Year Book 1983*, p. 91.

49. British Military Administration (Malaya), monthly report, no. 5, January 1946: "Refugees and Displaced Persons," p. 9.

Chapter 14

1. Inaugural address of Manuel L. Quezon, November 15, 1935, in *At the Helm of the Nation: Inaugural Addresses of the Presidents of the Philippine Republic and Commonwealth,* pp. 12–13, comp. Consuelo V. Fonacier (Manila: National Media Production Center, 1973). For labor unions, see Melinda Tria Kerkvliet, *Manila Workers' Unions, 1900–1950* (Quezon City: New Day, 1992). The *1946 Yearbook of Philippine Statistics* (Manila: Bureau of Printing, 1947), chap. 7, has statistics on strikes and wage claims, and lists of the number of labor organizations prior to the war.

2. Kerkvliet, *Manila Workers' Unions,* pp. 131–32; Benedict J. Kerkvliet, *The Huk Rebellion: A Study of Peasant Revolution in the Philippines* (Berkeley: University of California Press, 1977), pp. 26–60. For a general summation of prewar conditions, see Army Service Forces, *Manual M 365–9 Civil Affairs Handbook Philippine Islands Section 9: Labor* (Washington, DC: Headquarters, Army Service Forces, 1944).

3. Commonwealth Act no. 600, the Emergency Powers Act, August 19, 1939.

4. *Sixth Annual Report of the U.S. High Commissioner to the Philippine Islands* (Washington, DC: Government Printing Office, 1943), p. 104.

5. Executive Order no. 335, April 1, 1941; *The Civilian Emergency Administration and Its Service to the People* (Manila: Bureau of Printing, 1941), passim. Preparations were slow compared with similar moves in Singapore and the Netherlands East Indies. Major Cyril Q. Marron, report, October 20, 1941, in *Sixth Annual Report of the U.S. High Commissioner to the Philippine Islands,* pp. 179–82.

6. Faustino Aguilar, *Nang Magdaan ang Daluyong* (When the tempest passed) (Manila: PSP Press, 1945), pp. 16–17; Executive Order nos. 378 and 392, Philippine Commonwealth *Official Gazette* 41, no. 1 (April 1945): 18–19.

7. Farmer-Labor Auxiliary Service (FLAS), *FLAS in War and in Peace* (Manila: Farmer-Labor Auxiliary Service, 1945), p. 3. The National Commission of Labor had no official link with the CEA, and voluntarily presented itself and its members for government service.

8. Aguilar, *Nang Magdaan ang Daluyong* (When the tempest passed), pp. 20–25.

9. Historical Section, G-2, GHQ, Far Eastern Command, Japanese Monograph (hereafter JM) 103, "Civil Administration in Occupied Territories," p. 1; Order 5, Guiding Principles of Administration, February 21, 1942, issued by the commander- in-chief of the Imperial Japanese Forces, stated: "In carrying out the administrative policies, the foremost preference shall be given to satisfying the demands of the Imperial Japanese Forces, and importance shall be attached to the maintenance of peace and order." Executive Commission, *Official Gazette* (hereafter EC *OG*) 1, no. 2 (February 1942): 30.

10. *Official Journal of the Japanese Military Administration* (hereafter OJJMA) 1 (March 1942): 3–5.

11. JM 103, "Philippines," pp. 35–39. By March 15, 1943, 1,960 factories were authorized to operate; 1,081 were connected with food, 99 produced iron and steel products, 87 manufactured miscellaneous goods, and 25 produced electrical apparatus. Foreign Broadcast Intelligence Service (hereafter FBIS), Radio Report on the Far East, no. 17, April 30, 1943, p. F2. Regarding the shift from sugar to cotton, Vargas was told: "You should realize that it is unavoidable for the Filipino people to suffer some of these losses." Instructions to the chairman of the Executive Committee and the Commissioner of Agriculture and Commerce regarding the Fundamental Policy on the Readjustment of the Sugar Industry and the increased production of cotton, EC *OG 1*, no. 8 (August 1942): 422. On cotton, see also Nagano Yoshiko, "Cotton Production under Japanese Rule, 1942–1945," and on mining see Ikehata Setsuho, "Mining Industry Development and Local Anti-Japanese Resistance," both in Ikehata and Jose, *The Philippines under Japan*, pp. 171-96 and 127-70. For additional information, see Charles Parsons, "Report on Conditions in the Philippine Islands," June 1943, p. 18, in U.S. National Archives (Philippine Archives Collection) RG 407); Magic Summary 382, SRS 933, April 12, 1943, in *The Magic Documents: Summaries and Translations of the Top-Secret Diplomatic Communications with Japan, 1938–1945* (microfilm); Office of Strategic Services, Research and Analysis (Branch) (R&A) 1928, "Japan's Wooden Ships," July 16, 1944. On food production, see Administrative Order 39, July 8, 1943, in EC *OG* 2, no. 7 (July 1943): 664–65; Executive Order no. 40, EC *OG* 1, no. 5 (May 1942): 224–25.

12. "Minutes of the Interview between the Representative of the Imperial Japanese Forces and Jorge B. Vargas," January 7, 1942, EC *OG* 1, no. 1 (January 1942): 18.

13. JMA order 1, January 23, 1942, EC *OG* 1, no. 1 (January 1942): 6–7. Executive Order no. 1, in ibid., 13, 15; Executive Order no. 4, EC *OG* 1, no. 2 (February 1942): 45; "Appointments," EC *OG* 1, no. 2 (February 1942): 52–54.

14. Theodore Friend, *The Blue-Eyed Enemy: Japan against the West in Java and Luzon* (Princeton, NJ: Princeton University Press, 1988), pp. 100–104.

15. Japanese Monograph No. 1, Philippine Operations Record, Phase 1, 6 November 1941–June 1942, microfilm copy in the Japanese Diet Library. Combat and action reports of the 16th and 48th Divisions on file in the National Institute for Defense Studies Archives, Tokyo. The EC *OG* for 1942 contains several orders from the director general, JMA, to Quintin Paredes, Commissioner of Public Works and Communications; "Workers shall be treated as civilians attached to the army." See, for example, Instructions 7 and 8, March 2 and 6, 1942, EC *OG* 1, no. 3 (March 1942): 70–71; U.S. Board of Economic Warfare, Enemy Branch, "Japanese Techniques of Occupation: Philippine Islands," January 15, 1943, p. 11; Commissioner of Public Works and Communications, *First Annual Report of the Department of Public Works and Communications to the Chairman of the Executive Commission for the Period from January 23, 1942 to March 31, 1943* (hereafter DPWC Report), pp. 4, 19.

16. FBIS, Radio Report on the Far East, no. 7, November 10, 1942, p. 14. The Japanese also used American POWs for construction and mining, and there are many accounts of the terrible conditions they endured.

17. *Shin Seiki* 1, 6 (March 1943): 20; Claro M. Recto, "Annual Report of the Commissioner of Education, Health and Public Welfare, from January 2, 1942 to March 31, 1943," *Historical Bulletin* 11, 4 (December 1967): 435; Ikehata, "Mining Industry Development," p. 153.

18. Executive Order no. 53, EC *OG* 1, no. 6 (June 1942): 333–34; "System of Forced Savings for all Employees, January 23, 1942," in EC *OG* 1, no. 1 (January

1942): 10; JMA Instruction no. 74, EC *OG* 1, no. 9 (September 1942): 539. On wages, see Executive Order no. 11, EC *OG* 1, no. 2 (February 1942): 50; Executive Order no. 12, EC *OG* 1, no. 3 (March 1942): 76–77; Executive Order no. 87, EC *OG* 1, no. 9 (September 1942): 550; "Announcement no. 1, Increase of the Wages of General Laborers," EC *OG* 2, no. 8 (August 1943): 737–38. The "standard wage" in 1942 was 80 centavos per day for men and 64 centavos per day for women, but the JMA had "not had the occasion to enforce" these rates. In August 1942, the maximum daily wage was fixed at 1.30 pesos, but no minimum wage was set. Wage scales did not apply to workers below the age of eighteen, or to those employed in mines, railroads, communications, and other strategic areas. Executive Order no. 58 formally nullified laws setting maximum working hours and minimum wages, although the JMA had already suspended these provisions in February 1942.

19. A.V.H. Hartendorp, *History of Industry and Trade of the Philippines* (Manila: American Chamber of Commerce, 1958), pp. 87–91; JMA Instruction no. 51, July 23, 1942, EC *OG* 1, no. 7 (July 1942): 369–70; Military Administration Order (Kanrei) no. 20, EC *OG* 2, no. 8 (August 1943): 739; Magic Summary SRS 775, November 13, 1942; JM 103, Philippines, pp. 38–39; *Tribune,* September 25, 1943.

20. See, for example, Instruction no. 133, EC *OG* 1, no. 5 (May 1942): 214.

21. OJJMA 1, 13; Administrative Order, October 15, 1942, EC *OG* 1, no. 10 (October 1942): 667–69; Vargas speech, in ibid., pp. 724–28.

22. *Kalibapi Workers Handbook* (Manila: Bureau of Printing, 1943), p. 15; "Kalibapi Training Institute," *Shin Seiki* 2 (1943): 15.

23. FBIS, Radio Report on the Far East, no. 10, December 14, 1942, p. H2; *Tribune,* September 12, 1943; Vargas speech in EC *OG* 2, no. 9 (September 1943), pp. 889–90; Vargas statement, EC *OG* 2, no. 1 (January 1943): 98.

24. Manila's population in August 1942 was 873,000, excluding Japanese. In June 1943, it was reported as more than a million. The prewar population was 623,492. *Tribune,* August 19, 1942, April 5 and June 25, 1943; *1946 Yearbook of Philippine Statistics,* p. 7.

25. Instruction no. 5, February 22, 1942, EC *OG* 1, no. 2 (February 1942): 36. FBIS, Radio Report on the Far East, no. 6, October 27, 1942, p. 14. Figures of those the office was able to assist are given in *Journal of Philippine Statistics* (June 1942), p. 10. A majority of the unskilled got jobs, but only a fraction of the skilled workforce could be placed.

26. FBIS, Radio Report on the Far East, no. 6, October 27, 1942, pp. 14–15; no. 10, December 22, 1942, pp. H2, H9; JMA Instruction no. 145, January 1943, OG *EC* 2, no. 1 (January 1943), p. 6; Announcement by the chief of the Department of Information, Imperial Japanese Forces in the Philippines, EC *OG* 1, no. 10 (October 1942): 662–63. The Japanese was Ekichi Imamura.

27. JMA Instruction no. 145, EC *OG* 2, no. 1 (January 1943), p. 6; FBIS, Radio Report on the Far East, no. 10, December 22, 1942, p. H9; Vargas report to Lieutenant General Shigenori Kuroda, June 2, 1943, in EC *OG* 2, no. 6 (June 1943): 583–84.

28. *Tribune,* February 14, 1943.

29. Executive Order no. 118, EC *OG* 2, no. 1 (January 1943): 14–16; Bureau of Employment Administrative Order, no. 1, EC *OG* 2, no. 9 (September 1943): 212–13. Appointments, EC *OG* 2, no. 1 (January 1943): 67. Tirona was considered a progressive in and out of government, and before the war a friend of labor. He had been a judge in the Court of Industrial Relations and had served as senator. Emiliano T. Tirona, interview with the U.S. Army's Counter-Intelligence Corps (CIC), in 457th

CIC Det (Area), memo for the OIC, June 8, 1945, in Emiliano T. Tirona file, People's Court papers, University of the Philippines.

30. The Commissioner of the Interior—at that time Jose P. Laurel—served as chair, while the Director of Employment was the vice chair. Eight other members were to be appointed by the chairman of the Executive Commission, but they were not named until a month later, perhaps indicating the low priority attached to the board. The appointed members were Faustino Aguilar, Rafael Corpus, Josefa Llanes-Escoda, Eulogio R. Lerum, Pablo Manlapit, Domingo Ponce, Jose Turiano Santiago, and Ysidro Vamenta. Aguilar was not consulted about this and only learned of his appointment when it was announced in the newspapers. Administrative Order, no. 23, EC *OG* 2, no. 3 (March 1943): 287; *Tribune,* March 16 and April 14, 1943; EC *OG* 2, no. 4 (April 1943): 397; Aguilar, *Nang Magdaan ang Daluyong* (When the tempest passed), pp. 172–75.

31. *Tribune,* "Labor in the Right Place," editorial, March 18, 1943.

32. *Tribune,* March 14, 1943.

33. Teodoro A. Agoncillo, *The Fateful Years: Japan's Adventure in the Philippines* (Quezon City: R.P. Garcia, 1965), 2:565.

34. For details on relief, see Recto, "Annual Report of the Commissioner of Education, Health and Public Welfare," p. 434; FBIS, Radio Report on the Far East, no. 6, October 27, 1942, p. 14. Despite the need for relief workers, however, some government employees involved in the relief effort were themselves laid off in Manila due to a lack of funds. *Tribune,* July 29, 1943.

35. FBIS, Radio Report on the Far East, no. 9, December 8, 1942, p. K6; no. 10, December 22, 1942, p. H1; JM 103, p. 2.

36. Hartendorp, *History of Industry and Trade,* p. 80; Magic Summary no. 546, SRS 1096, September 25, 1943.

37. U.S. Office of Strategic Services, Board of Economic Warfare, Enemy Branch, "Japanese Techniques of Occupation: Philippine Islands," p. 12 (January 15, 1943), in US National Archives Record Group 226.

38. Agoncillo, *Fateful Years,* 2:565; Hartendorp, *History of Industry and Trade,* p. 81.

39. Isidoro P. Azarias, "The Free Press Saved My Life," *Philippines Free Press* (February 7, 1948): 30.

40. 1943 Constitution, in EC *OG* 2, no. 9-A (September 4, 1943): 40, 43–44.

41. Jose P. Laurel, Inaugural Address, in Republic of the Philippines *Official Gazette* (hereafter RP *OG*) 1, no. 1 (October 14–31, 1943): 68.

42. Documents in Ministry of Foreign Affairs, *Bulletin 1*, no. 1 (October 14, 1943–February 15, 1944).

43. RP *OG* 1, no. 1 (October 14–31, 1943): 13.

44. FBIS Radio Report on the Far East, no. 56 (October 13, 1944), pp. GA 5–6; Republic of the Philippines, Office of the President, Proclamation 29, September 21, 1944—mimeograph copy in Mauro P. Garcia collection, Sophia University, Tokyo.

45. "Basic Principles and Policies," in A.V.H. Hartendorp, *The Japanese Occupation of the Philippines* (Manila: Bookmark, 1967), 2:87–89.

46. RP *OG* 1, no. 6, (March 1944): 631; RP *OG* 1, no. 4 (January 1944): 391; RP *OG* 1, no. 5 (February 1944): 462; Executive Order no. 24; OSS R&A 2440, "The Programs of Japan in the Philippines," Assemblage 33, Supplement no. 1 (July 29, 1944), pp. 275–76; Executive Order Providing for the Reorganization of the Government of the Republic of the Philippines (Executive Order no. 39) for the Fiscal Period

January 1 to December 31, 1944 (Manila: Bureau of Printing, 1943), pp. 152–53; *Tribune,* January 28, 1944. The first conference on labor problems was held in November 1943. FBIS, Radio Report on the Far East, no. 33 (November 10, 1943), p. E12.

47. Act no. 2, RP *OG* 1, no. 1 (October 14–31, 1943), p. 31; OSS, "Programs of Japan in the Philippines," Supplement no. 1, p. 297.

48. *Tribune,* December 28 and 29, 1943.

49. Manila's population had soared to 1.5 million by January 1944. OSS, R&A Branch, "Manpower in Japan and Occupied Areas," Assemblage 45 (August 26, 1944), p. 292; "Minutes of the December 16, 1943, Cabinet Meeting," Japanese Occupation Papers, University of the Philippines; Executive Order no. 93; FBIS, Radio Report on the Far East, no. 40, March 2, 1944, p. E3; OSS, "Programs of Japan in the Philippines," Supplement no. 1, p. 276.

50. The 14th Army Field Freight Depot complained that because of persons leaving Manila, it was hard-pressed to recruit laborers to unload rice from ships. Allied Translator and Interpreter Section, Enemy Publication no. 311: 14th Army Field Freight Depot Duty Report for January 1944, p. 35; FBIS, Radio Report on the Far East, no. 40, March 2, 1944, p. E3; OSS, "Programs of Japan in the Philippines," Supplement no. 1, p. 276.

51. Act no. 7, RP *OG* 1, no. 1 (October 14–31, 1943): 34–35; OSS, "Programs of Japan in the Philippines," Supplement no. 2, p. 393. For wages and bonuses, see Executive Order nos. 66, 76, 77, 87, 101, 107, and Act nos. 20, 23, Garcia collection.

52. On the day that had been set, a typhoon hit Manila and flooded the city for three days, necessitating a postponement. Proclamation no. 2, RP *OG 1,* no. 1 (October 14–31, 1943), p. 7; *Tribune,* November 4, 6, 11–14, 19–21, 25, and December 4, 1943; FBIS, Radio Report on the Far East, no. 40 (March 2, 1944), p. E10.

53. Act no. 39, RP *OG* 1, no. 5 (February 1944), pp. 492–94.

54. OSS, "Programs of Japan in the Philippines," Supplement no. 1, p. 275–76; Ministry of Agriculture and Natural Resources, Ministry Administrative Order, no. 42, RP *OG* 1, no. 5 (February 1944), pp. 560–61. Executive Order no. 37, RP *OG* 1, no. 5 (February 1944), pp. 458–59; Armando J. Malay, "The Labor Corps in Action," *Pillars* 1, no. 3 (March 1944), pp. 1–5.

55. Act no. 12; Proclamation no. 17, RP *OG* 1, no. 8 (May 1944), p. 853.

56. FBIS, Radio Report on the Far East, no. 44 (April 27, 1944), pp. F11–12; Ibid., no. 45 (May 11, 1944), p. F11; OSS, "Programs of Japan in the Philippines," Supplement no. 2, p. 393. Hartendorp (in his *Japanese Occupation,* 2:276) commented, "Only one class of Filipinos remained: slaves."

57. *Tribune,* May 10, 11, 13, 14, 15, and June 9, 1944.

58. *Tribune,* May 15, 19, and June 9, 1944; Edwin Andrews to Douglas MacArthur, Radiogram no. 4, July 8, 1944, and no. 8, July 25, 1944, Courtney Whitney Papers, MacArthur Memorial; Hartendorp, *Japanese Occupation,* 2:277; Hartendorp, *History of Industry and Trade,* pp. 133–34.

59. *Tribune,* October 28, 31, and December 8, 1943, and January 10, and February 3, 5, 1944; Andrews to MacArthur, no. 266, April 17, 1944, Whitney Papers; former neighborhood association head, Author's interview with neighborhood association head Lazaro Vergara on February 23, 1991, in Apalit, Pampanga, Philippines; employment ads placed by the army, navy, and Japanese firms, *Tribune,* early 1944; Wati [Wachi] to Laurel, February 1944, "Asking Cooperation of the Government Concerning the Enlistment of Personnel in the Philippines," quoted in Friend, *Blue-Eyed Enemy,*

pp. 166–67. In February 1944, the Japanese army sought more than 7,000 laborers in various provinces.

60. April brought a request for 30,000 more laborers. OSS, "Programs of Japan in the Philippines," Supplement no. 2, p. 389.

61. Details concerning the creation of the LRA are found in the Tirona People's Court file, particularly the Information; 457th CIC Det (Area), memo for the OIC, June 8, 1945, p. 3; Labor Organization for the Army and Navy, "Working Plan and Minutes of Conference on the Recruitment of Laborers for the Imperial Japanese Army and Navy," March 20, 1944; Executive Order no. 47, RP *OG* 1, no. 7 (April 1944), pp. 750–51.

62. RP *OG* 1, no. 8 (May 1944), p. 864; FBIS, Radio Report on the Far East, no. 44 (April 27, 1944), pp. F10–11, and no. 45 (May 11, 1944), p. F12; Executive Order no. 47, RP *OG* 1, no. 7 (April 1944), pp. 750–51.

63. FBIS, Radio Report on the Far East, no. 44 (April 27, 1944), pp. F10–11; Hartendorp, *Japanese Occupation,* 2:274; *Tribune,* May 26, 1944.

64. For Japanese wants and LRA results, see Pablo Manlapit, "General Report of the Activities of the Labor Recruitment Agency from April 1, 1944 to September 30, 1944," in *Historical Bulletin* 11, no. 1 (March 1967), pp. 76–77. See also *Tribune,* June 1, 1944.

65. Manlapit, "General Report," p. 79; Mauro P. Garcia, ed., *Documents on the Japanese Occupation of the Philippines* (Manila: Philippine Historical Association, 1965), p. 78.

66. Manlapit, "General Report," pp. 80–81, 90–92ff; Elmer Lear, *The Japanese Occupation of the Philippines, Leyte 1941–1945* (Ithaca, NY: Cornell University Southeast Asia Program, 1961), pp. 101, 104; "Maltreatment of Filipinos by the Japanese," unsigned memo for HE The President of the Republic of the Philippines, undated [mid 1944], Mauro P. Garcia Collection Papers, Sophia University, Tokyo; Recto to Lieutenant General T. Wati, June 20, 1944, Garcia Collection.

67. Lear, *Leyte,* pp. 101, 104; Recto to Ambassador Syozo Murata, July 14, 1944, Garcia papers.

68. Magic Summary 802, June 5, 1944, SRS 1324; Magic Summary 879, August 21, 1944, SRS 1401.

69. Telegram, Teofilo Sison to Military Governor, Military District no. 6, City of Cebu, October 12, 1944, reproduced in GR-L 398, *People of the Philippines vs. Teofilo Sison—Brief for the Appellee* (Manila: Bureau of Printing, 1947), pp. 100–101. Similar telegrams were sent to the other military governors, with orders to recruit a total of 54,470 workers. Ibid., pp. 156–57. Sison later said the Japanese drafted these orders and he was made to sign them. Ibid., p. 158.

70. The Japanese army and navy representatives were Colonel Naokata Utsunomiya and Captain Hideo Hiraide. The compulsory labor order was Executive Order no. 100. 1945 Statement of Emilio Abello, former Executive Secretary, Republic of the Philippines, Exhibit I in Emilio Abello File, People's Court records, University of the Philippines Main Library, Quezon City; Emilio Abello, "Statement on Conscription of Labor," Jose P. Laurel Memorial Library. See also Friend, *Blue-Eyed Enemy,* p. 168. Although some Japanese officers favored military conscription of Filipinos, many others opposed the idea, realizing that the Filipinos were strongly anti-Japanese.

71. Philip Buencamino diary, entry for November 22, 1944.

72. Eliseo Quirino, *A Day to Remember* (Manila: Benipayo Press, 1961), pp. 240–41; Author's interview with Mr. and Mrs. Dizon, October 11, 1982, Angeles, Pampanga,

and with Lazaro Vergara, former neighborhood association head, February 23, 1991, Apalit, Pampanga.

73. Buencamino diary, entry for November 17, 1944. Buencamino wrote: "This labor conscription gives the lie to Laurel's main boast that he won't permit any conscription." Conscription through district and neighborhood associations continued in Manila until the end of 1944. See "Consolidated Report on Peace and Order of the Military Governor of the City of Manila," December 31, 1944, in Garcia, *Documents,* pp. 149–51.

74. *People of the Philippines vs. Jose P. Laurel,* Information; *People of the Philippines vs. Teofilo Sison,* Criminal Case no. 1, Information; *People of the Philippines vs. Emiliano T. Tirona,* Information.

Chapter 15

1. For more information on Phạm Công Tắc, see Trần Mỹ-Vân, "Vietnam's Cao Daism, Independence and Peace: The Life and Work of Pham Cong Tac" (PROSEA Research Paper 38, Taipei, September 2000), pp. 1–32.

2. *Đại Đạo Tam Kỳ Phổ Độ, Hồi Ký Trần Quang Vinh và Lịch Sử Quân Đội Cao Đài* (repr., North Potomac, MD: Thánh Thất vùng Hoa Thịnh Đốn, 1997), p. 125 (hereafter *Hồi Ký Trần Quang Vinh*); Trần Quang Vinh, *Tờ Phúc Trình* [report], p. 10. The report, which was written in 1946 for Phạm Công Tắc upon his return from exile, dealt with the political and military affairs of the Cao Đài religion during the period of Japanese occupation. It was later published as *Lịch Sử Quân Đội Cao Đài Trong Thời Kỳ Phục Quốc 1940–1946* (Saigon: published by the author, 1967) (hereafter *Tờ Phúc Trình*). Page references are to a copy of the *Tờ Phúc Trình* in my possession.

3. For example, the May 6, 1941, agreement granted privileges to Japanese firms and ships, including free access to exports and unlimited entry to Indochina; the Darlan-Kako Agreement (July 29, 1941) allowed a Japanese force of 35,000 men to make use of eight airfields and two naval bases for their conquest of Southeast Asia, including a payment of 400,000 French francs from the French authorities for their troops.

4. For more information on the Hòa Hảo during the Japanese occupation, see Trần Mỹ-Vân, "Beneath the Japanese Umbrella: Vietnam's Hoa Hao During and After the Pacific War," *Crossroads* 17, no. 1 (2003), pp. 60–107.

5. Matsushita came to Vietnam in 1913. From 1917 to 1922 he worked for Mitsui Bussan. He then established his own company, Dainan Koshi, with its head office in Hanoi and a branch in Saigon. In 1928 he moved the head office to Saigon, where he also resided. He further expanded his commercial activities to encompass Cambodia and Thailand.

6. See Takeshi Shiraishi and Moto Furuta, "Two Features of Japan's Indochina Policy during the Pacific War," in *Indochina in the 1940s and 1950s,* ed. Takeshi Shiraishi and Motoo Furuta (Ithaca, NY: Cornell University Southeast Asia Program, 1992), pp. 59–61; Minami Yoshizawa, "The Nishihara Mission in Hanoi, July 1940," in ibid., 48–49; Yukichida Tabuchi, "Indochina's Role in Japan's Greater East Asia Co-Prosperity Sphere: A Food-Procurement Strategy," in ibid., pp. 96–100.

7. *Hồi Ký Trần Quang Vinh,* p. 207.

8. Ibid.

9. Ibid., p. 217.

10. Tabuchi, "Indochina's Role," p. 102.

11. See appendix 12 in Pham Cao Duong, *Vietnamese Peasants under French Domination, 1861–1945,* Monograph Series 24 (Berkeley, CA: Center for South and Southeast Asia Studies, 1985), pp. 181–83.

12. See Trần Huy Liệu, *Xã Hội Việt Nam Trong Thời Pháp Nhật* (Vietnamese Society during the French and Japanese Period) (Hà Nội: Văn Sử Địa, 1957), pp. 77–85.

13. Kyoichi Tachikawa, "Independence Movement in Vietnam and Japan during WWII," *NIDS Security Reports,* no. 2 (March 2001), p. 109.

14. Piasters refers to Vietnamese *đồng.*

15. Quoted from Nguyễn Phan Quang, *Góp Thêm Tư Liệu Sài Gòn -Gia Định từ 1859–1945* (Hồ Chí Minh City: Trẻ, 1998), pp. 195–97.

16. For information on the background to food shortages and the famine, see Nguyen The Anh, "Japanese Food Policies and the 1945 Great Famine in Indochina," and Motoo Furuta, "A Survey of Village Conditions during the 1945 Famine in Vietnam," in *Food Supplies and the Japanese Occupation in South East Asia,* ed. Paul. H. Kratoska (Houndmills: Macmillan Press, 1998), pp. 208–37; and Bui Minh Duong, "Japan's Role in the Vietnamese Starvation," *Modern Asian Studies 29,* no. 3 (March 1995): 573–618; Văn Tạo and Furuta Moto, *Nạn Đói Năm 1945 ở Việt Nam* (Hà Nội: Viện Sử Học Việt Nam, 1995), pp. 1–90.

17. *Tờ Phúc Trình,* p. 27; *Hồi Ký Trần Quang Vinh,* p. 220.

18. *Hồi Ký Trần Quang Vinh,* p. 222.

19. Ibid., p. 104.

20. Ibid., p. 112.

21. Nguyễn Ngọc Hòa, interview with the author, Japan, April 10, 2001; Nguyễn Ngọc Hòa, *Hồi Ký, Đời Tôi giữa thế kỷ 20* (Diary, My Life in the mid-20th Century) (Tokyo: Việt á Văn Xả, 1998), p. 285. I would like to thank Nguyễn Ngọc Hòa for giving me access to his diary before its publication.

22. Ibid.

23. For information on this coup, known as Operation Akika, and the establishment of the Trần Trọng Kim government, see Kyoko Kurusu Nitz, "Independence without Nationalists? The Japanese and Vietnamese Nationalism during the Japanese Period, 1940–1945," *Journal of Southeast Asian Studies* 15, no. 1 (March 1984): 108–33, and R.B. Smith, "The Japanese in Indochina and the Coup of March 1945," *Journal of Southeast Asian Studies* 8, no. 2 (September 1977). Concerning Japanese plans for governing Vietnam, see Masaya Shiraishi, "Background to the Formation of Trần Trọng Kim Cabinet in April 1945: Japanese Plans for Governing Vietnam," in Takeshi and Furuta, *Indochina in the 1940s and 1950s,* pp. 113–41. See also David Marr, *Vietnam 1945: The Quest for Power* (Berkeley: University of California Press, 1995), pp. 110–12.

24. Nguyễn Ngọc Hòa, *Hồi Ký,* pp. 304–12, and Hòa interview.

25. Unbeknownst to the Vietnamese nationalists, General Tsuchihashi had already stated his refusal to have Prince Cường Đễ return as early as February 1945 to an envoy from the Tokyo Ministry of Foreign Affairs: "Send him, but understand that as soon as he arrives in Saigon airport I'll pack him off to Poulo Condore prison." Quoted in Shiraishi, "Background to the Formation of Trần Trọng Kim Cabinet," p. 135.

26. Bảo Đại, *Con Rồng Việt Nam: Hồi Ký 1913–1987* (The Dragon of Vietnam: Diary 1913–1987) (n.p.: Nguyễn Phước Tộc, 1990), pp. 174–75.

27. Trần Kỳ Nam, *Hồi Ký 1925–1964,* vol. 2 (Saigon: Dân Chủ Mới, 1964), p. 137.

28. Nguyễn Văn Hoa and Phạm Hồng Việt, eds., *Hiểu Thêm Lịch Sử Qua Các Hồi Kí* (Understanding History through Diaries) (Hà Nội: Giáo Dục, 1997), p. 109.

29. Trần Kỳ Nam, *Hồi Ký*, p. 165.

30. Quoted from Nguyễn Phan Quang, *Góp thêm tu liệu Sài Gòn-Gia Định từ 1959–1945*, p. 252.

31. Nguyễn văn Hầu, *Thất Sơn Mầu Nhiệm* (The Miraculous Seven Mountain Ranges) (Los Alamitos: Xuân Thu, 1995), pp. 247–259; Vương Kim, *Đức Huỳnh Giáo Chủ* (The Venerable Master Huynh) (Saigon, 1975), pp. 122–27; *Đuốc Từ Bi* (November 1, 1986), p. 70.

32. See Annex no. 111 by De la Croix, *Phật Giáo Hòa Hảo*, p. 102, in File 10 H 644, Service Historique de l'Armée de Terre (SHAT), Vincennes.

33. Ibid., note 1.

34. Tabuchi, "Indochina's Role," p. 103.

Chapter 16

I am grateful to Sarah Teasley for her editorial assistance and Ted Fowler and Kota Inoue for invaluable help with romanization of Japanese terms.

1. When the problem of military sexual slavery was first exposed in the late 1980s, the Korean media used the term *chŏngsindae*; a civil organization formed to address this problem in 1990 called itself Hanguk Chŏngsindae Munje Daech'aek Hyŏbŭihoe (Korean Council for the Women Drafted for Military Sexual Slavery by Japan).

2. The first clause of the order for the women's voluntary corps for labor (*joshi teishin kinrŏ rei*) reads, "The Women's Voluntary Corps for Labor will hereafter be referred to as the Women's Voluntary Corps." *Chōsen Sōtokufu Kanpō mokuroku* (A catalogue of the journal of colonial government of Korea), August 1944.

3. In 1944 an official of the colonial government named Tahara Minoru said, "Until now mobilization of the Women's Voluntary Corps has been made by government guidance, and this will remain the same as before." *Kokumin chōyō no kaisetsu* (Explanation of citizen mobilization) (Seoul: Kokumin Soryoku Chōsen Renmei, 1994).

4. Jūgun Ianfu Hyakutōban Henshū Iinkai, ed., *Jūgun ianfu hyakutōban* (Military comfort women hotline 110) (Tokyo: Akashi Shoten, 1992).

5. Yoshida Seiji, *Nanun chosōnsaramūl irŏke jabagatta* (I captured the Koreans in this way), trans. Hyŏndae sahoe yŏnguhoe (Seoul: Ch'ŏnggye Yŏnguso, 1989), p. 105.

6. For example, *Maeil sinbo* or *Kyŏngsŏng ilbo*.

7. See Takaki Ken'ichi, *Jūgun ianfu to sengo hoshō* (Military comfort women and postwar compensation) (Tokyo: San'ichi Shobō, 1992), p. 3.

8. This was decided at the First Asian Women's Solidarity Forum on Military Sexual Slavery by Japan held in Seoul in August 1992.

9. For instance, *Maeil sinbo*, October 27, 1944, and November 1, 1944.

10. Yoshimi Yoshiaki pointed this out at a joint symposium of the Korean Council and the Japanese War Responsibility Data Center (hereafter Data Center) in August 1993.

11. Kang Man-gil, "Ilbongun sŏngnoyemunjeŭi yŏksahakjŏk jŏbgŭn" (Historical approaches to the problem of Japanese military sexual slavery) (paper given at the Ilbongun Wianbu Munje Hail Hapdong Symposium [Korea–Japan Joint Symposium on Military Sexual Slavery by Japan] at the Korean Council and the Data Center, Seoul, December 1993).

12. "Iljeha ilbongunwianbue daehan saenghwalanjŏng jiwŏnbŏp" (An act to pro-

vide financial security for the Japanese military comfort women under Japanese colonial rule), 1993.

13. Suzuki Yūko et al., eds., *Onna, tennōsei, sensō* (Women, emperor system, and war) (Tokyo: Origin Sentā, 1989), pp. 7–16.

14. Tsunoda Yukiko, "Seibōryoku to tennōsei" (Sexual assault and the emperor system), in ibid., 197.

15. Fukae Masako, "Baishun seido to tennōsei" (The prostitution system and the emperor system), in ibid., pp. 202–5.

16. Saitō Yasuaki, "Heiryoku rōdōryoku no dōin to haichi" (Mobilization and deployment of the military and labor power), in *Taiheiyō sensō ka no rōdōsha kitai* (The state of the laborers during the Pacific war), ed. Daigen Shakai Mondai Kenkyūjo (Tokyo: Tōyō Keizai Shinpō Sha, 1964), pp. 23–26.

17. Suzuki Yūko, *Joseishi o hiraku* (Opening women's history) (Tokyo: Mirai Shu, 1989), pp. 53–73; Yŏ Sun-ju, "Iljemalgi chŏsŏnin yŏjakŭllo chŏngsidaeŭi silt'aee gwanhan yŏngu" (The reality of the Korean women's voluntary labor corps toward the end of Japanese colonial rule) (M.A. thesis, Ewha Women's University, 1993).

18. In 1910 there were 171,543 Japanese residing in Korea, which was 1.3 percent of the Japanese population. By 1940 this number increased to 689,790 (2.9 percent of the Japanese population). Chōsen Sōtokufu, *Chōsen ni okeru jinkō ni kansuru sōtōkei* (Census statistics in Korea), 1943, p. 27. In 1930 in an area of 122 irrigation associations, sixty-five of seventy-seven landowners with more than 245 acres were Japanese. There were many more Japanese landowners with holdings smaller than 245 acres. *Tonga ilbo* (Tonga newspaper), January 1, 1932.

19. In 1931 the Japanese colonial government established a policy to send some 20 percent of Korean landowning farmers to Manchuria. Ko Sŭng-je, *Hanguk iminsa yŏngu* (History of Korean emigration) (Seoul: Changmungak, 1973), p. 99.

20. Pak Kyŏng-sik, *Ilbon jegukchuŭiŭi chosŏn jibae* (Japanese colonial rule in Korea) (Seoul: Ch'ŏnga, 1973), p. 99.

21. James B. Crowley, *Japan's Quest for Autonomy* (Princeton, NJ: Princeton University Press, 1966), 4–8; and Chen I-te, "Japanese Colonialism in Korea and Formosa: A Comparision of Its Effects upon the Development of Nationalism" (Ph.D. diss., University of Pennsylvania, 1968), pp. 71–90.

22. Nippon Tokubetsu Kōtō Keisatsu, *Tokkō geppō* (Special police force monthly) (1930, 1944).

23. Miyata Setsuko, *Chōsengun gaiyōshi* (General history of Korean soldiers) (Tokyo: Fumi, 1990).

24. Hyōgo Chōsen Kankei Kenkyūkai, *Chika kōjō to chōsenjin kyōsei renkō* (Underground factories and forced laborers from Korea) (Tokyo: Akashi Shōten, 1990).

25. Oe Shinobu, ed., *Heishi kara no Nichi-Ro sensō: Gohyaku tsū no jūgun yūbin kara* (The Russo–Japanese war from the perspective of soldiers: From five hundred military letters) (Tokyo: Asahi Shimbun Sha, 1988).

26. Kŭm Pyŏng-dong, "Kaisetsu" (Interpretation), in *Senjō nisshi ni miru jūgun ianfu kokuni shiryōshū* (Tokyo: Rokuin Shobo, 1992), p. 3.

27. Inaba Masao, ed., *Okamura Yasujirō Taishō shiryō* (Materials of General Okamura Yasujirō), vol. 1, quoted in "Ajia Taiheiyō sensō kankoku giseisha hoshō seikyū jiken" (A suit by Korean victims of the Asia Pacific War), *Sojō* (Bill of complaint) (1992), pp. 24–25.

28. When the Manchurian Affair occurred, the Japanese navy sent troops to south China, and additional forces followed in October 1931 and January 1932. Fujiwara

Akira, *Ilbon gunsasa* (History of the Japanese military), trans. Ŏm Su-hyŏn (Seoul: Sisayŏngŏsa, 1994), pp. 209–10.

29. Okabe Naosaburō, *Okabe Naosaburō Taishō no nikki* (Diaries of General Okabe Naosaburō) (Tokyo: Fuyō Shoten, 1982), p. 23.

30. Zai Shanhai Sōryōjikan, *Shōwa jūnen zai Shanhai sōrōjikan keisatsu jimu jōkyō* (Police affair in Shanghai [Japanese] consulate) (1935).

31. Konsei Daijūshi Ryodan Shireibu, *Eisei gyōmu junpō* (Ten-day report of hygiene work), March 8, 1933.

32. Japan invaded China in July 1937 and occupied Nanjing in December 1937.

33. Nankin Senshi Henshū Iinkai, ed., *Nankin senshi shiryō sha* (Historical data regarding the Nanjing war) (Tokyo: Kaigyōsha, 1989), pp. 211, 220.

34. Rikugunshō Heimukyoku Heimuka kian (draft), "Gun'iansho jūgyōfu boshū ni kansuru ken" (Issues regarding the recruitment of [female] military comfort station workers), April 1938.

35. Zai Shanhai sōryōjikan, "Zairyū hōjin no kakushu eigyō kyoka oyobi torishimari ni kansuru rikukaigai sanshō kankeisha kaidō kettei jikō" (Decisions of the personnel related to army, navy, and three other departments regarding an assortment of business permits and the supervision of Japanese living in the area), April 16, 1938.

36. Kyōiku Sōkanbu, "Senji fukumu teiyō" (Rules of wartime duties), May 25, 1938.

37. *Kanemoto Setsuzō gyōmu nisshi tekiroku* (Kanemoto Setsuzō work journal), sono sanno ha (3 ha), July 26, 1941; Taiwangun, "Nanpō haken tokōsha ni kansuru ken" (Issues regarding the sailing personnel dispatched to South Asia), March 1942.

38. Senda Kako, *Jūgun ianfu, seihen* (Military comfort women, a true compilation) (Tokyo: San'ichi Shobō, 1978), p. 104.

39. *Kanemoto Setsuzō gyōmu tekiroku* (Kanemoto Setsuzō work journal) *2*, no. 5.1 (September 3, 1942).

40. On the provision of condoms, see Rikugunshō Keirikyoku Kenchikuka, *Riku-A mitsudai nikki* (Grand secret journal of the army in Asia), 1942. On financial support, see U.S. National Archives, May 1944; and Japanese War Responsibility Data Center, *Sensō sekinin kenkyu* (War responsibility study), no. 1 (Fall 1993), p. 34.

41. Naimushō keihōkyokucho, "Shina tokō fujo no toriatsukai ni kansuru ken" (Issues regarding women who sail to China), February 23, 1938.

42. Nihon Naimushō Keihōkyoku, "Chōsenjin rōdōsha boshū ni kansuru ken tsūchō" (Notice regarding recruitment of Korean laborers), quoted in Pak Kyŏng-sik, *Zainichi Chōsenjin kankei shiryō shūsei* (Compilation of historical data on Koreans in Japan), vol. 1 (Tokyo: San'ichi Shobō, 1983).

43. Chōsen Sōtokufu Keimukyokuchō, "Shinahōjin no torishimari ni kansuru ken" (Issues regarding supervision of Japanese nationals in China), March 19, 1942.

44. Taiwan Sōtokufu, "Nan'yō hōmen senryōchi ni okeru ianjo kaisetsu ni kansuru ken" (Issues regarding the opening of comfort stations in the occupied territories in the south sea), January 1942.

45. Dokuritsu kōjō jūhohei dai 2 daitaicho, "Jōkyō hōkoku" (Reports on the situation), January 20, 1939.

46. "Showa 13 nen 7 katsu 5 nichi fu zai Shanhai sōreishi hassin zai Nankin sōreishi ate tsūhō yōsi" (Major reports from the consulate in Shanghai to the consulate in Nanjing on July 5, 1938).

47. Asō Tetsuo, "Karyūbyō no sekkyoku-teki yobōhō" (Methods of aggressive prevention of venereal disease), June 26, 1939.

48. Dai 21gun Shireibu, "Sensi junpō" (Ten-day wartime report), April 1939, pp. 11–20.

49. Taiwan Sōtokufu, "Tosi jijū shōmeisho nado no toriyose funō to mitomeraruru taigan ehiiki heno tokōsha no toriatsukau ni kansuru ken" (On the treatment of persons who can or cannot get permission to go to south China), 1940.

50. Hido Gunseikanpu Bizaya Sifu Iroiro Shutchōjo, "Ianjo kitei sōfu no ken" (On sending the rules of the military comfort station), February 1943.

51. Sebu Kenpe Buntaichō/Takuroban Kenpe Buntaichō, "Gun'ian narabi goraku setsubi jōkyō chōsa no ken" (On the investigation of the situation of military equipment for comfort and recreation), August 1948. This case concerns one of the comfort women, Kim Pok-dong.

52. Yōsai Kenchiku Kinro Dai 6 Tsudai, "Jinchū nisshi" (Military camp journal), May–June 1944.

53. Asō Tetsuo, Karyūbyō; Senda Kakō, Jūgen ianfu, seihan; and many Japanese army records. See also Jūgun Ianfu Hyakutōban Henshū Iinkai, ed., Jūgun ianfu hyakutōban (Military comfort women hotline 110). For the testimony of victims, see Keith Howard, ed., True Stories of the Korean Comfort Women (London: Cassell, 1995).

54. Shina Hagengun Sōshireibu, "Fukukan gōdō jisshi no ken" (On the joint enforcement of adjutants), October 1942; Nankin Daijūgo Shiclan Ibu, "Gokuhi Shōwa jūhachinen nigatsu eisei gyōmu yōhō" (Important top secret notice regarding sanitation work in February 1943).

55. See Jūgun Ianfu Hyakutōban Henshū Iinkai, ed., Jūgun ianfu hyakutōban (Military comfort women hotline 110).

56. Dokuritsu Sanhōhei Daisan Rentai, "Jinchū nisshi" (Military camp journal), April 1–6, 1941.

57. In Korea the minimum age was supposed to be seventeen. See Yamashida Yŏngae, "Hanguk gūndae gongch'angjedo silsie gwanhan yŏngu" (A Study of the Execution of Korea's Modern Licensed Prostitution) (M.A. thesis, Ewha Women's University, 1991), p. 50.

58. See, for example, recruitment advertisements in Maeil sinbo.

59. And of course, it was the army who had made the original decision that the army should be in charge of the selection of women to be mobilized. See Rikugunshō Heimukyoku Heimuka kian (draft), "Gun ianjo jūgyōfunado boshū ni kansuru ken" (Issues regarding the recruitment of [female] workers and others for the military comfort station), April 1938.

60. "Shina Jihen ni saishi hōjin no toshi seigen narabi torishimari kankei zantei shori yōkō," (Temporary measure for age control and supervision of Japanese at the time of the China Incident.) May 1940.

61. "Regulations of the brothels should be strictly observed," in Dokuritsu Konsei Daijūgo Rentai Honbu, Jinchū nisshi, October 1935.

62. Dokuritsu Shubi Hohei Daisanjūgo Daitai, Jinchū nisshi, April 1941.

63. "2A Shireibu, Daini-gun jōkyō gaiyō" (General situation of the Second Army), December 10, 1938.

64. Dokuritsu Kōjō Jūhōhei Daini Daitai, "Ianjo kitei" (Comfort station rule), March 1938. See also Tokusetsu Butai, Tokusetsu Kansen, "Shina jihen dai-hachi kai kō-teki gaiken hyō, kaigun mukō chōsa" (Eighth compilation of the overview of the war with China), April 11, 1940, and others.

65. Yun Chŏng-ok, "Chŏngsindae; muŏsi munjeinga" (Chŏngsindae: What is at issue?), in Chŏngsindae munje charyojip, vol. 1, ed. Korean Council (1991).

66. Most of the Japanese military records related to military sexual slavery were classified as top secret. One recently discovered record reads, "Intact materials are rarely found because they were destroyed on the orders of the higher officers and any remnants were submitted to the Australian Army." "Dai yonjūhachi shidan senshi shiryō narabi shūusen jōkyō" (Historical data of the Forty-eighth Combat Division and the situation at the end of the war), July 1946.

67. Takagi Ken'ichi, *Chŏnhu bosangŭi nolli* (Thesis on the postwar compensation), trans. Ch'oe Yong-gi (Seoul: Hanul, 1995), p. 19.

68. Nishino Rumiko, "Japanese Military Comfort Station Policy and Managers of the Comfort Station" (paper presented at the Ilbongun Wianbu Munje Hail Hapdong Symposium [Korea–Japan Joint Symposium on Military Sexual Slavery by Japan] at the Korean Council and the Data Center, Seoul, December 1993).

69. Takagi Ken'ichi, *Chŏnhu bosangŭi nolli* (Thesis on the postwar compensation), p. 23.

70. Chŏng In-sŏp, "Kangje chonggunwianbu munjee daehan ilbonŭi ch'aegimihaeng bangan" (Suggestions for Japan's execution of responsibility toward forced military comfort women), in Korean Council, *Chŏngsindae munje charyojip,* 4:57.

71. The association provided a space for seven to eight victims to live for several years, and in December 1995 it built a house for the victims in Kwangju, a satellite city of Seoul.

72. Korean Council and Korean Research Group, eds., *Chunggŭkŭi chosŏnin kunwianbudŭl* (Korean military comfort women in China) (Seoul: Hanul, 1994).

73. It is unusual for an individual to demand an apology in the court. This victim, Song Sin-do, is supported by a large number of Koreans living in Japan as well as some Japanese, who formed a group called the "Association Supporting Song Sin-do's Suit."

74. Totsuka Etsurō, "Kankokujin higaisha-ra gojūnen-buri ni kokuso, kokuhatsu" (The Korean victims indictment and accusations after fifty years), *Hōgaku seminā* (Law Seminar), no. 472 (April 1994): 104.

75. In 1977 the Japanese government enacted a special Law for the Allowance of Condolence Money to Taiwanese Dead Soldiers (Taiwanjin senbotsusha nado ni taisuru chōikin shikyū hōritsu). This was also a product of public pressure. Earlier, the bereaved Taiwanese families had brought the issue before a Japanese court, but this effort failed.

76. E/CN.4/Sub.2/1998/13. On development at the Sub-Commission see Chinsung Chung, "Unesoui Ilbongun songnoye munje" (The issue of Japanese military sexual slavery at the UN) in Chinsung Chung, *Ilbongun Sungnoyeje* (The Japanese Sexual Slavery) (Seoul: Seoul National University Press, 2004).

77. On developments at the UN, see Totsuka Etsurō, "Military Sexual Slavery by Japan and Issues in Law," in Howard, *True Stories.*

78. For details, see Yun Mi-hyang, "Yuenesŏ yŏsŏnginkwŏnundongŏro jegidoen ilbongun wianbu munje" (The Japanese military comfort women issue brought to the UN as a women's human rights issue); Korean Council and PCA Korean–Japanese Lawyers Association, eds., *Ilbongunwianbuŭi gukjebŏpjok haegyŏrŭl wihayŏ* (Toward the international legal solution of the Japanese military comfort women issue) (Seoul: Korean Council, 1995).

79. Korean Democratic Lawyers Association and Korean Council, "Human Rights and Japanese War Responsibility: Counter Report to the Human Rights Committee on the Japanese Government's Third Periodic Report Submitted under Article 40 of

the International Covenant on Civil and Political Rights," October 1993. In 1996 the Human Rights Committee of the UN investigated the fulfillment of this covenant. Countries subscribing to this covenant must submit a first report upon joining, and further reports every five years thereafter. The UN also receives counterreports from other organizations. The 1993 report by the Japanese government was its third.

80. UNCHR announced that it "welcomes the activities and takes note of the report of the Special Rapporteur on violence against women." See UNCHR document, E/CN.4/1996/53 and Add. 1 and 2.

81. On developments at the ILO, see Chinsung Chung, "The issue of Japanese military sexual slavery and the International Labor Organization," Korea National Commission for UNESCO, *Korea Journal* 42, 1 (Spring, 2002).

82. International Commission of Jurists (ICJ), *Comfort Women: An Unfinished Ordeal* (Geneva: ICJ, 1994).

83. Asian Department, Korean Ministry of Foreign Affairs, "Miyajawa ilbon ch'ongni banghangyŏlgwa" (The outcome of Japanese prime minister Miyazawa's visit to Korea), 16–18, January 1992.

84. The victims receive initial lump-sum payments of about 6,000 (US) dollars and a monthly stipend of about 650 dollars. They also receive medical insurance and priority in renting a government-run apartment.

85. In response to Motooka Shōji's proposition in June 1990, Shimizu Yoshio, chief of the Employment Bureau of the Japanese Ministry of Labor said, "The establishment of brothels for the soldiers and the mobilization of the women were done by civilians, and an investigation of the government is out of the question." The Japanese Ministry of Labor expressed its position that the government did not engage in military sexual slavery (*Asahi Shinbun,* April 1991). Katō Kōichi, director of the Japanese Cabinet Secretariat also said that the Japanese government would not consider the compensation issue (*Asahi Shinbun,* December 1991).

86. *Shūkan posuto* (Weekly Post), March 7, 1992.

87. *Hankyŏre sinmun* (Hankyore Daily Newspaper), December 7, 1994.

88. Oral statements by Kim Sun-dŏk, Kang Tŏk-kyŏng, and Filipino victims at the Third Asian Womens Solidarity Forum on Military Sexual Slavery by Japan, Seoul, February 27, 1995.

89. Debate along these lines occurred during the joint symposium held in Seoul by the Korean Council and the Data Center in December 1993.

90. One example is a group of persons who help the government take action through the Asia Women's Fund, while filing suits in the district courts in Japan.

91. Nishioka Tsutomu, "Jūgun'ianfu mondai towa nandattanoka?" (What was the problem of comfort women?), *Bungeishunshū* (April 1992): 310–12. Tanaka Akira and Saitō Katsurmi, "Shazaisuru hodo warukunaru nikkankanke" (Japan–Korea relations worsen as Japan apologizes), *Bungeishunshu* (March 1992): 135–37.

92. Kamisaka Fuyuko, "Shinbun no jūgun ianfu hōdō tte okashikuarunasenka" (Aren't the reports of the newspapers on the comfort women issue ridiculous?), *Shūkan posuto,* February 28, 1992.

93. Arai Sawako, "Jūgun ianfu mondai ni omou" (Thinking of the military comfort women issue), *Gendai koria* (January 1992), p. 20; Arai Sawako, "Daremo kakanakatta jūgun ianfu mondai no kakushin bubun" (The core part of the problem of comfort wornen that no one wrote on), *Shūkan jiji,* February 1, 1992, pp. 14–17; Saito Kazuhide, "Ianfu to sekaishi" (Comfort women and world history), *Seiron* (June 1992), p. 198.

94. Kuroda Katsuhiro, "Nikkan gassaku ianfu seiji ketchaku no uchimaku" (The inside story of the political cooperation between Japan and Korea on comfort women), *Shōkun* (October 1993), p. 123.

95. Uesugi Chitoshi, "Kokuren tokubetsu hokokusha e no ikensho" (Opinion on the UN special rapporteur), *Jiyū* (May 1994), p. 63.

96. Nishioka, "Jūgun'ianfu mondai," pp. 60–61. They also criticize Japanese who work for this cause.

97. Tanaka Saitō, "Shazaisuru hodo," (Apology is not needed.) p. 140; Nishioka, "Jūgun'ianfu mondai," p. 300; Kamisaka, "Shinbun no jūgun ianfu hōdō tte okashikuarunasenka" (Aren't the reports of the newspapers on the comfort women issue ridiculous?), p. 219.

Chapter 17

1. Former POWs were quick to point out that Lean's film did not adequately portray the horrible conditions along the line and gave the false impression that escape was a viable possibility. From their perspective, however, the film's worst misrepresentation was its portrayal of a British officer going beyond minimal cooperation to assist the Japanese in building a bridge. Some former POWs insist that, in fact, they sabotaged the construction at every opportunity. See Ernest Gordon, *Through the Valley of the Kwai* (New York: Harper & Brothers, 1962), p. 70; Cornelis B. Evers, *Death Railway* (Bangkok: Craftsman Press, 1993), p. 12; and Eric Lomax, *Railway Man* (New York: W.W. Norton, 1995), pp. 96–97, 232.

2. A more balanced study, in Japanese, is Yoshiwara Toshiharu's *Tai-Men Tetsudō* (The Thailand–Burma railway) (Tokyo: Dōbunkan, 1994).

3. Hiroike Toshio, *Tai-Men Tetsudō* (The Thailand–Burma railway) (Tokyo: Yomiuri Shimbunsha, 1971), pp. 37–38; and Lionel Wigmore, *The Japanese Thrust* (Canberra: Australian War Memorial, 1957), p. 545.

4. *Bangkok Times Weekly Mail,* April 3, 1934.

5. Hiroike, *Tai-Men Tetsudō* (The Thailand–Burma railway), pp. 45–46 and; Byōdō Tsūshō and Byōdō Shōshin, *Waga ya no Nittai tsūshin* (Our family correspondence between Japan and Thailand) (Tokyo: Indogaku Kenkyūjo, 1979), p. 6.

6. *Japan Times and Advertiser,* June 17, 1942.

7. Hiroike, *Tai-Men Tetsudō* (The Thailand–Burma railway), pp. 114, 166–67, 198–99; Iwai Ken, *C56 Nampō senjo o iku* (The C56 locomotive goes to the southern battlefields) (Tokyo: Jiji Tsūshinsha, 1978), pp. 7, 116, 140; Tominaga Kametarō, *Chototsu hachijūnen* (Eighty reckless years) (Tokyo: Aato Kōpansha, 1987), pp. 188–92; and Evers, *Death Railway,* pp. 89–90.

8. Evers, *Death Railway,* pp. 89–90; Hiroike, *Tai-Men Tetsudō* (The Thailand–Burma railway), pp. 112–15, 198–99; Iwai, *C56 Nampō senjō o iku* (The C56 locomotive goes to the southern battlefields), pp. 136–37; and "POW in Siam," August 28, 1943, HS1/71, British Public Record Office (hereafter PRO), Kew. Tominaga Kametarō, a staff officer with the Thailand Garrison Army, very specifically laid the blame for the tragedy on the staff officers at Imperial General Headquarters and the Southern Army (*Chototsu hachijūnen* [Eighty reckless years], pp. 196–97) for their callous disregard of the realities of the situation on the ground.

9. On the Thai railways, see Virginia Thompson, *Thailand: The New Siam* (1941; repr., New York: Paragon Books, 1967), pp. 497–506; and Ian Brown, *The Elite and the Economy in Siam c. 1890–1920* (Singapore: Oxford University Press, 1988), pp. 15, 41.

10. Tsubokami to Tokyo, July 6 and July 23, 1942, A700 9–63, Japan Foreign Ministry Archives (hereafter JFMA), Tokyo.

11. The details of the agreement are contained in Viboon Leesuwan et al., *Kanchanaburi, Spirit of the Death Railway and the River Kwai Bridge* (Nonthaburi, Thailand: Indoor Design Co., 1987), pp. 20–22.

12. B.V.A. Roling and C.F. Ruter, eds., *The Tokyo Judgement* (Amsterdam: University Press Amsterdam, 1977), p. 414; Evers, *Death Railway,* pp. 6–7; and Gavan Daws, *Prisoners of the Japanese* (New York: William Morrow, 1994), pp. 222–23. Hiroike (*Tai-Men Tetsudō* [The Thailand–Burma railway], p. 133) notes that in July 1942 Attaché Moriya gave him a copy of the Geneva Conventions on POWs. "I was surprised there were so many restrictions . . . ," he wrote. "Since we couldn't comply, there was nothing to do but overlook them."

13. Evers, *Death Railway,* p. 51.

14. Hiroike, *Tai-Men Tetsudō* (The Thailand–Burma railway), p. 243.

15. Intelligence Report ZM 2351, Folder ZM 2300, Box 403, Entry 108, Record Group (hereafter RG) 226, U.S. National Archives, College Park, Maryland (hereafter USNA).

16. Evers, *Death Railway,* pp. 50–51; and Lomax, *Railway Man,* 105–6.

17. E.E. Dunlop, *The War Diaries of Weary Dunlop* (1986; repr., Ringwood, Vic., Australia: Penguin, 1990), p. 244.

18. Ibid., p. 303.

19. Arthur Lane, *Lesser Gods, Greater Devils* (Stockport, Cheshire, UK: Lane Publishers, 1993), 163, 217.

20. Ibid., pp. 171–72, 216–17.

21. Ibid., pp. 173–77.

22. Maya Maruko, "Death Railway Damages Sought," *Japan Times,* August 14, 1991. I am indebted to Lersak Tejayan, William Swan, and Larry Harris for supplying me with copies of many of the newspaper articles from Bangkok and Tokyo cited in this chapter.

23. Evers, *Death Railway,* p. 51; and Hiroike, *Tai-Men Tetsudō* (The Thailand–Burma railway), pp. 177–78, 237, 243–47. Hiroike described the Thai workers as "the ones with the worst character" (p. 243). He quoted Japanese reports on their performance (p. 244). One noted: "Compared to the Burmese the Thais are generally lazy. Even when recruited, the applicants are few and even those who come are unable to do heavy work and flee." Another stated: "Laborers are used from both Thailand and Burma, but the Thai have strong vanity and many are cunning. When they get their contract money in hand, they flee from the station."

24. Hiroike, *Thai-Men Tetsudō* (The Thailand–Burma railway), pp. 143, 246–47. Another Japanese railway officer, Iwai (*C56 Nampō senjo o iku* [The C56 locomotive goes to the southern battlefields], pp. 123, 135–36), painted an equally negative picture of relations with the Thai. On the Ban Pong incident, see E. Bruce Reynolds, *Thailand and Japan's Southern Advance, 1940–1945* (New York: St. Martin's Press, 1994), pp. 138–39.

25. Bangkok to Tokyo, April 1, 1943, SRDJ 34729, and Bangkok to Tokyo, May 22, 1943, SRDJ 37282, RG 457, USNA.

26. Bangkok to Tokyo, April 1, 1943, SRDJ 34729, RG 457, USNA. For more on the difficult position of the Chinese in Thailand and these negotiations, see E. Bruce Reynolds, "'International Orphans'—The Chinese in Thailand During World War II," *Journal of Southeast Asian Studies* 28 (September 1997): 365–88; Panee Bualek, "Botbat khong phokha bon sen thang say marana" (The role of merchants on the

"Death Railway"), *Thammasat University Journal* 21 (May–August 1995): 41–87; and Murashima Eiji, "Nittai Dōmei to Tai kakyō" (The Thai-Japanese alliance and the overseas Chinese in Thailand), *Keisei Daigaku Ajia-Taiheiyō Kenkyū* (Keisei University Asian-Pacific Research) 19 (1996): 43–71. The latter article has been translated as Eiji Murashima, "The Thai-Japanese Alliance and the Chinese of Thailand," in *Southeast Asian Minorities in the Wartime Japanese Empire,* ed. Paul H. Kratoska (London: RoutledgeCurzon, 2002), pp. 192–222.

27. Bangkok to Tokyo, May 22, 1943, SRDJ 37282, RG 457, USNA; and *Bangkok Chronicle,* July 28, 1943.

28. Bangkok to Tokyo, August 20, 1943, SRDJ 42607, RG 457, USNA.

29. Bangkok to Tokyo, October 25, 1944, SRDJ 76479, RG 457, USNA; and "Taikoku kakkyō genjō oyobi dō" (The circumstances and activities of overseas Chinese in Thailand), *Jōhō* (Intelligence) 27 (July 1, 1944): 85, A700 9-9-4, JFMA.

30. "Nittai gumpi kyōtei gaiyō" (Summary of Japanese-Thai military expenditures agreements) and "Shinchū gumpi mondai" (Military expenditures of the garrison army), A700 9-3-2, JFMA, Tokyo.

31. "Nittai gumpi kyōtei gaiyō," A700 9-3-2, JFMA, Tokyo; and Aoki to Bangkok, January 7 and February 4, 1943, SRDJ 030297 and 031212, RG 457, USNA.

32. Tokyo to Bangkok, May 8, 1943, SRDJ 36503, RG 457, USNA.

33. Tokyo to Bangkok, June 9, 1943, SRDJ 38203, RG 457, USNA.

34. Bangkok to Tokyo, December 24, 1943, SRDJ 48007, RG 457, USNA.

35. Ba Maw, *Breakthrough in Burma* (New Haven, CT: Yale University Press, 1968), p. 290.

36. Ibid., p. 293; and Evers, *Death Railway,* p. 51.

37. Ba Maw, *Breakthrough in Burma,* pp. 292–94; and Hiroike, *Tai-Men Tetsudō* (The Thailand–Burma railway), pp. 245–47. Railway officer Abe Hiroshi indicates in Haruko T. Cook and Theodore F. Cook, *Japan at War: An Oral History* (New York: New Press, 1992), that the Burmese were paid one rupee per day, while elephants cost two rupees per day. "Everyone took good care of the elephants," he wrote. "Even Japanese soldiers who beat up Burmese never took it out on the elephants" (p. 100).

38. M. Siviram, *Road to Delhi* (Tokyo: Charles E. Tuttle, 1966), pp. 101–2.

39. Ibid., pp. 104–5.

40. Ibid., p. 101.

41. Ram Singh Rawal, *I.N.A. Saga* (Allahabad: K.P. Khattri, 1946), pp. 165–66.

42. "They Ran Away," May 27, 1945, Folder 309, Box 29, Entry 110, RG 226, USNA.

43. GRASP Operational Report, September 24, 1945, Folder 1, Box 61, Entry 99, RG 226, USNA.

44. Andrew Gilchrist, *Bangkok Top Secret* (London: Hutchinson, 1970), pp. 224.

45. Ibid., pp. 224–25; and "Operation PRIEST/TWILL," Gilchrist to Pointon, undated, HS1/59, PRO, Kew.

46. Report by Captain R.H. Heptinstall, November 11, 1945, HS1/58, PRO, Kew.

47. "Operation PRIEST/TWILL," Gilchrist to Pointon, undated, HS1/59, PRO, Kew.

48. Quoted in the *Straits Times,* December 4, 1945. The paper identified Lieutenant Colonel James, "well-known Negri [Sembilan] planter and sportsman," as the leader of the group. Others involved included Captain T.F. Carey, Captain T.W. Barys, Captain Dubull, and Lieutenant V.P. Perkins.

49. *Straits Times,* November 23 and December 1, 1945.

50. *Straits Times,* December 1 and 3, 1945.

NOTES TO CHAPTER 17 417

51. W. Stanley Moss, *A War of Shadows* (London: T.V. Boardman, 1952), p. 214.

52. Yoshiharu Fujiwara, "Homecoming for a Forced Laborer," *Daily Yomiuri*, August 15, 1995. Boontum told an Australian journalist: "I received a salary and medical treatment from the Japanese army. I do not think I was treated badly." However, his memories of his wartime experience may have been influenced by his subsequent success in finding a new life in Thailand and possibly by the fact that his 1995 return trip to Java was paid for by the Japan-based River Kwai Foundation.

53. Dunlop, *The War Diaries of Weary Dunlop*, pp. 384–85.

54. Evers, *Death Railway*, p. 60.

55. Lomax, *The Railway Man*, p. 268.

56. Ibid., p. 249.

57. "Mass Grave Found close to Thai Rail Site," *San Jose Mercury News*, November 19, 1990.

58. Abe Hiroshi quoted in Cook and Cook, *Japan at War*, p. 421.

59. Byōdō and Byōdō, *Waga ya no Nittai tsūshin* (Our family correspondence between Japan and Thailand), p. 313.

60. Kenneth Harrison, *The Brave Japanese* (Adelaide: Rigby, 1966), p. 195. There are vivid descriptions of physical discipline in the Japanese army in Hanama Tasaki, *Long the Imperial Way* (1949; repr., Westport, CT: Greenwood Press, 1970), pp. 32–45; and Moss, *A War of Shadows*, pp. 219–21. The account of a Korean who guarded POWs on the railway, Mun Tae Pok, appears in Naoya Sugio, "Koreans Tried as War Criminals Denied Damages," *Japan Times*, August 9, 1991.

61. Testimony by British private Richard A. Brown in "They Ran Away," Folder 309, Box 29, Entry 110, RG 226, USNA.

62. Affidavit by Charles Mott, August 21, 1945, Folder ZM 1800, Box 400, Entry 108, RG 226, USNA.

63. Daws, *Prisoners of the Japanese*, pp. 220–21; and Byōdō and Byōdō, *Waga ya no Nittai tsūshin* (Our family correspondence between Japan and Thailand), p. 313.

64. Harrison, *The Brave Japanese*, p. 195. According to Tominaga (*Chototsu hachijūnen* [Eighty reckless years], p. 191), even the Japanese officers along the railway were undernourished.

65. Hiroshi Abe, quoted in Cook and Cook, *Japan at War*, p. 100.

66. Julian Ryall, "I Didn't Do Anything Wrong" and "Doctor's Diaries Paint Different Picture," *The Nation* (Bangkok), February 8, 1988.

67. "Allied POWs, Japanese Captors Plan Peace Walk over River Kwai Bridge," *Daily Yomiuri*, August 15, 1995, and Will Bennett, "The Legacy of War: To Forgive or Not to Forgive," *Daily Yomiuri*, August 20, 1995.

68. Ibid.

69. Micool Brooke, "Haunting Hatred Burns Like a Fire for Some POWs," *Bangkok Post*, December 5, 1993.

70. Quoted in Bennett, "The Legacy of War," *Daily Yomiuri*, August 20, 1995.

71. Maya Maruko, "Death Railway Damages Sought," *Japan Times*, August 14, 1991. The verdict rendered in October 1999 by a Japanese court in a compensation suit brought by Chinese war victims likewise cited postwar international settlements as having decided such matters.

72. Ryall, "I Didn't Do Anything Wrong."

73. George Hicks, *Japan's War Memories: Amnesia or Concealment?* (Aldershot, UK: Ashgate Publishing, 1997), p. 80. See also chapter 16, by Chin Sung Chung, in this volume.

74. Lomax, *The Railway Man.*

75. Peter Eng, "Hatred Built at River Kwai Lives On," *Japan Times,* May 31, 1998.

76. Ibid.

77. Brooke, "Japanese Return to River Kwai to Atone for their War Crimes," *Bangkok Post,* November 21, 1993; and "Return to the River Kwai," *Bangkok Post,* December 5, 1993. Nagase contends that the Japanese have exaggerated in claiming that 1,000 of their own soldiers died during the railway construction. He estimates the Japanese death toll at less than 100.

78. Eng, "Hatred Built at River Kwai Lives On."

79. Hicks, *Japan's War Memories,* pp. 65–66.

80. Fukui Fumiyoshi, "Tai-Menka rensetsu tetsudō" (The railroad connecting Thailand and Burma), in Taikoku Nihonjinkai (Japanese Association in Thailand), *Sōritsu gojū shōnen kinengo* (Fiftieth anniversary commemorative volume) (Bangkok: Shuryōsha, 1963), p. 72.

81. Tsuge Kunio, in *Gensui Terauchi Hisaichi* (Field Marshal Terauchi Hisaichi), ed. Jōhō Hayao (Tokyo: Fuyō Shobō, 1978), p. 409.

82. Nakamura Aketo, *Hotoke no shireikan* (The buddha's commander) (Tokuo: Shūhōsha, 1958), p. 64. On Nakamura's service in Thailand, see E. Bruce Reynolds, "General Nakamura Aketo—A Khaki-Clad Diplomat in Wartime Thailand," in *Thai-Japanese Relations in Historical Perspective,* ed. E. Bruce Reynolds and Chaiwat Khamchoo (Bangkok: Chulalongkorn University Institute of Asian Studies, 1988), pp. 161–202.

83. Ibid., p. 44, 60. Hiroike refers to 32 soldiers executed for war crimes as "sacrificial victims" (*Tai-Men Tetsudō* [The Thailand–Burma railway], pp. 32–33).

84. Pravit Rojanaphruk, "50 Years: A Time to Reflect," *The Nation* (Bangkok), August 17, 1995.

85. Byōdō and Byōdō, *Waga ya no Nittai tsūshin* (Our family correspondence between Japan and Thailand), p. 6.

86. William F. Nimmo, *Behind a Curtain of Silence: Japanese in Soviet Custody, 1945–1956* (Westport, CT: Greenwood Press, 1988).

87. In English: Aida Yūji, *Prisoner of the British,* trans. Hide Ishiguro and Louis Allen (London: Cresset Press, 1968). The Japanese-language original was titled *Aron Shūyōjo* (The Ahlone concentration camp) (Tokyo: Chūkō Shinsho, 1962). A recent Japanese commentary on the significance of Aida's work is Hirakawa Sukehito, "Prisoners in Burma," *Japan Echo* 26, no. 6 (December 1999): 43–50.

88. Tim Large, "Japanese Internees Recall Postwar Hardships," *Daily Yomiuri,* July 15, 2000. In the interview, Oba does not deny Japanese misdeeds, but states: "My basic concept is that in order to make reconciliation, we have to start from a mutual recognition of what (both sides) did during and after the war."

89. Daws, *Prisoners of the Japanese,* pp. 377, 389.

90. Hicks, *Japan's War Memories,* pp. viii–ix, 44–46.

91. The campaign to raise the issue of the Rape of Nanking has attained considerable momentum in the United States and elsewhere because of the best-selling book *The Rape of Nanking* (New York: Basic Books, 1997) by the Chinese American writer Iris Chang. Chang's popular polemic has been widely criticized by historians in Japan and in the West for its reliance on sources of dubious value and its oversimplification of complex issues. An excellent review article summarizing the historiography is Daqing Yang, "Convergence or Divergence? Recent Historical Writings on the Rape

of Nanking," *American Historical Review* 104 (June 1999): 842–65. Insightful articles by Yang and other scholars are included in Joshua A. Fogel, ed., *The Nanjing Massacre in History and Historiography* (Berkeley: University of California Press, 2000).

92. For a commentary on Chinese president Jiang Zemin's use of the "war guilt" card during a November 1998 visit to Tokyo, see Tanaka Akihiko, "Obuchi Diplomacy: How to Follow a Successful Start," *Japan Echo* 26, no. 2 (April 1999): 9.

93. Daws, *Prisoners of the Japanese*, p. 370.

94. In her book *The Rapprochement of Malaya and Japan, 1945–61* (New York: St. Martin's Press, 2000), p. 229, Tomaru Junko points out that because colonial overlord Great Britain had made the postwar settlement with Japan on behalf of Malaya and Singapore, after independence there were demands for payment of Japan's "blood debt" to its war victims. Japan reached a financial settlement with Singapore in 1966 and Malaysia in 1967, deals that did not involve payments to individual victims.

95. Eng, "Hatred Built at River Kwai Lives On."

96. On the nationalistic tone of East Asian textbooks, see Matsumoto Ken'ichi, "East Asian Countries Begin to Rewrite History," *Japan Echo* 28, no. 6 (December 2001): 56–60.

97. The Smithsonian exhibit came under fire because in its original form it raised uncomfortable questions about the American use of atomic bombs against Japanese cities.

98. Quoted in Ian Buruma, *The Wages of Guilt* (New York: Farrar Straus Giroux, 1994), p. 228.

99. Benjamin R. Barber, *Jihad vs. McWorld,* 2nd ed. (New York: Ballantine Books, 2001), p. 167.

About the Editor and Contributors

Chin-Sung Chung is Professor of Sociology, Seoul National University. She has written extensively on issues relating to women's rights, and particularly on forced prostitution during the Pacific War. In August 2004 she was appointed to a post with the United Nations Sub-Commission on the Promotion and Protection of Human Rights.

Henk Hovinga was born in 1931 in The Netherlands. He specialized as a historian of the Japanese occupation in Southeast Asia, particularly in the Indonesian archipelago, and has reported, written and produced radio and TV documentaries extensively on this subject. His book: *Eindstation Pakan Baroe 1943–1945*, about the construction of the Pakan Baroe railroad on Sumatra by Allied POW's and Javanese laborers, has been reprinted four times in the Netherlands. An English translation entitled *Final Destination Pakan Baroe* is available on CD-ROM from the author (henk.hovinga @tiscali.nl).

Ricardo T. Jose is currently professor in the Department of History, University of the Philippines. He obtained his Ph.D. from the Tokyo University of Foreign Studies in 1995, and does research on World War II with a focus on the Japanese occupation of the Philippines.

Ju Zhifen is a researcher at the Chinese Academy of Social Sciences. Her research concentrates on Japanese wartime activities in China, with an emphasis on labor.

Paul H. Kratoska is Publishing Director for Singapore University Press. His publications relating to the Pacific War include *The Japanese Occupation of Malaya* (C. Hurst, 1998) and two edited books, *Food Supplies and the Japanese Occupation of Southeast Asia* (Macmillan, 1998), and *Southeast Asian Minorities in the Wartime Japanese Empire* (RoutledgeCurzon, 2002). He is also editor of a 6-volume collection of documents entitled *The Thai-*

land-Burma Railway (Routledge, 2005). He is a former editor of the *Journal of Southeast Asian Studies*, and a regional editor for the *International Journal of Asian Studies*.

Kaori Maekawa is a Research Associate at the Institute of Japanese Literature. She has been a research fellow with the Japan Society for the Promotion of Science, a visiting scholar at the Institute of Asian Cultures, Sophia University, and a visiting fellow of Australian National University. Her Ph.D. dissertation on Indonesian *heiho* is nearing completion.

Naitou Hisako is a Lecturer in Japanese History at Keisen Women's University, and a Research Associate with the School of Literature and Language at Waseda University. Her specialization is the History of Modern Japanese Media and Literature, with a particular interest in the presentation of Koreans in Japan. Her article "Senngo-Katuzi-Media ni okeru Zainichi-Chousenjin" [Images of Koreans in Japan as reported in weekly magazines in the 1950s"] appeared in *Zainichi-Chousenjin-shi Kenkyuu* ["Historical Research on Korean Residents of Japan"] in 2002.

Michiko Nakahara recently retired from Waseda University's Center for International Education, where she taught courses dealing with Southeast Asia studies. She has written widely on the Pacific War, and has been an active participant in Violence against Women in War—Network Japan, and in the Women's International War Crimes Tribunal on Japan's Military Sexual Slavery.

Harry A. Poeze is Director of KITLV Press, Leiden, The Netherlands. His research focuses on the history of the Indonesian national movement from 1900 till 1950. He has published a number of monographs on this subject, and is in the final stages of work on an extensive history of the left during the Indonesian Revolution, with his biography of Tan Malaka (*Tan Malaka, strijder voor Indonesië's vrijheid, Levensloop 1897–1945*, 's-Gravenhage: Nijhoff, 1976), as its centerpiece.

Trần Mỹ-Vân is Associate Professor and Program Director for International and Asian Studies at the University of South Australia. She has been awarded the Order of Australia Medal (OAM) in recognition of her service to Australia-Asia Relations and the Order of Australia (AM) for her service to the Vietnamese community in Australia. Her research deals with the wartime experiences of religious and political organizations in the south, and more broadly with the history of Vietnam-Japan relations. Her book, *A Vietnamese Royal Exile in Japan: Prince Cuong De, 1882–1951,* is forthcoming from RoutledgeCurzon.

Hui-yu Caroline Ts'ai is currently working on Japanese colonial administration in Taiwan, 1895–1945. Her major research includes work on local administration including the *hokō* (Chinese: *pao-chia*) system, and wartime mobilization in colonial Taiwan. During the 1990s she conducted a series of oral history projects on colonial administration and Taiwanese veterans, resulting in publication of two Chinese-language books in 1997.

David Tucker is Visiting Assistant Professor of History at the University of Iowa. He has written "Learning from Dairen, Learning from Shinkyo: Japanese Colonial City Planning and Postwar Reconstruction," in Carola Hein, Jeffrey Diefendorf & Ishida Yorifusa, eds., *The Postwar Reconstruction of Urban Japan* (London: Palgrave, 2003), and "City Planning Without Cities" Utopian Order in Manchukuo," in Mariko Tamanoi, ed., *Crossed Histories: Manchuria in the Age of Empire* (Honolulu: University of Hawaii Press, 2005).

Remco Raben is a Researcher at the Netherlands Institute for War Documentation in Amsterdam. He publishes on the premodern and modern history of Indonesia, Thailand, Sri Lanka and the Netherlands, and is the author (with Ulbe Bosma) of a Dutch-language book entitled *De oude Indische wereld, 1500–1920* [The Old World of the Indies, 1500–1920] (Amsterdam: Bert Bakker, 2003). In 1999 he published an edited volume entitled *Representing the Japanese Occupation of Indonesia. Personal Testimonies and Public Images in Indonesia, Japan, and the Netherlands* (Zwolle: Waanders, and Amsterdam: Netherlands Institute for War Documentation).

E. Bruce Reynolds is Professor of History and Director of the East Asian Materials and Resources Center (EARMARC) at San Jose State University. His books include *Thailand and Japan's Southern Advance* (St. Martin's Press, 1994), *Thailand's Secret War: OSS, SOE and the Free Thai Underground During World War II* (Cambridge University Press, 2005), and the edited volume *Japan in the Fascist Era* (Palgrave Macmillan, 2004).

Shigeru Sato teaches in the School of Language and Media, The University of Newcastle, Australia. He has written one book and a number of articles on topics related to Indonesia during World War Two, and is preparing a few more books and editing an encyclopedia in the same field.

Utsumi Aiko is professor in the Faculty of Humanities at Keisen University in Tokyo. She has published 14 Japanese-language books, many of them dealing with Japan's activities in Korea and Indonesia during the Pacific War. Her recent research has explored issues relating to war crimes and sexual violence, war compensation, and peace activities by war criminals. In 2005 her book *Nihongun no Horyo Seisaku* (The POW Policies of the Japanese Military) was published in Tokyo by Aoki Shoten.

Index